D0190368

From Genesis to Revelations

Hidden
Bible Dates
Revealed

By: Sir William L. Smith Ph.D.

I

Introduction

Hidden Bible Dates Revealed is a history book on the Bible, it covers over four hundred events that are recorded in the Holy Bible, the Torah, the Dead Sea Scrolls, and other Ancient writings, ranging from before the creation of Adam the first perfect man, through the beginning of the Catholic Church under Constantine the Great. Until Israel became a nation once more. This manuscript assigns dates to important Biblical events. This book is broken up into twelve chapters, one for each month of the year to show when exactly important Biblical events took place. It is designed to appeal to readers interested in the history of the events that are recorded in the modern Bibles.

This book includes the years in which Cain and Abel were born, the dates of the ten plagues of Egypt, the day when Jesus walked on water, and when Michael went to war in Heaven against the Dragon and his armies, as these events are recorded in the scriptures. At the start of each chapter, readers will find a description of the Angel who presides over that month, the tribe associated with that month, and information about Biblical figures who were born during the month mentioned. I spent years studying many different Bibles in churches, seeing dates that were repeatedly mentioned in all of them, but whenever I inquired about them, it seemed that no one knew or cared to know when they had actually taken place.

Consequently, I started searching out these events to find more accurate information about them. It seemed to me that if these events were important enough for God to have them recorded, then it was important for me to find out when they might have actually occurred. What started out as a hobby turned into a passion. My specially is ancient and dead languages; I study Hebrew writings (pre-Babylonia), Aramaic, Latin, Greek, Samaritan, Babylonian, Akkadian, Egyptian hieroglyphics, and some Sanskrit. Being a student of languages, I understand the difficulty of translating from one language to another. So often meanings are lost, even between two languages that are very similar. So I have done the best I can to use the original Hebrew and Aramaic texts to create a accurate English translation of what was written. (I refused to let some of the Church's doctrines, politics, or opinion's of what should be know and taught, and what should be kept secrete, to influence the writings in this book).

Over the years I have a chance to study at some of the best collages, among them the University of Jerusalem where I studied Ancient Hebrew History and Harvard, where I took a class in Greek theology. In 2014 I received my Ph.D. in Theology and Biblical Counseling. I have spent several years studying with the Catholics to be a Priest, a couple of years to be a Minister, I have spent almost a year with the free Masons, then started studding to be a Rabbi. (Please note: I am not a Priest, a Minister, or a Rabbi. I am only a simple man who loves and wanted to know more about God, nothing more). That is why this book is so important, because it offers information about key scriptural dates to those who cannot read the old languages in which key religious texts were originally written. Such information could help readers build their own interpretations of the meaning of the religious texts and events as well as challenge the interpretations of the traditional English translations.

This book offers not only the dates of events but also where the dates were recorded and where the text were found. I have included this information so that readers may search it out for themselves, so to take away any doubt about what is written in this book. In creating this book, I have gone to the oldest writings that were found in Cairo, Jerusalem, Athens, Rome, and St. Petersburg and focused only on the dates recorded and the words actually written in the original text. The oldest writings of the New Testament were found in St. Petersburg, after the collapse of the U.S.S.R. They were written in Hebrew and Aramaic, not Greek and Latin. Among these writings was a letter that stated "we translated the letters as best we could, into Greek from the Aramaic and Hebrew text. To reset the the months as accurately as possible, I went back and found when the three calendars-Hebrew, Julian,and Georgian- lined up and then because the Hebrew calendar has only 360 days I placed 5 extra days to the end of the month of Adar (six in case of a leap year), bringing the year from 360 days to 365 days we have now.

I myself have been blessed more that I would have ever imagined while researching and writing this book. God showed me many things I never though I would ever see or had ever imagined. I never knew that the grave of Adam and Eve was in Hebron, about 16 miles from Jerusalem, or that the Garden of Eden was about 200 miles south of Baghdad. I truly hope this book will be a blessing to all who read it. I have found other dates in the Bible and other ancient writing, that were not record in this book. Inside you will find over 475 events that have been recorded, the others I left out for those who wish to search out and find some of the hidden treasures, that God placed in his Book. For it is written; **(Proverbs 25:2)** ***It is to the Glory of God to conceal a matter; but to the Honor of Kings to search out what is hidden.***

Note: Whenever the words in this book are highlighted in: Red text: These represent the words that were spoken by Jesus. Also Jesus was born about 3 miles outside of Bethlehem, in a cave used by herders for their livestock in winter.

Note: More about the actual name of Jesus of Nazareth

Jesus actual name was (Yahoshua), changed around +/- 200 A.D. by the Orthodox Church to: (Yeshua) which means Joshua; (Yahweh is our salvation) Later when the Gentiles tried to transliterate his name into Greek, they came up with (ιησουν) or "Iesous". Then when Iesous was transliterated into Latin, it became "Iesus", which was then carried over into English it became our modern day "Jesus" when the letter "J" was developed, and given its own unique sound somewhere between (1478-1550 C.E.) It was first found in Bibles that were printed after the 17th. Century.

More about the beginning of the Orthodox Church

The first Christian Churches were Jewish, held in homes of believers then later some of the Rabbi's would hold the services for them in the Synagogs. It was in the early centuries of the Church's existence, while fighting to safeguard the true doctrines of Christ, that the Christian Church officially took on the name "Orthodox." The word Orthodox literally means "straight teaching" or "straight worship," being derived from two Greek words: Orthos, "straight," and Doxa, "teaching" or "worship." The first Orthodox Church was built in Antioch, Turkey also called (Antakya) in the 2nd. century A.D. Where the first Bible's were formed.

Index

Month **Hebrew** **Page**

Chapter 1: January - Tevet

Tevet is the tenth month on the Hebrew calendar. The first of Tevet falls on December 27th.
In Hebrew this month is called: Tevet, which means:(Good)
Tribe of Asher, means:
(In our good fortune, they will call us blessed)
The stone of (Lavender Jade) represents this tribe.
Asher:(The 2nd.)Son of Zilpah, the hand maiden of Leah.
(Was believed to have been born in this month.)
(Spirit of Justice)

+/- January 1st. (Tevet 6th.)

The Year +/- 3228 B.C. Noah sent out a Dove the second Time.

(Geneses 8:10-11) 10:And he stayed yet other seven days; and again he sent forth the dove out of the ark; 11:And the dove came in to him in the evening; and look, in her mouth was an olive leaf: so Noah knew that the waters were abated from off the earth.

+/- January 5th. (Tevet 10th.)

The year +/- 582 B.C. The King of Babylon invades Jerusalem.

(Ezekiel 24:1-14) 1:On the tenth day of the tenth month, in the ninth year,the word of the Lord came to me; 2:Son of man wright down this date today, for this very day the King of Babylon has invested Jerusalem. 3:Propose this parable to the rebellious house; This says the Lord God. Set up the pot, set it up, then pour in some water, 4:put in some peaces of meat all good peaces, thigh and shoulder. Fill it with the choicest joints, 5:taken from the pick of the flock. Then pile the wood beneath it: bring to a boil these pieces and the joints that are with it.

6:Take out its pieces, one by one,with out casting lots for it. Therefore this says the Lord God: Woe to the bloody city, a pot containing rust,- whose rust has not been removed. 7:For the blood she has shed is in her mist; she poured it on the bare rock;she did not pour it out on the earth, to be covered with dust. 8:To work up my wrath, to excite my vengeance, she put her blood on the bare rock, not to be covered. 9;:Therefore this says the Lord God; I too, will heap up a great bonfire, 10:piling on the wood and kindling the fire. Till the meat has been cooked, till the broth has been boiled. 11:Then I will set the pot empty on the coals till its metal glows red hot, till the impurities in it melt, and its rust disappears. 12:Yet not even with fire will its great rust be removed. 13:Because you have sullied yourself with lewdness when I would have purified you,and you refused to be purified of your uncleanness, therefore you shall not be purified until I wreak my fury on you. 14:I the Lord, have spoken; By your conduct and your deeds, you shall be judged, says the Lord God.

+/- January 5th. (Tevet 10th.)

The year +/- 592 B.C. Nebuchadnezzar and his army.

(2 Kings 25:1) 1:In the tenth month on the ninth year on the tenth day of the month, Nebuchadnezzar, King of Babylon, and his whole army advanced against Jerusalem, encamped around it and built siege walls on every side.

(As written in the Book of Jeremiah)

Nebuchadnezzar King of Babylon, came against Jerusalem

(Jeremiah 39:1) 2: The ninth year of Zedekiah King of Judah, in the tenth month, again came Nebuchadnezzar King of Babylon and all his army against Jerusalem, and they besieged it.

+/- January 5th. (Tevet 10th.)

The Lord changed some of the days of (Fasting and Sorrow to days of Feasting and Joy).

(Zechariah 8:18-19) 18:This word of the Lord of hosts came to me: 19:This says the Lord of host; The fast days of the fourth, the fifth,the seventh, and the tenth months shall become occasions of joy and gladness, cheerful festivals for the house of Judah.

+/- January 7th. (Tevet 12th.)

The year +/- 581 B.C. Ezekiel prophesies against Pharaoh.

(Ezekiel 29:1-16) 1:On the twelfth day of the tenth month in the tenth year, the word of the Lord came to me; 2:Son of man, set your face against Pharaoh, King of Egypt, and prophesy against him and against all Egypt. 3:Say this to him: This says the Lord God: See! I am coming at you, Pharaoh, King of Egypt. Great crouching monster amidst your Niles; Who say; The Niles are mine; it is I who made them!
4: I will put hooks in your jaws and make the fish of your Niles stick to your scales.
5: I will cast you into the desert, you and all the fish of the Niles,

you shall fall upon the open field, you shall not be taken up or buried. To the beasts of the earth and the birds of the air I give you as food. 6;That all who dwell in Egypt may know that I am the Lord. Because you have been a reed staff for the house of Israel. 7:When they held you in hand, you splintered, throwing every shoulder out of joint. When they leaned on you, you broke bringing each one of them down headlong, 8:therefore this says the Lord God: See! I will bring a sword against you and cut off from you both man and beast. 9:The land of Egypt shall become a desolate waste; this they shall know that I am the Lord. Because you said,The Niles are mine:it is I who made them. 10:Therefore see! I am coming at you and against your Niles; I will make the land of Egypt a waste and a desolation from Migdol to Syene, and even to the frontier of Ethiopia. 11:No foot of man or beast shall pass through it; they shall not pass through it, and it will be uninhabited for forty years. 12: I will make the land of Egypt the most desolate of lands, and its cities shall be most deserted of cities for forty years, and I will scatter the Egyptians among the nations and strew them over foreign lands. 13:Yet this says the Lord God:At the end of forty years I will gather the Egyptians from the peoples among whom they are scattered, 14:and I will restore Egypt's fortune, bringing them back to the land of Pharaohs, the land of their origin where it will be the lowliest 15:of kingdoms, never more to set itself above the nations. I will make them few, that they may not dominate the nations. 16:No longer shall they be for the house of Israel to trust in, but the living reminder of the guilt for having turned to fallow after them. This way they shall know that; I am the Lord.

+/- January 8th. (Tevet 13th.)

Noah again sent out a dove.

(Genesis 8:12) 12:He had waited still another 7 days and then released the dove once more; and this time it did not come back.

+/- January 18th. (Tevet 23th.)

The year +/- 1357 B.C. Moses went up the mountain and met God:

(Exodus 3:1-4:18) 1: Mean while Moses was tending the flock of his father-in-law Jethro, the priest of Midian. Leading the flock across the desert, he came to Horeb, the mountain of God. 2:There a angel of the Lord appeared to him in a fire flaming out of a bush. As he look on, he was surprised to see that the bush, though on fire, was not consumed. 3:So Moses decided; “I must to look at this remarkable sight,and see why the bush is not burned.” 4:When the Lord saw him coming over to look at it more closely, God called out to him from the bush,“Moses! Moses!”He answered here I am. 5:God said, Come no nearer! Remove the sandals from your feet, for the place where you stand is holy ground. 6:“I am the God of your father, the God of Abraham, the God of Isaac, the God of Jacob.” Moses hid his face, for he was afraid to look at God. 7:But the Lord said, “ I have seen the affliction of my people in Egypt and have heard their cry’s of complaints against their slave drivers, so I know well what they are suffering. 8:Therefore I have come down to rescue them from the hands of the Egyptians and lead them out of that land into a good and spacious land, a land flowing with milk and meat, the country of the Canaanites, Hittites, Amorites, Perizzites, Hivites, and Jebusites.

9:So indeed the cry of the Israelites has reached me, and I have truly noted that the Egyptians are oppressing them. 10:Come now! I will send you to Pharaoh to lead my people, the Israelites out o Egypt. 11:But Moses said to God, "Who am I that I should go to Pharaoh and lead the Israelites out of Egypt?"12:He answered, "I will be with you, and this shall be your proof that;it is I who have sent you: when you bring back my people out of Egypt. You will worship God on this very mountain." 13:But said Moses to God ,when I go to the Israelites and say to them,"The God of your fathers has sent me to you"if they ask me, what is your name? What am I to tell them. 14:God replied;"I am, who I am" Then he added "I AM"sent me to you. 15:God spoke further to Moses, This shall you say to the Israelites: The Lord, the God of your fathers, the God of Abraham, the God of Isaac, the God of Jacob, has sent me to you. This is my name forever; this is my title for all generations. 16:"Go and assemble the elders of the Israelites, and tell them: The Lord the God of your fathers, the God of Abraham, Isaac, and Jacob, has appeared to me and said:I am concerted about you and about the way you have being treated in Egypt.

17:So I have decided to lead you up out of the misery of Egypt into the land of the Canaanites, Hittites, Amorites, Perizzites, Hivites and Jebusites, a land flowing with milk and meat. 18:This they will heed the message. Then you and the elders of Israel shall go to the King of Egypt and say to him: The Lord , the God of the Hebrews, has sent us word. Permit us, then, to go a three-days journey in the desert, that we may offer sacrifice to the Lord, our God. 19:Yet I know the king of Egypt will not let you go unless he is forced. 20: I will stretch out my hand, therefore and strike Egypt by doing all kings of wondrous deeds there. After that he will send you away. 21: I will even make the Egyptians so well-disposed towards this people that, when you leave, you will not go empty-handed. 22:Every woman shall ask her neighbor and her house guest for silver and gold articles and for clothing to put on your sons and daughters. This you will tell to the Egyptians.

4:1: But objected Moses, "Suppose they will not believe me, nor listen to my plea? For they may say, "The Lord did not appear to you." 2:The Lord therefore asked him: What is that in your hand?"A staff" he answered. 3:The Lord then said, "throw it on the ground. "When he threw it on the ground it was changed into a serpent. And Moses ran away from it. 4:"Now, put out your hand" the Lord said to him, and take hold of its tale. So he put out his hand and laid hold of it, and it became a stall in his hand. 5:"This will take place so that they may believe," he continued; The Lord the God of their fathers, the God of Abraham, the God of Isaac, the God of Jacob, did appear to you. 6:Again the Lord said to him,"Put your hand in your bosom,"He put in his bosom, and when he with drew it, to his surprise his hand was leprous, like snow. 7:The Lord then said to him:"Now, put you hand back in your bosom."Moses put his hand back in his bosom, and when he withdrew it,to his surprise it was again like the rest of his body.

8:If they will not believe you, nor heed the message of the first sign, they should believe the message of the second. 9:And if they will not believe even these two signs, nor heed your plea, take some water and from the river and pour it on the dry land. The water you take from the river will become blood on the dry ground. 10:Moses however, said to the Lord, If you please Lord, I have never been eloquent, neither in the past, nor recently, nor now that you have spoken with your servant; but I am slow of speech and tongue. 11:The Lord said to him,"Who gives one man speech and another deaf and dumb? Or who gives sight to one and makes another blind? Is it not I?the Lord. 12:Go then! It is I who will assist you in speaking and will teach you what you are to say. 13:Yet he insisted "If you please Lord send someone else! 14:Then the Lord became angry with Moses and said, Have you not your brother, Aaron the Levite? I know that he is an eloquent speaker. Besides he is now on his way to meet you. 15:When he sees you, his heart will be glad. You are to speak to him then, and put the words in his mouth. I will assist both you and him in speaking and will teach the two of you what you are to do. 16:He shall speak to the people for you; he shall be your profit, and you shall be as God to him. 17:Take this staff in your hand; with it you are to perform the signs. 18:After this Moses returned to his father-in-law Jethro ans said to him, "Let me go back please to my kinsman in Egypt, to see whether they are still living. Jethro replied, "Go in peace.

Mount Sinai: Where it is said that: Moses left after speaking with God, and went back to his father-in-law Jethro's house At the base is St. Catherine's Monastery, that is set below the high point of the Mountain.

+/- January 19th. (Tevet 24th.)

The year +/- 1357 B.C. Moses went back to his father-in-laws house.

(Exodus 4:18-23) 18:And Moses went and returned to Jethro his father in law, and said to him, Let me go, I ask you, and return to my brethren which are in Egypt, and see whether they are still alive. 19:And Jethro said to Moses, Go in peace.

And the Lord said to Moses in Midian, Go, return into Egypt: for all the men are dead which sought your life. 20:And Moses took his wife and his sons, and set them upon an ass, and he returned to the land of Egypt: and Moses took the rod of God in his hand. 21:And the Lord said to Moses, When you go to return into Egypt, see that you do all those wonders before Pharaoh, which I have put in your hand: but I will harden his heart, that he shall not let the people go. 22:And you shall say to Pharaoh, This says the Lord, Israel is my son, even my first born. 23:And I say to you, Let my son go, that he may serve me: and if you refuse to let them go, behold I will even slay your son, even to your firstborn.

+/- January 19th. (Tevet 24th.)

The year +/- 325 B.C. Esther was made Queen.

(Esther 2:15-18)15:Now when the turn of Esther, the daughter of Abihail the uncle of Mordecai, who had taken her for his daughter, was come to go in to the King, she asked for nothing but what Hegai the King's chamberlain, the keeper of the women, appointed. And Esther obtained favor in the sight of all them that looked upon her. 16:So Esther was taken to king Ahasuerus into his house royal in the 10th. month, which is the month Tevet, in the 7th year of his reign. 17:And the King loved Esther above all the women, and she obtained grace and favor in his sight more than all the virgins; so that he set the royal crown upon her head, and made her queen instead of Vashti. 18:Then the King made a great feast to all his princes and his servants, even Esther's feast; and he made a release the provinces, and gave gifts, according to the state of the King.

+/- January 21st. (Tevet 26th.)

The year +/- 1357 B.C. God told Aaron to go in to the desert and meet Moses,

(Exodus 4:27-28) 27;And the Lord said to Aaron, Go into the wilderness to meet Moses. And he went, and met him in the mount of God, and kissed him. 28;And Moses told Aaron all the words of the Lord who had sent him, and all the signs which he had commanded him.

+/- January 26th. (Shevat / Astec 1st.)

The year +/- 1317 B.C. Moses gives his last testimony to the Hebrews:

(Deuteronomy 1:1-33:29) 1:These are the words which Moses spoke to all Israel on this side Jordan in the wilderness, in the plain over against was the finale farewell address at the Red Sea, between Paran, and Tophel, and Laban, and Hazeroth, and Dizahab. 2:There are eleven days journey from Horeb by the way of mount Seir to Kadeshbarnea. 3:And it came to pass in the fortieth year, in the eleventh month, on the first day of the month, that Moses spoke to the children of Israel, according to all that the Lord had given him in commandment to them. 4:After he had slain Sihon the king of the Amorites, which dwelt in Heshbon, and Og the king of Bashan, which dwelt at Astaroth in Edrei. 5:On this side Jordan, in the land of Moab, began Moses to declare this law, saying,

6:The Lord our God spoke to us in Horeb, saying, You have dwelt long enough in this mount. 7:Turn you, and take your journey, and go to the mount of the Amorites, and to all the places near to the plains, in the hills, and in the vale, and in the south, and by the sea side, to the land of the Canaanites, and to Lebanon, to the great river, the river Euphrates. 8:Behold, I have set the land before you: go in and possess t he land which the Lord promised to your fathers, Abraham, Isaac, and Jacob, to give to them and to their seed after them. 9:And I spoke to you at that time, saying, I am not able to bear you myself alone. 10:The Lord your God has multiplied you, and, behold, you are this his day as the stars of heaven for multitude. 11:The Lord God of your fathers make you a thousand times so many more as you are, as he has bless you, as he has promised you! 12:How can I myself alone bear your encumbrance, and your burden, and your strife? 13:Take you wise men, and understanding, and known among your tribes and I will make them rulers over you. 14:And you answered me, and said, The thing which you have spoken is good for us to do.

15:So I took the chief of your tribes, wise men, and known, and made them heads over you, captains over thousands, and captains over hundreds, and captains over fifties, and captains over tens, and officers among your tribes. 16:And I charged your judges at that time, saying, Hear the causes between your brethren, and judge righteously between every man and his brother, and the stranger that is with him. 17:You shall not respect persons in judgment; but you shall hear the small as well as the great; you shall not be afraid of the face of man; for the judgment is God's: and the cause that is too hard for you, bring it to me, and I will hear it. 18:And I will commanded you at that time all the things which you should do. 19:And when we departed from Horeb, we went through all that great and terrible wilderness, which you saw by the way of the mountain of the Amorites, as the Lord our God commanded us; and we came to Kadeshbarnea. 20:And I said to you, You have come to the mountain of the Amorites, which the Lord our God does give to us. 21:Behold, the Lord your God has set the land before you. Go up and possess it, as the Lord God of your fathers has said to you; fear not, neither be discouraged. 22:And you come close to me everyone of you, and said, We will send men before us, and they shall search us out the land,and bring us word again by what way we must go up, and into what cities we shall come. 23:And the saying pleased me well: and I took twelve men of you, one of a tribe. 24:And they turned and went up into the mountain, and came to the valley of Eshcol, and searched it out.

25:And they took of the fruit of the land in their hands, and brought it down to us, and brought us word again, and said; It is a good land which the Lord our God does give to us. 26:Not trusting you would not go up, but rebelled against the commandment of the Lord your God. 27:And you murmured in your tents, and said, Because the Lord hates us, he has brought us forth out of the land of Egypt, to deliver us into the hand of the Amorites, to destroy us. 28:Where shall we go? Our brethren have discouraged our heart, saying, The people is greater and taller than we; the cities are great and walled up to heaven; and more over we have seen the sons of the Anakims there. 29:Then I said to you; Dread not, neither be afraid of them. 30:The Lord your God which go's before you, he shall fight for you, according to all that he did for you in Egypt before your eyes. 31:And in the wilderness, where you have seen how that the Lord your God cared for you,

as a man does care for his son, in all the way that you went, until you came to this
place. 32:Yet in this thing you did not believe the Lord your God. 33:Who went in
the way before you, to search you out a place to pitch your tents, in fire by night, to
showed you by what way you should go, and in a cloud by day. 34:And the Lord
heard the voice of your words, and was wroth, and swore, saying;
35:Surely there shall not one of these men of this evil generation see that good land,
which I swore to give to your fathers. 36:Save Caleb the son of Jephunneh; he shall
see it, and to him will I give the land that he has trodden upon, and to his children,
because he has wholly followed the Lord. 37:Also the Lord was angry with me for
your sakes, saying, You also shall not go in to it. 38:But Joshua the son of Nun,
which stands before you, he shall go in closer: encourage him: for he shall cause
Israel to inherit it. 39:Moreover your little ones, which you said should be a prey,
and your children, which in that day had no knowledge between good and evil, they
shall go in closer, and to them will I give it, and they shall possess it. 40:But as for
you, turn you, and take your journey into the wilderness by the way of the Red sea.

41:Then you answered and said to me, We have sinned against the Lord, we will go
up and fight, according to all that the Lord our God commanded us. And when you
had girded on every man his weapons of war, you were ready to go up into the hill.
42:And the Lord said to me, Say to them; Do not go up, nor fight; for I am not
among you; lest you be struck before your enemies. 43:So I spoke to you; and you
would not hear, but rebelled against the commandment of the Lord, and went
presumptuously up to the hill. 44:And the Amorites, which dwelt in that mountain,
came out against you, and chased you, as bees do, and destroyed you in Seir, even
to Hormah. 45:And you returned and wept before the Lord; but the Lord would not
listen to your voice, nor give ear to you. 46:So you stayed in Kadesh many days,
according to the days that you stayed there.

2:1 Then we turned, and took our journey into the wilderness by the way of the
Red Sea, as the Lord spoke to me: and we compassed mount Seir many days. 2:And
the Lord spoke to me, saying; 3:You have encompassed this mountain long enough:
turn you northward. 4:And command you the people, saying, You are to pass
through the coast of your brethren the children of Esau, which dwell in Seir; and
they shall be afraid of you: take you good heed to yourselves therefore. 5:Meddle
not with them; for I will not give you their land, not so much as a foot hold; because
I have given mount Seir to Esau for a possession. 6:You shall buy meat from them
for money, that you may eat; and you shall also buy water of them, for money, that
you may drink.

7:For the Lord your God has blessed you in all the works of your hands: he knows
about your walking through this great wilderness: these forty years the Lord your
God had been with you; you have lacked for nothing. 8:And when we passed by
from our brethren the children of Esau, which dwelt in Seir, through the way of the
plain from Elath, and from Eziongaber, we turned and passed by the way of the
wilderness of Moab. 9:And the Lord said to me, Distress not the Moabites, neither
contend with them in battle: for I will not give to you their land for a possession;
because I have given Ar, to the children of Lot for a possession.10:The Emims
dwelt there in times past, a people great, and many, and tall, as the Anakims;

11:Which also were accounted giants, as the Anakims; but the Moabites call them Emims. 12:The Horims also dwelt in Seir before time; but the children of Esau succeeded them, when they had destroyed them from before them, and dwelt in their stead; as Israel did to the land of his possession, which the Lord gave to them. 13:Now rise up, said I, and get you over the brook Zered. And we went over the brook Zered. 14:And the space in which we came from Kadeshbarnea, until we were come over the brook Zered, was thirty and eight years; until all the generation of the men of war were wasted out from among the host, as the Lord swore to them. 15:For indeed the hand of the Lord was against them, to destroy them from among the host, until they were consumed.16:So it came to pass, when all the men of war were consumed and dead from among the people, 17:That the Lord spoke to me, saying, 18:You are to pass over through Ar, the coast of Moab, this day: 19:And when you come near to cross over against the children of Ammon, distress them not, nor meddle with them: for I will not give you of the land of the children of Ammon any possession; because I have given it to the children of Lot for a possession.

20:(That also was accounted a land of giants: giants dwelt therein in old time; and the Ammonites call them Zamzummims) 21:A people great, and many, and tall, as the Anakims; but the Lord destroyed them before them; and they succeeded them, and dwelt in their stead: 22:As he did to the children of Esau, which dwelt in Seir, when he destroyed the Horims from before them; and they succeeded them, and dwelt in their stead even to this day: 23:And the Avims which dwelt in Hazerim, even to Azzah, the Caphtorims, which came forth out of Caphtor, destroyed them, and dwelt in their stead. 24:Rise up you, and take your journey, and passover the river Arnon: behold, I have given into your hands, Sihon the Amorite, King of Heshbon, and his land: begin to possess it, and contend with him in battle. 25:This day will I begin to put the dread of you and the fear of you upon the nations that are under the whole heaven, who shall hear report of you, and shall tremble, and be in anguish because of you. 26:And I sent messengers out of the wilderness of Kedemoth to Sihon king of Heshbon with words of peace, saying, 27:Let me pass through your land: I will go along by the high way, I will neither turn to the right hand nor to the left. 28:You shall sell me meat for money, that I may eat; and give me water for money, that I may drink: only I will pass through on my feet;

29:(As the children of Esau which dwell in Seir, and the Moabites which dwell in Ar, did to me;) until I shall pass over the Jordan to the land which the Lord our God gives us. 30:But Sihon King of Heshbon would not let us pass by him: for the Lord your God hardened his spirit, and made his heart obstinate, that he might deliver him into your hands, as it seems this day. 31:And the Lord said to me, Behold, I have begun to give Sihon and his land before you: begin to possess, that you may inherit his land. 32:Then Sihon came out against us, he and all his people, to fight at Jahaz. 33:And the Lord our God delivered him before us; and we struck him, and his sons, and all his people. 34:And we took all his cities at that time, and utterly destroyed the men, and the women, and the little ones, of every city, we left none to remain: 35:Only the cattle we took for a prey to ourselves, and the spoil of the cities which we took. 36:From Aroer, which is by the brink of the river of Arnon, and from the city that is by the river, even to Gilead, there was not one city too strong for us: the Lord our God delivered all to us:

37:Only to the land of the children of Ammon you came not, nor to any place of the
river Jabbok, nor to the cities in the mountains, nor to what soever the Lord our God
said we should not go.

3:1: Then we turned, and went up the way to Bashan: and Og the King of Bashan
came out against us, he and all his people, to battle at Edrei. 2:And the Lord said to
me, fear him not: for I will deliver him, and all his people, and his land, into your
hand; and you shall do to him as you did to Sihon King of the Amorites, which
dwelt at Heshbon. 3:So the Lord our God delivered into our hands Og also, the King
of Bashan, and all his people: and we struck him until none was left to him
remaining. 4:And we took all his cities at that time, there was not a city which we
took not from them, threescore cities, all the region of Argob, the kingdom of Og in
Bashan. 5:All these cities were fenced with high walls, gates, and bars; beside
unwalled towns a great many. 6:And we utterly destroyed them, as we did to Sihon
King of Heshbon, utterly destroying the men, women, and children, of every city.
7:But all the cattle, and the spoil of the cities, we took for a prey to ourselves. 8:And
we took at that time out of the hand of the two Kings of the Amorites the land that
was on this side Jordan, from the river of Arnon to mount Hermon. 9:(Which
Hermon the Sidonians call Sirion; and the Amorites call it Shenir;) 10:All the cities
of the plain, and all Gilead, and all Bashan, to Salchah and Edrei, cities of the
kingdom of Og in Bashan.

11:For only Og King of Bashan remained of the remnant of giants; behold, his
bedstead was a bedstead of iron; is it not in Rabbath of the children of Ammon?
nine cubits was the length thereof, and four cubits the breadth of it, after the cubit of
a man. 12:And this land, which we possessed at that time, from Aroer, which is by
the river Arnon, and half mount Gilead, and the cities thereof, gave I to the
Reubenites and to the Gadites. 13:And the rest of Gilead, and all Bashan, being the
kingdom of Og, gave I to the half tribe of Manasseh; all the region of Argob, with
all Bashan, which was called the land of Giants. 14:Jair the son of Manasseh took
all the country of Argob to the coasts of Geshuri and Maachathi; and called them
after his own name, Bashanhavothjair, to this day. 15:And I gave Gilead to Machir.
16:And to the Reubenites and to the Gadites I gave from Gilead even to the river
Arnon half the valley, and the border even to the river Jabbok, which is the border
of the children of Ammon; 17:The plain also, and Jordan, and the coast thereof,
from Chinnereth even to the sea of the plain, even the salt sea, under Ashdothpisgah
eastward. 18:And I commanded you at that time, saying, The Lord your God has
given you this land to possess it: you shall pass over armed before your brethren the
children of Israel, all that are ment for the war.

19:But your wives, and your little ones, and your cattle, (for I know that you have
much cattle,) shall abide in your cities which I have given you. 20:Until the Lord
have given rest to your brethren, as well as to you, and until they also possess the
land which the Lord your God has given them beyond Jordan: and then shall you
return every man to his possession, which I have given you. 21:And I commanded
Joshua at that time, saying; Your eyes have seen all that the Lord your God has done
to these two Kings: so shall the Lord do to all the kingdoms where you pass. 22:You
shall not fear them: for the Lord your God he shall fight for you.

23:And I besought the Lord at that time saying; 24:O Lord God, you have begun to
show your servant your greatness, and your might? 25:I pray you, let me go over,
and see the good land that is beyond Jordan, that goodly mountain, and Lebanon.
26:But the Lord was angry with me for your sakes, and would not hear me: and the
Lord said to me, Let it suffice, that you speak no more to me of this matter. 27:Get
up and go to the top of Pisgah, and lift up your eyes westward, and northward, and
southward, and eastward, and behold it with your eyes: for you shall not go over
this Jordan. 28:But charge Joshua, and encourage him, and strengthen him: for he
shall go over before this people, and he shall cause them to inherit the land which
you shall see. 29:So we abode in the valley over against Bethpeor.

4:1: Now therefore hearken, O Israel, to the statutes and to the judgments, which
I teach you, for to dothem , that you may live, and go in and possess the land which
the Lord God of your fathers has given you. 2:You shall not add to the word which I
command you, neither shall you diminish from it, that you may keep the
commandments of the Lord your God which I command you. 3:Your eyes have seen
what the Lord did because of Baalpeor: for all the men that followed Baalpeor, the
Lord your God has destroyed them from among you. 4:But you that did cleave to
the Lord your God are alive every one of you this day. 5:Behold, I have taught you
statutes and judgments, even as the Lord my God commanded me, that you should
do so in the land whither you go to possess it. 6:Keep therefore and do them for this
is your wisdom and your understanding in the sight of the nations, which shall hear
all these statutes, and say, Surely this great nation is a wise and understanding
people. 7:For what nation is there so great, who has God so close to them, as the
Lord our God is in all things that we call upon him for? 8:And what nation is there
so great, that has statutes and judgments so righteous as all this law, which I set
before you this day? 9:Only take heed to yourself, and keep your soul diligently,
lest you forget the things which your eyes have seen, and lest they depart from your
heart all the days of your life: but teach them to your sons, and grand sons.

10:Especially the day that you stood before the Lord your God in Horeb, when the
Lord said to me, Gather me the people together, and I will make them hear my
words, that they may learn to fear me all the days that they shall live upon the earth,
and that they may teach their children. 11:And you came near and stood under the
mountain; and the mountain burned with fire to the midst of heaven, with darkness,
clouds, and thick darkness. 12:And the Lord spoke to you out of the midst of the
fire: you heard the voice of the words, but saw no form; only you heard a voice.
13:And he declared to you his covenant, which he commanded you to perform, even
ten commandments; and he wrote them upon two tables of stone. 14:And the Lord
commanded me at that time to teach you statutes and judgments, that you might go
into the land where you are going to possess it. 15:Take you therefore good heed to
yourselves; for you saw no manner of form on the day that the Lord spoke to you in
Horeb out of the midst of the fire: 16:Lest you corrupt yourselves, and make you a
graven image, the form of any figure, the likeness of male or female. 17:The
likeness of any beast that is on the earth, the likeness of any winged fowl that flies
in the air. 18:The likeness of any thing that creeps on the ground, the likeness of any
fish that is in the waters beneath the earth: 19:And lest you lift up your eyes to
heaven, and when you see the sun, and the moon, and the stars,

even all the host of heaven, should be driven to worship them, and serve them, which the Lord your God has divided to all nations under the whole heaven. 20:But the Lord has taken you, and brought you forth out of the iron furnace, even out of Egypt, to be to him a people of inheritance, as you are this day. 21:Furthermore the Lord was angry with me for your sakes, and swore that I should not go over Jordan, and that I should not go in to that good land, which the Lord your God gives you for an inheritance. 22:But I must die in this land, I must not go over Jordan: but you shall go over, and possess that good land. 23:Take heed to yourselves, lest you forget the covenant of the Lord your God, which he made with you, and make you a graven image, or the likeness of any thing, which the Lord your God has forbidden you. 24:For the Lord your God is a consuming fire, even a jealous God. 25:When you shall have children, and your children, have children, and you shall have remained long in the land, and shall corrupt your self's, and make a graven image, or the likeness of anything, and shall do evil in the sight of the Lord your God, to provoke him to anger: 26:I call heaven and earth to witness against you this day, that you shall soon utterly perish from off the land where to you go over Jordan to possess it; you shall not prolong yours days upon it, but shall utterly be destroyed.

27;And the Lord shall scatter you among the nations, and you shall be left few in number among the heathen, whither the Lord shall lead you. 28:And there you shall serve other gods, the work of man's hands, wood and stone, which neither see, nor hear, nor eat, nor smell. 29:But if from there you shall seek the Lord your God, you shall find him, if you seek him with all your heart and with all your soul. 30:When you are in tribulation, and all these things are come upon you, even in the latter days, if you turn to the Lord your God, and shall be obedient to his voice. 31:(For the Lord your God is a merciful God;) he will not forsake you, neither destroy you, nor forget the covenant of your fathers which he swore to them. 32:For ask now of the days that are past, which were before you, since the day that God created man upon the earth, and ask from the one side of heaven to the other, whether there has been any such thing as this great thing is, or has been heard like it? 33:Has ever any people heard the voice of God speaking out of the midst of the fire, as you have heard, and lived? 34:Or has God assayed to go and take him a nation from the midst of another nation, by temptations, by signs, and by wonders, and by war, and by a mighty hand, and by a stretched out arm, and by great terrors, according to all that the Lord your God did for you in Egypt before your eyes?

35:To you it was showed, that you might know that the Lord he is God; there is none else beside him. 36:Out of heaven he made you to hear his voice, that he might instruct you, and upon earth he showed you his great fire; and you heard his words out of the midst of the fire. 37:And because he loved your fathers, therefore he chose their seed after them, and brought you out in his sight with his mighty power out of Egypt; 38;To drive out nations from before you greater and mightier than you are, to bring you in, to give you their land for an inheritance, as it is this day. 39:Know therefore this day, and consider it in your heart, that the Lord he is God in heaven above, and upon the earth beneath: there is none else. 40:You shall keep therefore his statutes, and his commandments, which I command you this day, that it may go well with you, and with your children after you, and that you may prolong your days upon the earth, which the Lord your God has given you.

41:Then Moses severed three cities on this side Jordan toward the Sunrise. 42:That the slayer might flee closer, which should kill his neighbor unawares, and did not hate him in times past; and that fleeing to one of these cities he might live: 43:Namely, Bezer in the wilderness, in the plain country, of the Reubenites; and Ramoth in Gilead, of the Gadites; and Golan in Bashan, of the Manassites. 44:And this is the law which Moses set before the children of Israel: 45:These are the testimonies, and the statutes, and the judgments, which Moses spoke to the children of Israel, after they came forth out of Egypt, 46:On this side Jordan, in the valley over against Bethpeor, in the land of Sihon King of the Amorites, who dwelt at Heshbon, whom Moses and the children of Israel struck, after they were come forth out of Egypt: 47:And they possessed his land, and the land of Og King of Bashan, two Kings of the Amorites, which were on this side Jordan toward the rising sun. 48:From Aroer, which is by the bank of the river Arnon, even to mount Sion, which is Hermon, 49:And all the plain on this side Jordan eastward, even to the sea of the plain, under the springs of Pisgah.

5:1: And Moses called all Israel, and said to them, Hear, O Israel, the statutes and judgments which I speak in your ears this day, that you may learn them, and keep them, and do them. 2:The Lord our God made a covenant with us in Horeb. 3:The Lord made not this covenant with our fathers, but with us, even us, who are all of us here alive this day. 4:The Lord talked with you face to face in the mount out of the midst of the fire. 5:(I stood between the Lord and you at that time, to show you the word of the Lord: for you were afraid by reason of the fire, and went not up into the mount;) saying, 6:I am the Lord your God, which brought you out of the land of Egypt, from the house of bondage. 7:You shall not have any false gods before me or mention any other gods names. 8:You shall not make for your self's any graven image, or any likeness of any thing that is in heaven above, or that is in the earth beneath, or that is in the waters beneath the earth: 9:You shall not bow down to them, nor serve them: for I the Lord your God am a Jealous God, visiting the iniquity of the fathers upon the children to the third and fourth generation of them that hate me. 10:And showing mercy to thousands of them that love me and keep my commandments. 11:You shall not take the Name of the Lord your God in vain: for the Lord will not hold him guiltless that takes his name in vain.

12:Keep the sabbath day to sanctify it, as the Lord your God has commanded you. 13:Six days you shall labor, and do all your work: 14:But the seventh day is the Sabbath of the Lord your God: in it you shall not do any work, you, nor your son, nor your daughter, nor your manservant, nor your maidservant, nor your ox, nor your ass, nor any of your cattle, nor your stranger that is within your gates; that your manservant and your maidservant may rest as well as you. 15:And remember that you were a servant in the land of Egypt, and that the Lord your God brought you out thence through a mighty hand and by a stretched out arm: therefore the Lord your God commanded you to keep the sabbath day. 16:Honor your father and your mother, as the Lord your God has commanded you; that your days may be prolonged, and that it may go well with you, in the land which the Lord your God gives you.17:You shall not kill. 18:Neither shall you commit adultery. 19:Neither shall you steal. 20:Neither shall you bear false witness against your neighbor. 21:Neither shall you desire your neighbor's wife, neither shall you covet your neighbor's house, his field, or his manservant, or his maidservant, his ox, or his ass, or any thing that is your neighbor's. 22:These words the Lord spoke to all your assembly in the mount out of the midst of the fire, of the cloud, and of the thick darkness, with a great voice: and he added no more. And he wrote them in two tables of stone, and delivered them to me. 23:And it came to pass, when you heard the voice out of the midst of the darkness, (for the mountain did burn with fire,) that you came near to me, even all the heads of your tribes, and your elders; 24:And you said, Behold, the Lord our God has showed us his glory and his greatness, and we have heard his voice out of the midst of the fire: we have seen this day that God did talk with man, and he lives.

25:Now therefore why should we die? for this great fire will consume us: if we hear the voice of the Lord our God any more, then we shall die. 26:For who is there of all flesh, that has heard the voice of the living God speaking out of the midst of the fire, as we have, and lived? 27:Go you near, and hear all that the Lord our God shall say: and speak you to us all that the Lord our God shall say to you; and we will hear it, and do it. 28:And the Lord heard the voice of your words, when you spoke to me; and the Lord said to me, I have heard the voice of the words of this people, which they have spoken to you: they have well said all that they have spoken.

29:O that there were such an heart in them, that they would fear me, and keep all my commandments always, that it might be well with them, and with their children forever! 30:Go say to them, Get you in to your tents again. 31:But as for you, stand you here by me, and I will speak to you all the commandments, and the statutes, and the judgments, which you shall teach them, that they may do them in the land which I give them to possess it. 32:You shall observe to do therefore as the Lord your God has commanded you: you shall not turn aside to the right hand or to the left. 33:You shall walk in all the ways which the Lord your God has commanded you, that you may live, and it may be well with you, that you may prolong your days in the land which you shall possess.

6:1;Now these are the commandments, the statutes, and the judgments, which the Lord your God commanded to teach you, that you might do them in the land whither you go to possess it. 2: That you might fear the Lord your God, to keep all his statutes and his commandments, which I command you, You, your son, and your son's son, all the days of your life; and that your days may be prolonged. 3:Hear therefore, O Israel, and observe to do it, that it may be well with you, and that you may increase mightily, as the Lord God of your fathers has promised you, in the land that flows with milk and meat.

4:Hear, O Israel: The Lord our God is one Lord, 5;And you shall love the Lord your God with all your heart, and with all your soul, and with all your might. 6:And these words, which I command you this day, shall be in your heart, 7:And you shall teach them diligently to your children, and shall talk of them when you sit in your house, and when you walk by the way, and when you lies down, and when you rise up. 8:And you shall bind them for a sign upon your hand, and they shall be as front between your eyes. 9:And you shall write them upon the posts of your house, and on your gates.

10:And it shall be, when the Lord your God shall have brought you into the land which he swore to your fathers, to Abraham, to Isaac, and to Jacob, to give you great and goodly cities, which you did not build. 11:And houses full of all good things, which you filled not, and wells dug which you did not dig, vineyards and olive trees, which you did not plant; when you shall have eaten and be full. 12:Then beware lest you forget the Lord, which brought you forth out of the land of Egypt, from the house of bondage. 13:You shall fear the Lord your God, and serve him, and shall swear by his name. 14:You shall not go after other gods, of the gods of the people which are round about you.

15:(For the Lord your God is a Jealous God among you) lest the anger of the Lord your God be kindled against you, and destroy you from off the face of the earth. 16:You shall not tempt the Lord your God, as you tempted him in Massah. 17:You shall diligently keep the commandments of the Lord your God, and his testimonies, and his statutes, which he has commanded you. 18:And you shall do that which is right and good in the sight of the Lord: that it may be well with you, and that you may go in and possess the good land which the Lord swore to your fathers,

19:To cast out all your enemies from before you, as the Lord has spoken. 20:And when your son ask you in time to come, saying, What means the testimonies, and the statutes, and the judgments, which the Lord our God has commanded you? 21:Then you shall say to your son, we were Pharaoh's bondmen in Egypt; and the Lord brought us out of Egypt with a mighty hand:

22:And the Lord showed signs and wonders, great and sore, upon Egypt, upon Pharaoh, and upon all his household, before our eyes. 23:And he brought us out from thence, that he might bring us in, to give us the land which he swore to our fathers. 24:And the Lord commanded us to do all these statutes, to fear the Lord our God, for our good always, that he might preserve us alive, as it is at this day. 25:And it shall be our righteousness, if we observe to do all these commandments before the Lord our God, as he has commanded us.

.

7:1: When the Lord your God shall bring you into the land whither you go to possess it, and has cast out many nations before you, the Hittites, and the Girgashites, and the Amorites, and the Canaanites, and the Perizzites, and the Hivites, and the Jebusites, seven nations greater and mightier than you. 2:And when the Lord your God shall deliver them before you; you shall strike them, and utterly destroy them; you shall make no covenant with them, nor show mercy to them. 3:Neither shall you make marriages with them; your daughter you shall not give to his son, nor his daughter shall you take to your son.

4:For they will turn away your son from following me, that they may serve other gods: so will the anger of the Lord be kindled against you, and destroy you suddenly. 5:But this shall you deal with them; you shall destroy their altars, and break down their images, and cut down their groves, and burn their graven images with fire. 6:For you are an holy people to the Lord your God: the Lord your God has chosen you to be a special people to himself, above all people that are upon the face of the earth.

7:The Lord did not set his love upon you, nor choose you, because you were more in number than any people; for you were the fewest of all people. 8:But because the Lord loved you, and because he would keep the oath which he had sworn to your fathers, has the Lord brought you out with a mighty hand, and redeemed you out of the house of bondmen, from the hand of Pharaoh king of Egypt. 9:Know therefore that the Lord your God, he is God, the faithful God, which keeps covenant and mercy with them that love him and keep his commandments to a thousand generations. 10:And repays them that hate him to their face, to destroy them: he will not be slack to him that hates him, he will repay him to his face. 11:You shall therefore keep the commandments, and the statutes, and the judgments, which I command you this day, to do them.

12:Wherefore it shall come to pass, if you hearken to these judgments, and keep, and do them, that the Lord your God shall keep to you the covenant and the mercy which he swore to your fathers. 13:And he will love you, and bless you, and multiply you: he will also bless the fruit of your womb, and the fruit of your land, your corn, and your wine, and your oil, the increase of your kind, and the flocks of your sheep, in the land which he swore to your fathers to give you. 14:You shall be blessed above all people: there shall not be male or female barren among you, or among your cattle.

15:And the Lord will take away from you all sickness, and will put none of the evil diseases of Egypt, which you know, never came upon you; but will lay them upon all them that hate you. 16:And you shall consume all the people which the Lord your God shall deliver you; your eye shall have no pity upon them: neither shall you serve their gods; for that will be a snare to you.

17:If you shall say in your heart, These nations are more than I; how can I dispossess them? 18:You shall not be afraid of them: but shall well remember what the Lord your God did to Pharaoh, and to all Egypt. 19:The great temptations which your eyes saw, and the signs, and the wonders, and the mighty hand, and the stretched out arm, whereby the Lord your God brought you out: so shall the Lord your God do to all the people of whom you are afraid.

20:Moreover the Lord your God will send the hornet among them, until they that are left, and hide themselves from you, be destroyed. 21:You shall not be afraid at the sight of them: for the Lord your God is among you, a mighty God and terrible. 22:And the Lord your God will put out those nations before you by little and little: you may not consume them at once, lest the beasts of the field increase upon you. 23:But the Lord your God shall deliver them to you, and shall destroy them with a mighty destruction,until they be destroyed. 24:And he shall deliver their Kings into your hand, and you shall destroy their name from under heaven: there shall no man be able to stand before you, until you have destroyed them. 25:The graven images of their gods shall you burn with fire: you shall not desire the silver or gold that is on them, nor take it to you, lest you be snared therein, for it is an abomination to the Lord your God. 26:Neither shall you bring an abomination into your house, lest you be a cursed thing like it: but you shall utterly detest it, and you shall utterly abhor it; for it is a cursed thing.

8:1;All the commandments which I command you this day shall you observe to do, that you may live, and multiply, and go in and possess the land which the Lord swore to your fathers. 2:And you shall remember all the way which the Lord your God led you these forty years in the wilderness, to humble you, and to prove you, to know what was in your heart, whether you would keep his commandments, or no. 3:And he humbled you, and suffered you to hunger, and fed you with manna, which you know not, neither did your fathers know; that he might make you know that man doth not live by bread only, but by every word that proceeds out of the mouth of the Lord does man live. 4:Your raiment waxed not old upon you, neither did your foot swell, these forty years. 5:You shall also consider in your heart, that, as a man chastises his son, so the Lord your God chastises you. 6:Therefore you shall keep the commandments of the Lord your God, to walk in his ways, and to fear him. 7:For the Lord your God brings you into a good land, a land of brooks of water, of fountains and depths that spring out of valleys and hills; 8:A land of wheat, and barley, and vines, and fig trees, and pomegranates; a land of oil olive, and meat.

9:A land where in you shall eat bread without scarceness, you shall not lack any thing in it, a land whose stones are iron, and out of whose hills you may dig brass. 10:When you have eaten and are full, then you shall bless the Lord your God for the good land which he has given you. 11:Beware that you forget not the Lord your God, in not keeping his commandments, and his judgments, and his statutes, which I command you this day: 12:Lest when you have eaten and are full, and have built goodly houses, and dwelt therein, 13:And when your herds and your flocks multiply, and your silver and your gold is multiplied, and all that you have is multiplied; 14:Then your heart be lifted up, and you forget the Lord your God, which brought you forth out of the land of Egypt, from the house of bondage.

15:Who led you through that great and terrible wilderness, wherein were fiery serpents, and scorpions, and drought, where there was no water; who brought you forth water out of the rock of flint. 16:Who fed you in the wilderness with manna, which your fathers knew not, that he might humble you, and that he might prove you, to do you good at your latter end. 17:And you say in your heart, My power and the might of mine hand has gotten me this wealth. 18:But you shall remember the Lord your God: for it is he that gives you power to get wealth, that he may establish his covenant which he swore to your fathers, as it is this day. 19:And it shall be, if you do at all forget the Lord your God, and walk after other gods, and serve them, and worship them, I testify against you this day that you shall surely perish. 20:As the nations which the Lord destroys before your face, so shall you perish; because you would not be obedient to the voice of the Lord your God.

9:1: Hear, O Israel: You are to pass over Jordan this day, to go in to possess nations greater and mightier than yourself, cities great and fenced up to heaven. 2:A people great and tall, the children of the Anakims,whom you know, and of whom you have heard say, Who can stand before the children of Anakims! 3:Understand therefore this day, that the Lord your God is he which go's over before you; as a consuming fire he shall destroy them, and he shall bring them down before your face: so shall you drive them out, and destroy them quickly, as the Lord has said to you. 4:Speak not you in your heart, after that the Lord your God has cast them out from before you, saying; For my righteousness the Lord has brought me in to possess this land: but for the wickedness of these nations the Lord does drive them out from before you. 5:Not for your righteousness, or for the uprightness of your heart, does you go to possess their land: but for the wickedness of these nations the Lord your God doth drive them out from before you, and that he may perform the word which the Lord swore to your fathers, Abraham, Isaac, and Jacob. 6:Understand therefore, that the Lord your God gives you not this good land to possess it for your righteousness; for you are a stiff necked people. 7:Remember, and forget not, how you provoked the Lord your God to wrath in the wilderness: from the day that you did depart out of the land of Egypt, until you came to this place, you have been rebellious against the Lord. 8:Also in Horeb you provoked the Lord to wrath, so that the Lord was angry with you to have destroyed you.

9:When I was gone up into the mount to receive the tables of stone, even the tables of the covenant which the Lord made with you, then I abode in the mount forty days and forty nights, I neither did eat bread nor drink water. 10:And the Lord delivered to me two tables of stone written with the finger of God; and on them was written according to all the words, which the Lord spoke with you in the mount out of the midst of the fire in the day of the assembly. 11:And it came to pass at the end of forty days and forty nights, that the Lord gave me the two tables of stone, even the tables of the covenant. 12:And the Lord said to me, Arise, get you down quickly from hence; for your people which you have brought forth out of Egypt have corrupted themselves, they are quickly turned aside out of the way which I commanded them; they have made them a molten image. 13:Furthermore the Lord spoke to me, saying, I have seen this people, and, behold, it is a stiff necked people: 14:Let me alone, that I may destroy them, and blot out their name from under heaven: and I will make of you a nation mightier and greater than they.

15:So I turned and came down from the mount, and the mount burned with fire: and the two tables of the covenant were in my two hands. 16:And I looked, and, behold, you had sinned against the Lord your God, and had made you a molten calf: you had turned aside quickly out of the way which the Lord had commanded you. 17:And I took the two tables, and cast them out of my two hands, and brake them before your eyes. 18:And I fell down before the Lord, as at the first, forty days and forty nights: I did neither eat bread, nor drink water, because of all your sins which you sinned, in doing wickedly in the sight of the Lord, to provoke him to anger. 19:For I was afraid of the anger and hot displeasure, wherewith the Lord was wroth against you to destroy you. But the Lord listened to me at that time also. 20:And the Lord was very angry with Aaron to have destroyed him: and I prayed for Aaron also the same time. 21:And I took your sin, the calf which you had made, and burnt it with fire, and stamped it, and ground it very small, even until it was as small as dust: and I cast the dust thereof into the brook that descended out of the mount.

22:And at Taberah, and at Massah, and at Kibroth-hattaavah, you provoked the Lord to wrath. 23:Likewise when the Lord sent you from Kadeshbarnea, saying, Go up and possess the land which I have given you; then you rebelled against the commandment of the Lord your God, and you believed him not, nor hearkened to his voice. 24:You have been rebellious against the Lord from the day that I knew you. 25:This I fell down before the Lord forty days and forty nights, as I fell down at the first; because the Lord had said he would destroy you. 26:I prayed therefore to the Lord, and said, O'Lord GOD, destroy not your people and your inheritance, which you have redeemed through your greatness, which you have brought forth out of Egypt with a mighty hand. 27:Remember your servants, Abraham, Isaac, and Jacob; look not to the stubbornness of this people, nor to their wickedness, nor to their sin. 28:Lest the land where you brought us out saying, Because the Lord was not able to bring them into the land which he promised them, and because he hated them, he has brought them out to slay them in the wilderness. 29:Yet they are your people and your inheritance, which you brought out by your mighty power and by your stretched out arm.

10:1; At that time the Lord said to me, Hew you two tables of stone like to the first, and come up to me into the mount, and make you an ark of wood. 2:And I will write on the tables the words that were in the first tables which you broke, and you shall put them in the ark. 3:And I made an ark of Shittim wood, and hewed two tables of stone like to the first, and went up into the mount, having the two tables in mine hand. 4:And he wrote on the tables, according to the first writing, the ten commandments, which the Lord spoke to you from the mount, out of the midst of the fire in the day of the assembly: and the Lord gave them to me. 5:And I turned myself and came down from the mount, and put the tables in the ark which I had made; and there they be, as the Lord commanded me. 6:And the children of Israel took their journey from Beeroth of the children of Jaakan to Mosera: there Aaron died, and there he was buried; and Eleazar his son ministered in the priest's office in his stead. 7:From thence they journeyed to Gudgodah; and from Gudgodah to Jotbath, a land of rivers of waters. 8:At that time the Lord separated the tribe of Levi, to bear the ark of the covenant of the Lord, to stand before the Lord to minister to him, and to bless in his name, to this day. 9:Wherefore Levi has no part nor inheritance with his brethren; the Lord is his inheritance, according as the Lord your God promised him. 10:And I stayed in the mount, according to the first time, forty days and forty nights; and the Lord hearkened to me at that time also, and the Lord would not destroy you. 11:And the Lord said to me, Arise, take your journey before the people, that they may go in and possess the land, which I swore to their fathers to give to them.

12:And now, Israel, what does the Lord your God require of you, but to fear the Lord your God, to walk in all his ways, and to love him, and to serve the Lord your God with all your heart and with all your soul. 13:To keep the commandments of the Lord, and his statutes, which I command you this day for your good? 14:Behold, the heaven and the heaven of heavens is the Lord your God's, the earth also, with all that therein is. 15:Only the Lord had a delight in your fathers to love them, and he chose their seed after them, even you above all people, as it is this day. 16:Circumcise therefore the foreskin of your heart, and be no more stiff necked. 17:For the Lord your God, is the God of gods, and Lord of lords, a great God, a mighty, and a terrible, which regards not a persons, nor takes reward: 18:He does execute the judgment of the fatherless and widow, and loves the stranger, in giving him food and raiment.

19:Love you therefore the stranger: for you were strangers in the land of Egypt.
20:You shall fear the Lord your God; him shall you serve, and to him shall you
cleave, and swear by his name. 21:He is your praise, and he is your God, that has
done for you these great and terrible things, which your eyes have seen. 22:Your
fathers went down into Egypt with threescore and ten persons; and now the Lord
your God has made you as the stars of heaven for multitude.

11:1;Therefore you shall love the Lord your God, and keep his charge, and his
statutes, and his judgments, and his commandments, always. 2:And know you this
day: for I speak not with your children which have not known, and which have not
seen the chastisement of the Lord your God, his greatness, his mighty hand, and his
stretched out arm, 3:And his miracles, and his acts, which he did in the midst of
Egypt to Pharaoh the king of Egypt, and to all his land. 4:And what he did to the
army of Egypt, to their horses, and to their chariots; how he made the water of the
Red sea to overflow them as they pursued after you, and how the Lord has
destroyed them to this day; 5:And what he did to you in the wilderness, until you
came into this place; 6:And what he did to Dathan and Abiram, the sons of Eliab,
the son of Reuben: how the earth opened her mouth, and swallowed them up, and
their households, and their tents, and all the substance that was in their possession,
in the midst of all Israel: 7:But your eyes have seen all the great acts of the Lord
which he did.

8:Therefore shall you keep all the commandments which I command you this day,
that you may be strong, and go in and possess the land, whither you go to possess it;
9:And that you may prolong your days in the land, which the Lord swore to your
fathers to give to them and to their seed, a land that flows with milk and meat.
10:For the land, when you go in to possess it, is not as the land of Egypt, from
whence you came out, where you sowed your seed, and watered it with your foot, as
a garden of herbs: 11:But the land, whither you go to possess it, is a land of hills and
valleys, and drink water of the rain of heaven: 12:A land which the Lord your God
cares for: the eyes of the Lord your God, are always upon it, from the beginning of
the year even to the end of the year. 13:And it shall come to pass, if you shall
hearken diligently to my commandments which I command you this day, to love the
Lord your God, and to serve him with all your heart and with all your soul.

14:That I will give you the rain of your land in his due season, the first rain and the
latter rain, that you may gather in your corn, and your wine, and your oil. 15:And I
will send grass in your fields for your cattle, that you may eat and be full. 16:Take
heed to yourselves, that your heart be not deceived, and you turn aside, and serve
other gods, and worship them; 17:And then the Lord's wrath be kindled against you,
and he shut up the heaven, that there be no rain, and that the land yield not her fruit;
and lest you perish quickly from off the good land which the Lord given you.
18:Therefore shall you lay up these my words in your heart and in your soul, and
bind them for a sign upon your hand, that they may be as a pendant between your
eyes. 19:And you shall teach them your children, speaking of them when you sit
down in your house, and when you walk by the way, when you lie down, and when
you rise up. 20:And you shall write them upon the door posts of your house, and
upon your gates:

21:That your days may be multiplied, and the days of your children, in the land
which the Lord swore to your fathers to give them, as the days of heaven upon the
earth. 22:For if you shall diligently keep all these commandments which I command
you, to do them, to love the Lord your God, to walk in all his ways, and to cleave to
him. 23:Then will the Lord drive out all these nations from before you, and you
shall possess greater nations and mightier than yourselves. 24:Every place whereon
the soles of your feet shall tread shall be yours: from the wilderness and Lebanon,
from the river, the river Euphrates, even to the uttermost sea shall your coast be.
25:There shall no man be able to stand before you: for the Lord your God shall lay
the fear of you and the dread of you upon all the land that you shall tread upon, as
he has said to you. 26:Behold, I set before you this day a blessing and a curse; 27:A
blessing, if you obey the commandments of the Lord your God, which I command
you this day. 28;And a curse, if you will not obey the commandments of the Lord
your God, but turn aside out of the way which I command you this day, to go after
other gods, which you have not known. 29:And it shall come to pass, when the Lord
your God has brought you in to the land where you go to possess it, that you shall
put the blessing upon mount Gerizim, and the curse upon mount Ebal. 30:Are they
not on the other side Jordan, by the way where the sun go down, in the land of the
Canaanites, which dwell in the country over against Gilgal, beside the plains of
Moreh? 31:For you shall pass over Jordan to go in to possess the land which the
Lord your God gives you, and you shall possess it, and dwell therein. 32:And you
shall observe to do all the statutes and judgments which I set before you this day.

12:1: These are the statutes and judgments, which you shall observe to do in the
land, which the Lord God of your fathers gave you to possess it, all the days that
you live upon the earth. 2:You shall utterly destroy all the places, wherein the
nations which you shall possess served their gods, upon the high mountains, and
upon the hills, and under every green tree. 3:And you shall overthrow their altars,
and break their pillars, and burn their groves with fire; and you shall hew down the
graven images of their gods,and destroy the names of them out of that place. 4:You
shall not do so the Lord your God. 5:But to the place which the Lord your God shall
choose out of all your tribes to put his name there, even to his habitation shall you
seek, and closer you shall come. 6:And nearer you shall bring your burnt offerings,
and your sacrifices, and your tithes, and heave offerings of your hand, and your
vows, and your freewill offerings, and the first lings of your herds and of your
flocks. 7:And there you shall eat before the Lord your God, and you shall rejoice in
all that you put your hand to, you and your households, wherein the Lord your God
has blessed you. 8:You shall not do after all the things that we do here this day,
every man whatsoever is right in his own eyes.

9:For you are not as yet come to the rest and to the inheritance, which the Lord your
God gives you. 10:But when you go over Jordan, and dwell in the land which the
Lord your God gives you to inherit, and when he gives you rest from all your
enemies round about, so that you dwell in safety. 11:Then there shall be a place
which the Lord your God shall choose to cause his name to dwell there; and closer
shall you bring all that I command you; your burnt offerings, and your sacrifices,
your tithes, and the heave offering of your hand, and all your choice vows which
you vow to the Lord:

12:And you shall rejoice before the Lord your God, you, and your sons, and your
daughters, and your menservants, and your maidservants, and the Levite that is
within your gates; for as much as he has no part nor inheritance with you. 13:Take
heed to yourself that you offer not your burnt offerings in every place that you see.
14:But in the place which the Lord shall choose in one of your tribes, there you
shall offer your burnt offerings, and there you shall do all that I command you.
15:Not with standing you may kill and eat flesh in all your gates, what soever your
soul lust after, according to the blessing of the Lord your God which he has given
you: the unclean and the clean may eat thereof, as of the roebuck, and as of the hart.
16:Only you shall not eat the blood; you shall pour it upon the earth as water.
17:You may not eat within your gates the tithe of your corn, or of your wine, or of
your oil, or the first lings of your herds or of your flock, nor any of your vows
which you vowed, nor your freewill offerings, or heave offering of your hand:

18:But you must eat them before the Lord your God in the place which the Lord
your God shall choose, you, and your son, and your daughter, and your manservant,
and your maid servant, and the Levite that is within your gates: and you shall rejoice
before the Lord your God in all that you put your hands to. 19:Take heed to yourself
that you forsake not the Levite as long as you livest upon the earth. 20:When the
Lord your God shall enlarge your border, as he has promised you, and you shall say,
I will eat flesh, because your heart longs to eat flesh; you may eat flesh, what so
ever your heart longs for. 21:If the place which the Lord your God has chosen to put
his name,there be too far from you, then you shall kill of your herd and of your
flock, which the Lord has given you, as I have commanded you, and you shall eat in
your gates whatsoever your soul lust after. 22:Even as the roebuck and the hart is
eaten, so you shall eat them: the unclean and the clean shall eat of them alike.
23:Only be sure that you eat not the blood: for the blood is the life; and you may not
eat the life with the flesh. 24:You shall not eat it; you shall pour it upon the earth as
water. 25:You shall not eat it; that it may go well with you, and with your children
after you when you shall do that which is right in the sight of the Lord.

26:Only your holy things which you have, and your vows, you shall take, and go to
the place which the Lord shall choose. 27:And you shall offer your burnt offerings,
the flesh and the blood, upon the altar of the Lord your God: and the blood of your
sacrifices shall be poured out upon the altar of the Lord your God, and you shall eat
the flesh. 28:Observe and hear all these words which I command you, that it may go
well with you, and with your children after you for ever, when you do that which is
good and right in the sight of the Lord your God.

29:When the Lord your God shall cut off the nations from before you, where ever
you go to possess them, and you succeed them, and dwell in their land. 30:Take
heed to yourself that you be not snared by following them, after that they be
destroyed from before you; and that you inquire not after their gods, saying, How
did these nations serve their gods? even so will I do likewise. 31:You shall not do so
to the Lord your God: for every abomination to the Lord, which he hates, have they
done to their gods; for even their sons and their daughters they have burnt in the fire
to their gods. 32:What thing soever I command you, observe to do it: you shall not
add thereto, nor diminish from it.

13:1: If there arise among you a prophet, or a dreamer of dreams, and gives you a sign or a wonder. 2:And the sign or the wonder come to pass, where of he speaks to you, saying, Let us go after other gods, which you have not known, and let us serve them. 3:You shall not listen to the words of that prophet, or that dreamer of dreams: for the Lord your God is watching you, to know whether you love the Lord your God with all your heart and with all your soul. 4:You shall walk after the Lord your God, and fear him, and keep his commandments, and obey his voice, and you shall serve him, and cleave to him. 5:And that prophet, or that dreamer of dreams, shall be put to death; because he has spoken to turn you away from the Lord your God, which brought you out of the land of Egypt, and redeemed you out of the house of bondage, to thrust you out of the way which the Lord your God commanded you to walk in. So shall you put the evil away from the midst of you. 6:If your brother, the son of your mother, or your son, or your daughter, or the wife of your bosom, or your friend, which is as your own soul, entice you secretly, saying, Let us go and serve other gods, which you have not known, you, nor your fathers.

7:Namely of the gods of the people which are round about you, near to you, or far off from you, from the one end of the earth even to the other end of the earth. 8:You shall not consent to him, nor hearken to him; neither shall your eye pity him, neither shall you spare, neither shall you conceal him: 9:But you shall surely kill him; your hand shall be first upon him to put him to death, and after wards the hand of all the people. 10:And you shall stone him with stones, that he die; because he has sought to thrust you away from the Lord your God, which brought you out of the land of Egypt, from the house of bondage. 11:And all Israel shall hear, and fear, and shall do no more any such wickedness as this is among you. 12:If you shall hear say in one of your cities, which the Lord your God has given you to dwell there, saying. 13:Certain men, the children of Belial, are gone out from among you, and have withdrawn the inhabitants of their city, saying, Let us go and serve other gods, which you have not known; 14:Then shall you inquire, and make search, and ask diligently; and, behold, if it be true, and the thing certain, that such abomination is wrought among you;

15:You shall surely strike the inhabitants of that city with the edge of the sword, destroying it utterly, and all that is therein, and the cattle thereof, with the edge of the sword. 16:And you shall gather all the spoil of it into the midst of the street thereof, and shall burn with fire the city, and all the spoil thereof every whit, for the Lord your God: and it shall be an heap for ever; it shall not be built again. 17:And you shall d nothing of the cursed thing to your hand: that the Lord may turn from the fierceness of his anger, and show you mercy, and have compassion upon you, and multiply you, as he has sworn to your fathers; 18:When you shall hearken to the voice of the Lord your God, to keep all his commandments which I command you this day, to do that which is right in the eyes of the Lord your God.

14:1: You are the children of the Lord your God: you shall not cut yourselves, nor make any baldness between your eyes for the dead. 2:For you are an holy people to the Lord your God, and the Lord has chosen you to be a peculiar people to himself, above all the nations that are upon the earth. 3:You shall not eat any abominable thing. 4:These are the beasts which you shall eat: the ox, the sheep, and the goat,

5:The hart, and the roebuck, and the fallow deer, and the wild goat, and the pygmy, and the wild ox, and the chamois. 6:And every beast that parted the hoof, and cloven the cleft into two claws, and chews the cud among the beasts, that you shall eat. 7:Nevertheless these you shall not eat of them that chew the cud, or of them that divide the cloven hoof; as the camel, and the hare, and the coney: for they chew the cud, but divide not the hoof; therefore they are unclean to you. 8;And the swine, because it divided the hoof, yet chews not the cud, it is unclean to you: you shall not eat of their flesh, nor touch their dead carcase. 9:These you shall eat of all that are in the waters: all that have fins and scales shall you eat. 10:And whatsoever has not fins and scales you may not eat; it is unclean to you. 11:Of all clean birds you shall eat. 12:But these are they of which you shall not eat: the eagle, and the saxifrage, and the osprey, 13:And the glide, and the kite, and the vulture after his kind, 14:And every raven after his kind, 15:And the owl, and the night hawk, and the cuckoo, and the hawk after his kind.

16:The little owl, and the great owl, and the swan, 17:And the pelican, and the gear eagle, and the cormorant, 18:And the stork, and the heron after her kind, and the lapwing, and the bat. 19:And every creeping thing that fliest is unclean to you: they shall not be eaten. 20:But of all clean fowls you may eat. 21;You shall not eat of any thing that dies of itself: you shall give it to the stranger that is in your gates, that he may eat it; or you may sell it to an alien: for you are an holy people to the Lord your God. You shall not cook a kid in his mother's milk. 22:You shall truly tithe all the increase of your seed, that the field brings forth year by year. 23:And you shall eat before the Lord your God, in the place which he shall choose to place his name there, the tithe of your corn, of your wine, and of your oil, and the yearlings of your herds and of your flocks; that you may learn to fear the Lord your God always. 24:And if the way be too long for you, so that you are not able to carry it; or if the place be too far from you, which the Lord your God shall choose to set his name there, when the Lord your God has blessed you.

25:Then shall you turn t into money, and bind up the money in your hand, and shall go to the place which the Lord your God shall choose. 26:And you shall bestow that money for whatsoever your soul lust after, for oxen, or for sheep, or for wine, or for strong drink, or for whatsoever your soul desires and you shall eat there before the Lord your God, and you shall rejoice, you, and your household, 27:And the Levite that is within your gates; you shall not forsake him; for he has no part nor inheritance with you. 28:At the end of three years you shall bring forth all the tithe of your increase the same year, and shall lay it up within your gates: 29:And the Levite, (because he has no part nor inheritance with you,) and the stranger, and the fatherless, and the widow, which are within your gates, shall come, and shall eat and be satisfied; that the Lord your God may bless you in all the work of your hand which you does.

15:1: At the end of every seven years you shall make a release. 2:And this is the manner of the release: Every creditor that lends out to his neighbor shall release it, he shall not exact it of his neighbor, or of his brother; because it is called the Lord's release. 3:Of a foreigner you may exact it again; but that which is your with your brother your hand shall release. 4:Save when there shall be no poor among you;

for the Lord shall greatly bless you in the land which the Lord your God gives you for an inheritance to possess it. 5:Only if you carefully listen to the voice of the Lord your God, to observe to do all these commandments which I command you this day. 6:For the Lord your God blesses you, as he promised you: and you shall lend to many nations, but you shall not borrow; and you shall reign over many nations, but they shall not reign over you.

7:If there be among you a poor man of one of your brethren within any of your gates in your land which the Lord your God given you, you shall not harden your heart, nor shut your hand from your poor brother. 8:But you shall open your hand wide to him, and shall surely lend him sufficient for his need, in that which he wants. 9:Beware that there be not a thought in your wicked heart, saying, The seventh year, the year of release, is at hand; and your eye be evil against your poor brother, and you gives him nothing; and he cry to the Lord against you, and it be sin to you. 10:You shall surely give him, and your heart shall not be grieved when you give to him: because that for this thing the Lord your God shall bless you in all your works, and in all that you put your hand into. 11:For the poor shall never cease out of the land: therefore I command you, saying; You shall open your hand wide to your brother, to your poor, and to your needy, in your land.

12:And if your brother, is an Hebrew man, or à Hebrew woman, be sold to you, and serve you six years; then in the seventh year you shall let him go free from you. 13:And when you send him out free from you, you shall not let him go away empty. 14:You shall furnish him liberally out of your flock, and out of your floor, and out of your wine press:of that where with the Lord your God has blessed you, you shall give to him. 15:And you shall remember that you were a bondman in the land of Egypt, and the Lord your God redeemed you: therefore I command you this thing to day. 16:And it shall be, if he say to you, I will not go away from you; because he loved you and your house, because he is well with you. 17:Then you shall take an maul, and thrust it through his ear to the door, and he shall be your servant for ever. And also to your maidservant you shall do likewise.

18:It shall not seem hard to you, when you sends him away free from you; for he has been worth a double hired servant to you, in serving you six years: and the Lord your God shall bless you in all that you do. 19:All the yearling males that come of your herd and of your flock you shall sanctify to the Lord your God: you shall do no work with the yearling of your your bullock, nor shear the yearling of y our sheep.

20:You shall eat it before the Lord your God year by year in the place which the Lord shall choose, you and your household. 21:And if there be any blemish therein, as if it be lame, or blind, or have any ill blemish, you shall not sacrifice it to the Lord your God. 22:You shall eat it within your gates: the unclean and the clean person shall eat it alike, as the roebuck, and as the hart. 23:Only you shall not eat the blood thereof; you shall pour it upon the ground as water.

16:1;Observe the month of Abib, and keep the passover to the Lord your God: for in the month of Abib the Lord your God brought you forth out of Egypt by night. 2:You shall therefore sacrifice the passover to the Lord your God, of the flock and the herd, in the place which the Lord shall choose to place his name there. 3:You shall eat no leavened bread with it, seven days shall you eat unleavened bread therewith, even the bread of affliction; for you came forth out of the land of Egypt in haste: that you may remember the day when you came forth out of the land of Egypt all the days of your life. 4:And there shall be no leavened bread seen with you in all your coast seven days; neither shall there any thing of the flesh, which you sacrificed the first day at even, remain all night until the morning. 5:You may not sacrifice the passover within any of your gates, which the Lord your God given you. 6:But at the place which the Lord your God shall choose to place his name in, there you shall sacrifice the passover at even, at the going down of the sun, at the season that you came forth out of Egypt.

7:And you shall roast and eat it in the place which the Lord your God shall choose: and you shall turn in the morning, and go to your tents. 8:Six days you shall eat unleavened bread: and on the seventh day shall be a solemn assembly to the Lord your God: you shall do no work there in. 9:Seven weeks shall you number to you: begin to number the seven weeks from such time as you begin to put the sickle to the corn. 10:And you shall keep the feast of weeks to the Lord your God with a tribute of a freewill offering of your hand, which you shall give to the Lord your God, according as the Lord your God has blessed you. 11:And you shall rejoice before the Lord your God, you, and your son, and your daughter, and your manservant, and your maidservant, and the Levite that is within your gates, and the stranger, and the fatherless, and the widow, that are among you, in the place which the Lord your God has chosen to place his name there.

12:And you shall remember that you were a bondman in Egypt: and you shall observe and do these statutes. 13:You shall observe the feast of tabernacles seven days, after that you have gathered in your corn and your wine. 14:And you shall rejoice in your feast, you, and your son, and your daughter, and your manservant, and your maidservant, and the Levite, the stranger, and the fatherless, and the widow, that are within your gates. 15:Seven days shall you keep a solemn feast to the Lord your God in the place which the Lord shall choose: because the Lord your God shall bless you in all your increase, and in all the works of your hands, therefore you shall surely rejoice. 16:Three times in a year shall all your males appear before the Lord your God in the place which he shall choose; in the feast of unleavened bread, and in the feast of weeks, and in the feast of tabernacles: and they shall not appear before the Lord empty:

17:Every man shall give as he is able, according to the blessing of the Lord your God which he has given you. 18:Judges and officers shall you make you in all your gates, which the Lord your God gives you, throughout your tribes: and they shall judge the people with just judgment. 19:You shall not wrest judgment; you shall not respect persons, neither take a gift: for a gift doth blind the eyes of the wise, and pervert the words of the righteous. 20:That which is altogether just shall you follow, that you may live, and inherit the land which the Lord your God gives you. 21:You shall not plant you a grove of any trees near to the altar of the Lord your God, which you shall make you. 22: Neither shall you set you up any image; which the Lord your God hates.

17:1: You shall not sacrifice to the Lord your God any bullock, or sheep, wherein is blemish, or any defects: for that is an abomination to the Lord your God. 2:If there be found among you, within any of your gates which the Lord your God gives you, man or woman, that has wrought wickedness in the sight of the Lord your God, in transgressing his covenant. 3:And has gone and served other gods, and worshiped them, either the sun, or moon, or any of the host of heaven, which I have not commanded; 4:And it be told you, and you have heard of it, and inquired diligently, and, behold, it to true and the thing certain, that such abomination is wrought in Israel. 5:Then shall you bring forth that man or that woman, which have committed that wicked thing, to your gates, even that man or that woman, and shall stone them with stones, till they die. 6:At the mouth of two witnesses, or three witnesses, shall he that is worthy of death be put to death; but at the mouth of one witness he shall not be put to death. 7:The hands of the witnesses shall be first upon him to put him to death, and afterward the hands of all the people. So you shall put the evil away from among you. 8:If there arise a matter too hard for you in judgment, between blood and blood, between plea and plea, and between stroke and stroke, being matters of controversy within your gates: then shall you arise, and get you up into the place which the Lord your God shall choose. 9:And you shall come to the priests the Levites, and to the judge that shall be in those days, and inquire; and they shall show you the sentence of judgment:

10:And you shall do according to the sentence, which they of that place which the Lord shall choose shall show you; and you shall observe to do according to all that they inform you. 11:According to the sentence of the law which they shall teach you, and according to the judgment which they shall tell you, you shall do: you shall not decline from the sentence which they shall show you to the right hand, nor to the left. 12:And the man that will do presumptuously, and will not hearken to the priest that standing to minister there before the Lord your God, or to the judge, even that man shall die: and you shall put away the evil from Israel. 13:And all the people shall hear, and fear, and do no more presumptuously.

14:When you are come to the land which the Lord your God gives you, and shall possess it, and shall dwell therein, and shall say, I will set a king over me, like as all the nations that are about me. 15:You shall in any wise set him King over you, whom the Lord your God shall choose: one from among your brethren shall you set King over you, you may not set a stranger over you, which is not your brother. 16;But he shall not multiply horses to himself, nor cause the people to return to Egypt, to the end that he should multiply horses: for as much as the Lord has said to you, You shall henceforth return no more that way. 17:Neither shall he multiply wives to himself, that his heart turn not away: neither shall he greatly multiply to himself silver and gold. 18:And it shall be, when he sitteth upon the throne of his kingdom, that he shall write him a copy of this law in a book, out of that which is before the priests the Levites. 19;And it shall be with him, and he shall read therein all the days of his life: that he may learn to fear the Lord his God, to keep all the words of this law and these statutes, to do them: 20:That his heart be not lifted up above his brethren, and that he turn not aside from the commandment, to the right hand, or to the left: to the end that he may prolong his days in his kingdom, he and his children, in the midst of Israel.

18:1;The priests the Levites, and all the tribe of Levi, shall have no part nor inheritance with Israel: they shall eat the offerings of the Lord made by fire, and his inheritance. 2:Therefore shall they have no inheritance among their brethren: the Lord is their inheritance, as he has said to them. 3:And this shall be the priest's due from the people, from them that offer a sacrifice, whether it be ox or sheep; and they shall give to the priest the shoulder, and the two cheeks, and the maw.4;The first fruit also of your corn, of your wine, and of your oil, and the first of the fleece of your sheep, shall you give him. 5:For the Lord your God has chosen him out of all your tribes, to stand to minister in the name of the Lord, him and his sons for ever. 6:And if a Levite come from any of your gates out of all Israel, where he sojourned, and come with all the desire of his mind to the place which the Lord shall choose;

7:Then he shall minister in the name of the Lord his God, as all his brethren the Levites do, which stand there before the Lord. 8:They shall have like portions to eat, beside that which comes of the sale of his patrimony. 9:When you are come into the land which the Lord your God gives you, you shall not learn to do after the abominations of those nations. 10:There shall not be found among you anyone that makes his son or his daughter to pass through the fire,or that uses divination, or an observer of times, or an enchanter, or a witch, 11:Or a charmer, or canceler with familiar spirits, or a wizard, or a necromancer. 12:For all that do these things are an abomination to the Lord, and because of these abominations the Lord your God doth drive them out from before you. 13:You shall be perfect with the Lord your God. 14:For these nations, which you shall possess, hearkened to observers of times, and to diviners: but as for you, the Lord your God has not suffered you so to do.

15:The Lord your God will raise up to you a Prophet from the midst of you, of your brethren, like to me; to him you shall hearken; 16:According to all that you desire of the Lord your God in Horeb in the day of the assembly, saying, Let me not hear again the voice of the Lord my God, neither let me see this great fire any more, that I die not. 17:And the Lord said to me, They have well spoken that which they have spoken. 18:I will raise them up a Prophet from among their brethren, like to you, and will put my words in his mouth; and he shall speak to them all that I shall command him. 19:And it shall come to pass, that whosoever will not hearken to my words, which he shall speak in my name, I will require it of him. 20:But the prophet, which shall presume to speak a word in my name, which I have not commanded him to speak, or that shall speak in the name of other gods, even that prophet shall die. 21:And if you say in your heart, How shall we know the word which the Lord has not spoken? 22:When a prophet speaks in the name of the Lord, if the thing follow not, nor come to pass, that is the thing which the Lord has not spoken, but the prophet has spoken it presumptuously: you shall not be afraid of him.

19:1: When the Lord your God has cut off the nations, whose land the Lord your God gives you, and you succeed them, and dwell in their cities, and in their houses. 2:You shall separate three cities for you in the midst of your land, which the Lord your God gives you to possess it. 3:You shall prepare you a way, and divide the coasts of your land which the Lord your God gives you to inherit, into three parts, that every slayer may flee closer. 4:And this is the case of the slayer, which shall flee closer, that he may live. Who so kills his neighbor ignorantly, whom he hated not in time past; 5:As when a man go's into the wood with his neighbor to hew wood, and his hand fetches a stroke with the ax to cut down the tree, and the head slips from the helve, and lands upon his neighbor, that he die; he shall flee to one of those cities, and live. 6:Lest the avenger of the blood pursue the slayer, while his heart is hot, and overtake him, because the way is long, and slay him; whereas he was not worthy of death, inasmuch as he hated him not in time past. 7:Wherefore I command you, saying: You shall separate three cities for you. 8:And if the Lord your God enlarge your coast, as he has sworn to your fathers, and give you all the land which he promised to give to your fathers.

9:If you shall keep all these commandments to do them, which I command you this day, to love the Lord your God, and to walk ever in his ways; then shall you add three cities more for you, beside these three. 10:That innocent blood be not shed in your land, which the Lord your God gives you for an inheritance, and so blood be upon you. 11:But if any man hate his neighbor, and lie in wait for him, and rise up against him, and struck him mortally that he die, and flees into one of these cities. 12;Then the elders of his city shall send and fetch him thence, and deliver him into the hand of the avenger of blood, that he may die. 13:Your eye shall not pity him, but you shall put away the guilt of innocent blood from Israel, that it may go well with you. 14:You shall not remove your neighbor's landmark, which they of old time have set in your inheritance, which you shall inherit in the land that the Lord your God gives you to possess it.

15:One witness shall not rise up against a man for any iniquity, or for any sin, in any sin that he sin's: at the mouth of two witnesses, or at the mouth of three witnesses, shall the matter be established. 16:If a false witness rise up against any man to testify against him that which is wrong. 17:Then both the men, between whom the controversy is, shall stand before the Lord, before the priests and the judges, which shall be in those days; 18:And the judges shall make diligent inquisition: and, behold, if the witness be a false witness, and has testified falsely against his brother. 19:Then shall you do to him, as he had thought to have done to his brother so shall you put the evil away from among you. 20:And those which remain shall hear, and fear, and shall henceforth commit no more any such evil among you. 21:And your eye shall not pity; but life shall go for life, eye for eye, tooth for tooth, hand for hand, foot for foot.

20:1: When you go's out to battle against your enemies, and see's horses, and chariots, and a people more than you, be not afraid of them: for the Lord your God is with you, which brought you up out of the land of Egypt. 2:And it shall be, when you are come near to the battle, that the priest shall approach and speak to the people. 3;And shall say to them, Hear, O Israel, you approach this day to battle against your enemies: let not your hearts faint, fear not, and do not tremble, neither be you terrified because of them. 4:For the Lord your God is he that go's with you, to fight for you against your enemies, to save you. 5:And the officers shall speak to the people, saying, What man is there that has built a new house, and has not dedicated it? let him go and return to his house, lest he die in the battle, and another man dedicate it. 6:And what man is he that has planted a vineyard, and has not yet eaten of it? Let him also go and return to his house, lest he die in the battle, and another man eat of it. 7:And what man is there that has betrothed a wife, and has not taken her? let him go and return to his house, lest he die in the battle, and another man take her. 8:And the officers shall speak further to the people, and they shall say, What man is there that is fearful and fainthearted? let him go and return to his house, lest his brethren heart faint as well as his heart. 9:And it shall be, when the officers have made an end of speaking to the people, that they shall make captains of the armies to lead the people. 10:When you comes near to a city to fight against it, then proclaim peace to it. 11:And it shall be, if it make you answer of peace, and open to you, then it shall be, that all the people that is found therein shall be tributaries to you, and they shall serve you. 12:And if it will make no peace with you, but will make war against you, then you shall besiege it. 13:And when the Lord your God has delivered it into your hands, you shall strike every male thereof with the edge of the sword.

14:But the women, and the little ones, and the cattle, and all that is in the city, even all the spoil thereof, shall you take to yourself; and you shall eat the spoil of your enemies, which the Lord your God has given you. 15:This shall you do to all the cities which are very far off from you, which are not of the cities of these nations. 16:But of the cities of these people, which the Lord your God doth give you for an inheritance, you shall save alive nothing that breathes: 17:But you shall utterly destroy them; namely, the Hittites, and the Amorites, the Canaanites, and the Perizzites, the Hivites, and the Jebusites; as the Lord your God has commanded you. 18:That they teach you not to do after all their abominations, which they have done to their gods; so should you sin against the Lord your God.19:When you shall besiege a city a long time, in making war against it to take it, you shall not destroy the trees thereof by forcing an ax against them: for you may eat of them, and you shall not cut them down (for the tree of the field is man's life)to employ them in the siege: 20:Only the trees which you know that they be not trees for meat, you shall destroy and cut them down; and you shall build bulwarks against the city that make war with you, until it be subdued.

21:1: If one be found slain in the land which the Lord your God gives you to possess it, lying in the field, and it be not known who has slain him. 2:Then your elders and your judges shall come forth, and they shall measure to the cities which are round about him that is slain. 3:And it shall be, that the city which is next to the slain man, even the elders of that city shall take an heifer, which has not been wrought with, and which has not drawn in the yoke, 4:and the elders of that city shall bring down the heifer to a rough valley, which is neither eared nor sown, and shall strike the heifer's neck there in the valley. 5:And the priests the sons of Levi shall come near; for them the Lord your God has chosen to minister to him, and to bless in the name of the Lord; and by their word shall every controversy and every stroke be tried. 6:And all the elders of that city, that are next to the slain man, shall wash their hands over the heifer that is beheaded in the valley. 7:And they shall answer and say, Our hands have not shed this blood, neither have our eyes seen it. 8:Be merciful, O Lord, to your people Israel, whom you have redeemed, and lay not innocent blood to your people of Israel's charge. And the blood shall be forgiven them. 9:So shall you put away the guilt of innocent blood from among you, when you shall do that which is right in the sight of the Lord. 10:When you go's forth to war against your enemies, and the Lord your God has delivered them into your hands, and you have taken them captive, 11;And sees among the captives a beautiful woman, and have a desire to her, that you would have her to your wife; 12:Then you shall bring her home to your house; and she shall shave her head, and pare her nails. 13:And she shall put the raiment of her captivity from off her, and shall remain in your house, and bewail her father and her mother a full month: and after that you shall go in to her, and be her husband, and she shall be your wife. 14:And it shall be, if you have no delight in her, then you shall let her go whither she will; but you shall not sell her at all for money, you shall not make merchandise of her, because you have humbled her.

15:If a man have two wives, one beloved, and another hated, and they have born him children, both the beloved and the hated; and if the firstborn son be hers that was hated. 16:Then it shall be, when he makes his sons to inherit that which he has, that he may not make the son of the beloved firstborn before the son of the hated, which is indeed the firstborn. 17:But he shall acknowledge the son of the hated for the firstborn, by giving him a double portion of all that he has, for he is the beginning of his strength; the right of the firstborn is his. 18:If a man have a stubborn and rebellious son, which will not obey the voice of his father, or the voice of his mother, and that, when they have chastened him, will not hearken to them.

19:Then shall his father and his mother lay hold on him, and bring him out to the elders of his city, and to the gate of his place, 20:and they shall say to the elders of his city: This our son is stubborn and rebellious, he will not obey our voice; he is a glutton, and a drunkard. 21:And all the men of his city shall stone him with stones, that he die: so shall you put evil away from among you; and all Israel shall hear, and fear. 22:And if a man have committed a sin worthy of death, and he be to be put to death, and you hang him on a tree. 23:His body shall not remain all night upon the tree, but you shall in any wise bury him that day; (for he that is hanged is accursed of God;) that your land be not defiled, which the Lord your God gives you for an inheritance.

22;1: You shall not see your brother's ox or his sheep go astray, and hide yourself from them: you shall in any case bring them again to your brother. 2:And if your brother be not nigh to you , or if you know him not, then you shall bring it to your own house, and it shall be with you until your brother seek after it, and you shall restore it to him again. 3:In like manner shall you do with his ass; and so shall you do with his raiment; and with all lost thing of your brother's, which he has lost, and you have found, shall you do likewise: you may not hide yourself. 4:You shall not see your brother's ass or his ox fall down by the way, and hide yourself from them: you shall surely help him to lift them up again. 5:The woman shall not wear that which pertain to a man, neither shall a man put on a woman's garment: for all that do so are abomination to the Lord your God. 6:If a bird's nest chance to be before you in the way in any tree, or on the ground, whether they be young ones, or eggs, and the dam sitting upon the young, or upon the eggs, you shall not take the dam with the young. 7:But you shall in any wise let the dam go, and take the young to you, that it may be well with you, and that you may prolong your days.

8:When you build a new house, then you shall make a battlement for your roof that you bring not blood upon your house, if any man fall from there. 9:You shall not sow your vineyard with divers seeds: lest the fruit of your seed which you have sown, and the fruit of your vineyard, be defiled. 10:You shall not plow with an ox and an ass together. 11:You shall not wear a garment of divers sorts, as of wool and linen together. 12:You shall make you fringes upon the four quarters of your vest, wherewith you cover yourself. 13:If any man take a wife, and go in to her, and hate her. 14:And give occasions of speech against her, and bring up an evil name upon her, and say, I took this woman, and when I came to her, I found her not a maid. 15:Then shall the father of the damsel, and her mother, take and bring forth the tokens of the damsel's virginity to the elders of the city in the gate. 16:And the damsel's father shall say to the elders, I gave my daughter to this man to wife, and he hates her; 17:and, look, he has given occasions of speech against her, saying, I found not your daughter a maid; and yet these are the tokens of my daughter's virginity. And they shall spread the cloth before the elders of the city.

18:And the elders of that city shall take that man and chastise him; 19:and they shall amerce him in an hundred shekels of silver, and give them to the father of the damsel, because he has brought up an evil name upon a virgin of Israel: and she shall be his wife; he may not put her away all his days. 20:But if this thing be true, and the tokens of virginity be not found for the damsel. 21:Then they shall bring out the damsel to the door of her father's house, and the men of her city shall stone her with stones that she die, because she has wrought folly in Israel, to play the whore in her father's house, so shall you put evil away from among you. 22:If a man be found lying with a woman married to an husband, then they shall both of them die, both the man that lay with the woman, and the woman: so shall you put away evil from Israel. 23:If a damsel that is a virgin be betrothed to an husband, and a man find her in the city, and lie with her.

24:Then you shall bring them both out to the gate of that city, and you shall stone them with stones that they die; the damsel, because she cried not, being in the city; and the man, because he has humbled his neighbor's wife: so you shall put away evil from among you. 25:But if a man find a betrothed damsel in the field, and the man force her, and lie with her: then the man only that lay with her shall die. 26:But to the damsel you shall do nothing; there is in the damsel no sin worthy of death: for as when a man rises against his neighbor, and slays him, even so is this matter. 27:For he found her in the field, and the betrothed damsel cried, and there was none to save her. 28:If a man find a damsel that is a virgin, which is not betrothed, and lay hold on her, and lie with her, and they be found. 29:Then the man that lay with her shall give to the damsel's father fifty shekels of silver, and she shall be his wife; because he has humbled her, he may not put her away all his days. 30:A man shall not take his father's wife, nor discover his father's skirt.

23:1: He that is wounded in the stones, or has his privy member cut off, shall not enter into the congregation of the Lord. 2:A bastard shall not enter into the congregation of the Lord; even to his tenth generation shall he not enter into the congregation of the Lord. 3:An Ammonite or Mobite shall not enter into the congregation of the Lord; even to their tenth generation shall they not enter, into the congregation of the Lord for ever. 4:Because they met you not with bread and with water in the way, when you came forth out of Egypt; and because they hired against you Balaam the son of Beor of Pethor of Mesopotamia, to curse you. 5:Nevertheless the Lord your God would not hearken to Balaam; but the Lord your God turned the curse into a blessing to you, because the Lord your God loved you. 6:You shall not seek their peace nor their prosperity all your days for ever. 7:You shall not abhor an Edomite; for he is your brother: you shall not abhor an Egyptian; because you were a stranger in his land. 8:The children that are begotten of them shall enter into the congregation of the Lord in their third generation. 9:When the host goeth forth against your enemies, then keep you from every wicked thing. 10:If there be among you any man, that is not clean by reason of uncleanness that chance him by night, then shall he go abroad out of the camp, he shall not come within the camp. 11:But it shall be, when evening comes on, he shall wash himself with water: and when the sun is down, he shall come into the camp again. 12:You shall have a place also with out the camp, whither you shall go forth abroad.

13:And you shall have a paddle upon your weapon; and it shall be, when you will ease yourself abroad, you shall dig therewith, and shall turn back and cover that which comes from you. 14:For the Lord your God walks in the midst of your camp, to deliver you, and to give up your enemies before you; therefore shall your camp be holy: that he see no unclean thing in you, and turn away from you. 15:You shall not deliver to his master the servant which has escaped from his master to you. 16:He shall dwell with you, even among you, in that place which he shall choose in one of your gates, where he it likes best: you shall not oppress him. 17:There shall be no whore of the daughters of Israel, nor a sodomite of the sons of Israel. 18:You shall not bring the hire of a whore, or the price of a dog, into the house of the Lord your God for any vow: for even both these are abomination to the Lord your God. 19:You shall not lend upon usury to your brother; usury of money, usury of victuals, usury of any thing that is lent upon usury. 20:To a stranger you may lend upon usury; but to your brother you shall not lend upon usury: that the Lord your God may bless you in all that you set your hand to in the land whither you go's to possess it. 21:When you shall vow a vow to the Lord your God, you shall not slack to pay it: for the Lord your God will surely require it of you, and it would be sin in you.

22:But if you refrain from making a vow, it shall be no sin in you. 23:That which is gone out of your lips you shall keep and perform; even a freewill offering, according as you have vowed to the Lord your God, which you have promised with your mouth. 24:When you comes into your neighbor's vineyard, then you may eat grapes your fill at your own pleasure; but you shall not put any in your vessel. 25:When you comes into the standing corn of your neighbor, then you may pluck the ears with your hand; but you shall not put a sickle to your neighbor's standing corn.

24:1: When a man has taken a wife, and married her, and it come to pass that she find no favor in his eyes, because he has found some uncleanness in her: then let him write her a bill of divorcement, and give it in her hand, and send her out of his house. 2:And when she is departed out of his house, she may go and be another man's wife. 3:And if the latter husband hate her, and write her a bill of divorcement, and gives it in her hand, and sends her out of his house; or if the latter husband die, which took her to be his wife. 4:Her former husband, which sent her away, may not take her again to be his wife, after that she is defiled; for that is abomination before the Lord: and you shall not cause the land to sin, which the Lord your God gives you for an inheritance. 5:When a man has taken a new wife, he shall not go out to war, neither shall he be charged with any business: but he shall be free at home one year, and shall cheer up his wife which he has taken. 6:No man shall take the nether or the upper millstone to pledge: for he takes a man's life to pledge. 7:If a man be found stealing any of his brethren of the children of Israel, and makes merchandise of him, or sells him; then that thief shall die; and you shall put evil away from among you. 8:Take heed in the plague of leprosy, that you observe diligently, and do according to all that the priests the Levites shall teach you: as I commanded them, so you shall observe to do. 9:Remember what the Lord your God did to Miriam by the way, after that you were come forth out of Egypt.

10:When you dost lend your brother any thing, you shall not go into his house to fetch his pledge. 11:You shall stand abroad, and the man to whom you dost lend shall bring out the pledge abroad to you. 12:And if the man be poor, you shall not sleep with his pledge. 13:In any case you shall deliver him the pledge again when the sun go's down, that he may sleep in his own raiment, and bless you, and it shall be righteousness to you before the Lord your God. 14:You shall not oppress an hired servant that is poor and needy, whether he be of your brethren, or of your strangers that are in your land within your gates. 15:At his day you shall give him his hire, neither shall the sun go down upon it; for he is poor, and sets his heart upon it: lest he cry against you to the Lord, and it be sin to you. 16:The fathers shall not be put to death for the children, neither shall the children be put to death for the fathers: every man shall be put to death for his own sin. 17:You shall not pervert the judgment of the stranger, nor of the fatherless; nor take a widow's raiment to pledge.

18:But you shall remember that you were a bondman in Egypt, and the Lord your God redeemed you thence: therefore I command you to do this thing. 19:When you cut down your harvest in your field, and have forgot a sheaf in the field, you shall not go again to fetch it: it shall be for the stranger, for the fatherless, and for the widow: that the Lord your God may bless you in all the work of your hands. 20:When you beat your olive tree, you shall not go over the boughs again: it shall be for the stranger, for the fatherless, and for the widow. 21:When you gathers the grapes of your vineyard, you shall not glean it afterward: it shall be for the stranger, for the fatherless, and for the widow. 22:And you shall remember that you were a bondman in the land of Egypt: therefore I command you to do this thing.

25:1: If there be a controversy between men, and they come to judgment, that the judges may judge them; then they shall justify the righteous, and condemn the wicked. 2:An d it shall be, if the wicked man be worthy to be beaten, that the judge shall cause him to lie down, and to be beaten before his face, according to his fault, by a certain number. 3:Forty stripes he may give him, and not exceed: lest, if he should exceed, and beat him above these with many stripes, then your brother should seem vile to you. 4:You shall not muzzle the ox when he treads out the corn..5:If brethren dwell together, and one of them die, and have no child, the wife of the dead shall not marry without to a stranger:her husband's brother shall go in to her, and take her to him to wife, and perform the duty of an husband's brother to her. 6:And it shall be, that the firstborn which she bears, shall succeed in the name of his brother which is dead, that his name be not put out of Israel. 7:And if the man like not to take his brother's wife, then let his brother's wife go up to the gate to the elders, and say, My husband's brother refuses to raise up to his brother a name in Israel, he will not perform the duty of my husband's brother. 8:Then the elders of his city shall call him, and speak to him: and if he stand to it, and say, I like not to take her; 9:Then shall his brother's wife come to him in the presence of the elders, and loose his shoe from off his foot, and spit in his face, and shall answer and say, So shall it be done to that man that will not build up his brother's house. 10:And his name shall be called in Israel, The house of him that has his shoe loosed. 11;When men strive together one with another, and the wife of the one draws near for to deliver her husband out of the hand of him that strikes him, and puts forth her hand, and takes him by his man hood.

12:Then you shall cut off her hand, your eye shall not pity her. 13:You shall not have in your bag divers weights, a great and a small. 14:You shall not have in your house divers measures, a great and a small. 15:But you shall have a perfect and just weight, a perfect and just measure shall you have: that your days may be lengthened in the land which the Lord your God gives you. 16:For all that do such things, and all that do unrighteousness , are an abomination to the Lord your God. 17:Remember what Amalek did to you by the way, when you were come forth out of Egypt. 18:How he met you by the way, and struck the hindmost of you, even all that were feeble behind you, when you were faint and weary; and he feared not God. 19:Therefore it shall be, when the Lord your God has given you rest from all your enemies round about, in the land which the Lord your God gives you for an inheritance to possess it, that you shall blot out the remembrance of Amalek from under heaven, you shall not forget it.

26:1: And it shall be, when you have come into the land which the Lord your God gives you for an inheritance, and posses it, and dwell therein. 2:That you shall take of the first of all the fruit of the earth, which you shall bring of your land that the Lord your God gives you, and shall put it in a basket, and shall go to the place which the Lord your God shall choose to place his name there. 3:And you shall go to the priest that shall be in those days, and say to him, I profess this day to the Lord your God, that I am come to the country which the Lord swore to our fathers for to give us. 4:And the priest shall take the basket out of your hand, and set it down before the altar of the Lord your God. 5:And you shall speak and say before the Lord your God, A Syrian ready to perish was my father, and he went down into Egypt, and sojourned there with a few, and became there a nation, great, mighty, and populous, 6:And the Egyptians evil entreated us, and afflicted us, and laid upon us hard bondage. 7:And when we cried to the Lord God of our fathers, the Lord heard our voice, and looked on our affliction, and our labor, and our oppression. 8:And the Lord brought us forth out of Egypt with a mighty hand, and with an outstretched arm, and with great terribleness, and with signs, and with wonders. 9:And he has brought us into this place, and has given us this land, even a land that flows with milk and meat. 10:And now, behold, I have brought the first fruits of the land, which you, O Lord, has given me. And you shall set it before the Lord your God, and worship before the Lord your God.11:And you shall rejoice in every good thing which the Lord your God has given to you , and to your house, you, and the Levite, and the stranger that is among you. 12:When you have made an end of tithing all the tithes of your increase the third year, which is the year of tithing, and have given it to the Levite, the stranger, the fatherless, and the widow, that they may eat within your gates, and be filled. 13;Then you shall say before the Lord your God, I have brought away the hallowed things out of mine house, and also have given them to the Levite, and to the stranger, to the fatherless, and to the widow, according to all your commandments which you have commanded me: I have not transgressed your commandments, neither have I forgotten them. 14:I have not eaten there of in my mourning, neither have I taken away anything there of, for any unclean use, nor given anything here, for the dead: but I have hearkened to the voice of the Lord my God, and have done according to all that you have commanded me.

15:Look down from your holy habitation, from heaven, and bless your people Israel, and the land which you have given us, as you swore to our fathers, a land that flows with milk and meat. 16;This day the Lord your God has commanded you to do these statutes and judgments: you shall therefore keep and do them with all your heart, and with all your soul. 17;You have avouched the Lord this day to be your God, and to walk in his ways, and to keep his statutes, and his commandments, and his judgments, and to hearken to his voice. 18:And the Lord has avouched you this day to be his peculiar people, as he has promised you, and that you should keep all his commandments. 19:And to make you high above all nations which he has made, in praise, and in name, and in honor; and that you may be an holy people to the Lord your God, as he has spoken.

27:1: And Moses with the elders of Israel commanded the people, saying, Keep all the commandments which I command you this day. 2:And it shall be on the day when you shall pass over Jordan to the land which the Lord your God gives you, that you shall set you up great stones, and plaster them with plaster. 3:And you shall write upon them all the words of this law, when you are passed over, that you may go in to the land which the Lord your God gives you, a land that flows with milk and meat; as the Lord God of your fathers has promised you. 4:Therefore it shall be when you be gone over Jordan, that you shall set up these stones, which I command you this day, in mount Ebal, and you shall plaster them with plaster. 5:And there shall you build an altar to the Lord your God, an altar of stones: you shall not lift up any iron tool upon them. 6:You shall build the altar of the Lord your God of whole stones: and you shall offer burnt offerings thereon to the Lord your God.

7:And you shall offer peace offerings, and shall eat there, and rejoice before the Lord your God. 8:And you shall write upon the stones all the words of this law very plainly. 9:And Moses and the priests the Levites spoke to all Israel, saying, Take heed, and hearken, O Israel; this day you are become the people of the Lord your God. 10:You shall therefore obey the voice of the Lord your God, and do his commandments and his statutes, which I command you this day. 11:And Moses charged the people the same day, saying, 12:These shall stand upon mount Gerizim to bless the people, when you are come over Jordan; Simeon, and Levi, and Judah, and Issachar, and Joseph, and Benjamin. 13:And these shall stand upon mount Ebal to curse; Reuben, Gad, and Asher, and Zebulun, Dan, and Naphtali. 14:And the Levites shall speak, and say to all the men of Israel with a loud voice. 15:Cursed be the man that makes any graven or molten image, an abomination to the Lord, the work of the hands of the craftsman, and puts it in a secret place. And all the people shall answer and say, Amen. 16:Cursed be he who dishonors his father or his mother. And all the people shall say, Amen. 17:Cursed be he that removes his neighbor's landmark. And all the people shall say, Amen. 18:Cursed be he that causes the blind to wander out of their way. And all the people shall say, Amen. 19:Cursed be he that perverts the judgment of the stranger, fatherless, and widow. And all the people shall say, Amen. 20:Cursed be he that lays with his father's wife; because he has uncovered his father's woman. And all the people shall say, Amen. 21:Cursed be he that lays with any manner of beast. And all the people shall say, Amen. 22:Cursed be he that lays with his sister, the daughter of his father, or the daughter of his mother. And all the people shall say, Amen. 23;Cursed be he that lays with his mother in law. And all the people shall say, Amen. 24:Cursed be he that strikes his neighbor secretly. And all the people shall say, Amen. 25:Cursed be he that takes reward to slay an innocent person. And all the people shall say, Amen. 26:Cursed be he that confirms not all the words of this law to do them. And all the people shall say, Amen.

28:1: And it shall come to pass, if you shall hearken diligently to the voice of the Lord your God, to observe and to do all his commandments which I command you this day, that the Lord your God will set you on high above all nations of the earth. 2:And all these blessings shall come on you, and overtake you, if you shall hearken to the voice of the Lord your God. 3:Blessed shall you be in the city, and blessed shall you be in the field. 4:Blessed shall be the fruit of your body, and the fruit of your ground, and the fruit of your cattle, the increase of your kine, and the flocks of your sheep. 5:Blessed shall be your basket and your store. 6:Blessed shall you be when you comes in, and blessed shall you be when you gos out. 7:The Lord shall cause your enemies that rise up against you to be smitten before your face: they shall come out against you one way, and flee before you seven ways.

8:The Lord shall command the blessing upon you in your storehouses, and in all that you sets your hand to; and he shall bless you in the land which the Lord your God gives to you. 9:The Lord shall establish you an holy people to himself, as he has sworn to you, if you shall keep the commandments of the Lord your God, and walk in his ways. 10:And all people of the earth shall see that you are called by the name of the Lord; and they shall be afraid of you. 11:And the Lord shall make you plenteous in goods, in the fruit of your body, and in the fruit of your cattle, and in the fruit of your ground, in the land which the Lord swore to your fathers to give you.12:The Lord shall open to you his good treasure, the heaven to give the rain to your land in his season, and to bless all the work of your hand: and you shall lend to many nations, and you shall not borrow. 13:And the Lord shall make you the head, and not the tail; and you shall be above only, and you shall not be beneath; if that you hearken to the commandments of the Lord your God, which I command you this day, to observe and to do them. 14:And you shall not go aside from any of the words which I command you this day, to the right hand, or to the left, to go after other gods to serve them. 15:But it shall come to pass, if you will not hearken to the voice of the Lord your God, to observe to do all his commandments and his statutes which I command you this day, that all these curses shall come upon you, and overtake you. 16;Cursed shall you be in the city, and cursed shall you be in the field. 17:Cursed shall be your basket and your store. 18:Cursed shall be the fruit of your body, and the fruit of your land, the increase of your kine, and the flocks of your sheep. 19:Cursed shall you be when you come in, and cursed shall you be when you go out. 20;The Lord shall send upon you cursing, vexation, and rebuke, in all that you set your hand to for to do, until you be destroyed, and until you perish quickly; because of the wickedness of your doings, whereby you have forsaken me. 21:The Lord shall make the pestilence cleave to you, until he have consumed you from off the land, whither you go to possess it.

22:The Lord shall strike you with a consumption, and with a fever, and with an inflammation, and with an extreme burning, and with the sword, and with blasting, and with mildew; and they shall pursue you until you perish. 23:And your heaven that is over your head shall be brass, and the earth that is under you shall be iron. 24:The Lord shall make the rain of your land powder and dust: from heaven shall it come down upon you, until you be destroyed. 25:The Lord shall cause you to be struck before your enemies: you shall go out one way against them, and flee seven ways before them: and shall be removed into all the kingdoms of the earth. 26:And your carcase shall be meat to all fowls of the air, and to the beasts of the earth, and no man shall fray them away. 27:The Lord will strike you with the botch of Egypt, and with the eczema, and with the scab, and with the itch, whereof you canst not be healed. 28:The Lord shall strike you with madness, and blindness, and astonishment of heart. 29:And you shall grope at noonday, as the blind groper in darkness, and you shall not prosper in your ways: and you shall be only oppressed and spoiled evermore, and no man shall save you. 30:You shall betroth a wife, and another man shall lie with her: you shall build an house, and you shall not dwell therein: you shall plant a vineyard, and shall not gather the grapes thereof.

31:Your ox shall be slain before your eyes, and you shall not eat thereof: your ass shall be violently taken away from before your face, and shall not be restored to you, your sheep shall be given to your enemies, and you shall have none to rescue them. 32:Your sons and your daughters shall be given to another people, and your eyes shall look, and fail with longing for them all the day long: and there shall be no might in your hand. 33:The fruit of your land, and all your labors, shall a nation which you knows not eat up; and you shall be only oppressed and crushed at all times. 34:So that you shall be mad for the sight of your eyes which you shall see. 35:The Lord shall strike you in the knees, and in the legs, with a sore botch that cannot be healed, from the sole of your foot to the top of your head. 36:The Lord shall bring you, and your King which you shall set over you, to a nation which neither you nor your fathers have known; and there shall you serve other gods, wood and stone. 37:And you shall become an astonishment, a proverb, and a byword, among all nations whither the Lord shall lead you. 38:You shall carry much seed out into the field, and shall gather but little in; for the locust shall consume it. 39:You shall plant vineyards, and dress them, but shall neither drink of the wine, nor gather the grapes, for the worms shall eat them.

40:You shall have olive trees throughout all your coasts, but you shall not anoint
yourself with the oil; for your olive shall cast its fruit. 41:You shall beget sons and
daughters, but you shall not enjoy them; for they shall go into captivity. 42:All your
trees and fruit of your land shall the locust consume. 43:The stranger that is with
you shall get up above you very high; and you shall come down very low. 44:He
shall lend to you, and you shall not lend to him: he shall be the head, and you shall
be the tail. 45:Moreover all these curses shall come upon you, and shall pursue you,
and overtake you, till you be destroyed; for you have not listened to the voice of the
Lord your God, to keep his commandments and his statutes which he commanded
you. 46:And they shall be upon you for a sign and for a wonder, and upon your seed
forever. 47;Because you serve not the Lord your God with joyfulness, and with
gladness of heart, for the abundance of all things. 48:Therefore shall you serve your
enemies which the Lord shall send against you, in hunger, and in thirst, and in
nakedness, and in want of all things, and he shall put a yoke of iron upon your neck,
until he have destroyed you.

49:The Lord shall bring a nation against you from far, from the end of the earth, as
swift as the eagle fly's; a nation whose tongue you shall not understand. 50:A nation
of fierce countenance, which shall not regard the person of the old, nor show favor
to the young. 51:And he shall eat the fruit of your cattle, and the fruit of your land,
until you be destroyed: which also shall not leave you either corn, wine, or oil, or
the increase of your kine, or flocks of your sheep, until he has destroyed you.
52:And he shall besiege you in all your gates, until your high and fenced walls come
down, where in you trust, throughout all your land: and he shall besiege you in all
your gates throughout all your land, which the Lord your God has given you.
53;And you shall eat the fruit of your own body, the flesh of your sons and of your
daughters, which the Lord your God has given you, in the siege, and in the
straightness, wherewith your enemies shall distress you. 54:So that the man that is
tender among you, and very delicate, his eye shall be evil toward his brother, and
toward the wife of his bosom, and toward the remnant of his children which he shall
leave. 55:So that he will not give to any of them of the flesh of his children whom
he shall eat: because he has nothing left him in the siege, and in the straightness,
wherewith your enemies shall distress you in all your gates.

56:The tender and delicate woman among you, which would not adventure to set the
sole of her foot upon the ground for delicateness and tenderness, her eye shall be
evil toward the husband of her bosom, and toward her son, and toward her daughter,
57:and toward her young one that comes out from between her feet, and toward her
children which she shall bear: for she shall eat them for want of all things secretly in
the siege and straightness, wherewith your enemy shall distress you in your gates.
58:If you will not observe to do all the words of this law that are written in this
book, that you may fear this glorious and fearful name of, **THE LORD YOUR
GOD.** 59:Then the Lord will make your plagues wonderful, and the plagues of
your seed, even great plagues, and of long continuance, and sore sicknesses, and of
long continuance. 60:Moreover he will bring upon you all the diseases of Egypt,
which you were afraid of; and they shall cleave to you. 61:Also every sickness, and
every plague, which is not written in the book of this law, them will the Lord bring
upon you, until you be destroyed.

62:And you shall be left few in number, whereas you were as the stars of heaven for multitude; because you would not obey the voice of the Lord your God. 63:And it shall come to pass, that as the Lord rejoiced over you to do you good, and to multiply you; so the Lord will rejoice over you to destroy you, and to bring you to nothing, and you shall be plucked from off the land, whither you go's to possess it. 64:And the Lord shall scatter you among all people, from the one end of the earth even to the other; and there you shall serve other gods, which neither you nor your fathers have known,even wood and stone. 65:And among these nations shall you find no ease, neither shall the sole of your foot have rest: but the Lord shall give you there a trembling heart, and failing of eyes, and sorrow of mind. 66:And your life shall hang in doubt before you; and you shall fear day and night, and shall have none assurance of your life. 67:In the morning you shall say, Would God it were even! and at even you shall say;Would God it were morning! for the fear of your heart wherewith you shall fear, and for the sight of your eyes which you shall see. 68:And the Lord shall bring you into Egypt again with ships, by the way whereof I spoke to you. You shall see it no more again: and there you shall be sold to your enemies for bondmen and bondwomen, and no man shall buy you.

29:1: These are the words of the covenant, which the Lord commanded Moses to make with the children of Israel in the land of Moab, beside the covenant which he made with them in Horeb. 2:And Moses called to all of Israel, and said to them. You have seen all that the Lord did before your eyes in the land of Egypt to Pharaoh, and to all his servants, and to all his land. 3:The great temptations which your eyes have seen, the signs, and those great miracles.4:Yet the Lord has not given you an heart to perceive, and eyes to see, and ears to hear, to this day. 5:And I have led you forty years in the wilderness: your clothes have not grown old upon you, and your shoes is not waxen old upon your foot. 6:You have not eaten bread, neither have you drank wine or strong drink: that you might know that I am the Lord your God. 7;And when you came to this place, Sihon, the King of Heshbon, and Og, the King of Bashan, came out against us to battle, and we struck them.

8:And we took their land, and gave it for an inheritance to the Reubenites, and to the Gadites, and to the half tribe of Manasseh. 9:Keep the words of this covenant, and do them, that you may prosper in all that you do. 10:You stand this day all of you before the Lord your God; your captains of your tribes, your elders, and your officers, with all the men of Israel. 11:Your little ones, your wives, and your stranger that is in your camp, from the hewer of your wood to the drawer of your water. 12:That you should enter into covenant with the Lord your God, and into his oath, which the Lord your God makes with you this day. 13:That he may establish you to day for a people to himself, and that he may be to you a God, as he has said to you, and as he has sworn to your fathers, to Abraham, to Isaac, and to Jacob. 14:Neither with you only do I make this covenant and this oath. 15:But with him that stands here with us this day before the Lord our God, and also with him that is not here with us this day. 16:(For you know how we have dwelt in the land of Egypt; and how we came through the nations which you passed by. 17:And you have seen their abominations, and their idols, wood and stone, silver and gold, which were among them.) 18:Lest there should be among you man, or woman, or family, or tribe, whose heart turns away this day from the Lord our God, to go and serve the gods of these nations; lest there should be among you a root that bears gall and wormwood. 19:And it come to pass, when he hears the words of this curse, that he bless himself in his heart, saying, I shall have peace, though I walk in the imagination of mine heart, to add drunkenness to thirst. 20:The Lord will not spare him, but then the anger of the Lord and his jealousy shall smoke against that man, and all the curses that are written in this book shall lie upon him, and the Lord shall blot out his name from under heaven. 21:And the Lord shall separate him to evil out of all the tribes of Israel, according to all the curses of the covenant that are written in this book of the law. 22:So that the generation to come of your children that shall rise up after you, and the stranger that shall come from a far land, shall say, when they see the plagues of that land, and the sicknesses which the Lord has laid upon it; 23:And that the whole land there of is brimstone, and salt, and burning, that it is not sown, nor bears, nor any grass grows therein, like the overthrow of Sodom, and Gomorrah, Admah, and Zeboim, which the Lord overthrew in his anger, and in his wrath.

24:Even all nations shall say, Wherefore has the Lord done this to this land? What means the heat of this great anger? 25:Then men shall say, Because they have forsaken the covenant of the Lord God of their fathers, which he made with them when he brought them forth out of the land of Egypt. 26:For they went and served other gods, and worshiped them, gods whom they knew not, and whom he had not given to them: 27:And the anger of the Lord was kindled against this land, to bring upon it all the curses that are written in this book, 28;and the Lord rooted them out of their land in anger, and in wrath, and in great indignation, and cast them into another land, as it is this day. 29:The secret things belong to the Lord our God: but those things which are revealed belong to us and to our children for ever, that we may do all the words of this law.

30:1: And it shall come to pass, when all these things are come upon you, the blessing and the curse, which I have set before you, and you shall call them to mind among all the nations, whither the Lord your God has driven you. 2:And shall return to the Lord your God, and shall obey his voice according to all that I command you this day, you and your children, with all your heart, and with all your soul. 3:That then the Lord your God will turn your captivity, and have compassion upon you, and will return and gather you from all the nations, whither the Lord your God has scattered you. 4:If any of your be driven out to the out most parts of heaven, from thence will the Lord your God gather you, and from thence will he fetch you. 5:And the Lord your God will bring you into the land which your fathers possessed, and you shall possess it; and he will do you good, and multiply you above your fathers.

6:And the Lord your God will circumcise your heart, and the heart of your seed, to love the Lord your God with all your heart, and with all your soul, that you may live. 7:And the Lord your God will put all these curses upon your enemies, and on them that hate you, which persecuted you. 8:And you shall return and obey the voice of the Lord, and do all his commandments which I command you this day. 9:And the Lord your God will make you plenteous in every work of your hand, in the fruit of your body, and in the fruit of your cattle, and in the fruit of your land, for good: for the Lord will again rejoice over you for good, as he rejoiced over your fathers. 10;If you shall hearken to the voice of the Lord your God, to keep his commandments and his statutes which are written in this book of the law, and if you turn to the Lord your God with all your heart, and with all your soul. 11:For this commandment which I command you this day, it is not hidden from you, neither is it far off. 12 :It is not in heaven, that you should say, Who shall go up for us to heaven, and bring it to us, that we may hear it, and do it? 13:Neither is it beyond the sea, that you should say, Who shall go over the sea for us and bring it to us, that we may hear it, and do it? 14:But the word is very nigh to you, in your mouth, and in your heart, that you may do it. 15:See, I have set before you this day life and good, and death and evil. 16:In that I command you this day, to love the Lord your God, to walk in his ways, and to keep his commandments and his statutes and his judgments, that you may live and multiply: and the Lord your God shall bless you in the land whither you go, to possess it.

17:But if your heart turn away, so that you will not hear, but shall be drawn away, and worship other gods, and serve them. 18: I denounce to you this day, that you shall surely perish, and that you shall not prolong your days upon the land, whither you pass over Jordan to go to possess it. 19:I call heaven and earth to record this day against you, that I have set before you life and death, blessing and cursing: therefore choose life, that both you and your seed may live. 20:That you may love the Lord your God, and that you may obey his voice, and that you may cleave to him: for he is your life, and the length of your days: that you may dwell in the land which the Lord swore to your fathers, to Abraham, to Isaac, and to Jacob, to give them.

31:1: And Moses went and spoke these words to all Israel. 2:And he said to them, I am an hundred and twenty years old this day; I can no more go out and come in: also the Lord has said to me, You shall not go over this Jordan. 3:The Lord your God, he will go over before you, and he will destroy these nations from before you, and you shall possess them: and Joshua, he shall go over before you, as the Lord has said. 4:And the Lord shall do to them as he did to Sihon and to Og, Kings of the Amorites, and to the land of them, whom he destroyed. 5:And the Lord shall give them up before your face, that you may do to them according to all the commandments which I have commanded you. 6:Be strong and of a good courage, fear not, nor be afraid of them: for the Lord your God, he it is that doth go with you, he will not fail you, nor forsake you.

7:And Moses called to Joshua, and said to him in the sight of all Israel, Be strong and of a good courage: for you must go with this people to the land which the Lord has sworn to their fathers to give them; and you shall cause them to inherit it. 8:And the Lord, he it is that doth go before you, he will be with you, he will not fail you, neither forsake you: fear not, neither be dismayed. 9:And Moses wrote this law, and delivered it to the priests the sons of Levi, which bare the ark of the covenant of the Lord, and to all the elders of Israel. 10:And Moses commanded them, saying, At the end of every seven years, in the solemnity of the year of release, in the feast of tabernacles. 11:When all Israel is come to appear before the Lord your God in the place which he shall choose, you shall read this law before all Israel in their hearing. 12:Gather the people together, men, and women, and children, and your stranger that is within your gates, that they may hear, and that they may learn, and fear the Lord your God, and observe to do all the words of this law: 13:And that their children, which have not known anything may hear, and learn to fear the Lord your God, as long as you live in the land whither you go over Jordan to possess it. 14:And the Lord said to Moses, Behold, your days approach that you must die, call Joshua, and present yourselves in the tabernacle of the congregation, that I may give him a charge. And Moses and Joshua went, and presented themselves in the tabernacle of the congregation.

15:And the Lord appeared in the tabernacle in a pillar of a cloud: and the pillar of the cloud stood over the door of the tabernacle. 16:And the Lord said to Moses, Behold, you shall sleep with your fathers; and this people will rise up, and go a whoring after the gods of the strangers of the land, whither they go to be among them, and will forsake me, and break my covenant which I have made with them.

17:Then my anger shall be kindled against them in that day, and I will forsake them, and I will hide my face from them, and they shall be devoured, and many evils and troubles shall befall them; so that they will say in that day, Are not these evils come upon us, because our God is not among us? 18:And I will surely hide my face in that day for all the evils which they shall have wrought, in that they are turned to other gods. 19:Now therefore write down this song for you, and teach it to the children of Israel: put it in their mouths, that this song may be a witness for me against the children of Israel.

20:For when I shall have brought them into the land which I swore to their fathers, that flows with milk and meat; and they shall have eaten and filled themselves, and waxen fat; then will they turn to other gods, and serve them, and provoke me, and break my covenant. 21:And it shall come to pass, when many evils and troubles are befallen them, that this song shall testify against them as a witness; for it shall not be forgotten out of the mouths of their seed: for I know their imagination which they go about, even now, before I have brought them into the land which I swore.

22:Moses therefore wrote this song the same day, and taught it the children of Israel. 23:And he gave Joshua the son of Nun a charge, and said, Be strong and of a good courage: for you shall bring the children of Israel into the land which I swore to them: and I will be with you. 24:And it came to pass, when Moses had made an end of writing the words of this law in a book, until they were finished.

25:That Moses commanded the Levites, which bare the ark of the covenant of the Lord, saying, 26:Take this book of the law, and put it in the side of the ark of the covenant of the Lord your God, that it may be there for a witness against you.

27:For I know your rebellion, and your stiff neck: behold, while I am yet alive with you this day, you have been rebellious against the Lord; and how much more after my death? 28:Gather to me all the elders of your tribes, and your officers, that I may speak these words in their ears, and call heaven and earth to record against them.

29:For I know that after my death you will utterly corrupt yourselves and turn aside from the way which I have commanded you;

and evil will befall you in the latter days; because you will do evil in the sight of the Lord, to provoke him to anger through the work of your hands. 30:And Moses spoke in the ears of all the congregation of Israel the words of this song, until they were ended.

32:1: Give ear, O you heavens, and I will speak; and hear, O earth, the words of my mouth. 2:My doctrine shall drop as the rain, my speech shall distil as the dew, as the small rain upon the tender herb, and as the showers upon the grass. 3:Because I will publish the name of the Lord: ascribe you greatness to our God. 4:He is the Rock, his work is perfect: for all his ways are judgment: a God of truth and without iniquity, just and right is he. 5:They have corrupted themselves, their spot is not the spot of his children: they are a perverse and crooked generation. 6:Do you this requite the Lord, O foolish people and unwise? is not he your father that has bought you? Have he not made you, and established you?

7:Remember the days of old, consider the years of many generations: ask your father, and he will show you; your elders, and they will tell you. 8:When the most High divided to the nations their inheritance, when he separated the sons of Adam, he set the bounds of the people according to the number of the children of Israel. 9:For the Lord's portion is his people; Jacob is the lot of his inheritance. 10:He found him in a desert land, and in the waste howling wilderness; he led him about, he instructed him, he kept him as the apple of his eye. 11:As an eagle stirs up her nest, flutters over her young, spreads abroad her wings, takes them, bearing them on her wings: 12:So the Lord alone did lead him, and there was no strange god with him.

13:He made him ride on the high places of the earth, that he might eat the increase of the fields; and he made him to suck meat out of the rock, and oil out of the flinty rock. 14:Butter of kine, and milk of sheep, with fat of lambs, and rams of the breed of Bashan, and goats, with the fat of kidneys of wheat; and you did drink the pure blood of the grape. 15:But Yeshurun grew fat, and kicked, you are very fat, you have grown thick, you are covered with fatness, after then he forsook God which made him, and lightly esteemed the Rock of his salvation.

16:They provoked him to jealousy with strange gods, with abominations provoked they him to anger. 17:They sacrificed to devils, not to God; to gods whom they knew not, to new gods that came newly up, whom your fathers feared not. 18:Of the Rock that begot you you are unmindful, and have forgotten God that formed you.

19:And when the Lord saw it, he abhorred them, because of the provoking of his sons, and of his daughters. 20:And he said, I will hide my face from them, I will see what their end shall be for they are a very froward generation, children in whom is no faith.

21:They have moved me to Jealousy with that which is not God; they have provoked me to anger with their vanities: and I will move them to jealousy with those which are not a people; I will provoke them to anger with a foolish nation. 22:For a fire is kindled in mine anger, and shall burn to the lowest hell,

and shall consume the earth with her increase, and set on fire the foundations of the
mountains. 23:I will heap mischief upon them; I will spend mine arrows upon them.
24:They shall be burnt with hunger, and devoured with burning heat, and with bitter
destruction: I will also send the teeth of beasts upon them, with the poison of
serpents of the dust.

25:The sword without, and terror within, shall destroy both the young man and the
virgin, the suckling also with the man of gray hairs. 26:I said, I would scatter them
into corners, I would make the remembrance of them to cease from among men.
27:Were it not that I feared the wrath of the enemy, lest their adversaries should
behave themselves strangely, and lest they should say, Our hand is high, and the
Lord has not done all this.

28:For they are a nation void of counsel, neither is there any understanding in them.
29:O that they were wise that they understood this, that they would consider their
latter end! 30:How should one chase a thousand, and two put ten thousand to flight,
except their Rock had sold them, and the Lord had shut them up? 31:For their rock
is not as our Rock, even our enemies themselves being judges. 32:For their vine is
of the vine of Sodom, and of the fields of Gomorrah: their grapes are grapes of gall,
their clusters are bitter.

33;Their wine is the poison of dragons, and the cruel venom of asps. 34:Is not this
laid up in store with me, and sealed up among my treasures? 35:To me belongs
vengeance, and recompense; their foot shall slide in due time: for the day of their
calamity is at hand, and the things that shall come upon them make haste. 36:For the
Lord shall judge his people, and repent himself for his servants, when he see that
their power is gone, and there is none shut up, or left.

37:And he shall say, Where are their gods, their rock in whom they trusted.
38:Which did eat the fat of their sacrifices, and drank the wine of their drink
offerings? Let them rise up and help you, and be your protection. 39:See now that I,
even I, am he, and there is no god with me: I take life, and I make alive; I wound,
and I heal: neither is there any that can deliver out of my hand. 40:For I lift up my
hand to heaven, and say, I live for ever.

41:If I whet my glittering sword, and mine hand take hold on judgment; I will
render vengeance to mine enemies, and will reward them that hate me. 42:I will
make mine arrows drunk with blood, and my sword shall devour flesh; and that with
the blood of the slain and of the captives, from the beginning of revenges upon the
enemy. 43:Rejoice, O you nations, with his people: for he will avenge the blood of
his servants, and will render vengeance to his adversaries, and will be merciful to
his land, and to his people. 44:And Moses came and spoke all the words of this song
in the ears of the people, he, and Joshua the son of Nun.

45:And Moses made an end of speaking all these words to all Israel. 46:And he
said to them, Set your hearts to all the words which I testify among you this day,
which you shall command your children to observe to do, all the words of this law.

47:For it is not a vain thing for you; because it is your life, and through this thing
you shall prolong your days in the land, whither you go over Jordan to possess it.
48:And the LORD spoke to Moses, that same day saying: 49:Get yourself up this
mountain here in Abram, to mount Nebo, which is in the land of Moab,

that is over against Jericho; and behold the land of Canaan, which I give to the
children of Israel for a possession. 50:And you will die on the mount where you are
going up, and be gathered to your people; as Aaron your brother died in mount Hor,
and was gathered to his people: 51:Because you trespassed against me among the
children of Israel at the waters of Meribah-Kadesh, in the wilderness of Zin;
because you sanctified me not in the midst of the children of Israel. 52:Yet you shall
see the land before you, but you shall not go closer have to the land which I give the
children of Israel.

33:1: And this is the blessing, wherewith Moses the man of God blessed the
children of Israel before his death. 2;And he said, The Lord came from Sinai, and
rose up from Seir to them; he shined forth from mount Paran, and he came with ten
thousands of saints: from his right hand went a fiery law for them. 3:But all his holy
ones were in his hand; they fallowed at his feet and he bore them up on his pinions.
4:Moses commanded us a law, even the inheritance of the congregation of Jacob.

5:And he was king in Jeshurun, when the heads of the people and the tribes of Israel
were gathered together.6:Let Reuben live, and not die; and let not his men be few.
7:And this is the blessing of Judah: and he said, Hear, Lord, the voice of Judah, and
bring him to his people: let his hands be sufficient for him; and be you an help to
him from his enemies. 8:And of Levi he said, let your Thummim and your Urim be
with your holy one, whom you did prove at Massah, and with whom you did strive
at the waters of Meribah.

9:Who said to his father and to his mother, I have not seen him; neither did he
acknowledge his brethren, nor knew his own children: for they have observed your
word, and kept your covenant. 10:They shall teach Jacob your judgments, and Israel
your law: they shall put incense before you, and whole burnt sacrifice upon your
altar. 11:Bless, Lord, his substance, and accept the work of his hands: strike through
the loins of them that rise against him, and of them that hate him, that they rise not
again.

12:And of Benjamin he said, The beloved of the Lord shall dwell in safety by him;
and the Lord shall cover him all the day long, and he shall dwell between his
shoulders. 13:And of Joseph he said, Blessed of the Lord be his land, for the
precious things of heaven, for the dew, and for the deep that couches beneath,

14:And for the precious fruits brought forth by the sun, and for the precious things
put forth by the moon. 15:And for the chief things of the ancient mountains, and for
the precious things of the lasting hills. 16:And for the precious things of the earth
and fulness thereof, and for the good will of him that dwelt in the bush: let the
blessing come upon the head of Joseph, and upon the top of the head of him that
was separated from his brethren.

17:His glory is like the yearling of his bullock, and his horns are like the horns of unicorns: with them he shall push the people together to the ends of the earth: and they are the ten thousands of Ephraim, and they are the thousands of Manasseh. 18:And of Zebulun he said, Rejoice, Zebulun, in your going out; and, Issachar, in your tents.

19:They shall call the people to the mountain; there they shall offer sacrifices of righteousness: for they shall suck of the abundance of the seas, and of treasures hid in the sand. 20;And of Gad he said, Blessed be he that enlarges Gad: he dwells as a lion, and tears the arm with the crown of the head. 21:And he provided the first part for himself, because there, in a portion of the lawgiver, was he seated; and he came with the heads of the people, he executed the justice of the Lord, and his judgments with Israel.

22:And of Dan he said, Dan is a lion's whelp: he shall leap from Bashan. 23:And of Naphtali he said, O Naphtali, satisfied with favor, and full with the blessing of the Lord: possess you the west and the south. 24:And of Asher he said, let Asherbe blessed with children; let him be acceptable to his brethren, and let him dip his foot in oil.

25:Your shoes shall be iron and brass; and as your days, so shall your strength be. 26:There is none like the God of Jeshurun, who rides upon the heaven with your help, and in his excellency on the sky. 27:The eternal God is your refuge, and underneath are the everlasting arms: and he shall thrust out the enemy from before you; and shall say, Destroy them.

28:Israel then shall dwell in safety alone: the fountain of Jacob shall be upon a land of corn and wine; also his heavens shall drop down dew. 29:Happy are you, O Israel: who is like to you, O people saved by the Lord, the shield of your help, and who is the sword of your excellency! and your enemies shall be found liars to you; and you shall tread upon their high places.

Please note in the Bible: where it is written (the land of milk and honey) was actually written as: (The land of milk and meat.)

(Then Moses Died:(Deuteronomy 34:1-7) 1:And Moses went up from the plains of Moab to the mountain of Nebo, to the top of Pisgah, that is over against Jericho. And the Lord showed him all the land of Gilead, to Dan, 2:And all Naphtali, and the land of Ephraim, and Manasseh, and all the land of Judah, to the utmost sea, 3:And the south, and the plain of the valley of Jericho, the city of palm trees, to Zoar.

4:And the Lord said to him. This is the land which I swore to Abraham, to Isaac, and to Jacob, saying, I will give it to your seed saying, I will give it to your seed: I have caused you to see it with your own eyes, but you shall not go over in to it. 5:So Moses the servant of the Lord died there in the land of Moab, according to the word of the Lord. 6:And he buried him in a valley in the land of Moab, over against Bethpeor: but where no man knows where to this day.

7:And Moses was an hundred and twenty years old when he died; his eye was not dim, nor his natural force abated.

Moses died on: +/- January 26, 1357 B.C.
Below are pictures from Mont Nebo.

Where you can see the promise land, and a Memorial to Moses. Both on top of Mt, Nebo.

+/- January 31st. (Shevat /Astec $6^{th.}$)

The year +/- 128 B.C. Simon and his men were Ambushed

(1 Maccabees 16:14-17) 14:As Simon was inspecting the cities of the country and providing for their needs, he and his sons Mattathias and Judas went down to Jericho in the year one hundred and seventy-seven in the eleventh month (that is the month of Shevat). 15:The son of Abubus gave them a delightful welcome in the little stronghold called Dok which he had built. While serving them a sumptouos banquet, he had his men hidden there.

16:Then when Simon and his sons had drunk freely, Ptolemy and his men sprang up,weapons in hand, rushed upon Simon in the banquet hall, and killed him, his two sons and some of his servants. 17:By this vicious act of treason he repaid good with evil.

The fallowing also happened during the month; of January-Shevat

The year +/-4780 B.C. (Genesis 3:1-24) Adam and Eve: were kicked out of the Garden of Eden:

1:Now the serpent was more cunning than any beast of the field which the Lord God had made. And he said to the woman, Yes, has God said, You shall not eat of every tree of the garden? 2:And the woman said to the serpent, we may eat of the fruit of the trees of the garden. 3:But of the fruit of the tree which is in the midst of the garden, God said, You shall not eat of it, neither shall you touch it, lest you die. 4:And the serpent said to the woman, You shall not surely die. 5:For God knows that in the day you eat the fruit, then your eyes shall be opened, and you shall be as gods, knowing good and evil. 6:And when the woman saw that the tree was good for food, and that it was pleasant to the eyes, and a tree to be desired to make one wise, she took the fruit and ate it, and also gave it to her husband with her; and he did eat. 7:And the eyes of them both were opened, and they knew that they were naked; and they sewed fig leaves together, and made themselves aprons. 8:And they heard the voice of the Lord God walking in the garden in the cool of the day: and Adam and his wife hid themselves from the presence of the Lord God amongst the trees of the garden. 9:And the Lord God called to Adam, and said to him, Where are you? 10:And he said, I heard your voice in the garden, and I was afraid, because I was naked; and I hid myself. 11:And he said, Who told you that you were naked? Have you eaten of the tree, where of I commanded you not to eat? 12:And the man said, The woman whom you gave to be with me, she gave me of the tree, and I did eat. 13:And the Lord God said to the woman. What is this that you have done? And the woman said, The serpent beguiled me, and I did eat. 14:And the Lord God said to the serpent, Because you have done this, you are cursed above all cattle, and above every beast of the field; upon your belly you shall go, and dust you shall eat all the days of your life. 15:And I will put enmity between you and the woman, and between your seed and her seed; it shall bruise your head, and you shall bruise his heel.

16:To the woman he said, I will greatly multiply your sorrow and you conception; in sorrow you shall bring forth children and your desire shall be for your husband, and he shall rule over you. 17:And to Adam he said, Because you have lessened to the voice of your wife, and have eaten of the tree, of which I commanded you, saying, You shall not eat of it, cursed is the ground for your sake; in sorrow you shall eat of it all the days of your life. 18:Thorns also and thistles shall it bring forth to you; and you shall eat the herb of the field; 19:By the sweat of your face shall you eat bread, till you return to the ground for out of it which you were taken:for dust you came and to dust shall you will return. 20:And Adam called his wife's name Eve; because she was the mother of all living. 21:To Adam also and to his wife did the Lord God make coats of skins, and clothed them. 22:And the Lord God said, Behold, the man is become as one of us, to know good and evil: and now, lest he put forth his hand, and take also of the tree of life, and eat, and live for ever. 23:Then the Lord God sent him out from the garden of Eden, to till the ground from where he was taken. 24:So he drove out the man; and he placed at the east of the garden of Eden Cherubim, and a flaming sword which turned every way, to guard the way to the tree of life.

(Please Note:) **Adam** (who's name means ***Dirt),*** and **Chavah** which in Hebrew means; to (**Breathe)** is what Adam first called out. When he saw the who would be called Eve. Then she took her first breath. Then he said; (this is woman, out of man.) Then later he called her;(**Eve**, **Mother of life**) after they were were kicked out of the: (Garden of Eden) which means:(**Fertile plain).** Which was located south of modern day Baghdad, Iraq. And then they returned to a cave at Hebron.
(Book of Jubilees 3:24-32 & Genesis 3:1-24)

The year +/- 4762 B.C. The birth of Seth:

(Genesis 4:25)25;And Adam knew his wife again; and she bare a son, and called his name Seth: For God, has appointed me another seed instead of Abel, whom Cain killed.

(Lots Daughters gave birth to his two sons)

(Genesis 19:36) 36;So were both the daughters of Lot with child by their father. The oldest gave birth to a son, whom she called Moab. The younger one gave birth to a son and called him: Benammi.

(Paul left the Island of Melita)

(Acts 28:7-11) 7:In the same quarters were possessions of the chief man of the island, whose name was Publius; who received us, and lodged us three days courteously. 8:And it came to pass, that the father of Publius lay sick of a fever and of a bloody flux: to whom Paul entered in, and prayed, and laid his hands on him, and healed him. 9:So when this was done, others also, which had diseases in the island, came, and were healed: 10:Who also honored us with many honors; and when we departed, they laded us with such things as were necessary. 11:And after three months we departed in a ship of Alexandria, which had wintered in the isle, whose sign was Castor and Pollux.

+/- 1582 C.E Pope Gregory the 13th. Started the Leap year, and Changed the New Year from April 1st to January 1st.

The Pope After learning the calendar was off by ten days, during the spring Equinox, ordered the removal of ten days from the Julian Calendar in the month of October in the year +/- 1582 C.E. Adding 1 day to February (29) every 4 years for calling it the leap year. Then ordered the New Year moved from April 1st. (Which was celebrated as the new year for thousands of years) to January 1st. in Rome and the rest of the Christian world. However the Protestants who lived in the newly founded "Americas" refused to change the New Year as ordered by the Catholic Church and continued to use April 1st. as their New Year. The Catholic Church considered them to be foolish, thus in England they started calling April 1st. "April fools Day." The leap year came to be, in around +/-1542C.E. The formula used to find this is. (1 day every 4 years x 10 days = 40 years. 1582 - 40 is 1542.)
Please Note: Some believe that Julius Cesar started the leap year in +/-46 B.C. However he did not discover the leap year but the 365 day year. The Julian calendar was formed around +/- 46-37 B.C. By Julius Caesar after adding the extra 10 days he changed the Calendar from 355 days to 365 days a year, which is in the Julian Calendar that we now use today.

51

(January / Tevet)

Below is the Island called Melita, where Paul was shipwrecked for three months.

Below a closer look at the side of the Island of Melita, where Paul was ship wrecked.

Chapter 2: February - Shevat /Astec

It is the eleventh Month of the Hebrew calendar
In Hebrew this month is called: Shevt /Astec,
which means: (Tree of life, / 11th. month)
Tribe of Issachar, means:(His reward)
The stone of (Amazonite) represents this tribe.
Issachar: (The 5th.) Son of Leah,
(Was believed to have been born during this month.)
(Spirit of Knowledge)

+/- February 1st. (Shevat /Astec 7th.)

The year +/- 661 B.C. Tobit was angry with Anna, his wife.

(Tobit 2:12-14) 12:When she sent back the goods to their owners, they would pay her. Late in winter she finished the cloth and sent it back to the owner. They paid her full salary and also gave her a young goat for the table. 13:On entering my house the goat began to bleat. I called my wife and said: Where did this goat come from" Perhaps it was stolen! Give it back to its owners; we have no right to eat stolen food! 14:But she said to me, "it was given to me as a bonus over and above my wages" yet I would not believe her; and told her to give it back to the owners. I became very angry with her over this. So she retorted; "Where are your virtuous acts? See! Your true character is finally showing itself!"

+/- February 2st. (Shevat /Astec 8th.)

The year +/- 1 B.C. (Removed from the modern Bibles);
Mary dedicates her self to God

After the 6 girls left the convent, the Priest came to them and said: it is time for you to go and find for your self's husbands. But, (**Mary** the daughter of Anna, who would become the: **Mother of Jesus**, and wife of **Joesph,** Said: No for I have dedicated my **Virginity** to God, and went on her way.
(The Kings James 1514, The St. Joseph 1611)

+/- February 18th. (Shevat /Astec 24th.)

The year +/- 513 B.C. God gives Zechariah a vision,

(Zechariah 1:7-6:15) 7:Upon the four and twentieth day of the eleventh month, which is the month Shevat, in the second year of Darius, came the word of the Lord to Zechariah, the son of Berechiah, the son of Iddo the prophet, saying, 8:I saw by night, and behold a man riding upon a red horse, and he stood among the myrtle trees that were in the bottom; and behind him were there red horses, speckled, and white. 9:Then said I, O my lord, what are these? And the angel that talked with me said to me, I will show you what these are.

10:And the man that stood among the myrtle trees answered and said; These are they whom the Lord has sent to walk to and fro through out the earth. 11:And they answered the angel of the Lord that stood among the myrtle trees, and said; We have walked to and fro through out the earth, and, behold, all the earth sitteth still, and is at rest. 12:Then the angel of the Lord answered and said, O Lord of hosts, how long will you not have mercy on Jerusalem and on the cities of Judah, against which you hast had indignation these threescore and ten years? 13:And the Lord answered the angel that talked with me with good words and comfortable words.

14:So the angel that communed with me said to me, Cry out you, saying, this says the Lord of hosts; I am jealous for Jerusalem and for Zion with a great jealousy. 15:And I am very exceedingly angry with the nations that are at ease: for I was but a little displeased, and they helped forward the affliction. 16:Therefore this says the Lord; I am returned to Jerusalem with mercies: my house shall be built in it, says the Lord of hosts, and a line shall be stretched forth upon Jerusalem. 17:Cry out saying, this says the Lord of hosts; My cities through prosperity shall yet be spread abroad; and the Lord shall yet comfort Zion, and shall yet choose Jerusalem.

18:Then lifted I up mine eyes, and saw, and behold four horns. 19:And I said to the angel that talked with me, What be these? And he answered me, These are the horns which have scattered Judah, Israel, and Jerusalem. 20:And the Lord showed me four carpenters. 21:Then said I, What come these to do? And he spake, saying, these are the horns which have scattered Judah, so that no man did lift up his head: And he spoke to me, saying, these are the horns which have scattered Judah, so that no man did lift up his head: but these are come to fray them, to cast out the horns of the Gentiles, which lifted up their horn over the land of Judah to scatter it.

2:1:I lifted up my eyes again, and looked, and behold a man with a measuring line in his hand. 2:Then said I, Where are you going? And he said to me, To measure Jerusalem, to see what is the breadth of it, and what is the length of it. 3:And, behold, the angel that talked with me went forth, and another angel went out to meet him, 4:And said to him, Run, speak to this young man, saying, Jerusalem shall be inhabited as are the towns without walls for the multitude of men and cattle therein. 5:For I, says the Lord, will be to her a wall of fire round about, and will be the glory in the midst of her. 6:Arise, arise, come out, and run from the land of the north, says the Lord: for I have spread you abroad as the four winds of the heaven, says the Lord. 7:Deliver yourself, O Zion, that dwells with the daughter of Babylon. 8:For this says the Lord of hosts; After the glory has he sent me to the nations which spoiled you: for he that touches you touches the apple of his eye.9:For, behold, I will shake mine hand upon them, and they shall be a spoil to their servants: and you shall know that the Lord of hosts has sent me.

10:Sing and rejoice, O daughter of Zion: for, look, I am coming, and I will live among you, says the Lord. 11:And many nations shall be joined to the Lord in that day, and so shall be my people: and I will live among you, and you shall know that the Lord of hosts has sent me to you. 12:And the Lord shall inherit Judah his portion in the holy land, and shall choose Jerusalem again. 13:Be silent, O all flesh, before the Lord: for he is raised up out of his holy habitation.

3:1;And he showed me Joshua the high priest standing before the angel of the Lord, and Satan standing at his right hand to resist him. 2:And the Lord said to Satan, The Lord rebuke you, O Satan; even the Lord that has chosen Jerusalem rebuke you: is not this a brand plucked out of the fire? 3:Now Joshua was clothed with filthy garments, and stood before the angel. 4:And he answered and spake to those that stood before him, saying, Take away the filthy garments from him. And to him he said, Behold, I have caused thine iniquity to pass from you, and I will clothe you with change of raiment.

5:And I said, Let them set a fair miter upon his head. So they set a fair miter upon his head, and clothed him with garments. And the angel of the Lord stood by. 6:And the angel of the Lord protested to Joshua, saying; 7:This says the Lord of hosts; If you will walk in my ways, and if you will keep my commandments, then you shall also judge my house, and shall also keep my courts, and I will give you places to walk among these that stand by. 8:Hear now, O Joshua the high priest, you, and your fellows that sit before you: for they are men wondered at: for, behold, I will bring forth my servant the Branch.

9:For behold the stone that I have laid before Joshua; upon one stone shall be seven eyes: behold, I will engrave the graving thereof, says the Lord of hosts, and I will remove the iniquity of that land in one day. 10:In that day, says the Lord of hosts, shall you call every man his neighbor under the vine and under the fig tree.

4:1:And the angel that talked with me came again, and waked with me, as a man that is wakened out of his sleep. 2:And said to me, What do you see? And I said, I have looked, and behold a candlestick all of gold, with a bowl upon the top of it, and his seven lamps thereon, and seven pipes to the seven lamps, which are upon the top thereof: 3:And two olive trees by it, one upon the right side of the bowl, and the other upon the left side thereof.

4:So I answered and said to the angel, that spoke with me, saying, What are these, my lord? 5:Then the angel that talked with me answered and said to me, do you know what these are? And I said, No, my lord. 6:Then he answered and spoke to me, saying, This is the word of the Lord to Zerubbabel, saying, Not by might, nor by power, but by my spirit, says the Lord of hosts.

7:Who are you, O great mountain? before Zerubbabel you shall become a plain: and
he shall bring forth the headstone there of with shouting, crying. Grace, grace to it.
8:Moreover the word of the Lord came to me, saying. 9:The hands of Zerubbabel
have laid the foundation of this house; his hands shall also finish it; and you shall
know that the Lord of hosts has sent me to you.

10:For who has despised the day of small things? for they shall rejoice, and shall see
the plummet in the hand of Zerubbabel with those seven; they are the eyes of the
Lord, which run to and fro through the whole earth. 11:Then answered I, and said to
him. What are these two olive trees upon the right side of the candlestick and upon
the left side thereof.

12:And I answered again, and said to him, What are these two olive branches which
through the two golden pipes empty the golden oil out of themselves? 13:And he
answered me and said, do you not know what these are? And I said; No, my lord.
14:Then said he, These are the two anointed ones, that stand by the Lord of the
whole earth.

5:1:Then I turned, and lifted up mine eyes, and looked, and behold a flying roll.
2:And he said to me; What do you see? And I answered, I see a flying roll; the
length thereof is twenty cubits, and the breadth thereof ten cubits. 3:Then said he to
me, This is the curse that go's forth over the face of the whole earth: for every one
that steals shall be cut off as on this side according to it; and every one that swears
shall be cut off as on that side according to it.

4:I will bring it forth, says the Lord of hosts, and it shall enter into the house of the
thief, and into the house of him that swears falsely by my name: and it shall remain
in the midst of his house, and shall consume it with the timber thereof and the
stones thereof. 5:Then the angel that talked with me went forth, and said to me, Lift
up now your eyes, and see what this is that go's forth. 6:And I said, What is it? And
he said, This is an ephah that go's forth. He said moreover, This is their resemblance
through all the earth. 7:And, behold, there was lifted up a talent of lead: and this is
a woman that sits in the midst of the ephah.

8:And he said, This is wickedness. And he cast it into the midst of the ephah; and
he cast the weight of lead upon the mouth thereof. 9:Then lifted I up mine eyes, and
looked, and, behold, there came out two women, and the wind was in their wings;
for they had wings like the wings of a stork: and they lifted up the ephah between
the earth and the heaven. 10:Then said I to the angel that talked with me, Whither
do these bear the ephah? 11:And he said to me, To build it an house in the land of
Shinar: and it shall be established, and set there upon her own base.

6:1;And I turned, and lifted up mine eyes, and looked, and, behold, there came four
chariots out from between two mountains; and the mountains were mountains of
brass. 2:In the first chariot were red horses; and in the second chariot black horse
horses. 3:And in the third chariot white horses; and in the fourth chariot grisled and
bay horses. 4:Then I answered and said to the angel that talked with me, What are
these, my lord? 5:And the angel answered and said to me,

These are the four spirits of the heavens, which go forth from standing before the Lord of all the earth. 6:The black horses which are therein go forth into the north country; and the white go forth after them; and the grisled go forth toward the south country. 7:And the bay went forth, and sought to go that they might walk to and fro through the earth: and he said, Get you hence, walk to and fro through the earth. So they walked to and fro through the earth.

8:Then cried he upon me, and spake to me, saying, Behold, these that go toward the north country have quieted my spirit in the north country. 9:And the word of the Lord came to me, saying; 10:Take of them of the captivity, even of Heldai, of Tobijah, and of Jedaiah, which are come from Babylon, and come you the same day, and go into the house of Josiah the son of Zephaniah;

11:Then take silver and gold, and make crowns, and set then upon the head of Joshua the son of Josedech, the high priest. 12:And speak to him, saying, this says the Lord of hosts: Behold there is a man whose name is The Branch; and he shall grow up out of his place, and he shall build the temple of the Lord:

13:Even he shall build the temple of the Lord; and he shall bear the glory, and shall sit and rule upon his throne; and he shall be a priest upon his throne: and the counsel of peace shall be between them both.14:And the crowns shall be to Helem, and to Tobijah, and to Jedaiah, and to Hen, the son of Zephaniah, for a memorial in the temple of the Lord. 15:And they that are far off shall come and build in the temple of the Lord, and you shall know that the Lord of hosts has sent me to you. And this shall truly come to pass, if you will diligently obey the voice of the Lord your God.

+/- February 21st. (Shevat /Astec 27th.)

John the Baptist gives his testimony

(John 1:19-28) 19:And this is the record of John, when the Jews sent priests and Levites from Jerusalem to ask him, Who are you? 20:And he confessed, and denied not; but confessed, I am not the Christ. 21:And they asked him, What then? Are you Elias? And he says; I am not. Are you that prophet? And he answered, No. 22:Then they asked him, Who are you? That we may give an answer to them that sent us. What do you say about yourself?

23:He said, I am the voice of one crying in the wilderness: Make straight the way of the Lord, as said by the prophet Elijah. 24:And they which were sent were of the Pharisees. 25:And they asked him, and said to him, Why are you baptizing then, if you are not the Christ, nor Elijah, neither that prophet? 26:John answered them, saying, I baptize with water: but there stands one among you, whom you do not know; 27:He it is, who coming after me is preferred before me, whose sandals I am not worthy to unloosen. 28:These things were done in Bethabarah beyond Jordan, where John was baptizing.

(As it was written in;Isaiah 40:3)

3;The voice of him that cries out in the wilderness; Prepare you the way of the Lord, make straight in the desert a highway for our God.

+/- February 22nd. (Shevat /Astec 28th.)

The year +/- 835 B.C. Obadiah meets with Elijah.

(1 Kings 18:7-46) 7:And as Obadiah was in the way, behold, Elijah met him: and he knew him, and fell on his face, and said, is that you my lord Elijah? 8:And he answered him, I am go, tell your lord, Behold, Elijah (is here) 9:And he said, What have I sinned, that you would deliver your servant into the hand of Ahab, to slay me? 10:As the Lord your God lives, there is no nation or kingdom, where my lord has not sent men to find you: and when they said, He is not there he took an oath of the kingdom and nation, that they could not find you.

11:And now you say, Go, tell my lord, Behold, Elijah is here. 12:And it shall come to pass, as soon as I am gone from you, that the Spirit of the Lord shall carry you whither I know not; and so when I come and tell Ahab, and he cannot find you, he shall kill me: but I your servant fears the Lord from my youth. 13:Was it not told my lord what I did when Jezebel slew the prophets of the Lord, how I hid an hundred men of the Lord's prophets by fifty in a cave, and fed them with bread and water?

14:And now you say, Go, tell your lord, Behold, Elijah is here; and he will kill me. 15:And Elijah sad, As the Lord of hosts lives, before whom I stand, I will surely show myself before him today. 16:So Obadiah went to meet Ahab, and told him: and Ahab went to meet Elijah. 17:And it came to pass, when Ahab saw Elijah, that Ahab said to him, Are you he that troubles Israel? 18:And he answered, I have not troubled Israel; but you, and your father's house, in that you have forsaken the commandments of the Lord, and you have followed Baalim.

19:Now therefore send, and gather to me all Israel to mount Carmel, and the prophets of Baal four hundred and fifty, and the prophets of the groves four hundred, which eat at Jezebel's table. 20:So Ahab sent to all the children of Israel, and gathered the prophets together to mount Carmel. 21:And Elijah came to all the people, and said, How long halt you between two opinions? if the Lord be God, follow him: but if Baal, then follow him. And the people answered him not a word.

22:Then said Elijah to the people, I, even I only, remain a prophet of the Lord; but Baal's prophets are four hundred and fifty men. 23:Let them therefore give us two bullocks; and let them choose one bullock for themselves, and cut it in pieces, and lay it on wood, and put no fire under it and I will dress the other bullock, and lay it on wood, and put no fire under it.

24:And you call on the name of your gods, and I will call on the name of the Lord: and the God that answers by fire, let him be God. And all the people answered and said, It is well spoken. 25:And Elijah said to the prophets of Baal, Choose you one bullock for yourselves, and dress it first; for you are many; and call on the name of your gods, but put no fire under it. 26:And they took the bullock which was given them, and they dressed it, and called on the name of Baal from morning even until noon, saying, O Baal, hear us. But there was no voice, nor any that answered. And they leaped upon the altar which was made.

27:And it came to pass at noon, that Elijah mocked them, and said, Cry aloud: for he is a god either he is talking, or he is pursuing, or he is in a journey, or maybe he is sleeping, and must be woke up. 28:And they cried aloud, and cut themselves after their manner with knives and lancets, till the blood gushed out upon them. 29:And it came to pass, when midday was past, and they prophesied until the time of the offering of the evening sacrifice, that there was neither voice, nor any to answer, nor any that regarded.

30:And Elijah said to all the people: come near to me. And all the people came near to him. And he repaired the altar of the Lord that was broken down. 31:And Elijah took twelve stones, according to the number of the tribes of the sons of Jacob, to whom the word of the Lord came, saying, Israel shall be your name. 32:And with the stones he built an altar in the name of the Lord: and he made a trench about the altar, as great as would contain two measures of seed.

33:And he put the wood in order, and cut the bullock in pieces, and laid him on the wood, and said, Fill four barrels with water, and pour it on the burnt sacrifice, and on the wood. 34:And he said, Do it the second time. And they did it the second time. And he said, Do it the third time. And they did it the third time. 35:And the water ran round about the altar; and he filled the trench also with water. 36:And it came to pass at the time of the offering of the evening sacrifice, that Elijah the prophet came near, and said, Lord God of Abraham, Isaac, and of Israel, let it be known this day that you are God in Israel, and that I am your servant, and that I have done all these things at your word.

37:Hear me, O Lord, hear me, that this people may know that you are the Lord God, and that you have turned their heart back again. 38:Then the fire of the Lord fell, and consumed the burnt sacrifice, and the wood, and the stones, and the dust, and licked up the water that was in the trench. 39;And when all the people saw it, they fell on their faces: and they said, The Lord, he is the God; the Lord, he is the God.

40:And Elijah said to them, Take the prophets of Baal; let not one of them escape. And they took them: and Elijah brought them down to the brook Kish on, and killed them there. 41:And Elijah said to Ahab, Get you up, eat and drink; for there is a sound of abundance of rain.

42:So Ahab went up to eat and to drink. And Elijah went up to the top of Carmel; and he cast himself down upon the earth, and put his face between his knees, 43:And said to his servant, Go up now, look toward the sea. And he went up, and looked, and said; There is nothing. And he said, Go again seven times.

44:And it came to pass at the seventh time, that he said, Behold, there is a little cloud out of the sea, like a man's hand. And he said, Go up, say to Ahab, Prepare your chariot, and get your self down, so that the rain does not stop you. 45:And it came to pass in the mean while, that the heaven was black with clouds and wind, and there was a great rain. And Ahab rode, and went to Jezreel. 46:And the hand of the Lord was on Elijah; and he girded up his loins, and ran before Ahab to the entrance of Jezreel

+/- February 22nd. (Shevat /Astec 28th.)

(Matthew 3:13-4:1) Jesus is baptized. 13;Then came Jesus from Galilee to Jordan to John, to be baptized from him. 14:But John tried to prevent him, saying It is I that should be baptized by you, and yet you are coming to me?

15:Jesus said to him in reply" Allow it now, Allow it now, for this is fitting for us to fulfill all righteousness.

Then he allowed him. 16:After Jesus was baptized, went up straightway out of the water: and behold, the heavens were opened for him, and he saw the Spirit of God descending like a dove, and lighting upon him: 17:And a voice from heaven, saying; This is my beloved Son, in whom I am well pleased. **4:1**;Then was Jesus led up of the Spirit into the wilderness, to be tempted by the Devil.

As written in Mark

(Mark 1:9-12) 9;And it came to pass in those days, that Jesus came from Nazareth of Galilee, and was baptized of John in Jordan. 10;And straightway coming up out of the water, he saw the heavens opened, and the Spirit like a dove descending upon him: 11;And there came a voice from heaven, saying,; You are my beloved Son, in whom I am well pleased. 12;And immediately the Spirit drove him into the wilderness.

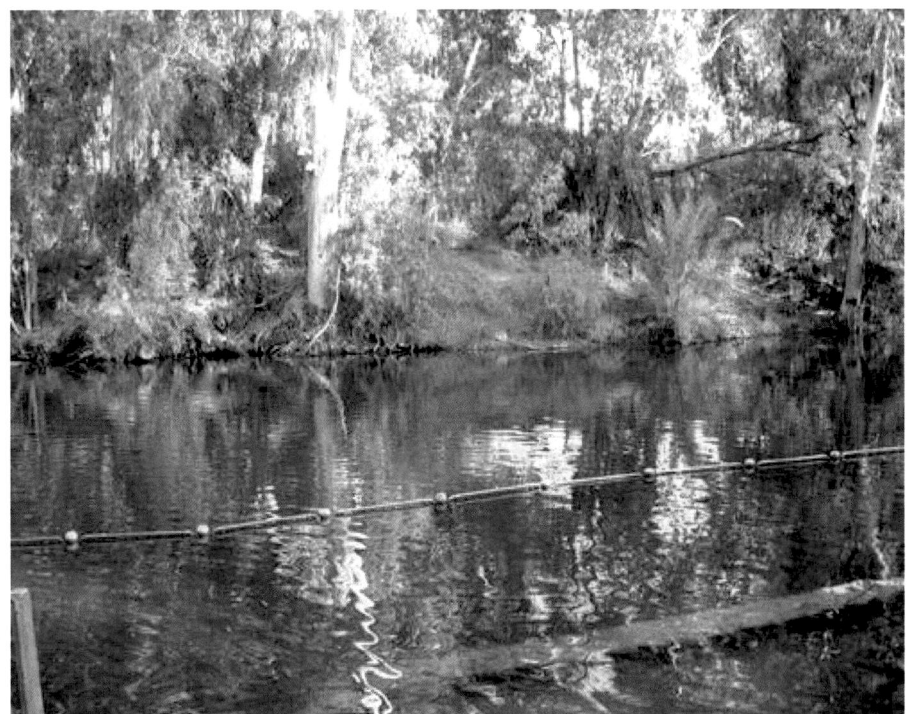

The location that is believed to be where Jesus was Baptized, by John the Baptist.

+/- February 23rd. (Shevat /Astec 29th.)

Goliath started taunting Israel for 40 days.

(1 Samuel 17:1-16) 1:Now the Philistines gathered together their armies to battle, and were gathered together at Shochoh, which belongs to Judah, and pitched between Shochoh and Azekah, in Ephesdammim.2:And Saul and the men of Israel were gathered together, and pitched by the valley of Elah, and set the battle in array against the Philistines. 3:And the Philistines stood on a mountain on the one side, and Israel stood on a mountain on the other side: and there was a valley between them. 4:And there went out a champion out of the camp of the Philistines, named Goliath, of Gath, whose height was six cubits and a span. 5:And he had an helmet of brass upon his head, and he was armed with a coat of mail; and the weight of the coat was five thousand shekels of brass. 6:And he had greaves of brass upon his legs, and a target of brass between his shoulders. 7:And the staff of his spear was like a weaver's beam; and his spear's head weighed six hundred shekels of iron: and one bearing a shield went before him. 8:And he stood and cried to the armies of Israel, and said to them: Why have you come out, and set yourself in battle array? Am not I a Philistine, and you servants to Saul? choose you a man for you, and let him come down to me. 9:If he be able to fight with me, and to kill me, then will we be your servants: but if I prevail against him, and kill him, then shall you be our servants, and serve us. 10:And the Philistine said, I defy the armies of Israel this day; give me a man, that we may fight together. 11:When Saul and all Israel heard those words of the Philistine, they were dismayed, and greatly afraid. 12:Now David was the son of that Ephrathite of Bethlehemjudah, whose name was Jesse; and he had eight sons: and the man went among men was an old man in the days of Saul. 13:And the three eldest sons of Jesse went and followed Saul to the battle: and the names of his three sons that went to the battle was Eliab the first born, and next to him Abinadab, and the third Shammah. 14:And David was the youngest: and the three eldest followed Saul. 15:But David went and returned from Saul to feed his father's sheep at Bethlehem. 16:And the Philistine drew near morning and evening,and presented himself forty days.

+/- February 24th. (Shevat /Astec 30th.)

Jezebel sent a message to Elijah

(1Kings 19:1-3)1:And Ahab told Jezebel all that Elijah had done, and withal how he had slain all the prophets with the sword. 2:Then Jezebel sent a messenger to Elijah, saying, So let the gods do to me, and more also, if I do not make your life as the life of one of them by tomorrow about this time. 3:And when he saw that, he arose, and went for his life, and came to Beersheba, which belongs to Judah, and left his servant there.

+/- February 25th. (Adar 1st.)

Go A angel fed Elijah under a juniper tree before his journey

(1Kings 19:4-8) 4:But he himself went a day's journey into the wilderness, and came and sat down under a juniper tree: and he requested for himself that he might die; and said, It is enough; now, O Lord, take away my life; for I am not better than my fathers. 5:And as he lay and slept under a juniper tree, behold, then an angel touched him, and said to him, Arise and eat. 6:And he looked, and, behold, a there was a cake that was baked on the coals, and a jug of water at his head. And he did eat and drink, and laid him down again. 7:And the angel of the Lord came again the second time, and touched him, and said, Get up and eat; because the journey is long way for you to travel. 8:And he arose, and did eat and drink, and went in the strength of that meat forty days and forty nights to Horeb the mount of God.

Above: Pictures of a juniper trees, similar to the one that: Elijah was sleeping under.

+/- February 25th. (Adar 1st.)

The year +/- 579 B.C. The Lord came to Ezekiel about Pharaoh.

(Ezekiel 32:1-16) 1:And it came to pass in the twelfth year, in the twelfth month, in the first day of the month, that he word of the Lord came to me, saying, 2:Son of man, take up a lamentation for Pharaoh King of Egypt, and say to him; You are like a young lion of the nations, and You are as a whale in the seas: and you came forth with your rivers, and troubled the waters with your feet, and fouled their rivers. 3:this says the Lord God; I will therefore spread out my net over you with a company of many people; and they shall bring you up in my net. 4:Then will I leave you upon the land, I will cast you upon the open field, and will cause all the fowls of the heaven to remain upon you, and I will fill the beasts of the whole earth with you. 5:And I will lay your flesh upon the mountains, and fill the valleys with your height. 6:I will also water with your blood the land wherein you swim, even to the mountains; and the rivers shall be full of you. 7:And when I shall put you out, I will cover the heaven, and make the stars thereof dark; I will cover the sun with a cloud, and the moon shall not give her light. 8:All the bright lights of heaven will I make dark over you, and set darkness upon your land, says the Lord God. 9:I will also vex the hearts of many people, when I shall bring you destruction among the nations, into the countries which you do not known. 10:I will make many people amazed at you, and their kings shall be horribly afraid for you, when I shall brandish my sword before them; and they shall tremble at every moment, every man for his own life, in the day of your fall. 11:For this says the Lord God; The sword of the King of Babylon shall come upon you.

12:By the swords of the mighty will I cause your multitude to fall, the terrible of the nations, all of them: and they shall spoil the pomp of Egypt, and all the multitude thereof shall be destroyed. 13:I will destroy also all the beasts there of from beside the great waters; neither shall be. 14:Then will I make their waters deep, and cause their rivers to run like oil, says the Lord God. 15:When I shall make the land of Egypt desolate, and the country shall be destitute of that whereof it was full, when I shall smite all them that dwell there, then shall they know that I am the Lord. 16:This is the lamentation wherewith they shall lament her: the daughters of the nations shall lament her: they shall lament for her, even for Egypt, and for all her multitude, says the Lord God

+/- February 27th. (Adar 3rd.)

The year +/- 1317 B.C. The Lord spoke to Joshua

(Joshua 1:1-2:4)1;Now after the death of Moses the servant of the Lord it came to pass, that the Lord spoke to Joshua the son of Nun, Moses's minister, saying, 2;Moses my servant is dead; now therefore arise, go over this Jordan, you, and all this people, to the land which I do give to them, even to the children of Israel. 3:Every place that the sole of your foot shall tread upon, that have I given to you, as I said to Moses. 4:From the wilderness and this Lebanon even to the great river, the river Euphrates, all the land of the Hittites, and to the great sea toward the going down of the sun, shall be your coast.

5:There shall not any man be able to stand before you all the days of your life: as I was with Moses, so I will be with you: I will not fail you, nor forsake you. 6:Be strong and of a good courage: for to this people shall you divide for an inheritance the land,which I swore to their fathers to give them. 7:Only you be strong and very courageous, that you may observe to do according to all the law, which Moses my servant commanded you: turn not from it to the right hand or to the left, that you may prosper where soever you go. 8:This book of the law shall not depart out of your mouth; but you shall meditate on it day and night, that you may observe to do according to all that is written therein: for then you shall make your way prosperous, and then you shall have good success. 9:Have not I commanded you? Be strong and of a good courage; be not afraid, neither be you dismayed: for the Lord your God is with you where so ever you go.

10:Then Joshua commanded the officers of the people, saying, 11;Pass through the host, and command the people, saying, Prepare you victuals; for within three days you shall pass over this Jordan, to go in to possess the land, which the Lord your God has given to you to possess. 12:And to the Reubenites, and to the Gadites, and to half the tribe of Manasseh, spoke Joshua, saying, 13:Remember the word which Moses the servant of the Lord commanded you, saying, The Lord your God has given you rest, and has given you this land. 14;Your wives, your little ones, and your cattle, shall remain in the land which Moses gave you on this side Jordan; but you shall pass before your brethren armed, all the mighty men of valor, and help them. 15:Until the Lord have given your brethren rest, as he has given you, and they also have possessed the land which the Lord your God given them: then you shall return to the land of your possession, and enjoy it, which Moses,

the Lord's servant gave you on this side Jordan toward the sun rise. 16;And they answered Joshua, saying, All that you commanded us we will do, and where so ever you send us, we will go. 17:According as we listen to Moses in all things, so will we listen to you only the Lord your God be with you, as he was with Moses. 18;Who so ever he be the one who rebel's against your commandments, and will not listen to your words in all that you command him, he shall be put to death,
only be strong and of a good courage.

2:1: And Joshua the son of Nun sent out of Shittim two men to spy secretly, saying, Go view the land, even Jericho. And they went, and came into an harlot's house, named Rahab, and lodged there. 2:And it was told the King of Jericho, saying, Behold, there came men here to stay the night of the children of Israel to search out the country. 3:And the King of Jericho sent to Rahab, saying, Bring forth the men that have come to you, which come to your home: for they have come to search out all the country. 4:And the woman took the two men, and hid them, and said this. There came men to me, but I do not know where they are.

+/- February 27th. (Adar 3rd.)

The year +/- 474 B.C.E. The house of the Lord was finished

(Ezra 6:15-18) 15;And this house was finished on the third day of the month Adar, which was in the sixth year of the reign of Darius the King. 6;And the children of Israel, the priests, and the Levites, and the rest of the children of the captivity, kept the dedication of this house of God with joy, 17;And offered at the dedication of this house of God an hundred bullocks, two hundred rams, four hundred lambs; and for a sin offering for all Israel, twelve he goats, according to the number of the tribes of Israel. 18;And they set the priests in their divisions, and the Levites in their courses, for the service of God, which is at Jerusalem; as it is written in the book of Moses.

(It was also during the month of February, Shevat /Astec)

An act of treason by Ptolemy.

(1 Maccabees 16:14-18) 14:the son of Abubus as Simon was inspecting the city's of the country and providing for their needs, he and his sons Mattathias and Judas went down to Jericho in the year one hundred and seventy seven, in the eleventh month, (the month of Shevat).

15:The son of Abubus gave them a deceitful welcome in the little stronghold called Dok which he had built. While serving them a banquet, he had his men hidden there. 16:Then when Simon and his sons had drunk freely, Ptolemy and his men sprang up, weapons in hand, rushed upon Simon in the banquet hall, and killed him, his two sons and some of his servants.

17:By this vicious act of treason he repaid good with evil. 18:Then Ptolemy wrote an account of this and sent it to the King, asking that troops be sent to help him, and that the country be turned over to him.

64
Paul sailed to Greece

(Acts 20:2-3) Paul sailed to Greece, 2:And when he had gone over those parts, and had given them much exhortation, he came into Greece, 3:And there abode three months. And when the Jews laid wait for him, as he was about to sail into Syria, he purposed to return through Macedonia.

On the left: is where Paul lived for 3 months while he was in Greece. On the right: a picture from the top looking in.

Chapter 3: March - Adar

It is the twelfth Month on the Hebrew Calendar
In Hebrew this month is called: Adar:
which means: (Strength) it is the 12th.month
Tribe of Zebulum means:(A Bridegroom's gift)
The stone of (Olivine) represents this tribe.
Zubulum: (The 6th.) Son of Leah,
(Was believed to have been born during this month.)
(Spirit of War)

+/- March 1$^{st.}$ (Adar 5$^{th.}$)

The year +/- 1317 B.C. The Hebrews crossed into the promised land

(Joshua 3:16-17) 16:That the waters which came down from above stood and rose up upon an heap very far from the city Adam, that is beside Zaretan: and those that came down toward the sea of the plain, even the salt sea, failed, and were cut off: and the people passed over right against Jericho. 17:And the priests that bare the ark of the covenant of the Lord stood firm on dry ground in the midst of Jordan, and all the Israelites passed over on dry ground, until all the people were passed clean over Jordan.

+/- March 1$^{st.}$ (Adar 5$^{th.}$)

The year +/- 835 B.C. Elijah was taken up to Heaven

(2 Kings 2:1-17) 1:And it came to pass, when the Lord would take up Elijah into heaven by a whirlwind, that Elijah went with Elisha from Gilgal. 2:And Elijah said to Elisha, stay here, I ask you; for the Lord has sent me to Bethel. And Elisha said to him, as the Lord lives, and as your soul lives, I will not leave you. So they went down to Bethel. 3:And the sons of the prophets that were at Bethel came forth to Elisha, and said to him, do you know that the Lord will take away your master from you on this day? And he said, Yes, I know, hold you, your peace. 4:And Elijah said to him, Elisha, stay here, I ask you; for the Lord had sent me to Jericho. And he said, as the Lord lives, and as your soul lives, I will not leave you.

So they came to Jericho. 5:And the sons of the prophets that were at Jericho came to Elisha, and said to him, do you know that the Lord will take away your master from you to day? And he answered, Yes, I know this, so hold you, your peace. 6:And Elijah said to him again, I ask you, stay here; for the Lord has sent me to Jordan. And he said, As the Lord lives, and as your soul lives, I will not leave your side. And they two went on. 7:And fifty men of the sons of the prophets went, and stood to view afar off: and they two stood by Jordan. 8:And Elijah took his mantle, and w rapped it together, and touched the waters, and they were divided hither and thither, so that they two went over on dry ground. 9:And it came to pass, when they were gone over, that Elijah said to Elisha, Ask what I shall do for you, before I am taken away from you. And Elisha said, I pray that you, let a double portion of your spirit be upon me. 10:And he said, You have asked a hard thing: nevertheless, if you see me when I am taken from you, it shall be so to you; but if not, it shall not be so. 11:And it came to pass, as they still went on, and talked, that, behold, there appeared a chariot of fire, and horses of fire, came between them both and Elijah went up, by a whirlwind into heaven.

12:And Elisha saw it, and he cried, My father, my father, the chariot of Israel, and the horsemen thereof. And he saw him no more: and he took hold of his own clothes, and tore them in two pieces. 13:He took up also the mantle of Elijah that fell from him, and went back, and stood by the bank of Jordan. 14:And he took the mantle of Elijah that fell from him, and touched the waters, and said, Where is the Lord God of Elijah? and when he also had touched the waters, they parted hither and thither: and Elisha went over. 15;And when the sons of the prophets which were to view at Jericho saw him, they said, The spirit of Elijah does rest on Elisha. And they came to meet him, and bowed themselves to the ground before him. 16:And they said to him, Behold now, there be with you servants fifty strong men; let them go, we ask you, and look for your master: lest perhaps the Spirit of the Lord has taken him up, and cast him upon some mountain, or into some valley. And he said, You shall not go. 17:And when they urged him till he was ashamed, he said, go then. They sent out fifty men; and they sought three days, but did not find him.

+/- March 3rd. (Adar 7th.)

The year +/- 1437 B.C. The birth of Moses

(Exodus 2:1-2) 2:And there was a man from the house of Levi, and he took a wife who was a daughter of Levi, 2:and the woman conceived, and gave birth and when she saw him that he was a male child, she hid him for three months.

+/- March 4th. (Adar 8th.)

The year +/- 835 B.C. Elisha told the men not to go

(2 Kings 2:18-22)18:And when they came again to him, (for he stayed at Jericho,) he said to them, Did I not say to you, Do not go? 19:And the men of the city said to Elisha, look, I ask you, the situation of this city is pleasant, as my lord you can see: but the water is no good, and the ground barren. 20:And he said, Bring me a new bowl, and put salt into it. And they brought it to him. 21:And he went forth to the spring of the waters,and cast the salt in there, and said, this you the Lord,

I have healed these waters. Never again will death or miscarriage spring from it. 22;So the waters were healed to this day, according to the saying of Elisha which he spoke.

+/- March 6th. (Adar 10th.)

Jesus spoke at the well with the Samaritan Woman,

(John 4:5-43) 5:Then he came to the a city of Samaria, which is called Sychar, near to the parcel of ground that Jacob gave to his son Joseph. 6:Now Jacob's well was there. Jesus therefore, being tired from his journey, sat down on the well: and it was about the sixth hour. 7:There came a woman of Samaria to draw water: Jesus you to her, Give me a drink. 8:(For his disciples have gone away in to the city to buy meat.) 9:Then the woman from Samaria said to him, How is it that you, being a Jew, ask for a drink from me, which I am a woman of Samaria? For the Jews have no dealings with the Samaritans. 10:Jesus answered and said to her, If you knew the gift of God, and whom it is that said to you, Give me a drink; you would have asked of him, and he would have given you living water. 11:The woman you to him, Sir, you have nothing to draw with, and the well is deep: from where then have you that living water? 12:Are you greater than our father Jacob, which gave us the well, and drank there of himself, and his children, and his cattle? 13:Jesus answered and said to her, Whosoever drinks of this water shall thirst again: 14:But whosoever drinks of the water that I will give him shall never thirst; but the water that I shall give him shall be in him a well of water springing up into everlasting life. 15;The woman said to him, Sir, give me this water, that I will not thirst, neither have to come here to draw. 16:Jesus said to her, Go, call your husband, and come draw. 17:The woman answered and said, I have no husband. Jesus said to her, You have well said, I have no husband: 18For you have had five husbands; and he whom you now live is not your husband: in that you spoke the truth. 19:The woman said to him, Sir, I perceive that you are a prophet. 20:Our fathers worshiped on this mountain; and you say, that in Jerusalem is the place where men ought to worship. 21:Jesus said to her: Woman, believe me the hour is coming, when you shall neither on this mountain, nor yet at Jerusalem, worship the Father. 22:You people worship you what you do not understand, we worship what we understand, because salvation is from the Jews. 23:But the hour is coming, and now is here, when the true worshipers shall worship the Father in spirit and in truth: for the Father longs for such; to worship him. 24:God is a Spirit: and they that worship him must worship him in spirit and in truth. 25:The woman said to him, I know that the one who is the Messiah is coming, who is called the Christ: when he comes, he will tell us all things. 26:Jesus said to her, I, the one speaking to you; am he. 27:And after this came his disciples, and marveled that he was talking with a woman: yet no man said, What are you looking for? or, Why are you speaking with her? 28:The woman then left her water pot, and went her way into the city, and said to the men. 29:Come, see a man, which told me all things that ever I did: is not this the Christ? 30:Then they went out of the city, and came to him. 31:In the mean while his disciples said to him, Master, eat. 32:But he said to them, I have meat to eat that you, do not know of. 33:Therefore the disciples said to one another, Has any man brought him something to eat? 34:Jesus said to them, My meat is to do the will of him that sent me, and to finish his work.

35:Say not you, There are yet four months, and then comes harvest? behold, I say to
you, Lift up your eyes, and look on the fields; for they are white already to harvest.
36:And he that the reapers receive their wages, and gathers fruit to life eternal: that
both he that sowed and he that reaps may rejoice together. 37;And herein is that
saying true, One sows and another reaps 38;I sent you to reap that where on you
bestowed no labor: other men labored, and you are entered into their labors. 39:And
many of the Samaritans of that city believed on him for the saying of the woman,
which testified, He told me all that ever I did. 40:So when the Samaritans were
coming to him, they sought him that he would stay with them: and he stay there two
days. 41:And many more believed because of his own word. 42:And said to the
woman, Now we believe, not just because of what you said: but we have heard him
ourselves, and know that this is indeed is the Christ, the Savior of the world.
43:Now after two days he departed thence, and went into Galilee.

The pictures above are of the Monastery where Jacob's well is located.

+/- March 8th. (Adar 12th.)

Jesus said: Go your way your son lives.

(John 4:45-50) 45:Then when he was come into Galilee, the Galileans received him, having seen all the things that he did at Jerusalem at the feast: for they also went to the feast. 46:So Jesus came again in to Cana of Galilee, where he made the water wine. And there was a certain nobleman, whose son was sick at Capernaum. 47:When he heard that Jesus was come out of Judea in to Galilee, he went to him, and he begged him that he would come down, and heal his son: for he was at the point of death. 48:Then said Jesus to him, Unless you see signs and wonders, you will not believe. 49:The nobleman said to him, Sir, come down or my child will die. 50:Jesus said to him, Go your way; your son lives. And the man believed the word that Jesus had spoken to him, and he went his way.

+/- March 9th. (Adar 13th.)

Between the years +/- 479-458 B.C. The Kings Command to kill Jews

(Esther 9:1-4)1:Now in the twelfth month, that is, the month Adar, on the thirteenth day of the same, when the King's commandment and his decree drew near to be put in execution, in the day that the enemies of the Jews hoped to have power over them,(though it was turned to the contrary, that the Jews had rule over them that hated them) 2:The Jews gathered themselves together in their cities throughout all the provinces of the king Ahasuerus, to lay hand on such as sought their hurt: and no man could withstand them; for the fear of them fell upon all people. 3:And all the rulers of the provinces, and the lieutenants,and the deputies, and officers of the King, helped the Jews; because the fear of Mordecai fell upon them. 4:For Mordecai was great in the King's house, and his fame went out throughout all the provinces: for this man Mordecai waxed greater and greater. 5:So did the Jews kill all their enemies with the stroke of the sword, and slaughter, and destruction, and did what they would to those that hated them. 6:And in Shushan the palace the Jews slew and destroyed five hundred men. 7:And Parshandatha, and Dalphon, and Aspatha. 8:And Poratha, and Adalia, and Aridatha. 9:And Parmashta, and Arisai, and Aridai, and Vajezatha, 10:The ten sons of Haman the son of Hammedatha, the enemy of the Jews, slew they; but on the spoil laid they not their hand. 11:On that day the number of those that were slain in Shushan the palace was brought before the King.

12:And the King told queen Esther: The Jews have slain and destroyed five hundred men in Shushan the palace, and the ten sons of Haman; what have they done in the rest of the King's provinces? Now what is your petition? And it shall be granted you: or what is your request further? and it shall be done. 13:Then said Esther, If it please the King, let it be granted to the Jews which are in Shushan to do tomorrow also according to this day's decree, and let Haman's ten sons be hanged upon the gallows. 14:And the king commanded it so to be done: and the decree was given at Shushan; and they hanged Haman's ten sons. 15:For the Jews that were in Shushan gathered themselves together on the fourteenth day also of the month Adar, and slew three hundred men at Shushan; but on the prey they laid not their hand. 16:But the other Jews that were in the king's provinces gathered themselves together, and stood for their lives, and had rest from their enemies, and slew of their foes seventy and five thousand, but they laid not their hands on the prey, 17:On the thirteenth day of the month Adar; and on the fourteenth day of the same they rested, and had a day of feasting and gladness.

+/- March 9th. (Adar 13th.)

(1st. Day of Purim)

(Esther 9:17) 17:On the thirteenth day of the month Adar; and on the fourteenth day of the same rested they, and made it a day of feasting and gladness.

+/- March 9th. (Adar 13th.)

The year +/- 134 B.C. The battle on the eve of Mordecai's day,

(2Maccabees 15:17-36) 17:Encouraged by Judas noble words, which had power to install valor and stir young harts to courage, the Jews determined not to delay, but to charge gallantly and decide the issue by hand to hand combat with the utmost courage, since their city and its temple with the sacred vessels were in danger.
18:They were not so much concerned about their wife's and children or their brothers and kinsmen; their first and foremost fear was for the consecrated sanctuary. 19:Those who remained in the city suffered a like agony, anxious as they were about the battle in the open country. 20:Everyone now awaited the decisive moment. The enemy already drawing near with their troops drawn up in a battle line, their elephants placed in strategic positions, and their cavalry stationed on the flanks. 21:Maccabees, contemplating the host before him, their elaborate equipment, and the fierceness of their elephants, stretched out his hands towards heaven and called on the Lord who works miracles; for he knew that it is not through arms but through the Lords decision that victory is won by those who deserve it. 22:He prayed to him this; You o Lord, sent your angel in the days of King Hezekiah of Judea, and he slew a 185,000 men of Sennacherib's army.
23:Sovereign of the heavens, send a good angel now to spread fear and dread before us. 24:By the might of your arm may those be struck down who have spoke blasphemously against you, and have come against your holy people. With this he ended his prayer. 25:Nicanor and his men advanced to the sound of trumpets and battle songs. 26:But Judas and his men met the army with supplication and prayer
27:Fighting with their hands and praying to God with their hearts, they laid low mat least 35,000 and rejoiced greatly over this manifestation of God's power. 28:When the battle was over and they were joyfully departing, they discovered Nicanor,lying there in all his Armour. 29:So they raised tumultuous shouts in their native tongue in praise of the divine Sovereign. 30:Then Judas, who was always in body and soul, the chief defender of his fellow citizens, and had maintained his from youth his affection for his countrymen, ordered Nicanor's head and whole right arm to be cut off and taken to Jerusalem. 31:When he arrived there, he assembled his countrymen, stationed the priest before the altar, and sent for those in the citadel. 32:He showed them the vile with Nicanor's head and the wretched blasphemer's arm that had been boastfully stretched out against the holy dwelling of the Almighty. 33:He cut out the tongue of the godless Nicanor, saying he would feed it piecemeal to the birds and would hang up the other wages of his folly opposite the temple. 34:At this, everyone looked towards heaven and praised the Lord who manifests his divine power,

saying "Blessed is he who has kept his own place undefiled!" 35:Judas hung up Nicanor's head on the wall of the citadel, a clear and evident proof to all of the Lords help. 36:By public vote it was unanimously decreed never to let this day pass unobserved, but to celebrate it on thirteenth day of the 12th.month, called Adar in Aramaic, the eve of Mordecai's Day.

+/- March 10th. (Adar 14th.)

The Year +/- 1438 B.C. (The Day Moses was Circumcised)

As it was commanded to Abraham in:

(Genesis 17:10-14) 10:This is my covenant, which you shall keep, between me and you and your seed after you; Every man child among you shall be circumcised. 11:And you shall circumcise the flesh of your foreskin; and it shall be a token of the covenant between me and you. 12:And he that is eight days old shall be circumcised among you, every man child in your generations, he that is born in the house, or bought with money of any stranger, which is not of your seed. 13:He that is born in your house, and he that is bought with your money, has to be circumcised: and my covenant shall be in your flesh for an everlasting covenant. 14:And the uncircumcised man child whose flesh of his foreskin is not circumcised, that soul shall be cut off from his people; he has broken my covenant.

+/- March 10th. (Adar 14th.)

Second Day of Purim

(Esther 9:17-22) 17:On the thirteenth day of the month Adar, and on the fourteenth day of the same rested they, and made it a day of feasting and gladness. 18:But the Jews that were at Shushan assembled together on the thirteenth day thereof, and on the fourteenth thereof; and on the fifteenth day of the same they rested, and made it a day of feasting and gladness. 19:Therefore the Jews of the villages, that dwelt in the unwalled towns, made the fourteenth day of the month Adar a day of gladness and feasting, and a good day, and of sending portions one to another. 20:And Mordecai wrote these things, and sent letters to all the Jews that were in all the provinces of the king Ahasuerus, both nigh and far. 21:To establish this among them, that they should keep the fourteenth day of the month Adar, and the fifteenth day of the same, yearly. 22:As the days wherein the Jews rested from their enemies, and the month which was turned to them from sorrow to joy, and from mourning into a good day, that they should make them days of feasting and joy, and of sending portions one to another, and gifts to the poor.

+/- March 10th. (Adar 14th.)

Jesus heals a man at the sheep gate

(John 5:1-6:1) 1:After this there was a feast of the Jews; and Jesus went up to Jerusalem. 2:Now there is at Jerusalem by the sheep market a pool, which is called in the Hebrew tongue Bethesda, having five porches. 3:In these lay a great multitude of impotent folk, of blind, halt, withered, waiting for the moving of the water. 4:For an angel went down at a certain season into the pool, and troubled the water: whosoever then first after the troubling of the water stepped in was made whole of whatsoever disease he had. 5:And a certain man was there, which had an infirmity thirty eight years. 6:When Jesus saw him lie, and knew that he had been now a long time in that place, so he said to him, Will you be made whole? 7:The impotent man answered him, Sir, I have no man, when the water is troubled, to put me into the pool, but while I am coming, another will step in before me. 8;Jesus said to him, Rise, take up your bed, and walk. 9:And immediately the man was made whole, and took up his bed, and walked: and on that day it was the sabbath. 10:The Jews therefore said to him that was cured, It is the sabbath day, it is not lawful for you to carry your bed with you. 11:He answered them, He that made me whole, the same said to me, Take up your bed, and walk. 12:Then asked they him, What man is that which said to you, Take up your bed, and walk? 13;And he that was healed did not know who it was: for Jesus had conveyed himself away, a multitude being in that place. 14:Afterward Jesus found the man in the temple, and said to him, Behold, you are made whole: sin no more, lest a worse thing come upon you. 15:The man then departed, and told the Jews that it was Jesus, which had made him whole. 16:And therefore the Jews wanted to persecute Jesus, and sought to kill him, because he had done these things on the sabbath day. 17:But Jesus answered them, My Father is at work until now, so and I at work. 18:Therefore the Jews sought the more to kill him, because he not only had broken the sabbath, but said also that God was his Father, making himself equal with God.

19;Then answered Jesus and said to them; Verily truly, I say to you, The Son can do nothing of himself, but what he sees his Father doing: for what things he does, his Son will do also. 20:For the Father loves the Son, and shows him every thing that he does: and he will show him greater works than these, that you may be amazed. 21:For as the Father raises up the dead, and gives life to them; even so also does the Son give life to whomever he wishes. 22:For the Father judges no man, but has committed all judgment to his Son: 23:That all should honor the Son, even as they honor the Father. He that honors not the Son, honors not the Father, which has sent him. 24:Verily truly, I say to you, He that hears my word, and believes on him that sent me, has everlasting life, and shall not come into condemnation; but is passed from death to life. 25:Verily truly, I say to you, The hour is coming, and now is here, when the dead shall hear the voice of the Son of God; and they that hear shall live. 26:For as the Father has life in himself; so has he given it to the Son, to have life in himself. 27:And has given him authority to execute judgment also, because he is the Son of Man. 28:Do not be amazed at this: for the hour is coming, in the which all that are in the graves shall hear his voice. 29:And shall come forth; they that have done good, to the resurrection of life; and they that have done evil, to the resurrection of damnation. 30:I can of mine own self do nothing: as I hear, I judge: and my judgment is just; because I seek not mine own will, but the will of the Father which has sent me. 31:If I bear witness of myself, my witness is not true. 32:There is another that bears witness of me; and I know that the testimony which he gives on my behalf is true. 33:You sent emissaries to John, and he testified to the truth. 34:But I receive not testimony from man: but these things I say, that you might be saved. 35:He was a burning and a shining lamp: and you were willing for a season to rejoice in his light. 36:But I have greater witness than that of John: for the works which the Father has given me to finish, the same works that I do, bear witness of me, that the Father has sent me. 37:And the Father himself, which has sent me, has borne witness of me. You have neither heard his voice at any time, nor seen his shape. 38:And you have not his word abiding in you: for whom he has sent, in him you do not believe. 39:Search the scriptures; for in them you think you have eternal life: and they are they which testify of me. 40:And you will not come to me, that you might have life. 41:I do not receive honor from men. 42:But I know you, that you have not the love of God in you. 43:I have come in my Father's name, and you do not receive me: if another shall come in his own name, him you would receive. 44:How can you believe, which receive honor one of another, and seek not the honor that comes only from God? 45;Do not think that I will accuse you to the Father: there is one that accuses you, even Moses, in whom you trust. 46:For had you believed Moses, you would have believed me: for he wrote of me. 47;But if you do not believe in his writings, how shall you believe my words? **6:1:**After these things Jesus went over the Sea of Galilee, which is also know as the Sea of Tiberias.

Below: The Pools of Bethesda

Please Note: This is where Jesus healed a man, waiting to go into the water. (John 5:8)

+/- March 10th. (Adar 14th.)

Jesus said your sins are forgiven you

(Luke 5:17-39) 17:And it came to pass on a certain day, as he was teaching, that there were Pharisees and doctors of the law sitting by, which were come out of every town of Galilee, Judea, and Jerusalem: and the power of the Lord was present to heal them. 18:And, behold, men brought in a bed, a man which was taken with a palsy: and they sought means to bring him in, and to lay him before him. 19:And when they could not find by what way they might bring him in because of the multitude, they went upon the housetop, and let him down through the tiling with his couch into the midst before Jesus. 20;And when he saw their faith, he said to him, Man, your sins are forgiven you. 21;And the scribes and the Pharisees began to reason, saying, Who is this which speaks blasphemies? Who can forgive sins, but God alone? 22;But when Jesus perceived their thoughts, he answering said to them; What are you thinking in your hearts? 23:Whether it is easier, to say, Your sins are forgiven you; or to say, Rise up and walk? 24:But that you may know that the Son of man has power upon the earth to forgive sins, (he said to the man who was paralyzed,) I say to you, Arise, and take up your couch, and go to your house. 25:And immediately he rose up before them, and took up that whereon he lay, and departed to his own house, glorifying God. 26:And they were all amazed, and they glorified God, and were filled with fear, saying, We have seen strange things today. 27:And after these things he went out, and saw a tax collector, named Levi, sitting at the custom post: and he said to him, Follow me. 28;And leaving everything behind, he got up, and followed him. 29;And Levi made him a great feast in his own house: and there was a great company of tax collectors and of others that sat down with them. 30:But their scribes and Pharisees murmured against his disciples, saying, Why do you eat and drink with tax collectors and sinners? 31;And Jesus answering said to them: They that are whole need not a physician; but they who are sick do. 32:I came not to call the righteous, but sinners to repentance. 33:And they said to him, Why do the disciples of John fast often, and make prayers, and likewise the disciples of the Pharisees; but yours eat and drink? 34:And he said to them, Can you make the wedding guest fast, while the bridegroom is with them? 35:But the days will come, when the bridegroom shall be taken away from them, and then shall they fast in those days. 36:And he spoke also a parable to them;No man tears a piece of a new garment to repair an old one; Otherwise, he will tear the new and the piece from it will not match the old cloak. 37:Likewise no man puts new wine in to old skins; else the new wine will burst the skins, and be spilled, and the skins will be ruined. 38:But new wine must be put into new skins; and both are preserved. 39:And No one who has been drinking old wine desires new, for he says, the old is better.

+/- March 11th. (Adar 15th.)

The year +/- 579 B.C. Ezekiel is told to cry for Egypt

(Ezekiel 32:17-32)17:It came to pass also in the twelfth year, in the fifteenth day of the month, that the word of the Lord came to me, saying, 18:Son of man, cry for the multitude of Egypt, and cast them down, even her, and the daughters of the famous nations, to the nether parts of the earth, with them that go down into the pit. 19:Whom do you excel in beauty? Come down, you and your allies, and lie with the uncircumcised. 20:They shall fall in the midst of them that are slain by the sword: she is delivered to the sword: draw her and all her multitudes. 21:The strong among the mighty shall speak to him out of the midst of hell with them that help him: they are gone down, they lie uncircumcised, slain by the sword. 22:Assyria is there and all her company: his graves are about him: all of them slain, fallen by the sword: 23:Whose graves are set in the sides of the pit, and her company is round about her grave: all of them slain, fallen by the sword, which caused terror in the land of the living. 24:There is Elam and all her multitude round about her grave, all of them slain, fallen by the sword, which are gone down uncircumcised into the nether parts of the earth, which caused their terror in the land of the living; yet have they borne their shame with them that go down to the pit. 25They have set her a bed in the midst of the slain with all her multitude: her graves are around about him: all of them uncircumcised, slain by the sword: though their terror was caused in the land of the living, yet have they borne their shame with them that go down to the pit: he is put in the midst of then that have been slain. 26:There is Meshech, Tubal, and all her multitude: her graves are around about him: all of them uncircumcised, slain by the sword, though they caused their terror in the land of the living. 27:And they shall not lie with the mighty that are fallen of the uncircumcised, which are gone down to hell with their weapons of war: and they have laid their swords under their heads, but their iniquities shall be upon their bones, though they were the terror of the mighty in the land of the living. 28:Yes, you shall be broken in the midst of the uncircumcised, and shall lie with them that are slain with the sword. 29:There is Edom, her kings, and all her princes, which with their might are laid by them that were slain by the sword: they shall lie with the uncircumcised, and with them that go down to the pit.30:There be the princes of the north, all of them, and all the Zidonians, which are gone down with the slain; with their terror they are ashamed of their might; and they lie uncircumcised with them that were slain by the sword, and bear their shame with them that go down to the pit. 31:Pharaoh shall see them,and shall be comforted over all his multitude, even Pharaoh and all his army slain by the sword, you the Lord God. 32:For I have caused my terror in the land of the living: and he shall be laid in the midst of the uncircumcised with them that are slain with the sword, even Pharaoh and all his multitude, says the Lord God.

+/- March 14th. (Adar 18th.)

The year +/- 1358 B.C. Moses and Aaron spoke to the Elders

(Exodus 4:29-31) 29:And Moses and Aaron went and gathered together all the elders of the children of Israel. 30:And Aaron spoke all the words which the Lord had spoken to Moses, and did the signs in the sight of the people. 31:And the people believed: and when they heard that the Lord had visited the children of Israel, and that he had looked upon their affliction, then they bowed their heads and worshiped.

+/- March 15th. (Adar 19th.)

The year +/- 1358 B.C. Moses and Aaron went again to speak to Pharaoh

(Exodus 5:1-13) 5:And afterward Moses and Aaron went in, and told Pharaoh, this you the Lord God of Israel, Let my people go, that they may hold a feast to me in the wilderness. 2:And Pharaoh said, Who is the Lord, that I should obey his voice to let Israel go? I know not the Lord, neither will I let Israel go. 3:And they said, The God of the Hebrews has met with us: let us go, we pray you, three days' journey into the desert, and sacrifice to the Lord our God; lest he fall upon us with pestilence, or with the sword. 4:And the king of Egypt said to them, Wherefore do you, Moses and Aaron, let the people from their works? get you to your burdens. 5:And Pharaoh said, Behold, the people of the land now are many, and you make them rest from their burdens.

6:And Pharaoh commanded the same day the taskmasters of the people, and their officers, saying; 7:You shall no more give the people straw to make brick, as from now on: let them go and gather straw for themselves. 8:And the quota of the bricks, which they hat to make before, you shall keep upon them; you shall not diminish the amount: for they are lazy; that is why they cry, saying, Let us go and sacrifice to our God. 9:Let there more work be laid upon the men, that they may labor therein; and let them not regard vain words. 10:And the taskmasters of the people went out, and their officers, and they spoke to the people, saying, this you Pharaoh, I will not give you straw. 11:Go you, get you straw where you can find it: yet none of your work quota shall be diminished. 12:So the people were scattered abroad throughout all the land of Egypt to gather stubble instead of straw. 13:And the taskmasters hasted them saying. Fulfill your works daily quota, as when there was straw.

+/- March 16th. (Adar 20th.)

The year +/- 1358 B.C. The Officers of the Jews were beaten

(Exodus 5:14-21) 14:And the officers of the children of Israel, which Pharaoh's taskmasters had set over them, were beaten, and were asked, Wherefore have you not fulfilled your task in making brick both yesterday and today, as before? 15:Then the officers of the children of Israel came and cried to Pharaoh, saying, Why do you treat your servants in this manner? 16:There is no straw given to your servants, and they say to us, Make brick, and, behold, your servants are beaten; it is you, "who are at fault. 17:But he said, You are lazy, you are idle: therefore you say, Let us go and do sacrifice to the Lord. 18:Off to work then! Straw shall not be provided for you, but you must still deliver your quota of bricks. 19:And the officers of the children of Israel did see that they were in evil case, after it was said, You shall not reduce from the number of bricks for your daily quota. 20:And they met Moses and Aaron, who stood in the way, as they came forth from Pharaoh. 21;And they said to them, The Lord look upon you, and judge! You have brought us into bad odor with Pharaoh and his servants, and have put a sword in their hands to slay us.

+/- March 17th. (Adar 21st.)

The year +/- 1358 B.C. Moses had Aaron throw down his staff

(Exodus 5:22-7:9) 22:And Moses returned to the Lord, and said, Lord, why do you treat these people so badly? 23:Ever since I went to Pharaoh to speak in your name, he has mistreated these people of yours, and you have done nothing to rescue them. **6:1:**Then the Lord said to Moses, Now shall you see what I will do to Pharaoh: for with a strong hand shall he let them go, and with a strong hand shall he drive them out of his land. 2:And God spoke to Moses, and said to him, I am the Lord: 3:And I appeared to Abraham, to Isaac, and to Jacob, by the name of God Almighty, but by my name YHVH was I not known to them. 4:And I have also established my covenant with them, to give them the land of Canaan, the land of their pilgrimage, wherein they were strangers. 5:And I have also heard the groaning of the children of Israel, whom the Egyptians keep in bondage; and I have remembered my covenant. 6:Wherefore say to the children of Israel, I am the Lord, and I will bring you out from under the burdens of the Egyptians, and I will rid you out of their bondage, and I will redeem you with a stretched out arm, and with great judgments.

7:And I will take you to me for a people, and I will be to you a God: and you shall know that I am the Lord your God, which brings you out from under the burdens of the Egyptians. 8:And I will bring you in to the land, concerning the which I did swear to give it to Abraham, to Isaac, and to Jacob; and I will give it you for an heritage: I am the Lord. 9:And Moses spoke so to the children of Israel: but they hearkened not to Moses for anguish of spirit, and for cruel bondage. 10:And the Lord spoke to Moses, saying, 11:Go in, speak to Pharaoh King of Egypt, that he let the children of Israel go out of his land. 12:And Moses spoke before the Lord, saying, Behold, the children of Israel have not hearkened to me; how then shall Pharaoh hear me, who am of uncircumcised lips? 13:And the Lord spoke to Moses and to Aaron, and gave them a charge to the children of Israel, and to Pharaoh king of Egypt, to bring the children of Israel out of the land of Egypt. 14:These be the heads of their fathers' houses: The sons of Reuben the firstborn of Israel; Hanoch, and Pallu, Hezron, and Carmi: these bethe families of Reuben. 15:And the sons of Simeon; Jemuel, and Jamin, and Ohad, and Jachin, and Zohar, and Shaul the son of a Canaanite woman: these are the families of Simon. 16:And these are the names of the sons of Levi according to their generations; Gershon, and Kohath, and Merari: and the years of the life of Levi were an hundred thirty and seven years. 17:The sons of Gershon; Libni, and Shimi, according to their families.

18:And the sons of Kohath; Amram, and Izhar, and Hebron, and Uzziel: and the years of the life of Kohath were an hundred thirty and three years. 19:And the sons of Merari; Mahali and Mushi: these are the families of Levi according to their generations. 20:And Amram took him Jochebed his father's sister to wife; and she bare him Aaron and Moses:and the years of the life of Amram were an hundred and thirty and seven years. 21:And the sons of Izhar; Korah, and Nepheg, and Zichri. 22:And the sons of Uzziel; Mishael, and Elzaphan, and Zithri. 23;And Aaron took him Elisheba, daughter of Amminadab, sister of Naashon, to wife; and she bare him Nadab, and Abihu, Eleazar, and Ithamar. 24:And the sons of Korah; Assir, and Elkanah, and Abiasaph: these are the families of the Korhites. 25:And Eleazar Aaron's son took him one of the daughters of Putiel to wife; and she bare him Phinehas: these are the heads of the fathers of the Levites according to their families. 26:These are that Aaron and Moses, to whom the Lord said, Bring out the children of Israel from the land of Egypt according to their armies. 27;These are they which spoke to Pharaoh King of Egypt, to bring out the children of Israel from Egypt:these are that Moses and Aaron. 28:And it came to pass on the day when the Lord spoke to Moses in the land of Egypt, 29:That the Lord spoke to Moses, saying, I am the Lord: speak you to Pharaoh king of Egypt all that I say to you. 30:And Moses said before the Lord, Behold, I am of uncircumcised lips, and how shall Pharaoh hearken to me? **7:1:**And the Lord said to Moses, See, I have made you a god to Pharaoh: and Aaron your brother shall be your prophet. 2:You shall speak all that I command you: and Aaron your brother shall speak to Pharaoh, that he send the children of Israel out of his land. 3:And I will harden Pharaoh's heart, and multiply my signs and my wonders in the land of Egypt. 4:But Pharaoh shall not hearken to you, that I may lay my hand upon Egypt, and bring forth mine armies, and my people the children of Israel, out of the land of Egypt by great judgments. 5:And the Egyptians shall know that I am the Lord, when I stretch forth mine hand upon Egypt, and bring out the children of Israel from among them.

6:And Moses and Aaron did as the Lord commanded them, so did they. 7:And Moses was fourscore years old, and Aaron fourscore and three years old, when they spoke to Pharaoh. 8:And the Lord spoke to Moses and to Aaron, saying, 9:When Pharaoh shall speak to you, saying, show us a miracle from you: then you shall say to Aaron, Take your rod, and cast it in front of Pharaoh, and it shall become a serpent. **(Note: the actual translation was into a crocodile, not a snake)**

+/- March 18th. (Adar 22nd.)

The year +/- 1358 B.C. Moses went back to see the Pharaoh

(Exodus 7:10-13) 10:And Moses and Aaron went in to Pharaoh, and they did so as the Lord had commanded: and Aaron cast down his rod before Pharaoh, and before his servants, and it became a serpent. 11:Then Pharaoh also called the wise men and the sorcerers: now the magicians of Egypt, they also did in like manner with their enchantments. 12:For they cast down every man his rod, and they became serpents: but Aaron's rod swallowed up their rods. 13:And he hardened Pharaoh's heart, that he hearkened not to them; as the Lord had said.

+/- March 19th. (Adar 23rd.)

The year +/- 1358 B.C. The water was turned into blood

(Exodus 7:14-24) 14:And the Lord said to Moses, Pharaoh's heart is hardened, he will refuse to let the people go. 15:Go to Pharaoh in the morning; see, he go's out to the water; and you shall stand by the river's bank where he will come and the rod which was turned to a serpent you shall take in your hand. 16:And you shall say to him, The Lord God of the Hebrews has sent me to you, saying, Let my people go, that they may serve me in the wilderness, and you would not listen.

17:This says the Lord, In this you shall know that I am the Lord: behold, I will strike with the rod that is in mine hand upon the waters which are in the river, and they shall be turned into blood. 18;And the fish that is in the river shall die,and the river shall stink; and the Egyptians shall hate to drink of the water of the river. 19:And the Lord spoke to Moses, Say to Aaron, Take your rod, and stretch out your hand upon the waters of Egypt, upon their streams, upon their rivers, and upon their ponds, and upon all their pools of water, that they may become blood; and that there may be blood throughout all the land of Egypt, both in vessels of wood, and in vessels of stone.

20:And Moses and Aaron did so, as the Lord commanded; and he lifted up the rod, and strike the waters that were in the river, in the sight of Pharaoh, and in the sight of his servants; and all the waters that were in the river were turned to blood. 21:And the fish that was in the river died; and the river stank, and the Egyptians could not drink of the water of the river; and there was blood throughout all the land of Egypt. 22:And the magicians of Egypt did so with their enchantments: and Pharaoh's heart was hardened, neither did he listen to them; as the Lord had said. 23:And Pharaoh turned and went into his house, neither did he set his heart to this also. 24:And all the Egyptians dug around about the river for water to drink; for they could not drink of the water of the river.

Below: The Nile river, that was turned into Blood, when Aron touched the water with Moses staff

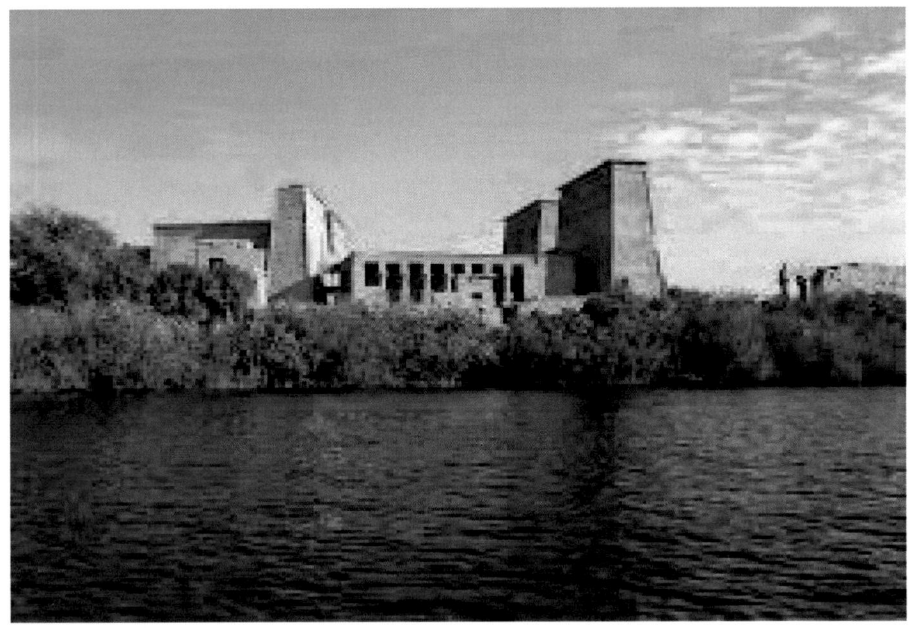

The Red Sea; is also known in the old writings as the sea of blood. Believed to be where Lilith lives. It is called this because the color of the water. When the Nile river turned Red it was believed that it was blood. Because all the fish died.

In China, the Yangtze River turned red, on September 7, 2012. Seen below: no one knows why.

+/- March 21th. (Adar 25th.)

The year +/- 576 B.C. Jehoiachin was released from prison

(Jeremiah 52:31-34) 52:And it came to pass in the seven and thirtieth year of the captivity of Jehoiachin king of Judah, in the twelfth month, in the five and twentieth day of the month, that Evilmerodach king of Babylon in the first year of his reign lifted up the head of Jehoiachin king of Judah, and brought him forth out of prison.

32:And spoke kindly to him, and set his throne above the throne of the kings that were with him in Babylon, 33:And changed his prison garments: and he did continually eat bread before him all the days of his life. 34:And for his diet, there was a continual diet given him of the king of Babylon, every day a portion until the day of his death, all the days of his life.

(Also as it is written in 2Kings)

(2Kings 25:27-30) 25:And it came to pass in the seven and thirtieth year of the captivity of Jehoiachin king of Judah, in the twelfth month, on the seven and twentieth day of the month, that Evilmerodach king of Babylon in the year that he began to reign did lift up the head of Jehoiachin King of Judah out of prison. 28:and he spoke kindly to him, and set his throne above the throne of the kings that were with him in Babylon; 29:And changed his prison garments: and he did eat bread continually before him all the days of his life. 30:And his allowance was a continual allowance given him of the King, a daily rate for every day, all the days of his life.

+/- March 25th. (Adar 29th.)

Jesus feeds about four thousand people

(Mark 8:1-9)1:In those days the multitude being very great, and having nothing to eat, Jesus called his disciples to him and said to them, 2:I have compassion on the multitude, because they have now been with me three days, and have nothing to eat: 3:And if I send them away fasting to their own houses, they will faint by the way: for divers of them came from far. 4:And his disciples answered him, From where can a man satisfy these men with bread here in the wilderness? 5:And he asked them, How many loaves do we have ? And they said, Seven. 6:And he commanded the people to sit down on the ground: and he took the seven loaves, and gave thanks, and brake, and gave to his disciples to set before them and they did set them out before the people. 7:And they had a few small fishes: and he blessed, and commanded to set them also before them. 8:So they did eat, and were filled: and they took up of the broken meat that was left seven baskets. 9:And they that had eaten were about four thousand: and he sent them away.

(Also as it is written in Mathew)

(Mathew 15:30-39) 30:And great multitudes came to him, having with them those that were lame, blind, dumb, maimed, and many others, and placed them down at Jesus' feet; and he healed them.31:Insomuch that the multitude wondered, when they saw the dumb to speak, the maimed to be whole, the lame to walk, and the blind to see: and they glorified the God of Israel. 32:Then Jesus called his disciples to him, and said, I have compassion on the multitude, because they continue with me now three days, and have nothing to eat: and I will not send them away fasting, lest they faint in the way. 33:And his disciples say to him, where should we have so much bread in the wilderness, as to fill so great a multitude? 34:And Jesus said to them, How many loaves have you? And they said, Seven, and a few little fishes. 35:And he commanded the multitude to sit down on the ground. 36:And he took the seven loaves and the fishes, and gave thanks, and brake them and gave to his disciples, and the disciples to the multitude.37:And they did all eat, and were filled: and they took up of the broken meat that was left seven baskets full.

38:And they that did eat were four thousand men, beside women and children. 39:And he sent away the multitude, and took ship, and came into the coasts of Magdala.

+/- March 26th. (Adar 30th.)

The year +/- 1358 B.C. And the Lord brought frogs to Egypt

(Exodus 7:25-8:7) 25:And seven days were fulfilled, after that the Lord had smitten the river. **8:1** And the Lord spoke to Moses, Go to Pharaoh, and say to him, this you the Lord, Let my people go, that they may serve me. 2:And if you refuse to let them go, behold, I will strike all your borders with frogs. 3:And the river shall bring forth frogs abundantly, which shall go up and come in to your house, and in to your bedchamber, and upon your bed, and in to the house of your servants, and upon your people, and in to their ovens, and in to your dreams. 4:And the frogs shall come up both on you, and upon your people, and upon all your servants.

5:And the Lord spoke to Moses, Say to Aaron, Stretch forth your hand with your rod over the streams, over the rivers, and over the ponds, and cause frogs to come up upon the land of Egypt. 6:And Aaron stretched out his hand over the waters of Egypt; and the frogs came up, and covered the land of Egypt. 7:And the magicians did so with their enchantments, and brought up frogs upon the land of Egypt.

+/- March 28th. (Adar 32nd.)

The year +/- 1358 B.C. Pharaoh ask Moses to take away the frogs

(Exodus 8:8-12) 8:Then Pharaoh called for Moses and Aaron, and said; Entreat the Lord, that he may take away the frogs from me, and from my people; and I will let the people go, that they may do sacrifice to the Lord. 9:And Moses said to Pharaoh, Glory over me: when shall I ask for you, and for your servants, and for your people, to destroy the frogs from you and your houses, that they may remain in the river only? 10:And he said, Tomorrow. And he said, Be it according to your word: that you may know that there is none like to the Lord our God. 11:And the frogs shall depart from you, and from your houses, and from your servants, and from your people; they shall remain in the river only. 12:And Moses and Aaron went out from Pharaoh: and Moses cried to the Lord because of the frogs, which he had brought against Pharaoh.

+/- March 29th. (Adar 33rd.)

The year +/- 1948 B.C. Isaac was born to Abraham

(Geneses 21:3) 3:And Abraham called the name of his son that was born to him, whom Sarah bare to him, Isaac.

+/- March 29th. (Adar 33rd.)

The year +/- 1358 B.C. The Lord killed all the frogs

(Exodus 8:13-15)13:And the Lord did according to the word of Moses; and the frogs died out of the houses, out of the villages, and out of the fields.

14:And they gathered them together upon heaps: and the land stank. 15:But when Pharaoh saw that there was respite, he hardened his heart, and hearkened not to them; as the Lord had said.

+/- March 30th. (Adar 34th.)

The year +/- 1358 B.C. Lice were sent upon the land

(Exodus 8:16-19) 16:And the Lord said to Moses, Say to Aaron, Stretch out your rod, and strike the dust of the land, that it may become lice throughout all the land of Egypt. 17:And they did so; for Aaron stretched out his hand with his rod, and struck the dust of the earth, and it became lice in man, and in beast; all the dust of the land became lice throughout all the land of Egypt. 18:And the magicians did so with their enchantments to bring forth lice, but they could not: so there were lice upon man, and upon beast. 19:Then the magicians said to Pharaoh, This is the finger of God: and Pharaoh's heart was hardened, and he hearkened not to them; as the Lord had said.

+/- March 31st. (Adar 35th.)

The year +/- 1358 B.C. The Lord said he would send swarms of flies:

(Exodus 8:20-23)20:And the Lord said to Moses, Rise up early in the morning, and stand before Pharaoh; look, when he comes forth to the water; and say to him, This says the Lord, Let my people go, that they may serve me. 21:Else, if you will not let my people go, behold, I will send swarms of flies upon you, and upon your servants, and upon your people, and into your houses: and the houses of the Egyptians shall be full of swarms of flies, and also the ground whereon they are. 22:And I will sever in that day the land of Goshen, in which my people dwell, that no swarms of flies shall be there; to the end you may know that I am the Lord in the midst of the earth. 23:And I will put a division between my people and your people: tomorrow shall this sign be.

(The fallowing also happened during the month of (March / Adar)

God spoke to Abraham and Blessed him

(Genesis 17:1-27) 1:And when Abram was ninety years old and nine, the Lord appeared to Abram, and said to him, I am the Almighty God; walk before me, and be you perfect. 2:And I will make my covenant between me and you, and will multiply you exceedingly. 3:And Abram fell on his face: and God talked with him, saying, 4:As for me, behold, my covenant is with you, and your shall be a father of many nations. 5:Neither shall your name any more be called Abram, but your name shall be Abraham; for a father of many nations have I made you. 6:And I will make you exceeding fruitful, and I will make nations of you, and kings shall come out of you. 7:And I will establish my covenant between me and you and your seed after you in their generations for an everlasting covenant, to be a God to you, and to your seed after you. 8:And I will give to you, and to your seed after you, the land wherein you are a stranger, all the land of Canaan, for an everlasting possession; and I will be their God. 9:And God said to Abraham, You shall keep my covenant before, you and your seed after you in their generations. 10:This is my covenant, which you shall keep, between me and you and your seed after you; Every man child among you shall be circumcised. 11:And you shall circumcise the flesh of your foreskin; and it shall be a token of the covenant between me and you. 12;And he that is eight days old shall be circumcised among you, every man child in your generations, he that is born in the house, or bought with money of any stranger, which is not of your seed. 13:He that is born in your house, and he that is bought with your money, must needs be circumcised: and my covenant shall be in your flesh for an everlasting covenant. 14:And the uncircumcised man child whose flesh of his foreskin is not circumcised, that soul shall be cut off from his people; he has broken my covenant. 15:And God said to Abraham, As for Sarai your wife, you shall not call her name Sarai, but Sarah shall her name be.16:And I will bless her, and give you a son also of her: yes, I will bless her, and she shall be a mother of nations; Kings of people shall be of her. 17:Then Abraham fell upon his face, and laughed, and said in his heart, Shall a child be born to him that is an hundred years old? and shall Sarah, that is ninety years old, bear? 18:And Abraham said to God, O that Ishmael might live before you! 19:And God said; Sarah your wife shall bear you a son indeed; and you shall call his name Isaac: and I will establish my covenant with him for an everlasting covenant, and with his seed after him. 20:And as for Ishmael, I have heard you: Behold, I have blessed him, and will make him fruitful, and will multiply him exceedingly; twelve princes shall he beget, and I will make him a great nation. 21;But my covenant will I establish with Isaac, which Sarah shall bear to you at this set time in the next year. 22:And he left off talking with him, and God went up from Abraham. 23:And Abraham took Ishmael I his son, and all that were born in his house, and all that were bought with his money, every male among the men of Abraham's house; and circumcised the flesh of their foreskin in the selfsame day, as God had said to him. 24:And Abraham was ninety years old and nine, when he was circumcised in the flesh of his foreskin. 25:And Ishmael his son was thirteen years old, when he was circumcised in the flesh of his foreskin. 26:On the same day that Abraham was circumcised, so was Ishmael his son. 27:And all the men of his house, born in the house, and bought with money of the stranger, were circumcised with him.

(During the beginning of the Barley Harvest)

David handed over seven to be hung

(2 Samuel 21:2-14) 2:And the King called the Gibeonites, and said to them; (now the Gibeonites were not of the children of Israel, but of the remnant of the Amorites; and the children of Israel had sworn to them: and Saul sought to slay them in his zeal to the children of Israel and Judah.) 3:Wherefore David said to the Gibeonites, What shall I do for you? and wherewith shall I make the atonement, that you may bless the inheritance of the Lord? 4:And the Gibeonites said to him, We will have no silver nor gold of Saul, nor of his house; neither for us shall you kill any man in Israel. And he said; What you shall say, that will I do for you. 5:And they answered the King, The man that consumed us, and that devised against us that we should be destroyed from remaining in any of the coasts of Israel. 6:Let seven men of his sons be delivered to us, and we will hang them up to the Lord in Gibeah of Saul, whom the Lord did choose. And the King said, I will give them.

7:But the King spared Mephibosheth, the son of Jonathan the son of Saul, because of the Lord's oath that was between them, between David and Jonathan the son of Saul. 8:But the King took the two sons of Rizpah the daughter of Aiah, whom she bare to Saul, Armoni and Mephibosheth; and the five sons of Michal the daughter of Saul, whom she brought up for Adriel the son of Barzillai the Meholathite. 9:And he delivered them into the hands of the Gibeonites, and they hanged them in the hill before the Lord: and they fell all seven together, and were put to death in the days of harvest, in the first days, in the beginning of barley harvest. 10:And Rizpah the daughter of Aiah took sackcloth, and spread it for her upon the rock, from the beginning of harvest until water dropped upon them out of heaven, and suffered neither the birds of the air to rest on them by day, nor the beasts of the field by night. 11:And it was told David what Rizpah the daughter of Aiah, the concubine of Saul, had done. 12:And David went and took the bones of Saul and the bones of Jonathan his son from the men of Jabeshgilead, which had stolen them from the street of Bethshan, where the Philistines had hanged them, when the of Jonathan his son; and they gathered the bones of them that were hanged. 14:And the bones of Saul and Jonathan his son buried they in the country of Benjamin in Zelah, in the sepulcher of Kish his father: and they performed all that the King commanded. And after that God granted relief to the land.

(Also during the Barley Harvest in the last part of this Month) Manasseh the husband of Judith dies

(Judith 8:2-5) 2:Her husband, Manasseh of her own tribe and clan, had died at the time of the Barley harvest. 3:While he was in the field, supervising those who bond the sheaves, he suffered a sunstroke. And was died from it, in Bethulia, his native city. He was buried with his forefathers in the field between Dothan and Balamon. 4:The widowed Judith remained three years and four mouths at home.5;where she set up a tent for herself on the roof of her house. She put on sackcloth about her loins and wore widow's weeds.

Above: A Picture of the barley harvest.

Above Barley, below a threshing floor. Below the floor there was another floor where the Barley would fall threw and could be gathered up and stored.

Zachariah was informed his wife would have a child.

(Luke 1:10-22)10:And the whole multitude of the people were praying without at the time of incense. 11:And there appeared to him an angel of the Lord standing on the right side of the altar of incense. 12:And when Zachariah saw him, he was troubled, and fear fell upon him. 13:But the Angel said to him, Fear not, Zachariah: for your prayer were heard; and your wife Elisabeth shall bear you a son, and you shall call his name John. 14:And you shall have joy and gladness; and many shall rejoice at his birth. 15:For he shall be great in the sight of the Lord, and shall drink neither wine nor strong drink; and he shall be filled with the Holy Ghost, even from his mother's womb.

16:And many of the children of Israel he shall turn back to the Lord their God. 17:And he shall go before him in the spirit and power of Elijah, to turn the hearts of the fathers to the children, and the disobedient to the wisdom of the just; to make ready a people prepared for the Lord. 18:And Zachariah said to the Angel, Why should I believe you? For I am an old man, and my wife well stricken in years.

19:And the Angel answering said to him, I am Gabriel, I am one who stands in the presence of God; and I was sent to speak to you, and to give you these glad tidings. 20:And, behold, you shall be dumb, and not be able to speak, until the day that these things shall be performed, because you did not believe my words, which shall be fulfilled in their season. 21:And the people waited for Zachariah, and marveled that he stayed so long in the temple. 22:And when he came out, he could not speak to them: and they perceived that he had seen a vision in the temple: for he beckoned to them, and remained speechless.

Extra notes:

Taken up to Heaven,

In a Chariot of Fire; Enoch in the year +/- 3898 B.C. (Genesis 5:24)

In a Whirlwind; Elijah in the year +/- 835 B.C. (2 King 2:11) Note: There is nothing ever mentioned of his parents, just that he was from the land of Gilead

In a Chariot of Light: Job's spirit was taken in June. (Note): Job was the 3rd. son of Issachar, who was the 5th. son born of Leah, Jacobs 1st wife Genesis 46:13

Received in the Clouds: Jesus in June at the beginning of the feast of weeks (Who died, then Returned, left and is coming back) (Mark 16:19, Luke 24:51)

On page 63: Jacobs well

It is said that anyone who drinks the water from this well will have a child, within three years.

On Page 68: The Sheep Gate

Also known as the Pool of Bethesda, is now kept drained. To stop the people from fighting over the water, when it starts to move, or get stirred up .

Note: On Page 71: The Task Masters

By the term officers; are today called: foremen, lead men, or group leaders. Some of them were also Hebrews slaves themselves, who were put in charge over the workers. So if they did not reach their quota for that day. In return they would be taken out and whipped. So they started whipping their fellow slaves, to keep from being beaten themselves.

Note: The Hebrew slaves were fed everyday they worked, in large eating areas, given meat, bread and wine, and were paid at the end of each month. According to their station, as in (Laborers, Stone Cutters, Water Carrier, Carpenters etc.)

Chapter 4:April - Nissan /Abib

It is the 1st. Month of the Hebrew calendar
In Hebrew this month is called: Nissan /Abib,
which means:(Their flight, a night to remember)
Tribe of Joseph, means:(He has given & He has taken away)
The stone of (Green Jade) represents this tribe.
Joseph: (The 1st.) Son of Rachel,
(Who is believed to have been born in this month,
in the year +/- 1796 B.C.E.)
(Spirit of War)

Note:(Exodus 12:2) 2:This month shall be to you,
the beginning of months.
(It shall be the first month of the year to you.)

+/- April 1st. (Nissan 1st.)

The year +/- 1357 B.C. God sent flies upon the land

(Exodus 8:24-29) 24:And the Lord did so; and there came a grievous swarm of flies into the house of Pharaoh, and into his servants' houses, and into all the land of Egypt: the land was corrupted by reason of the swarm of flies. 25:And Pharaoh called for Moses and for Aaron, and said, Go you, sacrifice to your God in the land. 26;And Moses said, It is not meet so to do; for we shall sacrifice the abomination of the Egyptians to the Lord our God: look, shall we sacrifice the abomination of the Egyptians before their eyes, and will they not stone us?

27:We will go three days' journey into the wilderness, and sacrifice to the Lord our God, as he shall command us. 28:And Pharaoh said, I will let you go, that you may sacrifice to the Lord your God in the wilderness; only you shall not go very far away: entreat for me. 29:And Moses said, Behold, I go out from you, and I will entreat the Lord that the swarms of flies may depart from Pharaoh, from his servants, and from his people, tomorrow: but let not Pharaoh deal deceitfully any more in not letting the people go to sacrifice to the Lord.

+/- April 1st. (Nissan 1st.)

They started to sanctify the house of the Lord

(2Chronicals 29:17) 17:Now they began on the first day of the first month to sanctify, and on the eighth day of the month came they to the porch of the Lord: so they sanctified the house of the Lord in eight days; and in the sixteenth day of the first month they made an end.

+/- April 1st. (Nissan 1st.)

Dream of Mordecai

(Esther A:1-11) 1:In the second year of the reign of the great King Alasuerus on the first day of Nissan, Mordecai the son of Jair, son of Shimei, son of Kish, of the tribe of Benjamin, had a dream. 2:He was a Hebrew residing in the city of Susa, a prominent man who served at the King's court, 3:and one of the captives whom Nebuchadnezzar, King of Babylon, had taken from Jerusalem with Jeconiah, King of Judah. 4:This was his dream; There was noise and therm oil, loud thunder then a earthquake, confusion upon the earth.

5:Two Great Dragons came out, both poised for combat. They uttered a mighty cry, 6:and at their cry every nation prepared for war., to fight against the race of the just. 7:it was a dark and gloomy day. Tribulation and distress, evil and great confusion, lay the earth. 8:The whole race the just were dismayed, of the evils of to come upon them, and were at the point of destruction. 9:Then they cried out to God, and as they cried, there appeared to come a great river, a flood of water from a little spring. 10:The light of the sun broke forth; the lowly were exalted and they and kept in mind devoured the nobles. 11:Having seen this dream and what God intended to do, Mordecai awoke. He kept it in mind, and tried in every way until night, to understand its meaning.

+/- April 1st. (Nissan 1st.)

The year +/- 452 B.C. Trip from Babylon

(Ezra 7:9) 9:For upon the first day of the first month began his journey to go up from Babylon to Jerusalem, and on the first day of the fifth month came he to Jerusalem, because the good hand of his God, was upon him.

+/- April 1st. (Nissan 1st.)

The year +/- 449 B.C. An end to the wrongful marriages

(Ezra 10:17-44) 17:And they made an end with all the men that had taken strange wives by the first day of the first month. 18:And among the sons of the priests there were found that had taken strange wives: namely; of the sons of Jeshua the son of Jozadak, and his brethren; Maaseiah, and Eliezer, and Jarib, and Gedaliah. 19:And they gave their hands that they would put away their wives; and being guilty, they offered a ram of the flock for their trespass. 20:And of the sons of Immer; Hanani, and Zebadiah.21:And of the sons of Harim; Maaseiah, and Elijah, and Shemaiah, and Jehiel, and Uzziah. 22:And of the sons of Pashur; Elioenai, Maaseiah, Ishmael,

Nethaneel, Jozabad, and Elasah. 23:Also of the Levites; Jozabad, and Shimei, and Kelaiah, (the same is Kelita,) Pethahiah, Judah, and Eliezer. 24:Of the singers also; Eliashib: and of the porters; Shallum, and Telem, and Uri. 25:Moreover of Israel: of the sons of Parosh; Ramiah, and Jeziah, and Malchiah, and Miamin, and Eleazar, and Malchijah, and Benaiah. 26:And of the sons of Elam; Mattaniah, Zechariah, and Jehiel, and Abdi, and Jeremoth, and Eliah. 27:And of the sons of Zattu; Elioenai, Eliashib, Mattaniah, and Jeremoth, and Zabad, and Aziza. 28:Of the sons also of Bebai; Jehohanan, Hananiah, Zabbai, and Athlai.

29:And of the sons of Bani; Meshullam, Malluch, and Adaiah, Jashub, and Sheal, and Ramoth. 30:And of the sons of Pahathmoab; Adna, and Chelal, Benaiah, Maaseiah, Mattaniah, Bezaleel, and Binnui, and Manasseh. 31:And of the sons of Harim; Eliezer, Ishijah, Malchiah, Shemaiah, Shimeon, 32:Benjamin, Malluch, and Shemariah. 33:Of the sons of Hashum; Mattenai, Mattathah, Zabad, Eliphelet, Jeremai, Manasseh, and Shimei. 34:Of the sons of Bani; Maadai, Amram, and Uel, 35:Benaiah, Bedeiah, Chelluh, 36:Vaniah, Meremoth, Eliashib, 37:Mattaniah, Mattenai, and Jaasau, 38:And Bani, and Binnui, Shimei, 39:And Shelemiah, and Nathan, and Adaiah, 40:Machnadebai, Shashai, Sharai, 41:Azareel, and Shelemiah, Shemariah, 42:Shallum, Amariah, and Joseph. 43:Of the sons of Nebo; Jeiel, Mattithiah, Zabad, Zebina, Jadau, and Joel, Benaiah. 44:All these had taken strange wives: and some of them had wives by whom they had children.

+/- April 1st. (Nissan 1st.)

The year +/- 580 B.C. God speaks Against the City of Tyre

(Ezekiel 26:1-21) 1:And it came to pass in the eleventh year, in the first day of the first month, that the word of the Lord came to me, saying, 2:Son of man, because that Tyrus, has spoke against Jerusalem, Aha, she is broken that was the gates of the people: she has turned to me: I shall be replenished, now she is laid waste. 3:Therefore this said the Lord God; Behold, I am against you, O Tyrus, and will cause many nations to come up against you, as the sea causes his waves to come up. 4:And they shall destroy the walls of Tyrus, and break down her towers: I will also scrape her dust from her, and make her like the top of a rock. 5;It shall be a place for the spreading of nets in the midst of the sea: for I have spoken it, said the Lord God: and it shall become a spoil to the nations. 6:And her daughters which are in the field shall be slain by the sword; and they shall know that I am the Lord.

7:For this says the Lord God; Behold, I will bring upon Tyrus Nebuchadrezzar King of Babylon, a King of kings, from the north, with horses, and with chariots, and with horsemen, and companies, and much people. 8:He shall slay with the sword your daughters in the field: and he shall make a fort against you, and cast a mount against you, and lift up the buckler against you. 9:And he shall set engines of war against your walls, and with his axes he shall break down your towers.10:By reason of the abundance of his horses their dust shall cover you: your walls shall shake at the noise of the horsemen, and of the wheels, and of the chariots, when he shall enter into your gates, as men enter into a city wherein is made a breach. 11:With the hoofs of his horses shall he tread down all your streets: he shall slay your people by the sword, and your strong garrisons shall go down to the ground.

12:And they shall make a spoil of your riches, and make a prey of your merchandise: and they shall break down your walls, and destroy your pleasant houses: and they shall lay your stones and your timber and your dust in the midst of the water. 13:And I will cause the noise of your songs to cease; and the sound of your harps shall be no more heard. 14:And I will make you like the top of a rock: you shall be a place to spread nets upon; you shall be built up no more: for I the Lord have spoken it, said the Lord God. 15;this says the Lord God to Tyrus; Shall not the isles shake at the sound of your fall, when the wounded cry, when the slaughter is made in the midst of you? 16:Then all the princes of the sea shall come down from their thrones, and lay away their robes, and put off their embroidered garments: they shall clothe themselves with trembling; they shall sit upon the ground, and shall tremble at every moment, and be astonished at you. 17:And they shall take up a lamentation for you, and say to you, How are you destroyed, that was inhabited of seafaring men, the renowned city, which wast strong in the sea, she and her inhabitants, which cause their terror to be on all that haunt it! 18:Now shall the isles tremble in the day of your fall; yes, the isles that are in the sea shall be troubled at your departure. 19:For this said the Lord God; When I shall make you a desolate city, like the cities that are not inhabited; when I shall bring up the deep upon you, and great waters shall cover you. 20:When I shall bring you down with them that descend into the pit, with the people of old time, and shall set you in the low parts of the earth, in places desolate of old, with them that go down to the pit, that all you be not inhabited; and I shall set glory in the land of the living; 21:I will make you a terror, and you shall be no more, though you be sought for yet shall you never be found again, said the Lord God.

+/- April 1st. (Nissan 1st.)

The year +/- 564 B.C. The Lord speaks of Nebuchadrezzar

(Ezekiel 29:17-21) 17;And it came to pass in the seven and twentieth year, in the first month,in the first day of the month, the word of the Lord came to me, saying, 18;Son of man, Nebuchadrezzar King of Babylon caused his army to serve a great service against Tyrus: every head was made bald, and every shoulder was peeled: yet had he no wages, nor his army, for Tyrus, for the service that he had served against it: 19;There fore this says the Lord God; Behold, I will give the land of Egypt to Nebuchadrezzar King of Babylon; and he shall take her multitude, and take her spoil, and take her prey; and it shall be the wages for his army. 20;I have given him the land of Egypt for his labor where he served against it, because they wrought for me, says the Lord God. 21;In that day will I cause the horn of the house of Israel to bud forth, and I will give you the opening of the mouth in the midst of them; and they shall know that I am the LORD.

+/- April 1st. (Nissan 1st.)

God speaks against the Syrians

(1Kings 20:26-28) 26:And it came to pass on the first of the year, that Benhadad numbered the Syrians, and went up to Aphek, to fight against Israel. 27:And the children of Israel were numbered, and were all present, and went against them: and the children of Israel pitched before them like two little flocks of kids;

but the Syrians filled the country. 28:And there came a man of God, and spoke to the King of Israel, and said, this says the Lord: Because the Syrians have said, The Lord is God of the hills, but he is not God of the valleys, therefore will I deliver all this great multitude in to your hands, and you shall know that I am the Lord.

+/- April 1st. (Nissan 1st.)

Jesus heals a blind man

(Mark 8:22-26) 22:And he came to Bethsaida; and they brought a blind man to him, and besought him to touch him. 23:And he took the blind man by the hand, and led him out of the town; and when he had spit on his eyes, and put his hands upon him, he asked him if he saw ought. 24:And he looked up, and said, I see men as trees, walking. 25:After that he put his hands again upon his eyes, and made him look up: and he was restored, and saw every man clearly. 26And he sent him away to his house, saying: Neither go into the town, nor tell it to any in the town.

+/- April 2nd. (Nissan 2nd.)

The year +/- 1357 God removed the flies

(Exodus 8:30-32)30:And Moses went out from Pharaoh, and entreated the Lord. 31:And the Lord did according to the word of Moses; and he removed the swarms of flies from Pharaoh, from his servants, and from his people; there remained not one. 32:And Pharaoh hardened his heart at this time also, neither would he let the people go.

+/- April 2nd. (Nissan 2nd.)

The plot to kill the King Discovered

(Esther A:12-17) 12: Mordecai lodged at the court with Bagathan and Thares, two eunuchs of the King who were court guards. 13: He overheard them plotting, investigated their plans, and discovered that they were preparing lay hands on King Ahasuerus. So he informed the King about them, and the King had the two eunuchs questioned and upon their confession, put to death. 15:Then the King had these things recorded; Mordecai , too, put them into writing. 16:The King also appointed Mordecai to serve at the court, and reward him for his actions. 17:Haman, however, son of Hammedatha the Agagite, who was in high honor with the King, sought to harm Mordecai and his people, because of the two eunuchs of the King.

+/- April 2nd. (Nissan 2nd.)

The Pharisees asked Jesus for a sign.

(Mathew 16:1-28) 1:The Pharisees also with the Sadducees came, and tempting desired him that he would show them a sign from heaven. 2:He answered and said to them, When it is evening, you say, it will be fair weather: for the sky is red. 3:And in the morning, It will be foul weather to day: for the sky is red and louring. O you hypocrites, you can discern the face of the sky; but can you do not discern the signs of the times? 4:A wicked and adulterous generation seek after a sign; and there shall be no sign given to you, but the sign of the prophet Jonas.

And he left them, and departed. 5:And when his disciples were come to the other side, they had forgotten to take bread. 6:Then Jesus said to them, Take heed and beware of the leaven of the Pharisees and of the Sadducees. 7:And they reasoned among themselves, saying, It is because we have taken no bread. 8:Which when Jesus perceived, he said to them, O you of little faith, why reason you among yourselves, because you have brought no bread? 9:Do you not yet understand, neither remember the five loaves, and the five thousand, and how many baskets you took up?, 10:Neither the seven loaves of the four thousand, and how many baskets you took up? 11:How is it that you do not understand that I speak, not to you concerning bread, that you should beware of the leaven of the Pharisees and of the Sadducees? 12:Then understood they how that he bade them not beware of the leaven of bread, but of the doctrine of the Pharisees and of the Sadducees. 13:When Jesus came into the coasts of Caesarea Philippi, he asked his disciples, saying, Whom do the men say that I the Son of man am? 14:And they said, Some say that you are John the Baptist: some, Elijah ; and others, Jeremiah, or one of the prophets. 15:He said to them, But whom do you say, that I am?

16:And Simon Peter answered and said; You are the Christ, the Son of the living God. 17:And Jesus answered and said to him; Blessed are you, Simon Baronage: for flesh and blood had not revealed this to you, but my Father which is in heaven. 18:And I say also to you, That you are Peter, and upon this rock I will build my church; and the gates of hell shall not prevail against it. 19:And I will give to you the keys of the kingdom of heaven: and whatsoever you shall bind on earth shall be bound in heaven: and whatsoever you shall loose on earth shall be loosed in heaven. 20:Then he charged his disciples that they should tell no man, that he was Jesus the Christ. 21:From that time on Jesus began to show his disciples, how that he must go to Jerusalem, and suffer many things of the elders and chief priests and scribes, and be killed, and be raised again the third day. 22:Then Peter took him, and began to rebuke him, saying, Be it far from you, Lord: this shall not be to you. 23:But he turned, and said to Peter, Get you behind me, Satan: you are an offense to me: for you want not the things that be of God, but those that be of men. 24:Then said Jesus to his disciples; If any man will come after me, let him deny himself, and take up his cross, and follow me. 25:For whosoever will try's to save his life shall lose it: and whosoever will lose his life for my sake shall find it. 26:For what is a man profited, if he shall gain the whole world, and lose his own soul? or what shall a man give in exchange for his soul? 27:For the Son of man shall come in the glory of his Father with his angels; and then he shall reward every man according to his works. 28:Verily truly;I say to you, There be some standing here, which shall not taste of death, till they see the Son of man coming in his kingdom.

+/- April 2nd. (Nissan 2nd.)

Jesus to his disciples about the Pharisees

(+/- 2nd Year of Jesus teaching)

(Mark 8:14 -38) 14:Now the disciples had forgotten to take bread, neither had they in the ship with them more than one loaf. 15:And he charged them, saying, Take heed, beware of the leaven of the Pharisees, and of the leaven of Herod. 16:And they reasoned among themselves, saying, It is because we have no bread.

17:And when Jesus knew it, he said to them; Why do you think, because we have no bread? Perceive you not yet,neither understand? have you let your hearts become hardened? 18:Having eyes, have you not seen? and having ears, have you not heard? and do you not remember? 19:When I brake the five loaves among five thousand, how many baskets full of fragments took you up? They said to him, Twelve. 20:And when the seven among four thousand, how many baskets full of fragments took you up? And they said seven. 21:And he said to them, How is it that you do not understand? 22:And he came to Bethsaida; and they brought a blind man to him, and asked him to touch him. 23:And he took the blind man by the hand, and led him out of the town; and when he had spit on his eyes, and put his hands upon him, he asked him what do you see? 24:And he looked up, and said, I see men as trees, walking. 25:After that he put his hands again upon his eyes, and made him look up: and he was restored, and saw every man clearly. 26;And he sent him away to his house, saying, Neither go into the town, nor tell it to any in the town. 27:And Jesus went out, and his disciples, to the towns of Caesarea Philippi: and by the way he asked his disciples, saying to them, Whom do men say that I am?

28:And they answered, John the Baptist: but some say,Elijah; and others, One of the prophets. 29:And he said to them, But whom do you say, that I am? And Peter answered and said to him, You are the Christ. 30:And he charged them that they should tell no man of him. 31:And he began to teach them, that the Son of man must suffer many things, and be rejected of the elders, and of the chief priests, and scribes, and be killed, and after three days rise again. 32:And he spoke that saying openly. And Peter took him, and began to rebuke him. 33:But when he had turned about and looked on his disciples, he rebuked Peter, saying, Get you behind me, Satan: for you do not want the things that are of God, but the things that are of men.

34:And when he had called the people to him with his disciples also, he said to them, Whosoever will come after me, let him deny himself, and take up his cross, and follow me. 35:For whosoever will save his life shall lose it; but whosoever shall lose his life for my sake and the gospel's, the same shall save it. 36:For what shall it profit a man, if he shall gain the whole world, and lose his own soul?37:Or what shall a man give in exchange for his soul? 38:Whosoever therefore shall be ashamed of me and of my words in this adulterous and sinful generation; of him also shall the Son of man be ashamed, when he comes in the glory of his Father with the holy angels.

+/- April 3rd. (Nissan 3rd.)

The year +/- 1317 B.C. Joshua sent out two spies,

(Joshua 2:1-4) 1:And Joshua the son of Nun sent out of Shittim two men to spy secretly, saying, Go view the land, even Jericho. And they went, and came into an harlot's house, named Rahab, and lodged there. 2:And it was told the King of Jericho, saying, Behold, there came men in hither to night of the children of Israel to search out the country. 3:And the King of Jericho sent to Rahab, saying, Bring to me the men that have come to you, which have entered into your house: for they have come to search out all the country. 4:And the woman, took the two men, and hid them, and said this, there came men to me, but I know not where they have gone.

+/- April 3rd. (Nissan 3rd.)

Daniel had a vision

(Daniel 10:1-3) 1:In the third year of Cyrus King of Persia a thing was revealed to Daniel, whose name was called Belteshazzar; and the thing was true, but the time appointed was long: and he understood the thing, and had understanding of the vision. 2:In those days I, Daniel was mourning three full weeks. 3:I ate no pleasant bread, neither came flesh nor wine in my mouth, neither did I anoint myself at all, till three whole weeks were fulfilled.

+/- April 4th. (Nissan 4th.)

The year +/- 1357 Moses told about the livestock dieing:

(Exodus 9:1-5) 1:Then the Lord said to Moses, Go in to Pharaoh, and tell him, This says the Lord God of the Hebrews, Let my people go, that they may serve me. 2:For if you refuse to let them go, and will hold them still. 3:Behold, the hand of the Lord is upon your cattle which is in the field, upon the horses, upon the asses, upon the camels, upon the oxen, and upon the sheep: there shall be a very grievous murrain. 4:And the Lord shall sever between the cattle of Israel and the cattle of Egypt: and there shall nothing die of all that is the children's of Israel. 5:And the Lord appointed a set time saying; Tomorrow the Lord shall do this thing in the land.

+/- April 4th. (Nissan 4th.)

The year +/- 1317 B.C. The two spies were let down in a basket

(Joshua 2:5-22) 5:And it came to pass about the time of shutting of the gate, when it was dark, that the men went out: where the men went I do not know: pursue after them quickly, for you shall overtake them. 6:But she had brought them up to the roof of the house, and hid them with the stalks of flax, which she had laid in order upon the roof. 7:And the men pursued after them the way to Jordan to the fords: and as soon as they which pursued after them were gone out, they shut the gate. 8:And before they were laid down, she came up to them upon the roof. 9:And she said to the men, I know that the Lord has given you the land, and that your terror is fallen upon us, and that all the inhabitants of the land are afraid because of you. 10:For we have heard how the Lord dried up the water of the Red sea for you, when you came out of Egypt; and what you did to the two Kings of the Amorites, that were on the other side Jordan, Sihon and Og, whom you utterly destroyed. 11:And as soon as we had heard these things, our hearts did melt, neither did there remain any more courage in any man, because of you: for the Lord your God, he is God in heaven above, and in earth beneath. 12:Now therefore, I pray you, swear to me by the Lord, since I have showed you kindness, that you will also show kindness to my father's house, and give me a truth token. 13:And that you will save the life of my Father, and my Mother, and my brothers, and my sisters, and all that they have, and deliver our lives from death. 14:And the men answered her, Our life for yours, if you utter not this our business. And it shall be, when the Lord has given us the land, that we will deal kindly and truly with you. 15:Then she let them down by a cord through the window: for her house was upon the town wall, and she dwelt upon the wall. 16:And she said to them, Get you to the mountain, lest the pursuers catch you;

and hide yourselves there three days, until the pursuers be returned:and afterward you may go your way. 17:And the men said to her, We will be true to this your oath which you have made us swear. 18:Behold, when we come into this land, you shall tie this line of scarlet thread in the window where you let us down by:and you shall bring your Father, and your Mother, and your brothers, and all your Father's household, home with you. 19:And it shall be, that whosoever shall go out of the doors of your house into the street, his blood shall be upon his head, and we will be guiltless: and whosoever shall be with you in the house, his blood shall be on our head, if any hand be upon him. 20:And if you utter this our business, then we will not be held to your oath, which you had made us swear to. 21:And she said, According to your words, so be it. And she sent them away, and they departed: and she bound the scarlet line in the window. 22;And they went, and came to the mountain, and abode there three days, until the pursuers were returned: and the pursuers sought them throughout all the way, but could not find them..

+/- April 4th. (Nissan 4th.)

The year +/- 48 C.E. Paul escaped from Nabatean the Governor.

(2Corinthians 11:32-33) 32:In Damascus the governor under Aretas the King kept the city of the Damascus with a garrison, desirous to apprehend me: 33:And through a window in a basket was I was let down by the wall, and escaped his hands.

+/- April 4th. (Nissan 4th.)

The Lord spoke to Elijah in a little voice in a cave

(1Kings 19:9-18) 9:And he then came upon a cave, and lodged there; and, behold, the word of the Lord came to him, and said to him, Why are you here, Elijah? 10:And he said, I have been very jealous for the Lord God of hosts: for the children of Israel have forsaken your covenant, thrown down your altars, and slain your prophets with the sword; and I, even I only, am left; and they seek my life, to take it away. 11:And he said, Go forth, and stand upon the mount before the Lord. And, behold, the Lord passed by, and a great and strong wind rent the mountains, and broke in pieces the rocks before the Lord; but the Lord was not in the wind: and after the wind an earthquake; but the Lord was not in the earthquake:

12:And after the earthquake a fire; but the Lord was not in the fire: and after the fire a still small voice. 13:And it was so,when Elijah heard it,that he wrapped his face in his mantle, and went out, and stood in the entering in of the cave. And, behold, there came a little voice to him, and said; What are you doing here, Elijah? 14:And he said, I have been very jealous for the Lord God of hosts: because the children of Israel have forsaken your covenant, thrown down thine altars, and slain your prophets with the sword; and I, even I only, am left; and they seek my life, to take it away. 15:And the Lord said to him, Go, return on your way to the wilderness of Damascus: and when you come to Hazael anoint him King over Syria. 16:And Jehu the son of Nimshi you shall anoint; to be King over Israel: and Elisha the son of Shaphat of Abelmeholah you shall anoint as prophet to succeed you. 17:And it shall come to pass, that him, that escapes the sword of Hazael shall Jehu slay: and him that escapes from the sword of Jehu shall Elisha slay.

18:Yet I have left me seven thousand in Israel, all the men who's knees have not bowed to Baal, and every mouth which has not kissed him.

+/- April 4th. (Nissan 4th.)

Satan tried to temp Jesus on the 40th. day

(Mathew 4:3-11) 3:And when the tempter came to him, he said, If you be the Son of God, command that these stones be made bread. 4:But he answered and said, It is written, Man shall not live by bread alone, but by every word that proceeds's out of the mouth of God. 5:Then the devil took him up in to the holy city, (Jerusalem): and sat him on a pinnacle of the temple, 6;And said to him; If you be the Son of God, cast yourself down, for it is written, He shall give his angels charge concerning you: and in their hands they shall bear you up, lest at any time you dash your foot against a stone. 7:Jesus said to him; It is written again, You shall not tempt the Lord your God. 8:Again, the devil took him up onto an exceeding high mountain, and showed him all the kingdoms of the world, and the glory of them; 9:And said to him, All these things will I give you, if you will fall down and worship me. 10:Then Jesus said to him, Get there behind me, Satan: for it is written, You shall worship the Lord your God, and him only shall you serve. 11:Then the devil left him, and behold angels came and ministered to him.

Please Note: 4:8: Originally was written as the kingdom that will rule the world. (It is believed that Satin had taken Jesus to the top of the mount of Olives, over looking Jerusalem)

(As it is written in the book of Mark 1:13)

(Mark 1:13) 13:And he was there in the wilderness forty days, then tempted by Satan; among the wild beasts; then the angels ministered to him.

+/- April 5th. (Nissan 5th.)

The year +/- 1948 B.C. Isaac was circumcised

(Genesis 21:4-7) 4:And Abraham circumcised his son Isaac being eight days old, as God had commanded him. 5:And Abraham was an hundred years old, when his son Isaac was born to him. 6:And Sarah said, God has made me to laugh, so that all that hear, will laugh with me. 7:And she said, Who would have said to Abraham, that Sarah should have given children suck? For now I have born him a son, in his old age.

+/- April 5th. (Nissan 5th.)

The year +/- 1357 All the cattle of Egypt died

(Exodus 9:6-12) 6:And the Lord did that thing on the next day, and all the cattle of Egypt died: but of the cattle of the children of Israel died not one. 7:And Pharaoh sent, and, behold, there was not one of the cattle of the Israelites dead. And the heart of Pharaoh was hardened, and he did not let the people go. 8:And the Lord said to Moses and to Aaron, Take to you handfuls of ashes of the furnace, and let Moses sprinkle it toward the heaven in the sight of Pharaoh.

9:And it shall become small dust in all the land of Egypt, and shall be a boil breaking forth with blistering upon man, and upon beast, throughout all the land of Egypt. 10:And they took ashes of the furnace, and stood before Pharaoh; and Moses sprinkled it up toward heaven; and it became a boil breaking forth with blistering upon man, and upon beast. 11:And the magicians could not stand before Moses because of the boils; for the boils was upon all of the magicians, and all the Egyptians. 12:And the Lord hardened the heart of Pharaoh, and he hearkened not to them; as the Lord had spoken to Moses.

+/- April 5th. (Nissan 5th.)

The year +/- 1011 B.C. David kills Goliath

(1Samuel 17:25-52) 24:And all the men of Israel, when they saw the man, fled from him, and were sore afraid. 25:And the men of Israel said, Have you ever seen this man that has come up to fight us? Surely to defy Israel he has come up: and it shall be, that the man who kills him, the King will enrich him with great riches, and will give him his daughter, and make his father's house free in Israel. 26:And David spoke to the men that stood by him, saying, What will be done to the man that kills this Philistine, and takes away the reproach from Israel? for who is this uncircumcised Philistine, that he should defy the armies of the living God? 27:And the people answered him in this manner, saying, So shall it be done to the man that kills him. 28:And Eliab his eldest brother heard when he was speaking to the men; and Eliab's anger was kindled against David, and he said, Why have you come down here? And with whom have you left those few sheep in the wilderness? I know your pride, and the evil of your heart; for you have come down that you might see the battle. 29:And David asked: What have I done now? Is there a reason or not?

30:And he turned from him toward another, and spoke in the same manner: and the people answered him again after the former manner. 31:And when the words were heard which David spoke, they went and told them to Saul: and he sent for him. 32:And David said to Saul, Let no man's heart fail because of him; your servant will go and fight with this Philistine. 33:And Saul said to David, you are not able to go against this Philistine to fight with him: for you are but a youth, and he a man of war from his youth. 34:And David said to Saul, your servant kept his father's sheep, and there came a lion, and a bear, and took a lamb out of the flock. 35:And I went out after him, and hit him, and delivered it out of his mouth: and when he arose against me, I caught him by his beard, and struck him, and killed him. 36:Your servant killed both the lion and the bear: and this uncircumcised Philistine shall be as one of them, seeing he has defied the armies of the living God. 37:David said moreover, The Lord that delivered me out of the paw of the lion, and out of the paw of the bear, he will deliver me out of the hand of this Philistine. And Saul said to David, Go, and the Lord be with you. 38;And Saul armed David with his armor, and he put an helmet of brass upon his head; also he armed him with a coat of mail. 39:And David girded his sword upon his armor. It was hard for him to walk, since he had never worn armor before (and was not use to the weight). And David said to Saul, I cannot go with these; for I have not used them before. And David took them off. 40: And he took his staff in his hand, and chose him five smooth stones out of the brook, and put them in a shepherd's bag which he had,

even in a scrip; and his sling was in his hand: and he drew near to the Philistine.
41:And the Philistine came on and drew near to David; and the man that bare the
shield went before him. 42:And when the Philistine looked about, and saw David,
he disdained him: for he was but a youth, and ruddy, and of a fair countenance.
43:And the Philistine said to David; Am I a dog, that you come to me with staff?
And the Philistine cursed David by his gods.

44:And the Philistine said to David, Come to me, and I will give your flesh to the
fowls of the air, and to the beasts of the field. 45:Then said David to the Philistine;
You come to me with a sword, and with a spear, and with a shield: but I come to you
in the name of the Lord of hosts, the God of the armies of Israel, whom you have
defied. 46:This day will the Lord deliver you into my hand; and I will strike you,
and take your head from you; and I will give the carcases of the host of the
Philistines this day to the fowls of the air, and to the wild beasts of the earth; that all
the earth may know that there is a God in Israel.

47:And all this assembly shall know that the Lord saves not with sword and spear:
for the battle is the Lord's, and he will give you into our hands. 48:And it came to
pass, when the Philistine arose, and came and drew nigh to meet David, that David
hasted,and ran toward the army to meet the Philistine. 49:And David put his hand in
his bag, and took thence a stone, and slang it, and hit the Philistine in his forehead,
that the stone sunk into his forehead; and he fell upon his face to the earth.

50:So David prevailed over the Philistine with a sling and with a stone, and struck
the Philistine, and killed him; but there was no sword in the hand of David.
51:Therefore David ran, and stood upon the Philistine, and took his sword, and drew
it out of the sheath thereof, and killed him, and cut off his head therewith. And when
the Philistines saw their champion was dead, they fled. 52:And the men of Israel
and of Judah arose, and shouted, and pursued the Philistines, until they came to the
valley, and to the gates of Ekron. And the wounded of the Philistines fell down on
the way to Shaaraim, even to Gath, and to Ekron.

+/- April 5th. (Nissan 5th.)

John the Baptist saw Jesus coming out of the wilderness

(John 1:35-42) 35:The next day that John (saw Jesus) he was with two of his
disciples, 36:and as he watched him walk by, and he said; Behold the lamb of God!
37:And the two disciples heard him speak, and they followed Jesus. 38:Then Jesus
turned, and saw them following him, and said to them; What are you looking for?
They said to him, Rabbi, (which in Hebrew, means, Teacher,) where are you
staying? 39:He said to them, Come and see. They came and saw where he lived,
and stayed with him that day: for it was about the tenth hour. 40:One of the two
which had heard John speak, and followed him, was Andrew, Simon Peter's brother.
41:He first found his own brother Simon, and said to him, We have found the
Messiah, which is, being interpreted, the Christ.

42:And he brought him to Jesus. And when Jesus saw him, he said, You are Simon
the son of Jona: you shall be called Peter, which is by interpretation, A stone.

+/- April 5th. (Nissan 5th.)

Jesus is told about Lazarus (+/- 8 days before he is killed)

(John 11:1-6) 1:Now a certain man was sick, named Lazarus, of Bethany, the town of Mary and her sister Martha. 2:(It was that Mary which anointed the Lord, with ointment, and wiped his feet with her hair, whose brother Lazarus was sick.) 3:Therefore his sisters sent to him, saying, Lord, behold, he whom you love is sick. 4:When Jesus heard that, he said, This sickness is not to death, but for the glory of God, that the Son of God might be glorified thereby. 5:Now Jesus loved Martha, her sister, and Lazarus. 6:When he had heard therefore that he was sick, he stayed there for two days more in the same place where he was.

+/- April 5th. (Nissan 5th.)

(Lazarus, of Bethany Died)

The brother of Martha and Mary; (Mary; who was the one who anointed the Lord with ointment, and wiped his feet with her hair), died and was laid in a tomb on this day.

+/- April 6th. (Nissan 6th.)

The year +/- 1357 Hail fell from Heaven

(Exodus 9:13-26) 13:And the Lord said to Moses, Rise up early in the morning, and stand before Pharaoh, and say to him, This says the Lord God of the Hebrews, Let my people go, that they may serve me. 14:For I will at this time send all my plagues upon your heart, and upon your servants, and upon your people; that you may know that there is none like me in all the earth. 15:For now I will stretch out my hand, that I may strike you and your people with pestilence; and you shall be cut off from the earth. 16:And in very deed for this cause have I raised you up, for to show in you my power; and that my name may be declared throughout all the earth. 17:As yet exalt you yourself against my people, that you will not let them go? 18:Behold, tomorrow about this time I will cause it to rain a very grievous hail, such as has not been in Egypt since the foundation thereof even until now. 19:Send therefore now, and gather your cattle, and all that you have in the field; for upon every man and beast which shall be found in the field, and shall not be brought home, the hail shall come down upon them, and they shall die. 20:He that feared the word of the Lord among the servants of Pharaoh made his servants and his cattle flee into the houses. 21:And he that regarded not the word of the Lord left his servants and his cattle in the field. 22:And the Lord said to Moses, Stretch forth your hand toward heaven, that there may be hail in all the land of Egypt, upon man, and upon beast, and upon every herb of the field, throughout the land of Egypt. 23:And Moses stretched forth his rod toward heaven: and the Lord sent thunder and hail, and the fire ran along upon the ground; and the Lord rained hail upon the land of Egypt. 24:So there was hail, and fire mingled with the hail, very grievous, such as there was none like it in all the land of Egypt since it became a nation. 25:And the hail struck all of the land of Egypt all that was in the field, both man and beast; and the hail struck every herb of the field, and broke every tree of the field. 26:Only in the land of Goshen, where the children of Israel were was there no hail.

+/- April 6$^{th.}$ (Nissan 6$^{th.}$)

The year +/- 1317 B.C. The two spies returned

(Joshua 2:23-24) 23;So the two men returned, and descended from the mountain, and passed over, and came to Joshua the son of Nun, and told him all things that befell them: 24:And they said to Joshua, Truly the Lord had delivered into our hands all the land; for even all the inhabitants of the country do grow faint because of us.

+/- April 6$^{th.}$ (Nissan 6$^{th.}$)

Jesus called Philip

(John 1:43-51) 43:The following day, (The 6th.) Jesus went into Galilee, and found Philip, and said to him, Follow me. 44:Now Philip was of Bethsaida, the city of Andrew and Peter. 45:Philip found Nathanael, and said to him, We have found him, of whom Moses in the law, and the prophets, did write, Jesus of Nazareth, the son of Joseph. 46:And Nathanael said to him, Can anything good come out of Nazareth? Philip said to him, Come and see. 47:Jesus saw Nathanael coming to him, and said of him, Behold an Israelite indeed, in whom is no guile! 48:Nathanael said to him, How do you know me? Jesus answered and said to him, Before Philip called you, when you were under the fig tree, I saw you. 49:Nathanael answered and said to him, Rabbi, you are the Son of God; you are the King of Israel. 50:Jesus answered and said to him, Because I said to you, I saw you under the fig tree, is that why you believe? You shall see greater things than these. 51:And he said to him, Verily truly, I say to you, Here after you shall see heaven open, and the angels of God ascending and descending upon the Son of man.

+/- April 7$^{th.}$ (Nissan 7$^{th.}$)

The year +/- 1357 B.C. Pharaoh called Moses about the Hail:

(Exodus 9:27-35) 27:And Pharaoh sent, and called for Moses and Aaron, and said to them, I have sinned this time: the Lord is righteous, and I and my people are wicked. 28:Entreat the Lord (for it is enough) that there be no more mighty thundering and hail; and I will let you go, and you shall stay no longer. 29:And Moses said to him, As soon as I am gone out of the city, I will spread abroad my hands to the Lord; and the thunder shall cease, neither shall there be any more hail; that you may know how that the earth is the Lord's.

30:But as for you and your servants, I know that you will not yet fear the Lord God. 31:And the flax and the barley was smitten: for the barley was in the ear, and the flax was boiled. 32:But the wheat and the rye were not struck: for they have not grown up. 33:And Moses went out of the city from Pharaoh, and spread abroad his hands to the Lord: and the thunders and hail ceased, and the rain was not poured upon the earth. 34:And when Pharaoh saw that the rain and the hail and the thunders were ceased, he sinned yet more, and hardened his heart, he and his servants.

35:And the heart of Pharaoh was hardened, neither would he let the children of Israel go; as the Lord had spoken by Moses.

+/- April 7th. (Nissan 7th.)

The year +/- 580 B.C. The day the Lord spoke against Egypt

(Ezekiel 30:20-26) 20:And it came to pass in the eleventh year, in the firs month, in the seventh day of the month, that the word of the Lord came to me, saying, 21:Son of man, I have broken the arm of Pharaoh King of Egypt; and, look, it shall not be bound up to be healed, to put a roller to bind it, to make it strong enough to hold the sword. 22:Therefore this said the Lord God; Behold, I am against Pharaoh King of Egypt, and will break his arms, the strong, and that which was broken; and I will cause the sword to fall out of his hand. 23:And I will scatter the Egyptians among the nations, and will disperse them through the countries. 24:And I will strengthen the arms of the King of Babylon, and put my sword in his hand: but I will break Pharaoh's arms, and he shall groan before him with the groaning, of a deadly wounded man. 25:But I will strengthen the arms of the King of Babylon, and the arms of Pharaoh shall fall down; and they shall know that I am the Lord, when I put my sword into the hand of the King of Babylon, and he shall stretch it out upon the land of Egypt. 26:And I will scatter the Egyptians among the nations, and disperse them among the countries; and they shall know that I am the Lord.

+/- April 7th. (Nissan 7th.)

Israel killed the Syrians

(1Kings 20:29-30) 29:And they pitched one over against the other seven days. And so it was, that in the seventh day the battle was joined: and the children of Israel killed of the Syrians an hundred thousand footmen in one day. 30:But the rest fled to Aphek, to the city; and there a wall fell upon twenty and seven thousand of the men that were left. And Benhadad fled, and came into the city, into an inner chamber.

+/- April 7th. (Nissan 7th.)

Jesus turned water in to wine (1st year of his teaching)

(John 2:1-11) 1:And the third day there was a marriage in Cana of Galilee; and the mother of Jesus was there. 2:And both Jesus was called, and his disciples, to the marriage. 3;And when they wanted wine, the mother of Jesus said to him, They have no wine. 4:Jesus said to her, Woman, what have I to do with this? my hour is not yet come. 5:His mother said to the servants, Whatsoever he says to you, do it. 6:And there were six water pots of stone sitting there, after the manner of the purifying of the Jews, each containing twenty to thirty gallons.

7:Jesus said to them, Fill the water pots with water. And they filled them up to the brim. 8:And he said to them, Draw out now, and take some to the governor of the feast. And they did as he said. 9:When the ruler of the feast had tasted the water that was made wine, and did not know where it came from : (But the servants which drew the water knew;) the governor of the feast called the bridegroom.
10:And said to him, Every man at the beginning first puts out his best wine; and when men have well drunk, then he brings out the lesser wine: but you have kept the best wine until now. 11:This beginning of miracles did Jesus in Cana of Galilee, and manifested forth his glory; and his disciples believed on him.

Below: is the church where it is believed that Jesus turned water into wine in Cana of Galilee

+/- April 8th. (Nissan 8th.)

The year +/- 1357 B.C. Moses stretched out his hand

(Exodus 10:1-15)1:And the Lord said to Moses, Go in to Pharaoh: for I have
hardened his heart, and the heart of his servants, that I might show these my signs
before him. 2:And that you may tell in the ears of your son, and of your son's son,
what things I have wrought in Egypt, and my signs which I have done among them;

that you may know how that I am the Lord. 3:And Moses and Aaron came in to Pharaoh, and said to him, This says the Lord God of the Hebrews, How long will you refuse to humble yourself before me? Let my people go, that they may serve me. 4:Else, if you refuse to let my people go, behold, to tomorrow I will bring the locusts to your coast. 5:And they shall cover the face of the earth, that one cannot be able to see the earth: and they shall eat the residue of that which is escaped, which remains to you from the hail, and shall eat every tree which grows for you out of the field. 6:And they shall fill your houses, and the houses of all your servants, and the houses of all the Egyptians; which neither your fathers, nor your fathers' fathers have seen, since the day that they were upon the earth to this day. And he turned himself, and went out from Pharaoh. 7:And Pharaoh's servants said to him, How long shall this man be a snare to us? Let the men go, that they may serve the Lord their God: know you not yet that Egypt is destroyed? 8:And Moses and Aaron were brought again to Pharaoh: and he said to them, Go, serve the Lord your God: but who are they that shall go? 9:And Moses said, We will go with our young and with our old, with our sons and with our daughters, with our flocks and with our herds will we go; for we must hold a feast to the Lord. 10:And he said to them, Let the Lord be so with you, as I will let you go, and your little ones: look to it, for evil is before you. 11:Not so: go now you that are men, and serve the Lord; for that you did desire. And they were driven out from Pharaoh's presence1 12:And the Lord said to Moses, Stretch out your hand over the land of Egypt for the locusts, that they may come up upon the land of Egypt, and eat every herb of the land, even all that the hail has left. 13:And Moses stretched forth his rod over the land of Egypt, and the Lord brought an east wind upon the land all that day, and all that night; and when it was morning, the east wind brought the locusts. 14:And the locusts went up over all the land of Egypt, and rested in all the coasts of Egypt: very grievous were they; before them there were no such locusts as they, neither after them shall be such. 15:For they covered the face of the whole earth, so that the land was darkened; and they did eat every herb of the land, and all the fruit of the trees which the hail had left: and there remained not any green thing in the trees, or in the herbs of the field, through all the land of Egypt.

+/- April 8th. (Nissan 8th.)

The year +/- 1317 B.C. Preparations for crossing the Jordan

(Joshua 3:1) 1:And Joshua rose early in the morning; and they moved from Shittim, and came to Jordan, he and all the children of Israel, and lodged there before they passed over.

+/- April 8th. (Nissan 8th.)

Benhadad sent his servants to Ahab to beg for his life

(1Kings 20:31-34) 31:And his servants said to him, Behold now, we have heard that the Kings of the house of Israel are merciful Kings: let us, I ask you, put sackcloth on our loins, and ropes upon our heads, and go out to the King of Israel: to see if he will spare your life. 32:So they girded sackcloth on their loins, and put ropes on their heads, and came to the King of Israel, and said, your servant Benhadad says, I pray that you, let me live. And he said, Is he still alive? He is my brother.

33:Now the men did diligently observe whether any thing good would come from him, and did quickly catch it; and they said, Your brother Benhadad. Then he said, Go you, bring him here . Then Benhadad came forth to him; and he caused him to come up into the chariot. 34:And Benhadad said to him, The cities, which my father took from your father, I will restore; and we will make streets for you in Damascus, as my father made in Samaria. Then said Ahab, I will send you away with this covenant. So he made a covenant with him, and sent him away.

+/- April 8th. (Nissan 8th.)

They finished sanctifying the Lords temple

(2Chroncles 29:17) 7:Now they began on the first day of the first month to sanctify, and on the eighth day of the month came they to the porch of the LORD: so they sanctified the house of the LORD for eight days; and in the sixteenth day of the first month they made an end.

+/- April 8th. (Nissan 8th.)

The Pharisees and Scribes murmured against Jesus

(+/- The 2nd. Year of his ministry)

(Luke 15:1-17:37) 1:Then drew near to him all the publicans and sinners to hear him. 2:And the Pharisees and Scribes murmured, saying, This man receives sinners, and eats with them. 3;And he spoke this parable to them, saying; 4:What man of you, having an hundred sheep, if he lose one of them, will not leave the ninety and nine in the wilderness, and go after that which is lost, until he find it? 5;And when he has found it, he carry's it on his shoulders, rejoicing. 6;And when he comes home, he calls together all his friends and neighbors, saying to them, Rejoice with me; for I have found my sheep which was lost. 7:I say to you, that likewise joy shall be in heaven over one sinner that repents, more than over ninety and nine just persons, which need no repentance. 8:Either what woman having ten pieces of silver, if she lose one piece, does not light a candle, and sweep the house, and seek diligently till she finds it.9:And when she has found it, she calls her friends and her neighbors together, saying, Rejoice with me; for I have found the piece which I had lost. 10:Likewise, I say to you, there is joy in the presence of the angels of God over one sinner that repents.

11:And he said, A certain man had two sons. 12:And the younger of them said to his father, Father, give me the portion of goods that fall to me. And he divided and gave to him his living. 13:And not many days after the younger son gathered all together, and took his journey to a far country, and there wasted his substance with riotous living. 14:And when he had spent all, there arose a mighty famine in that land; and he began to be in want.

15:And he went to work for a citizen of that country; and he sent him into his fields to feed swine. 16:And he would have been happy to fill his belly with the husks that the swine did eat: but no man gave any to him. 17:And when he came to himself, he said, How many hired servants of my father's have bread enough to spare, and I perish with hunger!

18:I will arise and go to my father, and will say to him, Father, I have sinned against
heaven, and before you. 19:And am no more worthy to be called your son: make me
as one of your hired servants. 20:And he arose, and came to his father. But when he
was yet a great way off, his father saw him, and had compassion, and ran,
and fell on his neck, and kissed him. 21:And the son said to him, Father, I have
sinned against heaven, and in your sight, and am no more worthy to be called your
son. 22:But the Father said to his servants, Bring forth the best robe, and put it on
him, and put a ring on his hand, and shoes on his feet: 23:And bring hither the fatted
calf, and kill it; and let us eat, and be merry.

24:For this my son was dead, and is alive again; he was lost, and is found. And they
began to be merry. 25:Now his elder son was in the field: and as he came and drew
nigh to the house, he heard music and dancing. 26:And he called one of the
servants, and asked what these things meant. 27:And he said to him;Your brother
has come home; and your Father has killed the fatted calf, because he has received
him safe and sound.

28:And he was angry, and would not go in: therefore his Father came out, and
asked him why he would not come in. 29:And he answering said to his Father, Lo,
all these many years did I serve you, neither transgressed I at any time your
commandment: and yet you never gave me a kid, that I might make merry with my
friends. 30;But as soon as this your son had come home, which has devoured your
living with harlots, you have killed for him a fatted calf. 31:And he said to him,
Son, you are always with me, and all that I have is yours. 32:It was meet that we
should make merry, and be glad: for this your brother was dead, and is alive again;
and was lost, and is found.

16:1: And he said also to his disciples; There was a certain rich man, which had a
steward; and the same was accused to him that he had wasted his goods. 2:And he
called him, and said to him, Why is it that I hear this about you? Give an account of
your stewardship; for you may be no longer my steward. 3:Then the steward said
within himself, What shall I do? for my lord is taking away from me the
stewardship: I cannot dig; to beg I am ashamed. 4:I am resolved what to do, that,
when I am put out of the stewardship, they may receive me into their houses.

5:So he called every one of his lord's debtors to him, and said to the first, How
much do you owe my lord? 6:And he said, An hundred measures of oil. And he said
to him, Take your bill, and sit down quickly, and write fifty. 7:Then said he to
another, And how much do you owe? And he said, An hundred measures of wheat.
And he said to him, Take your bill, and write fourscore.

8:And the lord commended the unjust steward, because he had done wisely: for the
children of this world are in their generation wiser than the children of light. 9:And I
say to you, Make to yourselves friends of the mammon of unrighteousness; that,
when you fail, they may receive you into everlasting habitations. 10:He that is
faithful in that which is least is faithful also in much: and he that is unjust in the
least is unjust also in much. 11:If therefore you have not been faithful in the
unrighteous mammon, who will commit to your trust the true riches?

12:And if you have not been faithful in that which is another man's, who shall give
you that which is your own, 13:No servant can serve two masters: for either he will
hate the one, and love the other; or else he will hold to the one, and despise the
other. You cannot serve God and mammon.
14:And the Pharisees also, who were covetous, heard all these things: and they
derided him.

15:And he said to them; You are they who justify yourselves before men; but God
knows your hearts:for that which is highly esteemed among men is abomination in
the sight of God. 16:The law and the prophets were until John: since that time the
kingdom of God is preached, and every man presses into it.17:And it is easier for
heaven and earth to pass, than one little letter of the law.

18:Whosoever divorce his wife, (for any other reason than sexual immorality) and
marries another, commits adultery: and whosoever marries her that is put away from
her husband, commits adultery. 19: There was a certain rich man, which was clothed
in purple and fine linen, and fared sumptuously every day. 20:And there was a
certain beggar named Lazarus, which was laid at his gate, full of sores.

21:And even wishing to be fed with the crumbs which fell from the rich man's table:
moreover the dogs came and licked his sores. 22:And it came to pass, that the
beggar died, and was carried by the angels into Abraham's bosom: the rich man also
died, and was buried. 23:And in hell he lift up his eyes, being in torments, and seen
Abraham afar off, and Lazarus in his bosom. 24:And he cried and said, Father
Abraham, have mercy on me, and send Lazarus, that he may dip the tip of his finger
in water, and cool my tongue; for I am tormented in this flame.

25:But Abraham said, Son, remember that you in your lifetime received your good
things, and likewise Lazarus evil things: but now he is comforted, and you are
tormented. 26:And beside all this, between us and you there is a great gulf fixed: so
that they which nothing can pass from here to you; neither can they pass to us, that
would come from there. 27:Then he said, I pray then therefore, father, that you
would send him to my father's house.

28:For I have five brethren; that he may testify to them, lest they also come into
this place of torment. 29:Abraham said to him, They had Moses and the prophets;
let them hear them. 30:And he said, No, Father Abraham: but if one went to them
from the dead, they will repent. 31;And he said to him, If they will not listen to
Moses and the prophets, neither will they be persuaded, though one rose from the
dead.

17:1;Then he said to the disciples, It is impossible not for sins to come in to this
world; but woe to him through whom they come! 2:It were better for him that a
millstone were hanged about his neck, and he cast into the sea, than that he should
offend one of these little ones. 3:Take heed to yourselves: If your brother trespass's
against you, rebuke him; and if he repent, forgive him.4:And if he trespass against
you seven times in a day, and seven times in a day turn again to you, saying, I
repent; you shall forgive him.

5:And the apostles said to the Lord, Increase our faith. 6:And the Lord said, If you had faith as a grain of mustard seed, you might say to this sycamore tree, Be you plucked up by the root, and be you planted in the sea; and it should obey you. 7:But which of you, having a servant plowing or feeding cattle, will say to him by and by, when he is come from the field, Go and sit down to eat some meat?

8:And will not rather you say to him, Make ready something for me to eat, and gird yourself, and serve me, till I have eaten and drunken; and afterward you shall eat and drink? 9:Does he thank the servant because he did the things that were commanded him? I think not.10:So likewise you, when you shall have done,all the things which are commanded you, say, We are unprofitable servants: we have done that which was our duty to do.

11:And it came to pass, as he went to Jerusalem, that he passed through the midst of Samaria and Galilee. 12:And as he entered to a certain village, there met him ten men that were lepers, which stood afar off. 13:And they lifted up their voices, and said, Jesus, Master, have mercy on us. 14:And when he saw them, he said to them, Go show yourselves to the priests. And it came to pass, that, as they went, they were cleansed.

15:And one of them, when he saw that he was healed, turned back, and with a loud voice glorified God,16:And fell down on his face at his feet, giving him thanks: and he was a Samaritan.

17:And Jesus answering said, Were there not ten cleansed? but where are the nine? 18:There are not found that returned to give glory to God, save this stranger. 19:And he said to him, Arise, go your way: your faith has made you whole.

20:And when he was demanded of the Pharisees, when the kingdom of God should come, he answered them and said, The kingdom of God comes not with observation: 21;Neither shall they say, Look here! or, look there! for, behold, the kingdom of God is within you.

22:And he said to the disciples, The days will come, when you shall desire to see one of the days of the Son of man, and you shall not see it. 23:And they shall say to you, See here; or, see there: go not after them, nor follow them. 24:For as the lightning flashes and lights up the shy from one side to another,; so shall also the Son of man be in his day. 25:But first must he suffer many things, and be rejected of this generation. 26:And as it was in the days of Noe, so shall it be also in the days of the Son of man. 27:They did eat, they drank, they married wives, they were given in marriage, until the day that Noah entered into the ark, and the flood came, and destroyed them all. 28;Likewise also as it was in the days of Lot; they did eat, they drank, they bought, they sold, they planted, they build.
29:But the same day that Lot went out of Sodom it rained fire and brimstone from heaven, and destroyed them all. 30:Even this shall it be in the day when the Son of man is revealed. 31:In that day, he which shall be upon the housetop, and his stuff in the house, let him not come down to take it away: and he that is in the field, let him likewise not return back. 32:Remember Lot's wife.

33:Whosoever shall seek to save his life shall lose it; and whosoever shall lose his life shall preserve it. 34:I tell you, in that night there shall be two men in one bed; the one shall be taken, and the other shall be left. 35:Two women shall be grinding together; the one shall be taken, and the other left. 36:Two men shall be in the field; the one shall be taken, and the other left. 37;And they answered and said to him, Where, Lord? And he said to them; Where so ever the body is, there also will the eagles be gathered together.

+/- April 8th. (Nissan 8th.)

Jesus transformed in front of Peter, James and John

(+/- 2nd. Year of his Ministry)

(Mathew 17:1-21) 1:And after six days Jesus took Peter, James, and John his brother, and brought them up to an high mountain apart. 2:And he was transfigured before them: and his face did shine as the sun, and his raiment was white as the light. 3:And, behold, there appeared to them Moses and Elijah talking with him. 4:Then answered Peter, and said to Jesus, Lord, it is good for us to be here: if you will let us make here, three tabernacles; one for you, and one for Moses, and one for Elijah. 5:While he was spoke, behold, a bright cloud overshadowed them: and behold a voice came out of the cloud, which said, This is my beloved Son, in whom I am well pleased; hear you him. 6:And when the disciples heard it, they fell on their face, and were sore afraid. 7:And Jesus came and touched them, and said, Arise, and be not afraid. 8:And when they had lifted up their eyes, they saw no one else, only Jesus. 9:And as they came down from the mountain, Jesus charged them, saying, Tell the vision to no man, until the Son of man be risen again from the dead.

10:And his disciples asked him, saying, Why then say the scribes that Elijah must first come? 11:And Jesus answered and said to them, Elijah truly shall first come, and restore all things. 12:But I say to you, That Elijah has come already, and they did not know him, but have done to him whatsoever they wanted. Likewise shall also the Son of man suffer of them. 13:Then the disciples understood that he spoke to them, of John the Baptist. 14:And when they were come to the multitude, there came to him a certain man, kneeling down to him, and saying, 15:Lord, have mercy on my son: for he is lunatic, and suffers severely: for ofttimes he falls into the fire, and often into the water. 16:And I brought him to your disciples, and they could not cure him. 17:Then Jesus answered and said, O faithless and perverse generation, how long shall I be with you? how long shall I suffer you? bring him hither to me. 18:And Jesus rebuked the devil; and he departed out of him: and the child was cured from that very hour. 19:Then came the disciples came to Jesus, and asked, Why could not we cast him out? 20;And Jesus said to them, Because of your unbelief: for verily I say to you, If you have faith as a grain of mustard seed, you shall say to this mountain, Remove yourself and go over there; and it shall remove; and nothing will be impossible for you. 21:However this kind is only cast out by;prayers and fasting.

(Also as it is written in Mark 9:2-50)

(Mark 9:2-50) 2;And after six days Jesus took with him Peter, and James, and John, and leaded them up to an high mountain apart by themselves: and he was transfigured before them.

3;And his raiment became shining, exceeding white as snow; so as no fuller on
earth can white them. 4:And there appeared to them Elijah with Moses: and they
were talking with Jesus. 5:And Peter answered and said to Jesus, Master, it is good
for us to be here: and let us make three tabernacles; one for you, and one for Moses,
and one for Elijah. 6:For he did not know what to say; for they were so afraid.

7:And there was a cloud that overshadowed them: and a voice came out of the
cloud, saying, This is my beloved Son: hear him. 8:And suddenly, when they had
looked round about, they saw no man any more, save Jesus only with themselves.
9:And as they came down from the mountain, he charged them that they should tell
no man what things they had seen, till the Son of man were risen from the dead.
10:And they kept that saying with themselves, questioning one with another what
the rising from the dead should mean. 11:And they asked him, saying, Why do the
scribes say that Elijah must first come?

12:And he answered and told them; Elijah does have to come first, and restored all
things; and how it is written of the Son of man, that he must suffer many things, and
be treated with contempt. 13:But I say to you, That Elijah has indeed already come,
and they have done to him whatsoever they wanted, as it is written of him.

14:And when he came to his disciples, he saw a great multitude about them, and the
scribes questioning with them. 15:And straightway all the people, when they beheld
him, were greatly amazed, and running to him to greet him. 16:And he asked the
scribes, What are you arguing with them about?

17:And one of the multitude answered and said, Master, I have brought to you my
son, which has a dumb spirit. 18:And where ever he seizes him, he throws him
down; and he foams, and gnashes with his teeth, and becomes rigid: and I spoke to
your disciples and asked if they would cast him out; but they could not. 19:He
answered him, and said, O faithless generation, how long shall I be with you? how
long shall I suffer you? bring him to me.

20:And they brought him to him: and when he saw him, straightway the spirit took
him; and he fell on the ground, and wallowed foaming. 21:And he asked his father,
How long has it been, since this came to him? And he said, sense he was a child.
22:And ofttimes it has cast him into the fire, and into the waters, to destroy him: but
if you can do anything, have compassion on us, and help us. 23:Jesus said to him, If
you can believe, all things are possible to him that believes.

24:And straightway the father of the child cried out, and said with tears, Lord, I
believe; please help me with my faith. 25:When Jesus saw that the people came
running together, he rebuked the foul spirit, saying to him, You dumb and deaf
spirit, I order you, come out of him, and never enter in to him again.

26:And the spirit cried, and tossed to the ground, and came out of him: and he was
as one dead; insomuch that many said, He is dead. 27;But Jesus took him by the
hand, and lifted him up; and he arose. 28:And when he came in to the house, his
disciples asked him privately, Why couldn't we cast him out?

29:And he said to them, This kind can only be brought out, by prayer and fasting.
30:And then they departed, and passed through Galilee; and he would not that any
man should know it. 31:For he taught his disciples, and said to them, The Son of
man is delivered into the hands of men, and they shall kill him; and after that he is
killed, he shall rise the third day.

32:But they understood not that saying, and were afraid to ask him. 33:And he came
to Capernaum: and being in the house he asked them, What was it that you disputed
among yourselves by the way? 34;But they held their peace: for by the way they
had disputed among themselves, who should be the greatest. 35;And he sat down,
and called the twelve, and said to them, If any man desire to be first, the same shall
be last of all, and servant of all.

36;And he took a child, and set him in the midst of them: and when he had taken
him in his arms, he said to them, 37:Whosoever shall receive one of such children in
my name, receive me: and whosoever shall receive me, receive not me, but him that
sent me. 38:And John answered him, saying, Master, we saw one casting out devils
in your name, and he does not follow us: and so we forbid him, because he was not
following us.

39:But Jesus said, Forbid him not: for there is no man which shall do a miracle in
my name, that can lightly speak evil of me. 40:For he that is not against us is on our
part. 41:For whosoever shall give you a cup of water to drink in my name, because
you belong to Christ, verily I say to you, he shall not lose his reward. 42:And
whosoever shall offend one of these little ones that believe in me, it is better for him
that a millstone were hanged about his neck, and he were cast into the sea. 43:And if
your hand offend you, cut it off: it is better for you to enter into life maimed, than
having two hands to go into hell, into the fire that never shall be quenched:
44:Where their worm do not die, and the fire is not quenched.

45:And if your foot offend you, cut it off: it is better for you to enter into life
without a foot, than having two feet to be cast into hell, into the fire that never shall
be quenched. 46:Where their worm do not die, and the fire is not quenched. 47:And
if your eye offend you, pluck it out: it is better for you to enter into the kingdom of
God with one eye, than having two eyes to be cast into hell fire: 48:Where their
worm never die, and the fire is not quenched. 49:For every one shall be salted with
fire, and every sacrifice shall be salted with salt. 50:Salt is good: but if the salt have
loses its flavor, what can you season with it? Have salt in yourselves, and have
peace one with another.

+/- April 8th. (Nissan 8th.)

Lazarus was raised from the grave

(John 11:7-53) 11;Then after that he said to his disciples, Let us go to Judea again.
8:His disciples said to him, Master, the Jews of late sought to stone you there; and
now you want to go back again? 9;Jesus said, Are there not twelve hours in the day?
If any man walk in the day, he does not stumble, because he can see the light of this
world.

10;But if a man walk in the night, he stumbles, because there is no light in him.
11:These things he said : and after that he said to them, Our friend Lazarus sleeps;
but I will go, that I may awake him out of sleep. 12;Then said his disciples, Lord, if
he sleep, he shall do well. 13:Though Jesus spoke of his death, but they thought
that he had spoken of taking of rest in sleep. 14:Then said Jesus to them plainly,
Lazarus is dead. 15:And I am glad for your sakes that I was not there, to the intent
you may believe; nevertheless let us go to him.

16:Then said Thomas, which is called Didymus, to his fellow disciples, Let us also
go, that we may die with him. 17:Then when Jesus came, he found that he had been
in the grave four days already. 18:Now Bethany was close to Jerusalem,
about fifteen furlongs off. 19:And many of the Jews came to Martha and Mary, to
comfort them concerning their brother.

20:Then Martha, as soon as she heard that Jesus was coming, went and met him: but
Mary sat still in the house. 21:Then said Martha to Jesus, Lord, if you had been
here, my brother would not have died. 22:But I know, that even now, what so ever
you will ask of God, God will give to you.

23:Jesus said to her, your brother shall rise again. 24:Martha said to him, I know
that he shall rise again in the resurrection at the last day. 25:Jesus said to her, I am
the resurrection, and the life: he that believes in me, though he were dead, yet shall
he live: 26:And whosoever lives and believes in me shall never die. Do you Believe
this?

27:She said to him, Yes, Lord: I believe that you are the Christ, the Son of God,
which should come into the world. 28:And when she had said this, she went her
way, and called Mary her sister secretly, saying, The Master has come, and calls for
you. 29;As soon as she heard that, she arose quickly, and came to him. 30;Now
Jesus has not yet, come in to the town, but was in that place where Martha met him.

31:The Jews then which were with her in the house, and comforted her, when they
saw Mary, that she rose up hastily and went out, followed her, saying, She is going
to the grave, to cry there. 32:Then when Mary had come to where Jesus was, and
saw him, she fell down at his feet, saying to him, Lord, if you had only been here,
my brother would not have died. 33:When Jesus saw her weeping, and the Jews also
weeping which came with her, he groaned in the spirit, and was troubled,

34:And said, Where have you laid him? They said to him, Lord, come and see.
35:Jesus wept. 36:Then said the Jews, Behold how he loved him! 37:And some of
them said, Could not this man, which opened the eyes of the blind, have caused that
even this man should not have died? 38:Jesus therefore again groaning in himself
came to the grave. It was a cave, and a stone lay upon it.

39:Jesus said, Take you, away the stone. Martha, the sister of him that was dead,
said to him, Lord, by this time he stinks: for he has been dead four days. 40:Jesus
said to her, Did I not say to you, that, if you would only believe, that you would see
the glory of God?

41:Then they took away the stone from the place, where he was laid. And Jesus lifted up his eyes, and said, Father, I thank you that you have heard me. 42:And I knew that you hear me always: but because of the people which stand by, I ask this so that they may believe that you have sent me. 43:And when he this had spoken, he cried with a loud voice, Lazarus, come here.

44:And he that was dead came forth, bound hand and foot with grave clothes: and his face was bound about with a napkin. Jesus said to them, Let him loose , and let him go. 45:Then many of the Jews which came to Mary, and had seen the things which Jesus did, believed on him. 46:But some of them went their ways to the Pharisees, and told them what things Jesus had done. 47:Then gathered the chief priests and the Pharisees a council, and said, What do we? for this man does many miracles.

48;If we let him alone, all men will believe on him: and the Romans shall come and take away both our place and nation. 49:And one of them, named;Caiaphas, being the high priest that same year, said to them, You know nothing at all. 50:Nor consider that it is expedient for us, that one man should die for the people, so that the whole nation may not perish.

51:And this he spoke not of himself: but being high priest that year, he prophesied that Jesus should die for that nation. 52:And not for that nation only, but that also he should gather together in one the children of God that were scattered abroad. 53:Then from that day forth they took counsel together, to find away for him, to be put to death.

Bethany 2 miles East of Jerusalem, from the mount of Olives.

Above is a picture of the tomb of Lazarus.

+/- April 8th. (Nissan 8th.)

Mary anointed Jesus feet

(John 12:1-8) 1:Then Jesus six days before the passover came to Bethany, where Lazarus was which had been dead, whom he raised from the dead. 2:There they made him a supper; and Martha served: but Lazarus was one of them that sat at the table with him. 3:Then took Mary a pound of ointment of aromatic perfume, very costly, and anointed the feet of Jesus, and wiped his feet with her hair: and the house was filled with the odor of the ointment. 4:Then said one of his disciples, Judas Iscariot, Simon's son, who will betray him. 5:Why was not this ointment sold for three hundred pence, and given to the poor? 6:Then he said, not that he cared for the poor; but because he was a thief, and had the bag, and stole from it some of what was put in it. 7:Then said Jesus, Let her alone: for the day of my burying has she kept this. 8:For the poor always you have with you; but me you will not always have.

+/- April 9th. (Nissan 9th.)

The year +/- 1357 B.C. God sent a wind to remove the Locust

(Exodus 10:16-23) 16:Then Pharaoh called for Moses and Aaron in haste; and he said, I have sinned against the Lord your God, and against you. 17:Now therefore forgive, I pray you, my sin only this once, and entreat the Lord your God, that he may take away from me this death only.

18:And he went out from Pharaoh, and entreated the Lord. 19:And the Lord turned a mighty strong west wind, which took away the locusts, and cast them into the Red sea; there remained not one locust in all the coasts of Egypt. 20:But the Lord hardened Pharaoh's heart, so that he would not let the children of Israel go. 21:And the Lord said to Moses, Stretch out your hand toward heaven, that there may be darkness over the land of Egypt, even darkness which may be felt. 22:And Moses stretched forth his hand toward heaven; and there was a thick darkness in all the land of Egypt three days. 23:They saw not one another, neither rose any from his place for three days: but all the children of Israel had light in their dwellings.

+/- April 9th. (Nissan 9th.)

The year +/- 728 B.C. The Levite went and spoke with his concubines father

(Judges 19:3-4) 3:And her husband arose, and went after her, to speak friendly to her, and to bring her again, having his servant with him, and a couple of asses: and she brought him into her father's house: and when the father of the damsel saw him, he rejoiced to meet him. 4:And his father in law, the damsel's father, retained him; and he stayed with him three days: so they did eat and drink, and lodged there.

+/- April 9th. (Nissan 9th.)

The Prophet spoke against the King

(1Kings 20:35-43) 35:And a certain man of the sons of the prophets said to his neighbor in the name of the Lord, Strike me, I beg you. And the man refused to strike him. 36:Then said he to him, Because you have not obeyed the voice of the Lord, behold, as soon as you depart from me, a lion shall kill you. And as soon as he departed from him, a lion found him, and killed him. 37:Then he found another man, and said, Strike me, I beg you. And the man struck him, so that in hitting him, he became wounded. 38:So the prophet departed, and waited for the King by the way, and disguised himself with ashes upon his face. 39:And as the King passed by, he cried out to the King: and he said, Your servant went out into the midst of the battle; and, behold, a man turned aside, and brought a man to me, and said, Keep this man: if by any means he come up missing, then your life will be, for his life, or you shall have to pay a talent of silver. 40:And as your servant was busy here and there, he was gone. And the King of Israel said to him, So shall your judgment be; you, yourself has decided it. 41:And he hurried, and took the ashes away from his face; and the King of Israel discerned, that he was one of the prophets. 42:And he said to the King, this says the Lord, Because you have let go out of your hands a man whom I appointed for utter destruction, therefore your life shall go for his life, and your people for his people. 43:And the King of Israel went to his house heavy and displeased, and came to Samaria.

+/- April 9th. (Nissan 9th.)

Jesus said go to the Village

(Mathew 21:1-11) 1:And when they drew near to Jerusalem, and had come to Bethphage, to the mount of Olives, then Jesus sent two disciples.

2:Saying to them, Go into the village over against you, and straightway you shall find an ass tied, and a colt with her: loose them, and bring them here to me. 3:And if any man ask you where are you going with them, you are to say to him, The Lord has need of him; and straightway he will send them. 4:All this was done, that it might be fulfilled which was spoken by the prophet, saying, 5:Tell the daughter Zion, Behold, your King comes to you, meek, and sitting upon an ass, and a colt the foal of an ass. 6:And the disciples went, and did as Jesus commanded them, 7:and brought the ass, and the colt, and put on them their clothes, and they set him up. 8:And a very great multitude spread their garments in the way; others cut down branches from the trees, and spread them in the way. 9:And the multitudes that went before, and that followed, cried, saying, Hosanna to the Son of David: Blessed is he that comes in the name of the Lord; Hosanna in the highest. 10:And when he was come into Jerusalem, all the city was moved, saying, Who is this? 11:And the multitude said, This is Jesus the prophet of Nazareth of Galilee.

+/- April 9th. (Nissan 9th.)

The Pharisees asked about divorce (+/- 2nd year of his teaching)

(Mark 10:2-45) 2:And the pharisees came to him, and asked him, is it lawful for a man to put away his wife for any reason? tempting him. 3:And he answered and said to them ,What did Moses command you? 4:And they said, Moses suffered to write a bill of divorce, and to put her away. 5:And Jesus answered and said to them, For the hardness of your heart he wrote you this precept. 6:But from the beginning of the creation God made them male and female. 7:For this cause shall a man leave his father and mother, and cleave to his wife; 8:And they come together and shall be one flesh: so then they are no more two, but one flesh. 9:What therefore what God has joined together, let not man put separate. 10;And in the house his disciples asked him again of the same matter. 11;And he said to them, Whosoever shall put away his wife, and marry another, commits adultery against her. 12:And if a woman shall put away her husband, and marry another, she commits adultery.

13:And they brought young children to him, that he should touch them: and his disciples stopped those that brought them. 14:But when Jesus saw it, he was very much displeased, and said to them, Let the little children come to me, and do not stop them: for such is the Kingdom of God. 15:Verily truly; I say to you, Who so ever shall not receive the Kingdom of God as a little child, he shall not enter therein. 16:And he took them up in his arms, put his hands upon them, and blessed them. 17:And he set out on his way towards Jerusalem on the way, there came a man running, and he knelt down to him, and asked him, Good Master, what shall I do that I may inherit eternal life? 18:And Jesus said to him, Why do you call me call good (perfect)? There is one, good (perfect) but one, that is God. 19:You know the commandments, Do not commit adultery, Do not kill, Do not steal, Do not bear false witness, Defraud no one, Honor your father and mother. 20:And he answered and said to him, Master, all these have I observed from my youth. 21:Then Jesus looking at him loved him, and said to him, One thing you lack: go your way, sell all of what you have, and give it to the poor, and you shall have such treasure in heaven: and come, take up your cross, and follow me. 22:And he was sad at that saying, and went away grieved: for he had great possessions.

23:And Jesus looked round about, and said to his disciples; How hard is it for them that have riches to enter into the kingdom of God! 24:And the disciples were astonished at his words. But Jesus answered again, and said to them, Children, how hard is it for them that trust in riches, to enter into the kingdom of God! 25:It is easier for a camel to go through the eye of a needle, than for a rich man to enter into the Kingdom of God. 26:And they were astonished out of measure, saying among themselves, Who then can be saved? 27:And Jesus looking upon them he said, With men it is impossible, but not with God: for with God all things are possible. 28:Then Peter began to say to him, Look, we have left all, and have followed you. 29:And Jesus answered and said, Verily truly; I say to you, There is no man that has left a house, or brothers, or sisters, or father, or mother, or wife, or children, or lands, for my sake, and the gospel's. 30:But he shall receive an hundredfold now in this time, houses, and brethren, and sisters, and mothers, and children, and lands, with persecutions; and in the world to come eternal life. 31:But many that are first shall be last; and the last first. 32:And they were on the way going up to Jerusalem; and Jesus went before them: and they were amazed, and as they followed, they were afraid. And he took again the twelve, and began to tell them what things that will happen to him. 33:Saying; Behold, we go up to Jerusalem; and the Son of man shall be delivered to the chief priests, and to the scribes; and they shall condemn him to death, and shall deliver him to the Gentiles. 34:And they shall mock him, and shall scourge him, and shall spit upon him, and shall kill him: and the third day he shall rise again. 35:And James and John, the sons of Zebedee, came to him, saying, Master, we want you to grant us whatever we ask of you? 36:And he said to them, What do you want, that I should do for you? 37:They said to him, Grant to us that we may sit, one on your right hand, and the other on your left hand, in your glory. 38:But Jesus said to them, You do not know what you are asking: can you drink of the cup that I drink of? and be baptized with the baptism that I am baptized with? 39:And they said to him, We can. And Jesus said to them, You shall indeed drink of the cup that I drink of; and with the baptism that I am baptized with all shall you be baptized. 40:But to sit on my right hand and on my left hand is not mine to give; but it shall be given to them for whom My Father has prepared.

41:And when the ten heard it, they began to be much displeased with James and John. 42:But Jesus called them to him, and said to them, You know that they which are accounted to rule over the Gentiles exercise lordship over them; and their great ones exercise authority upon them. 43:But so shall it not be among you: but whosoever will be great among you, shall be the least. 44:And whosoever of you will be the chiefest, shall be servant of all. 45:For even the Son of man came not to be served to, but to serve, and to give his life as a ransom for many.

+/- April 9th. (Nissan 9th.)

Jesus passed through Jericho

(Luke 19:1-28) 1:And Jesus entered and passed through Jericho. 2:And, behold, there was man named Zacchaeus, which was the chief among the republicans, and he was rich. 3:And he sought to see Jesus who he was; and could not for the press, because he was little of stature. 4:And he ran before, and climbed up into a sycamore tree to see him: for he was to pass that way.

5:And when Jesus came to the place, he looked up, and saw him, and said to him, Zacchaeus, hurry up, and come down; for to day I will visit and eat at your house. 6:And he hurried, and came down, and received him joyfully. 7:And when they saw it, they all murmured, saying, That he has gone to be a guest with a man that is a sinner. 8:And Zacchaeus stood, and said to the Lord; Behold, Lord, half of my goods I will give to the poor; and if I have taken any thing from any man, by false accusation, I restore him fourfold. 9:And Jesus said to him, This day salvation has come to this house, for so much as he also is a son of Abraham. 10:For the Son of man is come to seek and to save that which was lost. 11;And as they heard these things, he added and spoke a parable, because he was close to Jerusalem, and because they thought that the kingdom of God should immediately appear.

12;He said therefore, A certain nobleman went into a far country to receive for himself a kingdom, and to return. 13:And he called his three servants, and gave to them one ten gold coins, and to the second five gold coins and to the third one gold coin, and said to them, Engage in trade with these until I return. 14:But his citizens hated him, and sent a message after him, saying, We do not want this man to be King over us.15:And it came to pass, that when he was returned, having received the kingdom, then he commanded the three servants to be called to him, to whom he had given the money, that he might know how much every man had gained by trading. 16:Then came the first, saying, Lord, you gave me ten gold coins, and I now have twenty gold coins for you. 17:And he said to him, Well done, you good servant: because you have been faithful in a very little, have you will have authority over ten cities. 18:And the second came, saying, Lord, you gave me five gold coins, and now I have, 10 gold coins for you. 19:And he said likewise to him, Well done, you good servant: because you have been faithful in a very little, have you will have authority over five cities. 20;And another came, saying, Lord, look, here is your gold coin, which I have kept laid up in a napkin: 21:For I feared you, because you are an austere man: you take up where you have not laid down, and reap that which you did not sow. And he said to him, 22:And he said to him, Out of your own mouth will I judge you; You wicked servant. You knew that I was an austere man, taking up that I did not lay down, and reaping that I did not sow: 23:Why did you not even put my money in the bank, that way at my coming I might have gotten interest on it? 24;And he said to them tho were standing by, Take from him the one gold coin, and give it to him that has ten. 25:And they said to him, Lord, he already has ten gold coins. 26:For I say to you, That to everyone which has increased, more shall be given him; and from him that has not, even that what he has shall be taken away from him. 27:But those enemies of mine, which will not have me reign over them, bring here, and slay them before me. 28:After speaking he went on, ascending up to Jerusalem.

+/- April 9th. (Nissan 9th.)

Jesus rode in to Jerusalem (+/- 4 days before his death)

(John 12:12-36)12:On the next day many people had come to the feast, and when they heard that Jesus was coming to Jerusalem, 13:Took branches of palm trees, and went forth to meet him, and cried, Hosanna: Blessed is the King of Israel that comes in the name of the Lord.

14:And Jesus, when he had found a young ass, he sat on it; as it was written in:

(Zachariah 9:9 ; Rejoice greatly, O daughter of Zion; shout, O daughter of Jerusalem: behold, your King comes to you: he is just, and having salvation; plane looking, and riding upon an ass, and upon a colt the foal of an ass.)

15:Fear not, daughter of Zion: behold, your King comes, sitting on an ass's colt.
16:These things understood not his disciples at the first: but when Jesus was
glorified, then remembered they that these things were written of him, and that they
had done these things to him. 17:The people therefore that was with him when he
called Lazarus out of his grave, and raised him from the dead, bare record. 18:For
this cause the people also met him, for that they heard that he had done this miracle.
19:The Pharisees therefore said among themselves, do you see that you are gaining
nothing? behold, the world is going after him. 20:And there were certain Greeks
among them that came up to worship at the feast: 21:The same came therefore to
Philip, which was of Bethsaida of Galilee, and desired him, saying, Sir, we would
like to see Jesus. 22:Philip cometh and telleth Andrew: and again Andrew and Philip
tell Jesus.

23:And Jesus answered them, saying, The hour is come, that the Son of man should
be glorified. 24:Verily, truly, I say to you, Except a corn of wheat fall into the
ground and die, it will remain a corn of wheat: but if it die, it brings forth much
fruit. 25:He that loves his life shall lose it; and he that hates his life in this world
shall keep it to life eternal. 26:If any man serve me, let him follow me; and where I
am, there shall also my servant be: if any man serve me, him will my Father honor.
27:Now is my soul troubled; and what shall I say? Father, save me from this hour:
but it is for this cause; I came into this hour. 28:Father, glorify your name.

Then came there a voice from heaven, saying: I have both glorified it, and will
glorify it again. 29:The people therefore, that stood by, and heard it, said that it
thundered: others said, An angel spoke to him. 30:Jesus answered and said, This
voice came not because of me, but for your sakes. 31:Now is the judgment of this
world: now shall the prince of this world be cast out. 32:And I, if I be lifted up from
the earth, will draw all men to me. 33:This he said, signifying what death he should
die. 34:The people answered him, We have heard out of the law that Christ remains
forever: and why do you say that, The Son of man must be lifted up? Who is this
Son of man? 35:Then Jesus said to them, Yet a little while longer the light will be
with you. Walk while you have the light, lest darkness comes upon you: for he that
walks in darkness does not know where he is going. 36:While you have light,
believe in the light, that you may be the children of light. These things Jesus spoke,
and then departed, and did hide himself from them.

+/- April 10th. (Nissan 10th.)

The year +/- 1318 B.C. The Death of Miriam, Daughter of Jochebed.

(Numbers 20:1) 20:Then came the children of Israel, even the whole congregation,
into the desert of Zin in the first month: and the people stayed in Kadesh; and
Miriam died there, and was buried there.

+/- April 10th. (Nissan 10th.)

The year +/- 1317 B.C. The Hebrews crossed into the promised land

(Joshua 3:6-17) 6:And Joshua spoke to the priests, saying, Take up the ark of the covenant, and pass over before the people. And they took up the ark of the covenant, and went before the people. 7:And the Lord said to Joshua, This day will I begin to magnify you in the sight of all Israel, that they may know that, as I was with Moses, so I will be with you. 8:And you shall command the priests that bear the ark of the covenant, saying, When you are coming to the edge of the water of Jordan, you shall stand still in Jordan. 9:And Joshua said to the children of Israel, Come close, and hear the words of the Lord our God. 10:And Joshua said, this way you shall know that the living God is among you, and that he will not fail to drive out from before you the Canaanites, and the Hittites, and the Hivites, and the Perizzites, and the Girgashites, and the Amorites, and the Jebusites. 11:Behold, the ark of the covenant of the Lord of all the earth, shall passes over before you, into Jordan. 12:Now therefore take you twelve men out of the tribes of Israel, out of every tribe a man. 13:And it shall come to pass, as soon as the soles of the feet of the priests that bear the ark of the Lord, the Lord of all the earth, shall rest in the waters of Jordan, that the waters of Jordan shall be cut off from the waters that come down from above; and they shall stand upon an heap. 14:And it came to pass, when the people removed from their tents, to pass over Jordan, and the priests bearing the ark of the covenant before the people. 15:And as they that carried the ark over to the Jordan, and the feet of the priests that bared the ark were dipped in the edge of the water, (for the Jordan would over flow all its banks all the time of harvest,) 16:That the waters which came down from above stood and rose up upon an heap very far from the city Adam, that is beside Zaretan: and those that came down toward the sea of the plain, even the salt sea, failed, and were cut off: and the people passed over right against Jericho. 17:And the priests that carried the ark of the covenant of the Lord stood firm on dry ground in the midst of Jordan, and all the Israelites passed over on dry ground, until all the people were passed clean over Jordan.

The Jordan river near Jericho, believed to be where they would have crossed.

+/- April 10th. (Nissan 10th.)

The year +/- 566 B.C. Ezekiel was shown the new Jerusalem (Ezekiel 40:1-48:35) 1:In the five and twentieth year of our captivity, in the beginning of the year, in the tenth day of the month, in the fourteenth year after that the city was smitten, in the selfsame day the hand of the Lord was upon me, and brought me close. 2:In the visions of God brought he me to the land of Israel, and set me upon a very high mountain, by which was as the frame of a city on the south.3:And he brought me closer, and, behold, there was a man, whose appearance was like the appearance of brass, with a line of flax in his hand, and a measuring reed; and he stood in the gate. 4:And the man said to me, Son of man, behold with your eyes, and hear with your ears, and set your heart upon all that I shall show you; for to the intent that I might show them to you that you are brought closer, declare all that you see to the house of Israel. 5:And behold a wall on the outside of the house round about, and in the man's hand a measuring reed of six cubits long by the cubit and an hand breadth: so he measured the breadth of the building, one reed; and the height, one reed. 6:Then he came to the gate which looked toward the east, and went up the stairs thereof, and measured the threshold of the gate, which was one reed broad; and the other threshold of the gate, which was one reed broad.

7;And every little chamber was one reed long, and one reed broad; and between the little chambers were five cubits; and the threshold of the gate by the porch of the gate with in was one reed. 8:He measured also the porch of the gate within, one reed. 9:Then he measured the porch of the gate, eight cubits; and the posts thereof, two cubits; and the porch of the gate was inward. 10:And the little chambers of the gate eastward were three on this side, and three on that side; they three were of one measure: and the posts had one measure on this side and on that side. 11:And he measured the breadth of the entry of the gate, ten were fifty cubits. 12:The space also before the little chambers was one cubit on this side, and the space was one cubit on that side: and the little chambers were six cubits on this side, and six cubits on that side. 13:He measured then the gate from the roof of one little chamber to the roof of another: the breadth was five and twenty cubits, door against door. 14:He made also posts of threescore cubits, even to the post of the court round about the gate. 15;And from the face of the gate of the entrance to the face of the porch,of the inner gate was one reed long, and one reed broad; and between the little chambers were five cubits; and the threshold of the gate by the porch of the gate within was one reed. 8:He measured also the porch of the gate within, one reed.

16:And there were narrow windows to the little chambers, and to their posts within the gate round about, and likewise to the arches: and windows were round about inward: and upon each post were palm trees. 17:Then brought he me into the outward court, and, look, there were chambers, and a pavement made for the court round about: thirty chambers were upon the pavement. 18:And the pavement by the side of the gates over against the length of the gates was the lower pavement. 19:Then he measured the breadth from the forefront of the lower gate to the front of the inner court about, an hundred cubits eastward and northward. 20;And the gate of the outward court that looked toward the north, he measured the length there, and the breadth of it.

21:And the little chambers thereof were three on this side and three on that side; and
the posts thereof, and the arches thereof were after the measure of the first gate: the
length thereof was fifty cubits, and the breadth five and twenty cubits. 22:And their
windows, and their arches, and their palm trees, were after the measure of the gate
that looks toward the east; and they went up to it by seven steps; and the arches
thereof were before them. 23:And the gate of the inner court was over against the
gate toward the north, and toward the east; and he measured from gate to gate an
hundred cubits. 24:After that he brought me toward the south, and behold a gate
toward the south: and he measured the posts thereof and the arches thereof
according to these measures. 25:And there were windows in it and in the arches
thereof round about, like those windows: the length was fifty cubits, and the breadth
five and twenty cubits. 26:And there were seven steps to go up to it, and the arches
thereof were before them: and it had palm trees, one on this side, and another on
that side, upon the posts thereof. 27:And there was a gate in the inner court toward
the south: and he measured from gate to gate toward the south an hundred cubits.
28:And he brought me to the inner court by the south gate: and he measured the
south gate according to these measures.

29:And the little chambers thereof, and the posts thereof, and the arches thereof,
according to these measures: and there were windows in it and in the arches thereof
round about: it was fifty cubits long, and five and twenty cubits broad. 30:And the
arches round about were five and twenty cubits long, and five cubits broad. 31:And
the arches thereof were toward the utter court; and palm trees were upon the posts
there: and the way up to it had eight steps. 32:And he brought me into the inner
court toward the east: and he measured the gate according to these measures.
33:And the little chambers there, and the posts there, and the arches there, were
according to these measures: and there were windows there and in the arches there
round about: it was fifty cubits long, and five and twenty cubits broad. 34:And the
arches thereof were toward the outward court; and palm trees were upon the posts
thereof, on this side, and on that side: and the going up to it had eight steps. 35:And
he brought me to the north gate, and measured it according to these measures;
36:The little chambers thereof, the posts thereof, and the arches thereof, and the
windows to it round about: the length was fifty cubits, and the breadth five and
twenty cubits. 37:And the posts thereof were toward the outer court; and palm trees
were upon the posts thereof, on this side, and on that side: and the going up to it had
eight steps. 38:And the chambers and the entries thereof were by the posts of the
gates, where they washed the burnt offering. 39:And in the porch of the gate were
two tables on this side, and two tables on that side, to slay there on the burnt
offering and the sin offering and the trespass offering.

40:And at the side without, as one goes up to the entry of the north gate, were two
tables; and on the other side, which was at the porch of the gate, were two tables.
41:Four tables were on this side, and four tables on that side, by the side of the gate;
eight tables, whereupon they killed their sacrifices. 42:And the four tables were of
hew stone for the burnt offering, of a cubit and an half long, and a cubit and an half
broad, and one cubit high: where upon also they laid the instruments wherewith they
killed the burnt offering and the sacrifice. 43;And within were hooks, an hand
broad, fastened round about: and upon the tables was the flesh of the offering.

44:And without the inner gate were the chambers of the singers in the inner court, which was at the side of the north gate; and their prospect was toward the south: one at the side of the east gate having the prospect toward the north. 45:And he said to me, This chamber, whose prospect is toward the south, is for the priests, the keepers of the charge of the house. 46:And the chamber whose prospect is toward the north is for the priests, the keepers of the charge of the altar: these are the sons of Zadok among the sons of Levi,which come near to the Lord to minister to him. 47:So he measured the court, an hundred cubits long, and an hundred cubits broad, foursquare; and the altar that was before the house. 48:And he brought me to the porch of the house, and measured each post of the porch, five cubits on this side, and five cubits on that side: and the breadth of the gate was three cubits on this side, and three cubits on that side. 49:The length of the porch was twenty cubits, and the breadth eleven cubits; and he brought me by the steps where they went up to it: and there were pillars by the posts, one on this side, and another on that side.

41:1: Afterward he brought me to the temple, and measured the posts, six cubits broad on the one side, and six cubits broad on the other side, which was the breadth of the tabernacle. 2:And the breadth of the door was ten cubits; and the sides of the door were five cubits on the one side, and five cubits on the other side: and he measured the length thereof, forty cubits: and the breadth, twenty cubits. 3:Then he went inward, and measured the post of the door, two cubits; and the door, six cubits; and the breadth of the door, seven cubits. 4:So he measured the length thereof, twenty cubits; and the breadth, twenty cubits, before the temple: and he said to me, This is the most holy place. 5:After he measured the wall of the house, six cubits; and the breadth of every side chamber, four cubits, round about the house on every side. 6:And the side chambers were three, one over another, and thirty in order; and they entered into the wall which was of the house for the side chambers round about, that they might have hold, but they had not hold in the wall of the house.7:And there was an enlarging, and a winding about still upward to the side chambers: for the winding about of the house went still upward round about the house: therefore the breadth of the house was still upward, and so increased from the lowest chamber to the highest by the midst.

8:I saw also the height of the house round about: the foundations of the side chambers were a full reed of six great cubits. 9:The thickness of the wall, which was for the side chamber without, was five cubits: and that which was left was he place of the side chambers that were within.10:And between the chambers was the wideness of twenty cubits round about the house on every side. 11:And the doors of the side chambers were toward the place that was left, one door toward the north, and another door toward the south: and the breadth of the place that was left was five cubits round about. 12:Now the building that was before the separate place at the end toward the west was seventy cubits broad; and the wall of the building was five cubits thick round about, and the length thereof ninety cubits. 13:So he measured the house, an hundred cubits long; and the separate place, and the building, with the walls thereof, an hundred cubits long. 14:Also the breadth of the face of the house, and of the separate place toward the east, an hundred cubits. 15:And he measured the length of the building over against the separate place which was behind it, and the galleries thereof on the one side and on the other side, an hundred cubits, with the inner temple, and the porches of the court. 16:The door posts, and the narrow windows, and the galleries round about on their three stories, over against the door, covered with wood all around, and from the ground up to the windows, and the windows were covered. 17:To that above the door, even to the inner house, and without, and by all the wall round about within and without, by measure. 18:And it was covered with cherubims and palm trees, so that a palm tree were between a cherub and a cherub; and every cherub had two faces. 19:So that the face of a man was toward the palm tree on the one side, and the face of a young lion toward the palm tree on the other side: it was made through all the house round about. 20:From the ground to above the door were cherubims and palm trees made, and on the wall of the temple.

21:The posts of the temple were squared, and the face of the sanctuary; the appearance of the one as the appearance of the other. 22:The altar of wood was three cubits high, and the length thereof two cubits; and the corners thereof, and the length thereof, and the walls thereof, were of wood: and he said to me, This is the table that is before the Lord. 23:And the temple and the sanctuary had two doors. 24:And the doors had two leaves apiece, two turning leaves; two leaves for the one door, and two leaves for the other door 25:And there were made on them, on the doors of the temple, cherubims and palm trees, like as were made upon the walls; and there were thick planks upon the face of the porch without. 26:And there were narrow windows and palm trees on the one side and on the other side, on the sides of the porch, and upon the side chambers of the house, and thick planks.

42:1: Then he brought me forth into the utter court, the way toward the north: and he brought me into the chamber that was over against the separate place, and which was before the building toward the north. 2:Before the length of an hundred cubits was the north door, and the breadth was fifty cubits. 3:Over against the twenty cubits which were for the inner court, and over against the pavement which was for the utter court, was gallery against gallery in three stories. 4:And before the chambers was a walk of ten cubits breadth inward, a way of one cubit; and their doors toward the north. 5:Now the upper chambers were shorter: for the galleries were higher than these, than the lower, and than the middle most of the building. 6:For they were in three stories, but had not pillars as the pillars of the courts: therefore the building was straitened more than the lowest and the middlemost from the ground. 7:And the wall that was without over against the chambers, toward the utter court on the forepart of the chambers, the length thereof was fifty cubits.

8:For the length of the chambers that were in the other court was fifty cubits: and, look, before the temple were an hundred cubits. 9:And from under these chambers was the entry on the east side, as one go's into them from the outer court. 10:The chambers were in the thickness of the wall of the court toward the east, over against the separate place, and over against the building. 11:And the way before them was like the appearance of the chambers which were toward the north, as long as they, and as broad as they: and all their goings out were both according to their fashions, and according to their doors. 12:And according to the doors of the chambers that were toward the south was a door in the head of the way, even the way directly before the wall toward the east, as one entered into them.

13:Then said he to me, The north chambers and the south chambers, which are before the separate place, they be holy chambers, where the priests that approach to the Lord shall eat the most holy things: there shall they lay the most holy things, and the meat offering, and the sin offering, and the trespass offering; for the place is holy. 14:When the priests enter therein, then shall they not go out of the holy place into the outer court, but there they shall lay their garments wherein they minister; for they are holy; and shall put on other garments, and shall approach to those things which are for the people. 15:Now when he had made an end of measuring the inner house, he brought me forth toward the gate whose prospect is toward the east, and measured it round about. 16:He measured the east side with the measuring reed, five hundred reeds, with the measuring reed round about. 17:He measured the north side, five hundred reeds, with the measuring reed round about. 18:He measured the south side, five hundred reeds, with the measuring reed. 19He turned about to the west side, and measured five hundred reeds with the measuring reed. 20:He measured it by the four sides: it had a wall round about, five hundred reeds long, and five hundred broad, to make a separation between the sanctuary and the profane place.

43:1: Afterward he brought me to the gate, even the gate that looks toward the east. 2:And, behold, the glory of the God of Israel came from the way of the east: and his voice was like a noise of many waters: and the earth shined with his glory. 3:And it was according to the appearance of the vision which I saw, even according to the vision that I saw when I came to destroy the city: and the visions were like the vision that I saw by the river Chebar; and I fell upon my face. 4:And the glory of the Lord came into the house by the way of the gate whose prospect is toward the east. 5:So the spirit took me up, and brought me into the inner court; and, behold, the glory of the Lord filled the house. 6:And I heard him speaking to me out of the house; and the man stood by me. 7:And he said to me, Son of man, the place of my throne, and the place of the soles of my feet, where I will dwell in the midst of the children of Israel for ever, and my holy name, shall the house of Israel no more defile, neither they, nor their kings, by their harlotry's, nor by the carcases of their kings in their high places. 8:In their setting of their threshold by my thresholds, and their post by my posts, and the wall between me and them, they have even defiled my holy name by their abominations that they have committed: wherefore I have consumed them in mine anger. 9:Now let them put away their harlotry, and the carcases of their kings, far from me, and I will dwell in the midst of them for ever.

10:You son of man, show the house to the house of Israel, that they may be ashamed of their iniquities: and let them measure the pattern. 11:And if they be ashamed of all that they have done, show them the form of the house, and the fashion thereof, and the goings out thereof, and the comings in thereof, and all the forms thereof, and all the ordinances thereof, and all the forms thereof, and all the laws thereof: and write it in their sight, that they may keep the whole form thereof, and all the ordinances thereof, and do them. 12:This is the law of the house; Upon the top of the mountain the whole limit thereof round about shall be most holy. Behold, this is the law of the house.13:And these are the measures of the altar after the cubits: The cubit is a cubit and an hand breadth; even the bottom shall be a cubit, and the breadth a cubit, and the border thereof by the edge thereof round about shall be a span, and this shall be the higher place of the altar.

14:And from the bottom upon the ground even to the lower settle shall be two cubits, and the breadth one cubit; and from the lesser settle even to the greater settle shall be four cubits, and the breadth one cubit. 15:So the altar shall be four cubits; and from the altar and upward shall be four horns. 16:And the altar shall be twelve cubits long, twelve broad, square in the four squares thereof. 17:And the settle shall be fourteen cubits long and fourteen broad in the four squares thereof; and the border about it shall be half a cubit; and the bottom thereof shall be a cubit about; and his stairs shall look toward the east. 18:And he said to me, Son of man, this said the Lord God; These are the ordinances of the altar in the day when they shall make it, to offer burnt offerings thereon, and to sprinkle blood thereon. 19:And you shall give to the priests the Levites that be of the seed of Zadok, which approach me, to minister to me, said the Lord God,a young bullock for a sin offering.

20:And you shall take of the blood thereof, and put it on the four horns of it, and on the four corners of the settle, and upon the border round about: this shall you cleanse and purge it. 21:You shall take the bullock also of the sin offering, and he shall burn it in the appointed place of the house, without the sanctuary. 22:And on the second day you shall offer a kid of the goats without blemish for a sin offering; and they shall cleanse the altar, as they did cleanse it with the bullock. 23:When you have made an end of cleansing it, you shall offer a young bullock without blemish, and a ram out of the flock without blemish. 24:And you shall offer them before the Lord, and the priests shall cast salt upon them, and they shall offer them up for a burnt offering to the Lord. 25:Seven days shall you prepare every day a goat for a sin offering: they shall also prepare a young bullock, and a ram out of the flock, without blemish. 26:Seven days shall they purge the altar and purify it; and they shall consecrate themselves. 27:And when these days are expired, it shall be, that upon the eighth day, and so forward, the priests shall make your burnt offerings upon the altar, and your peace offerings; and I will accept you, said the Lord God.

44:1;Then he brought me back the way of the gate of the outward sanctuary which looks toward the east; and it was shut. 2;Then said the Lord to me; This gate shall be shut, it shall not be opened, and no man shall enter in by it; because the Lord, the God of Israel, has entered in by it, therefore it shall be shut. 3;It is for the prince; the prince, he shall sit in it to eat bread before the Lord; he shall enter by the way of the porch of that gate, and shall go out by the way of the same. 4;Then brought he me the way of the north gate before the house: and I looked, and, behold, the glory of the Lord filled the house of the Lord: and I fell upon my face. 5;And the Lord said to me, Son of man, mark well, and behold with thine eyes, and hear with thine ears all that I say to you concerning all the ordinances of the house of the Lord, and all the laws thereof; and mark well the entering in of the house, with every going forth of the sanctuary. 6;And you shall say to the rebellious, even to the house of Israel, This said the Lord God; O you house of Israel, let it suffice you of all your abominations.

7:In that you have brought into my sanctuary strangers, uncircumcised in heart, and uncircumcised in flesh, to be in my sanctuary, to pollute it, even my house, when you offer my bread, the fat and the blood, and they have broken my covenant because of all your abominations.

8:And you have not kept the charge of mine holy things: but you have set keepers of my charge in my sanctuary for yourselves. 9:This said the Lord God; No stranger, uncircumcised in heart, nor uncircumcised in flesh, shall enter into my sanctuary, of any stranger that is among the children of Israel. 10:And the Levites that are gone away far from me, when Israel went astray, which went astray away from me after their idols; they shall even bear their iniquity. 11:Yet they shall be ministers in my sanctuary, having charge at the gates of the house, and ministering to the house: they shall slay the burnt offering and the sacrifice for the people, and they shall stand before them to minister to them. 12:Because they ministered to them before their idols, and caused the house of Israel to fall into iniquity; therefore have I lifted up mine hand against them, said the Lord God, and they shall bear their iniquity.

13:And they shall not come near to me, to do the office of a priest to me, nor to come near to any of my holy things, in the most holy place; but they shall bear their shame, and their abominations which they have committed. 14:But I will make them keepers of the charge of the house, for all the service thereof, and for all that shall be done therein. 15:But the priests the Levites, the sons of Zadok, that kept the charge of my sanctuary when the children of Israel went astray from me, they shall come near to me to minister to me, and they shall stand before me to offer to me the fat and the blood, said the Lord God. 16:They shall enter into my sanctuary, and they shall come near to my table, to minister to me, and they shall keep my charge.

17:And it shall come to pass, that when they enter in at the gates of the inner court, they shall be clothed with linen garments; and no wool shall come upon them, whiles they minister in the gates of the inner court, and within. 18:They shall have linen bonnets upon their heads, and shall have linen breeches upon their loins; they shall not gird themselves with any thing that cause sweat. 19:And when they go forth into the utter court, even into the utter court to the people, they shall put off their garments wherein they ministered, and lay them in the holy chambers, and they shall put on other garments; and they shall not sanctify the people with their garments. 20:Neither shall they shave their heads, nor suffer their locks to grow long; they shall only poll their heads. 21:Neither shall any priest drink wine, when they enter into the inner court. 22:Neither shall they take for their wives a widow, nor her that is put away: but they shall take maidens of the seed of the house of Israel, or a widow that had a priest before.

23:And they shall teach my people the difference between the holy and profane, and cause them to discern between the unclean and the clean. 24:And in controversy they shall stand in judgment; and they shall judge it according to my judgments, and they shall keep my laws and my statutes in all mine assemblies; and they shall hallow my Sabbath's. 25:And they shall come at no dead person to defile themselves: but for father, or for mother, or for son, or for daughter, for brother, or for sister that has had no husband, they may defile themselves. 26:And after he is cleansed, they shall reckon to him seven days. 27:And in the day that he go's into the sanctuary, to the inner court, to minister in the sanctuary, he shall offer his sin offering, said the Lord God. 28:And it shall be to them for an inheritance: I am their inheritance: and you shall give them no possession in Israel: I am their possession. 29:They shall eat the meat offering, and the sin offering, and the trespass offering;

and every dedicated thing in Israel shall be theirs. 30:And the first of all the first fruits of all things and every oblation of all, of every sort of your oblations, shall be the priest's: you shall also give to the priest the first of your dough, that he may cause the blessing to rest in thine house. 31:The priests shall not eat of any thing that is dead of itself, or torn, whether it be fowl or beast.

45:1;Moreover, when you shall divide by lot the land for inheritance, you shall offer an oblation to the Lord, an holy portion of the land: the length shall be the length of five and twenty thousand reeds, and the breadth shall be ten thousand. This shall be holy in all the borders thereof round about. 2;Of this there shall be for the sanctuary five hundred in length, with five hundred in breadth, square round about; and fifty cubits round about for the suburbs thereof. 3;And of this measure shall you measure the length of five and twenty thousand, and the breadth of ten thousand: and in it shall be the sanctuary and the most holy place.

4;The holy portion of the land shall be for the priests the ministers of the sanctuary, which shall come near to minister to the Lord: and it shall be a place for their houses, and an holy place for the sanctuary. 5;And the five and twenty thousand of length, and the ten thousand of breadth, shall also the Levites, the ministers of the house, have for themselves for a possession for twenty chambers. 6:And you shall appoint the possession of the city five thousand broad, and five and twenty thousand long, over against the oblation of the holy portion: it shall be for the whole house of Israel. 7:And a portion shall be for the prince on the one side, and on the other side of the oblation of the house portion, and of the possession of the city, before the oblation of the holy portion, and before the possession of the city, from the west side westward, and from the east side eastward: and the length shall be over against one of the portions, from the west border to the east border.

8:In the land shall be his possession in Israel: and my princes shall no more oppress my people; and the rest of the land shall they give to the house of Israel according to their tribes. 9:This said the Lord God; Let it suffice you, O princes of Israel: remove violence and spoil, and execute judgment and justice, take away your evictions from my people, said the Lord God. 10:You shall have just balances, and a just ephah, and a just bath. 11:The ephah and the bath shall be of one measure, that the bath may contain the tenth part of an homer, and the ephah the tenth part of an homer: the measure thereof shall be after the homer. 12:And the shekel shall be twenty gerahs: twenty shekels, five and twenty shekels, fifteen shekels, shall be your maneh.

13:This is the oblation that you shall offer; the sixth part of an ephah of an homer of wheat, and you shall give the sixth part of an ephah of an homer of barley: 14:Concerning the ordinance of oil, the bath of oil, you shall offer the tenth part of a bath out of the cor, which is an homer of ten baths; for ten baths are an homer. 15:And one lamb out of the flock, out of two hundred, out of the fat pastures of Israel; for a meat offering, and for a burnt offering, and for peace offerings, to make reconciliation for them, said the Lord God. 16:All the people of the land shall give this oblation for the prince in Israel. 17:And it shall be the prince's part to give burnt offerings, and meat offerings, and drink offerings, in the feasts, and in the new moons, and in the sabbaths, in all solemnities of the house of Israel: he shall prepare the sin offering, and the meat offering, and the burnt offering, and the peace offerings, to make reconciliation for the house of Israel. 18:This said the Lord God; In the first month, in the first day of the month, you shall take a young bullock without blemish, and cleanse the sanctuary. 19:And the priest shall take of the blood of the sin offering, and put it upon the posts of the house, and upon the four corners of the settle of the altar, and upon the posts of the gate of the inner court. 20:And so you shall do the seventh day of the month for every one that errs, and for him that is simple: so shall you reconcile the house. 21:In the first month, in the fourteenth day of the month, you shall have the passover, a feast of seven days; unleavened bread shall be eaten.

22:And upon that day shall the prince prepare for himself and for all the people of the land,a bullock for a sin offering. 23:And seven days of the feast he shall prepare a burnt offering to the Lord, seven bullocks and seven rams without blemish daily the seven days; and a kid of the goats daily for a sin offering. 24:And he shall prepare a meat offering of an ephah for a bullock, and an ephah for a ram, and an hin of oil for an ephah. 25:In the seventh month, in the fifteenth day of the month, shall he do the like in the feast of the seven days, according to the sin offering, according to the burnt offering, and according to the meat offering, and according to the oil.

46:1: This said the Lord God; The gate of the inner court that look toward the east shall be shut,the six working days; but on the sabbath it shall be opened, and in the day of the new moon it shall be opened. 2:And the prince shall enter by the way of the porch of that gate without, and shall stand by the post of the gate, and the priests shall prepare his burnt offering and his peace offerings, and he shall worship at the threshold of the gate: then he shall go forth; but the gate shall not be shut until the evening. 3:Likewise the people of the land shall worship at the door of this gate before the Lord,in the sabbaths and in the new moons. 4:And the burnt offering that the prince shall offer to the Lord in the sabbath day shall be six lambs without blemish, and a ram without blemish. 5:And the meat offering shall be an ephah for a ram, and the meat offering for the lambs as he shall be able to give, and an hin of oil to an ephah. 6:And in the day of the new moon it shall be a young bullock without blemish, and six lambs, and a ram: they shall be without blemish.

7:And he shall prepare a meat offering, an ephah for a bullock, and an ephah for a ram, and for the lambs according as his hand shall attain to, and an hin of oil to an ephah. 8:And when the prince shall enter, he shall go in by the way of the porch of that gate, and he shall go forth by the way thereof. 9:But when the people of the land shall come before the Lord in the solemn feasts, he that enters in by the way of the north gate to worship shall go out by the way of the south gate; and he that enters by the way of the south gate shall go forth by the way of the north gate: he shall not return by the way of the gate whereby he came in, but shall go forth over against it. 10:And the prince in the midst of them, when they go in, shall go in; and when they go forth,shall go forth. 11:And in the feasts and in the solemnities the meat offering shall be an ephah to a bullock, and an ephah to a ram, and to the lambs as he is able to give, and an hin of oil to an ephah.

12:Now when the prince shall prepare a voluntary burnt offering or peace offerings
voluntarily to the Lord, one shall then open him the gate that looks toward the east,
and he shall prepare his burnt offering and his peace offerings, as he did on the
sabbath day: then he shall go forth; and after his going forth are shall shut the gate.
13:You shall daily prepare a burnt offering to the Lord of a lamb of the first year
without blemish: you shall prepare it every morning. 14:And you shall prepare a
meat offering for it every morning, the sixth part of an ephah, and the third part of
an hin of oil, to temper with the fine flour; a meat offering continually by a
perpetual ordinance to the Lord. 15:This shall they prepare the lamb, and the meat
offering, and the oil, every morning for a continual burnt offering.

16:This said the Lord God; If the prince give a gift to any of his sons, the
inheritance thereof shall be his sons'; it shall be their possession by inheritance.
17:But if he give a gift of his inheritance to one of his servants, then it shall be his to
the year of liberty; after it shall return to the prince: but his inheritance shall be his
sons' for them. 18:Moreover the prince shall not take of the people's inheritance by
oppression, to thrust them out of their possession; but he shall give his sons
inheritance out of his own possession: that my people be not scattered every man
from his possession. 19:After he brought me through the entry, which was at the
side of the gate, into the holy chambers of the priests, which looked toward the
north: and, behold, there was a place on the two sides westward.

20:Then said he to me, This is the place where the priests shall boil the trespass
offering and the sin offering, where they shall bake the meat offering; that they bear
them not out into the utter court, to sanctify the people. 21:Then he brought me
forth into the utter court, and caused me to pass by the four corners of the court;
and, behold, in every corner of the court there was a court. 22:In the four corners of
the court there was courts joined of forty cubits long and thirty broad: these four
corners were of one measure. 23:And there was a row of building round about in
them, round about them four, and it was made with boiling places under the rows
round about. 24:Then said he to me, These are the places of them that boil, where
the ministers of the house shall boil the sacrifice of the people.

47:1: Afterward he brought me again to the door of the house; and, behold, waters
issued out from under the threshold of the house eastward: for the forefront of the
house stood toward the east, and the waters came down from under from the right
side of the house, at the south side of the altar. 2:Then brought he me out of the way
of the gate northward, and led me about the way without to the utter gate by the way
that looks eastward; and, behold, there ran out waters on the right side. 3:And when
the man that had the line in his hand went forth eastward, he measured a thousand
cubits, and he brought me through the waters; the waters were to the ankles.

4:Again he measured a thousand, and brought me through the waters; the waters
were to the knees. Again he measured a thousand, and brought me through; the
waters were to the loins. 5:Afterward he measured a thousand; and it was a river
that I could not pass over: for the waters were risen, waters to swim in, a river that
could not be passed over. 6:And he said to me, Son of man, have you seen this?
Then he brought me, and caused me to return to the brink of the river.

7:Now when I had returned, behold, at the bank of the river were very many trees on the one side and on the other. 8:Then said he to me, These waters issue out toward the east country, and go down into the desert, and go into the sea: which being brought forth into the sea, the waters shall be healed. 9:And it shall come to pass, that every thing that lives, which moves, Where so ever the rivers shall come, shall live: and there shall be a very great multitude of fish, because these waters shall come closer: for they shall be healed; and every thing shall live where the river flows. 10:And it shall come to pass, that the fishers shall stand upon it from Engedi even to Eneglaim; they shall be a place to spread forth nets; their fish shall be according to their kinds, as the fish of the great sea, exceeding many.

11:But the miry places thereof and the marshes thereof shall not be healed; they shall be given to salt. 12:And by the river upon the bank thereof, on this side and on that side, shall grow all trees for meat, whose leaf shall not fade, neither shall the fruit thereof be consumed: it shall bring forth new fruit according to his months, because their waters they issued out of the sanctuary: and the fruit thereof shall be for meat, and the leaf thereof for medicine. 13:This say the Lord God; This shall be the border, where by you shall inherit the land according to the twelve tribes of Israel: Joseph shall have two portions. 14:All of you shall have a like portion in this land which I swore to give to your fathers, that it might fall to you as your inheritance. 15:And this shall be the border of the land toward the north side, from the great sea, the way of Hethlon, as men go to Zedad. 16:Hamath, Berothah, Sibraim, which is between the border of Damascus and the border of Hamath; Hazarhatticon, which is by the coast of Hauran.

17:And the border from the sea shall be Hazarenan, the border of Damascus, and the north northward, and the border of Hamath. And this is the north side. 18:And the east side you shall measure from Hauran, and from Damascus, and from Gilead, and from the land of Israel by Jordan, from the border to the east sea. And this is the east side. 19:And the south side southward, from Tamra even to the waters of strife in Kadesh, the river to the great sea. And this is the south side southward. 20:The west side also shall be the great sea from the border, till a man come over against Hamath. This is the west side. 21:So shall you divide this land to you according to the tribes of Israel. 22:And it shall come to pass, that you shall divide it by lot for an inheritance to you, and to the strangers that sojourner among you, which shall beget children among you: and they shall be to you as born in the country among the children of Israel; they shall have inheritance with you among the tribes of Israel. 23:And it shall come to pass, that in what tribe the stranger sojourner, there shall you give him his inheritance, said the Lord God.

48:1: Now these are the names of the tribes. From the north end to the coast of the way of Hethlon, as one go's to Hamath, Hazarenan, the border of Damascus northward, to the coast of Hamath; for these are his sides east and west; a portion for Dan. 2:And by the border of Dan, from the east side to the west side, a portion for Asher. 3:And by the border of Asher, from the east side even to the west side, a portion for Naphtali. 4:And by the border of Naphtali, from the east side to the west side, a portion for Manasseh. 5:And by the border of Manasseh, from the east side to the west side, a portion for Ephraim. 6:And by the border of Ephraim,

from the east side even to the west side, a portion for Reuben. 7:And by the border
of Reuben, from the east side to the west side, a portion for Judah. 8:And by the
border of Judah, from the east side to the west side, shall be the offering which you
shall offer of five and twenty thousand reeds in breadth, and in length as one of the
other parts, from the east side to the west side: and the sanctuary shall be in the
midst of it. 9:The oblation that you shall offer to the Lord shall be of five and
twenty thousand in length, and of ten thousand in breadth.

10:And for them, even for the priests, shall be this holy oblation; toward the north
five and twenty thousand in length, and toward the west ten thousand in breadth,
and toward the east ten thousand in breadth, and toward the south five and twenty
thousand in length: and the sanctuary of the Lord shall be in the midst thereof. 11:It
shall be for the priests that are sanctified of the sons of Zadok; which have kept my
charge, which went not astray when the children of Israel went astray, as the Levites
went astray.

12:And this oblation of the land that is offered shall be to them a thing most holy by
the border of the Levites. 13:And over against the border of the priests the Levites
ten thousand in breadth: all the length shall be five and twenty thousand, and the
breadth ten thousand. 14:And they shall not sell of it, neither exchange, nor alienate
the first fruits of the land: for it is holy to the Lord. 15:And the five thousand, that
are left in the breadth over against the five and twenty thousand, shall be a profane
place for the city, for dwelling, and for suburbs: and the city shall be in the midst
thereof. 16:And these shall be the measures thereof; the north side four thousand
and five hundred, and the south side four thousand and five hundred, and on the east
side four thousand and five hundred, and the west side four thousand and five
hundred.

17:And the suburbs of the city shall be toward the north two hundred and fifty, and
toward the south two hundred and fifty, and toward the east two hundred and fifty,
and toward the west two hundred and fifty. 18:And the residue in length over
against the oblation of the holy portion shall be ten thousand eastward, and ten
thousand westward: and it shall be over against the oblation of the holy portion, and
the increase thereof shall be for food to them,that serve the city. 19:And they that
serve the city shall serve it out of all the tribes of Israel. 20:All the oblation shall be
five and twenty thousand by five and twenty thousand: you shall offer the holy
oblation foursquare, with the possession of the city.

21:And the residue shall be for the prince, on the one side and on the other of the
holy oblation, and of the possession of the city, over against the five and twenty
thousand of the oblation toward the east border, and westward over against the five
and twenty thousand toward the west border, over against the portions for the
prince: and it shall be the holy oblation; and the sanctuary of the house shall be in
the midst thereof. 22:Moreover from the possession of the Levites, and from the
possession of the city, being in the midst of what which is the prince's, between the
border of Judah and the border of Benjamin, shall be for the prince. 23:As for the
rest of the tribes, from the east side to the west side, Benjamin shall have a portion.
24:And by the border of Benjamin, from the east side to the west side,

Simeon shall have a portion. 25:And by the border of Simeon, from the east side to the west side, Issachar a portion. 26:And by the border of Issachar, from the east side to the west side, Zebulun a portion. 27:And by the border of Zebulun, from the east side to the west side, Gad a portion. 28:And by the border of Gad, at the south side southward, the border shall be even from Tamra to the waters of strife in Kadesh, and to the river toward the great sea. 29:This is the land which you shall divide by lot to the tribes of Israel for inheritance, and these are their portions, said the Lord God. 30:And these are the goings out of the city on the north side, four thousand and five hundred measures.

31:And the gates of the city shall be after the names of the tribes of Israel: three gates northward; one gate of Reuben, one gate of Judah, one gate of Levi. 32:And at the east side four thousand and five hundred: and three gates; and one gate of Joseph, one gate of Benjamin, one gate of Dan. 33:And at the south side four thousand and five hundred measures: and three gates; one gate of Simeon, one gate of Issachar, one gate of Zebulun. 34:At the west side four thousand and five hundred, with their three gates; one gate of Gad, one gate of Asher, one gate of Naphtali. 35:It was round about eighteen thousand measures; and the name of the city from that day shall be; The LORD is there.

+/- April 10th. (Nissan 10th.)

Jesus healed a blind man on the way out of Jericho

(+/- 2nd. Year of his teaching)

(Mark 10:46-52) 46:And they came to Jericho: and as he went out of Jericho with his disciples and a great number of people, blind Bartimaeus, the son of Timaeus, sat by the highway side begging. 47:And when he heard that it was Jesus of Nazareth, he began to cry out, and say, Jesus, You Son of David, have mercy on me. 48:And many charged him that he should hold his peace: but he cried the more a great deal, you Son of David, have mercy on me. 49:And Jesus stood still, and commanded him to be called. And they call the blind man, saying to him, Be of good comfort, rise; he calls for you. 50:And he, casting away his garment, rose, and came to Jesus.

51:And Jesus answered and said to him: What do you me to do for you? The blind man said to him, Lord, that I might receive my sight. 52:And Jesus said to him, Go your way; your faith has made you whole. And immediately he received his sight, and followed Jesus in the way.

+/- April 11th. (Nissan 11th.)

The year +/- 1357 B.C. Pharaoh told Moses to go but leave his flocks

(Exodus 10:24-29) 24:And Pharaoh called to Moses, and said, Go you, serve the Lord; only let your flocks and your herds be stayed: let your little ones also go with you. 25:And Moses said; You must give us also sacrifices and burnt offerings, that we may sacrifice to the Lord our God. 26:Our cattle also shall go with us; there shall not an hoof be left behind; for thereof must we take to serve the Lord our God; and we know not with what we must serve the Lord, until we come near.

27:But the Lord hardened Pharaoh's heart, and he would not let them go. 28:And Pharaoh said to him, Get you from me, take heed to yourself, see my face no more; for in that day you see my face, you shall die. 29:And Moses said; You have spoken well, I will see your face again no more.

+/- April 11th. (Nissan 11th.)

The year +/- 1318 B.C. All the men were circumcised:

(Joshua 4:21-5:9) 21:And he spoke to the children of Israel, saying, When your children shall ask their fathers in time to come, saying, What do these stones mean? 22:Then you shall let your children know, saying, Israel came over this Jordan on dry land. 23:For the Lord your God dried up the waters of Jordan from before you, until we passed over it, as the Lord your God did to the Red sea, which he dried up from before us, until we were gone over: 24:That all the people of the earth might know the hand of the Lord, that it is mighty, that you might fear the Lord your God for ever.

5:1: And it came to pass, when all the kings of the Amorites, which were on the side of Jordan westward, and all the kings of the Canaanites, which whereby the sea, heard that the Lord had dried up the waters of Jordan from before the children of Israel, until we were passed over, that their heart melted, neither was there spirit in them any more, because of the children of Israel. 2:At that time the Lord said to Joshua, Make you sharp knives, and circumcise again the children of Israel the second time. 3:And Joshua made him sharp knives, and circumcised the children of Israel at the hill of the foreskins. 4:And this is why Joshua did circumcise: All the people that came out of Egypt, that were males, even all the men of war, died in the wilderness by the way, after they came out of Egypt. 5:Now all the people that came out were circumcised: but all the people that were born in the wilderness by the way as they came forth out of Egypt, them they had not circumcised. 6:For the children of Israel walked forty years in the wilderness, till all the people that were men of war, which came out of Egypt, were consumed, because they obeyed not the voice of the Lord: to whom the Lord swore that he would not show them the land, which the Lord swore to their fathers that he would give us, a land that flowing with milk and honey. 7:And their children, whom he raised up in their stead, them Joshua circumcised: for they were uncircumcised, because they had not circumcised them by the way. 8:And it came to pass, when they had done circumcising all the men, that they abode in their places in the camp, till they were whole. 9:And the Lord said to Joshua, This day have I rolled away the reproach of Egypt from off you. Wherefore the name of the place is called Gilgal to this day.

+/- April 11th. (Nissan 11th.)

Jesus asked about the greatest commandment

(Mathew 21:18-22:46)18:Now in the morning as he returned into the city, he hungered. 19:And when he saw a fig tree on the way, he came to it, and found nothing on it, but leaves only, and said to it, Let no fruit grow on you henceforward for ever. And presently the fig tree withered away. 20:And when the disciples saw it, they marveled, saying, How soon is the fig tree withered away!

21:Jesus answered and said to them, Verily I say to you, If you have faith, and doubt not, you shall not only do this which is done to the fig tree, but also if you shall say to this mountain, Be you removed, and be you cast into the sea; it shall be done. 22:And all things, whatsoever you shall ask in prayer, believing, you shall receive.

23:And when he was come into the temple, the chief priests and the elders of the people came to him as he was teaching, and said, By what authority do you do these things? And who gave you this authority? 24:And Jesus answered and said to them, I also will ask you one thing, which if you tell me, I in like wise will tell you by what authority I do these things. 25:The baptism of John, where was it? from heaven, or of men?

And they reasoned with themselves, saying, If we shall say, From heaven; he will say to us, Why did you not then believe him? 26:But if we shall say, Of men; we fear the people; for all hold John as a prophet. 27:And they answered Jesus, and said, We cannot tell. And he said to them, Neither tell I you by what authority I do these things. 28:But what think you? A certain man had two sons; and he came to the first, and said, Son, go work to day in my vineyard. 29:He answered and said, I will not: but afterward he repented, and went. 30:And he came to the second, and said likewise. And he answered and said, I go,sir: and went not. 31:Which one of them did the will of his father? They said to him, The first. Jesus said to them, Verily truly,I say to you, That the publicans and the harlots go into the kingdom of God before you. 32:For John came to you in the way righteousness, and you believed him not: but the publicans and the harlots believed him: and you, when you had seen it, repented not afterward, that you might believe him. 33:Hear another parable: There was a certain householder, which planted a vineyard, and hedged it round about, and dug a wine-press in it, and built a tower, and let it out to tenants, and went into a far country. 34:And when the time of the fruit drew near, he sent his servants to the tenants, that they might receive the fruits of it.

35:And the husband men took his servants, and beat one, and killed another, and stoned yet another. 36:Again, he sent other servants more than the first: and they did to them likewise. 37:But last of all he sent to them his son, saying, They will reverence my son. 38:But when the husbandmen saw the son, they said among themselves, This is the heir; come, let us kill him, and let us seize on his inheritance. 39:And they caught him, and cast him out of the vineyard, and killed him. 40:When the lord therefore of the vineyard cometh, what will he do to those husbandmen?

41:They say to him, He will miserably destroy those wicked men, and will let out his vineyard to other husbandmen, which shall render him the fruits in their seasons. 42:Jesus said to them, Did you never read in the scriptures, The stone which the builders rejected, the same is become the head of the corner:this is the Lord's doing, and it is marvelous in our eyes? 43:Therefore say I to you, The kingdom of God shall be taken from you, and given to a nation bringing forth the fruits thereof. 44:And whosoever shall fall on this stone shall be broken: but on whomsoever it shall fall, it will grind him to powder. 45:And when the chief priests and Pharisees had heard his parables, they perceived that he spoke of them.

46;But when they sought to lay hands on him, they feared the multitude, because
they took him for a prophet. **22:1:**And Jesus answered and spoke to them again by
parables, and said; 2:The kingdom of heaven is like to a certain King, which made a
marriage for his son. 3:And sent forth his servants to call them, that were bidden to
the wedding: and they would not come. 4:Again, he sent forth other servants,
saying, Tell them which are bidden, Behold, I have prepared my dinner: my oxen
and my fat-lings are killed, and all things are ready: come to the marriage. 5:But
they made light of it, and went their ways, one to his farm, another to his
merchandise: 6:And the remnant took his servants, and entreated them spitefully,
and killed them. 7:But when the King heard of it, he was wroth: and he sent forth
his armies, and destroyed those murderers, and burned up their city. 8:Then said he
to his servants, The wedding is ready, but they which were bidden were not worthy.
9:Go you therefore into the highways, and as many as you shall find, bid to the
marriage. 10:So those servants went out into the highways, and gathered together all
as many as they found, both bad and good: and the wedding was furnished with
guests. 11:And when the King came in to see the guests, he saw there a man which
had not on a wedding garment: 12:And he said to him, Friend, how came you in
hither not having a wedding garment? And he was speechless. 13:Then said the
King to the servants, Bind him hand and foot, and take him away, and cast him into
outer darkness; there shall be weeping and gnashing of teeth. 14:For many are
called, but few are chosen.

15:Then went the Pharisees, and took counsel how they might entangle him in his
talk. 16:And they sent out to him their disciples with the Herodians, saying, Master,
we know that you are true, and teaches the way of God in truth, neither cares you
for any man; for you regard no man. 17:Tell us therefore, What do you think? Is it
lawful to give tribute to Caesar, or not? 18:But Jesus perceived their wickedness,
and said, Why tempt you me, you hypocrites? 19:Show me the tribute money. And
they brought to him a penny. 20:And he said to them, Whose image and
superscription is on it? 21:They say to him, Caesar's. Then said he to them, Render
therefore to Caesar the things which are Caesar's; and to God the things that are
God's.

22:When they had heard these words, they marveled, and left him, and went their
way. 23:The same day came to him the Sadducees, which say that there is no
resurrection, and asked him. 24:Saying, Master, Moses said, If a man die, having no
children, his brother shall marry his wife, and raise up seed to his brother. 25:Now
there were with us seven brethren: and the first, when he had married a wife,
deceased, and, having no issue, left his wife to his brother. 26:Likewise the second
also, and the third, to the seventh. 27:And last of all the woman died also.
28:Therefore in the resurrection whose wife shall she be of the seven? for they all
had her. 29:Jesus answered and said to them, You are misled, not knowing the
scriptures, nor the power of God. 30:For in the resurrection they neither marry, nor
are given in marriage, but are as the angels of God in heaven. 31:But as touching the
resurrection of the dead, have you not read that which was spoken to you by God,
saying, 32:I am the God of Abraham, and the God of Isaac, and the God of Jacob?
God is not the God of the dead, but of the living.

33:And when the multitude heard this, they were astonished by his doctrine.

34:But when the Pharisees had heard that he had put the Sadducees to silence, they were gathered together. 35:Then one of them, which was a lawyer, asked him a question, tempting him, and saying, 36:Master, which is the greatest commandment in the law? 37:Jesus said to him, you shall love the Lord your God with all your heart, and with all your soul, and with all your mind. 38:This is the first and great commandment. 39;And the second is like to it, you shall love your neighbor as thyself. 40;On these two commandments hang all the law and the prophets. 41;While the Pharisees were gathered together, Jesus asked them, 42;Saying, What think you of Christ? whose son is he? They say to him, The Son of David. 43;He said to them, How then doth David in spirit call him Lord, saying, 44;The LORD said to my Lord, Sit you on my right hand, till I make thine enemies your footstool? 45;If David then call him Lord, how is he his son? 46;And no man was able to answer him a word, neither durst any man from that day forth,
ask him any more questions.

+/- April 11th. (Nissan 11th.)

Satan went to Judas Iscariot

(Luke 22:3-6) 3:Then entered Satan into Judas Iscariot, being of the number of the twelve. 4:And he went his way, and communed with the chief priests and captains, how he might betray him to them. 5:And they were glad, and covenanted to give him money. 6:And he promised, and sought opportunity to betray him, to them in the absence of the multitude.

+/- April 12th. (Nissan 12th.)

The year +/-1357 B.C. God tells Moses about the last Plague

(Exodus 11:1-10) 1:And the Lord said to Moses, Yet will I bring one plague more upon Pharaoh, and upon Egypt; after wards he will let you go, when he shall let you go, he shall surely thrust you out hence altogether. 2:Speak now in the ears of the people, and let every man ask of his neighbor, and every woman of her neighbor, for jewels of silver, and jewels of gold. 3;And the Lord gave the people favor in the sight of the Egyptians. Moreover the man Moses was very great in the land of Egypt, in the sight of Pharaoh's servants, and in the sight of the people. 4;And Moses said, This is what the Lord says: About midnight will I go out into the midst of Egypt: 5;And all the firstborn in the land of Egypt shall die, from the firstborn of Pharaoh that sitteth upon his throne, even to the firstborn of the maidservant that is behind the mill; and all the firstborn of beasts. 6;And there shall be a great cry throughout all the land of Egypt, such as there was none like it, nor shall be like it any more. 7:But against any of the children of Israel shall not a dog move his tongue, against man or beast: that you may know how that the Lord does put a difference between the Egyptians and Israel. 8:And all these your servants shall come down to me, and bow down themselves to me, saying, Get you out, and all the people that follow you: and after that I will go out. And he went out from Pharaoh in a great anger. 9;And the Lord said to Moses, Pharaoh shall not hearken to you; that my wonders may be multiplied in the land of Egypt. 10:And Moses and Aaron did all these wonders before Pharaoh: and the Lord hardened Pharaoh's heart, so that he would not let the children of Israel,go out of his land.

+/- April 12th. (Nissan 12th.)

The year +/- 428 B.C. Ezra and the others went to Jerusalem

(Ezra 8:31) 31:Then we departed from the river of Ahava on the twelfth day of the first month, to go up to Jerusalem: and the hand of our God was upon us, and he delivered us from the hand of the enemy.

+/- April 12th. (Nissan 12th.)

The year +/- 728 B.C. The Levite and his concubine left her fathers house

(Judges 19:5-7) 5:And it came to pass on the fourth day, when they arose early in the morning, that he rose up to depart, and the damsel's father said to his son in law, Comfort thine heart with a morsel of bread, and afterward go your way. 6:And they sat down, and did eat and drink both of them together: for the damsel's father had said to the man, Be content, I pray you, and tarry all night, and let thine heart be merry. 7:And when the man rose up to depart, his father in law urged him: therefore he lodged there again.

+/- April 12th. (Nissan 12th.)

Jesus washes his disciples feet

(John 13:1-17:26) 1;Now before the feast of the passover, when Jesus knew that his hour was come that he should depart out of this world to the Father, having loved his own which were in the world, he loved them to the end. 2:And supper being ended, the devil having now put into the heart of Judas Iscariot, Simon's son, to betray him. 3:Jesus knowing that the Father had given all things into his hands, and that he was come from God, and went to God. 4:He rose from supper, and laid aside his garments; and took a towel, and girded himself. 5:After that he poured water into a basin, and began to wash the disciples' feet, and to wipe them with the towel wherewith he was girded. 6:Then cometh he to Simon Peter: and Peter said to him, Lord, do you wash my feet? 7:Jesus answered and said to him, What I do you know not now; but you shall know hereafter. 8:Peter said to him, you shall never wash my feet. Jesus answered him, If I wash you not, you have no part with me. 9:Simon Peter said to him, Lord, not my feet only, but also my hands and my head. 10;Jesus said to him, He that is washed need not save to wash his feet, but is clean every whit: and you are clean, but not all. 11:For he knew who should betray him; therefore said he, you are not all clean. 12:So after he had washed their feet, and had taken his garments, and was set down again, he said to them, Know you what I have done to you? 13:You call me Master and Lord: and you say well; for so I am. 14:If I then, your Lord and Master, have washed your feet; you also should wash the feet of each another. 15:For I have given you an example, that you should do as I have done to you. 16;Verily, truly, I say to you; The servant is not greater than his lord; neither he that is sent greater than he that sent him.17:If you know these things, happy are you if you do them. 18;I speak not of you all: I know whom I have chosen: but that the scripture may be fulfilled, He that eats bread with me has lifted up his heel against me. 19:Now I tell you before it come, that, when it is come to pass, you may believe that I am he.

20:Verily, truly, I say to you he that receives whom ever I send receives me: and he that receives me receives him who sent me. 21:When Jesus had this said, he was troubled in spirit, and testified, and said, Verily, truly, I say to you, that one of you shall betray me. 22:Then the disciples looked one on another, doubting of whom he spoke. 23:Now there was leaning on Jesus' bosom one of his disciples, whom Jesus loved. 24:Simon Peter therefore beckoned to him, that he should ask who it should be of whom he spoke. 25:He then lying on Jesus breast and said to him, Lord, who is it? 26:Jesus answered; It is he, to whom I shall give a sop, when I have dipped it. And when he had dipped the bread, he gave it to Judas Iscariot, the son of Simon. 27:And after the sop. Then Satan entered into him. Then said Jesus to him, That what you are about to do, do quickly.

28:Now no man at the table knew for what intent he said this to him. 29:For some of them thought, because Judas had the bag, that Jesus had said to him, Buy those things that we have need of against the feast; or, that he should give something to the poor. 30:He then having received the sop went immediately out: and it was night.

31:Therefore, when he was gone out, Jesus said, Now is the Son of man glorified, and God is glorified in him. 32:If God be glorified in him, God shall also glorify him in himself, and shall straightway glorify him. 33:Little children, yet a little while I am with you. you shall seek me: and as I said to the Jews, Where I go, you cannot come; so now I say to you. 34:A new commandment I give to you, That you love one another; as I have loved you, that you also love one another. 35:By this shall all men know that you are my disciples, if you have love one to another.

36:Simon Peter said to him, Lord, where are you going? Jesus answered him, Where I go, you canst not follow me now; but you shall follow me afterwords. 37:Peter said to him, Lord, why cannot I follow you now? I will lay down my life for your sake. 38:Jesus answered him, will you lay down your life for my sake? Verily, verily, I say to you, The cock shall not crow, till you have denied me thrice.

14;1: Let not your heart be troubled: you believe in God, believe also in me. 2:In my Father's house are many mansions: if it were not so, I would have told you. I go to prepare a place for you. 3:And if I go and prepare a place for you, I will come again, and receive you to myself; that where I am, there you may be also. 4;And Where I go you know, and the way you know. 5:Thomas said to him, Lord, if we do not know not where you are going; how can we know the way? 6;Jesus said to him; I am the way, the truth, and the life: no man cometh to the Father, but by me. 7;If you had known me, you should have known my Father also: and from henceforth you know him, and have seen him.

8:Philip said to him, Lord, show us the Father, and it will be sufficient for us. 9:Jesus said to him, Have I been so long time with you, and yet have you not known me, Philip? he that has seen me has seen the Father; and why do you say then, show us the Father? 10;Believes you not that I am in the Father, and the Father in me? The words that I speak to you I speak not of myself: but the Father that dwells in me, he does the works.

11:Believe me that I am in the Father, and the Father in me: or else believe me for
the very works' sake. 12:Verily, truly, I say to you, He that believes on me, the
works that I do shall he do also; and greater works than these shall he do; because I
go to my Father. 13:And whatsoever you shall ask in my name, that will I do, that
the Father may be glorified in the Son. 14:If you shall ask any thing in my name, I
will do it. 15;If you love me, keep my commandments. 16:And I will pray the
Father, and he shall give you another Comforter, that he may abide with you for
ever; 17:Even, the Spirit of truth; whom the world cannot receive, because it sees
him not, neither knows him: but you know him; for he dwells with you, and shall be
in you. 18;I will not leave you comfortless: I will come to you. 19:Yet a little while,
and the world sees me no more; but you see me: because I live, you shall live also.
20:At that day you shall know that I am In my Father, and you are in me, and I in
you. 21:He that has my commandments, and keeps them, he it is that loves me: and
he that loves me shall be loved of my Father, and I will love him, and will manifest
myself to him.

22:Judas said to him, not Iscariot, Lord, how is it that you will manifest yourself to
us, and not to the world? 23:Jesus answered and said to him; If a man loves me, he
will keep my words: and my Father will love him, and we will come to him, and
make our abode with him. 24:He that loves me not keeps not my sayings: and the
word which you hear is not mine, but the Father's which sent me. 25:These things
have I spoken to you, being yet present with you. 26:But the Comforter, which is
the Holy Ghost, whom the Father will send in my name, he shall teach you all
things, and bring all things to your remembrance, whatsoever I have said to you.
27;Peace I leave with you, my peace I give to you: not as the world gives, give I to
you. Let not your heart be troubled, neither let it be afraid. 28:You have heard how I
said to you, I go away, and come again to you. If you loved me, you would rejoice,
because I said, I go to the Father: for my Father is greater than I. 29:And now I have
told you before it come to pass, that, when it is come to pass, you might believe.
30:Hereafter I will not talk much with you: for the prince of this world cometh, and
has nothing in me. 31:But that the world may know that I love the Father; and as the
Father gave me commandment, even so I do.

15:1; Arise, let us go hence. I am the true vine, and my Father is the husbandman.
2;Every branch in me that bears not fruit he will be taken away: and every branch
that bears fruit, he trims it, that it may bring forth more fruit. 3;Now you are clean
through the word which I have spoken to you. 4;Abide in me, and I in you. As the
branch cannot bear fruit of itself, except it abide in the vine; no more can you,
except you abide in me. 5;I am the vine, you are the branches: He that abides in me,
and I in him, the same brings forth much fruit: for without me you can do nothing.

6;If a man abide not in me, he is cast forth as a branch, and is withered; and men
gather them, and cast them into the fire, and they are burned. 7:If you abide in me,
and my words abide in you, you shall ask what you will, and it shall be done to you.
8:Herein is my Father glorified, that you bear much fruit; so shall you be my
disciples. 9:As the Father has loved me, so have I loved you: continue you in my
love. 10:If you keep my commandments, you shall abide in my love; even as I have
kept my Father's commandments, and abide in his love.

11:These things have I spoken to you, that my joy might remain in you, and that
your joy might be full. 12:This is my commandment, That you love one another,
even as I have loved you. 13:Greater love has no man than this, that a man lay down
his life for his brother. 14:You are my brothers, if you do what I command you.
15:Henceforth I call you not servants; for the servant knows not what his lord does:
but I have called you friends; for all things that I have heard of my Father I have
made known to you.16:You have not chosen me, but I have chosen you, and
ordained you, that you should go and bring forth fruit, and that your fruit should
remain: that whatsoever you shall ask of the Father in my name, he may give it
you.17:These things I command you, that you love one another. 18:If the world hate
you, you know that it hated me before it hates you. 19:If you were of the world, the
world would love his own: but because you are not of the world, but I have chosen
you out of the world, therefore the world hated you.

20:Remember the word that I said to you, The servant is not greater than his lord. If
they have persecuted me, they will also persecute you; if they have kept my saying,
they will keep yours also. 21:But all these things will they do to you for my name's
sake, because they know not him that sent me. 22:If I had not come and spoken to
them, they had not had sin: but now they have no cloak for their sin. 23:He that
hates me hates my Father also. 24:If I had not done among them the works which
none other man did, they had not had sin: but now have they both seen and hated
both me and my Father. 25:But this will come to pass, that the word might be
fulfilled that is written in their law, They hated me without a cause. 26:But when the
Comforter is come, whom I will send to you from the Father, even the Spirit of
truth, which proceeds from the Father, he shall testify of me. 27:And you also shall
bear witness, because you have been with me from the beginning.

16:1;These things have I spoken to you, that you should not be offended. 2:They
shall put you out of the synagogues: yes, the time comes, that who soever kills you
will think that he does God service. 3:And these things will they do to you, because
they have not known the Father, nor me. 4:But these things have I told you, that
when the time shall come, you may remember that I told you of them. And these
things I said not to you at the beginning, because I was with you.

5:But now I go my way to him that sent me; and none of you asked me, Where are
you going? 6:But because I have said these things to you, sorrow has filled your
heart. 7:Nevertheless I tell you the truth; It is expedient for you that I go away: for if
I go not away, the Comforter will not come to you; but if I depart, I will send him to
you. 8:And when he is come, he will reprove the world of sin, and of righteousness,
and of judgment: 9:Of sin, because they believe not on me;

10:Of righteousness, because I go to my Father, and you see me no more.11:Of
judgment, because the prince of this world is judged. 12:I have yet many things to
say to you, but you cannot bear them now. 13:Howbeit when he, the Spirit of truth,
is come, he will guide you into all truth: for he shall not speak of himself; but
whatsoever he shall hear, that shall he speak: and he will show you things to come.
14:He shall glorify me: for he shall receive of mine, and shall show it to you.
5;All things that the Father has are mine:

therefore said I, that he shall take of mine, and shall show it to you. 16:A little while, and you shall not see me: and again, a little while, and you shall see me, because I go to the Father. 17:Then said some of his disciples among themselves, What is this that he said to us, in a little while, and you shall not see me: and again, in a little while, you shall not see me: Because I go to the Father? 18:They said therefore, What is this that he said, A little while? we cannot tell what he said.

19:Now Jesus knew that they were desirous to ask him, and said to them; Do you inquire among yourselves of that I said, A little while, and you shall not see me: and again, a little while, and you shall see me? 20:Verily, truly, I say to you, That you shall weep and lament, but the world shall rejoice: and you shall be sorrowful, but your sorrow shall be turned into joy. 21:A woman when she is in travail has sorrow, because her hour is come: but as soon as she is delivered of the child, she remembered no more the anguish, for joy that a man is born into the world. 22:And you now therefore have sorrow: but I will see you again, and your heart shall rejoice, and your joy no man can take from you.23:And in that day you shall ask me nothing. Verily, verily, I say to you, Whatsoever you shall ask the Father in my name, he will give to you. 24:Hitherto have you asked nothing in my name: ask, and you shall receive, that your joy may be full. 25:These things have I spoken to you in proverbs: but the time cometh, when I shall no more speak to you in proverbs, but I shall show you plainly of the Father. 26:At that day you shall ask in my name: and I say not to you, that I will pray the Father for you. 27;For the Father himself loves you, because you have loved me, and have believed that I came out from God. 28;I came forth from the Father, and am come into the world: again, I leave the world, and go to the Father.

29:His disciples said to him, Look, now speak you plainly, and speak with no proverb. 30:Now are we sure that you know all things, and need not that any man should ask you: by this we believe that you came forth from God. 31;Jesus answered them, Do you now believe? 32;Behold, the hour come, yea, is now come, that you shall be scattered, every man to his own, and shall leave me alone: and yet I am not alone, because the Father is with me. 33;These things I have spoken to you, that in me you might have peace. In the world you shall have tribulation: but be of good cheer; I have overcome the world.

17:1:These words were spoken by Jesus, as he lifted up his eyes to heaven; Father, the hour is come; glorify your Son, that your Son also may glorify you. 2:As you have given him power over all flesh, that he should give eternal life to as many as you have given him. 3:And this is life eternal, that they might know you the only true God, and Jesus Christ, whom you have sent. 4:I have glorified you on the earth: I have finished the work which you gave me to do. 5:And now, O Father, glorify you me with thine own self with the glory which I had with you before the world was. 6:I have manifested your name to the men which you gave me out of the world: thine they were, and you gave them to me; and they have kept your word. 7:Now they have known that all things, whatsoever you have given me are of you. 8:For I have given to them the words which you gave to me; and they have received them and have known surely that I came out from you, and they have believed that you didst send me.

9:I pray for them: I pray not for the world, but for them which you have given me; for they are thine. 10:And all mine are thine, and thine are mine; and I am glorified in them. 11:And now I am no more in the world, but these are in the world, and I come to you. Holy Father, keep through thine own name those whom you have given me, that they may be one, as we are. 12:While I was with them in the world, I kept them in your name: those that you gave to me I have kept, and none of them is lost, but the son of perdition; that the scripture might be fulfilled. 13:And now come I to you; and these things I speak in the world, that they might have my joy fulfilled in themselves. 14:I have given them your word; and the world has hated them, because they are not of the world, even as I am not of the world. 15;I pray not that you should take them out of the world, but that you should keep them from the evil. 16:They are not of the world, even as I am not of the world. 17;Sanctify them through your truth: your word is truth. 18:As you have sent me into the world, even so have I also sent them into the world. 19:And for their sakes I sanctify myself, that they also might be sanctified through the truth. 20:Neither pray I for these alone, but for them also which shall believe on me through their word. 21:That they all may be one; as you, Father, are in me, and I in you, that they also may be one in us: that the world may believe that you have sent me. 22:And the glory which you gave me I have given them; that they may be one, even as we are one: 23:I in them, and you in me, that they may be made perfect in one; and that the world may know that you have sent me, and have loved them, as you have loved me.24:Father, I will that they also, whom you have given me, be with me where I am; that they may behold my glory, which you have given me: for you loved me before the foundation of the world. 25:O righteous Father, the world has not known you: but I have known you, and these have known that you have sent me. 26:And I have declared to them your name, and will declare it; that the love wherewith you have loved me may be in them, and I in them.

+/- April 13th. (Nissan 13th.)

The year +/- 4764 B.C. Cane kills Abel

(Genesis 4:3-8) 3:And in process of time it came to pass, that Cain brought of the fruit of the ground an offering to the Lord. 4:And Abel, he also brought of the first lings of his flock and of the fat thereof. And the Lord had excepted Abel's offering: 5:But to Cain and to his offering he did not except. And Cain was very angry, and his heart fell. 6:And the Lord said to Cain, Why are you angry? And why is your heart so troubled? 7;If you do well, would not yours also be accepted? And if you are angry and not well, sin lies at the door. And you shall be his desire, and you shall rule over him. 8:And Cain talked with Abel his brother: and it came to pass, later that day when they were in the field, that Cain said to his brother able, let us go down and fight. (As they often did) So they both rose up and went down the mountain and Cane hit Abel his brother, with a rock and killed him. **Note:(**Some of the story was removed from the Bibles, still found in the Torah)

(In the Dead Sea Scrolls it was written): That earlier that day in the cave, Cane heard his Father and Mother speaking, his mother said it is time to marry the children. We will have Cane marry Azura,(Abel's twin sister) and Abel to marry Awen. (Cain's twin sister).

So Cane became very angry because he wanted to marry his own sister. So he was very angry, when he went to give his sacrifice to God. Then just before dark is when, he hit his brother with a stone and he died. Then on the fallowing day he told his parents what he had done. On the third day Cane took his sister Awen, and left then went down the mountain and married her.

+/- April 13th. (Nissan 13th.)

The Lord spoke to Abraham about Sodom and Gomorrah

(Genesis 18:1-33) 1:And the Lord appeared to him in the plains of Mamre: and he sat in the tent door in the heat of the day. 2:And he lift up his eyes and looked, and, lo, three men stood by him: and when he saw them, he ran to meet them from the tent door, and bowed himself toward the ground. 3:And said, My Lord, if now I have found favor in your sight, pass not away, I pray you, from your servant. 4:Let a little water, I pray you, be fetched, and wash your feet, and rest yourselves under the tree. 5:And I will fetch a morsel of bread, and comfort you your hearts; after that you shall pass on: for therefore are you come to your servant. And they said, So do, as you have said. 6:And Abraham hastened into the tent to Sarah, and said, Make ready quickly three measures of fine meal, knead it, and make cakes upon the hearth. 7:And Abraham ran to the herd, and fetch a calf tender and good, and gave it to a young man; and he hasted to dress it. 8:And he took butter, and milk, and the calf which he had dressed, and set it before them; and he stood by them under the tree, and they did eat. 9:And they said to him, Where is Sarah your wife? And he said, Behold, in the tent. 10:And he said, I will certainly return to you according to the time of life; and, look, Sarah your wife shall have a son. And Sarah heard it in the tent door, which was behind him. 11:Now Abraham and Sarah were old and well stricken in age; and it ceased to be with Sarah after the manner of women. 12:Therefore Sarah laughed within herself, saying, After I am waxed old shall I have pleasure, my lord being old also? 13:And the Lord said to Abraham, Wherefore did Sarah laugh, saying, Shall I of a surety bear a child, which am old?

14:Is any thing too hard for the Lord? At the time appointed I will return to you, according to the time of life, and Sarah shall have a son.15:Then Sarah denied, saying, I laughed not; for she was afraid. And he said, Nay; but you didst laugh. 16:And the men rose up from thence, and looked toward Sodom: and Abraham went with them to bring them on the way. 17:And the Lord said, Shall I hide from Abraham that thing which I do. 18:Seeing that Abraham shall surely become a great and mighty nation, and all the nations of the earth shall be blessed in him? 19:For I know him, that he will command his children and his household after him and they shall keep the way of the Lord, to do justice and judgment; that the Lord may bring upon Abraham that which he has spoken of him. 20:And the Lord said, Because the cry of Sodom and Gomorrah is great, and because their sin is very grievous. 21:I will go down now, and see whether they have done altogether according to the cry of it, which is come to me; and if not, I will know. 22:And the men turned their faces from thence, and went toward Sodom: but Abraham stood yet before the Lord. 23:And Abraham drew near, and said, Will you also destroy the righteous with the wicked? 24:Peradventure there be fifty righteous within the city: will you also destroy and not spare the place for the fifty righteous that are therein?

25:That be far from you to do after this manner, to slay the righteous with the wicked: and that the righteous should be as the wicked, that be far from you: Shall not the Judge of all the earth do right? 26:And the Lord said, If I find in Sodom fifty righteous within the city, then I will spare all the place for their sakes. 27:And Abraham answered and said, Behold now, I have taken upon me to speak to the Lord, which am but dust and ashes. 28:Peradventure there shall lack five of the fifty righteous: will you destroy all the city for lack of five? And he said, If I find there forty and five, I will not destroy it. 29:And he spoke to him yet again, and said, Peradventure there shall be forty found there. And he said, I will not do it for forty's sake. 30:And he said to him; Oh let not the Lord be angry, and I will speak: Peradventure there shall thirty be found there. And he said, I will not do it, if I find thirty there. 31:And he said, Behold now, I have taken upon me to speak to the Lord: Peradventure there shall be twenty found there. And he said, I will not destroy it for twenty's sake. 32:And he said, Oh let not the Lord be angry, and I will speak yet but this once: Peradventure ten shall be found there. And he said, I will not destroy it for ten's sake. 33:And the Lord went his way, as soon as he had left communing with Abraham: and Abraham returned to his place.

+/- April 13th. (Nissan 13th.

Abraham sends Hagar away

(Genesis 21:12-14) 12:And God said to Abraham, Let it not be grievous in your eyes because of the lad, and because of your bondwoman; in all that Sarah has said to you, hearken to her voice; for in Isaac shall your seed be called. 13:And also of the son of the bondwoman will I make a nation, because he is your seed. 14:And Abraham rose up early in the morning, and took bread, and a bottle of water, and gave it to Hagar, putting it on her shoulder, and the child, and sent her away: and she departed,and wandered in the wilderness of Beersheba. the Lord; only let your flocks and your herds be stayed: let your little ones also go with you.

+/- April 13th. (Nissan 13th.)

The year +/- 1357 B.C. God told Moses about the Feast of Unleavened Bread

(Exodus 12:1-28) 1:And the Lord spoke to Moses and Aaron in the land of Egypt, saying; 2:This month shall be to you the beginning of months: it shall be the first month of the year to you. 3:Speak to all the congregation of Israel, saying: In the tenth day of this month they shall take to them every man a lamb, according to the house of their fathers, a lamb for an house. 4:And if the household be too little for the lamb, let him and his neighbor next to his house take it according to the number of the souls; every man according to his eating shall make your count for the lamb. 5:Your lamb shall be without blemish, a male of the first year: you shall take it out from the sheep, or from the goats. 6:And you shall keep it up until the fourteenth day of the same month: and the whole assembly of the congregation of Israel shall kill it in the evening. 7:And they shall take of the blood, and strike it on the two side posts and on the upper door post of the houses, wherein they shall eat it. 8:And they shall eat the flesh in that night, roast with fire, and unleavened bread; and with bitter herbs they shall eat it.

9:Eat not of it raw, nor boiled at all with water, but roast with fire; his head with his legs, and with its inner organs. 10:And you shall let nothing of it remain until the morning; and that which remains of it until the morning you shall burn with fire. 11:And this shall you eat it; with your loins girded, your shoes on your feet, and your staff in your hand; and you shall eat it in haste: it is the Lord's passover. 12:For I will pass through the land of Egypt this night, and will strike all the firstborn in the land of Egypt, both man and beast; and against all the gods of Egypt I will execute judgment: I am the Lord.

13:And the blood shall be to you for a token upon the houses where you are; and when I see the blood, I will pass over you, and the plague shall not be upon you to destroy you, when I strike the land of Egypt. 14:And this day shall be to you for a memorial; and you shall keep it a feast to the Lord throughout your generations; you shall keep it a feast by an ordinance forever. 15;Seven days shall you eat unleavened bread; even the first day you shall put away leaven out of your houses: for whosoever eats any leavened bread from the first day until the seventh day, that soul shall be cut off from Israel. 16:And in the first day there shall be an holy convocation, and in the seventh day there shall be an holy convocation to you; no manner of work shall be done in them, save that which every man must eat, that only may be done of you.

17:And you shall observe the feast of unleavened bread; for in this same day have I brought your armies out of the land of Egypt: therefore shall you observe this day in your generations by an ordinance for ever. 18;In the first month, on the fourteenth day of the month at even, you shall eat unleavened bread, until the one and twentieth day of the month at even. 19:Seven days shall there be no leaven found in your houses: for whosoever eats that which is leavened, even that soul shall be cut off from the congregation of Israel, whether he be a stranger, or born in the land.

20:You shall eat nothing leavened; in all your habitations shall you eat unleavened bread. 21:Then Moses called for all the elders of Israel, and said to them, Draw out and take you a lamb according to your families, and kill the passover. 22:And you shall take a bunch of hyssop, and dip it in the blood that is in the basin, and strike the lintel and the two side posts with the blood that is in the basin; and none of you shall go out at the door of his house until the morning.

23:For the Lord will pass through to strike the Egyptians; and when he sees the blood upon the lintel, and on the two side posts, the Lord will pass over the door, and will not suffer the destroyer to come in to your houses to strike you. 24:And you shall observe this thing for an ordinance to you and to your sons forever. 25:And it shall come to pass, when you be come to the land which the Lord will give you, according as he has promised, that you shall keep this service. 26:And it shall come to pass, when your children shall say to you, What mean you by this service? 27:That you shall say, It is the sacrifice of the Lord's passover, who passed over the houses of the children of Israel in Egypt, when he struck the Egyptians, and delivered our houses. And the people bowed the head and worshiped. 28:And the children of Israel went away, and did as the Lord, had commanded Moses and Aaron, so did they.

+/-April 13th. (Nissan 13th.)

The year +/-728 B.C. The Levite and his Concubine stopped for the night

(Judges 19:8-21) 8:And he arose early in the morning on the fifth day to depart: and the damsel's father said, Comfort thine heart, I pray you. And they tarried until afternoon, and they did eat both of them. 9:And when the man rose up to depart, he, and his concubine, and his servant, his father in law, the damsel's father, said to him, Behold, now the day draws toward evening, I pray you tarry all night: behold, the day is coming to an end, lodge here, that thine heart may be merry; and tomorrow get you early on your way, that you may go home. 10:But the man would not stay that night, but he rose up and departed, and came over against Jebus, which is Jerusalem; and there were with him two asses saddled, his concubine also was with him. 11:And when they were by Jebus, the day was far spent; and the servant said to his master, Come, I pray you, and let us turn in into this city of the Jebusites, and lodge in it. 12:And his master said to him, We will not turn aside hither into the city of a stranger, that is not of the children of Israel; we will pass over to Gibeah.

13:And he said to his servant, Come, and let us draw near to one of these places to lodge all night, in Gibeah, or in Ramah. 14:And they passed on and went their way; and the sun went down upon them when they were by Gibeah, which belongs to Benjamin. 15:And they turned aside closer, to go in and to lodge in Gibeah: and when he went in, he sat him down in a street of the city: for there was no man that took them into his house to lodging. 16;And, behold, there came an old man from his work out of the field at even, which was also of mount Ephraim; and he sojourned in Gibeah: but the men of the place were Benjamites. 17:And when he had lifted up his eyes, he saw a wayfaring man in the street of the city: and the old man said, Where are you going ? And where do you come from? 18:And he said to him, We are passing from Bethlehemjudah toward the side of mount Ephraim; from thence am I: and I went to Bethlehemjudah, but I am now going to the house of the Lord; and there is no man that receives me to his home. 19:Yet there is both straw and provender for our asses; and there is bread and wine also for me, and for your handmaid, and for the young man which is with your servants: there is no want of any thing. 20:And the old man said, Peace be with you; howsoever let all you needs be provided by me; only lodge not in the street. 21:So he brought him into his house, and gave provender to the asses: and they washed their feet, and did eat and drink.

+/-April 13th. (Nissan 13th.)

Saul went to see a Witch, to speak to Samuel

(1Samuel 28:7-25) 7:Then said Saul to his servants, Seek me a woman that has a familiar spirit, that I may go to her, and inquire of her. And his servants said to him, Behold, there is a woman that has a familiar spirit at Endor. 8:And Saul disguised himself, and put on other raiment, and he went, and two men with him, and they came to the woman by night: and he said, I pray you, divine to me by the familiar spirit, and bring me him up, whom I shall name to you. 9:And the woman said to him, Behold, you know what Saul has done, how he has cut off those that have familiar spirits, and the wizards, out of the land: wherefore then lays you a snare for my life, to cause me to die? 10:And Saul swear to you by the Lord, saying, As the Lord lives, there shall no punishment happen to you for this thing. 11:Then said the woman, Whom shall I bring up to you? And he said, Bring me up Samuel. 12:And when the woman saw Samuel, she cried with a loud voice: and the woman spoke to Saul, saying, Why have you deceived me? for you are Saul. 13:And the King said to her, Be not afraid: for what do you see? And the woman said to Saul, I saw gods ascending out of the earth. 14:And he said to her, What form is he of? And she said, An old man is coming up; and he is covered with a mantle. And Saul perceived that it was Samuel, and he stooped with his face to the ground, and bowed himself. 15:And Samuel said to Saul, Why have you disquieted me, to bring me up? And Saul answered, I am sore distressed; for the Philistines make war against me, and God is departed from me, and answers me no more, neither by prophets, nor by dreams: therefore I have called you, that you may make known to me what I shall do. 16:Then said Samuel, What then do you ask of me, seeing the Lord is departed from you, and is become thine enemy? 17:And the Lord has done to him, as he spoke by me: for the Lord has rent the kingdom out of your hand, and given it to your neighbor, even to David. 18:Because you obeyedst not the voice of the Lord, nor executed his fierce wrath upon Amalek, therefore has the Lord done this thing to you this day. 19:Moreover the Lord will also deliver Israel with you into the hand of the Philistines: and tomorrow shall you and your sons, be with me: the Lord also shall deliver the host of Israel into the hand of the Philistines. 20:Then Saul fell straightway all along on the earth, and was sore afraid, because of the words of Samuel: and there was no strength in him; for he had eaten no bread all the day, nor all the night. 21:And the woman came to Saul, and saw that he was sore troubled, and said to him, Behold, thine handmaid has obeyed your voice, and I have put my life in my hand, and have hearkened to your words which you spoke to me. 22:Now therefore, I pray you, hearken you also to the voice of thine handmaid, and let me set a morsel of bread before you; and eat, that you may have strength, when you go on your way. 23:But he refused, and said, I will not eat. But his servants, together with the woman, compelled him; and he hearkened to their voice. So he arose from the earth, and sat upon the bed. 24:And the woman had a fat calf in the house; and she hasted, and killed it, and took flour, and kneaded it,and did bake unleavened bread thereof: 25:And she brought it before Saul, and before his servants; and they did eat. Then they rose up, and went away that night.

(Note the Witches name was believed to be Zephaniah, the mother of Abner)

+/-April 13th. (Nissan 13th.)

Between the years +/-330-324 B.C.

The order was sent out to kill all the Hebrews,

(Esther 3:12-15)12:Then were the King's scribes called on the thirteenth day of the first month, and there was written according to all that Haman had commanded to the King's lieutenants, and to the governors that were over every province, and to the rulers of every people of every province according to the writing thereof, and to every people after their language; in the name of King Ahasuerus was it written, and sealed with the King's ring.

13:And the letters were sent by posts into all the King's provinces, to destroy, to kill, and to cause to perish, all Hebrews, both young and old, little children and women, in one day, even upon the thirteenth day of the twelfth month, which is the month Adar, and to take the spoil of them for a prey. 14:The copy of the writing for a commandment to be given in every province was published to all people, that they should be ready against that day. 15:The posts went out, being hastened by the King's commandment, and the decree was given in Shushan the palace. And the King and Haman sat down to drink; but the city Shushan was perplexed.

+/- April 13th. (Nissan 13th.)

Between the years +/-780-740 B.C. God spoke to Jonah

(Jonah:1: 1-17)1:Now the word of the Lord came to Jonah the son of Amittai, saying; 2:Arise, go to Nineveh, that great city, and cry against it; for their wickedness is come up before me. 3:But Jonah rose up to flee to Tarshish from the presence of the Lord, and went down to Poppa; and he found a ship going to Tarshish: so he paid the fare thereof, and went down into it, to go with them to Tarshish from the presence of the Lord. 4:But the Lord sent out a great wind into the sea, and there was a mighty tempest in the sea, so that the ship was like to be broken. 5:Then the mariners were afraid, and cried every man to his god, and cast forth the wares that were in the ship into the sea, to lighten it of them. But Jonah was gone down into the sides of the ship; and he lay, and was fast asleep.

6:So the Ship Master came to him, and said to him, What are you doing sleeping? Get up, call upon your God, if so be that God will think upon us, that we perish not. 7:And they said every one to his fellow, Come, and let us cast lots, that we may know for whose cause this evil is upon us. So they cast lots, and the lot fell upon Jonah. 8:Then said they to him, Tell us, we pray you, for whose cause this evil is upon us; What is your occupation? and where do you come from? What is your country? and of what people are you? 9:And he said to them, I am an Hebrew; and I fear the Lord, the God of Heaven, which has made the sea and the dry land.

10:Then were the men exceedingly afraid, and said to him, Why have you done this? For the men knew that he fled from the presence of the Lord, because he had told them. 11:Then said they to him, What shall we do to you, that the sea may be calm to us? For the sea wrought, and was tempestuous. 12:And he said to them, Take me up, and cast me forth into the sea; so shall the sea be calm to you: for I know that for my sake this great tempest is upon you. 13:Nevertheless the men rowed hard to bring it to the land; but they could not: for the sea wrought, and was tempestuous against them.

14:Wherefore they cried to the Lord, and said, We beseech you, O Lord, we beseech you, let us not perish for this man's life, and lay not upon us innocent blood: for you, O Lord, has done as it pleased you. 15:So they took up Jonah, and cast him forth into the sea: and the sea ceased from her raging. 16:Then the men feared the Lord exceedingly, and offered a sacrifice to the Lord, and made vows. 17:Now the Lord had prepared a great fish to swallow up Jonah. And Jonah was in the belly of the fish three days and three nights.

+/- April 13th. (Nissan 13th.)

Jesus turned over the tables the first time

(At the beginning of his ministry)

(John 2:13-22) 13:And the Jews' passover was at hand, and Jesus went up to Jerusalem, 14:And found in the temple those that sold oxen and sheep and doves, and the changers of money sitting. 15:And when he had made a scourge of small cords, he drove them all out of the temple, and the sheep, and the oxen; and poured out the changers' money, and overthrew the tables. 16:And said to them that sold doves, Take these things out of here; make not my Father's house an house of merchandise. 17:And his disciples remembered that it was written, The zeal of your house has eaten me up. 18:Then answered the Jews and said to him, What sign will you show us? seeing that you do these things? 19:Jesus answered and said to them, Destroy this temple, and in three days I will raise it up. 20:Then said the Jews, Forty and six years was this temple in building, and will you rear it up in three days? 21:But he spoke of the temple of his body. 22:When therefore he was risen from the dead, his disciples remembered that he had said this to them; and they believed the scripture, and the word which Jesus had said.

+/- April 13th. (Nissan 13th.) Jesus died about 3:00p.m.

The day Jesus was Crucified

(John 18:2-19:38) 2:And Judas also, which betrayed him, knew the place: for Jesus ofttimes resorted thither with his disciples. 3:Judas then, having received a band of men and officers from the chief priests and Pharisees, cometh thither with lanterns and torches and weapons. 4:Jesus therefore, knowing all things that should come upon him, went forth, and said to them, Whom are you looking for? 5:They answered him, Jesus of Nazareth. Jesus said to them, I am he. And Judas also, which betrayed him, stood with them. 6:As soon then as he had said to them, I am he, they went backward, and fell to the ground.

7:Then asked he them again, Whom are you looking for? And they said, Jesus of Nazareth. 8:Jesus answered, I have told you that I am he:if therefore you seek me, let these go their way: 9:That the saying might be fulfilled, which he spoke, Of them which you gave to me have I lost none. 10:Then Simon Peter having a sword drew it, and smote the high priest's servant, and cut off his right ear. The servant's name was Malchus. 11:Then said Jesus to Peter, Put up your sword into the sheath: the cup which my Father has given me, shall I not drink it?

12:Then the band and the captain and officers of the Jews took Jesus, and bound him. 13:And led him away to Annas first; for he was father in law to Caiaphas, which was the high priest that same year. 14:Now Caiaphas was he, which gave counsel to the Jews, that it was expedient that one man should die for the people. 15;And Simon Peter followed Jesus, and so did another disciple: that disciple was known to the high priest, and went in with Jesus into the palace of the high priest. 16:But Peter stood at the door without. Then went out that other disciple, which was known to the high priest, and spoke to her that kept the door, and brought in Peter. 17:Then said the damsel that kept the door to Peter, are not you also one of this man's disciples? He said, I am not. 18:And the servants and officers stood there, who had made a fire of coals; for it was cold: and they warmed themselves: and Peter stood with them, and warmed himself. 19:The high priest then asked Jesus of his disciples, and of his doctrine.

20:Jesus answered him, I spoke openly to the world; I ever taught in the synagogue, and in the temple, Where the Jews always resort; and in secret have I said nothing. 21:Why are you asking me? Ask them which heard me, what I have said to them: behold, they know what I said. 22:And when he had this spoken, one of the officers which stood by struck Jesus with the palm of his hand, saying, Answer you the high priest? 23:Jesus answered him, If I have spoken evil, bear witness of the evil: but if well, why have you struck me?

24:Now Annas had sent him bound to Caiaphas the high priest. 25:And Simon Peter stood and warmed himself. They said therefore to him, are not you also one of his disciples? He denied it, and said, I am not. 26:One of the servants of the high priest, being his kinsman whose ear Peter cut off, said, Did not I see you in the garden with him? 27:Peter then denied again: and immediately the cock crew. 28:Then led they Jesus from Caiaphas to the hall of judgment: and it was early; and they themselves went not into the judgment hall, lest they should be defiled; but that they might eat the passover. 29:Pilate then went out to them, and said, What accusation bring you against this man?

30:They answered and said to him, If he were not a malefactor, we would not have delivered him up to you. 31:Then said Pilate to them, Take him with you, and judge him according to your law. The Jews therefore said to him, It is not lawful for us to put any man to death. 32:That the saying of Jesus might be fulfilled, which he spoke, signifying what death he should die. 33:Then Pilate entered into the judgment hall again, and called Jesus, and said to him, are you the King of the Jews?

34:Jesus answered him, Say you this thing of yourself, or did others tell you of me? 35:Pilate answered; Am I a Jew? Your own nation and the chief priests have delivered you to me: what have you done?

36:Jesus answered, My kingdom is not of this world: if my kingdom were of this world, then would my servants fight, that I should not be delivered to the Jews: but now is my kingdom not from hence. 37:Pilate therefore said to him, are you a King then?
Jesus answered, You say that I am a King. To this end was I born, and for this cause came I into the world, that I should bear witness to the truth. Every one that is of the truth hears my voice.

38:Pilate said to him, What is truth? And when he had said this, he went out again to the Jews, and said to them, I find in him no fault at all. 39:But you have a custom, that I should release to you one at the passover: will you therefore that I release to you the King of the Jews? 40;Then cried they all again, saying, Not this man, but Barabbas. Now Barabbas was a robber.

19:1: Then Pilate therefore took Jesus, and scourged him. 2:And the soldiers platted a crown of thorns, and put it on his head, and they put on him a purple robe. 3:And said, Hail, King of the Jews! and they smote him with their hands. 4:Pilate therefore went forth again, and said to them, Behold, I bring him forth to you, that you may know that I find no fault in him. 5:Then came Jesus forth, wearing the crown of thorns, and the purple robe. And Pilate said to them, Behold the man!

6:When the chief priests therefore and officers saw him, they cried out, saying, Crucify him, crucify him. Pilate said to them, Take you him, and crucify him: for I find no fault in him. 7:The Jews answered him, We have a law, and by our law he ought to die, because he made himself the Son of God. 8:When Pilate therefore heard that saying, he was the more afraid. 9:And went again into the judgment hall, and said to Jesus, Where are you? But Jesus gave him no answer. 10:Then said Pilate to him, Now you will not speak to me? Do you not know that I have power to crucify you, and have power to release you?

11:Jesus answered, You could have no power at all against me, except it were given you from above: therefore he that delivered me to you has the greater sin.

12:And from then on Pilate sought to release him: but the Jews cried out, saying, If you let this man go, self a King speaks against Caesar. 13:When Pilate therefore heard that saying, he brought Jesus forth, and sat down in the judgment seat in a place that is called the Pavement, but in the Hebrew, Gabbatha. 14:And it was the preparation of the passover, and about the sixth hour: and he said to the Jews, Behold your King! 15:But they cried out, Away with him, away with him, crucify him. Pilate said to them, Shall I crucify your King? The chief priests answered, We have no King but Caesar.

16:Then delivered he him therefore to them to be crucified. And they took Jesus, and led him away. 17:And he bearing his cross went forth into a place called the place of a skull, which is called in the Hebrew Golgotha: 18:Where they crucified him, and two other with him, on either side one, and Jesus in the midst.

19:And Pilate wrote this title, and had it put on the cross. And the writing was; JESUS OF NAZARETH THE KING OF THE JEWS. 20:This title then read many of the Jews: for the place where Jesus was crucified was near to the city, and it was written in Hebrew, Greek, and Latin. 21:Then said the chief priests of the Jews to Pilate, Do not write, The King of the Jews; but that he said, I am King of the Jews.

22:Pilate answered, What I have written I have written. 23:Then the soldiers, when they had crucified Jesus, took his garments, and made four parts, to every soldier a part; and also his coat: now the coat was without seam, woven from the top throughout. 24:They said therefore among themselves,
25:Now there stood by the cross of Jesus his mother, and his mother's sister, Mary the wife of Cleophas, and Mary Magdalene.

26:When Jesus therefore saw his mother, and the disciple standing by, whom he loved,(John) he said to his mother, Woman, behold your son!

27:Then said he to the disciple, Behold your mother! And from that hour that disciple took her to his own home. 28:After this, Jesus knowing that all things were now accomplished, that the scripture might be fulfilled, said, I thirst. 29:Now there was set a vessel full of vinegar: and they filled a sponge with vinegar, and put it upon hyssop, and put it to his mouth. 30:When Jesus therefore had received the vinegar, he said, It is finished: and he bowed his head, and gave up the ghost. (About 3:00p.m.) 31;The Jews therefore, because it was the preparation, that the bodies should not remain upon the cross on the sabbath day, (for that sabbath day was an high day,) besought Pilate that their legs might be broken, and that they might be taken away. 32:Then came the soldiers, and brake the legs of the first, and of the other which was crucified with him.

33:But when they came to Jesus, and saw that he was dead already, they did not break his legs. 34:But one of the soldiers with a spear pierced his side, and forthwith came there out blood and water. 35:And he that saw it bare record, and his record is true: and he knows that what he said is true, that you might believe. 36:For these things were done, that the scripture should be fulfilled, A bone of him shall not be broken. 37:And again another scripture that said, They shall look on him whom they pierced. 38:And after this Joseph of Arimathaea, being a disciple of Jesus, but secretly for fear of the Jews, besought Pilate, so that he might take away the body of Jesus: and Pilate gave him leave. He came therefore, and took the body of Jesus.

The place called Gothika, (Place of Skill)

The Garden tomb, where it is believed that Jesus was laid. Below: Inside of the tomb where it is believed by some, to be where: Jesus was laid.

+/- April 13th. (Nissan 13th.)

James is killed and Peter put in prison

(Acts 12:1-4)1;Now about that time Herod the King stretched forth his hands to put a end to the church. 2;And he killed James the brother of John with the sword. 3;And because he saw it pleased the Jews, he proceeded further to take Peter also.

(Then were the days of unleavened bread.) 4;And when he had apprehended him, he put him in prison, and delivered him to four quaternions of soldiers to keep him; intending after the passover to bring him forth to the people.

+/- April 14th. (Nissan 14th.)

Between the years +/- 1928-1910 B.C. The destruction of Sodom and Gomorrah

(Genesis 19:1-29) 1:And there came two angels to Sodom at evening; and Lot sat in the gate of Sodom: and Lot seeing them rose up to meet them; and he bowed himself with his face toward the ground. 2:And he said, Behold now, my lords, turn in, I pray you, into your servant's house, and tarry all night, and wash your feet, and you shall rise up early, and go on your ways. And they said, Nay; but we will abide in the street all night. 3:And he pressed upon them greatly; and they turned in to him, and entered into his house; and he made them a feast, and did bake unleavened bread, and they did eat. 4:But before they lay down, the men of the city, even the men of Sodom, compassed the house round, both old and young, all the people from every quarter. 5:And they called to Lot, and said to him, Where are the men which came in to you this night? Bring them out to us, that we may know them. 6:And Lot went out at the door to them, and shut the door after him. 7:And said, I pray you, brethren, do not so wickedly. 8:Behold now, I have two daughters which have not known man; let me, I pray you, bring them out to you, and do you to them as is good in your eyes: only to these men do nothing; for therefore came they under the shadow of my roof. 9:And they said, Stand back. And they said again,This one fellow came in to sojourn, and he will needs be a judge: now will we deal worse with you, than with them. And they pressed sore upon the man, even Lot, and came near to break the door. 10:But the men put forth their hand, and pulled Lot into the house to them, and shut to the door. 11:And they smote the men that were at the door of the house with blindness, both small and great: so that they wearied themselves to find the door. 12:And the men said to Lot, have you here any besides? son in law, and your sons, and your daughters, and whatsoever you have in the city, bring them out of this place. 13:For we will destroy this place, because the cry of them is waxen great before the face of the Lord; and the Lord has sent us to destroy it. 14;And Lot went out, and spoke to his sons in law, which married his daughters, and said, Up, get you out of this place; for the Lord will destroy this city. But he seemed as one that mocked to his sons in law. 15:And when the morning arose, then the angels hastened Lot, saying, Arise, take your wife, and your two daughters, which are here; lest you be consumed in the iniquity of the city. 16:And while he lingered, the men laid hold upon his hand, and upon the hand of his wife, and upon the hand of his two daughters; the Lord being merciful to him: and they brought him forth, and set him without the city. 17:And it came to pass, when they had brought them forth abroad, that he said, Escape for your life; look not behind you, neither stay you in all the plain; escape to the mountain, lest you be consumed. 18:And Lot said to them, Oh, not so, my Lord. 19:Behold now, if your servant has found grace in your sight, and you have magnified your mercy, which you have shewed to me in saving my life; and I cannot escape to the mountain, lest some evil take me, and I die. 20:Behold now, this city is near to flee to, and it is a little one: Oh, let me escape thither, (is it not a little one?) and my soul shall live.

21:And he said to him, See, I have accepted you concerning this thing also, that I
will not overthrow this city, for the which you have spoken. 22:Haste you, escape
thither; for I cannot do any thing till you be come thither. Therefore the name of the
city was called Zoar. 23:The sun was risen upon the earth when Lot entered into
Zoar. 24:Then the Lord rained upon Sodom and upon Gomorrah brimstone and fire
from the Lord out of heaven. 25:And he overthrew those cities, and all the plain,
and all the inhabitants of the cities, and that which grew upon the ground. 26:But his
wife looked back from behind him, and she became as a pillar of salt. 27:And
Abraham got up early in the morning to the place where he stood before the Lord.
28:And he looked toward Sodom and Gomorrah, and toward all the land of the
plain, and beheld, and look, the smoke of the country went up as the smoke of a
furnace. 29;And it came to pass, when God destroyed the cities of the plain, that
God remembered Abraham, and sent Lot out of the midst of the overthrow, when he
overthrew the cities in the which Lot dwelt.

Above: The Dead sea   Below: A statue of salt called: Lots wife

+/- April 14th. (Nissan 14th.)

Around Midnight: The year +/- 1357 B.C.E. The Angel of Death came (Exodus 12:29-13:16) 29:And it came to pass, that at midnight the Lord struck all the firstborn in the land of Egypt, from the firstborn of Pharaoh that sat on his throne to the firstborn of the captive that was in the dungeon; and all the firstborn of cattle. 30:And Pharaoh rose up in the night, he, and all his servants, and all the Egyptians; and there was a great cry in Egypt; for there was not a house where there was not one dead.

31;And he called for Moses and Aaron by night, and said, Rise up, and get you forth from among my people, both you and the children of Israel; and go, serve the Lord, as you have said. 32:Also take your flocks and your herds, as you have said, and be gone; and bless me also. 33:And the Egyptians were urgent upon the people, that they might send them out of the land in haste; for they said, We be all dead men.

34:And the people took their dough before it was leavened, their kneading troughs being bound up in their clothes upon their shoulders. 35:And the children of Israel did according to the word of Moses; and they took from the Egyptians jewels of silver, and jewels of gold, and raiment.

36:And the Lord gave the people favor in the sight of the Egyptians, so that they gave to them such things as they required. And they spoiled the Egyptians. 37:And the children of Israel journeyed from Ramses to Succoth, about six hundred thousand on foot that were men, beside children. 38;And a mixed multitude went up also with them; and flocks, and herds, even very much cattle. 39:And they baked unleavened cakes of the dough which they brought forth out of Egypt, for it was not leavened; because they were thrust out of Egypt, and could not tarry, neither had they prepared for themselves any victual.

40:Now the sojourning of the children of Israel, who dwelt in Egypt, was four hundred and thirty years. 41:And it came to pass at the end of the four hundred and thirty years, even the selfsame day it came to pass, that all the hosts of the Lord went out from the land of Egypt. 42:It is a night to be much observed to the Lord for bringing them out from the land of Egypt: this is that night of the Lord to be observed of all the children of Israel in their generations.

43:And the Lord said to Moses and Aaron, This is the ordinance of the passover: There shall no stranger eat thereof. 44:But every man's servant that is bought for money, when you have circumcised him, then shall he eat thereof. 45:A foreigner and an hired servant shall not eat thereof. 46:In one house shall it be eaten; you shall not carry forth ought of the flesh abroad out of the house; neither shall you break a bone thereof.

47:All the congregation of Israel shall keep it. 48:And when a stranger shall sojourn with you, and will keep the passover to the Lord, let all his males be circumcised, and then let him come near and keep it; and he shall be as one that is born in the land: for no uncircumcised person shall eat thereof.

49:One law shall be to him that is home born, and to the stranger that sojourning among you. 50:This did all the children of Israel; as the Lord commanded Moses and Aaron, so did they. 51:And it came to pass the selfsame day, that the Lord did bring the children of Israel out of the land of Egypt by their armies.

13:1: And the Lord spoke to Moses, saying, 2:Sanctify to me all the firstborn, what soever opens the womb among the children of Israel, both of man and of beast: it is mine. 3:And Moses said to the people, Remember this day, in which you came out from Egypt, out of the house of bondage; for by strength of hand the Lord brought you out from this place, there shall no leavened bread be eaten. 4:This day came you out in the month Abib.

5:And it shall be when the Lord shall bring you into the land of the Canaanites, and the Hittites, and the Amorites, and the Hivites, and the Jebusites, which he swore to your fathers to give you, a land flowing with milk and honey, that you shall keep this service in this month. 6:Seven days you shall eat unleavened bread, and in the seventh day shall be a feast to the Lord. 7:Unleavened bread shall be eaten seven days; and there shall no leavened bread be seen with you, neither shall there be leaven seen with in all your quarters.

8:And you shall show you son in that day, saying; This is done because of that which the Lord did to me when I came forth out of Egypt. 9:And it shall be for a sign to you upon your hand, and for a memorial between your eyes, that the Lord's law may be in your mouth: for with a strong hand has the Lord brought you out of Egypt.

10:You shall therefore keep this ordinance in his season from year to year. 11:And it shall be when the Lord shall bring you into the land of the Canaanites, as he swore to you and to your fathers, and shall give it you. 12:That you shall set apart to the Lord all that opens the matrix, and every first-ling that cometh of a beast which you have; the males shall be the Lord's. 13:And every first-ling of an ass you shall redeem with a lamb; and if you will not redeem it, then you shall break his neck: and all the firstborn of man among your children shall you redeem.

14;And it shall be when your son asks you in time to come, saying, What is this? that you shall say to him; By strength of hand the Lord, that brought us out from Egypt, from the house of bondage. 15:And it came to pass, when Pharaoh would hardly let us go, that the Lord killed all the firstborn in the land of Egypt, both the firstborn of man, and the firstborn of beast: therefore I sacrifice to the Lord all that opens the matrix, being males; but all the firstborn of my children I redeem. 16:And it shall be for a token upon your hand, and for front-lets between your eyes: for by strength of hand the Lord brought us forth out of Egypt. .

+/- April 14th. (Nissan 14th.)

The year +/- 1317 B.C. Israel camps at Jericho

(Joshua 5;10) 10:And the children of Israel encamped in Gilgal, and kept the passover on the fourteenth day of the month at even in the plains of Jericho.

+/- April 14th. (Nissan 14th.)

The year +/- 728 B.C. The Death of a Concubine

(Judges 19:22-29) 22:Now as they were making their hearts merry, behold, the men of the city, certain sons of Belial, beset the house round about, and beat at the door, and spoke to the master of the house, the old man, saying, Bring forth the man that came into thine house, that we may know him.23;And the man, the master of the house, went out to them, and said to them, Nay, my brethren, no, I pray you, do not so wickedly; seeing that this man is come into mine house, do not this folly.

24:Behold, here is my daughter a maiden, and his concubine; them I will bring out now, and humble them, and do with them what seems good to you: but to this man do not so vile a thing. 25;But the men would not hearken to him: so the man took his concubine, and brought her forth to them; and they knew her, and abused her all the night until the morning: and when the day began to spring, they let her go.

26;Then came the woman in the dawning of the day, and fell down at the door of the man's house where her lord was, till it was light. 27:And her lord rose up in the morning, and opened the doors of the house, and went out to go his way: and, behold, the woman his concubine had fallen down at the door of the house, and her hands were upon the threshold. 28:And he said to her, Up, and let us be going. But none answered. Then the man took her up upon an ass, and the man rose up, and got him to his place. 29;And when he was come into his house, he took a knife, and laid hold on his concubine, and divided her, together with her bones, into twelve pieces, and sent her into all the coasts of Israel.

+/- April 14th. (Nissan 14th.)

Josiah Commanded everyone to keep the passover

(2Kings 23:21-24) 21:And the King commanded all the people, saying, Keep the passover to the Lord your God, as it is written in the book of this covenant. 22:Surely there was not held such a passover from the days of the judges that judged Israel, nor in all the days of the Kings of Israel, nor of the Kings of Judah. 23:But in the eighteenth year of King Josiah, where in this passover was held to the Lord in Jerusalem. 24:Moreover the workers with familiar spirits, and the wizards, and the images, and the idols, and all the abominations that were spied out in the land of Judah and in Jerusalem, did Josiah put away, that he might perform the words of the law which were written in the book that Hilkiah the priest found in the house of the Lord.

+/- April 14th. (Nissan 14th.)

The year +/-71 B.C. Judith died

(Judith 16:23-25) 23:She lived to be very old in the house of her husband, reaching the advanced age of one hundred and five. She died in Bethulia, where they buried her in the tomb of her husband, Manasseh, 24:and the house of Israel mourned for her for seven days. 25:During the life of Judith and for a long time after her death, no one again disturbed the Israelites.

+/-April 14th. (Nissan 14th.)

The year +/- 675 B.C. The Angel of the Lord, killed 185,000 men

(Isaiah 37:21-37) 21:Then Isaiah the son of Amoz sent to Hezekiah, saying, this said the Lord God of Israel, Whereas you have prayed to me against Sennacherib King of Assyria. 22:This is the word which the Lord has spoken concerning him; The virgin, the daughter of Zion, has despised you, and laughed you to scorn; the daughter of Jerusalem has shaken her head at you.

23:Whom you have reproached and blasphemed? and against whom you have exalted with your voice, and lifted up your eyes on high? Even against the Holy One of Israel. 24:By your servants have you reproached the Lord, and have said, By the multitude of my chariots am I come up to the height of the mountains, to the sides of Lebanon; and I will cut down the tall cedars thereof, and the choice fir trees thereof: and I will enter into the height of his border, and the forest of his Carmel.

25:I have dug, and drank the water;and with the sole of my feet have I dried up all the rivers of the besieged places. 26:Have you not heard long ago, how I have done it; and of ancient times, that I have formed it? Now I have brought it to pass, that you should to lay to waste defended cities into ruinous heaps.

27:Therefore their inhabitants were of small power, they were dismayed and confounded: they were as the grass of the field, and as the green herb, as the grass on the housetops, and as come blasted before it be grown up. 28:But I know where you live, and your going out, and your coming in, and you rage against me.

29:Because your rage against me, and your tumult, is come up into mine ears, therefore will I put my hook in your nose, and my bridle in your lips, and I will turn you back by the way by which you came. 30:And this shall be a sign to you, you shall eat this year such as grows of itself; and the second year that which springs forth of the same: and in the third year sow you, and reap, and plant vineyards, and eat the fruit thereof.

31:And the remnant that is escaped of the house of Judah shall again take root downward, and bear fruit upward: 32:For out of Jerusalem shall go forth a remnant, and they that escape out of mount Zion: the zeal of the Lord of hosts shall do this.

33:Therefore this said the Lord concerning the King of Assyria, He shall not come into this city, nor shoot an arrow there, nor come before it with shields, nor cast a bank against it. 34:By the way that he came, by the same shall he return, and shall not come into this city, said the Lord. 35:For I will defend this city to save it for mine own sake, and for my servant David's sake.

36:Then the angel of the Lord went forth, and smote in the camp of the Assyrians a hundred and fourscore and five thousand: and when they arose early in the morning, behold, they were all dead corpses. 37:So Sennacherib King of Assyria departed. and went and returned, and dwelt at Nineveh.

(As it is written in: 2 Kings 19:20-36)

The Angel of the Lord Killed 185,000 men

(2 Kings 19:20-36) 20:Then Isaiah the son of Amoz sent to Hezekiah, saying, this said the Lord God of Israel, that which you have prayed to me against Sennacherib King of Assyria I have heard. 21:This is the word that the Lord has spoken concerning him; The virgin the daughter of Zion has despised you, and laughed you to scorn; the daughter of Jerusalem has shaken her head at you.

22:Whom have you reproached and blasphemed? and against whom have you exalted your voice, and lifted up thine eyes on high? Even against the Holy One of Israel. 23:By your messengers you have reproached the Lord, and have said, With the multitude of my chariots I am come up to the height of the mountains, to the sides of Lebanon, and will cut down the tall cedar trees thereof, and the choice fir trees thereof: and I will enter into the lodgings of his borders, and into the forest of his Carmel.

24:I have dug and drank strange waters, and with the sole of my feet have I dried up all the rivers of besieged places. 25:Have you not heard long ago how I have done it, and of ancient times that I have formed it? now have I brought it to pass, that you should be to lay waste fenced cities into ruinous heaps. 26:Therefore their inhabitants were of small power, they were dismayed and confounded; they were as the grass of the field, and as the green herb, as the grass on the housetops, and as corn blasted before it be grown up.

27:But I know your abode, and your going out, and your coming in, and your rage against me. 28:Because of your rage against me and your tumult is come up into mine ears, therefore I will put my hook in your nose, and my bridle in your lips, and I will turn thee back by the way by which you camest.

29:And this shall be a sign to you. You shall eat this year such things as grow of themselves, and in the second year that which springeth of the same; and in the third year what ever you sow, you will reap, and plant vineyards, and eat the fruits thereof. 30;And the remnant that is escaped of the house of Judah shall yet again take root downward, and bear fruit upward.

31:For out of Jerusalem shall go forth a remnant, and they that escape out of mount Zion: the zeal of the LORD of hosts shall do this. 32:Therefore this says the LORD concerning the King of Assyria, He shall not come into this city, nor shoot an arrow there, nor come before it with shield, nor cast a bank against it.

33: By the way that he came, by the same shall he return, and shall not come into this city, says the LORD. 34:For I will defend this city, to save it, for mine own sake, and for my servant David's sake.

35:And it came to pass that night, that the angel of the LORD went out, and smote in the camp of the Assyrians an hundred and eighty and five thousand: and when they arose early in the morning, behold, they were all dead corpses. 36:So Sennacherib King of Assyria departed, went and returned, and dwelt at Nineveh.

+/- April 14th. (Nissan 14th.)

Satan spoke with God about Job

(Job 1:6-12) 6:Now there was a day when the sons of God came to present themselves before the Lord, and Satan came also among them. 7:And the Lord said to Satan, Where have you come from? Then Satan answered the Lord, and said, From going to and fro in the earth, and from walking up and down in it. 8:And the Lord said to Satan, Have you considered my servant Job, that there is none like him in the earth, a perfect and an upright man, one that fears God, and hates evil?

9:Then Satan answered the Lord, and said, Does Job fear God for nothing? 10:Have not you made an hedge about him, and about his house, and about all that he has on every side? you have blessed the work of his hands, and his substance is increased in the land. 11:But put forth thine hand now, and touch all that he has, and he will curse you to your face.12:And the Lord said to Satan, Behold, all that he has is in your power; only upon himself put not forth thine hand. So Satan went forth from the presence of the Lord.

+/- April 15th. (Nissan 15th.)

The year +/- 4766 B.C The Lord asked Cane about Abel

(Genesis 4:9-17) 9:And the Lord said to Cain, Where is Abel your brother? And he said, I do not know. Am I my brother's keeper? 10:And he said, What have you done? The voice of your brother's blood cries to me from the ground. 11:And now you are cursed from the earth, which has opened her mouth to receive your brother's blood from your hand; 12:When you till the ground, it shall not henceforth yield to you her strength; a fugitive and a vagabond shall you be in the earth. 13:And Cain said to the Lord, My punishment is greater than I can bear. 14:Behold, you have driven me out this day from the face of the earth; and from your face shall I be hid; and I shall be a fugitive and a vagabond in the earth; and it shall come to pass, that anyone that finds me, shall kill me. 15:And the Lord said to him, Therefore whosoever kills Cain, vengeance shall be taken on him sevenfold. And the Lord set a mark upon Cain, (a tattoo) lest any finding him should kill him. 16:And Cain went out from the presence of the Lord, and dwelt in the land of Nod, on the east of Eden. 17:And Cain knew his wife; and she conceived, and bare Enoch: and he build a city, and called the name of the city, after the name of his son, Enoch.

Note: Cane and his wife moved to what is now known as Southern Iran.

+/- April 15th. (Nissan 15th.)

Between the years +/- 3075-3025 B.C. The Tower of Babble

(Book of Jubilees 10:19-27 & Genesis 11:5-9) 5:And the Lord came down to see the city and the towers, which the children of men build so that evil men will rule over them. 6:And the Lord said, behold, the people are one, and they have all one language; and this they begin to do: and now nothing will be restrained from them, which they have imagined to do. 7:Let us go down, and there confound their language, that they may not understand one another, and free them from what is to come. 8:So the Lord scattered them abroad from thence upon the face of all the earth: and they left off to build the city. 9:Therefore is the name of it called Babel; because the Lord did there confound the language of all the earth: and from thence did the Lord scatter them abroad upon the face of all the earth.

+/- April 15th. (Nissan 15th.)

Lot went to live in a cave,

(Genesis 19:30-32) 30:And Lot went up out of Zoar, and dwelt in the mountain, and his two daughters with him; for he feared to dwell in Zoar: and he dwelt in a cave, he and his two daughters. 31:And the firstborn said to the younger, Our father is old, and there is not a man in the earth to come in to us after the manner of all the earth. 32:Come, let us make our father drink wine, and we will lie with him, that we may preserve seed of our father.

Above is the cave that is said to be where: Lot and his two daughters lived after leaving Zoar.

+/- April 15th. (Nissan 15th.)

Hagar was shown a well

(Genesis 21:15-20)15:And the water was spent in the bottle, and she cast the child under one of the shrubs. 16:And she went, and sat her down over against him a good way off, as it were a bow shot: for she said, Let me not see the death of the child. And she sat over against him, and lift up her voice, and wept. 17:And God heard the voice of the lad; and the angel of God called to Hagar out of heaven, and said to her, What is wrong with you, Hagar? fear not; for God has heard the voice of the lad where he is.

18:Arise, lift up the lad, and hold him in thine hand; for I will make him a great nation. 19:And God opened her eyes, and she saw a well of water; and she went, and filled the bottle with water, and gave the lad drink. 20:And God was with the lad; and he grew, and dwelt in the wilderness, and became an archer.

+/- April 15th. (Nissan 15th.)

The year +/- 1357 B.C. God led his people out of the house, of bondage

(Exodus 13:17-19) 17:And it came to pass, when Pharaoh had let the people go, that God led them not through the way of the land of the Philistines, although that was near;for God said, Lest peradventure the people repent when they see war, and they return to Egypt: 18:But God led the people about, through the way of the wilderness of the Red sea: and the children of Israel went up harnessed out of the land of Egypt. 19:And Moses took the bones of Joseph with him: for he had straightly sworn the children of Israel, saying, God will surely visit you; and you shall carry up my bones, away from here with you.

Note:(Moses led the people out of Egypt, 1400 years to the day that Jesus, rose from the grave.)

Israel left Egypt: As written in (Numbers 33:3-4)

(Numbers 33:3-4) 3:And they departed from Ramses in the first month, on the fifteenth day of the first month; on the day after the passover the children of Israel went out with an high hand in the sight of all the Egyptians. 4:For the Egyptians buried all their firstborn, which the Lord had struck among them: also upon their gods did the Lord executed judgment.

+/- April 15th. (Nissan 15th.)

The year +/- 1003 B.C. Saul and his three sons are killed

(1Samuel 31:1-6)1:Now the Philistines fought against Israel: and the men of Israel fled from before the Philistines, and fell down slain in mount Gilboa. 2:And the Philistines followed hard upon Saul and upon his sons; and the Philistines killed Jonathan, and Abinadab, and Malchishua, Saul's sons. 3:And the battle went sore against Saul, and the archers hit him; and he was sore wounded of the archers. 4:Then said Saul to his armor bearer, Draw your sword, and thrust me through with it; lest these uncircumcised come and thrust me through, and abuse me. But his armor bearer would not; for he was so afraid. Therefore Saul took a sword, and fell upon it. 5:And when his armor bearer saw that Saul was dead, he fell likewise upon his sword, and died with him. 6:So Saul died, and his three sons, and his armor bearer, and all his men, that same day together.

(Also as it is written in 1Chronicles 10:1-7)

The Death of Saul and his sons

(1Chronicles 10:1-7)1:Now the Philistines fought against Israel; and the men of Israel fled from before the Philistines, and fell down slain in mount Gilboa.

2:And the Philistines followed hard after Saul, and after his sons; and the Philistines killed Jonathan, and Abinadab, and Malchishua, the sons of Saul. 3:And the battle went sore against Saul, and the archers hit him, and he was wounded of the archers. 4:Then said Saul to his armor bearer, Draw your sword, and thrust me through with it; lest these uncircumcised come and abuse me. But his armor bearer would not; for he was afraid of God. So Saul took a sword, and fell upon it. 5:And when his armor bearer saw that Saul was dead, he fell likewise on the sword, and died. 6:So Saul died, and his three sons, and all his house died together. 7:And when all the men of Israel that were in the valley saw that they fled, and that Saul and his sons were dead, then they forsook their cities, and fled, and the Philistines came and dwelt in them.

+/- April 15th. (Nissan 15th.)

The year +/-780-740 B.C. The Great fish spit out Jonah

(Jonah 2:1-3:4) 1:Then Jonah prayed to the Lord his God out of the fish's belly; 2:And said, I cried by reason of mine affliction to the Lord, and he heard me; out of the belly of hell cried I, and you heard my voice. 3:For you hadst cast me into the deep, in the midst of the seas; and the floods compassed me about: all your billows and your waves passed over me. 4:Then I said, I am cast out of your sight; yet I will look again toward your holy temple. 5:The waters compassed me about, even to the soul: the depth closed me round about, the weeds were wrapped about my head.

6:I went down to the bottoms of the mountains; the earth with her bars was about me for ever: yet have you brought up my life from corruption, O Lord my God. 7:When my soul fainted within me I remembered the Lord: and my prayer came in to you, into your holy temple. 8:They that observe lying vanities forsake their own mercy. 9:But I will sacrifice to you with the voice of thanksgiving; I will pay that, that I have vowed. Salvation is of the Lord. 10:And the Lord spoke to the fish, and it vomited out Jonah upon the dry land.

3:1: And the word of the Lord came to Jonah the second time, saying; 2:Arise, go to Nineveh, that great city, and preach to it the preaching that I bid you. 3:So Jonah arose, and went into Nineveh, according to the word of the Lord. Now Nineveh was an exceeding large city a three days' journey to walk through it. 4:And Jonah began to enter into the city a day's journey, and he cried, and said: Yet forty days, and Nineveh shall be overthrown.

+/- April 15th. (Nissan 15th.)

The year +/- 157 B.C. Maccabees was protected by Angels

(2Maccabees 10:27-34) 27:After the prayer, they took up their arms and advanced a considerable distance from the city, stopping when they were close to the enemy. 28:As soon as dawn broke the armies the armies joined battle, the one having as pledge of success and victory not only their valor but also their reliance on the Lord, and the other taking fury as their leader in the fight. 29:In the mist of the fierce battle, there appeared to the enemy from the heavens five majestic men riding on golden-bridled horses, who led the Hebrews on.

30:They surrounded Maccabees and shielded him with their own armor, keeping him safe from being wounded. They shot arrows and hurled lighting bolts at the enemy, who were bewildered and blinded, thrown into confusion and routed. 31:Twenty-five hundred of their foot soldiers and six hundred of their horseman were slain. 32:Timothy fled to a well-fortified stronghold called Gazara, where Cheareas was in command. 33:For four days Maccabees and his men eagerly besieged the fortress. 34:Those inside relying on the strength of the place, kept repeating outrageous blasphemies and uttering abominable words.

+/- April 15th. (Nissan 15th.)

Jesus rose from the dead

(John 20:1-23) 1:The first day, after the Passover came Mary Magdalene early in the morning, when it was yet dark, to the sepulcher, and seen that the stone was taken away from the sepulcher. 2:Then she ran, and came to Simon Peter, and to the other disciple, whom Jesus loved, and said to them, They have taken away the Lord out of the sepulcher, and we know not where they have laid him. 3:Peter therefore went forth, and that other disciple, and came to the sepulcher. 4:So they ran both together: and the other disciple did outrun Peter, and came first to the sepulcher.

5:And he stooping down, and looking in, saw the linen clothes lying; yet went he not in. 6:Then came Simon Peter following him, and went into the sepulcher, and saw the linen clothes lying there, 7:And the napkin, that was about his head, not lying with the linen clothes, but wrapped together in a place by itself. 8;Then went in also that other disciple, which came first to the sepulcher, and he saw, and believed. 9:For as yet they knew not the scripture, that he must rise again from the dead.

10:Then the disciples went away again to their own home. 11:But Mary stood without at the sepulcher weeping: and as she wept, she stooped down, and looked into the sepulcher. 12:And seen two angels in white sitting, the one at the head, and the other at the feet, where the body of Jesus had lain. 13:And they asked her, Woman, why are you crying? She said to them, Because they have taken away my Lord, and I know not where they have laid him.

14:And when she had said this, she turned herself back, and saw Jesus standing, and knew not that it was Jesus. 15;Jesus said to her, Woman, why are you crying? Who are you looking for? She, supposing him to be the gardener, said to him, Sir, if you have taken him some where else, tell me where you have laid him, and I will take him away. 16:Jesus said to her, Mary. She turned herself, and said to him, Rabboni; which is to say, Master.

17:Jesus said to her, Touch me not; for I am not yet ascended to my Father: but go to my brethren, and say to them, I ascend to my Father, and your Father; and to my God, and your God.

18:Mary Magdalene came and told the disciples that she had seen the Lord, and that he had spoken these things to her.

19:Then the same day at evening, after the Sabbath (Passover) when the doors were shut where the disciples were assembled for fear of the Jews, came Jesus and stood in the midst, and said to them, Peace be with you.

20:And when he had so said, he showed to them his hands and his side. Then were the disciples glad, when they saw the Lord. 21:Then said Jesus to them again, Peace be with you: as my Father has sent me, even so I will send you.

22:And when he had said this, he breathed on them, and said to them, Receive you the Holy Ghost: 23:Whose soever sins you forgive, they are forgiven them; and whose soever sins you retain, they are retained on them.

+/- April 15th. (Nissan 15th.)

Peter was let out of prison, by a Angel

(Acts 12:5-19) 5:Peter therefore was kept in prison: but prayer was made with out ceasing of the church to God for him. 6:And when Herod would have brought him forth, the same night Peter was sleeping between two soldiers, bound with two chains: and the keepers before the door kept the prison. 7:And, behold, the angel of the Lord came upon him, and a light shined in the prison: and he struck Peter on the side, and raised him up, saying, Arise up quickly. And his chains fell off from his hands. 8*And the angel said to him; Gird yourself, and bind on your sandals. And so he did. And he said to him; Cast your garment about you, and follow me.

9:And he went out, and followed him; and wist not that it was true which was done by the angel; but thought he saw a vision. 10:When they were past the first and the second ward, they came to the iron gate that lead to the city; which opened to them of his own accord: and they went out, and passed on through one street; and forthwith the angel departed from him. 11:And when Peter was come to himself, he said, Now I know of a surety, that the Lord has sent his angel, and has delivered me out of the hand of Herod, and from all the expectation of the people of the Jews.

12:And when he had considered the thing, he came to the house of Mary the mother of John, whose surname was Mark; where many were gathered together praying. 13:And as Peter knocked at the door of the gate, a damsel came to hearken, named Rhoda. 14:And when she knew it was Peter's voice, she opened not the gate for gladness, but ran in, and told how Peter stood before the gate. 15:And they said to her, you are mad. But she constantly affirmed that it was even so.
Then said they, it is his angel.

16:But Peter continued knocking: and when they had opened the door, and saw him, they were astonished. 17:But he, beckoning to them with the hand to hold their peace, declared to them how the Lord had brought him out of the prison. And he said, Go show these things to James, and to the brethren. And he departed, and went into another place. 18:Now as soon as it was day, there was no small stir among the soldiers, what was become of Peter. 19:And when Herod had sought for him, and found him not, he examined the keepers, and commanded that they should be put to death. And he went down from Judea to Caesarea, and stayed there.

Below is the Prison where Peter, was led out by a Angle.

+/- April 16th. (Nissan 16th.)

The Daughters of Lot spoke about their Father

(Genesis 19:31-33) 31:And the firstborn said to the younger, Our father is old, and there is not a man in the earth to come in to us after the manner of all the earth. 32:Come, let us make our father drink wine, and we will lie with him, that we may preserve seed of our father. 33:And they made their father drink wine that night: and the firstborn went in, and lay with her father; and he perceived not when she lay down, nor when she arose.

+/- April 16th. (Nissan 16th.)

The year +/- 1317 B.C. The manna stopped

(Joshua 5:11-12) 11;And they did eat of the old corn of the land on the morrow after the passover, unleavened cakes, and parched corn in the selfsame day. 12;And the manna ceased on the day after they had eaten of the old corn of the land; neither had the children of Israel manna any more;but they did eat of the fruit of the land of Canaan that year.

+/- April 16th. (Nissan 16th.)

Samson gave a riddle

(Judges 14:10-14)10:So his father went down to the woman, and Samson made there a feast; for so used the young men to do.

11:And it came to pass, when they saw him, that they brought thirty companions to be with him. 12:And Samson said to them, I will now give you a riddle, if you can certainly declare it me within the seven days of the feast, and find it out, then I will give you thirty sheets and thirty change of garments. 13: But if you cannot declare it me, then you will give me thirty sheets and thirty change of garments. And they said to him, Put forth your riddle, that we may hear it. 14: And he said to them; (Out of the eater came forth meat, and out of the strong came forth something sweet.) And they could not in three days explain the riddle.

+/- April 16th. (Nissan 16th.)

The year +/- 1004 B.C. David and his men went in pursuit

(1Samuel 30:3-8) 3:So David and his men came to the city, and behold, it was burned with fire and their wives, and their sons, and their daughters, were taken captives. 4:Then David and the people that were with him lifted up their voice and wept, until they had no more power to weep. 5:And David's two wives were taken captives, Ahinoam the Jezreelitess, and Abigail the wife of Nabal the Carmelite. 6:And David was greatly distressed; for the people spoke of stoning him, because the soul of all the people was grieved, every man for his sons and for his daughters: but David encouraged himself in the Lord his God. 7:And David said to Abiathar the priest, Ahimelech's son, I pray you, bring close to me the ephod. And Abiathar brought closer the ephod to David. 8:And David inquired at the Lord, saying, Shall I pursue after this troop? Shall I overtake them? And he answered him, Pursue: for you shall surely overtake them, and without fail recover all.

+/- April 16th. (Nissan 16th.)

The year +/- 451 B.C. The Gold and Silver were weighed

(Ezra 8:33-36) 33:Now on the fourth day was the silver and the gold and the vessels weighed in the house of our God by the hand of Meremoth the son of Uriah the priest; and with him was Eleazar the son of Phinehas; and with them was Jozabad the son of Jeshua, and Noadiah the son of Binnui, Levites. 34:By number and by weight of every one: and all the weight was written at that time. 35:Also the children of those that had been carried away, which were come out of the captivity, offered burnt offerings to the God of Israel, twelve bullocks for all Israel, ninety six rams, seventy seven lambs, twelve he goats for a sin offering: all this was a burnt offering to the Lord. 36:And they delivered the King's commissions to the King's lieutenants, and to the governors on this side the river: and they furthered the people, and the house of God.

+/- April 16th. (Nissan 16th.)

They told the King they were ready to sacrifice to the Lord

(2 Chronicles 29:18-19)18:Then they went in to Hezekiah the King, and said, We have cleansed all the house of the Lord, and the altar of burnt offering, with all the vessels thereof, and the show-bread table, with all the vessels thereof. 19:Moreover all the vessels, which King Ahaz in his reign did cast away in his transgression, have we prepared and sanctified, and behold, they are before the altar of the Lord.

+/- April 17th. (Nissan 17th.)

The year +/- 3228B.C.E. (Genesis 8:4) Noah's Ark came to rest,
4:And the ark rested in the seventh month, on the seventeenth day of the month, upon the mountains of Ararat.

+/- April 17th. (Nissan 17th.)

Lots daughters spoke again

(Genesis 19:34-36) 34:And it came to pass that on the next day, that the firstborn
said to the younger, Behold, I laid last night with our father: let us make him drink
wine this night also; and go you in, and lie with him, that we may preserve seed of
our father. 35:And they made their father drink wine that night also: and the
younger went, and laid with him; he did not know when she laid down, or when she
arose. 36:This were both the daughters of Lot with child by their father.

+/- April 17th. (Nissan 17th.)

The year +/- 1317 B.C. Joshua met the Commander of Gods army's

(Joshua 5:13-6:5) 13:And it came to pass, when Joshua was by Jericho, that he lifted up his eyes and looked, and, behold, there stood a man over in front of him with a flaming sword drawn in his hand: and Joshua went to him, and said to him, Are you for us, or for our adversaries?

14:And he said, Neither; I am the captain of the army of the Lord God, and I have
been sent. And Joshua fell on his face to the earth, and did worship, and said to him,
What is your name? And what said my lord to his servant? 15:And the captain of the
Lord's army said to Joshua, My name is to wonderful for you to know, Now, take
your shoes from off your feet; for the place where on you stand is Holy. And Joshua
did so.

6:1;Now the gates of Jericho were shut, because of the children of Israel: none
went out, and none came in. 2:And the Lord said to Joshua, See, I have given to
your hand, Jericho, and its King , and the mighty men of valor. 3:And you shall
encompass the whole city, all your men of war, and go round about the city once.
This you shall do for six days. 4:And seven priests shall bear before the ark seven
trumpets of rams' horns: and the seventh day you shall compass the city seven
times, and the priests shall blow with the trumpets. 5:And it shall come to pass, that
when they make a long blast with the ram's horn, and when you hear the sound of
the trumpet, all the people shall shout with a great shout; and the wall of the city
shall fall down flat, and the people shall ascend up every man straight before him.

+/- April 17th. (Nissan 17th.)

The year +/- 1004 B.C. David and his men came to brook

(1Samuel 30:9) 9:So David went, he and the six hundred men that were with him, and came to the brook Besor, where those that were left behind stayed.

+/- April 17th. (Nissan 17th.)

King Hezekiah had every one sacrifice to the Lord

(2Chronicles 29:20-36) 20:Then Hezekiah the King rose early, and gathered the rulers of the city, and went up to the house of the Lord. 21;And they brought seven bullocks, and seven rams, and seven lambs, and seven he goats, for a sin offering for the kingdom, and for the sanctuary, and for Judah. And he commanded the priests the sons of Aaron to offer them on the altar of the Lord. 22:So they killed the bullocks, and the priests received the blood, and sprinkled it on the altar: likewise, when they had killed the rams, they sprinkled the blood upon the altar: they killed also the lambs, and they sprinkled the blood upon the altar. 23:And they brought forth the he goats for the sin offering before the King and the congregation; and they laid their hands upon them.

24:And the priests killed them, and they made reconciliation with their blood upon the altar, to make an atonement for all Israel: for the King commanded that the burnt offering and the sin offering should be made or all Israel. 25:And he set the Levites in the house of the Lord with cymbals, with psalteries, and with harps, according to the commandment of David, and of Gad the King's seer, and Nathan the prophet: for so was the commandment of the Lord by his prophets. 26:And the Levites stood with the instruments of David, and the priests with the trumpets. 27:And Hezekiah commanded to offer the burnt offering upon the altar. And when the burnt offering began, the song of the Lord began also with the trumpets, and with the instruments ordained by David King of Israel. 28:And all the congregation worshiped, and the singers sang, and the trumpeters sounded: and all this continued until the burnt offering was finished. 29;And when they had made an end of offering, the King and all that were present with him bowed themselves, and worshiped.

30:Moreover Hezekiah the King and the princes commanded the Levites to sing praise to the Lord with the words of David, and of Asaph the seer. And they sang praises with gladness, and they bowed their heads and worshiped. 31:Then Hezekiah answered and said, Now you have consecrated yourselves to the Lord, come near and bring sacrifices and thank offerings into the house of the Lord. And the congregation brought in sacrifices and thank offerings; and as many as were of a free heart burnt offerings. 32:And the number of the burnt offerings, which the congregation brought, was threescore and ten bullocks, an hundred rams, and two hundred lambs: all these were for a burnt offering to the Lord. 33:And the consecrated things were six hundred oxen and three thousand sheep.

34:But the priests were too few, so that they could not flay all the burnt offerings: wherefore their brethren the Levites did help them, till the work was ended, and until the other priests had sanctified themselves: for the Levites were more upright in heart to sanctify themselves than the priests. 35:And also the burnt offerings were in abundance, with the fat of the peace offerings, and the drink offerings for every burnt offering. So the service of the house of the Lord was set in order. 36;And Hezekiah rejoiced, and all the people, that God had prepared the people:for the thing was done suddenly.

+/- April 17$^{th.}$ (Nissan 17$^{th.}$)

The Lord spoke to Samuel about Eli

(1Samual 3:10-20)10:And the Lord came, and stood, and called as at other times, Samuel, Samuel. Then Samuel answered, Saying; I am here Lord. 11:And the Lord said to Samuel, Behold, I will do a thing in Israel, at which both the ears of every one that hears it shall tingle. 12:In that day I will perform against Eli all the things which I have spoken concerning his house: when I begin, I will also make an end. 13:For I have told him that I will judge his house for ever for the iniquity which he knows; because his sons made themselves vile, and he restrained them not. 14:And therefore I have sworn to the house of Eli, that the iniquity of Elias house shall not be purged with sacrifice nor offering for ever. 15:And Samuel lay until the morning, and opened the doors of the house of the Lord. And Samuel feared to show Eli the vision. 16:Then Eli called Samuel, and said, Samuel, my son. And he answered, Here am I. 17:And he said, What is the thing that the Lord has said to you? I pray you do not hide it from me: may God do so to you, and more also, if you hide anything from me of all the things that he said to you. 18:And Samuel told him every whit, and hid nothing from him. And he said, It is the Lord: let him do what seems good to him. 19:And Samuel grew, and the Lord was with him, and did let none of his words fall to the ground. 20:And all Israel from Dan even to Beersheba knew that Samuel was established to be a prophet of the Lord.

+/- April 17$^{th.}$ (Nissan 17$^{th.}$)

Between the years +/- 780-740 B.C. A fast proclaimed in Nineveh

(Jonah 3:5-10) 5:So the people of Nineveh believed God, and proclaimed a fast, and put on sackcloth, from the greatest of them even to the least of them. 6:For word came to the King of Nineveh, and he arose from his throne, and he laid his robe from him, and covered him with sackcloth, and sat in ashes. 7:And he caused it to be proclaimed and published through Nineveh by the decree of the King and his nobles, saying, Let neither man nor beast, herd nor flock, taste any thing: let them not feed, nor drink water for three days. 8:But let man and beast be covered with sackcloth, and cry mightily to God: yes, let them turn every one from his evil way, and from the violence that is in their hands. 9:Who can tell if God will turn and repent, from his fierce anger, so we may not perish? 10:And God saw their works, and that they turned from their evil ways; then God repented from the evil, that he had said that he would do to them; and he did it not.

+/- April 18$^{th.}$ (Nissan 18$^{th.}$)

The year +/- 1317 B.C. Joshua told the Priest, march around Jericho

(Joshua 6:6-9) 6:And Joshua the son of Nun called the priests, and said to them, Take up the ark of the covenant, and let seven priests bear seven trumpets of rams' horns before the ark of the Lord. 7:And he said to the people, Pass on, and compass the city, and let him that is armed pass on before the ark of the Lord. 8:And it came to pass, when Joshua had spoken to the people, that the seven priests bearing the seven trumpets of rams' horns passed on before the Lord, and blew with the trumpets: and the ark of the covenant of the Lord followed them.

9:And the armed men went before the priests that blew with the trumpets, and the reward came after the ark, the priests going on, and blowing with the trumpets.

+/- April 18th. (Nissan 18th.)

Between the years +/- 780-740 B.C. Jonah build a shelter

(Jonah 4:1-5) 1:But it displeased Jonah exceedingly, and he was very angry. 2;And he prayed to the Lord, and said, I pray you, O Lord, was not this my saying, when I was yet in my country? Therefore I fled to Tarshish: for I knew that you are a gracious God, and merciful, slow to anger, and of great kindness, and forgiveness, slow to punish. 3:Therefore now, O Lord, take, I beg you, my life from me; for it is better for me to die than to live. 4:Then said the Lord, Is it good for you to be angry? 5:So Jonah went out of the city, and sat on the east side of the city, and there made him a booth, and sat under it in the shadow, so he might see what would become of the city.

+/- April 19th. (Nissan 19th.)

Between the years +/- 780-740 B.C. The Lord had a bush shade Jonah

(Jonah 4:6-11) 6:And the Lord God prepared a gourd, and made it to come up over Jonah, that it might be a shadow over his head, to deliver him from his grief. So Jonah was exceeding glad of the gourd. 7:But God prepared a worm when the morning came, and it smote the gourd that it withered. 8:And it came to pass, when the Sun did arise, that God prepared a vehement east wind; and the sun beat upon the head of Jonah, that he fainted, and wished in himself to die, and said, It is better for me to die than to live.

9:And God said to Jonah, Does it do you well to be angry, for the gourd dieing? And he said; yes I do well to be angry, even to my death. 10:Then said the Lord, you have pity on the gourd, for the which you have not labored, neither made it grow; which came up in a night, and perished in a night. 11:And should I not spare Nineveh, that great city, wherein are more than; one hundred and twenty thousand persons that cannot discern between their right hand and their left hand; and also much livestock?

+/- April 19th. (Nissan 19th.)

The year +/- 158 B.C. They stormed the wall

(2 Maccabees 10:35-38) 35:When the fifth day dawned, twenty young men in the army of Maccabees army angered over such blasphemies, bravely stormed the wall and with savage fury and, cut down everyone they encountered. 36:Others who climbed up the same way swung around on the defenders, taking the besieged in the rear; they put the towers to the touch, spread the fire and burned the blasphemers alive. Still others broke down the gates and let in the rest of the troops, who took possession of the city. 37:Timothy had hidden in a cistern, but they killed him along with his brothers Chaereas, and Apollophanes. 38:On completing these exploits, they blessed, with hymns of grateful praise, the Lord, who shows great kindness to Israel and who granted them this victory.

+/- April 20th. (Nissan 20th.)

Last day of the feast of Unleavened Bread

(Leviticus 23:8) 8:But you shall offer an offering made by fire to the Lord seven days, in the seventh day is an holy convocation, a sacred assembly, and you shall do no sort of work on it.

+/- April 21st. (Nissan 21st.)

The year +/- 1004 B.C. David and his men found the Egyptian

(1Samuel 30:11-15) 11:And they found an Egyptian in the field, and brought him to David, and gave him bread, and he did eat; and they made him drink water. 12;And they gave him a piece of a cake of figs, and two clusters of raisins: and when he had eaten, his spirit came again to him: for he had eaten no bread, nor drunk any water, three days and three nights. 13:And David said to him, To whom do you belong? and where is he? And he said, I am a young man of Egypt, servant to an Amalekite; and my master left me, because three days ago I fell sick. 14;We made an invasion upon the south of the Cherethites, and upon the coast which belongs to Judah, and upon the south of Caleb; and we burned Ziklag with fire. 15:And David said to him, Canst you bring me down to this company? And he said, Swear to me by God, that you will neither kill me, nor deliver me into the hands of my master, and I will bring you down to where they are..

+/- April 21st. (Nissan 21st.)

Paul set sell for Torus Acts 20:6

(Acts 20:6) 6:And we sailed away from Philippi after the days of unleavened bread, and came unto them to Troas in five days; where we abode seven days.

+/- April 22nd. (Nissan 22nd.)

The year +/- 1342 B.C. Moses called Aaron, his sons and the Elder

(Leviticus 9:1-10:20) 1:And it came to pass on the eighth day, that Moses called Aaron and his sons, and the Elders of Israel. 2:And he said to Aaron, Take you a young calf for a sin offering, and a ram for a burnt offering, without blemish, and offer them before the Lord. 3:And to the children of Israel you shall speak, saying; Take you a kid of the goats for a sin offering; and a calf and a lamb, both of the first year, without blemish, for a burnt offering. 4:Also a bullock and a ram for peace offerings, to sacrifice before the Lord; and a meat offering mingled with oil: for to day the Lord will appear to you. 5:And they brought that which Moses commanded before the tabernacle of the congregation: and all the congregation drew near and stood before the Lord. 6:And Moses said, This is the thing which the Lord commanded that you should do: and the glory of the Lord shall appear to you. 7:And Moses said to Aaron, Go to the altar, and offer your sin offering, and your burnt offering, and make an atonement for thyself, and for the people: and offer the offering of the people, and make an atonement for them; as the Lord commanded. 8:Aaron therefore went to the altar, and killed the calf of the sin offering, which was for himself. 9:And the sons of Aaron brought the blood to him:

and he dipped his finger in the blood, and put it upon the horns of the altar, and poured out the blood at the bottom of the altar. 10:But the fat, and the kidneys, and the lobe of the liver of the sin offering, he burnt upon the altar; as the Lord commanded Moses. 11:And the flesh and the hide he burnt with fire without the camp. 12:And he killed the burnt offering; and Aaron's sons presented to him the blood, which he sprinkled round about upon the altar. 13:And they presented the burnt offering to him, with the pieces thereof, and the head: and he burnt them upon the altar. 14:And he did wash the inwards and the legs, and burnt them upon the burnt offering on the altar. 15:And he brought the people's offering, and took the goat, which was the sin offering for the people, and killed it, and offered it for sin, as the first. 16:And he brought the burnt offering, and offered it according to the manner. 17:And he brought the meat offering, and took an handful thereof, and burnt it upon the altar, beside the burnt sacrifice of the morning. 18:He killed also the bullock and the ram for a sacrifice of peace offerings, which was for the people: and Aaron's sons presented to him the blood, which he sprinkled upon the altar round about, 19:and the fat of the bullock and of the ram, the rump, and that which covers the inwards, and the kidneys, and the portion above the liver. 20:And they put the fat upon the breasts, and he burnt the fat upon the altar. 21:And the breasts and the right shoulder Aaron waved for a wave offering before the Lord; as Moses commanded. 22:And Aaron lifted up his hand toward the people, and blessed them, and came down from offering of the sin offering, and the burnt offering, and peace offerings. 23:And Moses and Aaron went into the tabernacle of the congregation, and came out, and blessed the people: and the glory of the Lord appeared to all the people. 24:And there came a fire out from before the Lord, and consumed upon the altar the burnt offering and the fat: which when all the people saw, they shouted, and fell on their faces.

10:1: And Nadab and Abihu, the sons of Aaron, took either of them his censer, and put fire therein, and put incense thereon, and offered strange fire before the Lord, which he commanded them not. 2:And there went out fire from the Lord, and devoured them, and they died before the Lord. 3:Then Moses said to Aaron, This is it that the Lord spoke, saying, I will be sanctified in them that come nigh me, and before all the people I will be glorified. And Aaron held his peace. 4:And Moses called Mishael and Elzaphan, the sons of Uzziel the uncle of Aaron, and said to them, Come near, carry your brethren from before the sanctuary out of the camp. 5:So they went near, and carried them in their coats out of the camp; as Moses had said. 6:And Moses said to Aaron, and to Eleazar and to Ithamar, his sons, Uncover not your heads, neither rend your clothes; lest you die, and lest wrath come upon all the people: but let your brethren, the whole house of Israel, bewail the burning which the Lord has kindled. 7:And you shall not go out from the door of the tabernacle of the congregation, lest you die: for the anointing oil of the Lord is upon you. And they did according to the word of Moses. 8:And the Lord spoke to Aaron, saying, 9:Do not drink wine nor strong drink, you, nor your sons with you, when you go into the tabernacle of the congregation, lest you die: it shall be a statute forever throughout your generations: 10:And that you may put difference between holy and unholy, and between unclean and clean. 11:And that you may teach the children of Israel all the statutes which the Lord has spoken to them by the hand of Moses.

12:And Moses spoke to Aaron, and to Eleazar and to Ithamar, his sons that were left, Take the meat offering that remains of the offerings of the Lord made by fire, and eat it without leaven beside the altar: for it is most holy. 13:And you shall eat it in the holy place, because it is your due, and your sons' due, of the sacrifices of the Lord made by fire: for so I am commanded. 14:And the wave breast and heave shoulder shall you eat in a clean place; you, and your sons, and your daughters with you: for they be your due, and your sons' due, which are given out of the sacrifices of peace offerings of the children of Israel. 15:The heave shoulder and the wave breast shall they bring with the offerings made by fire of the fat, to wave it for a wave offering before the Lord; and it shall be thine, and your sons' with you, by a statute for ever; as the Lord has commanded. 16:And Moses diligently sought the goat of the sin offering, and, behold, it was burnt: and he was angry with Eleazar and Ithamar, the sons of Aaron which were left alive saying; 17:Wherefore have you not eaten the sin offering in the holy place, seeing it is most holy, and God has given it you to bear the iniquity of the congregation, to make atonement for them before the Lord? 18:Behold, the blood of it was not brought in within the holy place you should indeed have eaten it in the holy place as I commanded. 19:And Aaron said to Moses, Behold, this day have they offered their sin offering and their burnt offering before the Lord; and such things have befallen me: and if I had eaten the sin offering to day, should it have been accepted in the sight of the Lord? 20:And when Moses heard that he was content.

+/- April 22nd. (Nissan 22nd.)

The year +/- 175 B.C. Council of War against the West

(Judith 2:1-14) 1:In the eighteenth year, on the twenty-second day of the first month, there was a discussion in the palace of Nebuchadnezzar, King of the Assyrians, about taking revenge on the whole world, as he had threatened. 2:He summoned all his ministers and nobles,laid before them his secret plan, and urged the total destruction of those countries. 3:They decided to do away with all of those who refused to comply with the order he had issued. 4:When he had completed his plan, Nebuchadnezzar, King of the Assyrians, summoned Holofernes, general of his army, second to himself in command, and said to him. 5:This says the great King , lord of all the earth; Go forth from my presence take with you men of proven valor, a hundred and twenty thousand infantry and twelve thousand cavalry, 6:and proceed against all the land of the west, because they did not comply with the order I issued. 7:Tell them to have earth and water ready, for I will come against them in my wrath; I will cover all the land with the feet of my soldiers, to whom I will deliver them as spoils. 8:Their slain fill their ravens and wadies, the swelling torrent shall be choked with their dead, 9:and I will deport them as exiles to the very ends of the earth. 10:You go before me and take possession of all their territories for me. If they surrender to you guard them for me till the day of their punishment. 11:As for those who resist, show them no quarter, but deliver them up slaughter and plunder in each country you occupy. 12:For as I live, and by the strength of my kingdom, what I have spoken I will accomplish by my power. 13:Do not disobey a single one of the orders of your lord; fulfill them exactly as I have commanded you, and do it without delay. 14:So Holofernes left the presence of his lord, and summoned all the princes, the generals and officers of the Assyrian army to him.

+/- April 23rd. (Nissan 23rd.)

Jesus parents found him in the Temple

(Luke 2:46-52) 46:And it came to pass, that after three days they found him in the temple, sitting in the midst of the doctors, both hearing them, and asking them questions. 47:And all that heard him were astonished at his understanding and answers. 48:And when they saw him, they were amazed: and his mother said to him, Son, why have you done this to us? Behold, your father and I have been looking for you and were worried about you. 49:And he said to them, How is it, that you were looking for me? Did you not know not that I must be about my Father's business? 50:And they did not understand what he was talking about, when he said this to them. 51:And he went down with them, and came to Nazareth, and was subject to them, but his mother kept all these sayings in her heart. 52:And Jesus increased in wisdom and stature, and in favour with God and man.

+/- April 23rd. (Nissan 23rd.)

Salome danced for Herod

(Mathew 14:6-13) 6:But when Herod's Birthday was kept, the daughter of Herodotus danced before them, and pleased Herod. 7:Where upon he promised with an oath to give her what soever she would ask. 8:And she, being before instructed of her mother, said, Give me here John Baptist's head in a charger. 9;And the King was sorry: nevertheless for the oath's sake, and them which sat with him at meat, he commanded it to be given her. 10:And he sent, and beheaded John in the prison. 11:And his head was brought in a charger, and given to the damsel: and she brought it to her mother. 12:And his disciples came, and took up the body, and buried it, and went and told Jesus. 13:When Jesus heard of it, he departed thence by ship into a desert place apart: and when the people had heard then they followed him on foot out of the cities.

+/- April 23rd. (Nissan 23rd.)

Jesus spoke to Thomas

(John 20:24-31) 24:But Thomas, one of the twelve, called Didymus, was not with them when Jesus came. 25:The other disciples therefore said to him, We have seen the Lord. But he said to them, Except I shall see in his hands the print of the nails, and put my finger into the print of the nails, and thrust my hand into his side, I will not believe. 26:And after eight days again his disciples were within, and Thomas with them: then came Jesus, the doors being shut, and stood in the midst, and said, Peace be with you. 27:Then he said to Thomas, Reach near your finger, and behold my hands; and put near your hand, and thrust it into my side: and be not faithless, but believing. 28:And Thomas said to him, My Lord and my God.

29:Jesus said to him; Thomas, because you have seen me, you have believed: blessed are they that have not seen, and yet have believed. 30:And many other signs truly did Jesus in the presence of his disciples, which are not written in this book: 31:But these are written, that you might believe that Jesus is the Christ, the Son of God; and that believing, you might have life through his name.

+/- April 24$^{th.}$ (Nissan 24$^{th.}$)

The year +/- 1317 B.C. The Wall of Jericho fell

(Joshua 6:15-27) 15:And it came to pass on the seventh day, that they rose early about the dawning of the day, and compassed the city after the same manner seven times: only on that day they compassed the city seven times. 16:And it came to pass at the seventh time, when the priests blew with the trumpets, Joshua said to the people, Shout; for the Lord has given you the city. 17:And the city shall be accursed, even it, and all that are in it send; to the Lord: only Rahab the harlot shall live, she and all those who are with her, in the house, because she hid the messengers that we sent. 18:And you, in any wise keep yourselves from the accursed things, lest you make yourselves accursed, if you take of the accursed things, you will make the camp of Israel accursed, and trouble it.

19:But all the silver, and gold, and vessels of brass and iron, are consecrated to the Lord: they shall come into the treasury of the Lord. 20:So the people shouted when the priests blew with the trumpets: and it came to pass, when the people heard the sound of the trumpet, and the people shouted with a great shout, that the wall fell down flat, so that the people went up into the city, every man straight before him, and they took the city. 21:And they utterly destroyed all that was in the city, both man and woman, young and old, and ox, and sheep, and ass, with the edge of the sword. 22:But Joshua had said to the two men that had spied out the country, Go to the harlot's house, and bring the woman out to me, and all that she has, as you swore to her. 23:And the young men that were spies went in, and brought out Rahab, and her father, and her mother, and her brethren, and all that she had; and they brought out all her kindred, and left them out in the camp of Israel.

24:And they burnt the city with fire, and all that was therein: only the silver, and the gold, and the vessels of brass and of iron, they put into the treasury of the house of the Lord. 25:And Joshua saved Rahab the harlot, and her father's household, and all that she had; and she dwells in Israel even to this day; because she hid the messengers, which Joshua sent to spy out Jericho. 26:And Joshua adjured them at that time, saying, Cursed be the man before the Lord, that rises up and builds this city Jericho again: he shall lay the foundation thereof in his firstborn, and in his youngest son shall he set up the gates of it. 27:So the Lord was with Joshua; and his fame was noised throughout all the country.

+/- April 24$^{th.}$ (Nissan 24$^{th.}$)

The year +/- 1004 B.C. The Egyptian showed David the camp

(1Samuel 30:16-20) 16:And when he had brought him down, behold, they were spread abroad upon all the earth, eating and drinking, and dancing, because of all the great spoil that they had taken out of the land of the Philistines, and out of the land of Judah. 17:And David struck them from the twilight even to the evening of the next day: and there escaped not a man of them, save four hundred young men, which rode upon camels, and fled. 18:And David recovered all that the Amalekites had carried away: and David rescued his two wives. 19:And there was nothing lacking to them, neither small nor great, neither sons nor daughters, neither spoil, nor any thing that they had taken to them: David recovered all. 20:And David took all the flocks and the herds, which they drove before those other cattle, and said, This is David's spoil.

+/- April 24th. (Nissan 24th.)

The Lord spoke to Daniel at the Tigris river

(Daniel 10:4-12:13) 4:And in the four and twentieth day of the first month, as I was by the side of the great river, which is called Hiddekel. 5:Then I lifted up mine eyes, and looked, and behold a certain man clothed in linen, whose loins were girded with fine gold of Uphaz. 6:His body also was like the beryl, and his face as the appearance of lightning, and his eyes as lamps of fire, and his arms and his feet like in color to polished brass, and the voice of his words like the voice of a multitude.

7:And I Daniel alone saw the vision: for the men that were with me saw not the vision; but a great quaking fell upon them, so that they fled to hide themselves. 8:Therefore I was left alone, and saw this great vision, and there remained no strength in me: for my comeliness was turned in me into corruption, and I retained no strength.

9:Yet heard I the voice of his words: and when I heard the voice of his words, then was I in a deep sleep on my face, and my face toward the ground. 10:And, behold, an hand touched me, which set me upon my knees and upon the palms of my hands. 11:And he said to me, O Daniel, a man greatly beloved, understand the words that I speak to you, and stand upright: for to you am I now sent. And when he had spoken this word to me, I stood trembling.

12:Then said he to me, Fear not, Daniel: for from the first day that you did set thine heart to understand, and to chasten thyself before your God, your words were heard, and I have come for your words. 13:But the prince of the kingdom of Persia withstood me one and twenty days: but, look, Michael, one of the chief princes, came to help me; and I remained there with the kings of Persia. 14:Now I have come to make you understand what shall befall your people in the latter days: for yet the vision is for many days. 15:And when he had spoken such words to me, I set my face toward the ground, and I became dumb.

16:And, behold, one like the similitude of the sons of men touched my lips: then I opened my mouth, and spoke, and said to him that stood before me, O my lord, by the vision my sorrows are turned upon me, and I have retained no strength. 17:For how can the servant of this my lord talk with this my lord? for as for me, straightway there remained no strength in me, neither is there breath left in me.

18:Then there came again and touched me one like the appearance of a man, and he strengthened me, 19;And said, O man greatly beloved, fear not: peace be to you, be strong, yes, be strong. And when he had said this to me, I was strengthened, and said, Let my lord speak; for you have strengthened me. Then said he, Know you why I have come to you? and now will I return to fight with the prince of Persia: and when I am gone forth, look, the prince of Grecian shall come.

21:But I will show you that which is noted in the scripture of truth and there is none that holds with me,in these things, but Michael your prince.

11:1: Also I in the first year of Darius the Medea, even I, stood to confirm and to strengthen him. 2:And now will I show you the truth. Behold, there shall stand up yet three kings in Persia; and the fourth shall be far richer than they all: and by his strength through his riches he shall stir up all against the realm of Grecian. 3:And a mighty King shall stand up, that shall rule with great dominion, and do according to his will. 4:And when he shall stand up, his kingdom shall be broken, and shall be divided toward the four winds of heaven; and not to his posterity, nor according to his dominion which he ruled: for his kingdom shall be plucked up, even for others beside those.

5:And the King of the south shall be strong, and one of his princes; and he shall be strong above him, and have dominion; his dominion shall be a great dominion. 6:And in the end of years they shall join themselves together; for the King's daughter of the south shall come to the King of the north to make an agreement: but she shall not retain the power of the arm; neither shall he stand, nor his arm: but she shall be given up, and they that brought her, and he that begot her, and he that strengthened her in these times. 7:But out of a branch of her roots shall one stand up in his estate, which shall come with an army, and shall enter into the fortress of the King of the north, and shall deal against them, and shall prevail.

8:And shall also carry captives into Egypt their gods, with their princes, and with their precious vessels of silver and of gold; and he shall continue more years than the King of the north. 9:So the King of the south shall come into his kingdom, and shall return into his own land. 10:But his sons shall be stirred up, and shall assemble a multitude of great forces: and one shall certainly come, and overflow, and pass through: then shall he return, and be stirred up, even to his fortress.

11:And the King of the south shall be moved with choler, and shall come forth and fight with him, even with the King of the north: and he shall set forth a great multitude; but the multitude shall be given into his hand. 12:And when he has taken away the multitude, his heart shall be lifted up; and he shall cast down as many as ten thousands: but he shall not be strengthened by it.

13:For the King of the north shall return, and shall set forth a multitude greater than the former, and shall certainly come after certain years with a great army and with much riches. 14:And in those times there shall many stand up against the King of the south: also the robbers of your people shall exalt themselves to establish the vision; but they shall fall.

15:So the King of the north shall come, and cast up a mount, and take the most fenced cities: and the arms of the south shall not withstand, neither his chosen people, neither shall there be any strength to withstand. 16:But he that cometh against him shall do according to his own will, and none shall stand before him;and he shall stand in the glorious land, which by his hand shall be consumed. 17:He shall also set his face to enter with the strength of his whole kingdom,

and upright ones with him; this shall he do: and he shall give him the daughter of
women, corrupting her: but she shall not stand on his side, neither be for him.
18:After this shall he turn his face to the isles, and shall take many: but a prince for
his own behalf shall cause the reproach offered by him to cease; without his own
reproach he shall cause it to turn upon him. 19:Then he shall turn his face toward
the fort of his own land: but he shall stumble and fall, and not be found. 20:Then
shall stand up in his estate a raiser of taxes in the glory of the kingdom: but within
few days he shall be destroyed, neither in anger, nor in battle. 21:And in his estate
shall stand up a vile person, to whom they shall not give the honor of the kingdom:
but he shall come in peaceably, and obtain the kingdom by flattery.

22:And with the arms of a flood shall they be overflown from before him, and shall
be broken; yea, also the prince of the covenant. 23:And after the league made with
him he shall work deceitfully: for he shall come up, and shall become strong with a
small people. 24:He shall enter peaceably even upon the fattest places of the
province; and he shall do that which his fathers have not done, nor his fathers'
fathers; he shall scatter among them the prey, and spoil, and riches: yes, and he shall
forecast his devices against the strong holds, even for a time.

25:And he shall stir up his power and his courage against the King of the south with
a great army; and the King of the south shall be stirred up to battle with a very great
and mighty army; but he shall not stand: for they shall forecast devices against him.
26:Yes, they that feed of the portion of his meat shall destroy him, and his army
shall overflow: and many shall fall down slain.

27:And both these Kings' hearts shall be set to do mischief, and they shall speak
lies at one table; but it shall not prosper: for yet the end shall be at the time
appointed. 28:Then shall he return into his land with great riches; and his heart shall
be against the holy covenant; and he shall do exploits, and return to his own land.

29:At the time appointed he shall return, and come toward the south; but it shall not
be as the former, or as the latter. 30:For the ships of Chittagong shall come against
him: therefore he shall be grieved, and return, and have indignation against the holy
covenant: so shall he do; he shall even return, and have intelligence with them that
forsake the holy covenant. 31:And arms shall stand on his part, and they shall
pollute the sanctuary of strength, and shall take away the daily sacrifices, and they
shall place the abomination that makes desolate.

32:And such as do wickedly against the covenant shall he corrupt by flattery: but
the people that do know their God shall be strong, and do exploits. 33:And they that
understand among the people shall instruct many: yet they shall fall by the sword,
and by flame, by captivity, and by spoil, many days. 34:Now when they shall fall,
they shall be Holden with a little help: but many shall cleave to them with flattery's.

35;And some of them of understanding shall fall, to try them, and to purge, and to
make them white, even to the time of the end: because it is yet for a time appointed.
36:And the King shall do according to his will; and he shall exalt himself, and
magnify himself above every god,

and shall speak marvelous things against the God of gods and shall prosper till the indignation be accomplished: for that that is determined shall be done. 37:Neither shall he regard the God of his fathers, nor the desire of women, nor regard any god: for he shall magnify himself above all. 38:But in his estate shall he honor the God of strongholds: and a god whom his fathers knew not, shall he honor with gold, and silver, and with precious stones, and pleasant things. 39;This shall he do in the most strong holds with a strange god, whom he shall acknowledge and increase with glory: and he shall cause them to rule over many, and shall divide the land for gain.

40:And at the time of the end shall the King of the south push at him: and the King of the north shall come against him like a whirlwind, with chariots, and with horsemen, and with many ships; and he shall enter into the countries, and shall overflow and pass over. 41;He shall enter also into the glorious land, and many countries shall be overthrown: but these shall escape out of his hand, even Edom, and Moab, and the chief of the children of Ammon.

42:He shall stretch forth his hand also upon the countries: and the land of Egypt shall not escape. 43:But he shall have power over the treasures of gold and of silver, and over all the precious things of Egypt: and the Libyans and the Ethiopians shall be at his steps. 44:But tidings out of the east and out of the north shall trouble him: therefore he shall go forth with great fury to destroy, and utterly to make away many. 45:And he shall plant the tabernacles of his palace between the seas in the glorious holy mountain; yet he shall come to his end, and none shall help him.

12:1: And at that time shall Michael stand up, the great prince which stands for the children of your people: and there shall be a time of trouble, such as never was since there was a nation even to that same time: and at that time your people shall be delivered, every one that shall be found written in the book. 2:And many of them that sleep in the dust of the earth shall awake, some to everlasting life, and some to shame and everlasting contempt.

3:And they that be wise shall shine as the brightness of the firmament; and they that turn many to righteousness as the stars for ever and ever. 4:But you, O Daniel, shut up the words, and seal the book, even to the time of the end: many shall run to and fro, and knowledge shall be increased. 5:Then I Daniel looked, and, behold, there stood other two, the one on this side of the bank of the river, and the other on that side of the bank of the river. 6:And one said to the man clothed in linen, which was upon the waters of the river, How long shall it be to the end of these wonders?

7:And I heard the man clothed in linen, which was upon the waters of the river, when he held up his right hand and his left hand to heaven, and swore by him that lives for ever that it shall be for a time, times, and an half; and when he shall have accomplished to scatter the power of the holy people, all these things shall be finished. 8:And I heard, but I understood not: then said I, O my Lord, what shall be the end of these things? 9:And he said, Go your way, Daniel: for the words are closed up and sealed till the time of the end.10:Many will be purified, and made white, and tried; but the wicked shall do wickedly:
and none of the wicked shall understand;

but the wise shall understand.11:And from the time that the daily sacrifice shall be taken away, and the abomination that makes desolate set up, there shall be a thousand two hundred and ninety days. 12:Blessed is he that waits, and comes to the one thousand three hundred and five and thirty days. 13:But go you, your way till the end, be for you shall rest, and stand in your lot at the end of the days.

Below a picture of the Tigris River in Modern Iraq

+/- April 24th. (Nissan 24th.)

Jesus was informed about John's death

(Matthew 14:12-13) 12:And his disciples came, and took up the body, and buried it, and went and told Jesus. 13:When Jesus heard of it, he departed thence by ship into a desert place apart: and when the people had heard of this, they followed him on foot out of the cities.

+/- April 25th. (Nissan 25th.)

(In the Aramaic writings: Jethro dies,)

Jethro, the Father-in law of Moses, lived a long and fruitful life then died on the fifth and twentieth day, of the month of Nissan

+/- April 25th. (Nissan 25th.)

Paul sailed to Troas,

(Acts 20:6) 6:And we sailed away from Philippi after the days of unleavened bread, and they came to Troas in five days; where we stayed seven days.

+/- April 26th. (Nissan 26th.)

Jesus fed five thousand Men, beside the Women and Children

(Matthew 14:13-23) 13:When Jesus heard of the news, about John the baptist death, he departed there by ship to a desert place apart: and when the people had heard about this they followed him on foot out of the cities. 14:As Jesus went forth, and saw a great multitude, and was moved with compassion toward them, and he healed their sick. 15:And when it was evening, his disciples came to him, saying, This is a desert place, and the time is now past; send the multitude away, that they may go into the villages, and buy themselves something to eat.

16:But Jesus said to them, They do not need to go away; give them something to eat. 17:And they said to him, We have here but five loaves, and two fishes. 18:He said, Bring them here to me. 19:And he commanded the multitude to sit down on the grass, and took the five loaves, and the two fishes, and looking up to heaven, he blessed it , and broke it, and gave the loaves to his disciples, and the disciples gave it to the multitude.

20:And they did all eat, and were filled: and they took up of the fragments that remained twelve baskets full. 21:And they that had eaten were about five thousand men, beside women and children. 22:And straightway Jesus told his disciples to get into a ship, and to go before him to the other side, while he sent the multitudes away. 23:And when he had sent the multitudes away, he went up into a mountain apart to pray: and when the evening was come, he was there alone.

+/- April 27th. (Nissan 27th.)

The year +/- 1004 B.C. David returned to the men left behind

(1 Samuel 30:21-25) 21:And David came to the two hundred men, which were so faint that they could not follow David, whom they had made also to abide at the brook Besor: and they went forth to meet David, and to meet the people that were with him: and when David came near to the people, he saluted them. 22:Then answered all the wicked men and men of Belial, of those that went with David, and said, Because they went not with us, we will not give them part of the spoils that we have recovered, except to every man his wife and his children, that they may lead them away, and depart. 23:Then said David; You shall not do so, my brethren, with that which the Lord has given us, who has preserved us, and delivered the company that came against us into our hand. 24:For who will listen to you on this matter? But as for his part that went down to the battle, so shall his part be that stayed by the stuff: they shall part alike. 25:And it was so from that day forward, that he made it a statute and an ordinance for Israel to this day.

+/- April 27th. (Nissan 27th.) About Midnight

Jesus walked on water to his disciples

(Matthew 14:24-32) 24:But the ship was now in the midst of the sea, tossed with waves: for the wind was contrary. 25:And in the fourth watch of the night Jesus went to them, walking on the sea.

26:And when the disciples saw him walking on the sea, they were troubled, saying,
It is a spirit; and they cried out for fear. 27:But straightway Jesus spoke to them,
saying, Be of good cheer; it is I; be not afraid. 28:And Peter answered him and said,
Lord, if it be you, bid me come to you on the water. 29:And he said, Come. And
when Peter was come down out of the ship, he walked on the water, to go to Jesus.
30:But when he saw the wind boisterous, he was afraid; and beginning to sink, he
cried, saying, Lord, save me. 31:And Jesus stretched out his hand, and caught him,
and said to him, O you of little faith, why do you doubt?

32:And when they had come to the ship, the wind ceased. 33:Then they that were in
the ship came and worshiped him, saying; It is true you are the Son of God. 34:And
when they were gone over, they came into the land of Gennesaret. (On the day of
the 25th.) 35:And when the men of that place had knowledge of him, they sent out
into all that country round about, and brought to him all that were diseased. 36:And
besought him that they might only touch the hem of his garment and as many as
touched were made perfectly whole.

15:1;Then came to Jesus scribes and Pharisees, which were of Jerusalem, saying;
2:Why do your disciples transgress the tradition of the Elders? for they wash not
their hands when they eat bread.

3:But he answered and said to them, Why do you also transgress the commandment
of God by your tradition? 4:For God commanded, saying, Honor your father and
mother: and, He that curses, his father or mother, let him be put to death. 5:But you
say, Whosoever shall say to his Father or his Mother, it is a gift, by what so ever you
might be profited by me. 6:And honor not his Father or his Mother, he shall be free,
this have you made the commandment of God of none effect by your tradition.
7:You hypocrites, well did Elijah prophesy of you, saying; 8:These people draw
near to me with their mouths, and honor me with their lips; but their heart is far
from me. 9:But in vain they do worship me, teaching for doctrines the
commandments of men.

10:And he called the multitude, and said to them, Hear, and understand. 11:It is not
that, which go's into the mouth defiles a man; but that which comes out of the
mouth, this defiles a man. 12:Then came his disciples, and said to him; do you
know that the Pharisees were offended, after they heard this saying. 13:But he
answered and said, Every plant, which my heavenly Father has not planted, shall be
rooted up. 14:Let them alone: they be blind leaders of the blind. And if the blind
lead the blind, both shall fall into the ditch.

15:Then answered Peter and said to him, Declare to us this parable. 16:And Jesus
said; Are you also yet without understanding? 17:Do not you, yet understand, that
what soever enters in at the mouth go's into the stomach and is cast out into the
drought? 18:But those things which proceed out of the mouth, come forth from the
heart; and they defile the man. 19:For out of the heart proceed evil thoughts,
murders, adulteries, fornication’s, thefts, false witness, blasphemies. 20:These are
the things which defile a man: but to eat with unwashed hands defile not a man.
21:Then Jesus went forth, and departed to the coasts of Tyre and Sidon.

+/- April 27th. (Nissan 27th.)

Jesus heals a Woman's daughter

(Matthew 15:1-28) 1:Then came to Jesus scribes and Pharisees, which were of Jerusalem, saying, 2: Why do your disciples transgress the tradition of the elders? For they wash not their hands when they eat bread.

3:But he answered and said to them, Why do you also transgress the commandment of God by your tradition? 4: For God commanded, saying, Honor your father and mother: and, He that cursed father or mother, let him die the death. 5: But you say, Whosoever shall say to his father or his mother, It is a gift, by whatsoever you might be profited by me; 6; And honor not his father or his mother, They shall be free. Thus have you made the commandment of God of none effect by your tradition. 7:You hypocrites, well did Elijah prophesy of you, saying, 8: This people draw near to me with their mouth, and honor me with their lips; but their heart is far from me. 9:But in vain they do worship me, teaching for doctrines the commandments of men

10:And he called the multitude, and said to them, Hear, and understand: 11: Not that which go's into the mouth defiles a man; but that which comes out of the mouth, this defiles a man.

12: Then came his disciples, and said to him, Know you that the Pharisees were offended, after they heard this saying?

13:But he answered and said, Every plant, which my heavenly Father hath not planted, shall be rooted up. 14:Let them alone: they be blind leaders of the blind. And if the blind lead the blind, both shall fall into the ditch.

15:Then answered Peter and said to him, Explain to us this parable.

16:And Jesus said, Are you also yet without understanding? 17:Do not you yet understand, that whatsoever enters in at the mouth gos in to the belly, and is cast out of the bawl? 18:But those things which proceed out of the mouth come forth from the heart; and they defile the man. 19: For out of the heart proceed evil thoughts, murders, adulteries, fornication's, thefts, false witness, blasphemies: 20:These are the things which defile a man: but to eat with unwashed hands defile not a man.

21: Then Jesus went thence, and departed into the coasts of Tyre and Sidon. 22: And, behold, a woman of Canaan came out of the same coasts, and cried to him, saying, Have mercy on me, O Lord, you Son of David; my daughter is grievously vexed with a devil. 23:But he answered her not a word. And his disciples came and besought him, saying, Send her away; for she cries after us.

24:But he answered and said, I am not sent but unto the lost sheep of the house of Israel.
25:Then came she and worshiped him, saying, Lord, help me. 26;But he answered and said, It is not meet to take the children's bread, and to cast it to dogs.

27:And she said, Truth, Lord: yet the dogs eat of the crumbs which fall from their masters' table. 28:Then Jesus answered and said unto her, O woman, great is your faith: be it unto thee even as you wilt. And her daughter was made whole from that very hour.

+/- April 28th. (Nissan 28th.)

The year +/- 1005 B.C. Saul tried to kill David,

(1Samuel 19:9-18) 9:And the evil spirit from the Lord was upon Saul, as he sat in his house with his javelin in his hand: and David played with his hand. 10:And Saul sought to strike David, even to pin him to the wall with the javelin; but he slipped away out of Saul's presence, and he threw the javelin into the wall: and David fled, and escaped that night. 11:Saul also sent messengers to David's house, to watch him, and to slay him in the morning: and Michael, David's wife told him, saying, If you save not your life to night, tomorrow you shall be slain. 12:So Michael let David down through a window: and he went, and fled, and escaped. 13:And Michael took an image, and laid it in the bed, and put a pillow of goats' hair for his bolster, and covered it with a cloth. 14:And when Saul sent messengers to take David, she said, He is sick. 15:And Saul sent the messengers again to see David, saying, Bring him up to me in the bed, that I may slay him. 16:And when the messengers were come in, behold, there was an image in the bed, with a pillow of goat's hair for his bolster. 17:And Saul said to Michael, Why have you deceived me so, and sent away mine enemy, that he is escaped? And Michael answered Saul, He said to me, Let me go; why should I kill you? (18:So David fled, and escaped, and came to Samuel in Ramah, and told him all that Saul had done to him. And he and Samuel went to stay in the sheds.)

+/- April 28th. (Nissan 28th.)

Jesus fed four thousand Men, beside Woman and Children

(Matthew 15:29-39) 29:And Jesus departed from thence, and came near to the sea of Galilee; and went up on a mountain, and sat down there. 30:And great multitudes came to him, having with them those that were lame, blind, dumb, maimed, and many others, and cast them down at Jesus' feet; and he healed them. 31:Insomuch that the multitude wondered, when they saw the dumb to speak, the maimed to be whole, the lame to walk, and the blind to see: and they glorified the God of Israel. 32:Then Jesus called his disciples to him, and said, I have compassion on the multitude, because they continue with me now three days, and have nothing to eat: and I will not send them away hungry, lest they faint on the way. 33:And his disciples say to him, Where could we find have so much bread in the wilderness, as to fill so great a multitude? 34:And Jesus said to them, How many loaves have you? And they said, Seven, and a few little fishes. 35:And he commanded the multitude to sit down on the ground. 36;And he took the seven loaves and the fishes, and gave thanks, and brake them, and gave to his disciples, and the disciples to the multitude. 37:And they did all eat, and were filled: and they took up of the broken meat that was left seven baskets full. 38:And they that did eat were four thousand men, beside women and children. 39;And he sent away the multitude, and took ship, and came into the coasts of Magdala.

+/- April 29th. (Nissan 29th.)

The year +/- 1005 B.C. Saul searched for David and Samuel

(1 Samuel 19:18-24) *18:So David fled, and escaped, and came to Samuel to Ramah, and told him all that Saul had done to him. And he and Samuel went and dwelt in Naioth.* 19:And it was told Saul, saying, Behold, David is at Naioth in Ramah. 20:And Saul sent messengers to take David: and when they saw the company of the prophets prophesying, and Samuel standing as appointed over them, the Spirit of God was upon the messengers of Saul, and they also prophesied. 21:And when it was told Saul, he sent other messengers, and they prophesied likewise. And Saul sent messengers again the third time, and they prophesied also. 22:Then went he also to Ramah, and came to a great well that is in Sechu: and he asked and said, Where are Samuel and David? And one said, Behold, they are at Naioth in Ramah. 23:And he went near to Naioth in Ramah: and the Spirit of God was upon him also, and he went on, and prophesied, until he came to Naioth in Ramah. 24:And he stripped off his clothes also, and prophesied before Samuel in like manner, and lay down naked all that day and all that night. Wherefore they say, is Saul also among the prophets?

+/- April 29th. (Nissan 29th.)

The year +/- 1004 B.C. David sent the spoil to Judah

(1Samuel 30:26-31) 26:And when David came to Ziklag, he sent of the spoil to the Elders of Judah, even to his friends, saying, Behold a present for you of the spoil of the enemies of the Lord. 27:To them which were in Bethel, and to them which were in south Ramoth, and to them which were in Jattir. 28:And to them which were in Aroer, and to Siphmoth, and to Eshtemoa, 29:And to them which were in Rachal, and to the cities of the Jerahmeelites, and to the cities of the Kenites, 30:And to them who were in Hormah, and to Chorashan, and to Athach. 31:Also to those in Hebron, and to all the places where David himself and his men were wont to haunt.

+/- April 30th. (Nissan 30th.)

The year +/- 1005 B.C. David and Jonathan swore a oath

(1Samuel 20:1-24) 1:And David fled from Naioth in Ramah, and came and said before Jonathan, What have I done? What is mine iniquity? And what is my sin before your father, that he seeks my life? 2:And he said to him, God forbid; you shall not die: behold, my father will do nothing either great or small, but that he tells it to me: and why should my father hide this thing from me? It is not so. 3:And David sware moreover, and said, Your father certainly knows that I have found grace in your eyes; and he says, Let not Jonathan know this, lest he be grieved: but truly as the LORD lives, and as your soul lives, there is but a step between me and death. 4:Then said Jonathan unto David, Whatsoever your soul desires, I will even do it for you. 5: And David said to Jonathan, Behold, tomorrow is the new moon, and I should not fail to sit with the King at meat: but let me go, that I may hide myself in the field unto the third day at evening. 6:If your father at all miss me, then say, David earnestly asked leave of me that he might run to Bethlehem his city: for there is a yearly sacrifice there for all the family.

7:If he say this, It is well; your servant shall have peace: but if he be very wroth, then be sure that evil is determined by him. 8:Therefore you shall deal kindly with your servant; for you have brought your servant into a covenant of the LORD with you: not with standing, if there be in me iniquity, slay me yourself; for why should you bring me to your father? 9:And Jonathan said, Far be it from you: for if I knew certainly that evil were determined by my father to come upon you, then would not I tell it you? 10:Then said: David to Jonathan, Who shall tell me? or what if you father answer you roughly? 11:And Jonathan said to David, Come, and let us go out into the field. And they went out both of them into the field. 12:And Jonathan said to David, O LORD God of Israel, when I have sounded my father about to morrow any time, or the third day and, behold, if there be good toward David, and I then send not to you, and show it to you; 13:The LORD do so and much more to Jonathan: but if it please my father to do you evil, then I will tell it to you, and send you away, that you may go in peace: and the LORD be with you, as he has been with my father. 14:And you shall not only while yet I live show me the kindness of the LORD, that I die not: 15:But also you shall not cut off your kindness from my house for ever: no, not when the LORD has cut off the enemies of David every one from the face of the earth. 16:So Jonathan made a covenant with the house of David, saying, Let the LORD even require it at the hand of David's enemies. 17:And Jonathan caused David to swear again, because he loved him: for he loved him as he loved his own soul. 18:Then Jonathan said to David, Tomorrow is the new moon: and you shall be missed, because your seat will be empty. 19:And when you have stayed three days, then you shall go down quickly, and come to the place where you did hide yourself when the business was in hand and shall remain by the stone Ezel. 20:And I will shoot three arrows on the side over there as though I shot at a mark. 21:And, behold, I will send a lad saying; Go, find out the arrows. If I expressly say unto the lad, Behold, the arrows are on this side of you, take them; then come you: for there is peace to you, and no hurt; as the LORD lives. 22:But if I say this to the young man, Behold, the arrows are beyond you; go your way: For the LORD has sent you away. 23:And as touching the matter which you and I have spoken of, behold, the LORD be between you and me for ever. 24:So David hid himself in the field: and when the new moon was come, the king sat him down to eat meat.

(The fallowing also happened during the month of April / Nissan)
(The Death of Sarah)

(Genesis 23:1-20) 1:And Sarah was an hundred and seven and twenty years old: these were the years of the life of Sarah. 2:And Sarah died in Kirjatharba; the Name is Hebron in the land of Canaan: and Abraham came to mourn for Sarah, and to weep for her. 3:And Abraham stood up from before his dead, and spoke to the sons of Heth, saying; 4:I am a stranger and a sojourner with you: give me a possession of a burying place with you, that I may bury my dead wife out of my sight. 5:And the children of Heth answered Abraham, saying to him. 6:Hear us, my lord: you are a mighty prince among us: in the choice of our sepulchers bury your dead; none of us shall withhold from you his sepulcher, but that you may bury your dead. 7:And Abraham stood up, and bowed himself to the people of the land, even to the children of Heth. 8:And he communed with them, saying, If it be your mind that I should bury my dead out of my sight; hear me, and entreat for me to Ephron the son of Zohar. 9:That he may give me the cave of Machpelah, which he has, which is in the end of his field; for as much money as it is worth he shall give it me for a possession of a burying place amongst you. 10:And Ephron dwelt among the children of Heth: and Ephron the Hittite answered Abraham in the audience of the children of Heth, even of all that went in at the gate of his city, saying, 11:Nay, my lord, hear me: the field I will give you and the cave that is there o top of it., I give it to you; in the presence of the sons of my people give I it to you: bury your dead. 12:And Abraham bowed down himself before the people of the land. 13:And he spoke to Ephron in the audience of the people of the land, saying, But if you will give it, I ask you, hear me: I will give you money for the field; take it of me, and I will bury my dead there.14:And Ephron answered Abraham, saying to him. 15:My lord, listen to me: the land is worth four hundred shekels of silver; what is that between me and you? Just go bury your dead. 16:And Abraham listened to Ephron; and Abraham weighed to Ephron the silver, which he had named in the audience of the sons of Heth, four hundred shekels of silver, current money with the merchant. 17:And the field of Ephron, which was in Machpelah, which was before Mamre, the field, and the cave which was therein, and all the trees that were in the field, that were in all the borders round about, were made sure,18:to Abraham for a possession in the presence of the children of Heth, before all that went in at the gate of his city. 19:And after this, Abraham buried Sarah his wife in the cave at the top of the field of Machpelah before Mamre: the name is Hebron in the land of Canaan. 20:And the field, and the cave that is there, were made sure to Abraham for a possession of a burying place by the sons of Heth.

Below: The entrance to Sarah Tomb

Sarah's Sepulcher

The year +/- 1357 B.C. The Lord spoke to Moses, a year after they left Egypt

(Numbers 9:1-14) 1:And the Lord spoke to Moses in the wilderness of Sinai, in the first month of the second year after they were come out of the land of Egypt, saying; 2:Let the children of Israel also keep the passover at his appointed season. 3:On the fourteenth day of this month, you shall keep it in his appointed season: according to all the rites of it, and according to all the ceremonies thereof, shall you keep it. 4:And Moses spoke to the children of Israel, saying they should keep the passover. 5:And they kept the passover on the fourteenth day of the first month at even in the wilderness of Sinai: according to all that the Lord commanded Moses, so did the children of Israel. 6:And there were certain men, who were defiled by the dead body of a man, that they could not keep the passover on that day: and they came before, Moses and before Aaron on that day. 7:And those men said to him, We are defiled by the dead body of a man: wherefore are we kept back, that we may not offer an offering of the Lord in his appointed season among the children of Israel? 8:And Moses said to them, stand still, and I will hear what the Lord will command concerning you. 9:And the Lord spoke to Moses, saying. 10:Speak to the children of Israel, saying, If any man of you or of your posterity shall be unclean by reason of a dead body, or be in a journey afar off, yet he shall keep the passover to the Lord. 11:The fourteenth day of the second month at even they shall keep it, and eat it with unleavened bread and bitter herbs. 12:They shall leave none of it to the morning, nor break any bone of it: according to all the ordinances of the passover they shall keep it. 13;But the man that is clean, and is not in a journey, and forbids to keep the passover, even the same soul shall be cut off from among his people: because he brought not the offering of the Lord in his appointed season,
that man shall bear his sin.

14:And if a stranger shall sojourn among you, and will keep the passover to the Lord; according to the ordinance of the passover, and according to the manner thereof, so shall he do: you shall have one ordinance, both for the stranger, and for him that was born in the land.

David was made King over Judah

(2 Samuel 2:1-7)1:And it came to pass after this, that David inquired of the Lord, saying, Shall I go up to any of the cities of Judah? And the Lord said to him, Go up. And David said, Where shall I go up? And he said, to Hebron. 2:So David went up thither, and his two wives also, Ahinoam the Jezreelitess, and Abigail Nabal's wife the Carmelite. 3:And his men that were with him did David bring up, every man with his household: and they dwelt in the cities of Hebron. 4:And the men of Judah came, and there they anointed David King over the house of Judah. And they told David, saying, that the men of Jabeshgilead were the ones that buried Saul. 5:And David sent messengers to the men of Jabeshgilead, and said to them, Blessed be you of the Lord, that you have showed this kindness to your lord, even to Saul, and have buried him. 6:And now the Lord will show kindness and truth to you: and I also will give you this kindness, because you have done this thing. 7:Therefore now let your hands be strengthened, and be you valiant: for your master Saul is dead, and also the house of Judah have anointed me King over them.

Israel killed one hundred thousand Syrians footmen in one day

(1Kings 20:26-43) 26:And it came to pass at the return of the year, that Benhadad numbered the Syrians, and went up to Aphek, to fight against Israel. 27:And the children of Israel were numbered, and were all present, and went against them: and the children of Israel pitched before them like two little flocks of kids; but the Syrians filled the country. 28:And there came a man of God, and spoke to the King of Israel, and said, this said the Lord, Because the Syrians have said, The Lord is only God of the hills, but he is not God of the valleys, therefore I will deliver all this great multitude into your hands, and you shall know that I am the Lord. 29:And they pitched one over against the other seven days. And so it was, that in the seventh day the battle was joined: and the children of Israel killed of the Syrians an hundred thousand footmen in one day. 30:But the rest fled to Aphek, into the city; and there a wall fell upon twenty and seven thousand of the men that were left. And Benhadad fled, and came into the city, into an inner chamber. 31;And his servants said to him, Behold now, we have heard that the Kings of the house of Israel are merciful Kings: let us, I pray you, put sackcloth on our loins, and ropes upon our heads, and go out to the King of Israel: peradventure he will save your life. 32:So they girded sackcloth on their loins,and put ropes on their heads, and came to the King of Israel, and said, your servant Benhadad said, I pray you, let me live. And he said, Is he yet alive? he is my brother. 33:Now the men did diligently observe whether any thing would come from him, and did hastily catch it, and they said; Your brother Benhadad. Then he said, Go you, and bring him to me. Then Benhadad came forth to him; and he caused him to come up into the chariot. 34:And Benhadad said to him, The cities, which my father took from your father, I will restore; and I shall make streets for you in Damascus, as my father made in Samaria. Then said Ahab; I will send you away with this covenant. So he made a covenant with him, and sent him away. 35:And a certain man of the sons of the prophets said to his neighbor in the word of the Lord, Strike me, I pray you. And the man refused to strike him. 36:Then said he to him, Because you have not obeyed the voice of the Lord, behold, as soon as you have departed from me, a lion shall kill you. And as soon as he was departed from him, a lion found him, and killed him. 37:Then he found another man, and said, Strike me, I pray you. And the man smote him, so that in smiting he wounded him. 38:So the prophet departed, and waited for the King by the way, and disguised himself with ashes upon his face. 39:And as the King passed by, he cried to the King: and he said, Your servant went out into the midst of the battle; and, behold, a man turned aside, and brought a man to me, and said, Keep this man: if by any means he be missing, then shall your life be for his life, or else you shall pay a talent of silver. 40:And as your servant was busy here and there, he was gone. And the King of Israel said to him, So shall your judgment be you , yourself has decided it. 41:And he hasted, and took the ashes away from his face; and the King of Israel discerned him that he was of the prophets. 42:And he said to him, this said the Lord, Because you have let go out of your hand a man whom I appointed to utter destruction, therefore your life shall go for his life, and your people for his people. 43:And the King of Israel went to his house heavy and displeased, and came to Samaria.

Josiah killed all the priests of false gods

(2Kings 23:1-23) 1:And the King sent, and they gathered to him all the elders of Judah and of Jerusalem. 2:And the King went up into the house of the Lord, and all the men of Judah and all the inhabitants of Jerusalem with him, and the priests, and the prophets, and all the people, both small and great: and he read in their ears all the words of the book of the covenant, which was found in the house of the Lord. 3:And the King stood by a pillar, and made a covenant before the Lord, to walk after the Lord, and to keep his commandments and his testimonies and his statutes with all their heart and all their soul, to perform the words of this covenant that were written in this book. And all the people stood to the covenant. 4:And the King commanded Hilkiah the high priest, and the priests of the second order, and the keepers of the door, to bring forth out of the temple of the Lord all the vessels that were made for Baal, and for the grove, and for all the host of heaven: and he burned them without Jerusalem in the fields of Kidder, and carried the ashes of them to Bethel. 5:And he put down the idolatrous priests, whom the Kings of Judah had ordained to burn incense in the high places in the cities of Judah, and in the places round about Jerusalem; them also that burned incense to Baal, to the sun, and to the moon, and to the planets, and to all the host of heaven. 6:And he brought out the grove from the house of the LORD, without Jerusalem, to the brook Kidron, and burned it at the brook Kidron, and stamped it small to powder, and cast the powder thereof upon the graves of the children of the people. 7: And he broke down the houses of the sodomites, that were by the house of the LORD, where the women wove hangings for the grove. 8:And he brought all the priests out of the cities of Judah, and defiled the high places where the priests had burned incense, from Geba to Beersheba, and brake down the high places of the gates that were in the entering in of the gate of Joshua the governor of the city, which were on a man's left hand at the gate of the city. 9;Nevertheless the priests of the high places, came not up to the altar of the Lord in Jerusalem, but they did eat of the unleavened bread among their brethren. 10:And he defiled Topheth, which is in the valley of the children of Hinnom, that no man might make his son or his daughter to pass through the fire to Molech. 11:And he took away the horses that the Kings of Judah had given to the sun, at the entering in of the house of the Lord, by the chamber of Nathanmelech the chamberlain, which was in the suburbs, and burned the chariots of the sun with fire. 12:And the altars that were on the top of the upper chamber of Ahaz, which the Kings of Judah had made, and the altars which Manasseh had made in the two courts of the house of the Lord, did the King beat down, and brake them down from thence, and cast the dust of them into the brook Kidron. 13:And the high places that were before Jerusalem, which were on the right hand of the mount of corruption, which Solomon the King of Israel had build for Ashtoreth the abomination, of the Zidonians, and for Chemosh the abomination of the Moabites, and for Milcom the abomination of the children of Ammon, did the King defile. 14:And he broke in pieces the images, and cut down the groves, and filled their places with the bones of men. 15:Moreover the altar that was at Bethel, and the high place which Jeroboam the son of Nebat, who made Israel to sin, had made, both that altar and the high place he brake down, and burned the high place, and stamped it small to powder, and burned the grove. 16:And as Josiah turned himself, he spied the sepulchers that were there in the mount, and sent, and took the bones out of the sepulchers, and burned them upon the altar, and polluted it, according to the word of the Lord which the man of God proclaimed, who proclaimed these words. 17:Then he said, What title is that that I see? And the men of the city told him, It is the sepulcher of the man of God, which came from Judah, and proclaimed these things that you have done against the altar of Bethel. 18:And he said, Let him alone; let no man move his bones. So they let his bones alone, with the bones of the prophet that came out of Samaria. 19:And all the houses also of the high places that were in the cities of Samaria, which the Kings of Israel had made to provoke the Lord to anger, Josiah took away, and did to them according to all the acts that he had done in Bethel. 20:And he killed all the priests of the high places that were there upon the altars, and burned all the men bones upon them, and returned to Jerusalem. 21:And the King commanded all the people, saying, Keep the passover to the Lord your God, as it is written in the book of this covenant. 22:Surely there was not held such a passover from the days of the Judges that judged Israel, nor in all the days of the Kings of Israel, or Kings of Judah. 23:But in the eighteenth year of King Josiah, where in this passover was held to the Lord in Jerusalem.

Nehemiah the son of Hachaliah went to rebuild Jerusalem

(Nehemiah 2:1-8) 1:And it came to pass in the month Nisan, in the twentieth year of Artaxerxes the King, that wine was before him: and I took up the wine, and gave it to the King. Now I have never before been sad in his presence. 2:Wherefore the King said to me, Why is your countenance sad, seeing you are not sick? This is nothing else but sorrow of heart. Then I was very much afraid.

3:And said to the King, Let the King live forever, why should not my countenance be sad, when the city, the place of my fathers' sepulchers, lies in waste, and the gates thereof are consumed with fire? 4:Then the King said to me, For what do you make request? So I prayed to the God of heaven.

5:And I said to the King, If it please the King, and if your servant have found favor in your sight, that you would send me to Judah, to the city of my fathers' sepulchers, that I may build it. 6:And the King said to me, (with the Queen also sitting by him,) For how long shall your journey be? And when will you return? So it pleased the King to send me; and I set him a time. 7:Moreover I said to the King, If it please the King, let letters be given me to the governors beyond the river, that they may convey me over till I come into Judah. 8:And a letter to Asaph the keeper of the King's forest, that he may give me timber to make beams for the gates of the palace which appertained to the house, and for the wall of the city, and for the house that I shall enter into. And the King granted me, according to the good hand of my God that is upon me.

+/- 477 B.C. Haman cast lots to destroy the Hebrews

(Esther 3:7-11)7:In the first month, that is, the month Nisan, in the twelfth year of King Ahasuerus, they cast Pur, that is the lot, before Haman from day to day, and from month to month, to the twelfth month, that is the month of Adar. 8: in all the provinces of your Kingdom; and their laws are diverse from all people; neither keep they the King's laws: therefore it is not for the King's profit to suffer them. 9:If it please the King, let it be written that they may be destroyed: and I will pay ten thousand talents of silver,to the hands of those that have the charge of the business, to bring it into the King's treasuries. 10:And the King took his ring from his hand, gave it to Haman the son of Hammedatha the Agagite, the Jew's enemy. 11:And the King said to Haman, The silver is given to you, the people also, to do with them as it seems good to you.

The Invasion of Judah

(1Maccabees 9:3-18) 3:In the first month of the year one hundred and fifty two, they encamped against Jerusalem. 4:Then they sent out for Berea with twenty thousand men and two thousand Calvary. 5:Judas with three thousand picked men, had camped at Elasa. 6:When his men saw the great number of troops, they were very much afraid, and many slipped away from the camp, until only eight hundred men remained.

7:As Judas saw his army was melting away just when the battle was imminent, he was panic-stricken, because he had no time to gather them together. 8:But in spite of his discouragement, he said to those who remained: let us go forward to meet our enemies; perhaps we can put up a good fight against them. 9:They tried to dissuade him saying “We certainly cannot”. Let us save our lives now and come back with our kinsmen, and then fight against them. Now we are too few. 10;But Judas said:Far be it for me to do such a thing as to flee from them! If our time has come, let us die bravely for our kinsmen and not leave a stain upon our glory!
11:Then the army of Bacchides moved out of camp and took its position for battle. The cavalry were divided into two squadrons, and the rock slingers and the archers came on ahead of the army, and all the valiant men were in the front line.
12:Bacchides was on the right wing. Flanked by the two squadrons, the phalanx attacked as they blew their trumpets. Those who were on Judas side also blew their trumpets.

13:The earth shook with the noise of the armies, and the battle raged from morning until evening. 14:Seeing that Bacchides was on the right with the main force of his army, Judas with all the most stouthearted rallying to him to 15:drive back the right wing and pursued as far as the mountain slopes. 16:But when the men on the left wing saw that the right wing was driven back, they turned and fallowed Judas and his men, taking them in the rear. 7:The battle was fought desperately, and many on both sides fell wounded. 18:Then Judas fell , and the rest fled.

Pictures of the place, where Jesus was taken to speak with Herod.
Jesus was led through Herod's gate, shown here below.

Pilates court yard where Jesus was brought to be judged.

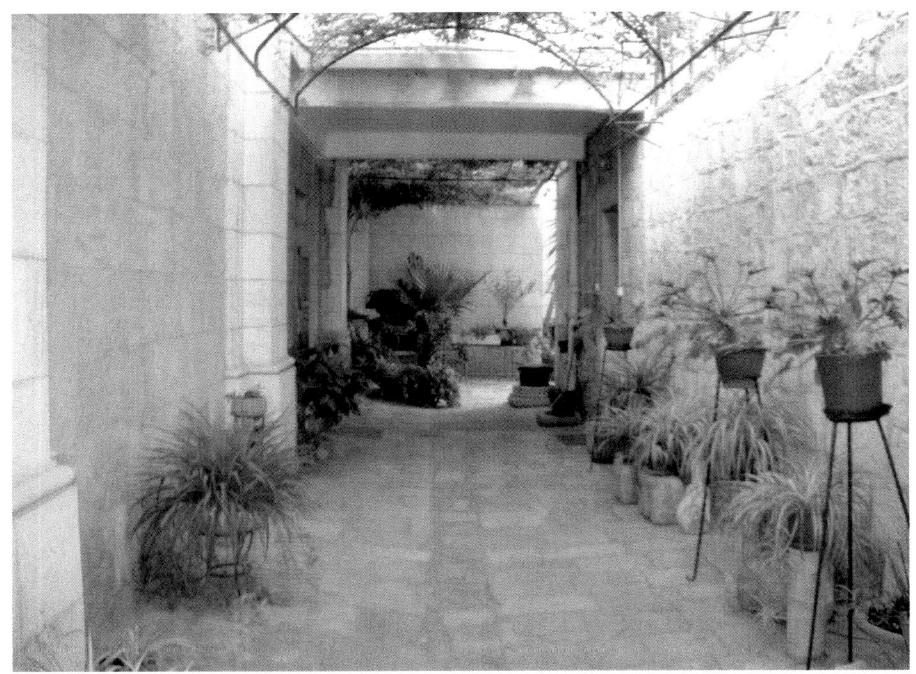

Above here:This is a picture of the court yard where, Pilate spoke alone with Jesus

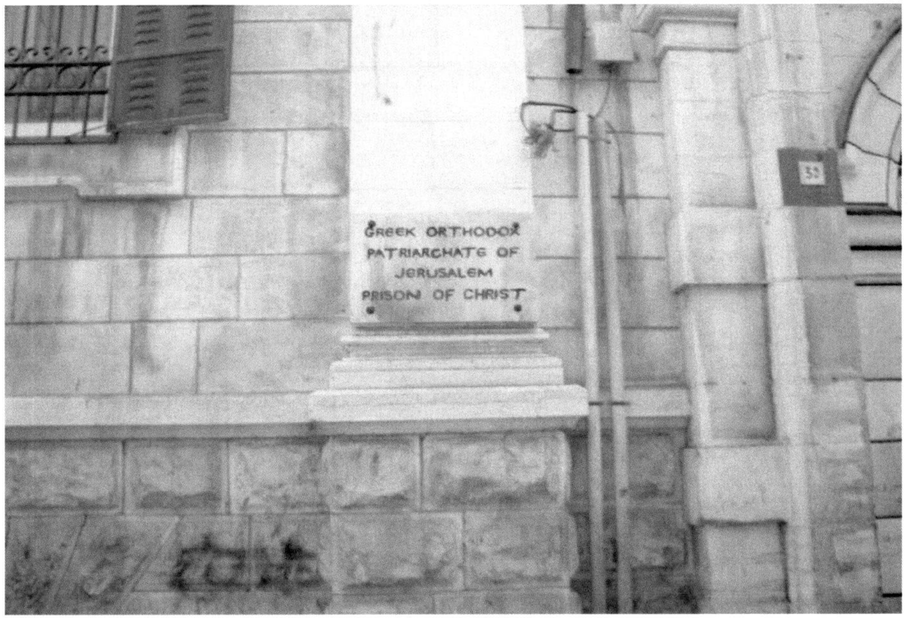

The Garrison shown here is where Jesus was taken, it is only about 50'ft. from Pilates Gate

Through the door, down the stairs on the left is the prison where Jesus was flogged, beaten and mocked.

Above on the left: Is part of the path where Jesus walked, carrying his cross being led to his death. On the Right: Is where the church says he was washed and wrapped to be placed in his tomb. Please Note: The path that was taken by passed most of the city, and was mostly a up hill journey. The streets are narrow and are made of stone. It is about a 20 minute walk up to where he would be crucified. If you just walk it casually. Along the way there are plaques that mark the spots where Jesus had fallen. Between the second and third time he had fallen it was only about 20 ft. or 7 meters. After he fell the third time, there was a man from Cyrene, who's name was Simon, was the man the soldiers took from the crowd and forced him to help carry the cross to the top of the hill.

Note: Each year Jesus and his parents would return to Jerusalem on the feast days of the Passover and Feast of Tabernacles or Booths.
As written in Leviticus 23:5, 23:43

Chapter 5:May - Iyar /Ziv

It is the second Month of the Hebrew calendar
In Hebrew this month is called: Iyar /Ziv, which means:
(Healing, Olive)
Tribe of Benjamin, means:(Sent out from the Fathers right hand, his first born)
The stone of (Lapis Lazuh) represents this tribe.
Benjamin: (The 2nd.) Son of Rachel,
(Who was believed to have been born during this month.)
(Spirit of Destruction)

+/- May 1st. (Iyar- Ziv 1st.)

The year +/- 1357 B.C. The first census done by Moses

(Numbers 1:1-54) 1:And the Lord spoke to Moses in the wilderness of Sinai, in the tabernacle of the congregation, on the first day of the second month, in the second year after they were come out of the land of Egypt, saying, 2:Take you the sum of all the congregation of the children of Israel, after their families, by the house of their fathers, with the number of their names, every male by their polls. 3:From twenty years old and upward, all that are able to go forth to war in Israel: you and Aaron shall number them by their armies. 4:And with you there shall be a man of every tribe; every one head of the house of his fathers. 5:And these are the names of the men that shall stand with you: of the tribe of Reuben; Elizur the son of Shedeur. 6:Of Simeon; Shelumiel the son of Zurishaddai. 7:Of Judah; Nahshon the son of Amminadab. 8:Of Issachar; Nethaneel the son of Zuar. 9:Of Zebulun; Eliab the son of Helon. 10:Of the children of Joseph: of Ephraim; Elishama the son of Ammihud: of Manasseh; Gamaliel the son of Pedahzur. 11:Of Benjamin; Abidan the son of Gideoni. 12:Of Dan; Ahiezer the son of Ammishaddai. 13:Of Asher; Pagiel the son of Ocran. 14:Of Gad; Eliasaph the son of Deuel. 15:Of Naphtali; Ahira the son of Enan. 16:These were the renowned of the congregation, princes of the tribes of their fathers, heads of thousands in Israel. 17:And Moses and Aaron took these men which are expressed by their names. 18:And they assembled all the congregation together on the first day of the second month, and they declared their pedigrees after their families, by the house of their fathers, according to the number of the names, from twenty years old and upward, by their polls. 19:As the Lord commanded Moses, so he numbered them in the wilderness of Sinai. 20:And the children of Reuben, Israel's eldest son, by their generations, after their families, by the house of their fathers, according to the number of the names, by their polls, every male from twenty years old and upward, all that were able to go forth to war.21:Those that were numbered of them, even of the tribe of Reuben, were forty and six thousand and five hundred. 22:Of the children of Simeon, by their generations, after their families, by the house of their fathers, those that were numbered of them, according to the number of the names, by their polls, every male from twenty years old and upward, all that were able to go forth to war. 23:Those that were numbered of them, even of the tribe of Simeon, were fifty and nine thousand and three hundred. 24: Of the children of Gad, by their generations, after their families, by the house of their fathers, according to the number of the names, from twenty years old and upward, all that were able to go forth to war; 25: Those that were numbered of them, even of the tribe of Gad, were forty and five thousand six hundred and fifty. 26:Of the children of Judah, by their generations, after their families, by the house of their fathers, according to the number of the names, from twenty years old and upward, all that were able to go forth to war; 27: Those that were numbered of them, even of the tribe of Judah, were threescore and fourteen thousand and six hundred. 28:Of the children of Issachar, by their generations, after their families, by the house of their fathers, according to the number of the names, from twenty years old and upward, all that were able to go forth to war; 29:Those that were numbered of them, even of the tribe of Issachar, were fifty and four thousand and four hundred. 30:Of the children of Zebulun, by their generations, after their families, by the house of their fathers, according to the number of the names, from twenty years old and upward, all that were able to go forth to war; 31:Those that were numbered of them, even of the tribe of Zebulun, were fifty and seven thousand and four hundred. 32:Of the children of Joseph, namely of the children of Ephraim, by their generations, after their families, by the house of their fathers, according to the number of the names, from twenty years old and upward, all that were able to go forth to war; 33: Those that were numbered of them, even of the tribe of Ephraim, were forty thousand and five hundred. 34: Of the children of Manasseh, by their generations, after their families, by the house of their fathers, according to the number of the names, from twenty years old and upward, all that were able to go forth to war; 35:Those that were numbered of them, even of the tribe of Manasseh, were thirty and two thousand and two hundred. 36: Of the children of Benjamin, by their generations, after their families, by the house of their fathers, according to the number of the names, from twenty years old and upward, all that were able to go forth to war; 37:Those that were numbered of them, even of the tribe of Benjamin, were thirty and five thousand and four hundred. 38: Of the children of Dan, by their generations, after their families, by the house of their fathers, according to the number of the names, from twenty years old and upward, all that were able to go forth to war; 39:Those that were numbered of them, even of the tribe of Dan, were threescore and two thousand and seven hundred. 40:Of the children of Asher, by their generations, after their families, by the house of their fathers, according to the number of the names, from twenty years old and upward, all that were able to go forth to war; 41:Those that were numbered of them, even of the tribe of Asher, were forty and one thousand and five hundred.

42:Of the children of Naphtali, throughout their generations, after their families, by the house of their fathers, according to the number of the names, from twenty years old and upward, all that were able to go forth to war; 43:Those that were numbered of them, even of the tribe of Naphtali, were fifty and three thousand and four hundred. 44 :These are those that were numbered, which Moses and Aaron numbered, and the princes of Israel, being twelve men: each one was for the house of his fathers. 45:So were all those that were numbered of the children of Israel, by the house of their fathers, from twenty years old and upward, all that were able to go forth to war in Israel; 46:Even all they that were numbered were six hundred thousand and three thousand and five hundred and fifty. 47:But the Levites after the tribe of their fathers were not numbered among them. 48;For the LORD had spoken unto Moses, saying, 49:Only you shall not number the tribe of Levi, neither take the sum of them among the children of Israel: 50:But you shall appoint the Levites over the tabernacle of testimony, and over all the vessels thereof, and over all things that belong to it: they shall bear the tabernacle, and all the vessels thereof; and they shall minister unto it, and shall encamp round about the tabernacle. 51:And when the tabernacle setteth forward, the Levites shall take it down: and when the tabernacle is to be pitched, the Levites shall set it up: and the stranger that cometh nigh shall be put to death. 52 :And the children of Israel shall pitch their tents, every man by his own camp, and every man by his own standard, throughout their hosts. 53:But the Levites shall pitch round about the tabernacle of testimony, that there be no wrath upon the congregation of the children of Israel: and the Levites shall keep the charge of the tabernacle of testimony. 54:And the children of Israel did according to all that the LORD commanded Moses, so did they.

+/- May1st. (Iyar- Ziv 1st.)

The year +/- 1005 B.C. Jonathan at the feast of the new moon

(1Samuel 20:25-26) 25:And the King sat upon his seat, as at other times, even upon a seat by the wall: and Jonathan arose, and Abner sat by Saul's side, and David's place was empty. 26:Nevertheless Saul spoke not any thing that day: for he thought, Something has befallen him,

+/- May1st. (Iyar- Ziv 1st.)

+/- (The 4th. Year of Paul ministry) Paul left for Troas

(Acts 20:4-6) 4:Sopater son of Pyrrhus from Berea, accompanied him, as did Aristarchus and Secundus from Thessalonia, Gaius from Trophimus from Asia, 5:who and waited for us at Troas. 6:We sailed from Philippi after the feast of Unleavened Bread, and rejoined them five days later in Troas, then we went on ahead to Thessalonians, where we stayed seven days.

+/- May1st. (Iyar- Ziv 1st.)

+/- (The 6th. Year of Paul ministry) Paul came to Rome

(Acts 28:15-16)15;And from there, when the brethren heard of us, they came to meet us as far as Appii forum, and The three taverns: whom when Paul saw, he thanked God, and took courage.

16;And when we came to Rome, the centurion delivered the prisoners to the captain of the guard: but Paul was suffered to dwell by himself with a soldier that kept him.

+/- May 2nd. (Iyar- Ziv 2nd.)

The year +/-1317 B.C. Joshua sets up around Ai

(Joshua 8:3-11) 3:So Joshua arose, and all the people of war, to go up against Ai, and Joshua chose out thirty thousand mighty men of valor, and sent them away by night. 4:And he commanded them, saying, Behold, you shall lie in wait against the city, even behind the city: go not very far from the city, but be you all ready. 5:And I, and all the people that are with me, will approach to the city: and it shall come to pass, when they come out against us, as at the first, that we will flee before them. 6:(For they will come out after us) till we have drawn them from the city; for they will say, They flee before us, as at the first: therefore we will flee before them. 7:Then you shall rise up from the ambush, and seize upon the city: for the Lord your God will deliver it into your hand. 8:And it shall be, when you have taken the city, that you shall set the city on fire: according to the commandment of the Lord shall you do. See, I have commanded you. 9:Joshua therefore sent them forth: and they went to lie in ambush, and abode between Bethel and Ai, on the west side of Ai: but Joshua lodged that night among the people. 10:And Joshua rose up early in the morning, and numbered the people, and went up, he and the elders of Israel, before the people to Ai. 11:And all the people, even the people of war that were with him, went up, and drew near, and came before the city, and pitched on the north side of Ai, now there was a valley between them and Ai.

+/- May 2nd. (Iyar- Ziv 2nd.)

The year +/- 1005 B.C. David said goodbye to Jonathan, his brother in law,

(1Samuel 20:27-21:15) 27:And it came to pass on the next day, which was the second day of the month, that David's place was empty: and Saul said to Jonathan his son, Wherefore cometh not the son of Jesse to meat, neither yesterday, nor to day? 28:And Jonathan answered Saul, David earnestly asked leave of me to go to Bethlehem. 29:And he said, Let me go, I pray you; for our family has a sacrifice in the city; and my brother, he has commanded me to be there, and now, if I have found favor in thine eyes, let me get away, I pray you, and see my brethren. Therefore he cometh not to the King's table. 30:Then Saul's anger was kindled against Jonathan, and he said to him, you son of the perverse rebellious woman, do not I know that you hast chosen the son of Jesse to thine own confusion, and to the confusion of your mother's nakedness? 31:For as long as the son of Jesse lives upon the ground, you shall not be established, nor your kingdom. Wherefore now send and fetch him to me, for he shall surely die. 32:And Jonathan answered Saul his father, and said to him, Wherefore shall he be slain? What has he done? 33:And Saul cast a javelin at him to strike him: where by Jonathan knew that it was determined of his father to slay David. 34:So Jonathan arose from the table in fierce anger, and did eat no meat the second day of the month: for he was grieved for David, because his father had done him shame. 35:And it came to pass in the morning, that Jonathan went out into the field at the time appointed with David, and a little lad with him. 36: And he said to his lad, Run, find out now the arrows which I shoot. And as the lad ran, he shot an arrow beyond him. 37:And when the lad was come to the place of the arrow which Jonathan had shot, Jonathan cried after the lad, and said: Is not the arrow beyond you? 38:And Jonathan cried after the lad, Make speed, haste, stay not. And Jonathan's lad gathered up the arrows, and came to his master. 39:But the lad knew not any thing: only Jonathan and David knew the matter. 40:And Jonathan gave his artillery to his lad, and said to him, Go, carry them to the city.

41:And as soon as the lad was gone, David arose out of the place toward the south, and fell on his face to the ground, and bowed himself three times: and they kissed one another, and wept one with another, until David exceeded. 42:And Jonathan said to David, Go in peace, for as much as we have sworn both of us in the name of the LORD, saying, The LORD be between me and you, and between my seed and your seed forever. And he arose and departed: and Jonathan went into the city.
“David went and picked up Goliath's sword”

21:1: Then came David to Nob to Ahimelech the priest: and Ahimelech was afraid at the meeting of David, and said to him, Why are you alone, and there is no man with you? 2:And David said to Ahimelech the priest, The King has commanded me a business, and has said to me, Let no man know any thing of the business where I am sending you, or what I have commanded you: and I have appointed my servants to do this and in such a place. 3:Now therefore what is under your hand? Hand over to me five loafs of bread here in my hand, or what ever you may have here. 4:And the priest answered David, and said; There is no common bread under my hand, but there is hallowed bread; if the young men have kept themselves from women.

5:And David answered the priest, and said to him, Of the truth women have been kept from us these three days, since I came out, and the vessels of the young men are holy, and the bread is in a manner common, yes, though it were sanctified this day in the vessel. 6:So the priest gave him hallowed bread for there was no bread there but the show bread, that was taken from before the LORD, to put hot bread in the day when it was taken away. 7:Now a certain man of the servants of Saul was there that day, detained before the LORD; and his name was Doeg, an Edomite, the chiefest of the herdsmen that belonged to Saul. 8:And David said to Ahimelech. And is there not here under your hand spear or sword? For I have neither brought my sword nor my weapons with me, because the King's business required haste.

9:And the priest said, The sword of Goliath the Philistine, whom you killed in the valley of Elah, behold, it is here wrapped in a cloth behind the ephod: if you will take that, take it, for there is no other one that that one here. And David said; There is none like that one; give it to me. 10:And David arose, and fled that day for fear of Saul, and went to Achish the King of Gath.

11:And the servants of Achish said to him; Is not this David the King of the land? Did they not sing one to another of him in dances, saying, Saul has slain his thousands, and David his ten thousands? 12:And David laid up these words in his heart, and was sore afraid of Achish the King of Gath.

13:And he changed his behavior before them, and feigned himself mad in their hands, and scrabbled on the doors of the gate, and let his spittle fall down upon his beard. 14;Then said Achish to his servants, Look, do you not see the man is mad: why then have you brought him here to me? 15:Do I have need of mad man? that you have brought this fellow to play the mad man in my presence? Shall this fellow come into my house?

+/- May 2nd. (Iyar- Ziv 2nd.)

The Solomon started to build the Lords House

(2Chroncles 3:1-17)1:Then Solomon began to build the house of the Lord at Jerusalem in mount Moriah, where the Lord appeared to David his father, in the place that David had prepared in the threshing floor of Ornan the Jebusite. 2:And he began to build in the second day of the second month, in the fourth year of his reign. 3:Now these are things that Solomon was instructed for the building of the house of God. The length by cubits after the first measure was threescore cubits, and the breadth twenty cubits.

4:And the porch that was in the front of the house, the length of it was according to the breadth of the house, twenty cubits, and the height was an hundred and twenty and he overlaid it within with pure gold. 5:And the greater house he circled with fir tree, which he overlaid with fine gold, and set thereon palm trees and chains. 6:And he garnished the house with precious stones for beauty: and the gold was gold of Parvaim. 7:He overlaid also the house, the beams, the posts, and the walls thereof, and the doors thereof, with gold; and graved cherubims on the walls.

8:And he made the most holy house, the length whereof was according to the breadth of the house, twenty cubits, and the breadth thereof twenty cubits: and he overlaid it with fine gold, amounting to six hundred talents. 9:And the weight of the nails was fifty shekels of gold. And he overlaid the upper chambers with gold. 10:And in the most holy house he made two cherubims of image work, and overlaid them with gold. 11:And the wings of the cherubims were twenty cubits long: one wing of the one cherub was five cubits, reaching to the wall of the house: and the other wing was likewise five cubits, reaching to the wing of the other cherub.

12:And one wing of the other cherub was five cubits, reaching to the wall of the house: and the other wing was five cubits also, joining to the wing of the other cherub. 13:The wings of these cherubims spread themselves forth twenty cubits: and they stood on their feet, and their faces were inward.

14:And he made the vale of blue, and purple, and crimson, and fine linen, and wrought cherubims thereon. 15:Also he made before the house two pillars of thirty and five cubits high, and the capital topping each was of five cubits. 16:And he made chains, as in the oracle, and put them on the heads of the pillars; and made an hundred pomegranates, and put them on the chains. 17:And he reared up the pillars before the temple, one on the right hand, and the other on the left; and called the name of that on the right hand Jachin, and the name of that on the left Boas.

Sense there are no pictures of the Lord temple. Here are two models of what the temple was described.

+/- May 3rd. (Iyar- Ziv 3rd.)

The year +/- 1005 B.C. David escaped to the cave of Adullam

(1Samuel 22:1-2) 22:1: David therefore departed thence, and escaped to the cave Adullam: and when his brethren and all his father's house heard it, they went down thither to him. 2:And every one that was in distress, and every one that was in debt, and every one that was discontented, gathered themselves unto him; and he became a captain over them: and there were with him about four hundred men.

+/- May 3rd. (Iyar- Ziv 3rd.)

The year +/- 1317 B.C. Joshua took the city Ai

(Joshua 8:12-29) 12:And he took about five thousand men, and set them to lie in ambush between Bethel and Ai, on the west side of the city. 13:And when they had set the people, even all the host that was on the north of the city, and they lied in wait on the west of the city, Joshua went that night into the midst of the valley. 14:And it came to pass, when the King of Ai saw it, that they hasted and rose up early, and the men of the city went out against Israel to battle, he and all his people, at a time appointed, before the plain; but he did not know that there were men laying in ambush against him behind the city. 15:And Joshua and all Israel made as if they were beaten before them, and fled by the way of the wilderness. 16:And all the people that were in Ai were called together to pursue after them: and they pursued after Joshua, and were drawn away from the city. 17:And there was not a man left in Ai or Bethel, that went not out after Israel: and they left the city open, and pursued after Israel. 18:And the Lord said to Joshua, Stretch out the spear that is in your hand toward Ai; for I will give it into your hand. And Joshua stretched out the spear that he had in his hand toward the city. 19:And the ambush arose quickly out of their place, and they ran as soon as he had stretched out his hand: and they entered into the city, and took it, and hasted and set the city on fire.

20:And when the men of Ai looked behind them, they saw, and, behold, the smoke of the city ascended up to heaven, and they had no power to flee this way or that way: and the people that fled to the wilderness turned back upon the pursuers.
21:And when Joshua and all Israel saw that the ambush had taken the city, and that the smoke of the city ascended, then they turned again, and slew the men of Ai.
22:And the other issued out of the city against them; so they were in the midst of Israel, some on this side, and some on that side: and they struck them, so that they let none of them remain or escape. 23:And the King of Ai they took alive, and brought him to Joshua. 24:And it came to pass, when Israel had made an end of slaying all the inhabitants of Ai in the field, in the wilderness wherein they chased them, and when they were all fallen on the edge of the sword, until they were consumed, that all the Israelites returned to Ai, and smote it with the edge of the sword. 25:And so it was, that all that fell that day, both of men and women, were twelve thousand, even all the men of Ai. 26:For Joshua drew not his hand back, wherewith he stretched out the spear, until he had utterly destroyed all the inhabitants of Ai. 27:Only the cattle and the spoil of that city Israel took for a prey to themselves, according to the word of the Lord, which he commanded Joshua.
28:And Joshua burnt Ai, and made it an heap for ever, even a desolation to this day.
29:And the king of Ai he hanged on a tree until eventide: and as soon as the sun was down, Joshua commanded that they should take his carcase down from the tree, and cast it at the entering of the gate of the city, and raise thereon a great heap of stones,that remain to this day.

+/- May 3rd. (Iyar- Ziv 3rd.)

+/- (The 4th. Year of Paul ministry) Paul brought a young man, back to life

(Acts 20:7-14) 7:And upon the first day of the week, when the disciples came together to break bread, Paul preached to them, ready to depart tomorrow; and continued his speech until midnight. 8:And there were many lights in the upper chamber, where they were gathered together. 9:And there sat in a window a certain young man named Eutychus, having fallen to sleep: and as Paul was long preaching, he sunk down with sleep, and fell down from the third loft, and was taken up dead.
10:And Paul went down, and fell on him, and holding him he said, Trouble not yourselves; for his life is in him.11:When he therefore was come up again, and had broken bread, and eaten, and talked a long while, even till break of day, so he departed. 12:And they brought the young man alive, and were not a little comforted.
13:And we went before to ship, and sailed to Assos, there intending to take in Paul: for so had he appointed, minding himself to go afoot. 14:And when he met with us at Assos, we took him in, and came to Mitylene.

+/- May 6th. (Iyar- Ziv 6th.)

The year +/- 1357 B.C. God told Moses to camp at the Red Sea

(Exodus 14:2-4) 2:And the Lord spoke to Moses, saying, 2;Speak to the children of Israel, that they turn and encamp before Pi-hahiroth, between Migdol and the sea, over against Baalzephon: before it shall you encamp by the sea. 3:For Pharaoh will say of the children of Israel, They are entangled in the land, the wilderness has shut them in. 4:And I will harden Pharaoh's heart, that he shall follow after them; and I will be honored upon Pharaoh, and upon all his host; that the Egyptians may know that, I am the Lord. And they did so.

+/- May 6th. (Iyar- Ziv 6th.)

+/- (The 4th. Year of Paul ministry) Paul says goodbye, knowing he will never see them again

(Acts 20:16-38)16:For Paul had determined to sail by Ephesus, because he would not spend the time in Asia: for he hasted, if it were possible for him, to be at Jerusalem the day of Pentecost. 17:And from Miletus he sent to Ephesus, and called the elders of the church. 18:And when they were come to him, he said to them, you know, from the first day that I came into Asia, after what manner I have been with you at all seasons. 19:Serving the Lord with all humility of mind, and with many tears, and temptations, which befell me by the lying in wait of the Jews. 20:And how I kept back nothing that was profitable to you, but have shewed you, and have taught you publicly, and from house to house.

21:Testifying both to the Hebrews, and also to the Greeks, repentance toward God, and faith toward our Lord Jesus Christ. 22:And now, behold, I go bound in the spirit to Jerusalem, not knowing the things that shall befall me there. 23:So that the Holy Ghost witnesses in every city, saying that bonds and afflictions abide me. 24:But none of these things move me, neither count I my life dear to myself, so that I might finish my course with joy, and the ministry, which I have received of the Lord Jesus, to testify the gospel of the grace of God. 25:And now, behold, I know that you all, among whom I have gone preaching the kingdom of God, shall see my face no more. 26:Wherefore I take you to record this day, that I am pure from the blood of all men. 27:For I have not shunned to declare to you all the counsel of God. 28:Take heed therefore to yourselves, and to all the flock, over the which the Holy Ghost has made you overseers, to feed the church of God, which he has purchased with his own blood. 29:For I know this, that after my departing shall grievous wolves enter in among you, not sparing the flock. 30:Also of your own selves shall men arise, speaking perverse things, to draw away disciples after them.

31:Therefore watch, and remember, that by the space of three years I ceased not to warn every one night and day with tears. 32:And now, brethren, I commend you to God, and to the word of his grace, which is able to build you up, and to give you an inheritance among all them which are sanctified. 33:I have coveted no man's silver, or gold, or apparel. 34:Yes, you yourselves know, that these hands have ministered to my necessities, and to them that were with me.

35:I have showed you all things, how that so laboring you ought to support the weak, and to remember the words of the Lord Jesus, how he said; It is more blessed to give than to receive. 36;And when he had spoken, he knelled down, and prayed with them all. 37:And they all wept sore, and fell on Paul's neck, and kissed him. 38:Sorrowing most of all for the words which he spoke, that they should see his face no more. and they accompanied him to the ship.

+/- May 7th. (Iyar- Ziv 7th.)

The year +/- 1357 B.C. Pharaoh came out after the Hebrews

(Exodus 14:5-19) 5:And it was told to the King of Egypt that the people fled: and the heart of Pharaoh and of his servants was turned against the people, and they said; Why have we done this, that we have let Israel go from serving us? 6:And he made ready his chariot, and took his people with him. 7:And he took six hundred chosen chariots, and all the chariots of Egypt, and captains over every one of them. 8:And the Lord hardened the heart of Pharaoh king of Egypt, and he pursued after the children of Israel: and the children of Israel went out with an high hand. 9:But the Egyptians pursued after them, all the horses and chariots of Pharaoh, and his horsemen, and his army, and overtook them encamping by the sea, beside Pi-hahiroth, before Baalzephon. 10:And when Pharaoh drew near, the children of Israel lifted up their eyes, and, behold, the Egyptians marched after them; and they were sore afraid: and the children of Israel cried out to the Lord. 11:And they said to Moses, Because there were no graves in Egypt, have you taken us away to die in the wilderness? Why have you dealt this way with us, to carry us forth out of Egypt? 12:Is not this the word that we did tell you in Egypt, saying, Let us alone, that we may serve the Egyptians? For it had been better for us to serve the Egyptians, than that we should die in the wilderness. 13:And Moses said to the people, Fear you not, stand still, and see the salvation of the Lord, which he will show to you to day: for the Egyptians whom you have seen to day, you shall see them again no more for ever. 14:The Lord shall fight for you, and you shall hold your peace. 15:And the Lord said to Moses, Why do you cry to me? speak to the children of Israel, that they go forward. 16:But lift you up your rod, and stretch out your hand over the sea, and divide it: and the children of Israel shall go on dry ground through the midst of the sea. 17:And I, behold, I will harden the hearts of the Egyptians, and they shall follow them: and I will get me honor upon Pharaoh, and upon all his host, upon his chariots, and upon his horsemen. 18:And the Egyptians shall know that I am the Lord, when I have gotten me honor upon Pharaoh, upon his chariots, and upon his horsemen. 19:And the angel of God, which went before the camp of Israel, removed and went behind them; and the pillar of the cloud went from before their faces, and stood behind them:

+/- May 7th. (Iyar- Ziv 7th.)

+/- (The 5th. Year of Paul ministry) Paul sailed by Coos

(Acts 21:1) 1:And it came to pass, that after we were gotten from them, and had launched, we came with a straight course to Coos, and the day following to Rhodes, and from there to Patrica:

+/- May 8th. (Iyar- Ziv 8th.)

The year +/- 1357 B.C. God parted the Red Sea,

(Exodus 14:20-15:21) 20:And it came between the camp of the Egyptians and the camp of Israel; and it was a cloud and darkness to the Egyptians, but it gave light by night to the Hebrews, so that the one came not near the other all the night. 21:And Moses stretched out his hand over the sea; and the Lord caused the sea to go back by a strong east wind all that night, and made the sea dry land,

and the waters were divided. 22:And the children of Israel went into the midst of the sea upon the dry ground and the waters were a wall to them on their right hand, and on their left. 23:And the Egyptians pursued, and went in after them to the midst of the sea, even all Pharaoh's horses, his chariots, and his horsemen. 24:And it came to pass, that in the morning watch the Lord looked to the host of the Egyptians through the pillar of fire and of the cloud, and troubled the host of the Egyptians. 25:And took off their chariot wheels, that they drove them heavily: so that the Egyptians said, Let us flee from the face of Israel; for the Lord fights for them against the Egyptians. 26:And the Lord said to Moses, Stretch out your hand over the sea, that the waters may come again upon the Egyptians, upon their chariots, and upon their horsemen. 27:And Moses stretched forth his hand over the sea, and the sea returned to his strength when the morning appeared; and the Egyptians fled against it; and the Lord overthrew the Egyptians in the midst of the sea. 28:And the waters returned, and covered the chariots, and the horsemen, and all the host of Pharaoh that came into the sea after them; there remained not so much as one of them. 29:But the children of Israel walked upon dry land in the midst of the sea; and the waters were a wall to them on their right hand, and on their left. 30:This the Lord saved Israel that day out of the hand of the Egyptians; and Israel saw the Egyptians dead upon the sea shore. 31:And Israel saw that great work which the Lord did upon the Egyptians: and the people feared the Lord, and believed the Lord, and his servant Moses. **15:1**:Then sang Moses and the children of Israel this song to the Lord, and spoke, saying, I will sing to the Lord, for he has triumphed gloriously: the horse and his rider has he thrown into the sea. 2:The Lord is my strength and song, and he is become my salvation: he is my God, and I will prepare him an habitation; my father's God, and I will exalt him. 3:The Lord is a man of war, the Lord is his name. 4:Pharaoh's chariots and his host has he cast into the sea: his chosen captains also are drowned in the Red sea. 5:The depths have covered them: they sank into the bottom as a stone. 6:your right hand, O Lord, is become glorious in power: your right hand, O Lord, has dashed in pieces the enemy. 7:And in the greatness of your excellency you have overthrown them that rose up against you: you sent forth your wrath, which consumed them as stubble. 8:And with the blast of your nostrils the waters were gathered together, the floods stood upright as an heap, and the depths were congealed in the heart of the sea. 9:The enemy said, I will pursue, I will overtake, I will divide the spoil; my lust shall be satisfied upon them; I will draw my sword, my hand shall destroy them. 10:You did blow with your wind, the sea covered them: they sank as lead in the mighty waters. 11:Who is like to you, O Lord, among the gods? Who is like you, glorious in holiness, fearful in praises, doing wonders? 12:You stretched out your right hand, the earth swallowed them. 13:You in your mercy has led forth the people which you have redeemed: you have guided them in your strength to your holy habitation. 14:The people shall hear, and be afraid: sorrow shall take hold on the inhabitants of Palestrina. 15:Then the dukes of Edom shall be amazed; the mighty men of Moab, trembling shall take hold upon them; all the inhabitants of Canaan shall melt away. 16:Fear and dread shall fall upon them; by the greatness of thine arm they shall be as still as a stone; till your people pass over, O Lord, till the people pass over, which you have purchased. 17:You shall bring them in, and plant them in the mountain of your inheritance, in the place, O Lord, which you have made for you to dwell in, in the Sanctuary, O Lord, which your hands have established.

18:The Lord shall reign for ever and ever. 19:For the horse of Pharaoh went in with his chariots and with his horsemen into the sea, and the Lord brought again the waters of the sea upon them; but the children of Israel went on dry land in the midst of the sea. 20:And Miriam the prophetess, the sister of Aaron, took a timbrel in her hand; and all the women went out after her with timbrels and with dances. 21;And Miriam answered them; Sing you to the Lord, for he has triumphed gloriously, the horse and his rider has he thrown into the sea.

Found in Nuweiba, Egypt in 1978 **Found on the Saudi, Arabia years later**

Both of theses have Phoenician writing on them.

Pictured above: The Red Sea, it seems to part it self every 1100 to 1400 years, for a few hours. Exposing a land bridge that is beneath the water. God had Moses used this land bridge to lead his people across the Red Sea.

The Red Sea parts every 1100 to 1400 years. For a few moments.

Note: Found in 1978, a Phoenician style column lying in the water. Then in 1984 a second granite column was found on the Saudi coastline opposite identical to the first, except on this one the inscription was still intact. In Phoenician letters: (Archaic Hebrew) it contained the words: Mizraim (Egypt); Solomon; Edom; death Pharaoh, Moses and Yahweh, indicating that King Solomon had set up these columns as a memorial to the miracle of the crossing of the sea. Saudi Arabia does not admit tourists, to this any longer and perhaps fearing unauthorized visitors, the Saudi Authorities have since removed this column, and replaced it with a flag marker where it once stood.

+/- May 8th. (Iyar - Ziv 8th.

+/- **(The 5th. Year of Paul ministry) Paul sailed to Phoenicia**

(Acts 21:2) 2:And finding a ship sailing over to Phoenicia, we went aboard, and set forth.

+/- May 9th. (Iyar- Ziv 9th.)

+/- **(The 5th. Year of Paul ministry) Paul landed in Cyprus**

(Acts 21: 3-4) 3:Now when we had discovered Cyprus, we left it on the left hand, and sailed into Syria, and landed at Tyre: for there the ship was to unload her burden. 4;And finding disciples, we tarried there seven days: who said to Paul through the Spirit, that he should not go up to Jerusalem.

+/- May 11th. (Iyar- Ziv 11th.)

The year +/- 1357 B.C. They came to Marah,

(Exodus 15:22-26) 22:So Moses brought Israel from the Red sea, and they went out into the wilderness of Shur; and they went three days in the wilderness, and found no water. 23:And when they came to Marah, they could not drink of the waters of Marah, for they were bitter: therefore the name of it was called Marah. 24:And the people murmured against Moses, saying, What shall we drink?

25:And he cried to the Lord; and the Lord showed him a tree, which when he had cast into the waters, the waters were made sweet: there he made for them a statute and an ordinance.

26:If you will diligently listen to the voice of the Lord your God, and will do that which is right in his sight, and will give ear to his commandments, and keep all his statutes, I will put none of these diseases upon you, which I have brought upon the Egyptians, for I am the Lord that heals you.

+/- May 12th. (Iyar - Ziv 12th.)

The year +/-1357 B.C. They came to Elim

(Exodus 15:27) And they came to Elim, where were twelve wells of water, and threescore and ten palm trees: and they encamped there by the waters.

+/- May 14th. (Iyar - Ziv 14th.)

(2nd Chance for Passover)

(Numbers 9:6-12) 6:And there were certain men, who were defiled by the dead body of a man, that they could not keep the passover on that day: and they came before Moses and before Aaron on that day. 7:And those men said to him, We are defiled by the dead body of a man: wherefore are we kept back, that we may not offer an offering of the Lord in his appointed season among the children of Israel? 8:And Moses said to them, Stand still, and I will hear what the Lord will command concerning you. 9:And the Lord spoke to Moses, saying; 10:Speak to the children of Israel, saying, If any man of you or of your posterity shall be unclean by reason of a dead body, or be in a journey afar off, yet he shall keep the passover to the Lord. 11:The fourteenth day of the second month at even they shall keep it, and eat it with unleavened bread and bitter herbs. 12;They shall leave none of it to the morning, nor break any bone of it, according to all the ordinances of the passover they shall keep it.

+/- May 14th. (Iyar- Ziv 14th.)

Hezekiah King of Judah held a passover feast

(2Chronicles 30:14-27)14:And they arose and took away the altars that were in Jerusalem, and all the altars for incense took they away, and cast them into the brook Kidron. 15:Then they killed the passover on the fourteenth day of the second month: and the priests and the Levites were ashamed, and sanctified themselves, and brought in the burnt offerings into the house of the Lord. 16:And they stood in their place after their manner, according to the law of Moses the man of God: the priests sprinkled the blood, which they received of the hand of the Levites. 17;For there were many in the congregation that were not sanctified: therefore the Levites had the charge of the killing of the passover for every one that was not clean, to sanctify them to the Lord. 18:For a multitude of the people, even many of Ephraim, and Manasseh, Issachar, and Zebulun, had not cleansed themselves, yet did they eat the passover otherwise than it was written. But Hezekiah prayed for them, saying, The good Lord pardon every one. 19;That prepared his heart to seek God, the Lord God of his fathers, though he be not cleansed according to the purification of the sanctuary. 20:And the Lord hearkened to Hezekiah, and healed the people. 21:And the children of Israel that were present at Jerusalem kept the feast of unleavened bread seven days with great gladness: and the Levites and the priests praised the Lord day by day, singing with loud instruments to the Lord. 22:And Hezekiah spoke comfortably to all the Levites that taught the good knowledge of the Lord, and they did eat throughout the feast seven days, offering peace offerings, and making confession to the Lord God of their fathers. 23:And the whole assembly took counsel to keep other seven days: and they kept other seven days with gladness. 24:For Hezekiah king of Judah did give to the congregation a thousand bullocks and seven thousand sheep; and the princes gave to the congregation a thousand bullocks and ten thousand sheep: and a great number of priests sanctified themselves. 25:And all the congregation of Judah, with the priests and the Levites, and all the congregation that came out of Israel, and the strangers that came out of the land of Israel, and that dwelt in Judah, rejoiced.

26:So there was great joy in Jerusalem: for since the time of Solomon the son of David king of Israel there was not the like in Jerusalem.27:Then the priests the Levites arose and blessed the people: and their voice was heard, and their prayer came up to his holy dwelling place, even to heaven.

+/- May 14th. (Iyar- Ziv 14th.)

In 1948 Israel, was returned as a Nation

(Ezekiel: 37:11-14) 11:Then he said to me, Son of man, these bones are the whole house of Israel: behold, they say, Our bones are dried, and our hope is lost: we are cut off for our parts. 12:Therefore prophesy and say to them, This says the Lord God; Behold, O my people, I will open your graves, and cause you to come up out of your graves, and bring you into the land of Israel. 13;And you shall know that I am the Lord, when I have opened your graves, O my people, and brought you up out of your graves, 14:And shall put my spirit in you, and you shall live, and I shall place you in your own land: then shall you know that I the Lord have spoken it, and will perform it, says the Lord.

+/- May 15th. (Iyar- Ziv 15th.)

The Lord came to Gideon

(Judges 6:11-26) 11:And there came an angel of the Lord, and sat under an oak which was in Oprah, that pertained to Josh the Abiezrite: and his son Gideon threshed wheat by the wine-press, to hide it from the Midianites. 12:And the angel of the Lord appeared to him, and said to him, The Lord is with you, you mighty man of valor. 13:And Gideon said to him, Oh my Lord, if the Lord be with us, why then is all this befallen us? And where be all his miracles which our fathers told us of, saying, Did not the Lord bring us up from Egypt? but now the Lord has forsaken us, and delivered us into the hands of the Midianites. 14:And the Lord looked upon him, and said, Go in this your might, and you shall save Israel from the hand of the Midianites: have not I sent you?

15:And he said to him, Oh my Lord, how shall I save Israel? behold, my family is poor in Manasseh, and I am the least in my father's house. . 16:And the Lord said to him, Surely I will be with you, and you shall strike the Midianites as one man. 17:And he said to him, If now I have found grace in your sight, then show me a sign that you talks with me.18;Depart not hence, I pray you, until I come to you, and bring forth my present, and set it before you. And he said,I will tarry until you come again. And Gideon went in, and made ready a kid, and unleavened cakes of an ephah of flour: the flesh he put in a basket, and he put the broth in a pot, and brought it out to him under the oak, and presented it.

20;And the Angel of God said to him, Take the flesh and the unleavened cakes, and lay them upon this rock, and pour out the broth. And he did so. 21:Then the angel of the Lord put forth the end of the staff that was in his hand, and touched the flesh and the unleavened cakes; and there rose up fire out of the rock, and consumed the flesh and the unleavened cakes. Then the angel of the Lord departed out of his sight. 22:And when Gideon perceived that he was an angel of the Lord,

Gideon said, Alas, O Lord God! For because I have seen an angel of the Lord face to face. 23:And the Lord said to him, Peace be to you; fear not: you shall not die. 24:Then Gideon built an altar there to the Lord, and called it Jehovah shalom: to this day it is yet in Ophrah of the Abiezrites.

25:And it came to pass the same night, that the Lord said to him, Take your father's young bull, even the second bull of seven years old, and tear down the altar of Baal, that your father has, and cut down the grove that is by it. 26:And build an altar to the Lord your God upon the top of this rock, in the ordered place, and take the second bullock, and offer a burnt sacrifice with the wood of the grove which you shall cut down

+/- May 15th. (Iyar- Ziv 15th.)

+/- (The 5th. Year of Paul ministry) Paul leaves Tyre

(Acts 21:5-6) 5:And when we had accomplished those days, we departed and went our way; and they all came with us, with wives and children, till we went out of the city, and we knelt down on the shore, and prayed. 6:And when we had taken our leave one of another, we took ship, and they returned home again.

+/- May 16th. (Iyar- Ziv 16th.)

Gideon did all he was commanded

(Judges 6:27) 27:Then Gideon took ten men of his servants, and did as the Lord had told him: and so it was, because he feared his father's household, and the men of the city, that he could not do it by day, so he did it at night.

+/- May 17th. (Iyar- Ziv 17th.)

The men found the alter destroyed,

(Judges 6:28-32) 28:And when the men of the city arose early in the morning, behold, the altar of Baal was cast down, and the grove was cut down that was by it, and the second bullock was offered upon the altar that was built. 29:And they said one to another, Who has done this thing? And when they inquired and asked, they said, Gideon the son of Joash has done this thing. 30:Then the men of the city said to Joash, Bring out your son, that he may die: because he has cast down the altar of Baal, and because he has cut down the grove that was by it. 31:And Joash said to all that stood against him, Will you plead for Baal? will you save him? he that will plead for him, let him be put to death while it is yet morning: if he be a god, let him plead for himself, because one has cast down his altar. 32:Therefore on that day,he called him Jeru-baal, saying, Let Baal plead against him, because he has thrown down his altar.

+/- May 17th. (Iyar- Ziv 17th.)

+/- (The 5th. Year of Paul ministry) Paul at Ptolemies

(Acts 21:7) 7;And when we had finished our course from Tyre, we came to Ptolemies, and saluted the brethren, and abode with them one day.

+/- May 19th. (Iyar- Ziv 19th.)

+/- (The 5th. Year of Paul ministry) **Paul comes to Caesarea**

(Acts 21:8-9)8:And the next day we that were of Paul's company departed, and came to Caesarea: and we entered into the house of Philip the evangelist, which was one of the seven; and abode with him. 9:And the same man had four daughters, virgins, which did prophesy.

+/- May 20th. (Iyar- Ziv 20th.)

The year +/- 1357 B.C. The Cloud was taken up from the Tabernacle

(Numbers 10:11-33) 11:And it came to pass on the twentieth day of the second month, in the second year, that the cloud was taken up from off the tabernacle of the testimony. 12;And the children of Israel took their journeys out of the wilderness of Sinai; and the cloud rested in the wilderness of Paran. 13:And they first took their journey according to the commandment of the Lord, by the hand of Moses. 14:In the first place went the standard of the camp of the children of Judah according to their armies: and over his host was Nahshon the son of Amminadab. 15:And over the host of the tribe of the children of Issachar was Nethaneel the son of Zuar. 16;And over the host of the tribe of the children of Zebulun was Eliab the son of Helon. 17:And the tabernacle was taken down; and the sons of Gershon and the sons of Merari set forward, bearing the tabernacle. 18;And the standard of the camp of Reuben set forward according to their armies: and over his host was Elizur the son of Shedeur. 19:And over the host of the tribe of the children of Simeon was Shelumiel the son of Zurishaddai. 20:And over the host of the tribe of the children of Gad was Eliasaph the son of Deuel. 21:And the Kohathites set forward, bearing the sanctuary: and the other did set up the tabernacle against they came. 22;And the standard of the camp of the children of Ephraim set forward according to their armies: and over his host was Elishama the son of Ammihud.

23:And over the host of the tribe of the children of Manasseh was Gamaliel the son of Pedahzur. 24:And over the host of the tribe of the children of Benjamin was Abidan the son of Gideoni. 25;And the standard of the camp of the children of Dan set forward, which was the reward of all the camps throughout their hosts: and over his host was Ahiezer the son of Ammishaddai. 26:And over the host of the tribe of the children of Asher was Pagiel the son of Ocran. 27:And over the host of the tribe of the children of Naphtali was Ahira the son of Enan. 28:This were the journey of the children of Israel according to their armies, when they set forward. 29:And Moses said to Jethro, the son of Raguel the Midianite, Moses' Father in law, We are journeying to the place of which the Lord said, I will give it you: come you with us, and we will do you good: for the Lord has spoken good concerning Israel. 30:And he said to him, I will not go; but I will depart to mine own land, and to my kindred. 31:And he said, Leave us not, I pray you; for as much as you know how we are to encamp in the wilderness, and you may be to us instead of eyes. 32:And it shall be, if you go with us, yes, it shall be, that what goodness the Lord shall do to us, the same will we do to you. 33:And they departed from the mount of the Lord a three day's journey: and the ark of the covenant of the Lord went before them for the three days' journey, to search out a resting place for them.

+/- May 23rd. (Iyar- Ziv 23rd.)

The year +/- 1357 B.C. The cloud of the Lord came on them.

(Numbers 10:34-36) 34:And the cloud of the Lord was upon them by day, when they went out of the camp. 35:And it came to pass, when the ark set forward, that Moses said, Rise up, Lord, and let thine enemies be scattered; and let them that hate you flee before you. 36:And when it rested, he said, Return, O Lord, to the many thousands of Israel.

+/- May 23rd. (Iyar- Ziv 23rd.)

The year +/- 135 B.C. A great enemy of Israel was destroyed

(1Maccabees 13:51-53) 51: On the twenty third day of the second month, in the year one hundred and seventy-one, the Hebrews entered the citadel with shouts on jubilation, waving of palm branches, the sound of harps and cymbals, lyres and the singing of hymns and canticles, because a great enemy of Israel had been destroyed. 52:Simon decreed that this day should be celebrated every year with rejoicing. He also strengthened the fortifications of the temple hill alongside the citadel, and he and his companions dwelt there. 53:Seeing that his son John was now a grown man, Simon made him commander of all his soldiers, with his residence in Gazara.

+/- May 25th. (Iyar- Ziv 25th.)

The Day that the Lord had set for destruction for Nineveh

(Jonah 3:4) 4:And Jonah began to enter into the city a day's journey, and he cried, and said; Yet in forty days, (the 25th.of Iyar) and Nineveh shall be overthrown.

+/- May 26th. (Iyar- Ziv 26th.)

+/- (The 5th. Year of Paul ministry) Agabus spoke with Paul,

(Acts 21:10-14)10:And as we stayed there many days, there came down from Judea a certain prophet, named Agabus. 11:And when he came to us, he took Paul's girdle, and bound his own hands and feet, and said, This says the Holy Ghost, So shall the Hebrews at Jerusalem bind the man, that owns this girdle, and shall deliver him to the hands of the Gentiles.

12:And when we heard these things, both we, and they of that place, begged him not to go up to Jerusalem. 13:Then Paul answered, What mean you to cry and break my heart? for I am ready not to be bound only, but also to die at Jerusalem for the name of the Lord Jesus.14:And when he would not be persuaded, we stopped, saying, The will of the Lord be done.

+/- May 28th. (Iyar- Ziv 28th.)

Samuel the prophet died

(1Samuel 28:3) 3:Now Samuel was dead, and all Israel had lamented him, and buried him in Ramah, even in his own city. And Saul had put away those that had familiar spirits, and the wizards, out of the land.

+/- May 28th. (Iyar- Ziv 28th.)

Between the years +/- 674-663 B.C. They destroyed all the alters.

(2Chronicles 31:1)1:Now when all this was finished, all that were present went out to the cities of Judah, and broke the images in pieces, and cut down the groves, and threw down the high places and the altars out of Judah and Benjamin, in Ephraim also and Manasseh, until they had utterly destroyed them all. Then all the children of Israel returned, every man to his possession, into their own cities.

+/- May 30th. (Iyar- Ziv 30th.)

+/- (The 5th. Year of Paul ministry) Paul and others went to Jerusalem

(Acts 21:15-17) 15:And after those days we took up our carriages, and went up to Jerusalem. 16:There went with us also certain of the disciples of Caesarea, and brought with them one Mason of Cyprus, an old disciple, with whom we should lodge. 17:And when we were come to Jerusalem, the brethren received us gladly.

+/- May 31st. (Sivan 1st.)

The year +/- 580 B.C.E. Ezekiel went and spoke to Pharaoh

(Ezekiel 31:1-18)1:And it came to pass in the twelfth year, in the twelfth month, in the first day of the month, that the word of the Lord came to me, saying; 2:Son of man, take up a lamentation for Pharaoh King of Egypt, and say to him; You are like a young lion of the nations, and you are as a whale in the seas: and you came forth with your rivers, and troubled the waters with your feet, and fouled their rivers. 3:This says the Lord God; I will therefore spread out my net over you with a company of many people; and they shall bring you up in my net. 4:Then will I leave you upon the land, I will cast you forth upon the open field, and will cause all the fowls of the heaven to remain upon you, and I will fill the beasts of the whole earth with you. 5:And I will lay your flesh upon the mountains, and fill the valleys with your height. 6:I will also water with your blood the land wherein you swim, even to the mountains; and the rivers shall be full of you. 7:And when I shall put you out, I will cover the heaven, and make the Stars dark; I will cover the Sun with a cloud, and the Moon shall not give her light. 8:All the bright lights of heaven will I make dark over you, and set darkness upon your land, says the Lord God. 9:I will also trouble the hearts of many people, when I shall bring your destruction among the nations, into the countries which you have not known. 10:Yes, I will make many people amazed at you, and their Kings shall be horribly afraid for you, when I shall brandish my sword before them; and they shall tremble at every moment, every man for his own life, in the day of your fall. 11:For this says the Lord God; The sword of the King of Babylon shall come upon you. 12:By the swords of the mighty will I cause your multitude to fall, the terrible of the nations, all of them: and they shall spoil the pomp of Egypt, and all the multitude thereof shall be destroyed. 13:I will destroy also all the beasts thereof from beside the great waters; neither shall the foot of man trouble them any more, nor the hoofs of beasts trouble them. 14:Then will I make their waters deep, and cause their rivers to run like oil, says the Lord God. 15:When I shall make the land of Egypt desolate, and the country shall be destitute of that whereof it was full, when I shall smite all them that dwell therein, then shall they know that I am the Lord. 16:This is the lamentation wherewith they shall lament her: the daughters of the nations shall lament her: they shall lament for her, even for Egypt, and for all her multitude, says the Lord God. 17: They also went down into hell with him to them that are slain with the sword; and they that were his arm, that dwelt under his shadow in the midst of the heathen. 18:To whom art you thus like in glory and in greatness among the trees of Eden? yet shall you be brought down with the trees of Eden unto the nether parts of the earth: you shall lie in the midst of the uncircumcised with them that are slain by the sword. This is Pharaoh and all his multitude, says the Lord GOD.

+/- May 31st. (Sivan 1st.)

+/- **(The 5th. Year of Paul ministry) Paul was asked about his teachings (Acts 21:18-25)** 18:And the day following Paul went in with us to James; and all the elders were present. 19:And when he had saluted them, he declared particularly what things God had wrought among the Gentiles by his ministry. 20:And when they heard it, they glorified the Lord, and said to him, You see, brother, how many thousands of Jews there are which believe; and they are all zealous of the law. 21:And they have been informed of you, that you teach all the Jews which are among the Gentiles to forsake Moses, saying that they ought not to circumcise their children, neither to walk after the customs. 22:What is this about? the multitude needs to come together: for they will hear that you have come. 23:Do therefore this that we say to you: We have four men which have a vow on them. 24:Them take, and purify thyself with them, and be at charges with them, that they may shave their heads: and all may know that those things, whereof they were informed concerning you, are nothing; but that you yourself also walks orderly, and keeps the law. 25:As touching the Gentiles which believe, we have written and concluded that they observe no such thing, save only that they keep themselves from things offered to idols, and from blood, and from strangled, and from fornication.

(It was also during this Month)(May- Iyar)

The year +/-1357 B.C. Then Moses struck the Rock,

(Numbers 20:1-22) 1:Then came the children of Israel, even the whole congregation, into the desert of Zin in the month after they left Egypt: and the people abode in Kadesh; and Miriam died there, and was buried there. 2:And there was no water for the congregation: and they gathered themselves together against Moses and against Aaron. 3:And the people held council against Moses, and spoke, saying, Would it not been better that we had died when our brethren before the Lord! 4:And why have you brought up the congregation of the Lord into this wilderness, that we and our cattle should die there? 5:And wherefore have you made us to come up out of Egypt, to bring us in to this evil place? it is no place of seed, or of figs, or of vines, or of pomegranates; neither is there any water to drink. 6:And Moses and Aaron went from the presence of the assembly to the door of the tabernacle of the congregation, and they fell upon their faces: and the glory of the Lord appeared to them. 7:And the Lord spoke to Moses, saying. 8:Take the rod, and gather you the assembly together, you, and Aaron your brother, and speak you to the rock before their eyes; and it shall give forth his water, and you shall bring forth to them water out of the rock: so you shall give the congregation and their beasts drink. 9:And Moses took the rod from before the Lord, as he commanded him. 10:And Moses and Aaron gathered the congregation together before the rock, and he said to them, Hear now, you rebels; must we fetch you water out of this rock? 11:And Moses lifted up his hand, and with his rod he struck the rock twice: and the water came out abundantly, and the congregation drank, and their beasts also. 12:And the Lord spoke to Moses and Aaron; Because you believed me not, to sanctify me in the eyes of the children of Israel, therefore you shall not bring this congregation into the land which I have given them. 13:This is the water of Meribah; because the children of Israel strove with the Lord, and he was sanctified in them. 14:And Moses sent messengers from Kadesh to the King of Edom. This says your brother Israel; you knowest all the travail that has befallen us. 15:How our fathers went down into Egypt, and we have dwelt in Egypt a long time; and the Egyptians vexed us, and our fathers. 16:And when we cried to the Lord, he heard our voice, and sent an angel, and has brought us forth out of Egypt: and, behold, we are in Kadesh, a city in the uttermost of your border: 17:Let us pass, I beg you, through your country: we will not pass through the fields, or through the vineyards, neither will we drink of the water of the wells: we will go by the King's high way, we will not turn to the right hand nor to the left, until we have passed your borders. 18:And Edom said to him, you shall not pass by me, lest I come out against you with the sword. 19:And the children of Israel said to him, We will go by the high way: and if I and my cattle drink of your water, then I will pay for it: I will only, without doing any thing else go through on my feet. 20:And he said, you shall not go through. And Edom came out against him with much people, and with a strong hand. 21:This Edom refused to give Israel passage through his border: wherefore Israel turned away from him. 22:And the children of Israel, even the whole congregation, journeyed from Kadesh, and came to mount Hor.

Believed to be the Rock that Moses struck

Left a picture of the rock. **Right a close up of the rock**

(May- Iyar)

The year +/- 514 B.C. The foundation of the Lords house was laid.
(Ezra 3:8-13) 8:Now in the second year of their coming to the house of God at Jerusalem, in the second month, began Zerubbabel the son of Shealtiel, and Jeshua the son of Jozadak, and the remnant of their brethren the priests and the Levites, and all they that were come out of the captivity to Jerusalem; and appointed the Levites, from twenty years old and upward, to set forward the work of the house of the Lord. 9:Then stood Jeshua with his sons and his brethren, Kadmiel and his sons, the sons of Judah, together, to set forward the workmen in the house of God: the sons of Henadad,with their sons and their brethren the Levites. 10:And when the builders laid the foundation of the temple of the Lord, they set the priests in their apparel with trumpets, and the Levites the sons of Asaph with cymbals, to praise the Lord, after the ordinance of David King of Israel. 11:And they sang together by course in praising and giving thanks to the Lord; because he is good, for his mercy endures for ever toward Israel. And all the people shouted with a great shout, when they praised the Lord, because the foundation of the house of the Lord was laid. 12:But many of the priests and Levites and chief of the fathers, who were ancient men, that had seen the first house, when the foundation of this house was laid before their eyes, wept with a loud voice; and many shouted aloud for joy: 13:So that the people could not discern the noise of the shout of joy from the noise of the weeping of the people: for the people shouted with a loud shout, and the noise was heard afar off.

Alcimus ordered the destruction of the work of the prophets, then died

(1 Maccabees 9:54-57) 54:In the year one hundred and fifty-three, in the second month, Alcimus ordered the wall on the inner court of the sanctuary to be torn down, This destroying the work of the prophets. But he only began to tear it down.55:Just at that time he had a stroke, and his work was interrupted: his month was closed and he was paralyzed, so that he could no longer utter a word to give orders concerning his house. 56:Finely he died in great agony. 57:Seeing that Alcimus was dead, Bacchides returned to the King, and the land of Judah was quite for two years.

The year +/- 544 B.C.

Daniel killed one of the Babylonians gods

(Daniel 14:1-41) 1:After King Astyages died he was laid with his fathers, Cyrus the Persian succeeded to his kingdom. 2:Daniel was the Kings favorite and was held in higher esteem than any of the friends of the King. 3:The Babylonians had an Idol called Bel, and everyday they provided for it six barrels of fine flour, forty sheep, and six measures of wine. 4:The King worshiped it and went every day to adore it; but Daniel adored only his God. 5:When the King asked him, "Why do you not adore Bel?" Daniel replied; "Because I worship not idols made with hands, but only the living God who made Heaven and Earth and has dominion over all mankind." 6:Then the King continued, "You do not think that Bel is living god?" Do you not see how much he eats and drinks every day? 7:Daniel began to laugh. "Do not be deceived, O King," he said; it is only clay on the inside and bronze on the out side; it has never taken any food or drink."

8:Enraged, the King called his priest and said to them, “Unless you tell me who it is
that consumes these provisions, you shall be put to death.” 9:But if you can show
that Bel consumes them, Daniel shall die for blaspheming Bel. Daniel said to the
King, “Let it be as you say!” 10:There were seventy priest of Bel, besides their
wives and children. When the King went with Daniel into the temple of Bel. 11:The
priest of Bel said;“See, we are going to leave. Do you, O King, set out the food and
prepare the wine; then shut the door and seal it with your ring. 12;If you do not find
that bel has eaten it all when you return in the morning, we are to die; otherwise
Daniel shall die for his lies against us.” 13:They were not worried, because under
the table they had made a secret entrance through which they always, came in to
consume the food. 14:After they departed the King set the food before Bel, while
Daniel ordered his servants to bring some ashes, which they scattered through the
whole temple, the King alone was present. Then they went outside, sealed the
closed door with the kings ring, and departed.

15:The priest entered that night as usual, with their wives and children, and they ate
and drank everything. 16:Early the next morning, the King came with Daniel.
17:“Are the seals unbroken, Daniel?” he asked And Daniel answered, “They are
unbroken, O King” 18:As soon as he had opened the door, the King looked at the
table and cried out aloud; “Great you are , O Bel; there is no trickery in you” 19:But
Daniel laughed and kept the King from entering. “Look at the floor” he said;
“Whose footprints are these?” 20;I see footprints of men, women and children!”
said the King. 21:The angry King arrested the priest, their wives and their children.
They showed him the secret door by which they used to enter to consume what was
on the table. 22:He put them to death, and handed Bel over to Daniel, who
destroyed it and its temple. 23:Then they went to Babylon, where there was a great
dragon which the Babylonians worshiped. 24:“Look !” said the King to Daniel, you
cannot deny that this is a living god, so adore it.”

25:But Daniel answered “I adore the Lord, my God, for he is the living God.
26:Give me permission, O King and I will kill this dragon with out a sword or a
club.” I give you permission the King said. 27:Then Daniel took some pitch, fat, and
hair; these he boiled together and made into cakes. He put them into the mouth of
the dragon, and when the dragon ate them, he burst asunder. This he said is what
you worshiped. 28:When the Babylonians heard this, they were angry and turned
against the King. “The King has become a Hebrew” They said he has destroyed Bel,
killed the dragon, and put the priest to death. 29:They went to the King and
demanded “Hand David over to us” or we will kill you and your family.” 30:When
he saw himself threatened with violence, the King was forced to hand Daniel over
to them. 31:They threw Daniel into a lions den where he remained six days.

32:In the den were seven Loins and two carcasses, and two sheep had been given to
them daily. But now they were giving nothing, so that they would devour Daniel.
33:In Judea there was a prophet, Habakkuk; he mixed some bread in a bowl with the
stew he had boiled, and was going to bring it to the reapers of the field, 34:when an
Angel of the Lord told him, “Take the lunch you have to Daniel who is in the lion's
den at Babylon.” 35:But Habakkuk answered saying; Babylon, sir I have never
seen, and I do not know the den!

36:The Angel of the Lord seized him by crown of his head, and carried him by the hair; with the speed of the wind, he set him down in Babylon above the den. 37:"Daniel, Daniel,"cried Haabakkuk, "take the lunch God has sent you." 38:"You have remembered me, O God" said Daniel; "You have have not forsaken those who love you." 39:While Daniel began to eat the Angel of the Lord at once brought Habakkuk back to his own place. 40;On the seventh day the King came to morn for Daniel, as he came to the den and looked in there was Daniel sitting there. 41:The King cried aloud, "You are great, O Lord, the God of Daniel, and there is no other besides you!" Then Daniel he took out of the Lions den, but those who tried to destroy him he had thrown into the den, and they were devoured in a moment before his eyes.

King David numbered the men of Israel:

(1Chroncles 21:1-14)1:And Satan stood up against Israel, and provoked David to number Israel. 2:And David said to Joab and to the rulers of the people, Go, number Israel from Beersheba even to Dan; and bring the number of them to me, that I may know it. 3:And Joab answered, The Lord make his people an hundred times so many more as they be, but, my lord the King, are they not all my lord's servants? why then doth my lord require this thing? why will he be a cause of trespass to Israel? 4:Nevertheless the King's word prevailed against Joab. Wherefore Joab departed, and went throughout all Israel, and came to Jerusalem. 5:And Joab gave the sum of the number of the people to David. And all they of Israel were a thousand thousand and an hundred thousand men that drew sword: and Judah was four hundred threescore and ten thousand men that drew sword. 6:But Levi and Benjamin counted he not among them: for the King's word was abominable to Joab.7:And God was displeased with this thing; therefore he struck Israel. 8:And David said to God, I have sinned greatly, because I have done this thing: but now, I ask you, do away the iniquity of your servant; for I have done very foolishly. 9:And the Lord spoke to Gad, David's seer, saying, 10:Go and tell David, saying, This says the Lord, I offer you three things, choose you one of them, that I may do it to you. 11:So Gad came to David, and said to him, This says the Lord, Choose you. 12:Either three years' famine; or three months to be destroyed before your foes, while that the sword of thine enemies overtake you, or else three days the sword of the Lord, even the pestilence, in the land, and the Angel of the Lord destroying throughout all the coasts of Israel. Now therefore advise yourself what word I shall bring again to him that sent me. 13:And David said to Gad, I am in a great strait: let me fall now into the hand of the Lord; for very great are his mercies: but let me not fall into the hand of man. 14;So the Lord sent pestilence upon Israel: and there fell of Israel seventy thousand men.

(It was also during the 3rd. week of this Month)

Samson slew a thousand men with the jawbone of a ass

(Judges 15:11-20) 11:Then three thousand men of Judah went to the top of the rock Etam, and said to Samson, do you not know that the Philistines are rulers over us? What is this that you have done to us? And he said to them, As they did to me, so have I done to them. 12:And they said to him, We are come down to bind you, that we may deliver you into the hand of the Philistines. And Samson said to them,

Swear to me, that you will not fall upon me yourselves. 13:And they spoke to him, saying, No; but we will bind you first, and deliver you to their hand: but surely we will not kill you. And they bound him with two new cords, and brought him up from the rock. 14:And when he came to Lehi, the Philistines shouted against him: and the Spirit of the Lord came mightily upon him, and the cords that were upon his arms became as flax that was burnt with fire, and his bands loosed from off his hands.

15:And he found a jawbone of an ass, and put forth his hand, and took it, and killed a thousand men with it. 16:And Samson said, With the jawbone of an ass, heaps upon heaps, with the jaw of an ass have I slain a thousand men.17:And it came to pass, when he had made an end of speaking, that he cast away the jawbone out of his hand, and called that place Ramath-lehi. 18:And he was sore athirst, and called on the Lord, and said, you hast given this great deliverance into the hand of your servant: and now shall I die for thirst, and fall into the hand of the uncircumcised?

19:But God carved an hollow place that was in the jaw, and there came water from it; and when he had drank, his spirit came again, and he revived: wherefore he called the name thereof En-hakkore, which is in Lehi to this day. 20:And he judged Israel in the days of the Philistines twenty years.

The picture is of Samson's tomb, where he and his Father are buried. Samson who's name means (Man of the Sun).

Chapter 6: June - Sivan

In Hebrew this month is called: Sivan,
which means:(Bright); it is the 3rd. Month
Tribe of Ruben, means:(Look a son)
The stone of (Emerald Jade) represents this tribe.
Ruben:(The 1st.) Son of Leah.
(Was believed to have been born in this month.)
(Spirit of Understanding)

+/- June 1st. (Sivan 2nd.)

Paul with four others went in to purify themselves

(Acts 21:26) 26:Then Paul took the men, and the next day purifying himself with them entered into the temple, to signify the accomplishment of the days of purification, until that an offering should be offered for every one of them.

+/- June 2rd. (Sivan 3th.)

David went to Ornan to buy his threshing floor

(1Chronicles 21:15-25) 15:And God sent an Angel to Jerusalem to destroy it: and as he was destroying, the Lord beheld, and he stopped him of the evil, and said to the Angel that destroyed, It is enough, stay now your hand. And the Angel of the Lord stood by the threshing floor of Ornan the Jebusite. 16:And David lifted up his eyes, and saw the Angel of the Lord stand between the earth and the heaven, having a drawn sword in his hand stretched out over Jerusalem. Then David and the elders of Israel, who were clothed in sackcloth, fell upon their faces. 17:And David said to God, is it not I that commanded the people to be numbered? Even I it is that have sinned and done evil indeed; but as for these sheep, what have they done? let your hand, I pray your, O Lord my God, be on me, and on my father's house; but not on your people, that they should be plagued. 18:Then the Angel of the Lord commanded Gad, to say to David, that David should go up, and set up an altar to the Lord in the threshing floor of Ornan the Jebusite. 19:And David went up at the saying of Gad, which he spoke in the name of the Lord. 20:And Ornan turned back, and saw the Angel; and his four sons with him hid themselves.

Now Ornan was threshing wheat. 21:And as David came to Ornan, Ornan looked and saw David, and went out of the threshing floor, and bowed himself to David with his face to the ground. 22:Then David said to Ornan, Grant me the place of this threshing floor, that I may build an altar therein to the Lord: your shall grant it me for the full price: that the plague may be stayed from the people. 23:And Ornan said to David, Take it to your, and let my lord the King do that which is good in his eyes: lo, I give your the oxen also for burnt offerings, and the threshing instruments for wood, and the wheat for the meat offering; I give it all. 24:And King David said to Ornan, Nay; but I will verily buy it for the full price: for I will not take that which is your for the Lord, nor offer burnt offerings without cost. 25:So David gave to Ornan for the place six hundred shekels of gold by weight.

+/- June 3rd. (Sivan 4th.)

The year +/- 1437 B.C. The Pharaoh's daughter found a Hebrew child in the River

(Exodus 2:3-10) 3:And when she could not longer hide him, she made for him an ark of bulrushes, and daubed it with slime and with pitch, and put the child therein; and she laid it in the flags by the river's brink. 4:And his sister stood afar off, to wit what would be done to him. 5:And the daughter of Pharaoh came down to wash herself at the river; and her maidens walked along by the river's side; and when she saw the ark among the flags, she sent her maid to fetch it. 6:And when she had opened it, she saw the child: and, behold, the babe wept. And she had compassion on him, and said, This is one of the Hebrews' children. 7:Then said his sister to the Pharaoh's daughter, Shall I go and call to your a nurse of the Hebrew women, that she may nurse the child for your? 8:And the Pharaoh's daughter said to her, Go. And the maid went and called the child's mother. 9:And Pharaoh's daughter said to her, Take this child away, and nurse it for me, and I will give your your wages. And the woman took the child, and nursed it. 10:And the child grew, and she brought him to Pharaoh's daughter, and he became her son. And she called his name Moses: and she said, Because I drew him out of the water.

+/- June 4th. (Sivan 5th.)

Satan spoke with God about Job

(Job 2:1-13) 1:Again there was a day when the sons of God came to present themselves before the Lord, and Satan came also among them to present himself before the Lord. 2:And the Lord said to Satan, where have you come from? And Satan answered the Lord, and said, From going to and fro in the earth, and from walking up and down in it. 3:And the Lord said to Satan, Have you considered my servant Job, that there is none like him in the earth, a perfect and an upright man, one that fears God, and hates evil? and still he holds fast his integrity, although you moved me against him, to destroy him without cause. 4:And Satan answered the Lord, and said, Skin for skin, yes, all that a man has will he give for his life. 5:But put forth your hand now, and touch his bone and his flesh, and he will curse your to your face. 6:And the Lord said to Satan, Behold, he is in your hand; but save his life. 7:So went Satan forth from the presence of the Lord, and smote Job with sore boils from the sole of his foot to his crown.

8:And he took him a potsherd to scrape himself withal; and he sat down among the ashes. 9:Then said his wife to him, Dost your still retain your integrity? Curse God, and die. 10:But he said to her, you speaks as one of the foolish women speaks. What? shall we receive good at the hand of God, and shall we not receive evil? In all this did not Job sin with his lips. 11:Now when Job's three friends heard of all this evil that was come upon him, they came every one from his own place; Eliphaz the Temanite, and Bildad the Shuhite, and Zophar the Naamathite, for they had made an appointment together to come to mourn with him and to comfort him. 12:And when they lifted up their eyes afar off, and knew him not, they lifted up their voice, and wept; and they rent every one his mantle, and sprinkled dust upon their heads toward heaven. 13:So they sat down with him upon the ground seven days and seven nights, and none spoke a word to him: for they saw that his grief was very great.

+/- June 4th. (Sivan)

Note:In the first part of this month is the Feast of Weeks

The feast of weeks is always 50 days after the first Sabbath -(Saturday), after the 14th. of Nissan (April). It can be as soon as the 4th. Or as late as the 11th. Of this month. It is the second time Men are to present them self's before God. It was on the +/-4th.of June, a Sunday the first day of this Feast of weeks, when it is written that: Jesus was received up in to the clouds.

+/- June 4th. (Sivan 5th.)

Jesus ascended in to heaven

(Acts 1:6-12) 6:When they therefore were come together, they asked of him, saying, Lord, will your at this time restore again the kingdom to Israel? 7:And he said to them, It is not for you to know the times or the seasons, which the Father has put in his own power. 8:But your shall receive power, after that the Holy Ghost is come upon you: and your shall be witnesses to me both in Jerusalem, and in all Judea, and in Samaria, and to the uttermost part of the earth. 9:And when he had spoken these things, while they beheld, he was taken up; and a cloud received him out of their sight. 10:And while they looked steadfastly toward heaven as he went up, behold, two men stood by them in white apparel. 11:Which also said, your men of Galilee, why stand your gazing up into heaven? this same Jesus, which is taken up from you into heaven, shall so come in like manner as you have seen him go into heaven. 12:Then returned they to Jerusalem from the mount called Olive, which is from Jerusalem a sabbath day's journey.

+/- June 5th. (Sivan 6th.)

Saul became King over Israel

(1Samuel 12:1-25) 1:And Samuel said to all Israel, Behold, I have hearkened to your voice in all that your said to me, and have made a King over you. 2:And now, behold, the King walks before you: and I am old and gray headed; and, behold, my sons are with you: and I have walked before you from my childhood to this day. 3:Behold, here I am witness; against me before the Lord, and before his anointed: whose ox have I taken? or whose ass have I taken? or whom have I defrauded? whom have I oppressed? or of whose hand have I received any bribe to blind mine eyes therewith? and I will restore it you. 4:And they said, your have not defrauded us, nor oppressed us, neither have your taken ought of any man's hand. 5:And he said to them, The Lord is witness against you, and his anointed is witness this day, that your have not found ought in my hand. And they answered, He is witness. 6:And Samuel said to the people, It is the Lord that advanced Moses and Aaron, and that brought your fathers up out of the land of Egypt. 7:Now therefore stand still, that I may reason with you before the Lord of all the righteous acts of the Lord, which he did to you and to your fathers. 8:When Jacob was come into Egypt, and your fathers cried to the Lord, then the Lord sent Moses and Aaron, which brought forth your fathers out of Egypt, and made them dwell in this place. 9:And when they forgot the Lord their God, he sold them into the hand of Sierra, captain of the host of Hazer, and into the hand of the Philistines, and into the hand of the king of Moab, and they fought against them.

10:And they cried to the Lord, and said, We have sinned, because we have forsaken the Lord, and have served Baalim and Ashtaroth: but now deliver us out of the hand of our enemies, and we will serve your. 11:And the Lord sent Jerubbaal, and Bedan, and Jephthah, and Samuel, and delivered you out of the hand of your enemies on every side, and your dwelled safe. 12:And when your saw that Nahash the King of the children of Ammon came against you, your said to me, Nay; but a King shall reign over us: when the Lord your God was your King. 13:Now therefore behold the King whom your have chosen, and whom your have desired! and, behold, the Lord has set a King over you. 14:If your will fear the Lord, and serve him, and obey his voice, and not rebel against the commandment of the Lord, then shall both your and also the King that reigns over you continue following the Lord your God. 15:But if your will not obey the voice of the Lord, but rebel against the commandment of the Lord, then shall the hand of the Lord be against you, as it was against your fathers. 16:Now therefore stand and see this great thing, which the Lord will do before your eyes.

17:Is it not wheat harvest today? I will call to the Lord, and he shall send thunder and rain; that your may perceive and see that your wickedness is great, which your have done in the sight of the Lord, in asking you a King. 18:So Samuel called to the Lord; and the Lord sent thunder and rain that day: and all the people greatly feared the Lord and Samuel. 19:And all the people said to Samuel, Pray for your servants to the Lord your God, that we die not: for we have added to all our sins this evil, to ask us a King. 20:And Samuel said to the people, Fear not, your have done all this wickedness: yet turn not aside from following the Lord, but serve the Lord with all your heart. 21:And turn your not aside: for then should you go after vain things, which cannot profit nor deliver; for they are vain. 22:For the Lord will not forsake his people for his great name's sake: because it has pleased the Lord to make you his people. 23:Moreover as for me, God forbid that I should sin against the Lord in ceasing to pray for you: but I will teach you the good and the right way. 24:Only fear the Lord, and serve him in truth with all your heart: for consider how great things he has done for you. 25;But if your shall still do wickedly, your shall be consumed, both you and your King.

+/- June 5th. (Sivan 6th.)

The prophecy of Amos was fulfilled

(Tobit 2:1-6) 1:This under King Esarhaddon I returned to my home, and my wife Anna and my son Tobit were restored to me. Then on the festival of Pentecost, the feast of weeks, a fine dinner was prepared for me, and I reclined to eat. 2:The table was set for me, and when many different dishes were placed before me, I said to my son Tobiah; My son, go out and try to find a poor man, from among our kinsmen exiled here in Nineveh. If he is a sincere worshiper of God, bring him back with you, so he can share this meal with me. Indeed son I will wait for you to come back. 3:Tobiah went to look for some poor kinsmen of ours. When he returned he said; "Father!" I said to him what is it son? He answered father one of our kinsmen have been murdered! His body lies in the market place, where he was just strangled! 4:I sprang to my feet, leaving the dinner untouched; and I carried the dead body from the street and put him in one of the rooms, so that I might bury him after sunset. 5:Returning to my own quarters, I washed and ate my food in sorrow. 6:I was reminded of the oracle pronounced by the prophet Amos against Bethel;""Your festivals shall be returned into mourning, and all you songs into lamentations".

"(Amos 8:10;And I will turn your feasts into mourning, and all your songs into lamentation; and I will bring up sackcloth upon all loins, and baldness upon every head; and I will make it as the mourning, of an only son, and the end thereof as a bitter day.)"

+/- June 6th. (Sivan 7th.)

Ruth worked the fields of Boaz

(Ruth 2:1-23)1:Naomi had a prominent kinsmen named Boaz, of the clan of her husband Elimelech. 2:Ruth the Moabite said to Naomi," let me go and glean ears of grain in the field of anyone who will allow me the favor." Naomi said ti her, "go my daughter" 3:and she went. The field she entered to glean after the harvesters happened to be the section belonging to Boaz of the clan of Elimelech. 4:Boaz him self came from Bethlehem and said to the harvesters; "The Lord be with you," and they replayed, The Lord bless you. 5:Boaz asked the overseer of his harvesters; "Who's girl is this?" 6:The overseer of the harvesters answered , "She is the Moabite girl who returned from the plateau of Moab with Naomi. 7:She asked for permission to gather the gleaning into sheaves after the harvesters; and ever since she came this morning she has remained here until now, with scarcely a moment's rest." 8:Boaz said to Ruth: "Listen my daughter! Do not glean anyone else's field; you are not to leave here. Stay here with my women servants. 9:Watch to see what field is to be harvested, and fallow them; I have commanded the young men to do you no harm. When you are thirsty, you can drink from the vessels the young men have filled." 10;Casting her self prostate upon the ground, she said to him;"Why should I , a foreigner, be favored with your notice?" 11:Boaz answered her ; "I have had a complete account of what you have done for your mother-in-law after your husbands death; you have left your father and your mother and the land of your birth, have come to a people you did not know previously. 12:May the Lord reward what you have done! May you receive a full reward from the Lord, the God of Israel, under whose wings you have come for refuge." 13:May I prove worthy of your kindness, my lord; you have comforted me, your servant, wit your consoling words, would indeed if I were a servant of yours! 14:At meal time Boaz said to her , "Come here and have some food; dip your bread in the sauce." Then as she sat near the reapers, he handed her some roasted grain and she ate her fill and had some left over. 15:She rose to glean, and Boaz instructed his servants to let her glean among the sheaves themselves without scolding her, 16:and even to drop some handfuls leave her to glean with out being told to stop. 17:She gleaned in the field until evening, and when she beat out what she had gleaned, it came to about an ephah of barley. 18:Which she took into the city and showed to her mother-in-law. Next she brought out,what she had left over from lunch. 19:So her mother-in-law asked her, "Where did you gleaned today? Where did you go to work? May he who took notice of you be blessed!"Then she told her mother-in-law whom she had worked, "The man whose place I worked today is named Boaz," she said. 20:"May he be blessed by the Lord who is ever merciful to the living and to the dead."Naomi explained to her daughter-in-law, " He is related to us, one of our next of kin. 21:"He even told me." said Ruth; that "I should stay with his servants until they complete his entire harvest." you would do well, my dear. 22:Naomi said, it will be good for you, to go out with his servants; for in someone else's field you might be insulted." 23;So she stayed gleaning with the servants of Boaz, until the end of the barley and wheat harvests.

+/- June 6th. (Sivan 7th.)

Tobit went out and buried a murdered man

(Tobit 2:7-10) 7:And I wept. Then at sunset I went out, dug a grave, and buried him. 8:The neighbors mocked me, saying to one another: "Will this man never learn! Once before he was hunted down for execution because of this very thing; yet now that he has escaped here he is again burying the dead." 9:That same night I bathed and went to sleep next to the wall of my courtyard. Because of the heat, I left my face uncovered. 10:I did not know that were birds perched on the wall above me, till their warm droppings settled in my eyes causing cataracts.

+/-June 7th. (Sivan 8th.)

Adrammelech was killed

(2 Kings 19:37) 37;And it came to pass, as he was worshiping in the house of Nisroch his god, that Adrammelech and Sharezer his sons smote him with the sword: and they escaped into the land of Armenia. And Esar-haddon his son reigned in his stead.

+/- June 8th. (Sivan 9th.)

Paul teaching in the Temple

(Acts 21:27-22:29) 27;And when the seven days were almost ended, the Jews which were of Asia, when they saw him in the temple, stirred up all the people, and laid hands on him. 28:Crying out, Men of Israel, help: This is the man, that teaches all men every where against the people, and the law, and this place:

and further brought Greeks also into the temple, and has polluted this holy place. 29:(For they had seen before with him in the city Trophimus an Ephesian, whom they supposed that Paul had brought into the temple.) 30:And all the city was moved, and the people ran together: and they took Paul, and drew him out of the temple: and forthwith the doors were shut. 31:And as they went about to kill him, tidings came to the chief captain of the band, that all Jerusalem was in an uproar. 32:Who immediately took soldiers and centurions, and ran down to them: and when they saw the chief captain and the soldiers, they stopped the beating of Paul. 33:Then the chief captain came near, and took him, and commanded him to be bound with two chains; and demanded who he was, and what he had done. 34:And some cried one thing, some another, among the multitude: and when he could not know the certainty for the tumult, he commanded him to be carried to the castle. 35:And when he came upon the stairs, so it was, that he was borne of the soldiers for the violence of the people. 36;For the multitude of the people followed after, crying, Away with him. 37;And as Paul was to be led into the castle, he said to the chief captain, May I speak to you? Who said, Can you speak Greek? 38;are not you that Egyptian, which before these days made an uproar, and led out into the wilderness four thousand men that were murderers? 39:But Paul said, I am a man who is a Jew of Tarsus, a city in Cilia, a citizen of no mean city: and, I ask you, let me to speak to the people. 40;And when he had given him license, Paul stood on the stairs, and beckoned with the hand to the people. And when there was made a great silence, he spoke to them in the Hebrew tongue, saying,

22:1: Men, brethren, and fathers, hear your my defense which I make now to you. 2:(And when they heard that he spoke in the Hebrew tongue to them, they kept the more silence: and he says,) 3:I am verily a man which am a Jew, born in Tarsus, a city in Cilia, yet brought up in this city at the feet of Gamaliel, and taught according to the perfect manner of the law of the fathers, and was zealous toward God, as you all are this day. 4:And I persecuted this way to the death, binding and delivering into prisons both men and women. 5:As also the high priest do bear me witness, and all the estate of the elders: from whom also I received letters to the brethren, and went to Damascus, to bring them which were there bound to Jerusalem, for to be punished. 6:And it came to pass, that, as I made my journey, and was come near to Damascus about noon, suddenly there shone from heaven a great light round about me. 7:And I fell to the ground, and heard a voice saying to me, Saul, Saul, why are you persecuting me? 8;And I answered, Who are you, Lord? And he said to me, I am Jesus of Nazareth, the one whom you persecute. 9;And they that were with me saw indeed the light, and were afraid; but they heard not the voice of him that spoke to me. 10:And I said, What shall I do, Lord? And the Lord said to me, Arise, and go into Damascus; and there it shall be told you of all things which are appointed for you to do. 11:And when I could not see for the glory of that light, being led by the hand of them that were with me, I came into Damascus. 12:And one Ananias, a devout man according to the law, having a good report of all the Jews which lived there. 13:Came to me, and stood, and said to me, Brother Saul, receive your sight. And the same hour I looked up upon him. 14;And he said, The God of our fathers has chosen you, that you should know his will, and see that Just One, and should hear the voice of his mouth. 15:For you shall be his witness to all men of what you have seen and heard. 16:And now why do you stay? arise, and be baptized, and wash away your sins, calling on the name of the Lord. 17;And it came to pass, that, when I was come again to Jerusalem, even while I prayed in the temple, I was in a trance. 18;And saw him saying to me, Make haste, and get your quickly out of Jerusalem: for they will not receive your testimony concerning me. 19:And I said, Lord, they know that I imprisoned and beat in every synagogue them that believed on your. 20:And when the blood of your martyr Stephen was shed, I also was standing by, and consenting to his death, and kept the raiment of them that slew him. 21;And he said to me, Depart: for I will send you far hence to the Gentiles. 22:And they gave him audience to this word, and them lifted up their voices, and said, Away with such a fellow from the earth: for it is not fit that he should live.

23:And as they cried out, and cast off their clothes, and threw dust into the air. 24:The chief captain commanded him to be brought into the castle, and bade that he should be examined by scourging; that he might know wherefore they cried so against him. 25:And as they bound him with thongs, Paul said to the centurion that stood by, Is it lawful for you to scourge a man that is a Roman, and not condemned? 26:When the centurion heard that, he went and told the chief captain, saying, Take heed what you do: for this man is a Roman. 27:Then the chief captain came, and said to him, Tell me, are your a Roman? He said, yes. 28:And the chief captain answered, With a great sum obtained I this freedom. And Paul said, But I was free born. 29:Then straightway they departed from him which should have examined him: and the chief captain also was afraid, after he knew that he was a Roman, and because he had bound him.

+/- June 9th. (Sivan 10th.)

The year +/- 581 B.C. They sent silver to Jerusalem

(Baruch 1:5-14) 5:After the wept and had fasted and prayed before the Lord, 6:and collected such funds as each could furnish. 7:these they sent to Jerusalem, to Jehoiakim, son of Hilkiah, son of Shallum, the priests, and all the who people who were with him in Jerusalem. 8:(This is when he received the vessels of the house of the Lord that had been removed from the temple, to restore them to the house of Judah, on the tenth of Sivan. These silver vessels Zedekiah, son of Josiah, King of Judah had made. 9:After Nebuchadnezzar, King of Babylon carried off Jeconiah, and the princes, the skilled workers, the nobles, and most of the people from the land of Jerusalem, as captives, and brought them to Babylon.

10:Their message was, we send you funds with which you are to procure holocausts, (Burnt Offerings), sin offerings, and frankincense, and to prepare cereal offerings. Offer these on the alter of the Lord our God. 11:Pray for the life of Nebuchadnezzar, King of Babylon, and Belshazzar, his son, that their lifetimes may equal the duration of the heavens above the earth. 12:That the lord may give us strength, and light to our eyes, that we may live under the protective shadow on Nebuchadnezzar, King of Babylon and that of Belshazzar his son, and serve them long, finding favor in their sight. 13:Pray for us also to the Lord our God, for we have have sinned against the Lord God, and his anger and wrath has not stopped, or withdrawn from us to this present day. 14:And read out publicly this scroll which we have sent you in the house of the Lord, on the feast day and during the assembly.

+/- June 9th. (Sivan 10th.)

+/- **(The 5th. Year of Paul ministry) The high Priest had Paul struck**

(Acts 22:30-23:11) 30:On the next day, because he would have known the certainty wherefore he was accused of the Jews, he loosed him from his bands, and commanded the chief priests and all their council to appear, and brought Paul down, and set him before them.

23:1: And Paul, earnestly beholding the council, said, Men and brethren, I have lived in all good conscience before God until this day. 2:And the high priest Ananias commanded them that stood by him to strike him on the mouth. Then said Paul to him, God shall strike you, you whited wall, for sitting there you to judge me after the law, and command me to be struck contrary to the law? 4:And they that stood by and said, will you revile God's high priest?

5:Then said Paul, I will not, brethren, that he was the high priest: for it is written, your shall not speak evil of the ruler of your people. 6:But when Paul perceived that the one part were Sadducees, and the other Pharisees, he cried out in the council, Men and brethren, I am a Pharisee, the son of a Pharisee: of the hope and resurrection of the dead I am called in question. 7:And when he had so said, there arose a dissension between the Pharisees and the Sadducees: and the multitude was divided. 8:For the Sadducees say that there is no resurrection, neither angel, nor spirit: but the Pharisees confess both. 9:And there arose a great cry: and the scribes that were of the Pharisees' part arose, and strove, saying, We find no evil in this man: but if a spirit or an angel has spoken to him, let us not fight against God.

10:And when there arose a great dissension, the chief captain, fearing lest Paul should have been pulled in pieces of them, commanded the soldiers to go down, and to take him by force from among them, and to bring him into the castle. 11:And the night following the Lord stood beside him, and said: Be of good cheer, Paul: for as you have testified of me in Jerusalem, so must you bear witness also at Rome.

+/- June 9th. (Sivan 10th.)

Jesus seated at the right hand of God

(Revelations 12:1-5) 1:And there appeared a great wonder in heaven; a woman clothed with the sun, and the moon under her feet, and upon her head a crown of twelve stars. 2:And she being with child cried, travailing in birth, and pained to be delivered. 3:And there appeared another wonder in heaven; and behold a great red dragon, having seven heads and ten horns, and seven crowns upon his heads. 4:And his tail drew the third part of the stars of heaven, and did cast them to the earth: and the dragon stood before the woman which was ready to be delivered, for to devour her child as soon as it was born. 5:And she brought forth a man child, who was to rule all nations with a rod of iron and her child was caught up to God, and to his throne.

(As it is written in Psalms 110:1)

(Psalm 110:1) 1:The Lord said to my Lord, Sit you at my right hand, until I make your enemies your footstool.

(As it is written in Matthew 26:64)

(Matthew 26:64) 64;Jesus said to him, you have said: nevertheless I say to you, Hereafter shall you see the Son of man sitting on the right hand of power, and coming in the clouds of heaven.

(As it is written in Mark 14:62)

(Mark 14:62) 62: And Jesus said, I am: and your shall see the Son of man sitting on the right hand of power, and coming in the clouds of heaven.

(As it is written in Luke 22:69)

(Luke 22:69) 69: Hereafter shall the Son of man sit on the right hand of the power of God.

(The Day of Pentecost)

The day of Pentecost Is the second time men are to present them self's before God. It comes at the end of the feast of weeks. A seven day celebration of the harvest. As it is written in: **(Leviticus 23:15-16)** 15:And you shall count for your self's from the day after the sabbath, from the day that you brought the sheaf of the wave offering; seven sabbaths shall be complete: 16:Even to the day after the seventh sabbath shall you number fifty days; and you shall offer a new meat offering to the LORD. Note: You, your children, your menservants, and maidservants, your neighbor, strangers, and Levite are to celebrate with you. It is a celebration that is on the last day of the feast of weeks, (Called feast of Pentecost in Grease). You are to eat all the food and drink all the wine your heart desires. So after the last day you will know the fear of the Lord God.

+/- June 10th. (Sivan 11th.)

The Day God Spoke to Job

(Job 3:1-42:17) 1:After this opened Job his mouth, and cursed his day. 2:And Job spoke, and said; 3:Let the day perish wherein I was born, and the night in which it was said, There is a man child conceived. 4:Let that day be darkness; let not God regard it from above, neither let the light shine upon it. 5:Let darkness and the shadow of death stain it; let a cloud dwell upon it; let the blackness of the day terrify it. 6:As for that night, let darkness seize upon it; let it not be joined to the days of the year, let it not come into the number of the months. 7:Look, let that night be solitary, let no joyful voice come therein. 8:Let them curse it that curse the day, who are ready to raise up their mourning. 9:Let the stars of the twilight thereof be dark; let it look for light, but have none; neither let it see the dawning of the day. 10:Because it shut not up the doors of my mother's womb, nor hid sorrow from mine eyes. 11:Why died I not from the womb? why did I not give up the ghost when I came out of the belly? 12:Why did the knees prevent me? or why the breasts that I should suck? 13:For now should I have lain still and been quiet, I should have slept: then had I been at rest. 14:With Kings and counselors of the earth, which built desolate places for themselves, 15:or with princes that had gold, who filled their houses with silver. 16:Or as an hidden untimely birth I had not been, as infants which never saw light. 17:There the wicked cease from troubling; and there the weary be at rest. 18:There the prisoners rest together; they hear not the voice of the oppressor. 19:The small and great are there; and the servant is free from his master. 20:Wherefore is light given to him that is in misery, and life to the bitter in soul. 21:Which long for death, but it does not come; and dig for it more than for hid treasures; 22:Which rejoice exceedingly, and are glad, when they can find the grave? 23:Why is light given to a man whose way is hid, and whom God has hedged in? 24:For my sighing comes before I eat, and my roaring's are poured out like the waters. 25:For the thing which I greatly feared is come upon me, and that which I was afraid of is come to me. 26:I was not in safety, neither had I rest, neither was I quiet; yet trouble came.

4:1;Then Eliphaz the Temanite answered and said: 2:If we assay to commune with your, will you be grieved? but who can withhold himself from speaking? 3:Behold, you have instructed many, and you have strengthened the weak hands. 4:Your words have up held him that was falling, and your have strengthened the feeble knees. 5:But now it is come upon your, and your faintest; it touches your, and your are troubled. 6:Is not this your fear, your confidence, your hope, and the uprightness of your ways? 7:Remember, I pray your, who ever perished, being innocent? Or where were the righteous cut off? 8:Even as I have seen, they that plow iniquity, and sow wickedness, reap the same. 9:By the blast of God they perish, and by the breath of his nostrils are they consumed. 10:The roaring of the lion, and the voice of the fierce lion, and the teeth of the young lions, are broken. 11:The old lion perish for lack of prey, and the stout lion's whelps are scattered abroad. 12:Now a thing was secretly brought to me, and mine ear received a little thereof. 13:In thoughts from the visions of the night, when deep sleep fallen on men, 14:Fear came upon me, and trembling, which made all my bones to shake. 15:Then a spirit passed before my face; the hair of my flesh stood up. 16:It stood still, but I could not discern the form thereof: an image was before mine eyes, there was silence, and I heard a voice, saying. 17:Shall mortal man be more just than God? shall a man be more pure than his maker? 18:Behold, he put no trust in his servants; and his angels he charged with folly: 19;How much less in them that dwell in houses of clay, whose foundation is in the dust, which are crushed before the moth? 20:They are destroyed from morning to evening: they perish forever without regarding it. 21;Does not their excellency which is in them go away? They die, even without wisdom. **5:1;**Call now, if there be any that will answer your; and to which of the saints will your turn? 2:For wrath kills the foolish man, and envy slays the silly one. 3:I have seen the foolish taking root: but suddenly I cursed his habitation. 4:His children are far from safety, and they are crushed in the gate, neither is there any to deliver them. 5:Whose harvest the hungry eats up, and takes it even out of the thorns, and the robber swallows up their substance. 6:Although affliction comes not forth of the dust, neither doth trouble spring out of the ground. 7:Yet man is born to trouble, as the sparks fly upward. 8:I would seek to find God, and to God would I commit my cause. 9:Which does great things and unsearchable; marvelous things without number. 10:Who gives rain upon the earth, and sends waters upon the fields. 11:To set up on high those that be low; that those which mourn may be exalted to safety. 12:He disappoints the devices of the crafty, so that their hands cannot perform their enterprise.

13:He takes the wise in their own craftiness: and the counsel of the froward is carried headlong. 14:They meet with darkness in the daytime, and grope in the noonday as in the night. 15:But he saves the poor from the sword, from their mouth, and from the hand of the mighty. 16:So the poor have hope, and iniquity shuts her mouth. 17:Behold, happy is the man whom God corrects: therefore despise not your the chastening of the Almighty. 18:For he makes sore, and binds up: he wound, and his hands make whole. 19:He shall deliver your in six troubles: yes, in seven there shall no evil touch your. 20:In famine he shall redeem your from death: and in war from the power of the sword. 21:your shall be hid from the scourge of the tongue, neither shall your be afraid of destruction when it comes. 22:At destruction and famine your shall laugh: neither shall your be afraid of the beasts of the earth. 23:For your shall be in league with the stones of the field:and the beasts of the field shall be at peace with your. 24:And your shall know that your tabernacle shall be in peace, and your shall visit your habitation, and shall not sin. 25;your shall know also that your seed shall be great, and your offspring as the grass of the earth. 26;your shall come to your grave in a full age, like as a shock of corn comes in in his season. 27;Look this, we have searched it, so it is; hear it,
and know you it for your good.

6:1:But Job answered and said: 2:Oh that my grief were thoroughly weighed, and my calamity laid in the balances together! 3:For now it would be heavier than the sand of the sea, therefore my words are swallowed up. 4;For the arrows of the Almighty are within me, the poison whereof drinks up my spirit: the terrors of God do set themselves in array against me. 5:Does the wild ass bray when he has grass? or low the ox over his fodder? 6;Can that which is unsavory be eaten without salt? or is there any taste in the white of an egg? 7:The things that my soul refused to touch are as my sorrowful meat. 8:Oh that I might have my request; and that God would grant me the thing that I long for! 9:Even that it would please God to destroy me; that he would let loose his hand, and cut me off! 10:Then should I yet have comfort; yes, I would harden myself in sorrow: let him not spare; for I have not concealed the words of the Holy One. 11:What is my strength, that I should hope? and what is mine end, that I should prolong my life? 12:Is my strength the strength of stones? or is my flesh of brass? 13:Is not my help in me? and is wisdom driven quite from me? 14:To him that is afflicted pity should be shewed from his friend; but he forsaken the fear of the Almighty. 15:My brethren have dealt deceitfully as a brook, and as the stream of brooks they pass away. 16:Which are blackish by reason of the ice, and wherein the snow is hid: 17:What time they wax warm, they vanish: when it is hot, they are consumed out of their place. 18:The paths of their way are turned aside; they go to nothing, and perish. 19:The caravans of Tema search, the companies of Sheba waited for them. 20:They were confounded because they had hoped; they came thither, and were ashamed. 21:For now your are nothing; your see my casting down, and are afraid. 22:Did I say, Bring to me? or, Give a reward for me of your substance? 23;Or, Deliver me from the enemy's hand? or, Redeem me from the hand of the mighty? 24:Teach me, and I will hold my tongue: and cause me to understand wherein I have erred. 25:How forcible are right words! But what does your arguing reprove? 26:Do your imagine to reprove words, and the speeches of one that is desperate, which are as wind? 27:Yes, your overwhelm the fatherless, and your dig a pit for your friend.

28:Now therefore be content, look upon me; for it is evident to you if I lie. 29:Return, I pray you, let it not be iniquity; yes, return again, my righteousness is in it. 30;Is there iniquity in my tongue? cannot my taste discern perverse things?

7:1: Is there not an appointed time to man upon earth? are not his days also like the days of an hireling? 2:As a servant earnestly desires the shadow, and as an hireling looks for the reward of his work. 3:So am I made to possess months of vanity, and wearisome nights are appointed to me. 4:When I lie down, I say, When shall I arise, and the night is gone? and I am full of tossing to and fro to the dawning of the day. 5:My flesh is clothed with worms and clods of dust; my skin is broken, and become loathsome. 6:My days are swifter than a weaver's shuttle, and are spent without hope. 7:O remember that my life is wind: mine eye shall no more see good. 8:The eye of him that has seen me shall see me no more your eyes are upon me, and I am not. 9:As the cloud is consumed and vanish away: so he that go's down to the grave shall come up no more. 10:He shall return no more to his house, neither shall his place know him any more. 11:Therefore I will not refrain my mouth; I will speak in the anguish of my spirit; I will complain in the bitterness of my soul. 12:Am I a sea, or a whale, that your sets a watch over me? 13:When I say, My bed shall comfort me, my couch shall ease my complaint. 14:Then your scares me with dreams, and terrifies me through visions. 15:So that my soul chooses strangling, and death rather than my life. 16:I loathe it; I would not live always: let me alone; for my days are vanity. 17:What is man, that you should magnify him? and that you should set your heart upon him? 18:And that you should visit him every morning, and try him every moment? 19:How long will your not depart from me, nor let me alone till I swallow down my spittle? 20:I have sinned; what shall I do to your, O your preserver of men? why have your set me as a mark against your, so that I am a burden to myself? 21:And why dost your not pardon my transgression, and take away mine iniquity? for now shall I sleep in the dust; and your shall seek me in the morning, but I shall not be.

8:1;Then answered Bildad the Shuhite and said, 2:How long will your speak these things? And how long shall the words of your mouth be like a strong wind? 3:Does God pervert judgment? or doth the Almighty pervert justice? 4:If your children have sinned against him, and he have cast them away for their transgression; 5:If your would seek to God, and make your supplication to the Almighty. 6:If your were pure and upright; surely now he would awake for your, and make the habitation of your righteousness prosperous. 7:Though your beginning was small, yet your latter end should greatly increase. 8:For inquire, I pray your, of the former age, and prepare thyself to the search of their fathers. 9:For we are but of yesterday, and know nothing, because our days upon earth are a shadow. 10:Shall not they teach your, and tell your, and utter words out of their heart? 11:Can the rush grow up without mire? can the flag grow without water? 12:Whilst it is yet in his greenness, and not cut down, it withered before any other herb. 13;So are the paths of all that forget God; and the hypocrite's hope shall perish. 14:Whose hope shall be cut off, and whose trust shall be a spider's web. 15:He shall lean upon his house, but it shall not stand: he shall hold it fast, but it shall not endure. 16:He is green before the sun, and his branch shootout forth in his garden. 17:His roots are wrapped about the heap, and senses the place of stones.

18:If he destroy him from his place, then it shall deny him, saying, I have not seen your. 19:Behold, this is the joy of his way, and out of the earth shall others grow. 20:Behold, God will not cast away a perfect man, neither will he help the evil doers. 21:Till he fill your mouth with laughing, and your lips with rejoicing. 22;:They that hate your shall be clothed with shame; and the dwelling place of the wicked, shall come to naught.

9:1:Then Job answered and said: 2:I know it is so of a truth: but how should man be just with God? 3:If he will contend with him, he cannot answer him one of a thousand. 4:He is wise in heart, and mighty in strength: who has hardened himself against him, and has prospered? 5:Which removed the mountains, and they know not: which overturn them in his anger. 6:Which shakes the earth out of her place, and the pillars thereof tremble. 7:Which commanded the sun, and it rise not; and seal up the stars. 8:Which alone spreads out the heavens, and treads upon the waves of the sea. 9:Which make Arcturus, Orion, and Pleiades's, and the chambers of the south. 10:Which does great things past finding out; yes, and wonders without number. 11:Look, he go's by me, and I see him not: he passes on also, but I perceive him not. 12:Behold, he takes away, who can hinder him? who will say to him, What have you done? 13:If God will not withdraw his anger, the proud helpers do stoop under him. 14;How much less shall I answer him, and choose out my words to reason with him? 15:Whom, though I were righteous, yet would I not answer, but I would make supplication to my judge. 16:If I had called, and he had answered me; yet would I not believe that he had hearkened to my voice. 17:For he breaks me with a tempest, and multiplies my wounds without cause. 18:He will not suffer me to take my breath, but fills me with bitterness. 19:If I speak of strength, look, he is strong: and if of judgment, who shall set me a time to plead? 20:If I justify myself, mine own mouth shall condemn me:If I say, I am perfect, it shall also prove me perverse. 21:Though I were perfect, yet would I not know my soul: I would despise my life. 22:This is one thing therefore I said it, He destroyed the perfect and the wicked. 23:If the scourge slay suddenly, he will laugh at the trial of the innocent. 24:The earth is given into the hand of the wicked: he covered the faces of the judges thereof; if not, where, and who is he? 25:Now my days are swifter than a post: they flee away, they see no good. 26:They are passed away as the swift ships: as the eagle that hasten to the prey. 27:If I say, I will forget my complaint, I will leave off my heaviness, and comfort myself. 28:I am afraid of all my sorrows, I know that your will not hold me innocent. 29:If I be wicked, why then labor I in vain? 30:If I wash myself with snow water, and make my hands never so clean. 31:Yet shall your plunge me in the ditch, and mine own clothes shall abhor me. 32:For he is not a man, as I am, that I should answer him, and we should come together in judgment. 33:Neither is there any days man betwixt us, that might lay his hand upon us both. 34:Let him take his rod away from me, and let not his fear terrify me. 35:Then would I speak, and not fear him; but it is not so with me.

10:1: My soul is weary you inquire after mine iniquity, and search after my sin? 2:I will say to God, Do not condemn me; show me wherefore your contend with me. 3:It is good to your that your should oppress, that your should despise the work of your hands, and shine upon the counsel of the wicked? 4:have your eyes of flesh? or sees your as man sees?

5:Are your days as the days of man? are your years as man's days. 6:That your inquires after mine iniquity, and searches after my sin? 7;your knowest that I am not wicked; and there is none that can deliver out of your hand. 8:our hands have made me and fashioned me together round about; yet your dost destroy me. 9:Remember, I beseech your, that your have made me as the clay; and will your bring me into dust again? 10:Have your not poured me out as milk, and curdled me like cheese? 11:You have clothed me with skin and flesh, and have fenced me with bones and sinews. 12:You have granted me life and favor, and your visitation has preserved my spirit. 13:And these things have you hid in your heart: I know that this is with your. 14:If I sin, then your mark me, and your will not acquit me from mine iniquity. 15:If I be wicked, woe to me; and if I be righteous, yet will I not lift up my head. I am full of confusion; therefore see your mine affliction. 16:For it increase. You hunt me as a fierce lion: and again your show thyself marvelous upon me. 17:You renew your witnesses against me, and increase your indignation upon me; changes and war are against me. 18:Wherefore then have your brought me forth out of the womb? Oh that I had given up the ghost, and no eye had seen me! 19:I should have been as though I had not been; I should have been carried from the womb to the grave. 20:Are not my days few? cease then, and let me alone, that I may take comfort a little. 21:Before I go when I shall not return, even to the land of darkness and the shadow of death; 22:A land of darkness, as darkness itself and of the shadow of death, without any order, and where the light is as darkness.

11:1;Then answered Zophar the Naamathite, and said: 2:Should not the multitude of words be answered? and should a man full of talk be justified? 3;Should your lies make men hold their peace? and when your mock, shall no man make your ashamed? 4:For your have said, My doctrine is pure, and I am clean in your eyes. 5:But oh that God would speak, and open his lips against your. 6:And that he would show your the secrets of wisdom, that they are double to that which is! Know therefore that God exact of your less than your iniquity deserve. 7:Canst your by searching find out God? canst your find out the Almighty to perfection? 8:It is as high as heaven; what canst your do? deeper than hell; what canst your know? 9:The measure thereof is longer than the earth, and broader than the sea. 10:If he cut off, and shut up, or gather together, then who can hinder him? 11:For he knows vain men: he sees wickedness also; will he not then considerate it? 12:For vain man would be wise, though man be born like a wild ass's colt. 13:If your prepare your heart, and stretch out your hands toward him. 14:If iniquity be in your hand, put it far away, and let not wickedness dwell in your tabernacles. 15:For then shall your lift up your face without spot; yes, your shall be steadfast, and shall not fear. 16:Because your shall forget your misery, and remember it as waters that pass away: 17:And your age shall be clearer than the noonday; your shall shine forth, your shall be as the morning. 18:And your shall be secure, because there is hope; yes, your shall dig about your, and your shall take your rest in safety. 19:Also your shall lie down, and none shall make your afraid; yes, many shall make suit to your. 20:But the eyes of the wicked shall fail, and they shall not escape, and their hope shall be as the giving up of the ghost.

12:1;And Job answered and said: 2:No doubt but you are the people, and wisdom shall die with you. 3;But I have understanding as well as you,

I am not inferior to you: yes, who knows not such things as these? 4:I am as one mocked of his neighbor, who calls upon God, and he answers him: the just upright man is laughed to scorn. 5:He that is ready to slip with his feet is as a lamp despised in the thought of him that is at ease. 6:The tabernacles of robbers prosper, and they that provoke God are secure; into whose hand God brings abundantly. 7:But ask now the beasts, and they shall teach your; and the fowls of the air, and they shall tell your. 8:Or speak to the earth, and it shall teach your: and the fishes of the sea shall declare to your. 9:Who knows not in all these that the hand of the Lord has wrought this? 10:In whose hand is the soul of every living thing, and the breath of all mankind. 11:Does not the ear try words? and the mouth taste his meat? 12:With the ancient is wisdom, and in length of days understanding. 13:With him is wisdom and strength, he has counsel and understanding.14:Behold, he breaks down, and it cannot be built again: he shuts up a man, and there can be no opening. 15:Behold, he with holds the waters, and they dry up: also he sends them out, and they overturn the earth. 16:With him is strength and wisdom: the deceived and the deceiver are his. 17:He leads counselors away spoiled, and makes the judges fools. 18:He looses the bond of Kings, and girds their loins with a girdle. 19:He leads princes away spoiled, and over throws the mighty. 20:He removes away the speech of the trusty, and takes away the understanding of the aged. 21:He pours contempt upon princes, and weakens the strength of the mighty. 22:He discovered deep things out of darkness, and brings out to light the shadow of death. 23:He increases the nations, and destroys them: he enlarges the nations, and straitens them again. 24:He takes away the heart of the chief of the people of the earth, and causes them to wander in a wilderness where there is no way. 25:They grope in the dark without light, and he makes them to stagger like a drunken man.

13:1: Look, mine eye has seen all this, mine ear has heard and understood it. 2:What your know, the same do I know also, I am not inferior to you. 3:Surely I would speak to the Almighty, and I desire to reason with God. 4:But your are forgers of lies, your are all physicians of no value. 5:O that your would altogether hold your peace! and it should be your wisdom. 6;Hear now my reasoning, and hearken to the pleadings of my lips. 7:Will your speak wickedly for God? and talk deceitfully for him? 8:Will your accept his person? will your contend for God? 9:Is it good that he should search you out? or as one man mocks another, do your so mock him? 10:He will surely reprove you, if your do secretly accept persons. 11:Shall not his excellency make you afraid? and his dread fall upon you? 12:Your remembrances are like to ashes, your bodies to bodies of clay. 13:Hold your peace, let me alone, that I may speak, and let come on me what will. 14:Wherefore do I take my flesh in my teeth, and put my life in mine hand? 15:Though he slay me, yet will I trust in him: but I will maintain mine own ways before him. 16:He also shall be my salvation, for an hypocrite shall not come before him. 17:Hear diligently my speech, and my declaration with your ears. 18:Behold now, I have ordered my cause; I know that I shall be justified. 19:Who is he that will plead with me? for now, if I hold my tongue, I shall give up the ghost. 20:Only do not two things to me: then will I not hide myself from your. 21:Withdraw your hand far from me: and let not your dread make me afraid. 22:Then call your, and I will answer: or let me speak, and answer your me. 23:How many are mine iniquities and sins? make me to know my transgression and my sin. 24:Wherefore hidden your your face,

and hold me for your enemy? 25:Will your break a leaf driven to and fro? and will
your pursue the dry stubble? 26:For your write bitter things against me, and makes
me, to possess the iniquities of my youth. 27:Your puts my feet also in the stocks,
and looks narrowly to all my paths, your sets a print upon the heels of my feet.
28:And he, as a rotten thing, consumes, as a garment that is moth eaten.

14:1: Man that is born of a woman is of few days, and full of trouble. 2:He comes
forth like a flower, and is cut down: he flees also as a shadow, and continues not.
3:And dost your open your eyes upon such an one, and brings me into judgment
with your? 4:Who can bring a clean thing out of an unclean? not one. 5:Seeing his
days are determined, the number of his months are with your, your have appointed
his bounds that he cannot pass; 6:Turn from him, that he may rest, till he shall
accomplish, as an hireling, his day. 7:For there is hope of a tree, if it be cut down,
that it will sprout again, and that the tender branch thereof will not cease. 8:Though
the root thereof wax old in the earth, and the stock thereof die in the ground. 9;Yet
through the scent of water it will bud, and bring forth boughs like a plant. 10:But
man dies, and wastes away: yes, man gives up the ghost, and where is he? 11:As the
waters fail from the sea, and the flood decays and dries up. 12:So man lies down,
and rises not: till the heavens be no more, they shall not awake, nor be raised out of
their sleep. 13:O that your woulds hide me in the grave, that your woulds keep me
secret, until your wrath be past, that your woulds appoint me a set time, and
remember me! 14:If a man die, shall he live again? all the days of my appointed
time will I wait, till my change come. 15:Your shall call, and I will answer your:
your will have a desire to the work of your hands. 16:For now your numbers my
steps: dost your not watch over my sin? 17:My transgression is sealed up in a bag,
and your stews up mine iniquity. 18:And surely the mountain falling comes to
naught, and the rock is removed out of his place. 19:The waters wear the stones:
your washes away the things which grow out of the dust of the earth; and your
destroy the hope of man. 20:Your prevail for ever against him, and he passes: your
change his countenance, and sends him away. 21:His sons come to honor, and he
knows it not; and they are brought low, but he perceived it not of them. 22:But his
flesh upon him shall have pain, and his soul within him shall mourn.

15:1:Then answered Eliphaz the Temanite, and said, 2:Should a wise man utter
vain knowledge, and fill his belly with the east wind. 3:Should he reason with
unprofitable talk? or with speeches wherewith he can do no good? 4:Yes, your cast
off fear, and restrain prayer before God. 5:For your mouth utters your iniquity, and
your choose the tongue of the crafty. 6:Your own mouth condemned your, and not I:
yes, your own lips testify against you. 7:Are your the first man that was born? Or
wast your made before the hills? 8:Have your heard the secret of God? And do your
restrain wisdom to yourself? 9:What knowest your, that we know not? What
understands you, which is not in us? 10:With us are both the gray headed and very
aged men, much elder than your father. 11:Are the consolations of God small with
your? Is there any secret thing with your? 12:Why doth your heart carry your away?
And what do your eyes wink at? 13:That your turn your spirit against God, and let
such words go out of your mouth? 14:What is man, that he should be clean? And he
which is born of a woman, that he should be righteous? 15:Behold, he puts no trust
in his saints; yes, the heavens are not clean in his sight.

16:How much more abominable and filthy is man, which drinks iniquity like water? 17:I will show your, hear me; and that which I have seen I will declare. 18:Which wise men have told from their fathers, and have not hid it. 19:To whom alone the earth was given, and no stranger passed among them. 20:The wicked man travails with pain all his days, and the number of years is hidden to the oppressor. 21:A dreadful sound is in his ears: in prosperity the destroyer shall come upon him. 22:He believes not that he shall return out of darkness, and he is waited for of the sword. 23:He wanders abroad for bread, saying, Where is it? he knows that the day of darkness is ready at his hand. 24:Trouble and anguish shall make him afraid; they shall prevail against him, as a king ready to the battle. 25:For he stretches out his hand against God, and strengthens himself against the Almighty. 26:He runs upon him, even on his neck, upon the thick bosses of his bucklers. 27:Because he covers his face with his fatness, and makes scollops of fat on his flanks. 28:And he dwells in desolate cities, and in houses which no man in habits, which are ready to become heaps. 29:He shall not be rich, neither shall his substance continue, neither shall he prolong the perfection thereof upon the earth. 30:He shall not depart out of darkness; the flame shall dry up his branches, and by the breath of his mouth shall he go away. 31:Let not him that is deceived trust in vanity: for vanity shall be his recompense. 32:It shall be accomplished before his time, and his branch shall not be green. 33:He shall shake off his unripe grape as the vine, and shall cast off his flower as the olive. 34:For the congregation of hypocrites shall be desolate, and fire shall consume the tabernacles of bribery. 35:They conceive mischief, and bring forth vanity, and their belly prepares deceit.

16:1:Then Job answered and said: 2:I have heard many such things: miserable comforters are your all. 3:Shall vain words have an end? or what embolden your that your answer? 4:I also could speak as your do, if your soul were in my soul's stead, I could heap up words against you, and shake mine head at you. 5:But I would strengthen you with my mouth, and the moving of my lips should be as waged as your grief. 6:Though I speak, my grief is not as waged: and though I forbear, what am I eased? 7:But now he has made me weary: your have made desolate all my company. 8:And your have filled me with wrinkles, which is a witness against me, and my leanness rising up in me bears witness to my face. 9:He tears me in his wrath, who hates me: he gnashes upon me with his teeth; mine enemy sharpened his eyes upon me. 10:They have gaped upon me with their mouth; they have smitten me upon the cheek reproachfully; they have gathered themselves together against me. 11:God has delivered me to the ungodly, and turned me over into the hands of the wicked. 12:I was at ease, but he has broken me asunder: he has also takes me by my neck, and shaken me to pieces, and set me up for his mark. 13:His archers compass me round about, he cleaves my reins asunder, and doth not spare; he pours out my gall upon the ground. 14:He breaks me with breach upon breach, he runs upon me like a giant. 15:I have sewed sackcloth upon my skin, and defiled my horn in the dust. 16:My face is foul with weeping, and on my eyelids is the shadow of death; 17:Not for any injustice in mine hands: also my prayer is pure. 18:O earth, cover not your my blood, and let my cry have no place. 19:Also now, behold, my witness is in heaven, and my record is on high. 20:My friends scorn me: but mine eye poured out tears to God. 21:O that one might plead for a man with God, as a man pleads for his neighbor!

22:When a few years are come, then I shall go the way where I shall not return.

17:1: My breath is corrupt, my days are extinct, the graves are ready for me. 2:Are
there not mockers with me? and doth not mine eye continue in their provocation?
3:Lay down now, put me in a surety with your; who is he that will strike hands with
me? 4:For your have hid their heart from understanding:therefore shall your not
exalt them. 5:He that speaks flattery to his friends, even the eyes of his children
shall fail. 6:He has made me also a byword of the people, their object lesson I have
become. 7:Mine eye also is dim by reason of sorrow, and all my members are as a
shadow. 8:Upright men shall be astonished at this, and the innocent shall stir up
himself against the hypocrite. 9:The righteous also shall hold on his way, and he that
has clean hands shall be stronger and stronger. 10:But as for you all, do your return,
and come now: for I cannot find one wise man among you. 11;My days are past, my
purposes are broken off, even the thoughts of my heart. 12:They change the night
into day: the light is short because of darkness. 13;If I wait, the grave is mine house:
I have made my bed in the darkness. 14:I have said to corruption, your are my
father, to the worm, your are my mother, and my sister. 15:And where is now my
hope? as for my hope, who shall see it? 16:They shall go down to the bars of the
pit, when our rest together is in the dust.

18:1:Then answered Bildad the Shuhite, and said: 2:How long will it be before
you make an end of words? mark, and after wards we will speak. 3:Wherefore are
we counted as beasts, and reputed vile in your sight? 4:He tears himself in his anger:
shall the earth be forsaken for your? and shall the rock be removed out of his place?
5:Yes, the light of the wicked shall be put out, and the spark of his fire shall not
shine. 6:The light shall be dark in his tabernacle, and his candle shall be put out with
him. 7:The steps of his strength shall be straitened, and his own counsel shall cast
him down. 8:For he is cast into a net by his own feet, and he walks upon a snare.
9:The gin shall take him by the heel, and the robber shall prevail against him.
10:The snare is laid for him in the ground, and a trap for him in the way. 11;Terrors
shall make him afraid on every side, and shall drive him to his feet. 12:His strength
shall be hunger bitten, and destruction shall be ready at his side. 13:It shall devour
the strength of his skin: even the firstborn of death shall devour his strength. 14:His
confidence shall be rooted out of his tabernacle, and it shall bring him to the king of
terrors. 15:It shall dwell in his tabernacle, because it is none of his: brimstone shall
be scattered upon his habitation. 16:His roots shall be dried up beneath, and above
shall his branch be cut off. 17:His remembrance shall perish from the earth, and he
shall have no name in the street. 18:He shall be driven from light into darkness, and
chased out of the world. 19:He shall neither have son nor nephew among his people,
nor any remaining in his dwellings. 20:They that come after him shall be astonished
at his day, as they who that went before were frighted. 21:Surely such are the
dwellings of the wicked, and this is the place of him that knows not God.

19:1:Then Job answered and said, 2:How long will your vex my soul, and break
me in pieces with words? 3:These ten times have your reproached me: your are not
ashamed that your make yourselves strange to me. 4:And be it indeed that I have
erred, mine error remains with myself. 5:If indeed your will magnify yourselves
against me, and plead against me my reproach.

6:Know now that God has overthrown me, and has compassed me with his net.
7:Behold, I cry out of wrong, but I am not heard: I cry aloud, but there is no
judgment. 8:He has fenced up my way that I cannot pass, and he has set darkness in
my paths. 9:He has stripped me of my glory, and taken the crown from my head.
10:He has destroyed me on every side, and I am gone: and mine hope has he
removed like a tree. 11:He has also kindled his wrath against me, and he counts me
to him as one of his enemies. 12:His troops come together, and raise up their way
against me, and encamp round about my tabernacle. 13:He has put my brethren far
from me, and mine acquaintance are verily estranged from me. 14:My kinsfolk have
failed, and my familiar friends have forgotten me. 15:They that dwell in mine
house, and my maids, count me for a stranger: I am an alien in their sight. 16:I
called my servant, and he gave me no answer; I entreated him with my mouth.
17:My breath is strange to my wife, though I entreated for the children's sake of
mine own body. 18:Yes, young children despised me, I arose, and they spoke
against me. 19:All my inward friends abhorred me: and they whom I loved are
turned against me. 20:My bone cleaves to my skin and to my flesh, and I am
escaped with the skin of my feet. 21:Have pity upon me, have pity upon me, O your
my friends; for the hand of God has touched me. 22:Why do your persecute me as
God, and are not satisfied with my flesh? 23:Oh that my words were now written!
oh that they were printed in a book! 24:That they were graven with an iron pen and
lead in the rock for ever! 25:For I know that my redeemer lives, and that he shall
stand at the latter day upon the earth. 26:And though after my skin worms destroy
this body, yet in my flesh shall I see God. 27:Whom I shall see for myself, and mine
eyes shall behold, and not another; though my reins be consumed within me. 28:But
your should say, Why persecute we him, seeing the root of the matter is found in
me? 29:Be your afraid of the sword: for wrath brings the punishments of the sword,
that your may know there is a judgment.

20:1;Then answered Zophar the Naamathite, and said: 2:Therefore do my
thoughts cause me to answer, and for this I make haste. 3:I have heard the check of
my reproach, and the spirit of my understanding causes me to answer. 4:Know your
not this of old, since man was placed upon earth. 5:That the triumphing of the
wicked is short, and the joy of the hypocrite but for a moment? 6:Though his
excellency mount up to the heavens, and his head reach to the clouds; 7:Yet he shall
perish for ever like his own dung: they which have seen him shall say, Where is he?
8:He shall fly away as a dream, and shall not be found: yes, he shall be chased away
as a vision of the night. 9:The eye also which saw him shall see him no more;
neither shall his place any more behold him. 10:His children shall seek to please the
poor, and his hands shall restore their goods. 11:His bones are full of the sin of his
youth, which shall lie down with him in the dust. 12:Though wickedness be sweet in
his mouth, though he hid it under his tongue. 13:Though he spare it, and forsake it
not; but keep it still within his mouth. 14:Yet his meat in his bowels is turned, it is
the gall of asps within him. 15:He has swallowed down riches, and he shall vomit
them up again: God shall cast them out of his belly. 16:He shall suck the poison of
asps: the viper's tongue shall slay him. 17:He shall not see the rivers, the floods, the
brooks of honey and butter. 18:That which he labored for shall he restore, and shall
not swallow it down: according to his substance shall the restitution be, and he shall
not rejoice therein.

19:Because he has oppressed and has forsaken the poor; because he has violently taken away an house which he did not build. 20:Surely he shall not feel quietness in his belly, he shall not save of that which he desired. 21:There shall none of his meat be left; therefore shall no man look for his goods. 22:In the fulness of his sufficiency he shall be in straits: every hand of the wicked shall come upon him. 23:When he is about to fill his belly, God shall cast the fury of his wrath upon him, and shall rain it upon him while he is eating. 24:He shall flee from the iron weapon, and the bow of steel shall strike him through. 25:It is drawn, and comes out of the body; yes, the glittering sword comes out of his gall: terrors are upon him. 26:All darkness shall be hid in his secret places: a fire not blown shall consume him; it shall go ill with him that is left in his tabernacle. 27:The heaven shall reveal his iniquity; and the earth shall rise up against him. 28:The increase of his house shall depart,and his goods shall flow away in the day of his wrath. 29:This is the portion of a wicked man from God, and the heritage appointed to him by God.

21;1But Job answered and said: 2:Hear diligently my speech, and let this be your consolations. 3:Suffer me that I may speak; and after that I have spoken, mock on. 4:As for me, is my complaint to man? and if it were so, why should not my spirit be troubled? 5:Mark me, and be astonished, and lay your hand upon your mouth. 6:Even when I remember I am afraid, and trembling takes hold on my flesh. 7:Wherefore do the wicked live, become old, yes, are mighty in power? 8:Their seed is established in their sight with them, and their offspring before their eyes. 9:Their houses are safe from fear, neither is the rod of God upon them. 10:Their bull gender, and fails not; their cow calves, and caste not her calve. 11:They send forth their little ones like a flock, and their children dance. 12:They take the timbrel and harp, and rejoice at the sound of the organ. 13:They spend their days in wealth, and in a moment go down to the grave. 14:Therefore they say to God, Depart from us; for we desire not the knowledge of your ways. 15:What is the Almighty, that we should serve him? and what profit should we have, if we pray to him? 16:Look, their good is not in their hand: the counsel of the wicked is far from me. 17:How oft is the candle of the wicked put out! and how often comes their destruction upon them! God distributes sorrows in his anger. 18:They are as stubble before the wind, and as chaff that the storm carries away. 19:God lays up his iniquity for his children: he rewards him, and he shall know it. 20:His eyes shall see his destruction, and he shall drink of the wrath of the Almighty. 21:For what pleasure has he in his house after him, when the number of his months is cut off in the midst? 22:Shall any teach God knowledge? seeing he judges those that are high. 23:One dies in his full strength, being wholly at ease and quiet. 24:His breasts are full of milk, and his bones are moistened with marrow. 25:And another dies in the bitterness of his soul, and never eats with pleasure. 26:They shall lie down alike in the dust, and the worms shall cover them. 27:Behold, I know your thoughts, and the devices which your wrongfully imagine against me. 28;For your say, Where is the house of the prince? and where are the dwelling places of the wicked? 29:Have your not asked them that go by the way? and do your not know their tokens. 30:That the wicked is reserved to the day of destruction? They shall be brought forth to the day of wrath. 31:Who shall declare his way to his face? and who shall repay him what he has done? 32:Yet shall he be brought to the grave, and shall remain in the tomb. 33:The clods of the valley shall be sweet to him, and every man shall draw after him, as there are innumerable before him. 34:How then comfort your me in vain, seeing in your answers there remains falsehood?

22:1:Then Eliphaz the Temanite answered and said, 2;Can a man be profitable to God, as he that is wise may be profitable to himself? 3:Is it any pleasure to the Almighty, that your are righteous? or is it gain to him, that your makes your ways perfect? 4:Will he reprove your for fear of your? will he enter with your into judgment? 5;Is not your wickedness great? and your iniquities infinite? 6:For you have taken a pledge from your brother for naught, and stripped the naked of their clothing. 7:You have not given water to the weary to drink, and your have with holding bread from the hungry. 8:But as for the mighty man, he had the earth; and the honorable man dwelt in it. 9:You have sent widows away empty, and the arms of the fatherless have been broken. 10;Therefore snares are around about your, and sudden fear troubled you. 11:Or darkness, that your canst not see; and abundance of waters cover you. 12:Is not God in the height of heaven? and behold the height of the stars, how high they are! 13:And your says, How does God know? Can he judge through the dark cloud? 14:Thick clouds are a covering to him, that he sees not; and he walks in the circuit of heaven. 15:Have you marked the old way which wicked men have trodden? 16:Which were cut down out of time, whose foundation was overflown with a flood. 17:Which said to God, Depart from us, and what can the Almighty do for them? 18;Yet he filled their houses with good things, but the counsel of the wicked is far from me. 19:The righteous see it, and are glad: and the innocent laugh them to scorn. 20:Whereas our substance is not cut down, but the remnant of them the fire consumes. 21:Acquaint now thyself with him, and be at peace: thereby good shall come to you. 22;Receive, I pray you, the law from his mouth, and lay up his words in your heart. 23:If your return to the Almighty, your shall be built up, your shall put away iniquity far from your tabernacles. 24:Then shall your lay up gold as dust, and the gold of Ophir as the stones of the brooks. 25Yes, the Almighty shall be your defense, and your shall have plenty of silver. 26:For then shall your have your delight in the Almighty, and shall lift up your face to God. 27:You shall make your prayer to him, and he shall hear you, and you shall pay your vows. 28;You shall also decree a thing, and it shall be established to you: and the light shall shine upon your ways. 29:When men are cast down, then your shall say, There is lifting up; and he shall save the humble person. 30:He shall deliver the island of the innocent: and it is delivered by the pureness of your hands.

23:1:Then Job answered and said, 2:Even to day is my complaint bitter my stroke is heavier than my groaning. 3:Oh that I knew where I might find him! that I might come even to his seat! 4:I would order my cause before him, and fill my mouth with arguments. 5:I would know the words which he would answer me, and understand what he would say to me. 6:Will he plead against me with his great power? No; but he would put strength in me. 7:There the righteous might dispute with him; so should I be delivered for ever from my judge. 8:Behold, I go forward, but he is not there, and backward, but I cannot perceive him. 9:On the left hand, where he doth work, but I cannot behold him, he hides himself on the right hand, that I cannot see him. 10:But he knows the way that I take, when he has tried me, I shall come forth as gold. 11:My foot has held his steps,
his way have I kept, and not declined.

12:Neither have I gone back from the commandment of his lips; I have esteemed the words of his mouth more than my necessary food. 13:But he is in one mind, and who can turn him? and what his soul desires, even that he does. 14:For he performs the thing that is appointed for me, and many such things are with him. 15:Therefore am I troubled at his presence: when I consider, I am afraid of him. 16:For God makes my heart soft, and the Almighty troubles me. 17:Because I was not cut off before the darkness, neither, has he covered the darkness from my face.

24:1: Why, seeing times are not hidden from the Almighty, do they that know him not see his days? 2:Some remove the landmarks; they violently take away flocks, and feed thereof. 3:They drive away the ass of the fatherless, they take the widow's ox for a pledge. 4:They turn the needy out of the way: the poor of the earth hide themselves together. 5:Behold, as wild asses in the desert, go they forth to their work; rising betimes for a prey: the wilderness yields food for them and for their children. 6:They reap every one his corn in the field, and they gather the vintage of the wicked. 7:They cause the naked to lodge without clothing, that they have no covering in the cold. 8:They are wet with the showers of the mountains, and embrace the rock for want of a shelter.

9:They pluck the fatherless from the breast, and take a pledge of the poor. 10;They cause him to go naked without clothing, and they take away the sheaf from the hungry. 11;Which make oil within their walls, and tread their wine presses, and suffer thirst. 12;Men groan from out of the city, and the soul of the wounded cries out: yet God lays not folly to them. 13:They are of those that rebel against the light; they know not the ways thereof, nor abide in the paths thereof. 14:The murderer rising with the light kills the poor and needy, and in the night is as a thief. 15:The eye also of the adulterer waits for the twilight, saying; No eye shall see me: and disguises his face. 16;In the dark they dig through houses,which they had marked for themselves in the daytime: they know not the light. 17:For the morning is to them even as the shadow of death: if one know them, they are in the terrors of the shadow of death. 18:He is swift as the waters; their portion is cursed in the earth: he holds not the way of the vineyards. 19:Drought and heat consume the snow waters: so does the grave those which have sinned. 20:The womb shall forget him; the worm shall feed sweetly on him; he shall be no more remembered; and wickedness shall be broken as a tree. 21;His evil entreats the barren that bear not: and does not good to the widow. 22:He draws also the mighty with his power: he rises up, and no man is sure of life. 23:Though it be given him to be in safety, whereon he rests; yet his eyes are upon their ways. 24:They are exalted for a little while, but are gone and brought low; they are taken out of the way as all other, and cut off as the tops of the ears of corn. 25:And if it be not so now, who will make me a liar, and make my speech nothing worth?

25:1:Then answered Bildad the Shuhite, and said, 2:Dominion and fear are with him, he makes peace in his high places. 3:Is there any number of his armies? and upon whom doth not his light arise? 4:How then can man be justified with God? or how can he be clean that is born of a woman? 5:Behold even to the moon, and it shines not; yes, the stars are not pure in his sight. 6;How much less man, this is a worm? and the son of man, which is a worm?

26:1;But Job answered and said: 2:How have you helped him that is without
power? how save your the arm that has no strength? 3:How have your counseled
him that has no wisdom? and how have your plentifully declared the thing as it is?
4:To whom have your uttered words? and whose spirit came from your? 5:Dead
things are formed from under the waters, and the inhabitants thereof. 6:Hell is
naked before him, and destruction has no covering. 7:He stretches out the north
over the empty place, and hangs the earth upon nothing. 8:He binds up the waters in
his thick clouds; and the cloud is not rent under them. 9:He holds back the face of
his throne, and spreads his cloud upon it. 10:He has compassed the waters with
bounds, until the day and night come to an end. 11:The pillars of heaven tremble
and are astonished at his reproof. 12:He divides the sea with his power,and by his
understanding he strikes through the proud. 13:By his spirit he has garnished the
heavens; his hand has formed the crooked serpent. 14:Look, these are parts of his
ways: but how little a portion is heard of him? but the thunder of his power
who can understand?

7:1;Moreover Job continued his parable, and said: 2:As God lives, who has
taken away my judgment; and the Almighty, who has vexed my soul. 3:All the
while my breath is in me, and the spirit of God is in my nostrils; 4:My lips shall not
speak wickedness, nor my tongue utter deceit. 5:God forbid that I should justify
you: till I die I will not remove mine integrity from me. 6:My righteousness I hold
fast, and will not let it go: my heart shall not reproach me so long as I live. 7:Let
mine enemy be as the wicked, and he that rises up against me as the unrighteous.
8:For what is the hope of the hypocrite, though he has gained, when God takes away
his soul? 9:Will God hear his cry when trouble comes upon him? 10:Will he delight
himself in the Almighty? will he always call upon God? 11:I will teach you by the
hand of God: that which is with the Almighty will I not conceal. 12:Behold, all your
yourselves have seen it why then are your This altogether vain? 13:This is the
portion of a wicked man with God, and the heritage of oppressors, which they shall
receive of the Almighty. 14:If his children be multiplied, it is for the sword: and his
offspring shall not be satisfied with bread. 15:Those that remain of him shall be
buried in death: and his widows shall not weep. 16:Though he heap up silver as the
dust, and prepare raiment as the clay; 17:He may prepare it but the just shall put it
on, and the innocent shall divide the silver. 18:He builds his house as a moth, and as
a booth that the keeper makes. 19:The rich man shall lie down, but he shall not be
gathered: he opens his eyes, and he is not. 20:Terrors take hold on him as waters, a
tempest steals him away in the night. 21:The east wind carries him away, and he
departs: and as a storm hurls him out of his place. 22:For God shall cast upon him,
and not spare: he would fain flee out of his hand. 23;Men shall clap their hands at
him, and shall hiss him out of his place.

28:1: Surely there is a vein for the silver, and a place for gold where they fine it.
2:Iron is taken out of the earth, and brass is molten out of the stone. 3:He sets an end
to darkness, and searches out all perfection: the stones of darkness, and the shadow
of death. 4:The flood breaks out from the inhabitant; even the waters forgotten of
the foot: they are dried up, they are gone away from men. 5:As for the earth, out of
it comes bread: and under it is turned up as it were fire. 6:The stones of it are the
place of sapphires: and it has dust of gold.

7:There is a path which no fowl knows, and which the vulture's eye has not seen. 8:The lion's whelps have not trodden it, nor the fierce lion passed by it. 9:He puts forth his hand upon the rock; he over turns the mountains by their roots. 10:He cuts out rivers among the rocks; and his eye sees every precious thing. 11:He binds the floods from overflowing; and the thing that is hid brings he forth to light. 12:But where shall wisdom be found? and where is the place of understanding? 13:Man knows not the price thereof; neither is it found in the land of the living. 14:The depth says, It is not in me: and the sea says, It is not with me. 15:It cannot be gotten for gold, neither shall silver be weighed for the price thereof. 16:It cannot be valued with the gold of Ophir, with the precious onyx, or the sapphire. 17:The gold and the crystal cannot equal it: and the exchange of it shall not be for jewels of fine gold. 18:No mention shall be made of coral, or of pearls: for the price of wisdom is above rubies. 19:The topaz of Ethiopia shall not equal it, neither shall it be valued with pure gold. 20:Where then does wisdom come? and where is the place of understanding? 21:Seeing it is hid from the eyes of all living, and kept close from the fowls of the air. 22:Destruction and death say, We have heard the fame thereof with our ears. 23:God understands the way thereof, and he knows the place thereof. 24:For he looks to the ends of the earth, and sees under the whole heaven. 25:To make the weight for the winds; and he weighed the waters by measure. 26:When he made a decree for the rain, and a way for the lightning of the thunder. 27:Then did he see it, and declare it; he prepared it, yes, and searched it out. 28;And to man he said, Behold, the fear of the Lord, that is wisdom, and to depart from evil is understanding.

29:1:(Job continued), 2:Oh that I were as in months past, as in the days when God preserved me. 3:When his candle shined upon my head, and when by his light I walked through darkness. 4:As I was in the days of my youth, when the secret of God was upon my tabernacle. 5:When the Almighty was yet with me, when my children were about me. 6:When I washed my steps with butter, and the rock poured me out rivers of oil; 7:When I went out to the gate through the city, when I prepared my seat in the street! 8:The young men saw me, and hid themselves: and the aged arose, and stood up. 9:The princes refrained from talking, and laid their hand on their mouth. 10:The nobles held their peace, and their tongue cleaved to the roof of their mouth. 11:When the ear heard me, then it blessed me; and when the eye saw me it gave witness to me. 12:Because I delivered the poor that cried, and the fatherless, and him that had none to help him. 13:The blessing of him that was ready to perish came upon me: and I caused the widow's heart to sing for joy. 14:I put on righteousness, and it clothed me: my judgment was as a robe and a diadem. 15:I was eyes to the blind, and feet was I to the lame. 16;I was a father to the poor: and the cause which I knew not I searched out. 17:And I brake the jaws of the wicked, and plucked the spoil out of his teeth. 18:Then I said, I shall die in my nest, and I shall multiply my days as the sand. 19: My root was spread out by the waters, and the dew lay all night upon my branch. 20:My glory was fresh in me, and my bow was renewed in my hand. 21:To me men gave ear, and waited, and kept silence at my counsel. 22:After my words they spoke not again; and my speech dropped upon them. 23:And they waited for me as for the rain; and they opened their mouth wide as for the latter rain. 24:If I laughed on them, they believed it not; and the light of my countenance they cast not down. 25:I chose out their way, and sat chief, and dwelt as a King in the army, as one that comforts the mourners.

30:1: But now they that are younger than I have me in derision, whose fathers I
would have disdained to have set with the dogs of my flock. 2:Yes, where to might
the strength of their hands profit me, in whom old age was perished? 3:For want and
famine they were solitary; fleeing into the wilderness in former time desolate and
waste. 4:Who cut up mallows by the bushes, and juniper roots for their meat.
5:They were driven forth from among men,. (they cried after them as after a thief;)
6:To dwell in the clefts of the valleys, in caves of the earth, and in the rocks.
7:Among the bushes they brayed; under the nettles they were gathered together.
8:They were children of fools, yes, children of base men: they were viler than the
earth. 9:And now am I their song, yes, I am their byword. 10:They abhor me, they
flee far from me, and spare not to spit in my face. 11:Because he has loosed my
cord, and afflicted me, they have also let loose the bridle before me. 12;Upon my
right hand rise the youth; they push away my feet, and they raise up against me the
ways of their destruction. 13:They mar my path, they set forward my calamity, they
have no helper. 14:They came upon me as a wide breaking in of waters in the
desolation they rolled themselves upon me. 15:Terrors are turned upon me: they
pursue my soul as the wind: and my welfare passes away as a cloud. 16:And now
my soul is poured out upon me; the days of affliction have taken hold upon me.
17:My bones are pierced in me in the night season and my sinews take no rest.
18:By the great force of my disease as my garment changed: it binded me about as
the collar of my coat. 19:He has cast me into the mire, and I am become like dust
and ashes. 20:I cry to your, and your dost not hear me: I stand up, and your regarded
me not. 21:You are become cruel to me: with your strong hand you opposes yourself
against me. 22:You lifted me up to the wind; you causes me to ride upon it, and
dissolves my substance. 23:For I know that your will bring me to death, and to the
house appointed for all living. 24:Howbeit he will not stretch out his hand to the
grave, though they cry in his destruction. 25:Did not I weep for him that was in
trouble? Was not my soul grieved for the poor? 26:When I looked for good, then
evil came to me and when I waited for light, there came darkness. 27:My bowels
boiled, and rested not: the days of affliction prevented me. 28:I went mourning
without the sun: Then I stood up, and I cried in the congregation. 29:I am a brother
to dragons, and a companion to owls. 30:My skin is black upon me, and my bones
are burned with heat. 31:My harp also is turned to mourning, and my organ into the
voice of them that weep.

31:1:I made a covenant with my eyes, why then should I think upon a maid? 2:For
what portion of God is there from above? and what inheritance of the Almighty
from on high? 3:Is not destruction to the wicked? And a strange punishments to the
workers of iniquity? 4:Does he not see my ways, and count all my steps? 5:If I have
walked with vanity, or if my foot has hasted to deceit. 6:Let me be weighed in an
even balance, that God may know mine integrity. 7:If my step has turned out of the
way, and mine heart walked after mine eyes, and if any blot has cleaved to mine
hands. 8:Then let me sow, and let another eat; yes, let my offspring be rooted out.
9;If mine heart have been deceived by a woman, or if I have laid wait at my
neighbor's door. 10:Then let my wife grind to another, and let others bow down
upon her. 11:For this is an heinous crime, yes, it is an iniquity to be punished by the
judges. 12:For it is a fire hat consumes to destruction, and would root out all mine
increase. 13:If I did despise the cause of my manservant or of my maidservant,

when they contended with me. 14:What then shall I do when God rises up? and
when he visits what shall I answer him? 15:Did not he that made me in the womb
make him? and did not one fashion us in the womb? 16:If I have with held the poor
from their desire, or have caused the eyes of the widow to fail. 17:Or have eaten my
morsel myself alone, and the fatherless has not eaten thereof. 18:(For from my
youth he was brought up with me, as with a father, and I have guided her from my
mother's womb;) 19:If I have seen any perish for want of clothing, or any poor
without covering. 20:If his loins have not blessed me, and if he were not warmed
with the fleece of my sheep. 21:If I have lifted up my hand against the fatherless,
when I saw my help in the gate. 22:Then let mine arm fall from my shoulder blade,
and mine arm be broken from the bone. 23:For destruction from God was a terror to
me, and by reason of his highness I could not endure. 24:If I have made gold my
hope, or have said to the fine gold, You are my confidence. 25:If I rejoiced because
my wealth was great, and because mine hand had gotten much. 26:If I beheld the
sun when it shined, or the moon walking in brightness. 27:And my heart has been
secretly enticed, or my mouth has kissed my hand. 28:This also were an iniquity to
be punished by the judge: for I should have denied the God that is above. 29:If I
rejoiced at the destruction of him that hated me, or lifted up myself when evil found
him. 30:Neither have I suffered my mouth to sin by wishing a curse to his soul.
31:If the men of my tabernacle said not, Oh that we had of his flesh! we cannot be
satisfied. 32:The stranger did not lodge in the street: but I opened my doors to the
traveler. 33:If I covered my transgressions as Adam, by hiding mine iniquity in my
bosom. 34:Did I fear a great multitude, or did the contempt of families terrify me,
that I kept silence, and went not out of the door? 35:Oh that one would hear me!
behold, my desire is, that the Almighty would answer me, and that mine adversary
had written a book. 36:Surely I would take it upon my shoulder, and bind it as a
crown to me. 37:I would declare to him the number of my steps; as a prince would I
go near to him. 38:If my land cry against me, or that the furrows likewise thereof
complain. 39:If I have eaten the fruits thereof without money, or have caused the
owners thereof to lose their life. 40;Let thistles grow instead of wheat,and cockle
instead of barley.

(Then the words of Job are ended.)

32:1:So these three men ceased to answer Job; because he was righteous in his
own eyes. 2:Then was kindled the wrath of Elihu the son of Barachel the Buzite, of
the kindred of Ram: against Job was his wrath kindled, because he justified himself
rather than God. 3:Also against his three friends was his wrath kindled, because
they had found no answer, and yet had condemned Job. 4:Now Elihu had waited till
Job had spoken, because they were elder than he. 5:When Elihu saw that there was
no answer in the mouth of these three men, then his wrath was kindled. 6:And Elihu
the son of Barachel the Buzite answered and said, I am young, and your are very
old; wherefore I was afraid, and durst not show you mine opinion. 7:I said, Days
should speak, and multitude of years should teach wisdom. 8:But there is a spirit in
man: and the inspiration of the Almighty given them understanding. 9:Great men
are not always wise: neither do the aged understand judgment. 10;Therefore I said,
Hearken to me; I also will show mine opinion. 11:Behold, I waited for your words; I
gave ear to your reasons, whilst your searched out what to say. 12:Yes, I attended to
you, and, behold, there was none of you that convinced Job,

or that answered his words. 13:Lest your should say, We have found out wisdom: God throw her down, but not man. 14:Now he has not directed his words against me: neither will I answer him with your speeches. 15:They were amazed, they answered no more: they left off speaking. 16:When I had waited, (for they spoke not, but stood still, and answered no more;) 17:I said; I will answer also my part, I also will show mine opinion. 18:For I am full of matter, the spirit within me constrains me. 19:Behold, my belly is as wine which has no vent; it is ready to burst like new bottles. 20:I will speak, that I may be refreshed: I will open my lips and answer. 21:Let me not, I pray you, accept any man's person, neither let me give flattering titles to man. 22:For I know not to give flattering titles; in so doing my maker would soon take me away.

33:1: Wherefore, Job, I pray your, hear my speeches, and hearken to all my words. 2:Behold, now I have opened my mouth, my tongue has spoken in my mouth. 3:My words shall be of the uprightness of my heart: and my lips shall utter knowledge clearly. 4:The Spirit of God has made me, and the breath of the Almighty has given me life. 5:If your canst answer me, set your words in order before me, stand up. 6;Behold, I am according to your wish in God's stead:I also am formed out of the clay. 7;Behold, my terror shall not make your afraid, neither shall my hand be heavy upon your. 8:Surely your have spoken in mine hearing, and I have heard the voice of your words, saying. 9:I am clean without transgression, I am innocent; neither is there iniquity in me. 10;Behold, he finds occasions against me, he counts me for his enemy. 11:He puts my feet in the stocks, he marks all my paths.

12:Behold, in this your are not just: I will answer your, that God is greater than man. 13:Why dost your strive against him? for he gives not account of any of his matters. 14:For God speaks once, yes twice, yet man perceives it not. 15:In a dream, in a vision of the night, when deep sleep falls upon men, in slumbering upon the bed. 16:Then he opens the ears of men, and seals their instruction. 17:That he may withdraw man from his purpose, and hide pride from man. 18:He keeps back his soul from the pit, and his life from perishing by the sword. 19:He is chastened also with pain upon his bed, and the multitude of his bones with strong pain. 20:So that his life ab-hordes bread, and his soul dainty meat. 21:His flesh is consumed away, that it cannot be seen; and his bones that were not seen stick out. 22:Yes, his soul draws near to the grave, and his life to the destroyers. 23:If there be a messenger with him, an interpreter, one among a thousand, to show to man his uprightness.

24:Then he is gracious to him, and says, Deliver him from going down to the pit: I have found a ransom. 25;His flesh shall be fresher than a child's: he shall return to the days of his youth. 26:He shall pray to God, and he will be favorable to him: and he shall see his face with joy, for he will render to man his righteousness. 27:He looks upon men, and if any say, I have sinned, and perverted that which was right, and it profited me not. 28:He will deliver his soul from going into the pit, and his life shall see the light. 29:Look, all these things work for God often times with man, 30:To bring back his soul from the pit, to be enlightened with the light of the living. 31:Mark well, O Job, hearken to me: hold your peace, and I will speak. 32:If your have any thing to say, answer me: speak, for I desire to justify your. 33:If not, hearken to me: hold your peace, and I shall teach your wisdom.

34:1:Furthermore Elihu answered and said: 2:Hear my words, O your wise men and give ear to me, your that have knowledge. 3:For the ear hears words, as the mouth taste meat. 4:Let us choose to us judgment: let us know among ourselves what is good. 5:For Job has said, I am righteous: and God has taken away my judgment. 6;Should I lie against my right? my wound is incurable without transgression. 7;What man is like Job, who drinks up scorning like water? 8:Which goeth in company with the workers of iniquity, and walks with wicked men. 9:For he has said, It profits a man nothing that he should delight himself with God. 10:Therefore hearken to me, your men of understanding: far be it from God, that he should do wickedness; and from the Almighty, that he should commit iniquity. 11:For the work of a man shall he render to him, and cause every man to find according to his ways. 12:Yes, surely God will not do wickedly, neither will the Almighty pervert judgment. 13:Who has given him a charge over the earth? or who has disposed the whole world? 14:If he set his heart upon man, if he gather to himself his spirit and his breath. 15:All flesh shall perish together, and man shall turn again to dust. 16:If now your have understanding, hear this: hearken to the voice of my words. 17:Shall even he that hate right government? and will your condemn him that is most just? 18:Is it fit to say to a King, your are wicked? And to princes, your are ungodly? 19:How much less to him that accepted not the persons of princes, nor regarded the rich more than the poor? For they all are the work of his hands. 20:In a moment shall they die, and the people shall be troubled at midnight, and pass away: and the mighty shall be taken away without hand. 21:For his eyes are upon the ways of man, and he sees all his goings. 22;There is no darkness, nor shadow of death, where the workers of iniquity may hide themselves. 23:For he will not lay upon man more than right, that he should enter into judgment with God. 24:He shall break in pieces mighty men without number, and set others in their stead. 25:Therefore he knows their works, and he over turns them in the night, so that they are destroyed. 26:He strikes them as wicked men in the open sight of others. 27:Because they turned back from him, and would not consider any of his ways. 28:So that they cause the cry of the poor to come to him, and he hears the cry of the afflicted. 29:When he gives quietness, who then can make trouble? and when he hides his face, who then can behold him? Whether it be done against a nation, or against a man only. 30:That the hypocrite reign not, lest the people be ensnared. 31:Surely it is meet to be said to God, I have borne chastisement, I will not offend any more. 32:That which I see not teach your me: if I have done iniquity, I will do no more. 33:Should it be according to your mind? he will recompense it, whether your refuse, or whether your choose; and not I: therefore speak what your knowest. 34:Let men of understanding tell me, and let a wise man hearken to me. 35:Job has spoken without knowledge, and his words were without wisdom. 36:My desire is that Job may be tried to the end because of his answers for wicked men. 37:For he adds rebellion to his sin, he claps his hands among us, and multiplies his words against God.

35:1:(Elihu continued speaking,) 2:Think your this to be right, that your said, My righteousness is more than God's? 3:For your said, what advantage will it be to your? And: What profit shall I have, if I be cleansed from my sin? 4:I will answer your, and your companions with your. 5:Look to the heavens, and see, and behold the clouds which are higher than you.

6:If you sins, what injury do you do against God? Or if your transgressions be multiplied, what does your to him? 7:If your be righteous, what give your him? Or what receive he of your hand? 8:your wickedness may hurt a man as your are, and your righteousness may profit the son of man. 9;By reason of the multitude of oppressions they make the oppressed to cry: they cry out by reason of the arm of the mighty. 10;But none says, Where is God my maker, who gives songs in the night; 11;Who teaches us more than the beasts of the earth, and makes us wiser than the fowls of heaven? 12;here they cry, but none gives answer, because of the pride of evil men. 13;Surely God will not hear vanity, neither will the Almighty regard it. 14;Although your says your shall not see him, yet judgment is before him; therefore trust your in him. 15;But now, because it is not so, he has visited in his anger; yet he knows it not in great extremity: 16;Therefore doth Job open his mouth in vain; he multiplies words without knowledge.

36:1;Elihu also proceeded talking, 2:Suffer me a little, and I will show your that I have yet to speak on God's behalf. 3:I will fetch my knowledge from afar, and will ascribe righteousness to my Maker. 4:For truly my words shall not be false: he that is perfect in knowledge is with your. 5:Behold, God is mighty, and despises not any, for he is mighty in strength and wisdom. 6:He preserves not the life of the wicked: but gives life to the poor. 7:He with draws not his eyes from the righteous: but with Kings are they on the throne? Yes, he does establish them forever, and they are exalted. 8:And if they be bound in fetters, and be held in cords of affliction. 9:Then he shows them their work, and their sins that they have exceeded. 10:He opens also their ear to discipline, and commands that they return from iniquity. 11:If they obey and serve him, they shall spend their days in prosperity, and their years in pleasures. 12:But if they obey not, they shall perish by the sword, and they shall die without knowledge. 13:But the hypocrites in heart heap up wrath: they cry not when he binds them. 14:They die in youth, and their life is among the unclean. 15:He delivers the poor in his affliction, and opens their ears in oppression. 16:Even so would he have removed your out of the strait into a broad place, where there is no straightness; and that which should be set on your table should be full of fatness. 17:But your have fulfilled the judgment of the wicked: judgment and justice take hold on your. 18:Because there is wrath, beware lest he take your away with his stroke: then a great ransom cannot deliver your. 19:Will he esteem your riches? no, not gold, nor all the forces of strength. 20:Desire not the night, when people are cut off in their place. 21:Take heed, regard not iniquity: for this have your chosen rather than affliction. 22:Behold, God exalts by his power: who teaches like him? 23:Who has enjoined him his way? or who can say, You have wrought iniquity? 24:Remember that your magnify his work, which men behold. 25:Every man may see it; man may behold it afar off. 26:Behold, God is great, and we know him not, neither can the number of his years be searched out. 27:He makes small the drops of water: they pour down rain according to the vapor thereof: 28:Which the clouds do drop and distil upon man abundantly. 29:Also can any understand the spreading of the clouds, or the noise of his tabernacle? 30:Behold, he spreads his light upon it, and covers the bottom of the sea. 31:For by them judges he the people; he gives meat in abundance. 32:With clouds he covers the light; and commands it not to shine by the clouds that come between. 33:The noise there of shows concerning it, the cattle also concerning the vapor.

37:1: At this also my heart trembles, and is moved out of his place. 2:Hear
attentively the noise of his voice, and the sound that go's out of his mouth. 3:He
directs it under the whole heaven, and his lightning to the ends of the earth. 4:After
it a voice roars: he thunders with the voice of his excellency; and he will not stay
them when his voice is heard. 5:God thunders marvelously with his voice; great
things does he, which we cannot comprehend. 6:For he says to the snow, Be your on
the earth; likewise to the small rain, and to the great rain of his strength. 7:He seals
up the hand of every man; that all men may know his work. 8:Then the beasts go
into dens, and remain in their places. 9:Out of the south comes the whirlwind:and
cold out of the north. 10:By the breath of God frost is given: and the breadth of the
waters is straitened. 11:Also by watering he wears the thick cloud: he scatters his
bright cloud. 12:And it is turned round about by his counsels: that they may do what
so ever he commands them upon the face of the world in the earth. 13:He causes it
to come, whether for correction, or for his land, or for mercy. 14:Hearken to this, O
Job: stand still, and consider the wondrous works of God. 15:Do you know when
God disposed them, and caused the light of his cloud to shine? 16:Do you know the
balancing of the clouds, the wondrous works of him which is perfect in knowledge?
17:How your garments are warm, when he quiets the earth by the south wind?
18;Have you with him spread out the sky, which is strong, and as a molten looking
glass? 19:Teach us what we shall say to him; for we cannot order our speech by
reason of darkness. 20:Shall it be told him that I speak? if a man speak, surely he
shall be swallowed up. 21:And now men see not the bright light which is in the
clouds: but the wind passes, and cleanses them. 22:Fair weather comes out of the
north: with God is terrible majesty. 23:Touching the Almighty, we cannot find him
out: he is excellent in power, and in judgment, and in plenty of justice: he will not
afflict. 24:Men do therefore fear him: he respects not any that are wise of heart.

38:1;Then the LORD spoke to Job out of the whirlwind, and said, 2:Who is this
that darkens counsel by words without knowledge? 3:Gird up now your loins like a
man; for I will demand of your, and answer your me. 4:Where wast your when I laid
the foundations of the earth? Declare if your have understanding 5:Who has laid the
measures thereof, if your knowest? or who has stretched the line upon it? 6:Where
upon are the foundations thereof fastened? or who laid the corner stone thereof.
7;When the morning stars sang together, and all the sons of God shouted for joy?
8:Or who shut up the sea with doors, when it brake forth, as if it had issued out of
the womb? 9;When I made the cloud the garment thereof, and thick darkness a
swaddling band for it, 10:And brake up for it my decreed place, and set bars and
doors. 11;And said, Hitherto shall your come, but no further, and here shall your
proud waves be stayed? 12:Have your commanded the morning since your days;
and caused the day spring to know his place. 13:That it might take hold of the ends
of the earth, that the wicked might be shaken out of it? 14;It is turned as clay to the
seal; and they stand as a garment. 15:And from the wicked their light is with held,
and the high arm shall be broken. 16:Have your entered into the springs of the sea?
or have your walked in the search of the depth? 17:Have the gates of death been
opened to your? or have your seen the doors of the shadow of death? 18:Have your
perceived the breadth of the earth? declare if your knowest it all. 19:Where is the
way where light dwells? and as for darkness, where is the place thereof. 20:That
your should take it to the bound thereof,

and that your should know the paths to he house thereof? 21:Knows you it because your was then born? Or because the number of your days is great? 22:Have your entered into the treasures of the snow? or have your seen the treasures of the hail. 23:Which I have reserved against the time of trouble, against the day of battle and war? 24:By what way is the light parted, which scattered the east wind upon the earth? 25:Who has divided a watercourse for the over flowing of waters, or a way for the lightning of thunder. 26:To cause it to rain on the earth, where no man is,on the wilderness, wherein there is no man. 27;To satisfy the desolate and waste ground, and to cause the bud of the tender herb to spring forth? 28:Has the rain a father? or who has begotten the drops of dew? 29:Out of whose womb came the ice? And the hoary frost of heaven, who has gendered it? 30:The waters are hid as with a stone, and the face of the deep is frozen. 31:Can your bind the sweet influences of Pleiades, or loose the belt of Orion? 32:Can your bring forth Mazzaroth in his season? Or can your guide Arcturus with his sons? 33:Knows your the ordinances of heaven? Can your set the dominion thereof in the earth? 34:Can your lift up your voice to the clouds, that abundance of waters may cover your? 35:Can your send lightnings, that they may go, and say to you, I have ran the path you have set before me. 36;Who has put wisdom in the inward parts? Or who has given understanding to the heart? 37:Who can number the clouds in wisdom? Or who can keep the bottles of heaven. 38:When the dust grows into hardness, and the clouds cleave fast together? 39:Will you hunt the prey for the lion? Or fill the appetite of the young lions, 40:When they couch in their dens, and abide in the covert to lie in wait? 41:Who provides for the raven his food? When his young ones cry to God, they wander for lack of meat.

39:1;Know your the time when the wild goats of the rock bring forth? Or can you mark when the hinds do calve? 2:Can you number the months that they fulfill? Or know you the time when they bring forth? 3:They bow themselves, they bring forth their young ones, they cast out their sorrows. 4:Their young ones are in good liking, they grow up with corn, they go forth, and return not to them. 5:Who has sent out the wild ass free? Or who has loosed the bands of the wild ass? 6:Whose house I have made the wilderness, and the barren land his dwellings. 7:He scorns the multitude of the city, neither regards he the crying of the driver. 8:The range of the mountains is his pasture, and he searches after every green thing. 9:Will the unicorn be willing to serve you, or abide by your crib? 10:Can your bind the unicorn with his band in the furrow? Or will he harrow the valleys after your? 11:Will your trust him, because his strength is great? Or will you leave your labor to him? 12:Will your believe him, that he will bring home your seed, and gather it into your barn? 13:Did you give the good wings to the peacocks? Or wings and feathers to the ostrich? 14:Which leaves her eggs in the earth, and warms them in dust, 15:And forgets that the foot may crush them, or that the wild beast may break them. 16:She is hardened against her young ones, as though they were not hers: her labor is in vain without fear. 17;Because God has deprived her of wisdom, neither has he imparted to her understanding. 18:What time she lifts up herself on high, she scorns the horse and his rider. 19:Have you given the horse strength? Have you clothed his neck with thunder? 20:Can you make him afraid as a grasshopper? The glory of his nostrils is terrible. 21:He pawed in the valley, and rejoiced in his strength, he go's on to meet the armed men.

22:He mocked at fear, and is not frighted, neither turns he back from the sword.
23:The quiver rattle against him, the glittering spear and the shield. 24;He swallows
the ground with fierceness and rage, neither believes he that it is the sound of the
trumpet. 25:He says among the trumpets, Ha, ha; and he smells the battle afar off,
the thunder of the captains, and the shouting. 26:Does the hawk fly by your wisdom,
and stretch her wings toward the south? 27;Do the eagle mount up at your
command, and make her nest on high? 28;She dwells and abides on the rock, upon
the crag of the rock, and the strong place. 29:From thence she seeks the prey, and
her eyes behold afar off. 30:Her young ones also suck up blood,
and where the slain are there is she.

40:1:Moreover the LORD said to Job: 2:Shall he that contends with the Almighty
instruct him? He that reproves God, let him answer it.

3:Then Job answered the LORD, and said: 4:Behold, I am vile; what shall I
answer your? I will lay mine hand upon my mouth. 5:Once have I spoken; but I will
not answer; yes twice, but I will proceed no further. 6;Then answered the LORD to
Job out of the whirlwind, and said; 7:Gird up your loins now like a man, I will
demand of your, and declare your to me. 8:Will your also dismiss my judgment?
Will your condemn me, that your may be righteous? 9:Have your an arm like God?
Or can you thunder with a voice like him? 10:Deck yourself now with majesty and
excellency; and array yourself with glory and beauty. 11:Cast abroad the rage of
your wrath, and behold every one that is proud, and abase him. 12:Look on every
one that is proud, and bring him low; and tread down the wicked in their place.
13;Hide them in the dust together; and bind their faces in secret. 14:Then will I also
confess to your that your own right hand can save your. 15:Behold now behemoth,
which I made with your; he eats grass as an ox. 16;Look now, his strength is in his
loins, and his force is in the navel of his belly. 17;He moves his tail like a cedar: the
sinews of his stones are wrapped together. 18:His bones are as strong pieces of
brass; his bones are like bars of iron. 19:He came at the beginning of God's ways, he
that made him can make his sword to approach to him. 20:Surely the mountains
bring him forth food, where all the beasts of the field play. 21:He lies under the
shady trees, in the covert of the reed, and fens. 22:The shady trees cover him with
their shadow; the willows of the brook compass him about. 23:Behold, he drinks up
a river, and haste not: he trust that he can draw up Jordan into his mouth. 24:He
takes it with his eyes: his nose pierce through snares. 41:1:Canst your draw out
leviathan with an hook? Or his tongue with a cord which your lays down? 2:Can
your put an hook into his nose? or bore his jaw through with a thorn? 3:Will he
make many supplications to your? Will he speak soft words to you? 4;Will he make
a covenant with you? Will you take him for a servant forever? 5:Will you play with
him as with a bird? Or will your bind him for your maidens? 6:Shall the
companions make a banquet of him? Shall they part him among the merchants?
7:Can you fill his skin with barbed irons? Or his head with fish spears? 8:Lay your
hand upon him, remember the battle, do no more.9:Behold, the hope of him is in
vain: shall not one be cast down even at the sight of him? 10:None is so fierce that
dare stir him up: who then is able to stand before me? 11:Who has prevented me,
that I should repay him? What soever is under the whole heaven is mine. 12:I will
not conceal his parts, nor his power, nor his comely proportion.

13:Who can discover the face of his garment? or who can come to him with his double bridle? 14:Who can open the doors of his face? his teeth are terrible round about. 15:His scales are his pride, shut up together as with a close seal. 16:One is so near to another, that no air can come between them. 17:They are joined one to another, they stick together, that they cannot be sundered. 18:By his sneezing a light doth shine, and his eyes are like the eyelids of the morning. 19:Out of his mouth go burning lamps, and sparks of fire leap out. 20:Out of his nostrils goeth smoke, as from a seething pot or caldron. 21:His breath kindles coals, and a flame goeth out of his mouth. 22:In his neck remains strength, and sorrow is turned into joy before him. 23:The flakes of his flesh are joined together, they are firm in themselves; they cannot be moved. 24:His heart is as firm as a stone; yes, as hard as a piece of the nether millstone. 25:When he raises up himself, the mighty are afraid, by reason of breaking they purify themselves. 26:The sword can not harm him: nor the spear, the dart, nor the harpoon. 27:He esteems iron as straw, and brass as rotten wood. 28;The arrow cannot make him flee: sling stones are turned with him into stubble. 29:Darts are counted as stubble: he laughs at the shaking of a spear. 30:Sharp stones are under him: he spreads sharp pointed things upon the mire. 31:He makes the deep to boil like a pot: he makes the sea like a pot of ointment. 32:He makes a path to shine after him; one would think the deep to be hoary. 33:Upon earth there is not his like, who is made without fear. 34:He beholds all high things he is the King, over all the children of pride.

Job 42:1 Then Job answered the LORD, and said: 2:I know that your can do anything, and that no thought can be with held from your. 3;Who is he that hides counsel without knowledge? Therefore have I uttered that I understood not, things too wonderful for me to know, which I knew not. 4:Hear, me I ask you, and I will speak, I will ask of you, and declare you to me. 5;I have heard of you by the hearing of the ear, but now with mine eyes, I have seen you. 6:Wherefore I abhor myself, and repent in dust and ashes.

42:7;After Job was finished speaking; The LORD said to Eliphaz the Temanite: My wrath is kindled against you, and against your two friends: for you have not spoken of me the things that are right, as my servant Job has. 8:Therefore take to you now seven bullocks and seven rams, and go to my servant Job, and offer up for yourselves a burnt offering, and my servant Job shall pray for you, for him will I accept. Lest I deal with you after your folly, in that you have not spoken of me the things that are right, like my servant Job. 9:So Eliphaz the Temanite and Bildad the Shuhite and Zophar the Naamathite went, and did according as the Lord commanded them, the Lord also accepted Job. 10:And the Lord turned the captivity of Job, when he prayed for his friends: also the Lord gave Job twice as much as he had before. 11:Then came there to him all his brethren, and all his sisters, and all they that had been of his acquaintance before, and did eat bread with him in his house, and they bemoaned him, and comforted him over all the evil that the Lord had brought upon him. Every man also gave him a piece of money, and every one an earring of gold. 12:So the Lord blessed the latter end of Job more than his beginning, for he had fourteen thousand sheep, and six thousand camels, and a thousand yoke of oxen, and a thousand she asses. 13:He had also seven sons and three daughters. 14:And he called the name of the first, Jemima;

and the name of the second, Kezia; and the name of the third, Keren-happuch.
15:And in all the land were no women found so fair as the daughters of Job: and
their father gave them inheritance among their brethren. 16:After this lived Job an
hundred and forty years, and saw his sons, and his sons' sons, even four generations.
17:So Job died, being old and full of days.

More about Job:

The book of Job; Job was originality written in Aramaic, Job, who was thought to be a Asian Chieftain who lived in the land of Uz (Modern Iran) the oldest book found was written in around the time around 600 B.C. according to the Vatican Archives. **His first family** names were: **1st.Wife:** Uzit, **His 7 Sons were ;** 1st.Agnor, 2nd.Thumel, 3rd.Goters, 4th.Hamel, 5th.Qigma, 6th.Dysta, 7th.Sidura. **His 3 Daughters;** names were;1st.Lugal, 2nd Ninsun, 3rd.Sidura.

(Job's second family names were)

Job's 2nd Wife; Dinah:(Vindicated), His **7 Sons were :**1st.Eigotu, 2nd.Dogia, 3rd.Famia, 4th.Hebasa, 5th.Kinoe, 6th.Niplata, 7th.Regnata, and his, **3 Daughters;** name were: 1st.Jemima:(Bright and beautiful day), 2nd.Kezia:(Cinnamon like bark), 3rd.Keren-happuch:(Fair colors)

(When he was tested, and when Job Died)

Vatican Archives: The Book of Job, and The Appendix to the Septuagint: When Job was struck with his test, he was believed to be 70 years of age, and after this God, doubled his years. When Job died at the age of one hundred and forty years, there with him were only his three daughters. Jemima who played the Lyre, Kezia who held the incense pan, and Keren-happuch who beat on the drum. **Note:** it is written that a Chariot of Light came for his soul.

The picture below is looking onto the front of Vatican City.

A picture looking out from Vatican City, towards Rome.

The Pictures above: left the Archives, right the Secret Archives found in the Vatican. He entrance is hidden in the wall, when closed it is imposable to see it.

+/- June $10^{th.}$ (Sivan $11^{th.}$)

Dositheus had his arm cut off at the shoulder

(2 Maccabees 12;32-37) 32:After the feast of Pentecost, they lost no time in
marching against Gorgias, governor of Idumea. 33:Who opposed them with three
thousand foot soldiers and four hundred horsemen. 34:In the ensuing battle, a few
of the Jews were slain. 35:A man called Dositheus,

a powerful horseman and one of Bacenor's men, caught hold of Gorgias, grasped his military cloak and dragged him along by main strength, intending to capture the vile wretch alive. When a Thracian horseman attacked Dositheus and cut off his arm at the shoulder. Then Gorgias fled to Marisa. 36:After Esdris and his men had been fighting for a long time and were weary, Judas called upon the Lord, to show himself their ally and leader in the battle. 37:Then raising a battle cry in his ancestral language, and with songs, he charged Gorgias men when they were not expecting it and put them to flight.

+/- June 10th. (Sivan 11th.)

They Baptized 3000 Souls

(Acts 2:1-41) 2:1: And when the day of Pentecost was fully come, they were all with one accord in one place. 2:And suddenly there came a sound from heaven as of a rushing mighty wind, and it filled all the house where they were sitting. 3:And there appeared to them cloven tongues like as of fire, and it sat upon each of them. 4:And they were all filled with the Holy Ghost, and began to speak with other tongues, as the Spirit gave them utterance. 5:And there were dwelling at Jerusalem Jews, devout men, out of every nation under heaven. 6:Now when this was noised abroad, the multitude came together, and were confounded, because that every man heard them speak in his own language. 7:And they were all amazed and marveled, saying one to another, Behold, are not all these which speak Galileans? 8:And how hear we every man in our own tongue, wherein we were born? 9:Parthians, and Medes, and Elamites, and the dwellers in Mesopotamia, and in Judea, and Cappuccino, in Pontus, and Asia. 10:Phrygia, and Pamphylia, in Egypt, and in the parts of Libya about Styrene, and strangers of Rome, Jews and proselytes. 11:Crete and Arabians, we do hear them speak in our tongues the wonderful works of God. 12:And they were all amazed, and were in doubt, saying one to another, What meaneth this? 13:Others mocking said, These men are full of new wine. 14:But Peter, standing up with the eleven, lifted up his voice, and said to them, your men of Judea, and all your that dwell at Jerusalem, be this known to you, and hearken to my words. 15:For these are not drunken, as your suppose, seeing it is but the third hour of the day. 16:But this is that which was spoken by the prophet Joel, 17:and it shall come to pass in the last days, says God, I will pour out of my Spirit upon all flesh: and your sons and your daughters shall prophesy, and your young men shall see visions, and your old men shall dream dreams. 18:And on my servants and on my handmaidens I will pour out in those days of my Spirit; and they shall prophesy. 19:And I will show wonders in heaven above, and signs in the earth beneath; blood, and fire, and vapor of smoke. 20:The sun shall be turned into darkness, and the moon into blood, before that great and notable day of the Lord come. 21:And it shall come to pass, that whosoever shall call on the name of the Lord shall be saved. 22:your men of Israel, hear these words: Jesus of Nazareth, a man approved of God among you by miracles and wonders and signs, which God did by him in the midst of you, as your yourselves also know. 23:Him, being delivered by the determinate counsel and foreknowledge of God, your have taken, and by wicked hands have crucified and slain. 24:Whom God has raised up, having loosed the pains of death: because it was not possible that he should be held of it. 25:For David spoke concerning him, I foresaw the Lord always before my face,

for he is on my right hand, that I should not be moved. 26:Therefore did my heart rejoice, and my tongue was glad; moreover also my flesh shall rest in hope. 27:Because your will not leave my soul in hell, neither will your suffer your Holy One to see corruption. 28:Your have made known to me the ways of life; your shall make me full of joy with your countenance. 29:Men and brethren, let me freely speak to you of the patriarch David, that he is both dead and buried, and his sepulcher is with us to this day. 30:Therefore being a prophet, and knowing that God had sworn with an oath to him, that of the fruit of his loins, according to the flesh, he would raise up Christ to sit on his throne. 31:He seeing this before spoke of the resurrection of Christ, that his soul was not left in hell, neither his flesh did see corruption. 32:This Jesus has God raised up, whereof we all are witnesses.
33:Therefore being by the right hand of God exalted, and having received of the Father the promise of the Holy Ghost, he has shed forth this, which your now see and hear. 34:For David is not ascended into the heavens: but he says himself, The Lord said to my Lord, Sit your on my right hand. 35:Until I make your foes your footstool. 36:Therefore let all the house of Israel know assuredly, that God hath made that same Jesus, whom you have crucified, both Lord and Christ. 37:Now when they heard this, they were pricked in their heart, and said to Peter and to the rest of the apostles, Men and brethren, what shall we do?
38:Then Peter said to them, Repent, and be baptized every one of you in the 36:Therefore let all the house of Israel know assuredly, that God has made that same Jesus, whom your have crucified, both name of Jesus Christ for the remission of sins, and your shall receive the gift of the Holy Ghost. 39:For the promise is to you, and to your children, and to all that are afar off, even as many as the Lord our God shall call. 40:And with many other words did he testify and exhort, saying, Save yourselves from this untoward generation. 41;Then they that gladly received his word were baptized, and the same day there were, added to them about three thousand souls.

+/- June 10th. (Sivan 11th.)

They planed to kill Paul

(Acts 23:12-31)12:And when it was day, certain of the Jews banded together, and bound themselves under a curse, saying that they would neither eat nor drink till they had killed Paul. 13:And they were more than forty which had made this conspiracy. 14:And they came to the chief priests and elders, and said, We have bound ourselves under a great curse, that we will eat nothing until we have slain Paul. 15:Now therefore your with the council signify to the chief captain that he bring him down to you to morrow, as though your would esquire something more perfectly concerning him: and we, or ever he come near, are ready to kill him.
16:And when Paul's sister's son heard of their lying in wait, he went and entered into the castle, and told Paul. 17:Then Paul called one of the centurions to him, and said, Bring this young man to the chief captain: for he has a certain thing to tell him.
18:So he took him, and brought him to the chief captain, and said, Paul the prisoner called me to him, and prayed me to bring this young man to your, who has something to say to your. 19:Then the chief captain took him by the hand, and went with him aside privately, and asked him, What is that your have to tell me? 20:And he said; The Jews have agreed to your desire, that you would bring Paul,

down tomorrow into the council, as though they would inquire somewhat of him more perfectly. 21:But do not your yield to them: for there lie in wait for him of them more than forty men, which have bound themselves with an oath, that they will neither eat nor drink till they have killed him: and now are they ready, looking for a promise from your. 22:So the chief captain then let the young man depart, and charged him, see your tell no man that you have, showed these things to me. 23:And he called to him two centurions, saying, Make ready two hundred soldiers to go to Caesarea, and horsemen threescore and ten, and spear men two hundred, at the third hour of the night. 24:And provide them beasts, that they may set Paul on, and bring him safe to Felix the governor. 25:And he wrote a letter after this manner: 26:Claudius Lysias to the most excellent governor Felix sends greeting. 27:This man was taken of the Jews, and should have been killed of them: then came I with an army, and rescued him, having understood that he was a Roman. 28:And when I would have known the cause wherefore they accused him, I brought him forth into their council. 29:Whom I perceived to be accused of questions of their law, but to have nothing laid to his charge worthy of death or of bonds. 30:And when it was told me how that the Jews laid in wait for the man, I sent straightway to you, and gave commandment to his accusers also to say before you what they had against him, Farewell. 31:Then the soldiers, as it was commanded them, took Paul, and brought him by night to Antipatris.

+/- June 11th. (Sivan 12th.)

The year +/- 1357 B.C. The people complained against Moses

(Exodus 15:23-25) The People complained against Moses. 23:And when they came to Marah, they could not drink of the waters of Marah, for they were bitter: therefore the name of it was called Marah. 24:And the people murmured against Moses, saying, What shall we drink? 25:And he cried to the Lord; and the Lord shewed him a tree, which when he had cast into the waters, the waters were made sweet: there he made for them a statute and an ordinance, and there he provided for them.

+/- June 11th. (Sivan 12th.)

Judas and his army purified themselves

(2 Maccabees 12:38) 38:Judas rallied his army and went to the city of Adullam. As the week was ending, they purified themselves according to custom, and kept the sabbath there.

+/- June 11th. (Sivan 12th.)

Paul was brought to Herod's judgment Hall

(Acts 23:32-35) 32:The next day they returned to the castle, leaving the horseman to complete the journey with him. 33:Who, when they came to Caesarea, and delivered the epistle to the governor, presented Paul also before him. 34:And when the governor had read the letter, he asked of what province he was. And when he understood that he was of Cilia; 35:I will hear your, said he, when your accusers are also come. And he commanded him to be kept in Herod's judgment hall.

+/- June 12th. (Sivan 13th.)

The year +/- 1357 B.C. They camped at Elim

(Exodus 15:27)27:And they came to Elim, where were twelve wells of water, and threescore and ten palm trees, and they encamped there by the waters.

+/- June 12th. (Sivan 13th.)

Judas did a Noble act

(2 Maccabees 12:39-46) 39:On the fallowing day, since the task had now become urgent, Judas and his men went to gather up the bodies of the slain and bury them with their kinsmen in their ancestral tombs. 40:But under the tunic of each of the dead they found amulets sacred to the idols of Jamnia, which the law forbids the Hebrews to wear. So it was clear to all that this is why these men had been slain. 41:They all therefore praised the ways of the Lord,the just judge who brings to light the things that are hidden. 42:Turning to supplication, they prayed that the sinful deed might be fully blotted out. The Nobel Judas warned the soldiers to keep themselves free from sin for they have seen with their own eyes what had happened because of the sin of those who have fallen.

43:He took up a collection among all his soldiers, amounting to two thousand silver drachmas, which he sent to Jerusalem to provide for an expiatory sacrifice. In dunning this he acted in a very excellent and noble way, inasmuch as he had spoken of the resurrection of the dead in view. 44:For if he did not expect the fallen to raise again, it would have been useless and foolish to pray for them in death. 45:But if he did this with a view to the splendid reward that awaits those who had gone to rest in godliness, it was a holy and pious thought. 46;This he made atonement for the dead, that they might be freed from this sin.

+/- June 14th. (Sivan 15th.)

The year +/- 1357 B.C. The children of Israel came into the wilderness of sin

(Exodus 16:1-6) 1:And they took their journey from Elim, and all the congregation of the children of Israel came to the wilderness of Sin, which is between Elim and Sinai, on the fifteenth day of the second month after their departing out of the land of Egypt. 2:And the whole congregation of the children of Israel murmured against Moses and Aaron in the wilderness. 3:And the children of Israel said to them, Would to God we had died by the hand of the Lord in the land of Egypt, when we sat by the flesh pots, and when we did eat bread to the full; for your have brought us forth into this wilderness, to kill this whole assembly with hunger. 4:Then said the Lord to Moses, Behold, I will rain bread from heaven for you; and the people shall go out and gather a certain rate every day, that I may prove them, whether they will walk in my law, or no. 5:And it shall come to pass, that on the sixth day they shall prepare that which they bring in; and it shall be twice as much as they gather daily. 6:And Moses and Aaron said to all the children of Israel, At even, then your shall know that the Lord, has brought you out from the land of Egypt.

+/- June 15th. (Sivan 16th.)

The year +/- 1357 B.C. God hears the murmurings of his children.

(Exodus 16:7-12) 7:And in the morning, then you shall see the glory of the Lord; for that he hears your murmurings against the Lord: and what are we, that your murmur against us? 8:And Moses said, This shall be, when the Lord shall give you in the evening flesh to eat, and in the morning bread to the full; for that the Lord hears your murmurings which you murmur against him: and what are we? Your murmurings is not against us, but against the Lord. 9:And Moses spoke to Aaron, Say to all the congregation of the children of Israel, Come near before the Lord: for he has heard your murmurings. 10:And it came to pass, as Aaron spoke to the whole congregation of the children of Israel, that they looked toward the wilderness, and, behold, the glory of the Lord appeared in the cloud. 11:And the Lord spoke to Moses, saying, 12:I have heard the murmurings of the children of Israel: speak to them, saying, At even your shall eat flesh, and in the morning your shall be filled with bread, and your shall know that, I am the Lord your God.

+/- June 16th. (Sivan 17th.)

The year +/- 1357 B.C.E. The Lord provided Meat and Manna

(Exodus 16:13-20) 13:And it came to pass, that at even the quails came up, and covered the camp: and in the morning the dew lay round about the host. 14:And when the dew that lay was gone up, behold, upon the face of the wilderness there lay a small round thing, as small as the hoar frost on the ground. 15:And when the children of Israel saw it, they said one to another, It is manna: for they wist not what it was. And Moses said to them, This is the bread which the Lord has given you to eat. 16:This is the thing which the Lord has commanded, Gather of it every man according to his eating, an omer for every man, according to the number of your persons; take your every man for them which are in his tents. 17:And the children of Israel did so, and gathered, some more, some less. 18:And when they did mete it with an omer, he that gathered much had nothing over, and he that gathered little had no lack; they gathered every man according to his eating. 19:And Moses said, Let no man leave of it till the morning. 20:Not with standing they hearkened not to Moses; but some of them left of it until the morning, and it bred worms, and stank, and Moses was angry with them.

+/- June 16th. (Sivan 17th.)

Mordecai told Queen Esther about the up coming slaughter

(Esther 4:1-46) 1:When Mordecai perceived all that was done, Mordecai rent his clothes, and put on sackcloth with ashes, and went out into the midst of the city, and cried with a loud and a bitter cry; 2:And came even before the King's gate: for none might enter into the King's gate clothed with sackcloth. 3:And in every province, whither so ever the King's commandment and his decree came, there was great mourning among the Hebrews, and fasting, and weeping, and wailing; and many lay in sackcloth and ashes. 4:So Esther's maids and her chamberlains came and told it her. Then was the queen exceedingly grieved; and she sent raiment to clothe Mordecai, and to take away his sackcloth from him: but he received it not.

5:Then called Esther for Hatach, one of the King's chamberlains, whom he had appointed to attend upon her, and gave him a commandment to Mordecai, to know what it was, and why it was. 6:So Hatach went forth to Mordecai to the street of the city, which was before the King's gate. 7:And Mordecai told him of all that had happened to him, and of the sum of the money that Haman had promised to pay from the King's treasuries for the Hebrews, to destroy them. 8:Also he gave him the copy of the writing of the decree that was given at Shushan to destroy them, to show it to Esther, and to declare it to her, and to charge her that she should go in to the King, to make supplication to him, and to make request before him for her people. 9:And Hatach came and told Esther the words of Mordecai. 10:Again Esther spoke to Hatach, and gave him commandment to Mordecai. 11:All the King's servants, and the people of the King's provinces, do know, that whosoever, whether man or woman, shall come to the King into the inner court, who is not called, there is one law of his to put him or her to death, except such to whom the King shall hold out the golden scepter, that he or she may live: but I have not been called to come in to the King these thirty days. 12:And they told to Mordecai Esther's words. 13:Then Mordecai commanded to answer Esther, think not with yourself that your shall escape in the King's house, more than all the Jews. 14:For if your altogether hold your peace at this time, then shall there enlargement and deliverance arise to the Hebrews from another place; but your and your father's house shall be destroyed: and who knows whether your are come to the kingdom for such a time as this? 15:Then Esther bade them return Mordecai this answer, 16:Go, gather together all the Jews that are present in Shushan, and fast your for me, and neither eat nor drink three days, night or day: I also and my maidens will fast likewise; and so will I go in to the King, which is not according to the law: and if I perish, I perish. 17:So Mordecai went his way, and did according to all that Esther had commanded him.

(Removed from some of the modern Bibles): 18:Recalling all that the Lord had done, he prayed to him, 19:and said: O Lord God, almighty King of all things are in your power, and there is no one to oppose you in your will to save Israel. 20;You made heaven and earth and every wonderful thing under the heaven. 21:You are Lord of all, and there is no one who can resist you, Lord. 22:You know all things, you know O Lord, that it was not out of insolence or pride or desire for fame that I acted This in not bowing down to the proud Haman. 23:Gladly would I have kissed the soles of his feet for the salvation of Israel. 24:But I acted as I did so as not to place the honor of man above that of God. I will not bow down to anyone but you, my Lord. It is not out of pride that I am acting this way. 25:And now Lord God of Abraham, spare your people, for our enemies plan out ruin and are bent upon destroying the inheritance that was yours from the beginning. 26:Do not spurn your portion, which you redeemed for yourself out of Egypt. 27:Hear my prayer; have pity on your inheritance and turn our sorrow into joy; This we shall live to sing praise to your name, "O Lord. Do not silence those who praise you" All Israel too, cried out with all their strength, for death was staring then in the face. 28:Queen Esther, seized with mortal anguish, likewise had recourse to the Lord. 29:Taking off her splendid garments, she put on garments of distress and mourning. In place of her precious ointments she covered her head with dirt and ashes. She afflicted her body severely; all her festive adornments were put aside, and her hair was wholly disheveled. 30:Then she prayed to the Lord, the God of Israel, saying; My Lord, our King, you alone are God. Help me, for I am alone and have no help but you, 31:for I am taking my life in my hands. 32:As a child I herd from the people of the land of my forefathers that you, O Lord;chose Israel from among all peoples, and our fathers from among all their ancestors, as a lasting heritage, and that you fulfilled all your promises to them. 33:But now we have sinned in your sight, and you have delivered us into the hands of our enemies, 34:because we worshiped their gods. You are just, O Lord. 35:But now they are not satisfied with our bitter servitude, but have undertaken. 36:To do away with the decree you have pronounced and to destroy your heritage; to close the mouths of those who praise you, and to extinguish the glory of your temple and your alter. 37:To open the mouths of the heathen to acclaim their false gods, and to extol an earthly king forever. 38:O Lord, do not relinquish your scepter, to those that are not worthy. Let them not gloat over our ruin, but turn their own counsel against them and make an example of our chief enemy. 39:Be mindful of us, O Lord, manifest yourself in the time of our distress and give me courage, King of the gods and ruler of every power. 40:Put in my mouth persuasive words in the presence of the lion and turn his heart to hatred for our enemy, so that he and those who are league with him may perish. 41:Save us by your power, and help me whom is alone and has no one but you, O Lord; You know all things. 42:You know I hate the glory of the pagans, and abhor the bet of the uncircumcised or of any foreigner. 43:You know that I am under constraint, that I abhor the sign of grandeur which rests on my head when I appear in public; abhor it like a polluted rag, and do not wear it in private. 44:I your handmaid, have never eaten at the table of Haman, nor have I graced the banquet of the king or drunk the wine of libations. 45:From the day I was brought here till now, your handmaid has had no joy except in you, O Lord, God of Abraham. 46:O God more powerful than all, hear the voice of those in despair. Save us from the power of the wicked, and deliver me from my fear.

+/- June 16$^{th.}$ (Sivan 17$^{th.}$)

The Jews started fasting and praying for Esther: Continually for three days. So she could go before the King, without being put to Death.

As written in (Esther 4:11;) All the King's servants, and the people of the King's provinces, do know, that whosoever, whether man or woman, shall come to the King into the inner court, who is not called, there is one law of his to put him or her to death, except such to whom the King shall hold out the golden scepter, that he or she may live.

+/- June 16$^{th.}$ (Sivan 17$^{th.}$)

The high Priest along with others complained against Paul

(Acts 24:1-22)1:And after five days Ananias the high priest descended with the elders, and with a certain orator named Tertullus, who informed the governor against Paul. 2:And when he was called forth, Tertullus began to accuse him, saying, Seeing that by your we enjoy great quietness, and that very worthy deeds are done to this nation by your providence. 3:We accept it always, and in all places, most noble Felix, with all thankfulness.

4:Notwithstanding, that I be not further tedious to your, I pray that you would hear us of your clemency a few words. 5:For we have found this man a pestilent fellow, and a mover of sedition among all the Jews throughout the world, and a ringleader of the sect of the Nazarenes. 6:Who also has gone about to profane the temple: whom we took, and would have judged according to our law. 7:But the chief captain Lysias came up on us, and with great violence took him away out of our hands. 8:Commanding his accusers to come to your: by examining of whom thyself may take knowledge of all these things, whereof we accuse him. 9:And the Jews also assented, saying that these things were so. 10:Then Paul, after that the governor had beckoned to him to speak. Answered: for as much as I know that your have been of many years a judge to this nation, I do the more cheerfully answer for myself: 11:Because that your may understand, that there are yet but twelve days since I went up to Jerusalem for to worship. 12:And they neither found me in the temple disputing with any man, neither raising up the people, neither in the synagogues, nor in the city. 13:Neither can they prove the things whereof they now accuse me. 14:But this I confess to your, that after the way which they call heresy, so worship I the God of my fathers, believing all things which are written in the law and in the prophets. 15:And have hope toward God, which they themselves also allow, that there shall be a resurrection of the dead, both of the just and unjust. 16:And herein do I exercise myself, to have always a conscience void of offense toward God, and toward men. 17:Now after many years I came to bring alms to my nation, and offerings. 18:Whereupon certain Jews from Asia found me purified in the temple, neither with multitude, nor with tumult. 19:Who ought to have been here before your, and object, if they had ought against me. 20:Or else let these same here say, if they have found any evil doing in me, while I stood before the council. 21:Except it be for this one voice, that I cried standing among them, Touching the resurrection of the dead I am called in question by you this day. 22:And when Felix heard these things, having more perfect knowledge of that way, he deferred them, and said, When Lysias the chief captain shall come down, I will know the uttermost of your matter.

+/- June 18th. (Sivan 19th.)

The day Queen Esther went before the King

(Esther 4:47-5:14) 47:On the third day, putting an end to her prayers, she took off her penitential garments and arrayed herself in her royal attire. 48:In making her state appearance, after invoking the all-seeing God, she took with her two maids, 49:on the one she leaned gently for support, 50:while the other followed her bearing her train. 51:She glowed with the perfection of her beauty and her countenance was as joyous as it was lovely, though her heart was shrunk with fear. 52:She passed through all the portals till she stood face to face with the King, who was seated on his royal throne, clothed in full robes of state, and covered with gold and precious stones, so that he inspired great awe. 53:As he looked up, his features ablaze with the height of majestic anger, the Queen staggered, changed color and leaned weakly against the head of the maid in front of her. 54:But God changed the King's anger to gentleness. In great anxiety he sprang from his throne, held her in his arms until she recovered, and comforted her with reassuring words. 55:"What is it Esther?" he said to her. I am your Husband take courage!

56:You shall not die because of this general decree of ours. 57:"Come near" 58:Raising the golden scepter, he touched her neck with it, embraced her, and said: "Speak to me" 59:She replied: "I saw you, my lord, as an angel of God, and my heart was troubled with fear of your majesty. 60:"For you are awesome, my lord, though your glance is full of kindness" 61:As she said this, she fainted. 62:The King became troubled and all his attendants tried to revive her. The King asked what was wrong with Esther? And her maidens told him she had not eaten nor drank for threedays or nights. 5:1:After Esther was revived, she was brought back into the Kings court. 2:And it was so, when the King saw Esther the queen standing in the court, that she obtained favor in his sight: and the King held out to Esther the golden scepter that was in his hand. So Esther drew near, and touched the top of the scepter.3:Then said the King to her, What will your, queen Esther? and what is your request? It shall be even given your to the half of the kingdom. 4:And Esther answered, If it seems good to the King, let the King and Haman come this day to the banquet that I have prepared for him. 5:Then the King said, Cause Haman to make haste, that he may do as Esther has said. So the King and Haman came to the banquet that Esther had prepared. 6:And the King said to Esther at the banquet of wine, What is your petition? and it shall be granted your: and what is your request? even to the half of the kingdom it shall be performed. 7:Then answered Esther, and said, My petition and my request is. 8:If I have found favor in the sight of the king, and if it please the king to grant my petition, and to perform my request, let the King and Haman come to the banquet that I shall prepare for them, and I will do tomorrow as the King has said. 9:Then went Haman forth that day joyful and with a glad heart: but when Haman saw Mordecai in the king's gate, that he stood not up, nor moved for him, he was full of indignation against Mordecai. 10:Nevertheless Haman refrained himself: and when he came home, he sent and called for his friends, and Zeresh his wife. 11:And Haman told them of the glory of his riches, and the multitude of his children, and all the things wherein the King had promoted him, and how he had advanced him above the princes and servants of the King. 12:Haman said moreover, yes, Esther the queen did let no man come in with the king to the banquet that she had prepared but myself; and to morrow am I invited to her also with the King. 13:Yet all this avail me nothing, so long as I see Mordecai the Jew sitting at the king's gate. 14:Then said Zeresh his wife and all his friends to him, Let a gallows be made of fifty cubits high, and tomorrow speak your to the King that Mordecai may be hanged thereon: then go your in merrily with the King to the banquet. And the thing pleased Haman; and he caused the gallows to be made.

+/- June 19th. (Sivan 20th.)

The Day Mordecai was honored

(Esther 6:1-8:1) 1:On that night could not the King sleep, and he commanded to bring the book of records of the chronicles; and they were read before the King. 2:And it was found written, that Mordecai had told of Bigthana and Teresh, two of the King's chamberlains, the keepers of the door, who sought to lay hand on the King Ahasuerus. 3:And the king said, What honor and dignity has been done to Mordecai for this? Then said the King's servants that ministered to him, said:There is nothing done for him. 4:And the king said, Who is in the court?

Now Haman was come into the outward court of the King's house, to speak to the King to hang Mordecai on the gallows that he had prepared for him. 5:And the King's servants said to him, Behold, Haman standing in the court. And the King said, Let him come in. 6:So Haman came in. And the King said to him, What shall be done to the man whom the King delights to honor? Now Haman thought in his heart, To whom would the King delight to do honor more than to myself? 7:And Haman answered the King, for the man whom the King delights to honor. 8:Let the royal apparel be brought which the King uses to wear, and the horse that the King rides upon, and the crown royal which is set upon his head. 9:And let this apparel and horse be delivered to the hand of one of the King's most noble princes, that they may array the man with whom the King delights to honor, and bring him on horseback through the street of the city, and proclaim before him; This shall it be done to the man whom the King delights to honor. 10:Then the King said to Haman, Make haste, and take the apparel and the horse, as you have said, and do even so to Mordecai the Hebrew, that sitteth at the King's gate: let nothing fail of all that your have spoken. 11:Then took Haman the apparel and the horse, and arrayed Mordecai, and brought him on horseback through the street of the city, and proclaimed before him, This shall it be done to the man whom the King delights to honor.12:And Mordecai came again to the king's gate. But Haman hasted to his house mourning, and having his head covered. 13:And Haman told Zeresh his wife and all his friends every thing that had befallen him. Then said his wise men and Zeresh his wife to him, If Mordecai be of the seed of the Hebrews, before whom your have begun to fall, your shall not prevail against him, but shall surely fall before him. 14:And while they were yet talking with him, came the King's chamberlains, and hasted to bring Haman to the banquet that Esther had prepared. **7:1;**So the king and Haman came to banquet with Esther the Queen. 2:And the King said again to Esther on the second day at the banquet of wine, What is your petition, Queen Esther? and it shall be granted your: and what is your request? and it shall be performed, even up to the half of the kingdom. 3:Then Esther the Queen answered and said, If I have found favor in your sight, O King, and if it please the King, let my life be given me at my petition, and my people at my request: 4:For we are sold, I and my people, to be destroyed, to be slain, and to perish. But if we had been sold for bondmen and bondwomen, I had held my tongue, although the enemy could not countervail the King's damage. 5:Then the King Ahasuerus answered and said to Esther the Queen, Who is he, and where is he, that durst presume in his heart to do so? 6:And Esther said, The adversary and enemy is this wicked man Haman. Then Haman was afraid before the King and the Queen. 7:And the King arising from the banquet of wine in his wrath went into the palace garden: and Haman stood up to make a request for his life to Esther the Queen; for evil was against him by the King. 8:Then the King returned out of the palace garden into the place of the banquet of wine; and Haman had fallen upon the bed onto Esther, She cried out for help. Then said the King, Will he force the Queen also in front of me in my own house? Guards! Guards! He called out, as the word went out of the King's mouth, they rushed in and tackled Haman and they covered his face. The King was enraged: what should be done with him? 9:And Harbonah, one of the chamberlains, said before the King, behold also, the gallows fifty cubits high, which Haman had made for Mordecai, who had spoken good for the King, stands in the house of Haman. Then the King said, Hang him on it.

10:So they hanged Haman on the gallows that he had prepared for Mordecai. Then was the King's wrath pacified. **8:1;**On that same day did the King Ahasuerus give the house of Haman to the Hebrews, the enemy to Esther the Queen. And Mordecai came before the King;for Esther had told who he was to her.

+/- June 20th. (Sivan 21st.)

The King put Mordecai in charge of this matter

(Esther 8:2-8) 2:And the King took off his ring, which he had taken from Haman, and gave it to Mordecai. And Esther set Mordecai over the house of Haman. 3:And Esther spoke yet again before the King, and fell down at his feet, and besought him with tears to put away the mischief of Haman the Agagite, and his device that he had devised against the Hebrews. 4:Then the King held out the golden scepter toward Esther. So Esther arose, and stood before the King,

5:And said, If it pleases the King, and if I have found favor in his sight, and the thing seems right before the King, and if I am pleasing in your eyes, let it be written to reverse the letters devised by Haman, the son of Hammedatha the Agagite, which he wrote to destroy the Hebrews which are in all the King's provinces. 6:For how can I endure to see the evil that shall come to my people? or how can I endure to see the destruction of my kindred? 7:Then the King Ahasuerus said to Esther the Queen and to Mordecai the Judean, Behold, I have given Esther the house of Haman, and him they have hanged upon the gallows, because he laid his hand upon the Hebrews. 8:Write your also for the Jews, as it pleases you, in the King's name, and seal it with the King's ring: for the writing which is written in the King's name, and sealed with the King's ring, may no man reverse.

+/- June 20th. (Sivan 21st.)

Paul spoke to Felix

(Acts 24:24-26) 24:And after certain days, when Felix came with his wife Drusilla, which was a Jewess, he sent for Paul, and heard him concerning the faith in Christ. 25:And as he reasoned of righteousness, temperance, and judgment to come, Felix trembled, and answered, Go your way for this time; when I have a convenient season, I will call for your. 26:He hoped also that money should have been given him of Paul, that he might loose him: wherefore he sent for him the oftener, and communed with him.

+/- June 21th. (Sivan 22nd.)

The year +/- 1357 B.C. On the sixth day there was twice as much manna

(Exodus 16:22-26) 22:And it came to pass, that on the sixth day they gathered twice as much bread, two omers for one man, and all the rulers of the congregation came and told Moses. 23:And he said to them, This is that which the Lord has said, Tomorrow is the rest of the holy sabbath to the Lord: bake that which you will bake for to day and eat what you will eat; and that which remains over lay up for you to be kept until the morning. 24:And they laid it up till the morning, as Moses has said: and it did not stink, neither was there any worm therein.

25:And Moses said: Eat that today; for tomorrow is a sabbath to the Lord:on that day you shall not find it in the field. 26:Six days you shall gather; but the seventh day, which is the sabbath, in it there shall be none.

+/- June 22nd. (Sivan 23rd.)

The year +/-1357 B.C. Some went out on the Sabbath to look for food

(Exodus 16:27-31) 27; And it came to pass, that there went out some of the people on the seventh day for to gather, and they found none. 28;And the Lord said to Moses, How long will they refuse to keep my commandments and my laws? 29;See, for that the Lord has given you the sabbath, therefore he gave you on the sixth day, the bread of two days; stay you every man in his own tent, let no man go out of his place on the seventh day. 30;So the people rested on the seventh day. 31;And the house of Israel called the name there of Manna: and it was like coriander seed, white; and the taste of it was like wafers made with honey.

(Please note; As written in the Torah): Its tasted like whatever you heart desired.

+/- June 22nd. (Sivan 23rd.)

The Kings scribes were called

(Esther 8:9-17) 9:Then were the King's scribes called at that time in the third month, that is the month Sivan, on the three and twentieth day there of; and it was written according to all that Mordecai commanded to the Hebrews, and to the lieutenants, and the deputies and rulers of the provinces which are from India to Ethiopia, an hundred twenty and seven provinces, to every province according to the writing thereof, and to every people after their language, and to the Jews according to their writing, and according to their language. 10:And he wrote in the King Ahasuerus' name, and sealed it with the King's ring, and sent letters by posts on horseback, and riders on mules, camels, and young dromedaries. 11:Wherein the king granted the Jews which were in every city to gather themselves together, and to stand for their life, to destroy, to slay, and to cause to perish, all the power of the people and province that would assault them, both little ones and women, and to take the spoil of them for a prey.

12:Upon one day in all the provinces of King Ahasuerus, namely, upon the thirteenth day of the twelfth month, which is the month Adar. 13:The copy of the writing for a commandment to be given in every province was published to all people, and that the Jews should be ready against that day to avenge themselves on their enemies. 14:So the posts that rode upon mules and camels went out, being hastened and pressed on by the King's commandment. And the decree was given at Shushan the palace. 15:And Mordecai went out from the presence of the king in royal apparel of blue and white, and with a great crown of gold, and with a garment of fine linen and purple: and the city of Shushan rejoiced and was glad. 16:The Jews had light, and gladness, and joy, and honor. 17:And in every province, and in every city, where soever the king's commandment and his decree came, the Jews had joy and gladness, a feast and a good day. And many of the people of the land became Jews; for the fear of the Jews fell upon them.

+/- June 25th. (Sivan 26th.)

Samson died on the first day of the Dragon Festival

(Judges 16:23-31) 23:Then the lords of the Philistines gathered together to offer a great sacrifice to Dagon their god, and to rejoice: for they said, Our god has delivered Samson our enemy into our hands. 24:And when the people saw him, they praised their god: for they said, Our god has delivered into our hands our enemy, and the destroyer of our country, which slew many of us.

25:And it came to pass, when their hearts were merry, that they said, Call for Samson, that he may make us sport. And they called for Samson out of the prison house; and he made them sport: and they set him between the pillars. 26:And Samson said to the lad that held him by the hand, Suffer me that I may feel the pillars whereupon the house stands, that I may lean upon them. 27:Now the house was full of men and women; and all the lords of the Philistines were there; and there were upon the roof about 3,000 men and women, that beheld while Samson made sport. 28:And Samson called to the Lord, and said, O LORD GOD, remember me, I pray you, and strengthen me, I pray you, only this once, O God, that I may be at once avenged of the Philistines for my two eye

29:And Samson took hold of the two middle pillars upon which the house stood, and on which it was borne up, of the one with his right hand, and of the other with his left. 30:And Samson said, Let me die with the Philistines. And he bowed himself with all his might; and the house fell upon the lords, and upon all the people that were therein. So the dead which he slew at his death were more than they which he slew in his life. 31:Then his brethren and all of the house of his father came down and took his body and brought him up and buried him between Zorah and Eshtaol in the burying place of Manoah his father. For he had judged Israel twenty years.

+/- June 30th. (Tammuz 1st.)

The tops of the Mountains were seen

(Geneses 8:5-9) 5:And the waters decreased continually until the tenth month: in the tenth month, on the first day of the month, were the tops of the mountains seen. 6:And it came to pass at the end of forty days, that Noah opened the window of the ark which he had made. 7:And he sent forth a raven, which went forth to and fro, until the waters were dried up from off the earth.

8:Also he sent forth a dove from him, to see if the waters were abated from off the face of the ground. 9:But the dove found no rest for the sole of her foot, and she returned to him into the ark, for the waters were on the face of the whole earth: then he put forth his hand, and took her, and pulled her in to him into the ark.

Please note: (Tishul / Ephraim, (Beginning) was originality the first of the months, It was the the month that it is believed that: God had started to form the world. It was changed to, **Nissan, (Their flight)** in **(Exodus 12:2)** When God said: **"This will now be the Beginning of months to you".**

Also in the Month: (June, Sivan) during the Wheat Harvest, during the first 11 days)

Leah bought Jacob for mandrakes

(Genesis 30:14-17)14:And Reuben went in the days of wheat harvest, and found mandrakes in the field, and brought them to his mother Leah. Then Rachel said to Leah, Give me, I pray your, of your son's mandrakes. 15:And she said to her, Is it a small matter that your have taken my husband? and would you take away my son's mandrakes also? And Rachel said; Therefore he shall lie with your to night for your son's mandrakes. 16:And Jacob came out of the field in the evening, and Leah went out to meet him, and said, You must come in to me; for surely I have hired your with my son's mandrakes. And he lay with her that night. 17:And God hearkened to Leah, and she conceived, and bare Jacob the fifth son. 18:And Leah said, God has given me my hire, because I have given my maiden to my husband: and she called his name Issachar.

(During the Wheat Harvest)

(Judges 15:1-8) Samson tied 300 foxes tails together: 1:But it came to pass within a while after, in the time of wheat harvest, that Samson visited his wife with a kid; and he said, I will go in to my wife into the chamber. But her father would not let him to go in to her. 2:And her father said, I verily thought that you had utterly hated her; therefore I gave her to your friend: is not her younger sister fairer than she? take her, I pray your, instead of her. 3:And Samson said concerning them, Now shall I be more blameless than the Philistines, though I do them a displeasure. 4:And Samson went and caught three hundred foxes, and took firebrands, and turned tail to tail, and put a firebrand in the midst between two tails. 5:And when he had set the brands on fire, he let them go into the standing corn of the Philistines, and burnt up both the shocks, and also the standing corn, with the vineyards and olives. 6:Then the Philistines said, Who has done this? And they answered, Samson, the son in law of the Timnite, because he had taken his wife, and given her to his companion. And the Philistines came up, and burnt her and her father with fire.
7:And Samson said to them, though your have done this, yet will I be avenged of you, and after that I will cease. 8:And he smote them hip and thigh with a great slaughter: and he went down and dwelt in the top of the rock Etam.

It was also during the wheat Harvest

(1Samuel 25:2-37) David and his meet with Abigail: 2:And there was a man in Maon, whose possessions were in Carmel; and the man was very great, and he had three thousand sheep, and a thousand goats: and he was shearing his sheep in Carmel. 3:Now the name of the man was Nabal; and the name of his wife Abigail: and she was a woman of good understanding, and of a beautiful countenance: but the man was churlish and evil in his doings; and he was of the house of Caleb.
4:And David heard in the wilderness that Nabal did shear his sheep. 5:And David sent out ten young men, and David said to the young men, Get you up to Carmel, and go to Nabal, and greet him in my name. 6:And This shall your say to him that lives in prosperity, Peace be both to you, and peace be to your house, and peace be to all that your have.

7:And now I have heard that you have shearers: now your shepherds which were with us, we hurt them not, neither was there ought missing to them,all the while they were in Carmel. 8;Ask your young men, and they will show you. Therefore let the young men find favor in your eyes, for we come in a good day: give, I pray your, whatsoever comes to your hand to your servants, and to your son David.
9:And when David's young men came, they spoke to Nabal according to all those words in the name of David, and ceased. 10:And Nabal answered David's servants, and said; Who is David? And who is the son of Jesse? there be many servants now a days that break away every man from his master. 11:Shall I then take my bread, and my water, and my flesh that I have killed for my shearers, and give it to men, whom I know not where they be? 12:So David's young men turned their way, and went again, and came and told him all those sayings. 13:And David said to his men, Gird your on every man his sword. And they girded on every man his sword; and David also girded on his sword: and there went up after David about four hundred men; and two hundred abode by the stuff. 14:But one of the young men told Abigail, Nabal's wife, saying, Behold, David sent messengers out of the wilderness to salute our master; and he railed on them. 15:But the men were very good to us, and we were not hurt, neither missed we any thing, as long as we were conversant with them, when we were in the fields. 16:They were a wall to us both by night and day, all the while we were with them keeping the sheep.

17:Now therefore know and consider what your will do; for evil is determined against our master, and against all his household: for he is such a son of Belial, that a man cannot speak to him. 18:Then Abigail made haste, and took two hundred loaves, and two bottles of wine, and five sheep ready dressed, and five measures of parched corn and an hundred clusters of raisins, and two hundred cakes of figs, and laid them on asses. 19:And she said to her servants, Go on before me; behold, I come after you. But she told not her husband Nabal. 20:And it was so, as she rode on the ass, that she came down by the covert of the hill, and, behold, David and his men came down against her; and she met them. 21:Now David had said, Surely in vain have I kept all that this fellow has in the wilderness, so that nothing was missed of all that pertained to him: and he has requited me evil for good. 22:So and more also do God to the enemies of David, if I leave of all that pertain to him by the morning light any that passes against the wall. 23:And when Abigail saw David, she hasted, and lighted off the ass, and fell before David on her face, and bowed herself to the ground. 24:And fell at his feet, and said, Upon me, my lord, upon me let this iniquity be, and let your handmaid, I pray your, speak in your audience, and hear the words of your handmaid.

25:Let not my lord, I pray your, regard this man of Belial, even Nabal: for as his name is, so is he; Nabal is his name, and folly is with him: but I your handmaid saw not the young men of my lord, whom you didst send. 26:Now therefore, my lord, as the Lord lives, and as your soul lives, seeing the Lord has with held your from coming to shed blood, and from avenging thyself with your own hand, now let your enemies, and they that seek evil to my lord, be as Nabal. 27:And now this blessing which your handmaid has brought to my lord, let it even be given to the young men that follow my lord.

28:I pray you, forgive the trespass of your handmaid: for the Lord will certainly make my lord a sure house; because my lord fights the battles of the Lord, and evil has not been found in you all your days. 29:Yet a man is risen to pursue your, and to seek your soul: but the soul of my lord shall be bound, in the bundle of life with the Lord your God; and the souls of your enemies, them shall he sling out, as out of the middle of a sling. 30:And it shall come to pass, when the Lord shall have done to my lord according to all the good that he has spoken concerning your, and shall have appointed your ruler over Israel. 31:That this shall be no grief to your, nor offense of heart to my lord, either that your have shed blood causeless, or that my lord has avenged himself: but when the Lord shall have dealt well with my lord, then remember your handmaid. 32:And David said to Abigail, Blessed be the Lord God of Israel, which sent your this day to meet me.

33:And blessed be your advice, and blessed be you, which have kept me this day from coming to shed blood, and from avenging myself with mine own hand. 34:For in very deed, as the Lord God of Israel lives, which has kept me back from hurting your, except your hadst hasted and come to meet me, surely there had not been left to Nabal by the morning light any that passes against the wall. 35:So David received of her hand that which she had brought him, and said to her, Go up in peace to your house; see, I have hearkened to your voice, and have accepted your person. 36:And Abigail came to Nabal; and, behold, he held a feast in his house, like the feast of a King; and Nabal's heart was merry within him, for he was very drunken: wherefore she told him nothing, less or more, until the morning light. 37:But it came to pass in the morning, when the wine was gone out of Nabal, and his wife had told him these things, that his heart died within him, and he became as a stone.

(Also during the Wheat Harvest)

Three of the mighty men of valor went and got David some water

(2Samuel 23:13-39) 13:And three of the thirty chief went down, and came to David in the harvest time to the cave of Adullam: and the troop of the Philistines pitched in the valley of Rephaim. 14:And David was then in an hold, and the garrison of the Philistines was then in Bethlehem. 15:And David longed, and said, Oh that one would give me drink of the water of the well of Bethlehem, which is by the gate! 16:And the three mighty men broke through the host, of the Philistines, and drew water out of the well of Bethlehem, that was by the gate, and took it and brought it to David: nevertheless he would not drink thereof, but poured it out to the Lord. 17:And he said, Be it far from me, O Lord, that I should do this: is not this the blood of the men that went in jeopardy of their lives? therefore he would not drink it. These things did these three mighty men. 18:And Abishai, the brother of Joab, the son of Zeruiah, was chief among three. And he lifted up his spear against three hundred, and slew them, and had the name among three. 19:Was he not most honorable of three? therefore he was their captain: howbeit he attained not to the first three. 20:And Benaiah the son of Jehoiada, the son of a valiant man, of Kabzeel, who had done many acts, he slew two lion like men of Moab: he went down also and slew a lion in the midst of a pit in time of snow. 21:And he slew an Egyptian, a giant man: and the Egyptian had a spear in his hand;

but he went down to him with a staff, and plucked the spear out of the Egyptian's hand, and slew him with his own spear. 22;These things did Benaiah the son of Jehoiada, and had the name among three mighty men. 23:He was more honorable than the thirty, but he attained not to the first three. And David set him over his guard. 24:Asahel the brother of Joab was one of the thirty; Elhanan the son of Dodo of Bethlehem. 25:Shammah the Harodite, Elika the Harodite. 26:Helez the Paltite, Ira the son of Ikkesh the Tekoite, 27:Abiezer the Anethothite, Mebunnai the Hushathite, 28:Zalmon the Ahohite, Maharai the Netophathite, 29:Heleb the son of Baanah, a Netophathite, Ittai the son of Ribai out of Gibeah of the children of Benjamin, 30:Benaiah the Pirathonite, Hiddai of the brooks of Gaash, 31:Abialbon the Arbathite, Azmaveth the Barhumite, 32:Eliahba the Shaalbonite, of the sons of Jashen, Jonathan, 33;Shammah the Hararite, Ahiam the son of Sharar the Hararite, 34:Eliphelet the son of Ahasbai, the son of the Maachathite, Eliam the son of Ahithophel the Gilonite, 35:Hezrai the Carmelite, Paarai the Arbite, 36:Igal the son of Nathan of Zobah, Bani the Gadite, 37:Zelek the Ammonite, Naharai the Beerothite, armourbearer to Joab the son of Zeruiah, 38:Ira an Ithrite, Gareb an Ithrite, 39:Uriah the Hittite: thirty seven in all.

(As it is written in 1Chronicles)

(1Chronicles 11:15-12:40) 15:Now three of the thirty captains went down to the rock to David, into the cave of Adullam; and the host of the Philistines encamped in the valley of Rephaim. 16:And David was then in the hold, and the Philistines' garrison was then at Bethlehem. 17:And David longed, and said, Oh that one would give me drink of the water of the well of Bethlehem, that is at the gate! 18:And the three brake through the host of the Philistines, and drew water out of the well of Bethlehem, that was by the gate, and took it, and brought it to David: but David would not drink of it, but poured it out to the Lord, 19:And said, My God forbid it me, that I should do this thing: shall I drink the blood of these men that have put their lives in jeopardy? for with the jeopardy of their lives they brought it. Therefore he would not drink it. These things did these three mightiest. 20:And Abishai the brother of Joab, he was chief of the three: for lifting up his spear against three hundred, he slew them and had a name among the three. 21:Of the three, he was more honorable than the two; for he was their captain: how be it he attained not to the first three. 22:Benaiah the son of Jehoiada, the son of a valiant man of Kabzeel, who had done many acts; he slew two lions like men of Moab: also he went down and slew a lion in a pit on a snowy day. 23:And he slew an Egyptian, a man of great stature, five cubits high; and in the Egyptian's hand was a spear like a weaver's beam; and he went down to him with a staff, and plucked the spear out of the Egyptian's hand, and slew him with his own spear. 24:These things did Benaiah the son of Jehoiada, and had the name among the three mightiest. 25:Behold, he was honorable among the thirty, but attained not to the first three: and David set him over his guard. 26:Also the valiant men of the armies were, Asahel the brother of Joab, Elhanan the son of Dodo of Bethlehem, 27:Shammoth the Harorite, Helez the Pelonite. 28:Ira the son of Ikkesh the Tekoite, Abiezer the Antothite, 29:Sibbecai the Hushathite, Ilai the Ahohite, 30:Maharai the Netophathite, Heled the son of Baanah the Netophathite. 31:Ithai the son of Ribai of Gibeah, that pertained to the children of Benjamin, Benaiah the Pirathonite.

32:Hurai of the brooks of Gaash, Abiel the Arbathite, 33:Azmaveth the Baharumite, Eliahba the Shaalbonite. 34:The sons of Hashem the Gizonite, Jonathan the son of Shage the Hararite, 35:Ahiam the son of Sacar the Hararite. Eliphal the son of Ur, 36:Hepher the Mecherathite, Ahijah the Pelonite, 37:Hezro the Carmelite, Naarai the son of Ezbai. 38:Joel the brother of Nathan, Mibhar the son of Haggeri, 39:Zelek the Ammonite, Naharai the Berothite, the armourbearer of Joab the son of Zeruiah, 40:Ira the Ithrite, Gareb the Ithrite, 41:Uriah the Hittite, Zabad the son of Ahlai, 42:Adina the son of Shiza the Reubenite, a captain of the Reubenites, and thirty with him, 43:Hanan the son of Maachah, and Joshaphat the Mithnite, 44:Uzzia the Ashterathite, Shama and Jehiel the sons of Hothan the Aroerite, 45:Jediael the son of Shimri, and Joha his brother, the Tizite, 46:Eliel the Mahavite, and Jeribai, and Joshaviah, the sons of Elnaam, and Ithmah the Moabite, 47:Eliel, and Obed, and Jasiel the Mesobaite.

12:1: Now these are they that came to David to Ziklag, while he yet kept himself close because of Saul the son of Kish: and they were among the mighty men, helpers of the war. 2:They were armed with bows, and could use both the right hand and the left in hurling tones and shooting arrows out of a bow, even of Saul's brethren of Benjamin. 3:The chief was Ahiezer, then Joash, the sons of Shemaah the Gibeathite; and Jeziel, and Pelet, the sons of Azmaveth; and Berachah, and Jehu the Antothite. 4:And Ismaiah the Gibeonite, a mighty man among the thirty, and over the thirty; and Jeremiah, and Jahaziel, and Johanan, and Josabad the Gederathite, 5:Eluzai, and Jerimoth, and Bealiah, and Shemariah, and Shephatiah the Haruphite, 6:Elkanah, and Jesiah, and Azareel, and Joezer, and Jashobeam, the Korhites, 7:And Joelah, and Zebadiah, the sons of Jeroham of Gedor. 8:And of the Gadites there separated themselves to David into the hold to the wilderness men of might, and men of war fit for the battle, that could handle shield and buckler, whose faces were like the faces of lions, and were as swift as the roes upon the mountains. 9:Ezer the first, Obadiah the second, Eliab the third, 10:Mishmannah the fourth, Jeremiah the fifth, 11:Attai the sixth, Eliel the seventh, 12:Johanan the eighth, Elzabad the ninth, 13:Jeremiah the tenth, Machbanai the eleventh.

14:These were of the sons of Gad, captains of the host: one of the least was over an hundred, and the greatest over a thousand. 15:These are they that went over Jordan in the first month, when it had overflown all his banks; and they put to flight all them of the valleys, both toward the east, and toward the west. 16:And there came of the children of Benjamin and Judah to the hold to David. 17:And David went out to meet them, and answered and said to them, If your be come peaceably to me to help me, mine heart shall be knit to you: but if you be come to betray me to mine enemies, seeing there is no wrong in mine hands, the God of our fathers look there on and rebuke it. 18:Then the spirit came upon Amasai, who was chief of the captains, and then said, your are we, David, and on your side, your son of Jesse: peace, peace be to you, and peace be to your helpers; for your God helps your. Then David received them, and made them captains of the band. 19:And there fell some of Manasseh to David, when he came with the Philistines against Saul to battle: but they helped them not: for the lords of the Philistines upon advisement sent him away, saying, He will fall to his master Saul to the jeopardy of our heads.

20:As he went to Ziklag, there fell to him of Manasseh, Adnah, and Jozabad, and Jediael, and Michael, and Jozabad, and Elihu, and Zilthai, captains of the thousands that were of Manasseh. 21:And they helped David against the band of the rovers for they were all mighty men of valor, and were captains in the host. 22:For at that time day by day there came to David to help him, until it was a great host, like the host of God. 23:And these are the numbers of the bands that were ready armed to the war, and came to David to Hebron, to turn the kingdom of Saul to him, according to the word of the Lord. 24:The children of Judah that bare shield and spear were six thousand and eight hundred, ready armed to the war. 25:Of the children of Simeon, mighty men of valor for the war, seven thousand and one hundred. 26:Of the children of Levi four thousand and six hundred.

27:And Jehoiada was the leader of the Maronite, and with him were three thousand and seven hundred, 28:And Zadok, a young man mighty of valor, and of his father's house twenty and two captains. 29:And of the children of Benjamin, the kindred of Saul, three thousand: for hitherto the greatest part of them had kept the ward of the house of Saul. 30:And of the children of Ephraim twenty thousand and eight hundred, mighty men of valor, famous throughout the house of their fathers. 31:And of the half tribe of Manasseh eighteen thousand, which were expressed by name, to come and make David King. 32:And of the children of Issachar, which were men that had understanding of the times, to know what Israel ought to do; the heads of them were two hundred; and all their brethren were at their commandment. 33:Of Zebulun, such as went forth to battle, expert in war, with all instruments of war, fifty thousand, which could keep rank: they were not of double heart. 34:And of Naphtali a thousand captains, and with them with shield and spear thirty and seven thousand. 35:And of the Danites expert in war twenty and eight thousand and six hundred. 36:And of Asher, such as went forth to battle, expert in war, forty thousand. 37:And on the other side of Jordan, of the Reubenites, and the Gadites, and of the half tribe of Manasseh, with all manner of instruments of war for the battle, an hundred and twenty thousand. 38:All these men of war, that could keep rank, came with a perfect heart to Hebron, to make David King over all Israel: and all the rest also of Israel were of one heart to make David King. 39:And there they were with David three days, eating, drinking: for their brethren had prepared for them. 40:Moreover they that were nigh them, even to Issachar and Zebulun and Naphtali, brought bread on asses, and on camels, and on mules, and on oxen, and meat, meal, cakes of figs, and bunches of raisins, and wine, and oil, and oxen, and sheep abundantly: for there was joy in Israel.

(It was during the second week of this Month)

They started building the LORD'S temple

(2Chronicles 31:7) 7:In the third month after the feast of weeks they began to lay the foundation of the heaps, and finished them in the seventh month.

Philip spoke with a Ethiopian eunuch

(Acts 8:26-40) 26:And the angel of the Lord spoke to Philip, saying, Arise, and go toward the south to the way that goeth down from Jerusalem to Gaza, which is desert. 27:And he arose and went: and, behold, a man of Ethiopia, an eunuch of great authority under Candace queen of the Ethiopians, who had the charge of all her treasure, and had come to Jerusalem to worship. 28:Was returning, and sitting in his chariot read Isaiah the prophet. 29:Then the Spirit said to Philip, Go near, and join thyself to this chariot. 30:And Philip ran closer to him, and heard him read the prophet Isaiah, and said, Do you understand what you are reading? 31:And he said, How can I, except some man should guide me? And he desired Philip that he would come up and sit with him. 32:The place of the scripture which he read was this, He was led as a lamb to the slaughter; and like a lamb dumb before his shearer, so he did not open his mouth. 33:In his humiliation his judgment was taken away: and who shall declare his generation? for his life is taken from the earth. 34:And the eunuch answered Philip, and said, I pray your, of whom speaks the prophet this? Of himself, or of some other man? 35:Then Philip opened his mouth, and began at the same scripture, and preached to him Jesus. 36:And as they went on their way, they came to a certain water: and the eunuch said, See, here is water; what doth hinder me from being baptized? 37:And Philip said, If your believe with all your heart, your may. And he answered and said, I believe that Jesus Christ is the Son of God. 38:And he commanded the chariot to stand still: and they went down both into the water, both Philip and the eunuch; and he baptized him. 39:And when they were come up out of the water, the Spirit of the Lord caught away Philip, that the eunuch saw him no more: and he went on his way rejoicing. 40:But Philip was found at Azotus: and passing through he preached in all the cities, till he came to Caesarea.

(It was during the third week of this Month)

Joshua prayed and the Sun stood still for a day

(Joshua 10:6-43) 6:And the men of Gibeon sent to Joshua to the camp to Gilgal, saying, Slack not your hand from your servants; come up to us quickly, and save us, and help us: for all the kings of the Amorites that dwell in the mountains are gathered together against us. 7:So Joshua ascended from Gilgal, he, and all the people of war with him, and all the mighty men of valor. 8:And the Lord said to Joshua, Fear them not: for I have delivered them into your hand; there shall not a man of them stand before your. 9:Joshua therefore came to them suddenly, and went up from Gilgal all night. 10:And the Lord discomfited them before Israel, and slew them with a great slaughter at Gibeon, and chased them along the way that goeth up to Bethhoron, and smote them to Azekah, and to Makkedah. 11:And it came to pass, as they fled from before Israel, and were in the going down to Bethhoron, that the Lord cast down great stones from heaven upon them to Azekah, and they died: they were more which died with hailstones, than they whom the children of Israel slew with the sword. 12:Then spoke Joshua to the Lord in the day when the Lord delivered up the Amorites before the children of Israel, and he said in the sight of Israel, Sun, stand your still upon Gibeon; and your, Moon, in the valley of Ajalon. 13:And the sun stood still, and the moon stayed, until the people had avenged themselves upon their enemies. Is not this written in the book of Jasher? So the sun stood still in the midst of heaven, and hasted not to go down about a whole day. 14:And there was no day like that before it or after it, that the Lord hearkened to the voice of a man: for the Lord fought for Israel. 15:And Joshua returned, and all Israel with him, to the camp to Gilgal. 16:But these five kings fled, and hid themselves in a cave at Makkedah. 17:And it was told Joshua, saying, The five Kings are found hid in a cave at Makkedah. 18:And Joshua said; Roll great stones upon the mouth of the cave, and set men by it for to keep them. 19:And stay your not, but pursue after your enemies, and strike the hindmost of them; suffer them not to enter into their cities: for the Lord your God has delivered them into your hand. 20:And it came to pass, when Joshua and the children of Israel had made an end of slaying them with a very great slaughter, till they were consumed, that the rest which remained of them entered into fenced cities. 21:And all the people returned to the camp to Joshua at Makkedah in peace: none moved his tongue against any of the children of Israel. 22:Then said Joshua, Open the mouth of the cave, and bring out those five Kings to me out of the cave. 23:And they did so, and brought forth those five Kings to him out of the cave, the king of Jerusalem, the King of Hebron, the King of Jarmuth, the King of Lachish, and the King of Eglon. 24:And it came to pass, when they brought out those kings to Joshua, that Joshua called for all the men of Israel, and said to the captains of the men of war which went with him, Come near, put your feet upon the necks of these kings. And they came near, and put their feet upon the necks of them. 25:And Joshua said to them, Fear not, nor be dismayed, be strong and of good courage: for This shall the Lord do to all your enemies against whom your fight.

26:And afterward Joshua smote them, and slew them, and hanged them on five trees: and they were hanging upon the trees until the evening. 27:And it came to pass at the time of the going down of the sun, that Joshua commanded, and they took them down off the trees, and cast them into the cave wherein they had been hid, and laid great stones in the cave's mouth, which remain until this very day. 28:And that day Joshua took Makkedah, and smote it with the edge of the sword, and the King thereof he utterly destroyed, them, and all the souls that were therein; he let none remain: and he did to the King of Makkedah as he did to the king of Jericho. 29:Then Joshua passed from Makkedah, and all Israel with him, to Libnah, and fought against Libnah. 30:And the Lord delivered it also, and the King thereof, into the hand of Israel; and he smote it with the edge of the sword, and all the souls that were therein; he let none remain in it; but did to the King thereof as he did to the King of Jericho.

31:And Joshua passed from Libnah, and all Israel with him, to Lachish, and encamped against it, and fought against it. 32:And the Lord delivered Lachish into the hand of Israel, which took it on the second day, and smote it with the edge of the sword, and all the souls that were therein, according to all that he had done to Libnah. 33:Then Horam King of Gezer came up to help Lachish; and Joshua struck him and his people, until he had left him none remaining. 34:And from Lachish Joshua passed to Eglon, and all Israel with him; and they encamped against it, and fought against it. 35:And they took it on that day, and smote it with the edge of the sword, and all the souls that were therein he utterly destroyed that day, according to all that he had done to Lachish. 36:And Joshua went up from Eglon, and all Israel with him, to Hebron; and they fought against it.

37:And they took it, and smote it with the edge of the sword, and the king thereof, and all the cities thereof, and all the souls that were therein; he left none remaining, according to all that he had done to Eglon; but destroyed it utterly, and all the souls that were therein. 38:And Joshua returned, and all Israel with him, to Debir; and fought against it. 39:And he took it, and the King thereof, and all the cities thereof; and they smote them with the edge of the sword, and utterly destroyed all the souls that were therein; he left none remaining: as he had done to Hebron, so he did to Debir, and to the King thereof; as he had done also to Libnah, and to her King. 40:So Joshua struck all the country of the hills, and of the south, and of the vale, and of the springs, and all their kings: he left none remaining, utterly destroyed all that breathed, as the Lord God of Israel commanded. 41:And Joshua smote them from Kadeshbarnea even to Gaza, and all the country of Goshen, even to Gibeon. 42:And all these kings and their land did Joshua take at one time, because the Lord God of Israel fought for Israel. 43:And Joshua returned, and all Israel with him, to the camp to Gilgal.

(During the last week of this Month)

Nabal died, and David took Abigail for a wife

(1Samuel 25:38-43) 38;And it came to pass about ten days after, that the Lord struck Nabal, that he died. 39;And when David heard that Nabal was dead, he said, Blessed be the Lord, that has pleaded the cause of my reproach from the hand of Nabal, and had kept his servant from doing evil: for the Lord has returned the wickedness of Nabal upon his own head. And David sent and communed with Abigail, to take her to him to wife. 40;And when the servants of David were come to Abigail to Carmel, they spoke to her, saying, David sent us to your, to take your to him to wife. 41;And she arose, and bowed herself on her face to the earth, and said, Behold, of the servants of my lord. 42;And Abigail hasted, and arose, and rode upon an ass, with five damsels of hers that went after her; and she went after the messengers of David, and became his wife. 43;David also took Ahinoam, of Jezreel; and they were also both of them his wives.

(Also during the last week of this Month)

Tobiah finds a Wife and Raphael binds a Demon

(Tobit 7:9-8:21) 9:Afterward, Raguel slaughtered a ram from the flock and gave them a cordial reception. After they had bathed and reclined to eat, Tobiah said to Raphael, "Brother Azariah , ask Raguel to marry my kinswoman Sarah." 10:Raguel overheard the words; so he said to the boy: "Eat and drink and be merry tonight, for no man is more entitled to marry my daughter Sarah than you, brother. Besides, not even have I the right to give her to anyone but you, because you are my closest relative. But I will explain the situation to you very frankly. 11:I have given her in marriage to seven men, all of whom were kinsmen of ours, and all died on the very night they approached her. But now son, eat and drink. I am sure the Lord will look after you both." Tobiah answered "I will not eat or drink anything until you have set aside what belongs to me." Raguel said to him: "I will do it.

She is yours according to the decree of the Book of Moses. Your marriage to her has been decided in heaven! Take your kinswoman from now you are her husband, and she is your wife. She is yours today and for ever after. And tonight, son may the Lord of heaven prosper you both. May he grant you mercy and peace" 12:Then Raguel called his daughter Sarah. He took her by the hand and gave her to Tobiah with these words:"Take her according to the law. According to the decree written in the Book of Moses she is your wife. Take her and bring her back safely to your father. And may the God of heaven grant both of you peace and prosperity." 13:He then called her Mother and told her to bring a scroll, so that he might draw up a marriage contract stating that he gave, Sarah to Tobiah as his wife, according to the decree of the Mosaic law. Her Mother brought the scroll, and he drew up the contract, to which they affixed their seals. 14:Afterward they began to eat and drink. 15:Later Raguel called his wife Edna ans said: "My love, prepare the other bedroom and bring the girl there." 16:She went and made the bed, in the room as she was told, and brought the girl there. After she had cried over her, she wiped away the tears and said; 17:"Be brave my daughter, may the Lord of heaven grant you joy in place of your grief. Courage, my daughter." Then she left.

8:1: When they had finished eating and drinking, the girl's parents wanted to retire. They brought the young man out of the dinning room and led him to the bedroom. 2:At this point Tobiah mindful of Raphael's instructions, took the fish's liver and heart from the bag which he had with him, and placed them on the embers for the incense. 3:The demon repelled by the order of the fish, fled to upper Egypt; Raphael chased him there and bound him hand and foot. Then Raphael returned immediately. 4:When the girl's parents left the bedroom and closed the door behind them, Tobiah got out of bed and said to his wife, "My love, get up. Let us pray and beg our Lord to have mercy on us, and to grant us deliverance." 5:She got up, and they started to pray that deliverance might be theirs. He began with these words: Blessed are you O God of our fathers, praised be your name forever and ever. Let the heavens and all of your creation praise you forever. 6:You made Adam and you gave him his wife Eve, to be his help and support, and it was from these two all of your people came forth. You said it is not good for man to be alone, I will make for him a help mate. 7:Lord you know that I take this wife of mine, not because of lust, but for a noble purpose. Call down your mercy on us, and allow us to live together to a happy old age." 8:They said together, "Amen, Amen" 9:And went to bed for the night. But Raguel got up and summoned his servants. With him they went out to dig a grave, 10:for he said; "I must do this, because if Tobiah should die we would be subjected to ridicule and insult." 11:When they had finished digging the grave, Raguel went back to the house and called his wife, 12:saying; "Send in one of the maids in to see if Tobiah is alive of dead, so that if necessary we may bury him without anyone knowing about it." 13:She sent the maid, who lit a lamp, opened the bedroom door, went in, and found them fast asleep together. 14:The maid went out and told the girls parents that Tobiah was alive, and that there was nothing wrong. 15:Then Raguel praised the God of Heaven in theses words: "Blessed are you, O God with every holy and pure blessing! Let all your chosen ones praise you; let them bless you forever! 16:Blessed are you, who have made me glad; what I feared did not happen. Rather you have dealt with us according to your great mercy.

17:Blessed are you, for you were merciful towards two, only children. Grant them, Master, mercy and deliverance and bring their to fulfillment with happiness and mercy." 18:Then he told his servants to go fill in the grave before dawn. 19:He asked his wife to bake many loaves of bread; he himself went out to the herd and picked out two steers and four rams, which he ordered to be slaughtered, So the servants began to prepare the feast. 20:He summed Tobiah and made a oath in his presence, saying:"For fourteen days you shall not stir from here, but shall remain here eating and drinking with me, and you shall bring joy to my daughter's sorrowing spirit. 21:Take to begin with, half of whatever I own, when you go back to your father; the other half will be yours when I and my wife die. Be of good cheer, my son! I am your father, and Edna is your mother; and we belong to you and to your beloved now and forever, So be happy son"

Below is Gilgal where Joshua prayed, and the Sun stood still for about a day (Spoken of on pages 279-281)

Extra notes on the Dragon Festival, from page 272

The Dragon festival has been held for over 4000 years, in some country's like Tibet, Main land China, Korea, Turkestan, Nepal, Bangladesh, Vietnam, Hong Kong, and Manchuria. It was during the first day of the Dragon festival, that they were going to kill Samson. To offer him as a sacrifice to their God: Dragon. Also know as Dagon

Chapter 7: July - Tammuz

It is the 4th. Month of the Hebrew calendar
In Hebrew this month is called: Tammuz,
which means:(Hidden giver of the vine) the 4th.Month
Tribe of Simon, means:(He heard)
The stone of (Citrine Quarts) represents this tribe.
Simon: (The 2nd.) Son of Leah.
(Was believed to have been born in this month.)
(Spirit of Wisdom)

+/- July 4th. (Tammuz 5th.)

The year +/- 586 B.C. The Lord showed Ezekiel a vision

(Ezekiel 1:1-3:14) 1:Now it came to pass in the thirtieth year, in the fourth month, in the fifth day of the month, as I was among the captives by the river of Chebar, that the heavens were opened, and I saw visions of God. 2:In the fifth day of the month, which was the fifth year of King Jehoiachin's captivity. 3:The word of the Lord came expressly to Ezekiel the priest, the son of Buzi, in the land of the Chaldeans by the river Chebar; and the hand of the Lord was there upon him. 4;And I looked, and, behold, a whirlwind came out of the north, a great cloud, and a fire infolding itself, and a brightness was about it, and out of the midst thereof as the color of amber, out of the midst of the fire. 5:Also out of the midst thereof came the likeness of four living creatures. And this was their appearance; they had the likeness of a man. 6:And every one had four faces, and every one had four wings. 7:And their feet were straight feet; and the sole of their feet was like the sole of a calf's foot: and they sparkled like the color of burnished brass. 8:And they had the hands of a man under their wings on their four sides; and they four had their faces and their wings. 9;:Their wings were joined one to another; they turned not when they went; they went every one straight forward. 10:As for the likeness of their faces, they four had the face of a man, and the face of a lion, on the right side: and they four had the face of an ox on the left side; they four also had the face of an eagle. 11:This were their faces: and their wings were stretched upward; two wings of every one were joined one to another, and two covered their bodies. 12:And they went every one straight forward: whither the spirit was to go, they went;

and they turned not when they went. 13:As for the likeness of the living creatures, their appearance was like burning coals of fire, and like the appearance of lamps: it went up and down among the living creatures; and the fire was bright, and out of the fire went forth lightning. 14:And the living creatures ran and returned as the appearance of a flash of lightning. 15:Now as I beheld the living creatures, behold one wheel upon the earth by the living creatures, with his four faces. 16:The appearance of the wheels and their work was like to the color of a beryl: and they four had one likeness: and their appearance and their work was as it were a wheel in the middle of a wheel. 17:When they went, they went upon their four sides: and they turned not when they went. 18:As for their rings, they were so high that they were dreadful; and their rings were full of eyes round about them four. 19:And when the living creatures went, the wheels went by them: and when the living creatures were lifted up from the earth, the wheels were lifted up. 20:Where ever the spirit was to go, they went, thither was their spirit to go; and the wheels were lifted up over against them: for the spirit of the living creature was in the wheels. 21:When those went, these went; and when those stood, these stood; and when those were lifted up from the earth, the wheels were lifted up over against them: for the spirit of the living creature was in the wheels. 22:And the likeness of the firmament upon the heads of the living creature was as the color of the terrible crystal, stretched forth over their heads above. 23:And under the firmament were their wings straight, the one toward the other: every one had two, which covered on this side, and every one had two, which covered on that side, their bodies. 24:And when they went, I heard the noise of their wings, like the noise of great waters, as the voice of the Almighty, the voice of speech, as the noise of an host: when they stood, they let down their wings. 25:And there was a voice from the firmament that was over their heads, when they stood, and had let down their wings. 26:And above the firmament that was over their heads was the likeness of a throne, as the appearance of a sapphire stone: and upon the likeness of the throne was the likeness as the appearance of a man above upon it. 27:And I saw as the color of amber, as the appearance of fire round about within it, from the appearance of his loins even upward, and from the appearance of his loins even downward, I saw as it were the appearance of fire, and it had brightness round about. 28:As the appearance of the bow that is in the cloud in the day of rain, so was the appearance of the brightness round about. This was the appearance of the likeness of the glory of the Lord. And when I saw it, I fell upon my face, and I heard a voice of one that spoke.

2:1: And he said to me, Son of man, stand upon your feet, and I will speak to you. 2:And the spirit entered into me when he spoke to me, and set me upon my feet, that I heard him that spoke to me. 3:And he said to me, Son of man, I send you to the children of Israel, to a rebellious nation that has rebelled against me: they and their fathers have transgressed against me, even to this very day. 4:For they are impudent children and stiff heart-ed. I do send you to them; and you shall say to them, this says the Lord your God. 5:And they, whether they will hear, or whether they will forbear, (for they are a rebellious house,) yet shall know that there has been a prophet among them. 6:And you, son of man, be not afraid of them, neither be afraid of their words, though briers and thorns be with you, and you do dwell among scorpions: be not afraid of their words, nor be dismayed at their looks, though they be a rebellious house.

7:And you shall speak my words to them, whether they will hear, or whether they will forbear: for they are most rebellious. 8:But you, son of man, hear what I say to you; Be not you rebellious like that rebellious house: open your mouth, and eat that I give you. 9:And when I looked, behold, an hand was sent to me; and, look, a roll of a book was therein. 10:And he spread it before me; and it was written within and without: and there was written therein lamentations, and mourning, and woe.

3:1: Moreover he said to me, Son of man, eat what you found; eat this roll, and go speak to the house of Israel. 2:So I opened my mouth, and he caused me to eat that roll. 3:And he said to me, Son of man, cause your belly to eat, and fill your bowels with this roll that I give you. Then did I eat it; and it was in my mouth as honey for sweetness. 4:And he said to me, Son of man, go, get you to the house of Israel, and speak with my words to them. 5:For you are not sent to a people of a strange speech and of an hard language, but to the house of Israel; 6:Not to many people of a strange speech and of an hard language, whose words you canst not understand. Surely, had I sent you to them, they would have hearkened to you. 7:But the house of Israel will not hearken to you; for they will not hearken to me: for all the house of Israel are impudent and hardhearted. 8:Behold, I have made your face strong against their faces, and your forehead strong against their foreheads. 9:As an adamant harder than flint have I made your forehead: fear them not, neither be dismayed at their looks, though they be a rebellious house. 10:Moreover he said to me, Son of man, all my words that I shall speak to you receive in your heart, and hear with your ears. 11:And go, get you to them of the captivity, to the children of your people, and speak to them, and tell them, this says the Lord God; whether they will hear, or whether they will forbear. 12:Then the spirit took me up, and I heard behind me a voice, of a great rushing, saying Blessed be the glory of the Lord from his place. 13:I heard also the noise of the wings of the living creatures that touched one another, and the noise of the wheels over against them, and a noise of a great rushing. 14:So the spirit lifted me up, and took me away, and I went in bitterness, in the heat of my spirit; but the hand of the Lord was strong upon me.

+/- July 6th. (Tammuz 7th.)

The year +/- 591 B.C. Ezekiel went to the river and stayed 7 days

(Ezekiel 3:15)15:Then I came to those who were in captivity at Tel abib, that dwelt by the river of Chebar, and I sat there with them, and I remained there astonished among them for seven days.

+/- July 8th. (Tammuz 9th.)

The year +/- 591 B.C. The Chaldeans capture the King of Jerusalem

(2Kings 25:3-7) 3:And on the ninth day of the fourth month the famine prevailed in the city, and there was no bread for the people of the land. 4:And the city was broken up, and all the men of war fled by night by the way of the gate between two walls, which is by the King's garden: (now the Chaldeans were against the city round about:) and the King, went the way toward the plain. 5:And the army of the Chaldeans pursued after the king, and overtook him in the plains of Jericho: and all his army were scattered from him.

6:So they took the king, and brought him up to the King of Babylon to Riblah; and they gave judgment upon him. 7:And they slew the sons of Zedekiah before his eyes, and put out the eyes of Zedekiah, and bound him with fetters of brass, and carried him to Babylon.

+/- July 8th. (Tammuz 9th.)

The year +/- 581 B.C. King Nebuchadnezzar slew the sons of Zedekiah

(Jeremiah 39:2-14) 2:And in the eleventh year of Zedekiah, in the fourth month, the ninth day of the month, the city was broken up. 3:And all the princes of the King of Babylon came in, and sat in the middle gate, even Nergalsharezer, Samgarnebo, Sarsechim, Rabsaris, Nergalsharezer, Rabmag, with all the residue of the princes of the King of Babylon. 4:And it came to pass, that when Zedekiah the King of Judah saw them, and all the men of war, then they fled, and went forth out of the city by night, by the way of the King's garden, by the gate betwixt the two walls: and he went out the way of the plain. 5:But the Chaldeans' army pursued after them, and overtook Zedekiah in the plains of Jericho, and when they had taken him, they brought him up to Nebuchadnezzar King of Babylon to Riblah in the land of Hamath, where he gave judgment upon him. 6:Then the King of Babylon slew the sons of Zedekiah in Riblah before his eyes: also the King of Babylon slew all the nobles of Judah. 7:Moreover he put out Zedekiah's eyes, and bound him with chains, to carry him to Babylon. 8:And the Chaldeans burned the King's house, and the houses of the people, with fire, and broke down the walls of Jerusalem. 9:Then Nebuzaradan the captain of the guard carried away captive into Babylon the remnant of the people that remained in the city, and those that fell away, that fell to him, with the rest of the people that remained. 10:But Nebuzaradan the captain of the guard left of the poor of the people, which had nothing, in the land of Judah, and gave them vineyards and fields at the same time. 11:Now Nebuchadrezzar King of Babylon gave charge concerning Jeremiah to Nebuzaradan the captain of the guard, saying. 12:Take him, and look well to him, and do him no harm; but do to him even as he shall say to you. 13:So Nebuzaradan the captain of the guard sent, and Nebushasban, Rabsaris, and Nergalsharezer, Rabmag, and all the King of Babylon's princes. 14:Even they sent, and took Jeremiah out of the court of the prison, and committed him to Gedaliah the son of Ahikam the son of Shaphan, that he should carry him home: so he dwelt among the people.

(Again recalled in Jeremiah 52:6-11)

The year +/- 581 B.C. 6:And in the fourth month, in the ninth day of the month, the famine was sore in the city, so that there was no bread for the people of the land. 7:Then the city was broken up, and all the men of war fled, and went forth out of the city by night by the way of the gate between the two walls, which was by the King's garden; (now the Chaldeans were by the city round about:) and they went by the way of the plain. 8:But the army of the Chaldeans pursued after the king, and overtook Zedekiah in the plains of Jericho; and all his army was scattered from him. 9;Then they took the King, and carried him up to the King of Babylon to Riblah in the land of Hamath; where he gave judgment upon him.

10:And the King of Babylon slew the sons of Zedekiah before his eyes: he slew also all the princes of Judah in Riblah. 11:Then he put out the eyes of Zedekiah; and the king of Babylon bound him in chains, and carried him to Babylon, and put him in prison till the day of his death.

+/- July 13th. (Tammuz 14th.)

The year +/- 597 B.C. God told Ezekiel, he has been made a watchman

(Ezekiel 3:16-5:17) 16:And it came to pass at the end of seven days, that the word of the Lord came to me, saying. 17:Son of man, I have made you a watchman to the house of Israel: therefore hear the word at my mouth, and give them warning from me. 18:When I say to the wicked, you shall surely die; and you gave him not warning, nor spoke to warn the wicked from his wicked way, to save his life; the same wicked man shall die in his iniquity; but his blood will I require at your hand. 19:Yet if you warn the wicked, and he turn not from his wickedness, nor from his wicked way, he shall die in his iniquity; but you hast delivered your soul. 20:Again, When a righteous man doth turn from his righteousness, and commit iniquity, and I lay a stumbling block before him, he shall die, because you hast not given him warning, he shall die in his sin, and his righteousness which he has done shall not be remembered; but his blood will I require at your hand. 21:Nevertheless if you warn the righteous man that the righteous sin not, and he doth not sin, he shall surely live, because he is warned; also you hast delivered your soul. 22:And the hand of the Lord was there upon me; and he said to me, Arise, go forth into the plain, and I will there talk with you. 23:Then I arose, and went forth into the plain: and, behold, the glory of the Lord stood there, as the glory which I saw by the river of Chebar: and I fell on my face. 24:Then the spirit entered into me, and set me upon my feet, and spoke with me, and said to me, Go, shut thyself within your house. 25:But you, O son of man, behold, they shall put bands upon you, and shall bind you with them, and you shall not go out among them. 26:And I will make your tongue cleave to the roof of your mouth, that you shall be dumb, and shall not be to them a reprove: for they are a rebellious house. 27:But when I speak with you, I will open your mouth, and you shall say to them, this says the Lord God; He that hears, let him hear; and he that forbears, let him forbear: for they are a rebellious house.

4:1:You also, son of man, take you a tile, and lay it before you, and portray upon it the city, even Jerusalem. 2:And lay siege against it, and build a fort against it, and cast a mount against it; set the camp also against it, and set battering rams against it round about. 3:Moreover take you to you an iron pan, and set it for a wall of iron between you and the city: and set your face against it, and it shall be besieged, and you shall lay siege against it. This shall be a sign to the house of Israel. 4:Lie you also upon your left side, and lay the iniquity of the house of Israel upon it: according to the number of the days that you shall lie upon it you shall bear their iniquity. 5:For I have laid upon you the years of their iniquity, according to the number of the days, three hundred and ninety days: so shall you bear the iniquity of the house of Israel. 6:And when you hast accomplished them, lie again on your right side, and you shall bear the iniquity of the house of Judah forty days: I have appointed you each day for a year.

7:Therefore you shall set your face toward the siege of Jerusalem, and your arm
shall be uncovered, and you shall prophesy against it. 8:And, behold, I will lay
bands upon you, and you shall not turn you from one side to another, till you hast
ended the days of your siege. 9:Take you also to you wheat, and barley, and beans,
and lentils, and millet, and fiches, and put them in one vessel, and make you bread
thereof, according to the number of the days that you shall lie upon your side, three
hundred and ninety days shall you eat thereof. 10:And your meat which you shall
eat shall be by weight, twenty shekels a day: from time to time shall you eat it.
11:You shall drink also water by measure, the sixth part of an hin: from time to time
shall you drink. 12:And you shall eat it as barley cakes, and you shall bake it with
dung that comes out of man, in their sight. 13:And the Lord said, Even this shall the
children of Israel eat their defiled bread among the Gentiles, whither I will drive
them. 14:Then said I, Ah Lord God! behold, my soul has not been polluted: for from
my youth up even till now have I not eaten of that which dies of itself, or is torn in
pieces; neither came there abominable flesh into my mouth. 15:Then he said to me,
Look, I have given you cow's dung for man's dung, and you shall prepare your
bread therewith. 16:Moreover he said to me, Son of man, behold, I will break the
staff of bread in Jerusalem, and they shall eat bread by weight, and with care; and
they shall drink water by measure, and with astonishment: 17:That they may want
bread and water, and be astonished one with another, and consume away for their
iniquity.

5:1: And you, son of man, take you a sharp knife, take you a barber's razor, and
cause it to pass upon your head and upon your beard: then take you balances to
weigh, and divide the hair. 2:You shall burn with fire a third part in the midst of the
city, when the days of the siege are fulfilled: and you shall take a third part, and
smite about it with a knife: and a third part you shall scatter in the wind; and I will
draw out a sword after them. 3:You shall also take thereof a few in number, and
bind them in your skirts. 4:Then take of them again, and cast them into the midst of
the fire, and burn them in the fire; for there of shall a fire come forth into all the
house of Israel. 5:This says the Lord God; This is Jerusalem: I have set it in the
midst of the nations and countries that are round about her. 6:And she has changed
my judgments into wickedness more than the nations, and my statutes more than the
countries that are round about her: for they have refused my judgments and my
statutes, they have not walked in them. 7:Therefore this says the Lord God; Because
you multiplied more than the nations that are round about you, and have not walked
in my statutes, neither have kept my judgments, neither have done according to the
judgments of the nations that are round about you, 8:Therefore this says the Lord
God; Behold, I, even I, am against you, and will execute judgments in the midst of
you in the sight of the nations. 9:And I will do in you that which I have not done,
and where to I will not do any more the like, because of all your abominations.
10:Therefore the fathers shall eat the sons in the midst of you, and the sons shall eat
their fathers; and I will execute judgments in you, and the whole remnant of you
will I scatter into all the winds. 11:Wherefore, as I live, says the Lord God; Surely,
because you hast defiled my sanctuary with all your detestable things, and with all
your abominations, therefore will I also diminish you, neither shall mine eye spare,
neither will I have any pity. 12:A third part of you shall die with the pestilence, and
with famine shall they be consumed in the midst of you:

and a third part shall fall by the sword round about you; and I will scatter a third part into all the winds, and I will draw out a sword after them. 13:This shall mine anger be accomplished, and I will cause my fury to rest upon them, and I will be comforted: and they shall know that I the Lord have spoken it in my zeal, when I have accomplished my fury in them. 14:Moreover I will make you waste, and a reproach among the nations that are round about you, in the sight of all that pass by. 15:So it shall be a reproach and a taunt, an instruction and an astonishment to the nations that are round about you, when I shall execute judgments in you in anger and in fury and in furious rebukes. I the Lord have spoken it. 16:When I shall send upon them the evil arrows of famine, which shall be for their destruction, and which I will send to destroy you: and I will increase the famine upon you, and will break your staff of bread. 17:So will I send upon you famine and evil beasts, and they shall bereave you; and pestilence and blood shall pass through you, and I will bring the sword upon you. I the Lord have spoken it.

+/- July 14th. (Tammuz 15th.)

The year +/- 1357 B.C. God spoke to Moses, in three days come to see me on the mountain

(Exodus 19:1-15)1:In the third month, when the children of Israel were gone forth out of the land of Egypt, the same day came they into the wilderness of Sinai. 2:For they were departed from Rephidim, and had come to the desert of Sinai, and had pitched in the wilderness; and there Israel camped before the mount. 3:And Moses went up to God, and the Lord called to him out of the mountain, saying, this shall you say to the house of Jacob, and tell the children of Israel. 4:You have seen what I did to the Egyptians, and how I bare you on eagles' wings, and brought you to myself. 5:Now therefore, if you will obey my voice indeed, and keep my covenant, then you shall be a peculiar treasure to me above all people: for all the earth is mine.

6:And you shall be to me a kingdom of priests, and an holy nation. These are the words which you shall speak to the children of Israel. 7:And Moses came and called for the elders of the people, and laid before their faces all these words which the Lord commanded him. 8:And all the people answered together, and said, All that the Lord has spoken we will do. And Moses returned the words of the people to the Lord. 9:And the Lord said to Moses, Look, I come to you in a thick cloud, that the people may hear when I speak with you, and believe you forever. And Moses told the words of the people to the Lord. 10:And the Lord said to Moses, Go to the people, and sanctify them today and tomorrow, and let them wash their clothes.

11:And be ready against the third day: for the third day the Lord will come down in the sight of all the people upon mount Sinai. 12:And you shall set bounds to the people round about, saying, Take heed to yourselves, that you go not up into the mount, or touch the border of it: who soever touches the mount shall be surely put to death. 13:There shall not an hand touch it, but he shall surely be stoned, or shot through; whether it be beast or man, it shall not live: when the trumpet sounds long, they shall come up to the mount. 14:And Moses went down from the mount to the people, and sanctified the people; and they washed their clothes. 15:And he said to the people, Be ready again the third day: and come not to your wives.

+/- July 17th. (Tammuz 18th.)

The year +/- 1357 B.C. God spoke to the Hebrews about the Laws

(Exodus 19:16-24:3) 16:And it came to pass on the third day in the morning, that there were thunders and lightnings, and a thick cloud upon the mount, and the voice of the trumpet exceeding loud; so that all the people that was in the camp trembled. 17:And Moses brought forth the people out of the camp to meet with God; and they stood at the nether part of the mount. 18:And mount Sinai was altogether on a smoke, because the Lord descended upon it in fire: and the smoke thereof ascended as the smoke of a furnace, and the whole mount quaked greatly. 19:And when the voice of the trumpet sounded long, and waxed louder and louder, Moses spoke, and God answered him by a voice. 20:And the Lord came down upon mount Sinai, on the top of the mount: and the Lord called Moses up to the top of the mount; and Moses went up. 21:And the Lord said to Moses, Go down, charge the people, lest they break through to the Lord to gaze, and many of them perish. 22:And let the priests also, which come near to the Lord,sanctify themselves, lest the Lord break forth upon them. 23:And Moses said to the Lord, The people cannot come up to mount Sinai: for you charged us, saying, Set bounds about the mount, and sanctify it. 24:And the Lord said to him, Away, get you down, and you shall come up, you, and Aaron with you: but let not the priests and the people break through to come up to the Lord, lest he break forth upon them. 25:So Moses went down to the people, and spoke to them.

20:1: And God spoke all these words, saying; 2:I am the Lord your God, which have brought you out of the land of Egypt, out of the house of bondage. 3:You shall say no other gods names before me. 4:You shall not make to you any graven image, or any likeness of any thing that is in heaven above, or that is in the earth beneath, or that is in the water under the earth. 5:You shall not bow down yourself to them, nor serve them, for I the Lord your God am a Jealous God, visiting the iniquity of the fathers upon the children to the third and fourth generation of them that hate me, 6:And showing mercy to thousands of them that love me, and keep my commandments. 7:You shall not take the name of the Lord your God in vain; for the Lord will not hold him guiltless that takes his name in vain. 8:Remember the sabbath day, to keep it holy. 9:Six days shall you labor, and do all your work: 10:But the seventh day is the sabbath of the Lord your God: in it you shall not do any work, you, nor your son, nor your daughter, your manservant, nor your maidservant, nor your cattle, nor your stranger that is within your gates. 11:For in six days the Lord made heaven and earth, the sea, and all that in them is, and rested the seventh day: wherefore the Lord blessed the sabbath day, and hallowed it. 12:Honor your Father and your Mother: that your days may be long upon the land which the Lord your God gives you. 13:You shall not kill. 14:You shall not commit adultery. 15:You shall not steal. 16:You shall not bear false witness against your neighbor. 17:You shall not covet your neighbor's house, you shall not covet your neighbor's wife, nor his manservant, nor his maidservant, nor his ox, nor his ass, nor any thing that is your neighbor's. 18:And all the people heard the thundering, and saw the lightning, and the noise of the trumpet, and the mountain smoking: and when the people saw it, they moved away, and stood far off. **The people spoke to Moses:** 19:And they said to Moses, Speak you with us, and we will hear: but let not God speak with us,

lest we die. 20:And Moses said to the people, Fear not: for God is come to prove
you, and that his fear may be before your faces, that you sin not. 21:And the people
stood afar off, and Moses drew near to the thick darkness where God was.
The Lord spoke to Moses again saying: 22:And the Lord said to Moses, this you
shall say to the children of Israel, You have seen that I have talked with you from
heaven. 23:You shall not make for your self's gods of silver, neither shall you make
for you self's gods of gold. 24:An altar of earth you shall make to me, and shall
sacrifice thereon your burnt offerings, and your peace offerings, your sheep, and
your oxen: in all places where I record my name I will come to you, and I will bless
you. 25:And if you will make me an altar of stone, you shall not build it of hew
stone: for if you lift up your tool upon it, you hast polluted it. 26:You shall not you
go up by steps to mine altar, that your nakedness be not discovered thereon.

21:1: Now these are the judgments which you shall set before them. 2:If you buy an
Hebrew servant, six years he shall serve: and in the seventh he shall go out free for
nothing. 3:If he came in by himself, he shall go out by himself: if he were married,
then his wife shall go out with him. 4:If his master have given him a wife, and she
have born him sons or daughters; the wife and her children shall be her master's,
and he shall go out by himself. 5:And if the servant shall plainly say, I love my
master, my wife, and my children; I will not go out free. 6:Then his master shall
bring him to the judges; he shall also bring him to the door, or to the door post; and
his master shall bore his ear through with an awl; and he shall serve him for ever.
7:And if a man sells his daughter to be a maidservant, she shall not go out as the
men servants do. 8:If she please not her master, who has betrothed her to himself,
then shall he let her be redeemed: to sell her to a strange nation he shall have no
power, seeing he has dealt deceitfully with her. 9:And if he have betrothed her to
his son, he shall deal with her after the manner of daughters. 10:If he take him
another wife, her food, her raiment, and her duty of marriage, shall he not diminish.
11:And if he do not these three to her, then shall she go out free without money.
12:He that strikes a man, so that he dies, shall be surely put to death. 13:And if a
man lie not in wait, but God deliver him into his hand; then I will appoint you a
place whither he shall flee. 14:But if a man come presumptuously upon his
neighbor, to slay him with guile; you shall take him from mine altar, that he may
die. 15:And he that strikes his father, or his mother, shall be surely put to death.
16:And he that steals a man, and sells him, or if he be found in his hand, he shall
surely be put to death. 17:And he that curses his father, or his mother, shall surely be
put to death. 18:And if men strive together, and one strikes another with a stone, or
with his fist, and he die not, but keeps in his bed: 19:If he rise again, and walks
abroad upon his staff, then shall he that struck him will go unpunished: only he shall
pay for the loss of his time, and shall cause him to be thoroughly healed. 20;And if a
man strikes his servant, or his maid, with a rod, and he die under his hand; he shall
be surely punished. 21:Not with standing, if he continue a day or two, he shall not
be punished: for he is his property. 22:If men strive, and hurt a woman with child,
so that her fruit depart from her, and yet no mischief follow: he shall be surely
punished, according as the woman's husband will lay upon him; and he shall pay as
the judges determine. 23:And if any mischief follow, then you shall give life for
life. 24:Eye for eye, tooth for tooth, hand for hand, foot for foot. 25:Burning for
burning, wound for wound, stripe for stripe.

26:And if a man strikes the eye of his servant, or the eye of his maid, that it perish; he shall let him go free for his eye's sake. 27:And if he strikes out his manservant's tooth, or his maidservant's tooth; he shall let him go free for his tooth's sake. 28:If an ox gore a man or a woman, that they die: then the ox shall be surely stoned,and his flesh shall not be eaten; but the owner of the ox shall go unpunished. 29:But if the ox were wont to push with his horn in time past, and it has been testified to his owner, and he has not kept him in, but that he has killed a man or a woman; the ox shall be stoned, and his owner also shall be put to death. 30:If there be laid on him a sum of money, then he shall give for the ransom of his life whatsoever is laid upon him. 31:Whether he have gored a son, or have gored a daughter, according to this judgment shall it be done to him. 32;If the ox shall push a manservant or a maidservant; he shall give to their master thirty shekels of silver, and the ox shall be stoned. 33;And if a man shall open a pit, or if a man shall dig a pit, and not cover it, and an ox or an ass fall therein. 34:The owner of the pit shall make it good, and give money to the owner of them; and the dead beast shall be his. 35:And if one man's ox hurt another's man's ox, that he dies; then they shall sell the live ox, and divide the money of it; and the dead ox also they shall divide. 36:Or if it be known that the ox has used to push in time past, and his owner has not kept him in; he shall surely pay ox for ox; and the dead shall be his own.

22:1: If a man shall steal an ox, or a sheep, and kill it, or sell it; he shall restore five oxen for an ox, and four sheep for a sheep. 2:If a thief be found breaking up, and be smitten that he die, there shall no blood be shed for him. 3:If the sun be risen upon him, there shall be blood shed for him; for he should make full restitution; if he have nothing, then he shall be sold for his theft. 4:If the theft be certainly found in his hand alive, whether it be ox, or ass, or sheep; he shall restore double. 5:If a man shall cause a field or vineyard to be eaten, and shall put in his beast, and shall feed in another man's field; of the best of his own field, and of the best of his own vineyard, shall he make restitution. 6:If fire break out, and catch in thorns, so that the stacks of corn, or the standing corn, or the field, be consumed there with; he that kindled the fire shall surely make restitution. 7:If a man shall deliver to his neighbor money or stuff to keep, and it be stolen out of the man's house; if the thief be found, let him pay double. 8:If the thief be not found, then the master of the house shall be brought to the judges, to see whether he have put his hand to his neighbor's goods. 9:For all manner of trespass, whether it be for ox, for ass, for sheep, for raiment, or for any manner of lost thing, which another challenge to be his, the cause of both parties shall come before the judges; and whom the judges shall condemn, he shall pay double to his neighbor. 10:If a man deliver to his neighbor an ass, or an ox, or a sheep, or any beast, to keep; and it die, or be hurt, or driven away, no man seeing it. 11:Then shall an oath of the Lord be between them both, that he has not put his hand to his neighbor's goods; and the owner of it shall accept there of, there of and he shall not make it good. 12:And if it be stolen from him, he shall make restitution to the owner thereof. 13:If it be torn in pieces, then let him bring it for witness, and he shall not make good that which was torn. 14:And if a man borrows a animal of his neighbor, and it becomes hurt, or dies, the owner there of being not with it, he shall surely make it good. 15:But if the owner there of it be with it, he shall not make it good: if it be an hired thing, it came for his hire. 16:And if a man entice a maid that is not betrothed, and lie with her, he shall surely endow her to be his wife.

17:If her father utterly refuse to give her to him, he shall pay money according to
the dowry of virgins. 18;You shall not suffer a witch to live. 19:Whosoever lies with
a beast shall surely be put to death. 20:He that sacrifices to any other god, other than
to the Lord, he shall be utterly destroyed. 21:You shall neither vex a stranger, nor
oppress him: for you were strangers in the land of Egypt. 22:You shall not afflict
any widow, or fatherless child. 23:If you afflict them in any wise, and they cry at all
to me, I will surely hear their cry. 24:And my wrath shall wax hot, and I will kill
you with the sword; and your wives shall be widows, and your children fatherless.
25:If you lend money to any of my people that is poor by you, you shall not be to
him as an usurer, neither shall you lay upon him usury. 26:If you at all take your
neighbor's raiment to pledge, you shall deliver it to him by that the sun goeth down.
27:For that is his covering only, it is his raiment for his skin: wherein shall he sleep?
and it shall come to pass, when he cries to me, that I will hear; for I am gracious.
28:You shall not revile the judges, nor curse the ruler of your people. 29:You shall
not delay to offer the first of your ripe fruits, and of your liquors: the firstborn of
your sons shall you give to me. 30:Likewise shall you do with your oxen, and with
your sheep: seven days it shall be with his dam; on the eighth day you shall give it
me. 31:And you shall be holy men to me: neither shall you eat any flesh that is torn
of beasts in the field; you shall cast it to the dogs.

23:1: You shall not raise a false report: or put not your hand in with the wicked to
be an unrighteous witness. 2:You shall not follow a multitude to do evil; neither
shall you speak in a cause to decline after many to pervert justice. 3:Neither shall
you countenance a poor man in his cause. 4:If you meet your enemy's ox or his ass
going astray, you shall surely bring it back to him again. 5:If you see the ass of him
that hates you lying under his burden, and would forbear to help him, you shall
surely help with him. 6:You shall not wrest the judgment of your poor in his cause.
7:Keep you far from a false matter; and the innocent and righteous slay you not: for
I will not justify the wicked. 8:And you shall take no gift: for the gift blinds the
wise, and perverts the words of the righteous. 9:Also you shall not oppress a
stranger: for you know the heart of a stranger, seeing you were strangers in the land
of Egypt. 10:And six years you shall sow your land, and shall gather in the fruits
thereof: 11:But the seventh year you shall let it rest and lie still; that the poor of
your people may eat: and what they leave the beasts of the field shall eat. In like
manner you shall deal with your vineyard, and with your olive yard. 12:Six days
you shall do your work, and on the seventh day you shall rest: that your ox and your
ass may rest, and the son of your handmaid, and the stranger, may be refreshed.
13:And in all things that I have said to you be circumspect: And make no mention of
the name of any other gods, neither let them be heard coming out of your mouth.
14:Three times you shall keep a feast to me in the year. 15:You shall keep the feast
of unleavened bread: (you shall eat unleavened bread seven days, as I commanded
you, in the time appointed of the month Abib; for in it you came out from Egypt:
and none shall appear before me empty) 16:And the feast of harvest, the first fruits
of your labors, which you hast sown in the field: and the feast of in-gathering,
which is in the end of the season, when you have gathered in your labors out of the
field. 17:Three times in the year all your males shall appear before the Lord God.
18:You shall not offer the blood of my sacrifice with leavened bread; neither shall
the fat of my sacrifice remain until the morning.

19:The first of the first fruits of your land you shall bring into the house of the Lord
your God. you shall not seethe a kid in his mother's milk. 20:Behold, I send an
Angel before you, to keep you in the way, and to bring you into the place which I
have prepared. 21:Beware of him, and obey his voice, provoke him not; for he will
not pardon your transgressions: for my name is in him. 22:But if you shall indeed
obey his voice, and do all that I speak; then I will be an enemy to your enemies, and
an adversary to your adversaries. 23:For mine Angel shall go before you, and bring
you in to the Amorites, and the Hittites, and the Perizzites, and the Canaanites, the
Hivites, and the Jebusites: and I will cut them off. 24:You shall not bow down to
their gods, nor serve them, nor do after their works: but you shall utterly overthrow
them, and quite break down their images. 25:And you shall serve the Lord your
God, and he shall bless your bread, and your water; and I will take sickness away
from the midst of you. 26:There shall nothing cast their young, nor be barren, in
your land: the number of your days I will fulfill. 27:I will send my fear before you,
and will destroy all the people to whom you shall come, and I will make all your
enemies turn their backs to you. 28:And I will send hornets before you, which shall
drive out the Hivite, the Canaanite, and the Hittite, from before you. 29:I will not
drive them out from before you in one year; lest the land become desolate, and the
beast of the field multiply against you. 30:By little and little I will drive them out
from before you, until you be increased, and inherit the land. 31:And I will set your
bounds from the Red sea even to the sea of the Philistines, and from the desert to the
river: for I will deliver the inhabitants of the land into your hand; and you shall
drive them out before you. 32:You shall make no covenant with them, nor with their
gods. 33:They shall not dwell in your land, lest they make you sin against me: for if
you serve their gods, it will surely be a snare to you. **24:1:**And he said to Moses,
Come up to the Lord, you, and Aaron, Nadab, and Abihu, and seventy of the elders
of Israel; and worship you afar off. 2:And Moses alone shall come near the Lord:
but they shall not come near; neither shall the people go up with him. 3:And Moses
came and told the people all the words of the Lord, and all the judgments: and all
the people answered with one voice, and said, All the words which the Lord has said
will we do.

+/- July 17th. (Tammuz 18th.)

Day of fasting turned into a day of Feasting:

(Zechariah 8:19) 19:This says the Lord of hosts; The fast of the (**Fourth month,**) and the fast of the fifth, and the fast of the seventh, and the fast of the tenth, shall be to the house of Judah joy and gladness, and cheerful feasts; therefore love the truth and peace.

+/-July 18th. (Tammuz 19th.)

The year +/- 1357 B.C. Moses wrote down the words of the Lord

(Exodus 24:4-16) 4:And Moses wrote down all the words of the Lord, and rose up
early in the morning, and build an altar under the hill, and twelve pillars, according
to the twelve tribes of Israel. 5:And he sent young men of the children of Israel,
which offered burnt offerings, and sacrificed peace offerings of oxen to the Lord.
6:And Moses took half of the blood, and put it in basin;

and half of the blood he sprinkled on the altar. 7:And he took the book of the covenant, and read in the audience of the people: and they said, All that the Lord has said will we do, and be obedient. 8:And Moses took the blood, and sprinkled it on the people, and said, Behold the blood of the covenant, which the Lord has made with you concerning all these words. 9:Then went up Moses, and Aaron, Nadab, and Abihu, and seventy of the elders of Israel: 10:And they saw the God of Israel: and there was under his feet as it were a paved work of a sapphire stone, and as it were the body of heaven in his clearness. 11:And upon the nobles of the children of Israel he laid not his hand: also they saw God, and did eat and drink. 12:And the Lord said to Moses, Come up to me into the mount, and be there: and I will give you tables of stone, and a law, and commandments which I have written; that you may teach them. 13:And Moses rose up, and his minister Joshua: and Moses went up into the mount of God. 14:And he said to the elders, you stay and wait here for us, until we come again to you: and, behold, Aaron and Hur are with you: if any man have any matters to do, let him come to them. 15:And Moses went up into the mount, and a cloud covered the mount. 16:And the glory of the Lord abode upon mount Sinai, and the cloud covered it for six days: and the seventh day, he called to Moses out of the midst of the cloud.

+/-July 23th. (Tammuz 24th.)

The year +/- 1357 B.C. The Lord called Moses in to the Cloud

(Exodus 24:16-18)16:And the glory of the Lord abode upon mount Sinai, and the cloud covered it for six days: and the seventh day he called into Moses out of the midst of the cloud. 17:And the sight of the glory of the Lord was like devouring fire on the top of the mount in the eyes of the children of Israel. 18:And Moses went into the midst of the cloud, and got him up into the mount: and Moses was in the mount forty days and forty nights.

Picture on the left: The top of Mount Sinai, where God spoke to Moses. It is surrounded by a fence, and is heavily guarded.

+/- July 26th. (Tammuz 27th.)

The year +/- 427 B.C. Nehemiah went to Jerusalem

(Nehemiah 2:11) 11: So I came to Jerusalem, and was there three days.

+/- July 29th. (Tammuz 30th.)

The year +/- 427 B.C. Nehemiah went to see the state of Jerusalem's walls

(Nehemiah 2:12) 12:And I arose in the night, I and a few men with me; neither told I any man what my God had put in my heart to do at Jerusalem: neither was there any beast with me, save the beast that I rode upon.

+/-July 30th. (Abba/ Av 1st.)

The year +/- 1317 B.C. Aaron Died on Mount Hor

(Numbers 33:38) 38;And Aaron the priest went up to mount Hor at the commandment of the Lord, and died there, in the fortieth year after the children of Israel had come out of the land of Egypt, in the first day of the fifth month, the month of Av. 39;And Aaron was an hundred and twenty and three years old when he died in mount Hor.

+/- July 30th. (Abba/ Av 1st.)

The year +/- 427 B.C. Nehemiah went out by night

(Nehemiah 2:13-14)b13;And I went out by night by the gate of the valley, even before the dragon well, and to the dung port, and viewed the walls of Jerusalem, which were broken down,and the gates thereof were consumed with fire. 14;Then I went on to the gate of the fountain, and to the King's pool: but there was no place for the beast that was under me to pass.

The Dung Gate

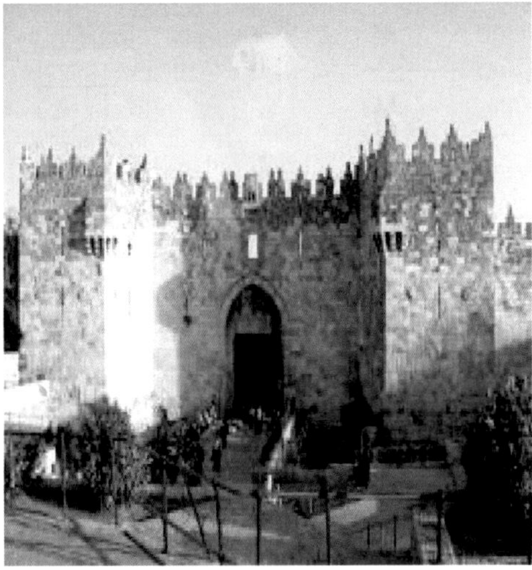

The Gate of the Valley

One of Jerusalem's outside walls

+/- July 30th. (Abba/ Av 1st.)

The year +/- 151 B.C. Achior told Holofernes about the Hebrews

(Judith 5:1-6:21) 1:It was reported to Holofernes, commander in chief of the Assyrian army, that the Israelites were ready for battle, and had blocked the mountain passes, fortified the summits of all the higher peaks, and placed roadblocks in the plains. 2:In great anger he summoned all the rulers of the Moabites, the generals of the Ammonites, and all the satraps of the seacoast, 3:and said to them: "Now tell me, you Canaanites, what sort of people is this that dwells in the mountains? Which city's do they inhabit? How large is their army? In what dies their power and strength consist? Who has set himself as their King and the leader of their army? 4:"Why have they refused to come out me along with all the other inhabitants of the west?" 5:Then Achior, the leader of all the Ammonites, said to him: My Lord, hear this account from your servant; I will the truth about thease people that live near you, that live in this mountain region; no lie shall escape your servant's lips. 6:These people are descendants of Chaldeans. 7:They formerly dwelt in Mesopotamia, for they did not not wish to follow the gods of their forefathers who were born in the land of Chaldeans. 8:Since they abandoned the way of their ancestors, and acknowledged with divine worship the God of heaven, their forefathers expelled them from the presence of their gods. So they fled to Mesopotamia dwelt their a long time. 9:Their God told them to leave their abode and proceed to the land of Canaan. Here they settled, and grew very rich in gold, silver, and a great abundance of livestock. 10:Later, when famine had gripped the whole land of Canaan, they went down into Egypt. They stayed there as long as they found sustenance, and grew into such a great multitude,that the number of their race could not be counted.

11:The King of Egypt however, rose up against them, shrewdly forced them into labor at brick making, oppressed and enslaved them. 12:But they cried to their God, and he struck the land of Egypt with plagues for which there was no remedy. When the Egyptians expelled them. 13:God dried up the Red Sea before them, 14:and led them along the route to Sinai and Kadesh-barnea. First they drove out all the inhabitants of the desert. 15Then they settled in the land of the Amorites, destroyed all the Heshbonites by main force, crossed the Jordan, and took possession of the whole mountain region. 16:They expelled the Canaanites, the Perizzites, the Jebusites, the Schematizes,and all the Gergesites; and they lived in these mountains a long time. 17:As long as the Israelites did not sin in the eyes of their God, they prospered. For their God who hates wickedness,was with them. 18:At this time the people fell prostate and worshiped God, and they cried out; 19:Lord God of Heaven, behold their arrogance! Have pity on the lowliness of our people, and look with favor on this day those who are consecrated to you. 20:Then they reassured Achior and praised him highly. 21:Uzziah took him from the assembly to his home, where he gave a banquet for the elders. That whole night they called on the God of Israel for help. 22:When Achior had finished his speech, all the people standing around the tent began to protest. Holofernes' own senior officers, as well as the Moabites and those from the Mediterranean coast, demanded that Achior be put to death. 23:Why should we be afraid of these Israelites? They asked. They are weak; they can't put up a strong defense. 24: Let's go ahead! General Holofernes, your great army will slaughter them easily.

6:1; When the noise of the crowd around the council had subsided, Holofernes spoke to Achior in front of the entire group, those from the Mediterranean coast, the Moabites, and the Ammonite mercenaries. 2: Achior, who do you think you are, acting like a prophet? Who are you to tell us not to go to war against the Israelites because some god will defend them? Nebuchadnezzar is our god, and that's all that matters. He will send his army and wipe these Israelites off the face of the earth. Their god can't help them. 3: But we serve Nebuchadnezzar, and we will beat them as easily as if their whole army were one man. They will not be able to hold their ground against our cavalry; 4: it will overwhelm them. The mountains will be soaked with their blood, and the valleys will be filled with their corpses. After our attack, they will be completely wiped out; not a trace of them will be left. This is the command of Nebuchadnezzar, the lord of the whole earth, and he doesn't speak idle words.5: Achior, you are nothing but an Ammonite mercenary, and you talk like a traitor. You will not see me again until I come and punish this race of runaway slaves. 6: And when I do, my soldiers will put you to death. You will be just another name on the casualty list. 7: Now my men will take you into the mountains and leave you in one of the Israelite towns, 8:and you will die with the people there. 9:Why look so worried, Achior? Don't you think the town can stand against me? I will carry out all my threats; you can be sure of that! 10: Then Holofernes ordered his men, who were waiting in his tent, to seize Achior, take him to Bethulia, and hand him over to the Israelites. 11:So the men seized Achior and took him out of the camp into the valley. From there they led him into the mountains, as far as the spring which was below Bethulia. 12: When the men of that town saw them approaching, they picked up their weapons and ran to the top of the hill. Every man who used a sling as a weapon rained stones down on Holofernes' soldiers, and this stopped them from coming any farther up the mountain. 13: The Assyrians were forced to take cover along the mountainside, where they tied Achior up and left him lying at the foot of the mountain. Then they returned to Holofernes. 14:Later, when the Israelites came down from Bethulia, they untied Achior, brought him into the town, and took him before the town officials, 15: who at that time were Uzziah son of Micah, of the tribe of Simeon, Chabris son of Gothoniel, and Charmis son of Melchiel. 16: The officials called together the town elders, and all the women and the young men also ran to the assembly. Achior was brought before the people, and Uzziah began questioning him. 17: Achior told them what had been said at Holofernes war council, what he himself had said to the Assyrian officers, and how Holofernes had boasted about what he would do to the Israelites. 18: When the people heard this, they fell on their knees and worshiped God. They prayed: 19: O Lord God of heaven, look how our boastful enemies have humiliated your people! Have pity on us and help us. 20: Then they reassured Achior and praised him for what he had done. 21: After the assembly was over, Uzziah took Achior home with him, and gave a banquet there for the elders. All that night they prayed to the God of Israel for help.

+/- July 31th. (Abba/ Av 2nd.)

The year +/- 427 B.C.E. Nehemiah stood by the brook:

(Nehemiah 2:15-16)15:Then went I up in the night by the brook, and viewed the wall, and turned back, and entered by the gate of the valley, and then returned. 16:And the rulers knew not whither I went, or what I did; neither had I as of yet, told any of the Hebrews, nor to the priests, nor to the nobles, nor to the rulers, nor to the rest that did the work.

+/- July 31th. (Abba/ Av 2nd.)

The year +/- 151 B.C. Holofernes army was on display

(Judith 7:1-5)1;The fallowing day Holofernes ordered his whole army, and all the allied troops that had come to his support, to move against Bethulia, seize the mountain passes, and engage the Israelites in battle. 2:That same day all their fighting men went into action. Their forces numbered a hundred and seventy thousand infantry and twelve thousand horsemen, not counting the baggage train or the men who accompanied it on foot, it was a very grate army. 3:They encamped at the spring in the valley near Bethulia, and spread out in breadth toward Dothan as far as Balbaim and in length from Bethulia to Cyamon, which faces Esdraelon. 4:When the Israelites saw how many there were, they said to one another in great dismay; "Soon they will devour the whole country. Neither the high mountains nor the valleys or the hills can support the mass of them." 5:Yet they all seized their weapons, lighted fires on their bastions, and kept watch throughout the night.

(Also it was during this Month of July / Tammuz)

David gathered all of Israel together

(1Chroncles 13:1-14) 1:And David consulted with the captains of thousands and hundreds, and with every leader. 2:And David said to all the congregation of Israel, If it seems good to you, and that it be of the Lord our God, let us send abroad to our brethren every where, that are left in all the land of Israel, and with them also to the priests and Levites which are in their cities and suburbs, that they may gather themselves to us. 3:And let us bring again the ark of our God to us: for we never inquired of it in all the days of Saul. 4:And all the congregation said that they would do so: for the thing was right in the eyes of all the people. 5:So David gathered all Israel together, from Shihor of Egypt even to the entering of Hemath, to bring the ark of God from Kirjathjearim.

6:And David went up, and all Israel, to Baalah, that is to Kirjathjearim, which belonged to Judah, to bring up the ark of the Lord God, that dwells between the cherubims, whose name is called on it. 7:And they carried the ark of God in a new cart out of the house of Abinadab: and Uzza and Ahio drove the cart. 8:And David and all Israel played before God with all their might, and with singing, and with harps, and with psalteries, and with timbrels, and with cymbals, and with trumpets. 9:And when they came to the threshing floor of Chidon, Uzza put forth his hand to hold the ark; for the oxen stumbled. 10:And the anger of the Lord was kindled against Uzza, and he struck him, because he put his hand to the ark: and there he died before God. 11:And David was displeased, because the Lord had made a breach upon Uzza: wherefore that place is called Perezuzza to this day. 12:And David was afraid of God that day, saying, How shall I bring the ark of God home to me? 13:So David brought not the ark home to himself to the city of David, but carried it aside to the house of Obededom the Gittite. 14:And the ark of God remained with the family of Obededom in his house three months. And the Lord blessed the house of Obededom, and all that he had.

Pictures of Kiriathjearim:

**Where the Ark was before David took it back to Jerusalem.
There is now a church in the place where,
Abinadab's house use to be.**

Chapter 8: August – Abba /Av

It is the 5th. month on the Hebrew calendar
In Hebrew this month is called: Abba / Av, which means:
(Father / A spiritual wedding to be held in Jerusalem)
Tribe of Levi, means:(He will become attached)
The stone of (Sadr) represents this tribe.
Levi: (The 3rd.) Son of Leah,
(Was believed to have been born in this month.)
(Spirit of Strength,)

+/-August 1st. (Abba/ Av 3rd.)

The year +/- 175 B.C. Holofernes seized their source of water

(Judith 7:6-7) 6:On the second day Holofernes led out all of his cavalry in the sight of the Israelites who were in Bethulia. 7He reconnoitered the approaches to their city and located their sources of water; these he seized, and stationed armed detachments around them, while he himself returned to his troops.

+/-August 1st. (Abba/ Av 3rd.)

The year +/- 160 B.C. The Martyrdom of a Mother & Her 7 Sons

(2Maccabees 7:1-42) 1:It also happened that seven brothers along with their mother were arrested and tortured with whips and scourges by the King, to force them to eat pork in violation of God's law. 2:The oldest brother, speaking out for the others asked; "What do you expect to achieve by torturing us? We are ready to die rather than transgress the laws of our ancestors." 3:At that the King in a fury, gave orders have pans and caldrons heated. 4:While they were being quickly heated, he commanded his executioners to cut out the tongue of the one who had spoken for the others, to scalp him and cut off his hands and feet, while the rest of his brothers and his mother watched. 5:When he was completely maimed but still breathing, the King ordered them to carry to the fire and and fry him. As a cloud of smoke spread from the pan, the brothers and their mother encouraged one another to die bravely, saying such words as these.

6:"The Lord god is watching,and he truly has compassion on us, as Moses declared in his canticle, when he protested openly with the words, And he will have pity on his servants." 7:When the first brother had died in this manner, they brought the second to be made sport of. After scalping him, they asked him, "Will you eat pork rather than have your body tortured limb by limb?" 8:Answering in the language of his forefathers, (Hebrew) he said; Never! So he too in turn suffered the same tortures as the first. 9:At the point of death he said: "You accursed friend, you are depriving us of this present life, but the King of the world will raise us up to live again forever. It is for his laws that we are dieing. 10:After him the third suffered their cruel sport. He cut out his tongue at once when told to do so, and bravely held out his hands, 11; as he spoke these noble words: "It was from Heaven I received these; for the sake of his laws I disdain them, from him I hope to receive them again." 12:Even the King and his attendants marveled at the young man's courage, because he regarded his suffering as nothing. 13: After he had died, they tortured and maltreated the fourth brother in the same way. 14:When he was near death, he said; "It is my choice at the hands of men with the God-given hope of being restored to life by him; but for you, there will be no resurrection to life." 15:They next brought forward the fifth brother and maltreated him. 16:Looking at the King he said: "Since you have power among men, mortal though you are, do what you please. But do not think that our nation is forsaken by God. 17:Only wait, and you will see how his great power will torment you and your descendants."

18:After him they brought the sixth brother. When he was about to die, he said: "have no illusions. We suffer these thing son our own account, because we have sinned against our God; that is why such astonishing things have happened to us. 19:Do not think, then, that you will go unpunished for having dared to fight against God." 20:Most admirable and worthy of everlasting remembrance was the mother; who had seen six of her sons already perish in one day, knowing the last one will also die, yet bore it courageously because of her trust in the Lord. 21:Filled with a noble spirit that stirred her womanly heart with manly courage, she exhorted each of them in the language of their forefathers, (Hebrew) with these words. 22:"I do not know how you came into existence my womb; it was not I who gave you the breath of life, nor was it I who set in order the elements of which each of you is composed. 23:Therefore, since it is the Creator of the heavens who shapes each man's beginning, as he brings about the origin of everything, he in his mercy, will give you back both breath and life, because you now disregard yourselves for the sake of his law." 24:Antiochus suspecting insult in her words, thought he was being ridiculed. So as the younger brother was still alive, the King appealed to him , not with mere words, but with promises on oath, to make him rich and happy if he would abandon his ancestral customs, and he would make him his friend, and entrust him with a high office. 25:When the youth paid no attention to him at all, the King appealed to the mother, urging her to advise her son to save his life. 26:After he had urged her for a long time, she went through the motions of persuading her son. 27:In derision of the cruel tyrant, she leaned over close to her son and spoke in her native language saying; "Son, have pity on me, who carried you in my womb for nine months, nursed you for three years, brought you up, educated and supported you to your present age. 28:I beg you child, to look at the heavens and the earth and see all that is in them. Then you will know that God did not make them out of existing things, and in the same way man kind came into existence. 29:Do not be afraid of this executioner, but be worthy of your brothers and accept death, so that in the time of mercy I may receive you again with them. 30:She had scarcely finished speaking when the youth said:"What are you waiting for? I will not obey the King's command. I obey the command of the law given to our forefathers through Moses. 31:But you who have contrived every kind of affliction for the Hebrews will not escape the hands of God. 32:We indeed are suffering because of our sins. 33:Though our living Lord treats us harshly for a little while to correct us with chastisements, he will again reconciled with his servants. 34:But you wretch, vilest of all men! Do not in your insolence, concern your self's with unfounded hopes,as you raise your hand against the children of Heaven. 35:You have not yet escaped the judgment of the almighty and all-seeing God. 36:My brothers, after enduring brief pain, have drunk of never-failing life, under God's covenant, but you, by the judgment of God, shall receive just punishments for your arrogance. 37:Like my brothers I offer up my body and my life for our ancestral laws, imploring God to show mercy soon to our nation, and by afflictions and blows to make you confess that he alone is God. 38:Through me and my brothers, may there be a end to the wrath of the almighty that has justly fallen on our whole nation." 39:At that the King became enraged and treated him even worse than the others, since he bitterly resented the boy's contempt. 40:This he too died undefiled, putting all his trust into the Lord. 41:The mother was the last to die after her sons. When she also would not defile her self, by eating pork, she was treated very harshly. But she would not give up her faith in the Lord God of heaven, and the laws that were given to her forefathers by Moses. 42:Enough has been said about the sacrificial meals and the excessive cruelties.

The Name of the Mother

Though not named in the Bibles, her name was Hannah, also spelled (Chanah). In some other areas, she is also called; Miriam, Solomonia, and Shmony. Which is most commonly translated as Grace. After watching her seven sons killed they turned and killed her as well. The Seven sons are often referred to as the seven pillars of wisdom. Note: She had the children without knowing a man. (For she knew not how they came about). **Please note:** It is the only other time it is written that a women had children without knowing a man. It was Antiochus IV Epiphanes, that had them killed. His name was changed when he ascended to the throne. He was born Mithradates. He died in the year +/- 158 B.C. 2 years after the killing.

+/-August 1st. (Abba/ Av 3rd.)

The year +/- 427 B.C. They got ready to start rebuilding the walls

(Nehemiah 2:17-20)17:Then said I to them, You see the distress that we are in, how Jerusalem lays in waste, and the gates thereof are burned with fire: come, and let us build up the wall of Jerusalem, that we be no more a reproach. 18:Then I told them of the hand of my God which was good upon me; as also the King's words that he had spoken to me. And they said, Let us rise up and build. So they strengthened their hands for this good word. 19:But when Sanballat the Horonite, and Tobiah the servant, the Ammonite, and Geshem the Arabian, heard it, they laughed at us to scorn, and despised us, and said, What is this thing that you are doing?

Will you rebel against the King? 20:Then I answered them, and said to them: The God of heaven, he will prosper us; therefore we his servants will arise and build: but you will have no portion, nor right, nor memorial, in Jerusalem.

+/-August 1st. (Abba/ Av 3rd.)

The year +/- 71 B.C. Judith Died

(Judith 16:23-25) 23:She lived to be very old in the house of her husband, reaching the age of one hundred and five. She died in Bethulia, where they buried her in the tomb of her husband, Manasseh; and the house of Israel mourned for her seven days. 24:Before she died, she distributed her goods to the relatives of her husband, Manasseh, and to her own relatives; and to the maid she gave her freedom. 25:During the life of Judith and for a long time after her death, no one again disturbed the Israelites.

+/-August 1st. (Abba/ Av 3rd.)

Fast turned into Feast

(Zechariah 8:19)19:This says the Lord of hosts; The Fast of the Fourth month, and the **Fast of the Fifth month**, and the Fast of the Seventh, and the Fast of the Tenth, shall be to the house of Judah joy and gladness, and cheerful feasts; therefore love the truth and peace.

+/-August 2nd. (Abba/ Av 4th.)

The year +/- 427 B.C. They started to repaired Jerusalem's walls

(Nehemiah 3:1-32)1:Then Eliashib the high priest rose up with his brethren the priests, and they build the sheep gate; they sanctified it, and set up the doors of it; even to the tower of Meah they sanctified it, to the tower of Hananeel. 2:And next to him build, the men of Jericho. And next to them build Zaccur the son of Imri. 3:But the fish gate did the sons of Hassenaah build, who also laid the beams thereof, and set up the doors thereof, the locks thereof, and the bars thereof. 4:And next to them repaired Meremoth the son of Urijah, the son of Koz. And next to them repaired Meshullam the son of Berechiah, the son of Meshezabeel. And next to them repaired Zadok the son of Baana.

5:And next to them the Tekoites repaired; but their nobles put not their necks to the work of their Lord. 6:Moreover the old gate repaired Jehoiada the son of Paseah, and Meshullam the son of Besodeiah; they laid the beams thereof, and set up the doors thereof, and the locks thereof, and the bars thereof. 7:And next to them repaired Melatiah the Gibeonite, and Jadon the Meronothite, the men of Gibeon, and of Mizar, to the throne of the governor on this side the river. 8:Next to him repaired Uzziel the son of Harhaiah, of the goldsmiths. Next to him also repaired Hananiah the son of one of the apothecaries, and they fortified Jerusalem to the broad wall. 9:And next to them repaired Rephaiah the son of Hur, the ruler of the half part of Jerusalem. 10:And next to them repaired Jedaiah the son of Harumaph, even over against his house. And next to him repaired Hattush the son of Hashabniah.

11:Malchijah the son of Harim, and Hashub the son of Pahathmoab, repaired the other piece, and the tower of the furnaces. 12:And next to him repaired Shallum the son of Halohesh, the ruler of the half part of Jerusalem, he and his daughters. 13:The valley gate repaired Hanun, and the inhabitants of Zanoah; they built it, and set up the doors thereof, the locks thereof, and the bars thereof, and a thousand cubits on the wall to the dung gate. 14:But the dung gate repaired Malchiah the son of Rechab, the ruler of part of Bethhaccerem; he built it, and set up the doors thereof, the locks thereof, and the bars thereof. 15:But the gate of the fountain repaired Shallun the son of Colhozeh, the ruler of part of Mizpah; he built it, and covered it, and set up the doors thereof, the locks thereof, and the bars thereof, and the wall of the pool of Siloah by the King's garden, and to the stairs that go down from the city of David.

16:After him repaired Nehemiah the son of Azbuk, the ruler of the half part of Bethzur, to the place over against the sepulchers of David, and to the pool that was made, and to the house of the mighty. 17:After him repaired the Levites, Rehum the son of Bani. Next to him repaired Hashabiah, the ruler of the half part of Keilah, in his part. 18:After him repaired their brethren, Bavai the son of Henadad, the ruler of the half part of Keilah. 19:And next to him repaired Ezer the son of Jeshua, the ruler of Mizpah, another piece over against the going up to the armory at the turning of the wall. 20:After him Baruch the son of Zabbai earnestly repaired the other piece, from the turning of the wall to the door of the house of Eliashib the high priest.

21:After him repaired Meremoth the son of Urijah the son of Koz another piece, from the door of the house of Eliashib even to the end of the house of Eliashib. 22:And after him repaired the priests, the men of the plain. 23:After him repaired Benjamin and Hashub over against their house. After him repaired Azariah the son of Maaseiah, the son of Ananiah by his house. 24:After him repaired Binnui the son of Henadad another piece, from the house of Azariah to the turning of the wall, even to the corner.

25:Palal the son of Uzai, over against the turning of the wall, and the tower which lies out from the King's high house, that was by the court of the prison. After him Pedaiah the son of Parosh. 26;Moreover the Nethinims dwelt in Ophel, to the place over against the water gate toward the east, and the tower that lies out. 27:After them the Tekoites repaired another piece, over against the great tower that lies out, even to the wall of Ophel.28:From above the horse gate repaired the priests, every one over against his house. 29:After them repaired Zadok the son of Immer over against his house. After him repaired also Shemaiah the son of Shechaniah, the keeper of the east gate.

30:After him repaired Hananiah the son of Shelemiah, and Hanun the sixth son of Zalaph, another piece. After him repaired Meshullam the son of Berechiah over against his chamber. 31:After him repaired Malchiah the goldsmith's son to the place of the Nethinims, and of the merchants, over against the gate Miphkad, and to the going up of the corner. 32:And from the corner to the sheep gate repairs were done by the goldsmiths and the merchants.

+/-August 4th. (Abba/ Av 6th.)

The year +/- 151 B.C. The commanders and Leaders spoke with Holofernes about their plan

(Judith 7:8-18)8:All the commanders of the Edomites and all the leaders of the ammonites, together with the generals of the seacoast, came to Holofernes and said: 9:"Sir, listen to what we have to say, that there may be no losses among your troops. 10:These Israelites do not rely on their spears, but on the height of the mountains where they dwell;it is not easy to reach the summit of their mountain. 11:Therefore, sir, do not attack them in regular formation; this not a single one of your troops will fall. 12:Stay in your camp, and spare all soldiers. Have some of your servants keep control of the source of water that flows out of the base of the mountain.

13:For that is where the inhabitants of Bethulia get their water. Then thirst will begin to carry them off, and they will surrender their city. Meanwhile, we and our men will go up to the summits of the nearby mountains, and encamp there to guard against anyone leaving the city. 14:They and their and their wives and children will languish with hunger, and even before the sword strikes them they will be laid low in the streets of their city. 15:This you will render them dire punishment for their rebellion and their refusal to meet you peacefully." 16:Their words pleased Holofernes and all his ministers, and he ordered their proposal to be carried out.

17:Thereupon the Moabites moved camp, together with five thousand Assyrians. They encamped in the valley, and held the water supply, and the springs of the Israelites.18:The Edomites and the Ammonites went up and encamped in the mountain region opposite Dothan, and and they sent some of their men to the south and to the east opposite Egrebel, near Chusi, which is on Wadi Mochmur. The rest of the Assyrian army was encamped in the plain, covering the whole countryside. Their enormous store of tents and equipment, was spread out in profusion everywhere.

August 5th. (Abba/ Av 7th.)

Between the years +/-1958-1948 B.C. Abram went to save Lot

(Genesis 14:16-24) 16:And he brought back all the goods, and also brought again his brother Lot, and his goods, and the women also, and the people. 17:And the King of Sodom went out to meet him after his return from the slaughter of Chedorlaomer, and of the Kings that were with him, at the valley of Shaveh, which is the King's dale. 18:And Melchizedek; the King of Salem brought forth bread and wine: and he was the: Priest of the most high God. 19:And he blessed him, and said, Blessed be Abram of the most high God, possessor of heaven and earth.

20:And blessed be the most high God, which has delivered thine enemies into your hand. And he gave him tithes of all. 21:And the King of Sodom said to Abram, Give me the persons, and take the goods to thyself. 22:And Abram said to the King of Sodom, I have lift up mine hand to the Lord, the most high God, the possessor of heaven and earth. 23:That I will not take from a thread even to a shoe latch, and that I will not take any thing that is thine, lest You should say, I have made Abram rich.

24:Save only that which the young men have eaten, and the portion of the men which, went with me, Amer, Eshcol, and Mamre; let them take their portion.

August 5th. (Abba/ Av 7th.)

King Nebuchadnezzar burned the house of the Lord

(2Kings 25:8-19) 8;And in the fifth month, on the seventh day of the month, which is the nineteenth year of King Nebuchadnezzar, King of Babylon, came Nebuzaradan, captain of the guard, a servant of the King of Babylon, to Jerusalem. 9:And he burnt the house of the Lord,and the King's house, and all the houses of Jerusalem, and every great man's house burnt he with fire. 10:And all the army of the Chaldean, that were with the captain of the guard, brake down the walls of Jerusalem round about. 11:Now the rest of the people that were left in the city, and the fugitives that fell away to the King of Babylon, with the remnant of the multitude, did Nebuzaradan the captain of the guard carry away. 12:But the captain of the guard left of the poor of the land to be vine-dressers and husbandmen. 13:And the pillars of brass that were in the house of the Lord, and the bases, and the brazen sea that was in the house of the Lord, the Chaldean broke into pieces, and carried the brass of them to Babylon.

14:And the pots, and the shovels, and the snuffers, and the spoons, and all the vessels of brass wherewith they ministered, took they away. 15:And the fire pans, and the bowls, and such things as were of gold, in gold, and of silver, in silver, the captain of the guard took away. 16:The two pillars, one sea, and the bases which Solomon had made for the house of the Lord; the brass of all these vessels was without weight. 17:The height of the one pillar was eighteen cubits, and the chapter upon it was brass: and the height of the chapter three cubits; and the wreath-en work, and pomegranates upon the chaperon round about, all of brass: and like unto these had the second pillar with wreath-en work. 18:And the captain of the guard took Seraiah the chief priest, and Zephaniah the second priest, and the three keepers of the door. 19:And out of the city he took an officer that was set over the men of war, and five men of them that were in the King's presence, which were found in the city, and the principal scribe of the host, which mustered the people of the land and threescore men of the people of the land that were found in the city.

Also written in Jeremiah 52:12-14,
the day was recorded as the 10th. instead of the 7th.

August 5th. (Abba/ Av 7th.)

The year +/- 581 B.C. Baruch read the scroll to the people, at the River Sud.

(Baruch 1:1-4) 1:Now these are the words of the scroll which Baruch, son of Neriah, son of Mahseiah, son of Zedekiah, son of Hasadiah, son of Hilkiah, wrote in Babylon. 2:In the fifth year, on the seventh day of the month Av, at the time when the Chaldeans took Jerusalem and burnt it with fire. 3:Baruch read the words of this scroll for Jeconiah, son of Jehoiakim, King of Judah, to hear it as well as all the people who came to the reading. 4;The Nobles the Kings sons the Elders, and the whole people, small and great alike, all who lived in Babylon by the river Sud.

August 6th. (Abba/ Av 8th.)

The year +/- 1357 B.C. They returned from searching the land

(Numbers 13:25-14:10) 25:And they returned from searching of the land after forty days. 26:And they went and came to Moses, and to Aaron, and to all the congregation of the children of Israel, to the wilderness of Paran, to Kadesh; and brought back word to them, and to all the congregation, and shewed them the fruit of the land. 27:And they told him, and said, We came to the land whither You sent us, and surely it flows with milk and honey; and this is the fruit of it. 28:Nevertheless the people be strong that dwell in the land, and the cities are walled, and very great: and moreover we saw the children of Anakim there.

29:The Amalekites dwell in the land of the south: and the Hittites, and the Jebusites, and the Amorites, dwell in the mountains: and the Canaanites dwell by the sea, and by the coast of Jordan. 30:And Caleb stilled the people before Moses, and said, Let us go up at once, and possess it; for we are well able to overcome it. 31:But the men that went up with him said, We be not able to go up against the people; for they are stronger than we. 32:And they brought up an evil report of the land which they had searched to the children of Israel saying ; The land through which we have gone to search it, is a land that eats up your inhabitants thereof; and all the people that we saw in it are men of a great stature. 33:And there we saw the giants, the sons of Amalek, which come from the giant race: and we were in our own sight as grasshoppers, and also we were in theirs.

14:1: And all the congregation lifted up their voice, and cried; and the people wept that night. 2:And all the children of Israel murmured against Moses and against Aaron: and the whole congregation said to them, Would only that we had died in the land of Egypt! or if we had died in this wilderness! 3:And why has the Lord brought us to this land, to fall by the sword, that our wives and our children should be a prey? were it not better for us to return to Egypt?

4:And they said one to another, Let us make a captain, and let us return into Egypt. 5:Then Moses and Aaron fell on their faces before all the assembly of the congregation of the children of Israel. 6:And Joshua the son of Nun, and Caleb the son of Jephunneh, which were of them that searched the land, rent their clothes.

7:And they spoke to all the company of the children of Israel, saying, The land, which we passed through to search it, is an exceeding good land. 8:If the Lord delights in us, then he will bring us into this land, and give it us; a land which flows with milk and honey. 9:Only rebel not you against the Lord, neither fear you the people of the land; for they are bread for us: their defenses is departed from them, and the Lord is with us: fear them not. 10:But all the congregation wanted to stone them with stones. And the glory of the Lord appeared, in the tabernacle of the congregation, before all the children of Israel.

Note: Below are pictures of Giant skeletons

Similar to those found in Egypt, in 1820, also found in Israel, Turkey, China, Iran, and Africa. They range from 34' to 36' ft. tall. In other country's such as Russia, Columbia. In other parts of America, they have found Giants skeletons that ranged from 9' to 28' ft. Skeletons like these have been found from the 1820's to present day. Here below are two different digs, in two different country's. These are believed to be some of the remains of the Amalekites.

August 7th. (Abba/ Av 9th.)

The year +/- 1357 B.C. God became angry with the people

(Numbers 14:11-25) 11:And the Lord said to Moses, How long will this people provoke me? And how long will it be before they believe me, for all the signs which I have showed them? 12:I will strike them with the pestilence, and disinherit them, and will make of you a greater nation and mightier than they. 13:And Moses said to the Lord, Then the Egyptians shall hear it, (for you brought up this people in your might from among them;) 14:And they will tell it to the inhabitants of this land: for they have heard that you Lord are among this people, that you Lord, are seen face to face, and that your cloud stands over them, and that you go's before them, by day time in a pillar of a cloud, and in a pillar of fire by night.

15:Now if you shall kill all this people as one man, then the nations which have heard the fame of you will speak, saying, 16:Because the Lord was not able to bring this people to the land which he swore to them, therefore he has slain them in the wilderness. 17:And now, I beg you, let the power of my Lord be great, according as you have spoken saying. 18:The Lord is long suffering, and of great mercy, forgiving iniquity and transgression, and by no means clearing the guilty, visiting the iniquity of the fathers upon the children to the third and fourth generation. 19:Pardon, I beg you, the iniquity of this people according to the greatness of your mercy, and as you have forgiven this people, from Egypt even until now. 20:And the Lord said, I have pardoned according to your word. 21:But as truly as I live, all the earth shall be filled with the glory of the Lord.

22:Because all those men which have seen my glory, and my miracles, which I did in Egypt and in the wilderness, and have tempted me now these ten times, and have not hearkened to my voice. 23:Surely they shall not see the land which I swore to their fathers, neither shall any of them that provoked me see it: 24:But my servant Caleb, because he had another spirit with him, and has followed me fully, him will I bring into the land where in he went; and his seed shall possess it. 25:(Now the Amalekites and the Canaanites dwelt in the valley.) Tomorrow turn you, and get you into the wilderness by the way of the Red sea.

+/- August 7th. (Abba/ Av 9th.)

The year +/- 619 B.C. The 1st. Destruction of Solomon's temple

(2Kings 24:10-15) 10:At that time the servants of Nebuchadnezzar King of Babylon came up against Jerusalem, and the city was besieged. 11:And Nebuchadnezzar King of Babylon came against the city, and his servants did besiege it. 12:And Jehoiachin the King of Judah went out to the King of Babylon, he, and his mother, and his servants, and his princes, and his officers: and the King of Babylon took him in the eighth year of his reign. 13:And he carried out thence all the treasures of the house of the Lord, and the treasures of the King's house, and cut in pieces all the vessels of gold which Solomon king of Israel had made in the temple of the Lord, as the Lord had said. 14:And he carried away all Jerusalem, and all the princes, and all the mighty men of valor, even ten thousand captives, and all the craftsmen and smiths: none remained, save the poorest sort of the people of the land. 15:And he carried away Jehoiachin to Babylon, and the king's mother, and the king's wives, and his officers, and the mighty of the land, those carried he into captivity from Jerusalem to Babylon.

(Destruction of Solomon's temple: As it is written in 2Chronicles)

King Nebuchadnezzar carried the vessels to Babylon

(2Chroncles 36:6-8) 6:Against him came Nebuchadnezzar King of Babylon, and bound him in fetters, to carry him to Babylon. 7:Nebuchadnezzar also carried of the vessels of the house of the Lord to Babylon, and put them in his temple at Babylon. 8:Now the rest of the acts of Jehoiakim, and his abominations which he did, and that which was found in him, behold, they are written in the book of the Kings of Israel and Judah: and Jehoiachin his son reigned in his stead.

+/-August 7th. (Abba/Av 9th.)

(Other times of sadness on this Day in History, for the Jews.)

In: **(70 C.E.) The Lords Temple was destroyed by the Romans, (132 C.E.)**The Romans crushed Bar Kokhba's revolt and destroyed the city of Betar, killing over 100,000 Hebrews. **(133 C.E.)** Fallowing the Roman siege of Jerusalem, the Roman commander Turnus Rufus plowed the Temple site and surrounding area. **(1095 C.E.)** The first Crusade was declared by Pope Urban 11, killing 10,000 Jews in its first month and annihilating Jewish Communities in France and the Rhineland. **(1290 C.E.)** King Edward 1st., Issued an edict expelling all Jews from England. **(1492 C.E.)** An edict of expulsion of the Jews in Spain was carried out. **(1914 C.E.)** World War 1, broke out, setting the stage for the later devastation of, World War 2, and the Holocaust. **(1942 C.E.)** On the eve of the 7th.of August, (which is the 9th.of Abba) the mass deportation of Jews from the Warsaw Ghetto to Hitler's Treblinka death camp began. **(1994 C.E.)** The bombing of the Jewish community in Buenos aires killed 86 and wounded 300 others. **(2005 C.E.)** More that 8,500 Jewish resident were expelled from Gaza as part of Israel's ill-fated disengagement plan. A desecrate bid for peace, designed to further relations with Palestinian Arabs.

+/-August 8th. (Abba/ Av 10th.)

The year +/- 1357 B.C. God told them for 40 years will you wonder

(Numbers 14:26-45) 26:And the Lord spoke to Moses and to Aaron, saying; 27:How long shall I bear with this evil congregation, which murmur against me? I have heard the murmurings of the children of Israel, which they murmur against me. 28:Say to them, As truly as I live, says the Lord, as you have spoken in mine ears, so will I do to you: 29:Your carcases shall fall in this wilderness; and all that were numbered of you, according to your whole number, from twenty years old and upward, which have murmured against me. 30:Doubtless you shall not come into the land, concerning which I swore to make you dwell therein, except Caleb the son of Jephunneh, and Joshua the son of Nun. 31:But your little ones, which you said should be a prey, them will I bring in, and they shall know the land which you have despised.

32:But as for you, your carcases, they shall fall in this wilderness. 33:And your children shall wander in the wilderness forty years, and bear your whoredoms, until your carcases be wasted in the wilderness. 34:After the number of the days in which you searched the land, even forty days, each day for a year, shall you bear your iniquities, even forty years, and you shall know my breach of promise. 35:I the Lord have said, I will surely do it to all this evil congregation, that are gathered together against me: in this wilderness they shall be consumed, and there they shall die. 36:And the men, which Moses sent to search the land, who returned, and made all the congregation to murmur against him, by bringing up a slander upon the land. 37:Even those men that did bring up the evil report upon the land, died by the plague before the Lord. 38:But Joshua the son of Nun, and Caleb the son of Jephunneh, which were of the men that went to search the land, lived still. 39:And Moses told these sayings to all the children of Israel: and the people mourned greatly.40:And they rose up early in the morning, and went up to the top of the mountain, saying, Look, we are here and will go up to the place which the Lord has promised: for we have sinned. 41:And Moses said, Why now do you transgress the commandment of the Lord? 42:Do not go up, for the Lord is not with you, or you will be killed before your enemies. 43;For the Amalekites and the Canaanites are there before you, and you shall fall by the sword: because you have turned away from the Lord, therefore the Lord will not be with you. 44:But they presumed to go up to the hill top: nevertheless the ark of the covenant of the Lord, and Moses, departed not out of the camp. 45Then the Amalekites came down, and the Canaanites which dwelt in that hill, and struck them, and discomfited them, even to Hormah.

+/- August 8th. (Abba/Av 10th.)

The year +/- 581 B.C. He burned the Lords house

(Jeremiah 52:12-14) 12:Now in the fifth month, on the tenth day of the month, which was the nineteenth year of Nebuchadrezzar King of Babylon, came Nebuzaradan captain of the guard, which served the King of Babylon, unto Jerusalem. 13:And burned the house of the Lord, and the King's house; and all the houses of Jerusalem, and all the houses of the great men, he burned with fire: 14;And all the army of the Chaldeans, that were with the captain of the guard, broke down all the walls of Jerusalem around it.

+/- August 8th. (Abba/Av 10th.)

The year +/- 584 B.C. God spoke to Ezekiel about his people

(Ezekiel 20:1-49)1:And it came to pass in the seventh year, in the fifth month the tenth day of the month, that certain of the elders of Israel came to inquire of the Lord, and sat before me. 2:Then came the word of the Lord to me, saying; 3:Son of man, speak to the elders of Israel, and say to them, This says the Lord God; Have you come to inquire of me? As I live, says the Lord God, I will not be inquired of by you. 4:Will you judge them, son of man, how will you judge them? Cause them to know the abominations of their fathers: 5:And say to them, This says the Lord God; In the day when I chose Israel, and lifted up mine hand to the seed of the house of Jacob, and made myself known to them in the land of Egypt, when I lifted up mine hand to them, saying, I am the Lord your God. 6:In the day that I lifted up, mine hand to them, to bring them forth of the land of Egypt into a land that I had espied for them, flowing with milk and honey, which is the glory of all lands. 7:Then said I to them, Cast you away every man the abominations of his eyes, and defile not yourselves with the idols of Egypt: I am the Lord your God. 8:But they rebelled against me, and would not hearken to me: they did not every man cast away the abominations of their eyes, neither did they forsake the idols of Egypt: then I said, I will pour out my fury upon them, to accomplish my anger against them in the midst of the land of Egypt. 9:But I wrought for my name's sake, that it should not be polluted before the heathen, among whom they were, in whose sight I made myself known to them, in bringing them forth out of the land of Egypt. 10:Wherefore I caused them to go forth out of the land of Egypt, and brought them into the wilderness. 11:And I gave them my statutes, and shewed them my judgments, which if a man do, he shall even live in them. 12:Moreover also I gave them my sabbaths, to be a sign between me and them, that they might know that I am the Lord that sanctify them. 13:But the house of Israel rebelled against me in the wilderness: they walked not in my statutes, and they despised my judgments, which if a man do, he shall even live in them; and my sabbaths they greatly polluted: then I said, I would pour out my fury upon them in the wilderness, to consume them. 14:But I wrought for my name's sake, that it should not be polluted before the heathen, in whose sight I brought them out.

15:Yet also I lifted up my hand to them in the wilderness, that I would not bring them into the land which I had given them flowing with milk and honey, which is the glory of all lands. 16:Because they despised my judgments, and walked not in my statutes, but polluted my sabbaths: for their heart went after their idols. 17:Nevertheless mine eye spared them from destroying them, neither did I make an end of them in the wilderness. 18:But I said to their children in the wilderness, Walk you not in the statutes of your fathers, neither observe their judgments, nor defile yourselves with their idols. 19:I am the Lord your God; walk in my statutes, and keep my judgments, and do them. 20:And hallow my sabbaths; and they shall be a sign between me and you, that you may know that I am the Lord your God. 21:Not with standing the children rebelled against me: they walked not in my statutes, neither kept my judgments to do them, which if a man do, he shall even live in them; they polluted my sabbaths: then I said, I would pour out my fury upon them, to accomplish my anger against them in the wilderness. 22:Nevertheless I withdrew mine hand, and wrought for my name's sake, that it should not be polluted in the sight of the heathen, in whose sight I brought them forth. 23:I lifted up mine hand to them also in the wilderness, that I would scatter them among the heathen, and disperse them through the countries. 24:Because they had not executed my judgments, but had despised my statutes, and had polluted my sabbaths, and their eyes were after their fathers' idols. 25:Wherefore I gave them also statutes that were not good, and judgments whereby they should not live. 26:And I polluted them in their own gifts, in that they caused to pass through the fire all that opened the womb, that I might make them desolate, to the end that they might know that I am the Lord. 27:Therefore, son of man, speak to the house of Israel, and say to them, This says the Lord God; Yet in this your fathers have blasphemed me, in that they have committed a trespass against me.

28:For when I had brought them into the land, for the which I lifted up mine hand
to give it to them, then they saw every high hill, and all the thick trees, and they
offered there their sacrifices, and there they presented the provocation of their
offering: there also they made their sweet savor, and poured out there their drink
offerings. 29:Then I said to them, What is the high place where you are going? And
the name thereof is called Bamah to this day. 30:Wherefore say to the house of
Israel: This says the Lord God; Are you polluted after the manner of your fathers?
and commit you whoredom after their abominations? 31:For when you offer your
gifts, when you make your sons to pass through the fire, you pollute yourselves with
all your idols, even to this day: and shall I be inquired of by you, O house of Israel?
As I live, says the Lord God, I will not be inquired of by you. 32:And that which
comes into your mind shall not be at all, that you say, We will be as the heathen, as
the families of the countries, to serve wood and stone. 33:As I live, says the Lord
God, surely with a mighty hand, and with a stretched out arm, and with fury poured
out, will I rule over you. 34:And I will bring you out from the people, and will
gather you out of the countries wherein you are scattered, with a mighty hand, and
with a stretched out arm, and with fury poured out. 35:And I will bring you into the
wilderness of the people, and there will I plead with you face to face.

36:Like as I pleaded with your fathers in the wilderness of the land of Egypt, so will
I plead with you, says the Lord God. 37:And I will cause you to pass under the rod,
and I will bring you into the bond of the covenant. 38:And I will purge out from
among you the rebels, and them that transgress against me: I will bring them forth
out of the country where they sojourn, and they shall not enter into the land of
Israel: and you shall know that I am the Lord. 39:As for you, O house of Israel, this
says the Lord God; Go you, serve you every one his idols, and hereafter also, if you
will not hearken to me: but pollute you my holy name no more with your gifts, and
with your idols. 40:For in my Holy mountain, in the mountain of the height of
Israel, says the Lord God, there shall all the house of Israel, all of them in the land,
serve me: there will I accept them, and there will I require your offerings, and the
first fruits of your oblations, with all your holy things. 41: I will accept you with
your sweet savor, when I bring you out from the people, and gather you out of the
countries,where in you have been scattered; and I will be sanctified in you before
the heathen. 42:And you shall know that I am the Lord, when I shall bring you into
the land of Israel, into the country for the which I lifted up mine hand to give it to
your fathers. 43:And there shall you remember your ways, and all your doings,
wherein you have been defiled; and you shall loathe yourselves in your own sight
for all your evils that you have committed. 44:And you shall know that I am the
Lord, when I have wrought with you for my name's sake, not according to your
wicked ways, nor according to your corrupt doings, O you house of Israel, says the
Lord God. 45:Moreover the word of the Lord came to me, saying; 46:Son of man,
set your face toward the south, and drop your words toward the south, and prophesy
against the forest of the south field. 47:And say to the forest of the south, Hear the
word of the Lord; This says the Lord God; Behold, I will kindle a fire in you, and it
shall devour every green tree in you, and every dry tree: the flaming flame shall not
be quenched, and all faces from the south to the north shall be burned therein.
48:And all flesh shall see that I the Lord have kindled it: it shall not be quenched.
49:Then said I, Ah Lord God! they say of me, Doth he not speak parables?

+/- August 9th. (Abba/Av 11th.)

The year +/- 151 B.C. The Israelites cried to their God

(Judith7:19)19:The Israelites cried to the Lord, their God for they were disheartened, since all their enemies had them surrounded, and there was no way of slipping through their lines.

+/- August 12th. (Abba/Av 14th.)

(Recorded in the Aramaic writings)The Death of the Virgin Mary

Mary, the wife of Joseph, who was the Mother of Jesus of Nazareth, the one called the Messiah. Died on the fourteenth day of the fifth month and was placed in her husband's tomb, at the foot of the Mount of Olives.

The entrance of Mary's tomb, and here are the steps going down to where Mary's Tomb is located. Below is Mary's tomb.

+/- August 12th. (Abba/Av 14th.)

The year +/- 70 C.E. Day of Great Understanding for the Christians

(John 2:19) Jesus spoke saying: Destroy this temple and in three days I will rebuild it. After three days of mourning and sadness. The followers of Jesus remembered his words and understood the New Temple of the Lord was in the hearts of men, not in a building of stone.

More on the tomb of the Blessed Virgin

Please note: When you are facing Mary's tomb to her left is her husband Joesph, and behind her are both of her parents, her Father: (Joaquin, also know as; Heli), and her Mother: (Anne) found in the Gospel of James.

+/- August 15st. (Abba/ Av 17th.)

(According to the Roman Catholic Church, written in the Vatican Archives; Mary received into Heaven

The book of: The Holy Virgin; On the seventeenth day, which is the third day after her death, Mary, the Holy Mother of God, was received into heaven.

+/- August 23rd. (Abba/Av 25th.)

The Year +/- 3995 B.C. The Death of Adam and Eve:

(Genesis 5:1-5)1:This is the book of the generations of Adam. In the day that God
created man, in the likeness of God. 2:Both male and female he created them; and
blessed them, and called their names; Adam in the day when they were created.
3:And Adam lived an hundred and thirty years, then begot another son in his own
likeness, after his image, through his mate Eve and called his name Seth. 4:And the
days of Adam after he had begotten Seth, were eight hundred and twenty years, and
he begot sons and daughters. 5:And all the days that Adam lived were a full nine
hundred and fifty years, then Adam and Eve his second wife, whom God created out
of man, died together and were buried in a cave at Hebron, the very ground that,
Adam was taken from.

Shown here above is Hebron, it means: (Friend). It is the grave site to Adam and Eve, Abraham and Sarah, Isaac, Rebecca, Jacob, Leah along with others.

Above on the left are the stairs going down to the entrance of the cave where Adam and Eve are. On the right is one of the more know entrances to the Caves.

(Also during this month)

(August / Abba)

After a vision in the sky, that lasted almost 40 days,

(2Maccabees 5:1-4) 1:About this time Antiochus sent his second expedition into Egypt. 2:It then happened that all over the city, for nearly forty days, there appeared horsemen charging in midair, clad in garments interwoven with gold-companies fully armed with lances 3:and drawn swords, squadrons of cavalry in battle array. Charging and counter charging on this side and that, with brandished shields and bristling spears, flights of arrows and flashes of gold ornaments, together with armor of every sort. 4:Therefore all prayed that this vision might be a good one.

God spoke to Jeremiah

(Jeremiah 1:1-19) 1:The words of Jeremiah the son of Hilkiah, of the priests that were in Anathoth in the land of Benjamin. 2:To whom the word of the Lord came in the days of Josiah the son of Amon King of Judah, in the thirteenth year of his reign. 3:It came also in the days of Jehoiakim the son of Josiah King of Judah, to the end of the eleventh year of Zedekiah the son of Josiah King of Judah, to the carrying away of Jerusalem captive in the fifth month.4:Then the word of the Lord came to me, saying; 5:Before I formed you in the belly I knew you; and before you came forth out of the womb I sanctified you, and I ordained you a prophet to the nations. 6:Then I said; Ah, Lord God! behold, I cannot speak: for I am a child. 7:But the Lord said to me, Say not, I am a child: for you shall go to all that I shall send you, and whatsoever I command you, you shall speak.

8:Be not afraid of their faces: for I am with you to deliver you, says the Lord.
9:Then the Lord put forth his hand, and touched my mouth. And the Lord said to
me, Behold, I have put my words in your mouth. 10:See, I have this day set you
over the nations and over the kingdoms, to root out, and to pull down, and to
destroy, and to throw down, to build, and to plant. 11:Moreover the word of the
Lord came to me, saying, Jeremiah, what do you see? And I said, I see a rod of an
almond tree. 12:Then said the Lord to me, You hast well seen: for I will hasten my
word to perform it. 13:And the word of the Lord came to me the second time,
saying, What do you see? And I said, I see a seething pot; and the face thereof is
toward the north. 14:Then the Lord said to me, Out of the north an evil shall break
forth upon all the inhabitants of the land. 15:For, look, I will call all the families of
the kingdoms of the north, says the Lord; and they shall come, and they shall set
every one his throne at the entering of the gates of Jerusalem, and against all the
walls thereof round about, and against all the cities of Judah. 16:And I will utter my
judgments against them touching all their wickedness, who have forsaken me, and
have burned incense to other gods, and worshiped the works of their own hands.
17:You therefore gird up your loins, and arise, and speak to them all that I command
you: be not dismayed at their faces, lest confound you before them.18:For, behold, I
have made you this day a defended city, and an iron pillar, and brazen walls against
the whole land, against the kings of Judah, against the princes thereof, against the
priests thereof, and against the people of the land. 19:And they shall fight against
you; but they shall not prevail against you; for I am with you, says the Lord, to
deliver you.

Hananiah son of Azur the prophet gave a false prophesy

(Jeremiah 28:1-29:18) 1:And it came to pass the same year, in the beginning of the
reign of Zedekiah King of Judah, in the fourth year, and in the fifth month, that
Hananiah the son of Azur the prophet, which was of Gibeon, spoke to me in the
house of the Lord, in the presence of the priests and of all the people, saying, 2:This
says the Lord of hosts, the God of Israel, saying, I have broken the yoke of the King
of Babylon. 3:Within two full years will I bring again into this place,all the vessels
of the Lord's house, that Nebuchadnezzar King of Babylon, took away from this
place, and carried them to Babylon. 4:And I will bring again to this place Jeconiah
the son of Jehoiakim King of Judah, with all the captives of Judah, that went into
Babylon, says the Lord: for I will break the yoke of the King of Babylon. 5:Then the
prophet Jeremiah said, to the prophet Hananiah in the presence of the priests, and in
the presence of all the people that stood in the house of the Lord.

6;Even the prophet Jeremiah said, Amen: the Lord do so: the Lord perform your
words which you hast prophesied, to bring again the vessels of the Lord's house,
and all that is carried away captive, from Babylon into this place. 7:Nevertheless
hear you now this word that I speak in thine ears, and in the ears of all the people.
8:The prophets that have been before me and before you of old prophesied both
against many countries, and against great kingdoms, of war, and of evil, and of
pestilence. 9:The prophet which prophesies of peace, when the word of the prophet
shall come to pass, then shall the prophet be known, that the Lord has truly sent
him.10:Then Hananiah the prophet took the yoke from off the prophet Jeremiah's
neck, and broke it.

11:And Hananiah spoke in the presence of all the people, saying, this says the Lord;
Even so will I break the yoke of Nebuchadnezzar King of Babylon from the neck of
all nations within the space of two full years. And the prophet Jeremiah went his
way. 12:Then the word of the Lord came to Jeremiah the prophet, after that
Hananiah the prophet had broken the yoke from off the neck of the prophet
Jeremiah, saying, 13:Go and tell Hananiah, saying, this says the Lord; You have
broken the yokes of wood; but you shall make for them yokes of iron.

14:For this says the Lord of hosts, the God of Israel; I have put a yoke of iron upon
the neck of all these nations, that they may serve Nebuchadnezzar King of Babylon;
and they shall serve him: and I have given him the beasts of the field also. 15:Then
said the prophet Jeremiah to Hananiah the prophet, Hear now, Hananiah; The Lord
has not sent you; but you make these people to trust in a lie. 16:Therefore this says
the Lord; Behold, I will cast you from off the face of the earth, this year you shall
die, because you have taught rebellion against the Lord. (17;So Hananiah the
prophet died the same year in the seventh month.)

29:1;Now these are the words of the letter that Jeremiah the prophet sent from
Jerusalem to the residue of the elders which were carried away captives, and to the
priests, and to the prophets, and to all the people whom Nebuchadnezzar had carried
away captive from Jerusalem to Babylon. 2:(After that Jeconiah the King, and the
Queen, and the eunuchs, the princes of Judah and Jerusalem, and the carpenters, and
the smiths, were departed from Jerusalem;) 3:By the hand of Elasah the son of
Shaphan, and Gemariah the son of Hilkiah, (whom Zedekiah King of Judah sent to
Babylon to Nebuchadnezzar King of Babylon) saying. 4:This says the Lord of
hosts, the God of Israel, to all that are carried away captives, whom I have caused to
be carried away from Jerusalem to Babylon.

5:Build you houses, and dwell in them and plant gardens, and eat the fruit of them.
6:Take you wives, and have sons and daughters; and take wives for your sons, and
give your daughters to husbands, that they may bear sons and daughters; that you
may be increased there, and not diminished. 7:And seek the peace of the city
whither I have caused you to be carried away captives, and pray to the Lord for it:
for in the peace thereof shall you have peace. 8:For this says the Lord of hosts, the
God of Israel; Let not your prophets and your diviners, that be in the midst of you,
deceive you, neither hearken to your dreams which you cause to be dreamed.

9:For they prophesy falsely to you in my name: I have not sent them, says the Lord.
10:For this says the Lord, That after seventy years be accomplished at Babylon I
will visit you, and perform my good word toward you, in causing you to return to
this place. 11:For I know the thoughts that I think toward you, says the Lord,
thoughts of peace, and not of evil, to give you an expected end. 12:Then shall you
call upon me, and you shall go and pray to me, and I will hearken to you. 13:And
you shall seek me, and find me, when you shall search for me with all your heart.

14:And I will be found of you, says the Lord: and I will turn away your captivity,
and I will gather you from all the nations, and from all the places whither I have
driven you, says the Lord; and I will bring you again into the place where,

I caused you to be carried away captive. 15:Because you have said, The Lord has raised us up prophets in Babylon; 16:Know that this says the Lord of the King that sitteth upon the throne of David, and of all the people that dwell in this city, with you into captivity. 17:This says the Lord of hosts; Behold, I will send upon them the sword, the famine, and the pestilence, and will make them like vile figs, that cannot be eaten, they are so evil. 18:And I will persecute them with the sword, with the famine, and with the pestilence, and will deliver them to be removed to all the kingdoms of the earth, to be a curse, and an astonishment, and an hissing, and a reproach among all the nations where I have driven them:

+/- August 29th. (Elul 1st.)

Haggai the prophet spoke to the people about the Lords house

(Haggai 1:1-14) 1:In the second year of Darius the King, in the sixth month, on the first day of the month, came the word of the Lord by Haggai, the prophet to Zerubbabel the son of Shealtiel, governor of Judah, and to Joshua the son of Josedech, the high priest, saying; 2:This says the Lord of Hosts, saying: These people say, The time has not come, that we should build the Lords house. 3:Then came the word of the Lord by Haggai the prophet, saying, 4:Is it time for you, O you, who dwell in your circled houses, and this house lies in waste? 5:Now therefore this says the Lord of Hosts; Consider your ways. 6:You have sowed much, and bring in little; you eat, but you have not enough; you drink, but you are not filled with drink; you clothe your self's, but there is none warm; and he that earns wages earns wages to put it into a bag with holes. 7:This says the Lord of Hosts; Consider your ways. 8:Go up to the mountain, and bring wood, and build the house; and I will take pleasure in it, and I will be glorified, says the Lord.

9:You looked for much, and, see, it came to little; and when you brought it home, I did blow upon it. Why? said the Lord of Hosts. Because of mine house, that is in waste, and you run every man to his own house. 10:Therefore the heaven over you is stayed from dew, and the earth is stayed from her fruit. 11:And I called for a drought upon the land, and upon the mountains, and upon the corn, and upon the new wine, and upon the oil, and upon that which the ground brings forth, and upon men, and upon cattle, and upon all the labor of the hands. 12:Then Zerubbabel the son of Shealtiel, and Joshua the son of Josedech, the high priest, with all the remnant of the people, obeyed the voice of the Lord their God, and the words of Haggai the prophet, as the Lord their God had sent him, and the people did fear before the Lord. 3:Then spoke Haggai the Lord's messenger, here is the Lord's message to his people, I am with you, says the Lord. 14:And the Lord stirred up the spirit of Zerubbabel the son of Shealtiel, governor of Judah, and the spirit of Joshua the son of Josedech, the high priest, and the spirit of all the remnant of the people; and they came and did work, in the house of the Lord of Hosts, their God,

Please Note: During the month Av / Abba +/- 135C.E. Rome changed the name of Israel to Palestine and outlawed circumcision for the Hebrews

Food for Thought

1: In Genesis 5:1; God made Man (Adam) in his form and likeness, God did make him. He was perfect in his form and being.
2: 1Chorinthians 15:45; The first man, Adam became a living being, and brought a The Last Adam who is the Christ, is a life giving Spirit.
3:John 12:45 When you look at me, you are seeing the one who sent me.

Below the shroud of Jesus, and below that is the face that is on it

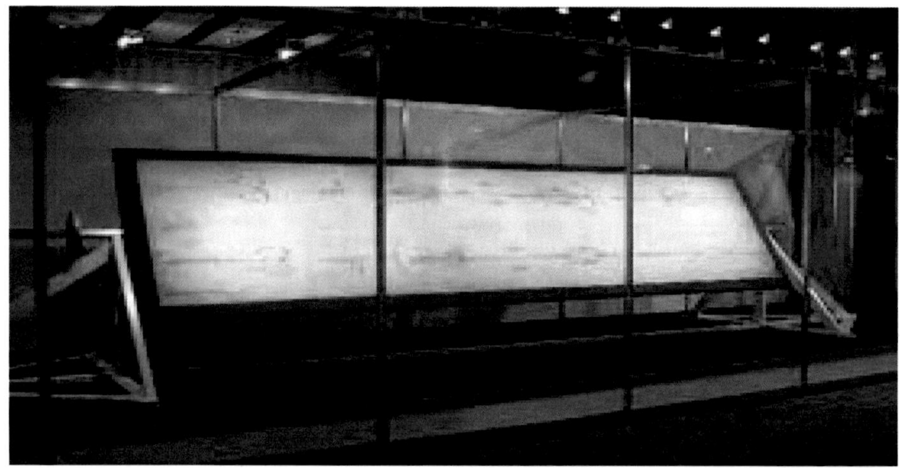

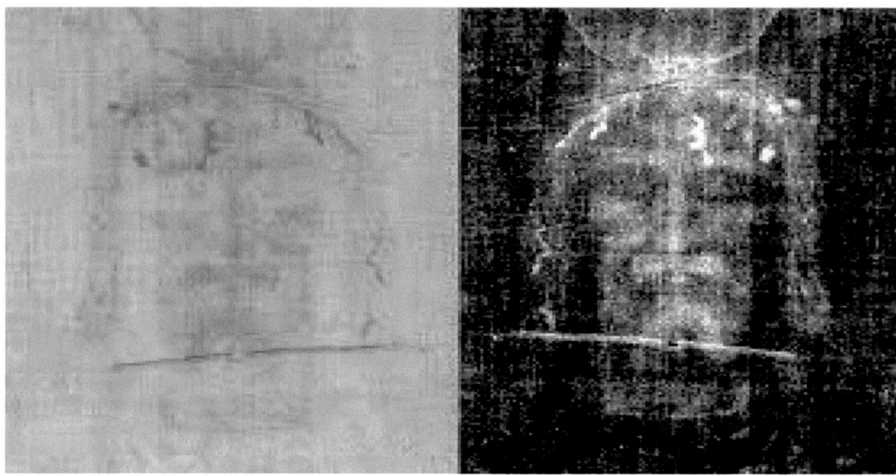

The oldest kept records of the shroud of Turin was from 1353-1357 when it was in the possession of a french knight by the name of Geoffroi de Charny who died in 1356. Pope John Paul II showed himself to be deeply moved by the image of the Shroud and arranged for public showings in 1998 and 2000. In his address at the Turin Cathedral on Sunday May 24, 1998. It is kept on display in the Chapel of the Cathedral of Saint John the Baptist in, Turin, Italy scene 1983.

Question:Could this be the face of our Lord Jesus of Natherith?
Would this actually be what Adam looked like?
Might this be the image or likeness of the (One True God)?

Chapter 9: September - Elul

It is the 6th. month on the Hebrew calendar
In Hebrew this month is called:Elul, which means:Repentance
Tribe of Judah, means:(We will give grateful praise)
The stone of (Sardonyn) represents this tribe.
Judah: (The 4th.) Son of Leah,
(Was believed to have been born in this month.)
(Spirit of Peace)

+/- September 1st. (Elul 4th.)

The year +/- 1357 B.C. Moses was given instructions from God

(Exodus 25:1-32:5)1:And the Lord spoke to Moses, saying; 2:Speak to the children of Israel, that they may bring me an offering: of every man that gives it willingly with his heart, you shall take my offering. 3:And this is the offering which you shall take of them; gold, and silver, and brass. 4:And blue, and purple, and scarlet, and fine linen, and goats hair. 5:And rams' skins dyed red, and badgers' skins, acacia wood. 6:Oil for the light, spices for anointing oil, and for sweet incense. 7:Onyx stones, and stones to be set in the ephod, and in the breastplate. 8:And let them make me a sanctuary; that I may dwell among them. 9:According to all that I show you, after the pattern of the tabernacle, and the pattern of all the instruments thereof, even so shall you make it. 10:And they shall make an ark of acacia wood: two cubits and a half shall be the length thereof, and a cubit and a half the breadth thereof, and a cubit and a half the height thereof. 11:And you shall overlay it with pure gold, within and without shall you overlay it, and shall make upon it a crown of gold round about. 12:And you shall cast four rings of gold for it, and put them in the four corners thereof; and two rings shall be in the one side of it, and two rings in the other side of it. 13:And you shall make poles of acacia wood, and overlay them with gold. 14:And you shall put the poles into the rings by the sides of the ark, that the ark may be borne with them. 15:The poles shall be in the rings of the ark: they shall not be taken from it. 16:And you shall put into the ark the testimony which I shall give you. 17:And you shall make a mercy seat of pure gold: two cubits and a half shall be the length thereof, and a cubit and a half the breadth thereof. 18:And you shall make two cherubims of gold, of beaten work shall you make them, in the two ends of the mercy seat. 19:And make one cherub on the one end, and the other cherub on the other end: even of the mercy seat shall you make the cherubims on the two ends thereof. 20:And the cherubims shall stretch forth their wings on high, covering the mercy seat with their wings, and their faces shall look one to another; toward the mercy seat shall the faces of the cherubims be. 21:And you shall put the mercy seat above upon the ark; and in the ark you shall put the testimony that I shall give you. 22:And there I will meet with you, and I will commune with you from above the mercy seat, from between the two cherubims which are upon the ark of the testimony, of all things which I will give you in commandment to the children of Israel. 23:You shall also make a table of acacia wood: two cubits shall be the length thereof, and a cubit the breadth thereof, and a cubit and a half the height thereof. 24:And you shall overlay it with pure gold, and make a crown of gold round about. 25:And you shall make to it a border of an hand breadth round about, and you shall make a golden crown to the border, thereof round about. 26:And you shall make for it four rings of gold, and put the rings in the four corners that are on the four feet thereof. 27:Over against the border shall the rings be for places of the poles to bear the table. 28:And you shall make the poles of acacia wood, and overlay them with gold, that the table may be borne with them. 29:And you shall make the dishes thereof, and spoons thereof, and covers thereof, and bowls thereof, to cover withal: of pure gold shall you make them. 30:And you shall set upon the table show bread before me always. 31:And you shall make a candlestick of pure gold: of beaten work shall the candlestick be made: his shaft, and his branches, his bowls, his knobs, and his flowers, shall be of the same. 32:And six branches shall come out of the sides of it; three branches of the candlestick out of the one side, and three branches of the candlestick out of the other side. 33:Three bowls made like to almonds, with a knob and a flower in one branch;and three bowls made like almonds in the other branch, with a knob and a flower: so in the six branches that come out of the candlestick. 34:And in the candlestick shall be four bowls made like to almonds, with their knobs and their flowers. 35:And there shall be a knob under two branches of the same, and a knob under two branches of the same, and a knob under two branches of the same, according to the six branches that proceed out of the candlestick. 36:Their knobs and their branches shall be of the same: all it shall be one beaten work of pure gold. 37:And you shall make the seven lamps thereof: and they shall light the lamps thereof, that they may give light over against it. 38:These as well as the trimming shears and trays, must be of pure gold. 39:Of a talent of pure gold shall he make it, with all these vessels. 40:And look that you make them after their pattern, which was showed you in the mount.

26:1: Moreover you shall make the tabernacle with ten curtains of fine twined linen, and blue, and purple, and scarlet: with cherubims of cunning work shall you make them. 2:The length of one curtain shall be eight and twenty cubits, and the breadth of one curtain four cubits: and every one of the curtains shall have one measure. 3:The five curtains shall be coupled together one to another; and other five curtains shall be coupled one to another. 4:And you shall make loops of blue upon the edge of the one curtain from the selvedge in the coupling; and likewise shall you make in the uttermost edge of another curtain, in the coupling of the second. 5:Fifty loops shall you make in the one curtain, and fifty loops shall you make in the edge of the curtain that is in the coupling of the second;

that the loops may take hold one of another. 6:And you shall make fifty clasps of gold, with which to join the two sets of sheets, so that the curtains come together and it shall be one tabernacle. 7:And you shall make curtains of goats hair to be a covering upon the tabernacle: eleven curtains shall you make. 8:The length of one curtain shall be thirty cubits, and the breadth of one curtain four cubits: and the eleven curtains shall be all of one measure. 9:And you shall couple five curtains by themselves, and six curtains by themselves, and shall double the sixth curtain in the forefront of the tabernacle. 10:And you shall make fifty loops on the edge of the one curtain that is out most in the coupling, and fifty loops in the edge of the curtain which couples the second. 11:And you shall make fifty latches of brass, and put the latches into the loops, and couple the tent together, that it may be one. 12:And the remnant that remains of the curtains of the tent, the half curtain that remains, shall hang over the backside of the tabernacle. 13:And a cubit on the one side, and a cubit on the other side of that which remains in the length of the curtains of the tent, it shall hang over the sides of the tabernacle on this side and on that side, to cover it. 14:And you shall make a covering for the tent of rams skins dyed red, and a covering above of badgers' skins. 15:And you shall make boards for the tabernacle of acacia wood standing up. 16:Ten cubits shall be the length of a board, and a cubit and a half shall be the breadth of one board. 17:Two tenons shall there be in one board, set in order one against another: This shall you make for all the boards of the tabernacle. 18:And you shall make the boards for the tabernacle, twenty boards on the south side southward. 19:And you shall make forty sockets of silver under the twenty boards; two sockets under one board for his two tenons, and two sockets under another board for his two tenons.

20:And for the second side of the tabernacle on the north side there shall be twenty boards. 21:And their forty sockets of silver; two sockets under one board, and two sockets under another board. 22:And for the sides of the tabernacle westward you shall make six boards. 23:And two boards shall you make for the corners of the tabernacle in the two sides. 24:And they shall be coupled together beneath, and they shall be coupled together above the head of it to one ring: This shall it be for them both; they shall be for the two corners. 25:And they shall be eight boards, and their sockets of silver, sixteen sockets; two sockets under one board, and two sockets under another board. 26:And you shall make bars of acacia wood; five for the boards of the one side of the tabernacle. 27:And five bars for the boards of the other side of the tabernacle, and five bars for the boards of the side of the tabernacle, for the two sides westward. 28:And the middle bar in the midst of the boards shall reach from end to end. 29:And you shall overlay the boards with gold, and make their rings of gold for places for the bars: and you shall overlay the bars with gold. 30:And you shall rear up the tabernacle according to the fashion thereof which was shewed you in the mount. 31:And you shall make a veil of blue, and purple, and scarlet, and fine twined linen of cunning work: with cherubims shall it be made. 32:And you shall hang it upon four pillars of acacia wood overlaid with gold: their hooks shall be of gold, upon the four sockets of silver. 33:And you shall hang up the veil under the clasps, that you may bring in closer within the veil the ark of the testimony: and the veil shall divide to you between the holy place and the most holy. 34:And you shall put the mercy seat upon the ark of the testimony in the most holy place. 35:And you shall set the table without the veil, and the candlestick over against the table on the side of the tabernacle toward the south: and you shall put the table on the north side. 36:And you shall make an hanging for the door of the tent, of blue, purple, and scarlet, and fine twined linen, wrought with needlework. 37:And you shall make for the hanging five pillars of acacia wood, and overlay them with gold, and their hooks, shall be of gold: and you shall cast five sockets of brass for them.

27:1: And you shall make an altar of acacia wood, five cubits long, and five cubits broad; the altar shall be foursquare: and the height thereof shall be three cubits. 2:And you shall make the horns of it upon the four corners thereof: his horns shall be of the same: and you shall overlay it with brass. 3:And you shall make his pans to receive his ashes, and his shovels, and his basins, and his flesh hooks, and his fire pans: all the vessels thereof you shall make of brass. 4:And you shall make for it a grate of network of brass; and upon the net shall you make four brass rings in the four corners thereof. 5:And you shall put it under the compass of the altar beneath, that the net may be even to the midst of the altar. 6:And you shall make poles for the altar, poles of acacia wood, and overlay them with brass. 7;And the poles shall be put into the rings, and the poles shall be upon the two sides of the altar, to bear it. 8:Hollow with boards shall you make it: as it was shewed you in the mount, so shall they make it. 9:And you shall make the court of the tabernacle: for the south side southward there shall be hangings for the court of fine twined linen of an hundred cubits long for one side. 10:And the twenty pillars thereof and their twenty sockets shall be of brass; the hooks of the pillars and their fillets shall be of silver. 11:And likewise for the north side in length there shall be hangings of an hundred cubits long, and his twenty pillars and their twenty sockets of brass; the hooks of the pillars and their fillets of silver. 12:And for the breadth of the court on the west side shall be hangings of fifty cubits: their pillars ten, and their sockets ten. 13:And the breadth of the court on the east side eastward shall be fifty cubits. 14:The hangings of one side of the gate shall be fifteen cubits: their pillars three, and their sockets three. 15:And on the other side shall be hangings fifteen cubits, their pillars three, and their sockets three. 16:And for the gate of the court shall be an hanging of twenty cubits, of blue, and purple, and scarlet, and fine twined linen, wrought with needlework: and their pillars shall be four, and their sockets four. 17:All the pillars round about the court shall be filleted with silver; their hooks shall be of silver, and their sockets of brass. 18:The length of the court shall be an hundred cubits, and the breadth fifty every where, and the height five cubits of fine twined linen, and their sockets of brass. 19:All the vessels of the tabernacle in all the service thereof, and all the pins thereof, and all the pins of the court, shall be of brass. 20:And you shall command the children of Israel, that they bring you pure oil olive beaten for the light, to cause the lamp to burn always. 21:In the tabernacle of the congregation without the veil, which is before the testimony, Aaron and his sons shall order it from evening to morning before the Lord, it shall be a statute for ever to their generations on the behalf of the children of Israel.

28:1: And take you to you Aaron your brother, and his sons with him, from among the children of Israel, that he may minister to me in the priest's office, even Aaron, Nadab and Abihu, Eleazar and Ithamar, Aaron's sons. 2:And you shall make holy garments for Aaron your brother for glory and for beauty.

3:And you shall speak to all that are wise heart-ed, whom I have filled with the
spirit of wisdom, that they may make Aaron's garments to consecrate him, that he
may minister to me in the priest's office. 4:And these are the garments which they
shall make; a breastplate, and an ephod, and a robe, and a embroidered coat, a miter,
and a girdle: and they shall make holy garments for Aaron your brother, and his
sons, that he may minister to me in the priest's office. 5:And they shall take gold,
and blue, and purple, and scarlet, and fine linen. 6:And they shall make the ephod of
gold, of blue, and of purple, of scarlet, and fine twined linen, with cunning work.
7:It shall have the two shoulder pieces there of joined at the two edges thereof; and
so it shall be joined together. 8:And the curious girdle of the ephod, which is upon
it, shall be of the same, according to the work thereof; even of gold, of blue, and
purple, and scarlet, and fine twined linen. 9:And you shall take two onyx stones, and
grave on them the names of the children of Israel. 10:Six of their names on one
stone, and the other six names of the rest, on the other stone, according to their
birth. 11:With the work of an engraver in stone, like the engravings of a signet,shall
you engrave the two stones with the names of the children of Israel: you shall make
them to be set in pouches of gold. 12:And you shall put the two stones upon the
shoulders of the ephod for stones of memorial to the children of Israel: and Aaron
shall bear their names before the Lord upon his two shoulders for a memorial.
13:And you shall make pouches of gold. 14:And two chains of pure gold at the
ends; and fasten the cord like chains to the pouches. 15:And you shall make the
breastplate of judgment with cunning work; after the work of the ephod you shall
make it; of gold, of blue, and of purple, and of scarlet, and of fine twined linen, shall
you make it. 16:Foursquare it shall be being doubled; a span shall be the length
thereof, and a span shall be the breadth thereof. 17:And you shall set in it settings of
stones, even four rows of stones, the first row shall be a Carnelian, a Topaz,

18:and a Emerald Jade, in the second row, a Garnet, a Sapphire, a Beryl, 19:And the
third row a Ligate, an Agate, and an Amethyst Quarts. 20:And the fourth row a
Chrysoprase, and an Onyx, and a Jasper: they shall be set in gold in their in
closings. 21:And the stones shall be with the names of the children of Israel, twelve,
according to their names, like the engravings of a signet; every one with his name
shall they be according to the twelve tribes. 22:And you shall make upon the
breastplate chains at the ends of wreathe work of pure gold. 23:And you shall make
upon the breastplate two rings of gold, and shall put the two rings on the two ends
of the breastplate. 24:And you shall put the two wreathe chains of gold in the two
rings which are on the ends of the breastplate. 25:And the other two ends of the two
wreathe chains you shall fasten in the two pouches, and put them on the shoulder
pieces of the ephod before it. 26:And you shall make two rings of gold, and you
shall put them upon the two ends of the breastplate in the border thereof, which is in
the side of the ephod inward. 27:And two other rings of gold you shall make, and
shall put them on the two sides of the ephod underneath, toward the forepart thereof,
over against the other coupling thereof, above the curious girdle of the ephod.
28:And they shall bind the breastplate by the rings thereof to the rings of the ephod
with a lace of blue, that it may be above the curious girdle of the ephod, and that the
breastplate be not loosed from the ephod. 29:And Aaron shall bear the names of the
children of Israel in the breastplate of judgment upon his heart, when he goeth in to
the holy places, for a memorial before the Lord continually.

30:And you shall put in the breastplate of judgment the Urim and the Thummim;
and they shall be upon Aaron's heart, when he goeth in before the Lord: and Aaron
shall bear the judgment of the children of Israel upon his heart before the Lord
continually. 31:And you shall make the robe of the ephod all of blue. 32:And there
shall be an hole in the top of it, in the midst thereof: it shall have a binding of woven
work round about the hole of it, as it were the hole of an haberdasher, that it be not
rent. 33:And beneath upon the hem of it you shall make pomegranates of blue, and
of purple, and of scarlet, round about the hem thereof; and bells of gold between
them round about. 34:A golden bell and a pomegranate, a golden bell and a
pomegranate, upon the hem of the robe round about. 35:And it shall be upon Aaron
to minister: and his sound shall be heard when he goeth in to the holy place before
the Lord, and when he comes out, that he die not. 36:And you shall make a plate of
pure gold, and grave upon it, like the engravings of a signet, HOLINESS TO THE
LORD. 37:And you shall put it on a blue lace, that it may be upon the miter; upon
the forefront of the miter it shall be. 38:And it shall be upon Aaron's forehead, that
Aaron may bear the iniquity of the holy things, which the children of Israel shall
hallow in all their holy gifts; and it shall be always upon his forehead, that they may
be accepted before the Lord. 39:And you shall embroider the coat of fine linen, and
you shall make the miter of fine linen, and you shall make the girdle of needlework.
40:And for Aaron's sons you shall make coats, and you shall make for them girdles,
and bonnets shall you make for them, for glory and for beauty. 41:And you shall put
them upon Aaron your brother, and his sons with him; and shall anoint them, and
consecrate them, and sanctify them, that they may minister to me in the priest's
office. 42:And you shall make them linen breeches to cover their nakedness; from
the loins even to the thighs they shall reach. 43:And they shall be upon Aaron, and
upon his sons, when they come in to the tabernacle of the congregation, or when
they come near to the altar to minister in the holy place, that they bear not iniquity,
and die: it shall be, a statute for ever to him and his seed after him.

29:1: And this is the thing that you shall do to them to hallow them, to minister to
me in the priest's office: Take one young bullock, and two rams without blemish,
2:And unleavened bread, and cakes unleavened tempered with oil, and wafers
unleavened anointed with oil, of wheat flour shall you make them. 3:And you shall
put them into one basket, and bring them in the basket, with the bullock and the two
rams. 4:And Aaron and his sons you shall bring to the door of the tabernacle of the
congregation, and shall wash them with water. 5:And you shall take the garments,
and put upon Aaron the coat, and the robe of the ephod, and the ephod, and the
breastplate, and gird him with the curious girdle of the ephod. 6:And you shall put
the miter upon his head, and put the holy crown upon the miter. 7:Then shall you
take the anointing oil, and pour it upon his head, and anoint him. 8:And you shall
bring his sons, and put coats upon them. 9:And you shall gird them with girdles,
Aaron and his sons, and put the bonnets on them: and the priest's office shall be
theirs for a perpetual statute: and you shall consecrate Aaron and his sons. 10:And
you shall cause a bullock to be brought before the tabernacle of the congregation:
and Aaron and his sons shall put their hands upon the head of the bullock. 11:And
you shall kill the bullock before the Lord, by the door of the tabernacle of the
congregation. 12:And you shall take of the blood of the bullock, and put it upon the
horns of the altar with your finger,

and pour all the blood beside the bottom of the altar. 13:And you shall take all the fat that covers the inwards, and the lobe that is above the liver, and the two kidneys, and the fat that is upon them, and burn them upon the altar. 14:But the flesh of the bullock, and his skin, and his dung, shall you burn with fire without the camp: it is a sin offering. 15:You shall also take one ram; and Aaron and his sons shall put their hands upon the head of the ram. 16:And you shall slay the ram, and you shall take his blood, and sprinkle it round about upon the altar. 17:And you shall cut the ram in pieces, and wash the inwards of him, and his legs, and put them to his pieces, and to his head. 18:And you shall burn the whole ram upon the altar: it is a burnt offering to the Lord: it is a sweet savor, an offering made by fire to the Lord. 19:And you shall take the other ram; and Aaron and his sons shall put their hands upon the head of the ram. 20:Then shall you kill the ram, and take of his blood, and put it upon the tip of the right ear of Aaron, and upon the tip of the right ear of his sons, and upon the thumb of their right hand, and upon the great toe of their right foot, and sprinkle the blood upon the altar round about. 21:And you shall take of the blood that is upon the altar, and of the anointing oil, and sprinkle it upon Aaron, and upon his garments, and upon his sons, and upon the garments of his sons with him: and he shall be hallowed, and his garments, and his sons, and his sons' garments with him. 22:Also you shall take of the ram the fat and the rump, and the fat that covers the inwards, and the lobe above the liver, and the two kidneys, and the fat that is upon them, and the right shoulder; for it is a ram of consecration: 23:And one loaf of bread, and one cake of oiled bread, and one wafer out of the basket of the unleavened bread that is before the Lord. 24:And you shall put all in the hands of Aaron, and in the hands of his sons; and shall wave them for a wave offering before the Lord. 25:And you shall receive them of their hands, and burn them upon the altar for a burnt offering, for a sweet savor before the Lord: it is an offering made by fire to the Lord.

26:And you shall take the breast of the ram of Aaron's consecration, and wave it for a wave offering before the Lord: and it shall be your part. 27:And you shall sanctify the breast of the wave offering, and the shoulder of the heave offering, which is waved, and which is heaved up, of the ram of the consecration, even of that which is for Aaron, and of that which is for his sons. 28:And it shall be Aaron's and his sons' by a statute for ever from the children of Israel: for it is an heave offering: and it shall be an heave offering from the children of Israel of the sacrifice of their peace offerings, even their heave offering to the Lord. 29:And the Holy garments of Aaron shall be his sons' after him, to be anointed therein, and to be consecrated in them. 30:And that son that is priest in his stead shall put them on seven days, when he comes into the tabernacle of the congregation to minister in the holy place. 31:And you shall take the ram of the consecration, and seethe his flesh in the holy place. 32:And Aaron and his sons shall eat the flesh of the ram, and the bread that is in the basket, by the door of the tabernacle of the congregation. 33:And they shall eat those things wherewith the atonement was made, to consecrate and to sanctify them: but a stranger shall not eat thereof, because they are holy. 34:And if ought of the flesh of the consecrations, or of the bread, remain to the morning, then you shall burn the remainder with fire: it shall not be eaten, because it is holy. 35:And This shall you do to Aaron, and to his sons, according to all things which I have commanded you: seven days shall you consecrate them.

36:And you shall offer every day a bullock for a sin offering for atonement: and you shall cleanse the altar, when you hast made an atonement for it, and you shall anoint it, to sanctify it. 37:Seven days you shall make an atonement for the altar, and sanctify it; and it shall be an altar most holy: what soever touches the altar shall be holy. 38:Now this is that which you shall offer upon the altar; two lambs of the first year day by day continually. 39:The one lamb you shall offer in the morning; and the other lamb you shall offer at even. 40:And with the one lamb a tenth deal of flour, mingled with the fourth part of an hin of beaten oil; and the fourth part of an hin of wine for a drink offering. 41:And the other lamb you shall offer at even, and shall do thereto according to the meat offering of the morning, and according to the drink offering thereof, for a sweet savor, an offering made by fire to the Lord. 42:This shall be a continual burnt offering throughout your generations, at the door of the tabernacle of the congregation before the Lord: where I will meet you, to speak there to you. 43:And there I will meet with the children of Israel, and the tabernacle shall be sanctified by my glory. 44:And I will sanctify the tabernacle of the congregation, and the altar: I will sanctify also both Aaron and his sons, to minister to me in the priest's office. 45:And I will dwell among the children of Israel, and will be their God. 46;And they shall know that I am the Lord their God, that brought them forth out of the land of Egypt, that I may dwell among them: I am the Lord their God.

30:1: And you shall make an altar to burn incense upon:of acacia wood shall you make it. 2:A cubit shall be the length thereof, and a cubit the breadth thereof; foursquare shall it be: and two cubits shall be the height thereof: the horns thereof shall be of the same. 3:And you shall overlay it with pure gold, the top thereof, and the sides thereof round about, and the horns thereof; and you shall make to it a crown of gold round about. 4:And two golden rings shall you make to it under the crown of it, by the two corners thereof, upon the two sides of it shall you make it and they shall be for places for the poles to bear it withal. 5:And you shall make the poles of acacia wood, and overlay them with gold. 6:And you shall put it before the vale that is by the ark of the testimony, before the mercy seat that is shall not give less than half a shekel, when they give an offering to the Lord, to make an atonement for your souls. 16:And you shall over the testimony, where I will meet with you. 7:And Aaron shall burn thereon sweet incense every morning: when he dresses the lamps, he shall burn incense upon it. 8:And when Aaron lights the lamps at even, he shall burn incense upon it, a perpetual incense before the Lord throughout your generations. 9:You shall offer no strange incense thereon, nor burnt sacrifice, nor meat offering; neither shall you pour drink offering thereon. 10:And Aaron shall make an atonement upon the horns of it once in a year with the blood of the sin offering of atonement's: once in the year shall he make atonement upon it throughout your generations: it is most holy to the Lord. 11:And the Lord spoke to Moses, saying; 12:When you takes the sum of the children of Israel after their number, then shall they give every man a ransom for his soul to the Lord, when you numbers them; that there be no plague among them, when you numbers them. 13:This they shall give, every one that passes among them that are numbered, half a shekel after the shekel of the sanctuary: (a shekel is twenty gerahs:) an half shekel shall be the offering of the Lord. 14:Every one that passes among them that are numbered, from twenty years old and above, shall give an offering to the Lord.

15:The rich shall not give more, and the poor take the atonement money of the children of Israel, and shall appoint it for the service of the tabernacle of the congregation; that it may be a memorial to the children of Israel before the Lord, to make an atonement for your souls. 17:And the Lord spoke to Moses, saying; 18:You shall also make a leaver of brass, and his foot also of brass, to wash with, and you shall put it between the tabernacle of the congregation and the altar, and you shall put water therein. 19:For Aaron and his sons shall wash their hands and their feet thereat 20:When they go into the tabernacle of the congregation, they shall wash with water, that they die not; or when they come near to the altar to minister, to burn offering made by fire to the Lord. 21:So they shall wash their hands and their feet, that they die not: and it shall be a statute for ever to them, even to him and to his seed throughout their generations. 22:Moreover the Lord spoke to Moses, saying; 23:Take you also to you principal spices, of pure myrrh five hundred shekels and of sweet cinnamon half so much, even two hundred and fifty shekels, and of sweet cane two hundred and fifty shekels, 24:And of cassia five hundred shekels, after the shekel of the sanctuary, and of oil olive an hin. 25:And you shall make it an oil of holy ointment, an ointment compound after the are of the apothecary: it shall be an holy anointing oil. 26:And you shall anoint the tabernacle of the congregation therewith, and the ark of the testimony. 27:And the table and all his vessels, and the candlestick and his vessels, and the altar of incense. 28:And the altar of burnt offering with all his vessels, and the laver and his foot. 29:And you shall sanctify them, that they may be most holy: whatsoever touches them shall be holy. 30:And you shall anoint Aaron and his sons, and consecrate them, that they may minister to me in the priest's office. 31:And you shall speak to the children of Israel, saying, This shall be an holy anointing oil to me throughout your generations. 32:Upon man's flesh shall it not be poured, neither shall you make any other like it, after the composition of it: it is holy, and it shall be holy to you. 33:Who soever compounds any like it, or who soever puts any of it upon a stranger, shall even be cut off from his people. 34:And the Lord said to Moses, Take to you sweet spices, storax, and onycha, and galbanum; these sweet spices with pure frankincense: of each shall there be a like weight. 35:And you shall make it a perfume, a confection after the are of the apothecary, tempered together, pure and holy. 36:And you shall beat some of it very small, and put of it before the testimony in the tabernacle of the congregation, where I will meet with you: it shall be to you most holy. 37:And as for the perfume which you shall make, you shall not make to yourselves according to the composition thereof: it shall be to you holy for the Lord. 38:Whosoever shall make like to that, to smell thereto, shall even be cut off from his people.

31:1: And the Lord spoke to Moses, saying; 2:See, I have called by name, Bezaleel the son of Uri, the son of Hur, of the tribe of Judah: 3:And I have filled him with the spirit of God, in wisdom, understanding, an in knowledge, and in all manner of workmanship. 4:To devise cunning works, to work in gold, and in silver, and in brass. 5:And in cutting of stones, to set them, and in carving of timber, to work in all manner of workmanship. 6:And I, behold, I have given with him Aholiab, the son of Ahisamach, of the tribe of Dan: and in the hearts of all that are wise hearted I have put wisdom, that they may make all that I have commanded you. 7:The tabernacle of the congregation, and the ark of the testimony, and the mercy seat that is thereupon, and all the furniture of the tabernacle.

8:And the table and his furniture, and the pure candlestick with all his furniture, and the altar of incense, 9:and the altar of burnt offering with all his furniture, and the laver and his foot. 10:And the cloths of service, and the holy garments for Aaron the priest, and the garments of his sons, to minister in the priest's office, 11:And the anointing oil, and sweet incense for the holy place, according to all that I have commanded you shall they do. 12:And the Lord spoke to Moses, saying; 13:Speak you also to the children of Israel, saying; Truly my sabbaths you shall keep: for it is a sign between me and you throughout your generations; that you may know that I am the Lord that doth sanctify you. 14:You shall keep the sabbath therefore; for it is holy to you, every one that defiles it shall surely be put to death: for whosoever does any work therein, that soul shall be cut off from among his people. 15:Six days may work be done; but in the seventh is the sabbath of rest, holy to the Lord: whosoever does any work in the sabbath day, he shall surely be put to death. 16:Wherefore the children of Israel shall keep the sabbath, to observe the sabbath throughout their generations, for a perpetual covenant.17:It is a sign between me and the children of Israel for ever: for in six days the Lord made heaven and earth, and on the seventh day he rested, and was refreshed. 18:And he gave to Moses, when he had made an end of communing with him upon mount Sinai, two tables of testimony, tables of stone, written with the finger of God.

32:1: And when the people saw that Moses delayed to come down out of the mount, the people gathered themselves together to Aaron, and said to him, Up, make us gods, which shall go before us; for as for this Moses, the man that brought us up out of the land of Egypt, we know not what has become of him. 2:And Aaron said to them, Break off the golden earrings, which are in the ears of your wives, your sons, and your daughters, and bring them to me. 3:And all the people broke off the golden earrings which were in their ears, and brought them to Aaron. 4:And he received them at their hand, and fashioned it with a graving tool, after he had made it a molten calf: and they said, These be your gods, O Israel, which brought you up out of the land of Egypt. 5:And when Aaron saw it, he built an altar before it; and Aaron made proclamation, and said: Tomorrow is a feast to the Lord.

+/- September 1st. (Elul 4th.)

Israel made a vow with the Lord

(Numbers 21:1-3) 1:And when King Arad, the Canaanite, which dwelt in the south, heard tell that Israel came by the way of the spies; then he fought against Israel, and took some of them prisoners. 2:And Israel vowed a vow to the Lord, and said, If you will indeed deliver this people into my hand, then I will utterly destroy their cities. 3;And the Lord hearkened to the voice of Israel, and delivered up the Canaanites; and they utterly destroyed them and their cities: and he called the name of the place Hormah.

+/- September 2nd. (Elul 5th.)

The year +/- 1357 B.C. They started to worshiping false gods of gold

(Exodus 32:6-29) 6:And they rose up early the next day, and offered burnt offerings, and brought peace offerings;and the people sat down to eat and to drink, and rose up to play. 7:And the Lord said to Moses, Go, get you down; for your people, which you brought out of the land of Egypt, have corrupted them self's. 8:They have turned aside quickly out of the way which I commanded them: they have made them a molten calf, and have worshiped it, and have sacrificed there too, and said, These be your gods, O Israel, which have brought you up out of the land of Egypt. 9:And the Lord said to Moses, I have seen this people, and, behold, it is a stiff necked people. 10:Now therefore let me alone, that my wrath may wax hot against them, and that I may consume them: and I will make of you a great nation.

11:And Moses besought the Lord his God, and said, Lord, why does your wrath wax hot against your people, which you have brought forth out of the land of Egypt with great power, and with a mighty hand? 12:Wherefore should the Egyptians speak, and say, For mischief did he bring them out, to slay them in the mountains, and to consume them from the face of the earth? Turn from your fierce wrath, and repent of this evil against your people. 13:Remember Abraham, Isaac, and Israel, your servants, to whom you swore by thine own self, and said to them, I will multiply your seed as the stars of heaven, and all this land that I have spoken of will I give to your seed, and they shall inherit it forever. 14:And the Lord repented of the evil which he thought to do to his people. 15:And Moses turned, and went down from the mount, and the two tables of the testimony were in his hand: the tables were written on both their sides; on the one side and on the other were they written. 16:And the tables were the work of God, and the writing was the writing of God, graven upon the tables. 17:And when Joshua heard the noise of the people as they shouted, he said to Moses, There is a noise of war in the camp. 18:And he said, It is not the voice of them that shout for mastery, neither is it the voice of them that cry for being overcome, but the noise of them that sing do I hear. 19:And it came to pass, as soon as he came nigh to the camp, that he saw the calf, and the dancing: and Moses' anger waxed hot, and he cast the tables out of his hands, and brake them beneath the mount. 20:And he took the calf which they had made, and burnt it in the fire, and ground it to powder, and strawed it upon the water, and made the children of Israel drink of it. 21:And Moses said to Aaron, What did this people do to you, that you have brought so great a sin upon them?

22:And Aaron said, Let not the anger of my lord wax hot: you knowest the people, that they are set on mischief. 23:For they said to me, Make us gods, which shall go before us: for as for this Moses, the man that brought us up out of the land of Egypt, we wot not what is become of him. 24:And I said to them, Whosoever has any gold, let them break it off. So they gave it me: then I cast it into the fire, and there came out this calf. 25:And when Moses saw that the people were naked. 26:Then Moses stood in the gate of the camp, and said, Who is on the Lord's side? Let him come to me. And all the sons of Levi gathered themselves together to him. 27;And he said to them, This says the Lord God of Israel, Put every man his sword by his side, and go in and out from gate to gate throughout the camp, and slay every man his brother, and every man his companion, and every man his neighbor. 28;And the children of Levi did according to the word of Moses: and there fell of the people that day about three thousand men. 29:For Moses had said, Consecrate yourselves to day to the Lord, even every man upon his son, and upon his brother; that he may bestow upon you a blessing this day.

Above: A fenced off area, where it is believed that the golden calf's alter was. Below: A statue similar to the Egyptian calf god that they use to pray and worship in Egypt.

+/- September 2st. (Elul 5th.)

The year +/- 585 B.C. God shows Ezekiel the abominations of the Churches

(Ezekiel 8:1-11;25) 1:And it came to pass in the sixth year, in the sixth month, in the fifth day of the month, as I sat in mine house, and the elders of Judah sat before me, that the hand of the Lord God fell there upon me.

2:Then I beheld, and lo a likeness as the appearance of fire: from the appearance of his loins even downward, fire; and from his loins even upward, as the appearance of brightness, as the color of amber. 3:And he put forth the form of an hand, and took me by a lock of mine head; and the spirit lifted me up between the earth and the heaven, and brought me in the visions of God to Jerusalem, to the door of the inner gate that looks toward the north; where there was the seat of the image of jealousy, which provoke to jealousy. 4:And, behold, the glory of the God of Israel was there, according to the vision that I saw in the plain. 5:Then he said to me, Son of man, lift up thine eyes now the way toward the north. So I lifted up mine eyes the way toward the north, and behold northward at the gate of the altar this image of jealousy in the entry. 6:He said furthermore to me, Son of man, do you see what they are doing? even the great abominations that the house of Israel commits here, that I should go far away from my sanctuary? but turn you yet again, and you shall see greater abominations. 7:And he brought me to the door of the court; and when I looked, behold a hole in the wall. 8:Then said he to me, Son of man, dig now in the wall: and when I had dug into the wall, behold a door. 9:And he said to me, Go in, and behold the wicked abominations that they do here. 10:So I went in and saw; and behold every form of creeping things, and abominable beasts, and all the idols of the house of Israel, portrayed upon the wall round about. 11:And there stood before them seventy men of the ancients of the house of Israel, and in the midst of them stood Jaazaniah the son of Shaphan, with every man his censer in his hand; and a thick cloud of incense went up. 12:Then said he to me, Son of man, have you seen what the ancients of the house of Israel do in the dark, every man in the chambers of his imagery? for they say; The Lord sees us not; the Lord has forsaken the earth. 13:He said also to me, Turn you yet again, and you shall see even greater abominations that they do. 14:Then he brought me to the door of the gate,of the Lord's house which was toward the north; and, behold, there sat women weeping for Tammuz. 15:Then said he to me, Have you seen this, O 'son of man? turn you yet again, and you shall see greater abominations than these. 16:And he brought me into the inner court of the Lord's house, and, behold, at the door of the temple of the Lord, between the porch and the altar, were about five and twenty men, with their backs toward the temple of the Lord, and their faces toward the east; and they worshiped the sun toward the east. 17;Then he said to me, Have you seen this, O son of man? Is it a light thing to the house of Judah that they commit the abominations which they commit here? For they have filled the land with violence, and have returned to provoke me to anger: and, look, they put the branch to their nose. 18:Therefore will I also deal in fury: mine eye shall not spare, neither will I have pity: and though they cry in mine ears with a loud voice, yet will I not hear them.

9:1: He cried also in mine ears with a loud voice, saying, Cause them that have charge over the city to draw near, even every man with his destroying weapon in his hand. 2;And, behold, six men came from the way of the higher gate, which lies toward the north, and every man a slaughter weapon in his hand; and one man among them was clothed with linen, with a writer's ink horn by his side: and they went in, and stood beside the brazen altar. 3;And the glory of the God of Israel was gone up from the cherub, whereupon he was, to the threshold of the house. And he called to the man clothed with linen, which had the writer's ink horn by his side;

4;And the Lord said to him, Go through the midst of the city, through the midst of
Jerusalem, and set a mark upon the foreheads of the men that sigh and that cry for
all the abominations that be done in the midst thereof. 5;And to the others he said in
mine hearing, go you after him through the city, and strike; let not your eye spare,
neither have you pity: 6;Slay utterly old and young, both maids, and little children,
and women: but come not near any man upon whom is the mark; and begin at my
sanctuary. Then they began at the ancient men which were before the house. 7;And
he said to them, Defile the house, and fill the courts with the slain: go you forth.
And they went forth, and slew in the city. 8;And it came to pass, while they were
slaying them, and I was left, that I fell upon my face, and cried, and said, Ah Lord
God! Will you destroy all the residue of Israel in your pouring out of your fury upon
Jerusalem? 9;Then said he to me, The iniquity of the house of Israel and Judah is
exceeding great, and the land is full of blood, and the city full of perverseness: for
they say; The Lord has forsaken the earth, and the Lord sees not. 10;And as for me
also, mine eye shall not spare, neither will I have pity, but I will recompense their
way upon their head. 11;And, behold, the man clothed with linen, which had the ink
horn by his side, reported the matter, saying, I have done as you hast commanded
me.

10:1: Then I looked, and, behold, in the firmament that was above the head of the
cherubims there appeared over them as it were a sapphire stone, as the appearance
of the likeness of a throne. 2:And he spoke to the man clothed with linen, and said,
Go in between the wheels, even under the cherub, and fill thine hand with coals of
fire from between the cherubims, and scatter them over the city. And he went in in
my sight. 3:Now the cherubims stood on the right side of the house, when the man
went in; and the cloud filled the inner court. 4;Then the glory of the Lord went up
from the cherub, and stood over the threshold of the house; and the house was filled
with the cloud, and the court was full of the brightness of the Lord's glory. 5:And
the sound of the cherubims' wings was heard even to the outer court, as the voice of
the Almighty God when he speaks. 6:And it came to pass, that when he had
commanded the man clothed with linen, saying, Take fire from between the wheels,
from between the cherubims; then he went in, and stood beside the wheels. 7:And
one cherub stretched forth his hand from between the cherubims to the fire that was
between the cherubims, and took thereof, and put it into the hands of him that was
clothed with linen: who took it, and went out. 8:And there appeared in the
cherubims the form of a man's hand under their wings. 9:And when I looked, behold
the four wheels by the cherubims, one wheel by one cherub, and another wheel by
another cherub: and the appearance of the wheels was as the color of a beryl stone.
10:And as for their appearances, they four had one likeness, as if a wheel had been
in the midst of a wheel. 11:When they went, they went upon their four sides; they
turned not as they went, but to the place whither the head looked they followed it;
they turned not as they went. 12:And their whole body, and their backs, and their
hands, and their wings, and the wheels, were full of eyes round about, even the
wheels that they four had. 13:As for the wheels, it was cried to them in my hearing,
O wheel. 14:And every one had four faces: the first face was the face of a cherub,
and the second face was the face of a man, and the third the face of a lion, and the
fourth the face of an eagle. 15:And the cherubims were lifted up. This is the living
creature that I saw by the river of Chebar.

16:And when the cherubims went, the wheels went by them: and when the
cherubims lifted up their wings to mount up from the earth, the same wheels also
turned not from beside them. 17:When they stood, these stood; and when they were
lifted up, these lifted up themselves also; for the spirit of the living creature was in
them. 18:Then the glory of the Lord departed from off the threshold of the house,
and stood over the cherubims. 19:And the cherubims lifted up their wings, and
mounted up from the earth in my sight: when they went out, the wheels also were
beside them, and everyone stood at the door of the east gate of the Lord's house; and
the glory of the God of Israel was over them above.

11:1: Moreover the spirit lifted me up, and brought me to the east gate of the Lord's
house, which looks eastward: and behold at the door of the gate five and twenty
men; among whom I saw Jaazaniah the son of Azur, and Pelatiah the son of
Benaiah, princes of the people. 2:Then said he to me, Son of man, these are the men
that devise mischief, and give wicked counsel in this city. 3:Which say, It is not
near; let us build houses: this city is the caldron, and we be the flesh. 4:Therefore
prophesy against them, prophesy, O son of man. 5:And the Spirit of the Lord fell
upon me, and said to me, Speak; This says the Lord; This have you said, O house of
Israel: for I know the things that come into your mind, everyone of them. 6:You
have multiplied your slain in this city, and you have filled the streets thereof with
the slain. 7;Therefore This says the Lord God; Your slain whom you have laid in the
midst of it, they are the flesh, and this city is the caldron: but I will bring you forth
out of the midst of it. 8:You have feared the sword; and I will bring a sword upon
you, says the Lord God. 9:And I will bring you out of the midst thereof, and deliver
you into the hands of strangers, and will execute judgments among you. 10:You
shall fall by the sword; I will judge you in the border of Israel; and you shall know
that I am the Lord. 11:This city shall not be your caldron, neither shall you be the
flesh in the midst thereof; but I will judge you in the border of Israel. 12:And you
shall know that I am the Lord: for you have not walked in my statutes, neither
executed my judgments, but have done after the manners of the heathen that are
round about you. 13:And it came to pass, when I prophesied, that Pelatiah the son of
Benaiah died. Then fell I down upon my face, and cried with a loud voice, and said,
Ah Lord God! will you make a full end of the remnant of Israel?

14:Again the word of the Lord came to me, saying; 15:Son of man, your brethren,
even your brethren, the men of your kindred, and all the house of Israel wholly, are
they to whom the inhabitants of Jerusalem have said, Get you far from the Lord: to
us is this land given in possession. 16:Therefore say, This says the Lord God;
Although I have cast them far off among the heathen, and although I have scattered
them among the countries, yet will I be to them as a little sanctuary in the countries
where they shall come. 17:Therefore say, This says the Lord God; I will even gather
you from the people, and assemble you out of the countries where you have been
scattered, and I will give you the land of Israel. 18:And they shall come closer, and
they shall take away all the detestable things thereof and all the abominations
thereof from here. 19:And I will give them one heart, and I will put a new spirit
within you; and I will take the stony heart out of their flesh, and will give them an
heart of flesh. 20:That they may walk in my statutes, and keep mine ordinances,
and do them: and they shall be my people, and I will be their God.

21:But as for them whose heart walks after the heart of their detestable things and their abominations, I will recompense their way upon their own heads, says the Lord God. 22:Then did the cherubims lift up their wings, and the wheels beside them; and the glory of the God of Israel was over them above. 23:And the glory of the Lord went up from the midst of the city, and stood upon the mountain which is on the east side of the city. 24:After wards the spirit took me up, and brought me in a vision by the Spirit of God into Chaldea, to them of the captivity. So the vision that I had seen went up from me. 25:Then I spoke to them of the captivity all the things, that the Lord had showed me.

+/- September 3st. (Elul 6th.)

The year +/- 1357 B.C. Moses pleaded to God for the people

(Exodus 32:30-34) 30;And it came to pass on the next day, that Moses said to the people, you have sinned a great sin, and now I will go up to the Lord; peradventure I shall make an atonement for your sins. 31;And Moses returned to the Lord, and said, Oh, this people have sinned a great sin, and have made for them self's gods of gold. 32;If you would only forgive their sin! If you will not, I pray then, blot me out of the book you have written. 33;And the Lord said to Moses, Who soever has sinned against me, him will I blot out of my book. 34;Therefore now go, lead the people to the place of which I have spoken to you: behold, mine Angel shall go before you: nevertheless in the day when I return, I will return their sin upon them.

+/- September 6st. (Elul 9th.)

The year +/- 1952 B.C. Ishmael was born

(Genesis 16:15-17:11) 15:And Hagar bare Abram a son: and Abram called his son's name, which Hagar bare, Ishmael. 16:And Abram was fourscore and six years old, when Hagar bare Ishmael to Abram.

17:1: And when Abram was ninety years old and nine, the Lord appeared to Abram, and said to him, I am the Almighty God; walk before me, and be you perfect. 2:And I will make my covenant between me and you, and will multiply you exceedingly. 3:And Abram fell on his face: and God talked with him, saying, 4;As for me, behold, my covenant is with you, and you shall be a father of many nations. 5:Neither shall your name any more be called Abram, but your name shall be Abraham; for a father of many nations have I made you. 6:And I will make you exceeding fruitful, and I will make nations of you, and kings shall come out of you.

7:And I will establish my covenant between me and you and your seed after you in their generations for an everlasting covenant, to be a God to you, and to your seed after you. 8:And I will give to you, and to your seed after you, the land wherein you are a stranger, all the land of Canaan, for an everlasting possession; and I will be their God. 9:And God said to Abraham, you shall keep my covenant therefore, you, and your seed after you in their generations. 10:This is my covenant, which you shall keep, between me and you and your seed after you; Every man child among you shall be circumcised. 11:And you shall circumcise the flesh of your foreskin; and it shall be a token of the covenant betwixt me and you.

+/- September 6st. (Elul 9th.)

A Angel of God spoke with Mary

(Luke 1:28-39) 28:And the angel came in to her, and said, Hail, you that are highly favored, the Lord is with you: blessed are you among women. 29;And when she saw him, she was troubled at his saying, and cast in her mind what manner of salutation this should be. 30:And the angel said to her, Fear not, Mary: for you have found favor with God. 31:And, behold, you shall conceive in your womb, and bring forth a son, and shall call his name; Jesus. 32:He shall be great, and shall be called the Son of the Highest: and the Lord God shall give to him the throne of his father David. 33:And he shall reign over the house of Jacob for ever; and of his kingdom there shall be no end. 34:Then said Mary to the angel, How shall this be, seeing I know not a man? 35:And the angel answered and said to her, The Holy Ghost shall come upon you, and the power of the Highest shall overshadow you: therefore also that holy thing which shall be born of you shall be called the Son of God. 36:And, behold, your cousin Elisabeth, she has also conceived a son in her old age, and this is the sixth month with her, who was called barren. 37:For with God nothing shall be impossible. 38:And Mary said, Behold the handmaid of the Lord; be it to me according to your word. And the angel departed from her. 39:And Mary arose in those days, and went into the hill country with haste, into a city of Judah.

+/- September 7th. (Elul 10th.)

Jephthah came home and found great sorrow

(Judges 11:34-38) 34:And Jephthah returned to Mizpah to his house, and, behold, his daughter came out to meet him with timbrels and dancing: for she was his only child; he had no other. 35:And it came to pass, when he saw her, that he rent his clothes, and said, Alas, my daughter! you have brought me much sorrow, and you are one of them that trouble me: for I have said to the Lord, and I cannot take it back.(That what ever comes out of my house first, I will sacrifice to him.) 36:And she said to him, My father, if you have promised this to the Lord, do to me according to that which you have said; for as much as the Lord has taken vengeance for you on your enemies, even of the children of Ammon. 37:And she said to her father, Let this thing be done for me: let me go out for two months, that I may go up and down upon the mountains, and bewail my virginity, I and my friends. 38:And he said:Go, and he sent her away for two months: and she went with her companions, and mourned her virginity upon the mountains.

+/- September 11th. (Elul 14th.)

The year +/- 151 B.C. Judith tells the elders of her Idea

(Judith 8;9-36) 9:When Judith, therefore, heard of the harsh words which the people, discouraged by their lack of water, had spoken against their ruler, and and all that Uzziah had said to them in reply, swearing that he would hand over the city to the Assyrians at the end of five days, 10:she sent the maid who was in charge of all her things to ask Uzziah, Chabris, and Charmis the elders of the city, to visit her. 11:When they came she said to them; "Listen to me , you rulers of the people of Bethulia. What you said to the people today is not proper.

When you promised to hand over the city to our enemies at the end of five days unless within that time the Lord comes to our aid, you interposed between God and yourselves this oath that you took. 12:Who are you then, that you should have put God to the test this day, setting yourselves in the place of God in human affairs? 13:It is the Lord Almighty for whom you are laying down conditions; will you never understand anything? 14:You can not plumb the depths of the human heart or grasp the workings of the human mind; how then can you fathom God, who has made all these things, discern his mind, and understand his plan? No my brothers do not anger the Lord our God. 15:For if he does not wish to come to our aid within the five days, he has it equally within his power to protect us at such time as he pleases, or to destroy us in the face of our enemies. 16:It is not up to you to make the Lord our God give surety for his plans "God is not a man that he should be moved by threats, nor human, that he may be given an ultimatum. 17:So while we wait for the salvation that comes from him, let let us call upon him to help us, and he will hear our cry; if it is his good pleasure. 18:For there has not risen among us in recent generations, nor does there exist today, any tribe, clan, town, or city of ours that worships gods made by hands, as happened in former days. 19:It was not for such conduct that our forefathers were handed over to the sword and pillaged, and fell with great destruction before our enemies. 20:But since we acknowledge no other god but the Lord, we hope that he will not disdain us or any of our people. 21:If we are taken, all Judea will fall, our sanctuary will be plundered and God make us pay for its profanation with our life's blood.

23:Our enslavement will not be turned to our benefit, but the Lord our God will maintain it to our disgrace. 24:Therefore my brothers, let us set an example for our kinsmen. Their lives depend on us, and the defense of the sanctuary, the temple, and the alter rests with us. 25:Beside all this, we should be grateful to our lord God, for putting us to the test, as he did our forefathers. 26:Recall how he dealt with Abraham, and how he tried Isaac, and all that happened to Jacob in Syrian Mesopotamia, while he was tending the flocks of Laban, his mother's brother. 27:Not for vengeance did the Lord put them in the crucible to try their hearts, nor has he done so with us. It is by the way of admonition that he chastises those who are close to him." (Uzziah's response) 28:Then Uzziah said: to her; "All that you have said was spoken with good sense, and no one can gainsay your words. 29:Not today only is your wisdom make evident, but from your earliest years all the people have recognized your prudence, which corresponds to the worthy dispositions of your heart. 30:The people however, were so tortured with thirst that they forced us to speak to them as we did, and to bind ourselves by an oath that we cannot break. 31:But now, God-fearing woman that you are, pray for us that the Lord may send rain to fill up our cisterns , lest we be weakened still further." 32:Then Judith said to them: "Listen to me I will do something that will go down from generation to generation among the descendents of our race. 33:Stand at the gate tonight and let me pass through with my maid; and within the days you have specified before you will surrender the city to our enemies, the Lord will rescue Israel by my hand. 34:You must not inquire into what I am doing, for I will not tell you until my plan has been accomplished." 35:Uzziah and the rulers said to her, "Go in peace, and may the Lord God go before you to take vengeance upon our enemies!" 36:Then they withdrew from the tent and returned to their post.

+/- September 12th. (Elul 15th.)

God tested Abraham

(Genesis 22:1-3)1:And it came to pass after these things, that God did tempt Abraham, and said to him: Abraham: and he said, Behold, here I am. 2:And he said, Take now your son. Abraham said; which one I have two sons? The son whom you love, Isaac, and go into the land of Moriah; and offer him there for a burnt offering upon one of the mountains which I will show you. 3:So Abraham rose up early in the morning, and saddled his ass, and took two of his young men with him, and Isaac his son, and took the wood, for the burnt offering, and rose up, and went to the place of which; God had told him.

+/- September 12th. (Elul 15th.)

The year +/- 151 B.C. Judith prayed to God for deliverance

(Judith 9;1-14)1:Judith threw herself down prostate, with ashes strewn upon her head, and wearing nothing over her except sackcloth. While the incense was being offered in the temple of God in Jerusalem that evening, Judith prayed to the Lord with a loud voice. 2:Lord, God of my forefather Simeon! You put a Sword into his hand to take revenge upon the foreigners, who had immodestly loosened the maiden's girdle, shamefully exposed her thighs, and disgracefully violated her body. This they did though you forbade it. 3:Therefore you had their rulers slaughtered; and you covered with their blood the bed in which they lay deceived, the same bed that had felt the shame of their own deceiving. You struck the slaves together with their princes, and the prince together with their servants. 4:Their wife's you handed over to plunder, and their daughters to captivity, and all the spoils you divided among your favored sons, who burned with zeal for you, but others in abhorrence of the defilement of their kinswoman, your sons called on you for help and you came. 5:"O God, my God, hear me also, a widow It is you who were the author of those events and of what preceded and fallowed them. The present and the future you have planed. Whatever you device comes into being, 6:the things you decide on come forward and say: Hear we are! All your ways are in readiness, and your judgment is made with foreknowledge. 7:Here are the Assyrians, a vast force, priding themselves on horse and rider, boasting of the power of their infantry, trusting in their shield and spear, bow and sling. They do not know that. 8;"You, the Lord, crush warfare; the Lord is your name." Shatter their strength in your might and crush their force with your in your wrath, for they have resolved to profane your sanctuary, to defile the tent where your glorious name resides, and to overthrow with iron the horns of your alter. 9:See their pride, and send forth your wrath upon their heads. Give me a widow, a strong hand to execute my plan.10;With the guile of my lips, smite the slave together with the ruler, the ruler together with his servant, crush their pride by a hand of a woman. 11:Your strength is not in numbers, nor does your power depend upon stalwart men; but you are the God of the lowly, the helper of the oppressed, the supporter of the weak, the protector of the forsaken, and the savior of those without hope. 12:"Please, please, God of my forefathers, god of of the heritage of Israel, Lord of the heavens and earth. The Creator of the waters, King of all you have created, hear my prayer! 13:Let my guileful speech bring wound and wale on those who have planned dire things against your covenant, your holy temple , Mount Zion and the homes your children have inherited." 14;Let your whole nation and all the tribes know clearly that you are the God of all power and might, and you alone who protect the people of Israel.

+/- September 13th. (Elul 16th.)

The year +/- 151 B.C.E. Judith went down to Holofernes camp

(Judith 10:1-12:4) 1:As soon as Judith had This concluded, and ceased her invocation to the God of Israel, 2:she rose from the ground. She called her maid and they went down into the house, which she used only on sabbaths and feast days. 3;She took off the sackcloth she had on, and laid aside the garments of her widowhood, washed her body with water, and anointed her self with costly perfume. She arranged her hair and bound it with a fillet, and put on the festive attire she had worn while her husband, Manasseh was living. 4:She chose sandals for her feet and put on her anklets, bracelets, rings, earrings, all her other jewelry. This she made her self very beautiful, to captivate the eyes of all the men who would see her. 5:She gave her maid a leather flask of wine and a cruse of oil. She filled a bag with roasted grain, fig cakes, bread and cheese, all these provisions she wrapped up and gave to her maid to carry. 6:Then they went out to the gate of the city of Bethulia and found Uzziah and the elders of the city, Chabris and Charmis, standing there. 7:When these men saw Judith transformed in looks and differently dressed, they were very much astounded at her beauty and said to her; 8:"May the God of our fathers bring you to favor, and make your undertaking a success, for for the glory of the Israelites and the exaltation of Jerusalem." Judith bowed down to God, Then she said to them. 9:"Order the gate of the city opened for me, that I may go carry out the business we discussed." So they ordered the youths to open the gate for her as she requested. 10:When they did so, Judith and her maid went out. The men of the city kept her in view as she went down the mountain and crossed the valley, then they lost sight of her. 11:As Judith and her maid walked directly across the valley, they encountered the Assyrian outpost. 12:The men took her into custody and asked her,"To what people do you belong? Where do you come from, and where are you going?" She replied: I am a daughter of the Hebrews, and I am fleeing from them, because there are about to be delivered up to you as pray. 13:I have come to see Holofernes the general in charge of your forces, to give him a trustworthy report; I will show him the route by which he can ascend and take possession of the whole mountain district without a single one of his men suffering injury of loss of life." 14:When the men heard her words and gazed upon her face, which appeared wondrously beautiful to them, they said to her; 1:;"By coming down this quickly to see our master, you have saved your life. Now go to his tent; some of our men will accompany you to present you to him. 16:When you stand before him, have no fear in you heart; give him the report you spoke of, and he will treat you well" 17:So they send a hundred of their men as a escort for her and her maid, and these took them to the tent of Holofernes. 18:When the news of her spread among the tents, a crowd gathered in the camp. They came and stood around her as she waited outside the tent of Holofernes, while he was being informed about her. 19:They marveled at her beauty, regarding the Israelites with wonder because of her, and they said to one another; "Who can despise this people that has such women among them? It would not be wise for us to leave even one of their men alive, for if any were spared they could beguile the whole world. 20:The guard of Holofernes and all his servants came out and ushered her into the tent. 21:Now Holofernes was reclining on his bed under a canopy with a netting of crimson and gold, emeralds and other precious stones. 22:When they announced her to him, he came out to the antechamber, preceded by silver lamps; 23:and when Holofernes and his servants beheld Judith, they all marveled at the beauty of her face. She threw herself down, prostrate before him, but his servants raised her up.

11:1;Then Holofernes said to her: "Take courage, lady; have no fear in your heart! Never have I harmed anyone who chose to serve Nebuchadnezzar, King of all the earth. 2:Nor would I have raised my spear against your people who dwell in these mountain region, had they not despised me and brought this among themselves. 3:But now tell me why you fled from them and came to us? In any case you have come to safety. Take courage! Your life is spared tonight and for the future. 4:No one at all will harm you. Rather, you will be well treated, as are all the servants of my lord, King Nebuchadnezzar." 5:Judith answered him: "Listen to the words of your servant, and let your handmaid speak in your presence. I will tell no lie to my lord this night, 6:and if you follow out the words of your handmaid, God will give you complete success and my lord will not fail in any of his undertaking. 7:By the life of Nebuchadnezzar, King of all the earth, and by the power of him who has sent you to set all creatures aright! Not only do men serve him through you; but even the wild beast and the cattle and the birds of the air, because of your strength, will live for Nebuchadnezzar and his whole house. 8:Indeed, we have heard of your wisdom and sagacity, and all the world is aware that throughout the kingdom you alone are competent, rich in experience, and distinguished in military strategy. 9:As for Achior's speech in your council, we have heard of it. When the men of Bethulia spared him, he told them all he had said to you. 10:So then, my lord and master, do you disregard his word, but bear in mind, for it is true. For our people are not punished, nor does the sword prevail against them, except when they sin against their God. 11:But now their guilt has caught up with them by which they bring the wrath of their God upon them whenever they do wrong; so that my lord will not be repulsed and fail, but death will overtake them. 12:Since their food gave out and their water ran low, they decided to kill their animals, and determined to consume all the things which God in his laws forbid them to eat. 13:They decreed that they would use up the first fruits of grain and the tithes of wine and oil which they had sanctified and reserved for the priest who minister in the presence of our God in Jerusalem; things which no layman should even touch with his hands. 14:They have sent messengers to Jerusalem to bring back to them authorization from the council of the elders; for the inhabitants there have also done these things. 15:On the very day when the response reaches them and they act upon It, they will be handed over to you for destruction. 16:"As soon as I your maid servant had learned of this, I fled from them. God has sent me to perform with you such deeds that people throughout the world will be astonished on hearing of them. 17:Your handmaid is, indeed a God-fearing woman, serving the God of heaven night and day. Now I will remain with you, my lord; but each night your handmaid will go out to the ravine and pray to God. He will tell me when the Israelites have committed their crimes. 18:Then I will come and let you know, so that you may go out with your whole force, and not one of them will be able to withstand you.

19:I will lead you through Judea, until you come to Jerusalem, and there I will set up your judgment seat. You will drive them like sheep that have no shepherd, and not even a dog will growl at you. This was told to me, and announced to me in advance, and I in turn have been sent to tell you." 20:Her words pleased Holofernes and all his servants; they marveled at her wisdom and proclaimed; 21:"There is not anther woman from one end of the world to the other, that looks so beautiful and speaks so wisely!" 22:Then Holofernes said to her; "God has done well in sending you ahead of your people, to bring victory to our arms, and destruction to those who have despised my lord. 23:You are fair to behold, and your words are well spoken. If you do as you have said, your God will be my God; you shall dwell in the palace of the King Nebuchadnezzar, and shall be renowned throughout the earth.

12:1;Then he ordered them to lead her into the room where his silverware was kept, and told them to set a table for her with his own delicacies to eat and his own wine to drink. 2;But Judith said: "I will not partake of them, lest it be a occasion of sin; but I shall be amply supplied from the things I brought with me." 3;Holofernes asked her; "But if your provisions give out, where shall we get more of the same to provide for you? None of your people are with us." 4;Judith answered him: "As surly as you, my lord, live, your handmaid will not use up her supplies till the Lord, accomplishes by my hand what he has determined."

+/- September 13th. (Elul 16th.)

The Lord sent serpents

(Numbers 21:5-6) 5:And the people spoke against God, and against Moses, wherefore have you brought us up out of Egypt to die in the wilderness? for there is no bread, neither is there any water; and our soul loathes this light bread. 6:And the Lord sent fiery serpents among the people, and they bit the people; and many of the people of Israel died. 7:Therefore the people came to Moses, and said, We have sinned, for we have spoken against the LORD, and against you; pray to the LORD, that he take away the serpents from us. And Moses prayed for the people. 8:And the LORD said to Moses, Make you a fiery serpent, and set it upon a pole: and it shall come to pass, that every one that is bitten, when they look upon it and believe, shall live.

+/- September 14th. (Elul 17th.)

The day the Hebrews believe the Universe, was called into Existence;

(Genesis 1:1) 1:And in the beginning, God created the Heaven's and the Earth.

+/- September 14th. (Elul 17th.)

+/-151 B.C. Judith went into her sleeping quarters

(Judith 1:5-7) Then the servants of Holofernes led her into the tent, where she slept until midnight. In the night watch just before dawn she rose, 6:and sent this message to Holofernes, "Give orders, my lord, to let your handmaid go out for prayer," 7:So Holofernes ordered his bodyguards not to stop her. She stayed there three days.

+/- September 14th. (Elul 17th.)

The year +/- 1 A.D. The Hebrew year 3752 The Birth of Jesus

(Matthew 2:1-11)1:Now when Jesus was born in Bethlehem of Judea in the days of Herod the King, behold, there came wise men from the east to Jerusalem. 2:Saying, Where is he that is born King of the Jews? For we have seen his star in the east, and are come to worship him. 3:When Herod the King had heard these things, he was troubled, and all Jerusalem with him. 4:And when he had gathered all the chief priests and scribes of the people together, he demanded of them where Christ should be born. 5:And they said to him, In Bethlehem of Judah: for This it is written by the prophet, 6:And you Bethlehem, in the land of Judah, are not the least among the princes of Judah: for out of you shall come a King, that shall rule my people Israel. 7:Then Herod, when he had privily called the wise men, inquired of them diligently what time the star appeared. 8:And he sent them to Bethlehem, and said; Go and search diligently for the young child; and when you have found him, bring me word again, that I may come and worship him also. 9:When they had heard the King, they departed; and, look, the star, which they saw in the east, went before them, till it came and stood over where the young child was. 10:When they saw the star, they rejoiced with exceeding great joy. 11:And when they were come into the house, they saw the young child with Mary his mother, and fell down, and worshiped him: and when they had opened their treasures, they presented to him gifts; of gold, frankincense, and myrrh.

Note:More about the Magi: It is written that they brought three gifts, not that there were just three wise men.

The word (Magi) means: someone who has knowledge of more than just what can be seen, but from a higher source. Their names were believed to be; Jasper, Melchior, and Balthasar, along with them was a Astrologer, named: Liu Shang, from Asia. They stayed through the feast of Booths then returned home.

Below in the town of Bethlehem, is the Church of the Nativity.

Above: the place believed to be the Birth place of Jesus

(Note: It was during this month when,
Gabriel told Mary she would give birth

(Luke 1:26-38) 26:And in the sixth month the angel Gabriel was sent from God to a city of Galilee, named Nazareth, 27:To a maiden who was engaged to a man whose name was Joseph, of the house of David; and the virgin's name was Mary. 28:And the angel came to her, and said, Hail, you that are highly favored, the Lord is with you: blessed are you among women. 29:And when she saw him, she was troubled at his saying, and thought in her mind what manner of greeting this might be.

30:And the angel said to her, Fear not, Mary: for you have found favor with God. 31:And behold, you shall conceive in your womb, and bring forth a son, and shall call his name Jesus. 32:He shall be great, and shall be called the Son of the Highest: and the Lord God shall give to him the throne of his father David. 33:And he shall reign over the house of Jacob for ever; and of his kingdom there shall be no end. 34:Then said Mary to the angel, How shall this be, seeing I have never known a man? 35:And the angel answered and said to her, The Holy Ghost shall come upon you, and the power of the Highest shall overshadow you: therefore also that Holy thing which shall be born of you shall be called the Son of God, around this time next year you shall give birth.

36:And, behold, your cousin Elisabeth, she has also conceived a son in her old age, and this is the sixth month with her, whom was called barren. 37:For with God nothing shall be impossible. 38;And Mary said; Behold the handmaid of the Lord; be it to me according to your words. And the angel departed from her.

Note: Written in the Gospel of James

The first visitor of Jesus

A woman named Salome was led in to see Mary by the midwife who helped deliver Mary's child. Salome also believed to be a mid wife was filled with faith when she saw that Mary was still a Virgin. (As it was written) As a Virgin you will conceive, as a virgin you will give birth, and as a virgin you will give suckle.

+/- September 15th. (Elul 18th.)

The year +/- 134 B.C. So they made inscription on bronze tablets

(1Maccabees 14:27-35) 27:The fallowing is a copy of the inscription:On the eighteenth day of Elul, in the year one hundred and seventy-two that is, the third year under Simon the high priest in Asaramel, 28:in a great assembly of the priest, people, rulers of the nation, and elders of the country, the fallowing proclamation was made. 29:"Since there has often been wars in our country, Simon son of the priest Mattathias, descendant of Joarib, and his brothers have out themselves in danger and resisted the enemies of their nation, so that their sanctuary and the law might be maintained, and they have. This brought great glory to their nation.

30:After Jonathan had rallied his nation and became their high priest, he was gathered to his kinsmen. 31:When the enemies of the Hebrews sought to invade and devastate their country and to lay hands on their temple. 32:Simon rose up and fought for his nation, spending large sums of his own money to equip the men of his nations armed forces and giving them their pay. 33:He fortified the cities of Judah, especially the frontier city of Bethzur, where he stationed a garrison of Hebrew soldiers, and where previously the enemy's arms had been stored. 34:He also fortified Joppa by the sea and Gazara on the border of Azotus, a place previously occupied by the enemy; these cities he resettled with Hebrews, and furnished them with all that was necessary for their restoration. 35:When the Hebrew people saw Simon's loyalty and the glory he planed to bring to his nation, they made him their leader and high priest because of all he had accomplished and the loyalty and justice he had shown his nation. In every way he sought to lift up his people.

+/- September 16th. (Elul 19th.)

The year +/-2891 B.C.E. (Genesis 11:18-19) Peleg died:

(Genesis 11:18-19)18:And Peleg lived thirty years, then begot Reu: 19:And Peleg lived after he begot Reu, two hundred and nine years, and he had sons and daughters. His was two hundred and thirty nine years of age when he died, on the nineteenth day of the twelfth month.

+/- September 16th. (Elul 19th.)

Abraham saw where he was to sacrifice his son

(Genesis 22:4-19) 4:Then on the third day Abraham lifted up his eyes, and saw the place afar off. 5:And Abraham said to his young men, Abide you here with the ass; and I and the lad will go yonder and worship, and come again to you. 6:And Abraham took the wood of the burnt offering, and laid it upon Isaac his son;

and he took the fire in his hand, and a knife; and they went both of them together. 7:And Isaac spoke to Abraham his father, and said, My father: and he said, Here I am, my son. And he said, Behold the fire and the wood: but where is the lamb for a burnt offering? 8:And Abraham said, My son, God will provide himself, a lamb for a burnt offering: so they went both of them together.

9:And they came to the place which God had told him; and Abraham built an altar there, and laid the wood in order, and bound Isaac his son, and laid him on the altar upon the wood. 10:And Abraham stretched forth his hand, and took the knife to slay his son.,,11:And the angel of the Lord called to him out of heaven, and said, Abraham, Abraham: and he said, Here I am.

12:And he said, Lay not thine hand upon the lad, neither do you any thing to him: for now I know that you fears God, seeing you have not withheld your son, thine only son from me. 13:And Abraham lifted up his eyes, and looked, and behold behind him a ram caught in a thicket by his horns: and Abraham went and took the ram, and offered him up for a burnt offering in the stead of his son.

14:And Abraham called the name of that place Jehovahjireh: as it is said to this day, In the mount of the Lord it shall be seen. 15:And the angel of the Lord called to Abraham out of heaven the second time. 16:And said, By myself have I sworn, says the Lord, for because you hast done this thing, and hast not withheld your son, thine only son.

17:That in blessing I will bless you, and in multiplying I will multiply your seed as the stars of the heaven, and as the sand which is upon the sea shore; and your seed shall possess the gate of his enemies. 18:And in your seed shall all the nations of the earth be blessed; because you hast obeyed my voice. 19:So Abraham returned to his young men, and they rose up and went together to Beersheba; and Abraham dwelt at Beersheba.

+/- September 16th. (Elul 19th.)

God told them to make a Fiery Serpent

(Numbers 21:7-8) 7:Therefore the people came to Moses, and said; We have sinned, for we have spoken against the Lord, and against you; pray to the Lord, that he takes away the serpents from among us. And Moses prayed for the people. 8:And the Lord said to Moses, Make you a fiery serpent, and set it upon a pole: and it shall come to pass, that every one that is bitten, if they touch it, or even look upon it, they shall live.

+/- September 17th. (Elul 20th.)

Moses put up the serpent in the wilderness

(Numbers 21:9) 9:So Moses made a serpent of brass, and put it upon a pole that stood on a mound, in the sixth month on the twentieth day, and it came to pass, if a serpent had bitten anyone, when they looked upon the serpent of brass, that was hung on the pole and believed, they lived.

(The Fiery Serpent's name was Nehushtan):

Which means; Despising the Grace of God Note: As spoken of by Jesus:
(John 3:14-15) 14: And as Moses lifted up the serpent in the wilderness, even so must the Son of man be lifted up. 15:That whosoever believes in him should not perish, but have eternal life.

Above:(Left) Mounted on Mount Nebo, a Serpent to represent the one that Moses erected in the wilderness. (Right) a picture of a copper snake on a pole.

Above: a picture of the Egyptian Copperheads, found in the area where the Hebrews were traveling through.

+/- September 17th. (Elul 20th.)

The year +/- 151 B.C. Judith prayed to God for help

(Judith 12:8-9) 8:After bathing, she prayed to the Lord God of Israel, to direct her way for the triumph of his people. 9:Then she returned purified to the tent, and remained there, until her food was brought to her towards evening.

+/- September 18th. (Elul 21st.)

The year +/- 151 B.C. Judith cut off the head of Holofernes

(Judith 12:10-14;19) 10:And in the fourth day Holofernes made a feast to his own servants only, and called none of the officers to the banquet. 11:Then he said to Bagoas the eunuch, who had charge over all that he had, Go now, and bring this Hebrew woman which is with you, that she may come join us, to eat and drink with us. 12:It would be a disgrace to have such a woman with us without enjoying her company. If we do not entice her, she will laugh at us to scorn. 13:Then went Bagoas from the presence of Holofernes, and came to her, and he said, Let not this fair damsel fear to come to my lord, and to be honored in his presence, to drink wine, and be merry with us and be made this day as one of the daughters of the Assyrians, which serve in the house of Nebuchadnezzar. 14:Then said Judith to him; Who am I, to refuse my lord? What ever is pleasing to him, I will do, and it shall be my joy to the day of my death. 15:So she arose, and decked herself with her apparel and all her woman's attire, and her maid went and laid soft skins on the ground for her over against Holofernes, which she had received of Bagoas for her daily use, that she might sit and eat upon them. 16:Now when Judith came in and sat down, Holofernes his heart was taken with her, and his mind was moved, and he desired greatly her company; for he waited a time to deceive her, from the day that he had seen her. 17:Then said Holofernes to her, Drink now, and be merry with us. 18:So Judith said, I will drink now, my lord, because my life is magnified in me this day more than any since I was born. 19:Then she took and ate and drank before him what her maid had prepared. 20:And Holofernes took great delight in her, and drank more wine than he had drank before, at any time in one day since he was born.

13;1: Now when the evening was come, his servants made haste to depart, and Bagoas shut his tent without, and dismissed the waiters from the presence of his lord; and they went to their beds: for they were all weary, because the feast had been long. 2:And Judith was left along in the tent, and Holofernes lying along upon his bed: for he was filled with wine. 3:Now Judith had commanded her maid to stand without her bedchamber, and to wait for her. coming forth, as she did daily: for she said she would go forth to her prayers, and she spoke to Bagoas according to the same purpose. 4:So all went forth and none was left in the bedchamber, neither little nor great. Then Judith, standing by his bed, said in her heart, O Lord God of all power, look at this present upon the works of mine hands for the exaltation of Jerusalem. 5:For now is the time to help your inheritance, and to execute your plan to the destruction of the enemies which are risen against us.6:Then she came to the pillar of the bed, which was at Holofernes' head, and took down his sword from there. 7:And approached his bed, and took hold of the hair of his head, and said, Strengthen me, O Lord God of Israel, this day. 8:And she struck twice on his neck with all her might, and she took away his head from him.

9:And tumbled his body down from the bed, and pulled down the canopy from the
pillars; and anon after she went forth, and gave Holofernes his head to her maid.
10:And she put it in her bag of meat: so they twain went together according to their
custom to prayer: and when they passed the camp, they compassed the valley, and
went up the mountain of Bethulia, and came to the gates thereof. 11:Then Judith
called while still afar off, to the watchmen at the gate, Open, open the gate now:
God, our God, is with us, to show his power yet in Jerusalem, and his forces against
the enemy, as he has done this day. 12:Now when the men of her city heard her
voice, they made haste to go down to the gate of their city, and they called the elders
of the city. 13:And then they ran all together, both small and great, for it was strange
to them that she was come: so they opened the gate, and received them, and made a
fire for a light, and stood round about them. 14:Then she said to them with a loud
voice, Praise, praise God, praise God, I say, for he has not taken away his mercy
from the house of Israel, but has destroyed our enemies by mine hands this night.
15:So she took the head out of the bag, and showed it, and said to them, behold the
head of Holofernes, the chief captain of the army of Assyrian army, and behold the
canopy, wherein he did lie in his drunkenness; and the Lord has smitten him by the
hand of a woman. 16:As the Lord lives, who has kept me in my way that I went, my
countenance has deceived him to his destruction, and yet has he not committed sin
with me, to defile and shame me. 17:Then all the people were wonderfully
astonished, and bowed themselves and worshiped God, and said with one accord,
Blessed be you, O our God, which has this day brought to not to the enemies of
your people. 18:Then Uzziah said to her, O daughter, blessed are you of the most
high God above all the women upon the earth; and blessed be the Lord God, which
has created the heavens and the earth, which has directed you to the cutting off of
the head of the chief of our enemies. 19:For this your confidence shall not depart
from the heart of men, which remember the power of God forever. 20:And God turn
these things to you for a perpetual praise, to visit you in good things because you
have not spared your life for the affliction of our nation, but have revenged our ruin,
walking a straight way before our God. And all the people said; So be it, so be it.

14:1: Then said Judith to them, Hear me now, my brethren, and take this head, and
hang it upon the highest place of your walls. 2:And so soon as the morning shall
appears, and the sun shall come forth upon the earth, take you every one his
weapons, and go forth every valiant man out of the city, and set yourself a captain
over them, as though you would go down into the field toward the watch of the
Assyrians; but go not down. 3:Then they shall take their armor, and shall go into
their camp, and raise up the captains of the army of Assyrians, and shall run to the
tent of Holofernes, but shall not find him: then fear shall fall upon them, and they
shall flee before your face. 4:So you, and all that inhabit the coast of Israel, shall
pursue them, and overthrow them as they go. 5:But before you do these things, call
me Achior the Ammonite, that he may see and know him that despised the house of
Israel, and that sent him to us as it were to his death. 6:Then they called Achior out
of the house of Uzziah, and when he had come, and saw the head of Holofernes, in a
man's hand in the assembly of the people, he fell down on his face, and his spirit
failed 7:But when they had recovered him, he fell at Judith's feet, and reverenced
her, and said, Blessed are you in all the tabernacles of Judah, and in all nations,
which hearing your name shall be astonished.

8:Now therefore tell me all the things that you have done in these days. Then Judith declared to him in the midst of the people all that she had done, from the day that she went forth until that hour she spoke to them. 9:And when she had left off speaking, the people shouted with a loud voice, and made a joyful noise in their city. 10:And when Achior had seen all that the God of Israel had done, he believed in God greatly, and circumcised the flesh of his foreskin, and was joined to the house of Israel to this day. 11:And as soon as the morning arose, they hanged the head of Holofernes upon the wall, and every man took his weapons, and they went forth by bands to the straits of the mountain. 12:But when the Assyrians saw them, they sent to their leaders, which came to their captains and tribunes, and to every one of their rulers. 13:So they came to Holofernes' tent, and said to him that had the charge of all his things, Waken now our lord: for the slaves have been bold to come down against us to battle, that they may be utterly destroyed.

14:Then went in Bagoas, and knocked at the door of the tent; for he thought that he had slept with Judith. 15:But because none answered, he opened it, and went into the bed chamber, and found him cast upon the floor dead, and his head was taken from him 16:Therefore he cried with a loud voice, with weeping, and sighing, and a mighty cry, and rent his garments. 17:After he went into the tent where Judith lodged: and when he found her not, he leaped out to the people, and cried. 18:These slaves have dealt treacherously; one woman of the Hebrews has brought shame upon the house of King Nebuchadnezzar: for, behold, Holofernes lies upon the ground without a head.19:When the captains of the Assyrians' army heard these words, they rent their coats and their minds were wonderfully troubled, and there was a cry and a very great noise throughout the camp.

+/- September 19th. (Elul 22nd.)

The year +/- 151 B.C. Israel attacked the Assyrians

(Judith 15;1-7) 1:And when they that were in the tents heard, they were astonished at the thing that was done. 2:And fear and trembling fell upon them, so that there was no man that durst abide in the sight of his neighbor, but rushing out all together, they fled into every way of the plain, and of the hill country. 3:They also that had camped in the mountains round about Bethulia fled away. Then the children of Israel, every one that was a warrior among them, rushed out upon them. 4:Then sent Uzziah to Betomasthaim, and to the whole country of Israel to report what had happened, and that all should rush forth upon their enemies to destroy them.

5:Now when the children of Israel heard it, they all fell upon them with one consent, and slew them to Choba: likewise also they that came from Jerusalem, and from all the hill country, (for men had told them what things were done in the camp of their enemies) and they that were in Gileadites, and in Galileans, chased them with a great slaughter, until they were past Damascus and the borders thereof. 6:And the residue that dwelt at Bethulia, fell upon the camp of Assyrians, and spoiled them, and were greatly enriched. 7:And the children of Israel that returned from the slaughter had that which remained; and the villages and the cities, that were in the mountains and in the plain, got many spoils: for the multitude was very great.

+/- September 20th. (Elul 23rd.)

The year +/- 151 B.C. And for 30 days they plundered

(Judith 15;8-11.) 8:Then Joakim the high priest, and the ancients of the children of Israel that dwelt in Jerusalem, came to behold the good things that God had done for Israel, and to see Judith, and to salute her. 9:And when they came to her, they blessed her with one accord, and said to her, You are the exaltation of Jerusalem, you are the great glory of Israel, you are the great rejoicing of our nation.

10:You have done all these things by your hand: you have done much good for Israel, and God is pleased therewith: blessed are you of the Almighty Lord for evermore. And all the people said, So be it. 11:And the people took the spoil's from the camp for thirty days: and they gave to Judith, Holofernes tent, and all his things that were in it, the plates, beds, vessels, and all his stuff: and she took it and laid it on her mules; and made ready her carts, and filled them with the things given her.

+/- September 21st. (Elul 24th.)

The year +/- 514 B.C. The Lord stirred them to work on his house

(Haggai 1:14-15)14:And the Lord stirred up the spirit of Zerubbabel the son of Shealtiel, governor of Judah, and the spirit of Joshua the son of Josedech, the high priest, and the spirit of all the remnant of the people; and they came and did work in the house of the Lord of hosts, their God. 15:In the four and twentieth day of the sixth month, in the second year of Darius the King.

+/- September 21st. (Elul 24th.)

The year +/- 15 B.C. (Believed to be the birthday of the Virgin Mary) Via:The Catholic Church: Vatican City, Italy.

I received a letter from the the Catholic Church: it stated this: The Church's settled on this date to celebrate the birth of the Most-Pure Mother of God. After many studies over several years. September 21st. Which is the 24th of Elul.

+/- September 21st. (Elul 24th.)

The year +/-1 A.D The day Jesus was circumcised and named (As spoken in the covenant given to Abraham by God.)

(Genesis 17:10-14) 10:This is my covenant, which you shall keep, between me and you and your seed after you; Every man child among you shall be circumcised. 11:And you shall circumcise the flesh of your foreskin; and it shall be a token of the covenant between me and you. 12:And he that is eight days old shall be circumcised among you, every man child in your generations, he that is born in the house, or bought with money of any stranger, which is not of your seed.

13:He that is born in your house, and he that is bought with your money, must needs be circumcised; and my covenant shall be in your flesh for an everlasting covenant. 14:And the uncircumcised man child whose flesh of his foreskin is not circumcised, that soul shall be cut off from his people, for he has broken my covenant.

(The Law given to Moses concerting Child Birth)

(Leviticus 12:1-8) God told Moses about child birth: 1:And the Lord spoke to Moses, saying; 2:Speak to the children of Israel, saying, If a woman have conceived seed, and born a man child: then she shall be unclean seven days; according to the days of the separation for her infirmity shall she be unclean. 3:And in the eighth day the flesh of his foreskin shall be circumcised. 4:And she shall then continue in the blood of her purifying three and thirty days; she shall touch no hallowed thing, nor come into the sanctuary, until the days of her purifying be fulfilled. 5:But if she bear a maid child, then she shall be unclean two weeks, as in her separation: and she shall continue in the blood of her purifying threescore and six days. 6:And when the days of her purifying are fulfilled, for a son, or for a daughter, she shall bring a lamb of the first year for a burnt offering, and a young pigeon, or a turtledove, for a sin offering, to the door of the tabernacle of the congregation, to the priest. 7:Who shall offer it before the Lord, and make an atonement for her; and she shall be cleansed from the issue of her blood. This is the law for her that has born a male or a female. 8:And if she be not able to bring a lamb, then she shall bring two turtles, or two young pigeons; the one for the burnt offering, and the other for a sin offering: and the priest shall make an atonement for her, and she shall be clean.

Jesus was Named

(Luke 2:21) 21:And when eight days were accomplished for the circumcising of the child, his name was called Jesus, which was so named of the angel before he was conceived in the womb.

+/- September 22nd. (Elul 25th.)

The year: +/- 166 B.C. Mattathias and his sons ran

(1Maccabees 2:15-30) 15:The officers of the King in charge of enforcing the apostasy came to the city of Modein to organize the sacrifices. 16:Many of Israel joined them, but Mattathias and his sons gathered in a group apart. 17:The the officers of the King addressed Mattathias; "You are a leader, an honorable and great man in this city, supported by sons and kinsmen. 18:Come now and be the first to obey the Kings command, as all the gentiles and the men of Judah and those who were left in Jerusalem have done. Then you and your sons will be numbered among the Kings friends, and shall be enriched with silver and gold and many gifts. 19:But Mattathias answered in a loud voice: "Although all the gentiles in the Kings realm obey him, so that each forsake the religion of their Fathers and consent to the Kings orders, 20:yet my sons and I along with my kinsmen will keep the covenant of our forefathers.21;God forbid that we should forsake the law and the commandments. 22:We will not obey the words of the King nor depart from our religion in the slightest degree." 23:As he finished saying these words, a certain Hebrew came forward in the sight of all, to offer sacrifice on the alter in Modein according to the Kings order. 24:When Mattathias saw him, he sprang forward and killed him on the alter. 25:At the same time, he also killed the messenger of the King who was forcing them to sacrifice, and he tore down the alter. 26:This he showed zeal for the law, just as Phinehas did with Zimri, son of Salu. 27:Then Mattathias went through the city shouting: "Let everyone who is Zealous for the law and who stands by the covenant follow after me!"

28:There upon he fled to the mountains with his sons, leaving behind in the city their possessions. 29:Many who sought to live according to righteousness and religious customs went out into the desert to settle there, 30:they and their sons, their wives and their cattle, because misfortunes pressed so hard on them.

+/- September 22nd. (Elul 25th.)

The year +/- 401 B.C. The walls were finished being rebuilt

(Nehemiah 6:15) 15;So the walls were finished in the twenty and fifth day of the month Elul, in fifty and two days.

On left a picture of the outside walls, on the right a picture of the walkway on the walls, that were used for defense of the city.

+/- September 24nd. (Elul 27th.)

The year +/- 162 B.C. A vision of the war in Heaven

(2Maccabees 5:1-4) 1:About this time Antochus sent his second expedition into Egypt. 2:It then happened that all over the city, for nearly forty days, there appeared horsemen charging in midair,clad in garments interwoven with gold, companies fully armed with lances, 3:and drawn swords; squadrons of cavalry in a battle array charging and counter-charges on this side and that, with brandished shields and bristling spears, flights of arrows and flashes of gold ornaments together with armor of every sort. 4;Therefore all prayed that this vision might be a good omen.

+/- September 27th. (Elul 30th.)

Jacob was told to return to his own kinsman

(Genesis 31:1-19)1:And he heard the words of Laban's sons, saying, Jacob has taken away all that was our father's; and of that which was our father's had, he gotten all this glory. 2:And Jacob beheld the countenance of Laban, and, behold, it was not toward him as before.

3:And the Lord said to Jacob, Return to the land of your fathers, and to your kindred; and I will be with you. 4:And Jacob sent and called Rachel and Leah to the field to his flock. 5:And said to them, I have seen your father's countenance, that it is not toward me as before; but the God of my father has been with me. 6:And you know that with all my power I have served your father. 7:And your father has deceived me, and changed my wages ten times; but God suffered him not to hurt me. 8:If he said This, The speckled shall be your wages; then all the cattle bare speckled: and if he said This, The streaked shall be your wages; then bare all the cattle bore streaked young. 9:This God has taken away the cattle of your father, and given them to me. 10:And it came to pass at the time that the cattle conceived, that I lifted up mine eyes, and saw in a dream, and, behold, the rams which leaped upon the cattle were streaked, speckled, and grisled. 11:And the angel of God spoke to me in a dream, saying Jacob: And I said, Here I am. 12:And he said, Lift up now thine eyes, and see, all the rams which leap upon the cattle are streaked, speckled, and grisled: for I have seen all that Laban does to you. 13:I am the God of Bethel, where you anointed the pillar, and where you vowed a vow to me: now arise, what is yours out from this land, and return to the land of your kindred. 14:And Rachel and Leah answered and said to him, is there yet any portion or inheritance for us in our father's house? 15:Are we not also counted as strangers by him? For he has sold us, and has quite devoured also all our money. 16:For all the riches which God has taken from our father, that is ours, and our children's: now then, what ever God has told you to do, do it quickly. 17:Then Jacob rose up, and set his sons and his wives upon camels. 18:And he carried away all his cattle, and all his goods which he had gotten, the cattle of his getting, which he had gotten in Paddan-aram, for to go to Isaac his father in the land of Canaan. 19:And Laban went to shear his sheep: and Rachel had stolen the images that were her father's.

+/- September 27th. (Elul 30th.)

The year: +/- 327 B.C. (At the end of 180 days)

The King held a feast for seven days

(Esther 1:5-9) 5:And when these days were expired, the King made a feast to all the people that were present in Shushan the palace, both to great and small, seven days, in the court of the garden of the King's palace. 6:There were white, green, and blue, hangings, fastened with cords of fine linen and purple to silver rings and pillars of marble: the beds were of gold and silver, upon a pavement of red, and blue, and white, and black, marble. 7:And they gave them drink in vessels of gold, (the vessels being diverse one from another,) and royal wine in abundance, according to the state of the King. 8:And the drinking was according to the law; none did compel: for so the King had appointed to all the officers of his house, that they should do according to every man's pleasure. 9:Also Vashti the Queen made a feast for the women, in the royal house which belonged to King Ahasuerus.

+/- September 27th. (Elul 30th.)

Paul was delivered to a centurion

(Acts 27:1-2)1:And when it was determined that we should sail into Italy, they delivered Paul and certain other prisoners to one named Julius, a centurion of Augustus' band. 2And entering into a ship of Adramyttium, we launched, meaning to sail by the coasts of Asia; one Aristarchus, a Macedonian of Thessalonica, being with us.

+/- September 28th. (Tishul /Ephraim 1st.)

As written in the Torah +/- (10K) 25,237,500,000 B.A.

The First day, was called; Yom Reeshone

(As it is translated from the Greek text)

(Genesis 1:2-5) The Beginning. 2:And the earth was without form, and void; and darkness was upon the face of the deep. And the Spirit of God hovered over the face of the waters. 3:And God spoke, **Let it begin** and the earth started to take form. 4:And God saw it form and saw it was pleasing to him and said that it was good: and God divided the light from the darkness. 5:And God called the light Day, and the darkness he called Night. And there was evening and morning. This is the very first day.

Translated from Hebrew

(Genesis 1:2-5) 1:2: And the earth was in chaos: and darkness was upon the face of the deep. And the Spirit of God hovers upon the face of the waters. 3:And God said, Let there be order: and there was order. 4:And God will see the light that is good, and God will separate between the light that is good and the darkness. 5:And God will call to the light day an to the darkness called night and will be evening and will be morning one day.

+/- September 28th. (Tishul /Ephraim 1st.)

God changed the beginning of the months

(Tishul /Ephraim); Was the original beginning of the year. It was changed to Nissan / Abib in **(Exodus 12:2)** When God said this will now be the beginning of the year to you.

+/- September 28th. (Tishul /Ephraim 1st.)

The year +/- 3228 B.C. Noah removed the covering from the Ark:

(Genesis 8:13) 13:And it came to pass in the six hundredth and first year, in the first month, the first day of the month, the waters were dried up from off the earth: and Noah removed the covering of the ark, and looked, and behold, the face of the ground was dry.

+/- September 28th. (Tishul /Ephraim 1st.)

The year +/-1357 B.C. God spoke of The Blowing of Trumpets

(Leviticus 23:23-36) 23: And the LORD spoke to Moses, saying: 24:Speak to the children of Israel, saying, In the seventh month, in the first day of the month, shall you have a sabbath, a memorial of blowing of trumpets, an holy convocation. 25:You shall do no servile work on this day, but you shall offer an offering made by fire to the LORD.

26:And the LORD spoke to Moses, saying: 27:Also on the tenth day of this seventh month there shall be a day of atonement: it shall be an holy convocation to you; and you shall afflict your souls, and offer an offering made by fire to the LORD.
28;And you shall do no work in that same day: for it is a day of atonement, to make an atonement for you before the LORD your God. 29:For whatsoever soul it be that shall not be afflicted in that same day, he shall be cut off from among his people.
30:And what soever soul it be that does any work in that same day, the same soul will I destroy from among his people. 31:You shall do no manner of work: it shall be a statute for ever throughout your generations in all your dwellings.

32:It shall be to you a sabbath of rest, and you shall afflict your souls: in the ninth day of the month at evening , from evening unto evening, shall you celebrate your sabbath. 33;And the Lord spoke to Moses, saying; 34:Speak to the children of Israel, saying, The fifteenth day of this seventh month shall be the feast of tabernacles for seven days to the Lord. 35:On the first day shall be an holy convocation: you shall do no kind of work on this day. 36:Seven days you shall offer an offering made by fire to the Lord: on the eighth day shall be an holy convocation to you; and you shall offer an offering made by fire to the Lord: for it is a solemn assembly; and you shall do no kind work on it.

+/- September 28th. (Tishul /Ephraim 1st.)

The year +/- 831 B.C. Jehoiada was made King

(2Kings 11:11-21) 11:And the guard stood, every man with his weapons in his hand, round about the King, from the right corner of the temple to the left corner of the temple, along by the altar and the temple. 12:And he brought forth the king's son, and put the crown upon him, and gave him the testimony; and they made him King, and anointed him; and they clapped their hands, and said, God save the King.
13:And when Athaliah heard the noise of the guard and of the people, she came to the people into the temple of the Lord. 14:And when she looked, behold, the King stood by a pillar, as the manner was, and the princes and the trumpeters by the King, and all the people of the land rejoiced, and blew with trumpets: and Athaliah rent her clothes, and cried, Treason, Treason. 15:But Jehoiada the priest commanded the captains of the hundreds, the officers of the host, and said to them; "Bring her forth without the ranges: and him that follows her kill with the sword. For the priest had said, Let her not be slain in the house of the Lord. 16:And they laid hands on her; and she went by the way by the which the horses came into the King's house: and there was she slain. 17:And Jehoiada made a covenant between the Lord, and the King, and the people that they should be the Lord's people; between the King also and the people. 18:And all the people of the land went into the house of Baal, and broke it down; his altars and his images brake they in pieces thoroughly, and slew Mattan the priest of Baal before the altars. And the priest appointed officers over the house of the Lord. 19;And he became the ruler over hundreds, and the captains, and the guard, and all the people of the land; and they brought down the king from the house of the Lord, and came by the way of the gate of the guard to the King's house. And he sat on the throne of the Kings. 20;And all the people of the land rejoiced, and the city was in quiet when they slew Athaliah with the sword beside the King's house. 21:Seven years old was Jehoiada when he began to reign.

+/- September 28th. (Tishul /Ephraim 1st.)

David prepared for the Blowing of Trumpets

(1Chronicles 15:1-16:37) 1:And David made him houses in the city of David, and prepared a place for the ark of God, and pitched for it a tent. 2:Then David said, None ought to carry the ark of God but the Levites: for they have been chosen by the Lord to carry the ark of God, and to minister to him for ever. 3:And David gathered all Israel together to Jerusalem, to bring up the ark of the Lord to his place, which he had prepared for it. 4:And David assembled the children of Aaron, and the Levites. 5:Of the sons of Kohath; Uriel the chief, and his brethren an hundred and twenty. 6:Of the sons of Merari; Asaiah the chief, and his brethren two hundred and twenty. 7:Of the sons of Gershom; Joel the chief, and his brethren an hundred and thirty. 8;Of the sons of Elizaphan; Shemaiah the chief, and his brethren two hundred. 9:Of the sons of Hebron; Eliel the chief, and his brethren fourscore.

10:Of the sons of Uzziel; Amminadab the chief, and his brethren an hundred and twelve. 11:And David called for Zadok and Abiathar the priests, and for the Levites, for Uriel, Asaiah, and Joel, Shemaiah, and Eliel, and Amminadab, 12:And said to them, you are the chief of the fathers of the Levites: sanctify yourselves, both you and your brethren, that you may bring up the ark of the Lord God of Israel to the place that I have prepared for it. 13:For because you did not not at the first, the Lord our God made a breach upon us, for that we sought him not after the due order. 14:So the priests and the Levites sanctified themselves to bring up the ark of the Lord God of Israel. 15:And the children of the Levites bare the ark of God upon their shoulders with the poles thereon, as Moses commanded according to the word of the Lord. 16:And David spoke to the chief of the Levites to appoint their brethren to be the singers with instruments of music, psalteries and harps and cymbals, sounding, by lifting up the voice with joy.

17:So the Levites appointed Heman the son of Joel; and of his brethren, Asaph the son of Berechiah; and of the sons of Merari their brethren, Ethan the son of Kushaiah. 18:And with them their brethren of the second degree, Zechariah, Ben, and Jaaziel, and Shemiramoth, and Jehiel, and Unni, Eliab, and Benaiah, and Maaseiah, and Mattithiah, and Elipheleh, and Mikneiah, and Obededom, and Jeiel, the porters. 19:So the singers, Heman, Asaph, and Ethan, were appointed to sound with cymbals of brass; 20;And Zechariah, and Aziel, and Shemiramoth, and Jehiel, and Unni, and Eliab, and Maasciah, and Benaiah, with psalteries on Alamoth, 21:and Mattithiah, and Elipheleh, and Mikneiah, and Obededom, and Jeiel, and Azaziah, with harps on the Sheminith to excel. 22:And Chenaniah, chief of the Levites, was for song: he instructed about the song, because he was skilful. 23:And Berechiah and Elkanah were doorkeepers for the ark.

24:And Shebaniah, and Jehoshaphat, and Nethaneel, and Amasai, and Zechariah, and Benaiah, and Eliezer, the priests, did blow with the trumpets before the ark of God: and Obededom and Jehiah were doorkeepers for the ark.25:So David, and the elders of Israel, and the captains over thousands, went to bring up the ark of the covenant of the Lord out of the house of Obededom with joy. 26:And it came to pass, when God helped the Levites that bare the ark of the covenant of the Lord, that they offered seven bullocks and seven rams. 27:And David was clothed with a robe of fine linen, and all the Levites that bare the ark,and the singers, and Chenaniah the master of the song with the singers: David also had upon him an ephod of linen. 28:This all Israel brought up the ark of the covenant of the Lord with shouting,

and with sound of the cornet, and with trumpets, and with cymbals, making a noise with psalteries and harps. 29:And it came to pass, as the ark of the covenant of the Lord came to the city of David, that Michal the daughter of Saul looking out at a window saw; King David dancing and playing: and she despised him in her heart.

16:1: So they brought the ark of God, and set it in the midst of the tent that David had pitched for it: and they offered burnt sacrifices and peace offerings before God. 2:And when David had made an end of offering the burnt offerings and the peace offerings, he blessed the people in the name of the Lords. 3:And he dealt to every one of Israel, both man and woman, to every one a loaf of bread, and a good piece of flesh, and a flagon of wine. 4:And he appointed certain ones of the Levites to minister before the ark of the LORD, and to record, and to thank and praise the LORD God of Israel.

5:Asaph the chief, and next to him Zechariah, Jeiel, and Shemiramoth, and Jehiel, and Mattithiah, and Eliab, and Benaiah, and Obededom: and Jeiel with psalteries and with harps; but Asaph made a sound with cymbals. 6:Benaiah also and Jahaziel the priests with trumpets continually, before the ark of the covenant of God. 7:Then on that day David delivered first this psalm to thank the Lord, and put it into the hand of Asaph and his brethren. 8:Give thanks to the Lord, call upon his name, make known his deeds among the people. 9:Sing to him, sing psalms to him, talk all of you of all his wondrous works.

10:Glory you in his holy name: let the heart of them rejoice that seek the Lord. 11:Seek the Lord and his strength, seek his face continually. 12:Remember his marvelous works that he has done, his wonders, and the judgments of his mouth. 13:O' you seed of Israel his servant, you children of Jacob, his chosen ones. 14:He is the Lord our God; his judgments are in all the earth.

15:Be you mindful always of his covenant; the word which he commanded to a thousand generations. 16:Even of the covenant which he made with Abraham, and of his oath to Isaac. 17:And has confirmed the same to Jacob for a law, and to Israel for an everlasting covenant; 18:Saying, to you will I give the land of Canaan, the lot of your inheritance. 19:When you were but few, even a few, and strangers in it.

20:And when they went from nation to nation, and from one kingdom to another people. 21:He suffered no man to do them wrong: yea, he reproved kings for their sakes. 22:Saying; Touch not mine anointed, and do my prophets no harm. 23:Sing to the Lord, all the earth; show forth from day to day his salvation. 24:Declare his glory among the heathen; his marvelous works among all nations.
25:For great is the Lord, and greatly to be praised: he also is to be feared above all gods.

26:For all the gods of the people are idols: but the Lord made the heavens. 27:Glory and honor are in his presence; strength and gladness are in his place. 28;Give to the Lord, you kindred of the people, give to the Lord glory and strength. 29:Give to the Lord the glory due to his name: bring an offering, and come before him: worship the Lord in the beauty of holiness.

30:Fear before him, all the earth: the world also shall be stable, that it be not moved. 31:Let the heavens be glad, and let the earth rejoice: and let men say among the nations, The Lord reigns. 32:Let the sea roar, and the fulness thereof: let the fields rejoice, and all that is therein. 33:Then shall the trees of the wood sing out at the presence of the Lord, because he comes to judge the earth. 34:O give thanks to the Lord; for he is good; and his mercy endures forever.

35;And say you, Save us, O God of our salvation, and gather us together, and deliver us from the heathen, that we may give thanks to your holy name, and glory in your praise. 36:Blessed be the Lord God of Israel for ever and ever. And all the people said, Amen, and praised the Lord.37:So he left there before the ark of the covenant of the Lord Asaph and his brethren, to minister before the ark continually, as every day's work required:

The Traditional trumpets used to bring in the New year: Tishul /Ephraim 1st.

+/- September 28th. (Tishul /Ephraim 1st.)

The year +/- 401 B.C. Ezra read from the Book of Moses

(Nehemiah 7:73-8:12) 73:So the priests, and the Levites, and the porters, and the singers, and some of the people, and the Nethinims, and all Israel, dwelt in their cities; and when the seventh month came, the children of Israel were in their cities. **8:1:**And all the people gathered themselves together as one man into the street that was before the water gate; and they spoke to Ezra the scribe to bring the book of the law of Moses, which the Lord had commanded to Israel.

2:And Ezra the priest brought the law before the congregation both of men and
women, and all that could hear with understanding, upon the first day of the seventh
month. 3:And he read therein before the street that was before the water gate from
the morning until midday, before the men and the women, and those that could
understand; and the ears of all the people were attentive to the book of the law.

4:And Ezra the scribe stood upon a pulpit of wood, which they had made for the
purpose; and beside him stood Mattithiah, and Shema, and Anaiah, and Urijah, and
Hilkiah, and Maaseiah, on his right hand; and on his left hand, Pedaiah, and
Mishael, and Malchiah, and Hashum, and Hashbadana, Zechariah, and Meshullam.
5:And Ezra opened the book in the sight of all the people; (for he was above all the
people;) and when he opened it, all the people stood up.

6:And Ezra blessed the Lord, the great God. And all the people answered, Amen,
Amen, with lifting up their hands: and they bowed their heads, and worshiped the
Lord with their faces to the ground. 7:Also Jeshua, and Bani, and Sherebiah, Jamin,
Akkub, Shabbethai, Hodijah, Maaseiah, Kelita, Azariah, Jozabad, Hanan, Pelaiah,
and the Levites, caused the people to understand the law: and the people stood in
their place. 8:So they read in the book in the law of God distinctly, and gave the
sense, and caused them to understand the reading.

9:And Nehemiah, which is the Tirshatha, and Ezra the priest the scribe, and the
Levites that taught the people, said to all the people, This day is holy to the Lord
your God; mourn not, nor weep. For all the people wept, when they heard the words
of the law. 10:Then he said to them, Go your way, eat the fat, and drink the sweet,
and send portions to them for whom nothing is prepared: for this day is holy to our
Lord: neither be you sorry; for the joy of the Lord is your strength.

11:So the Levites stilled all the people, saying, Hold your peace, for the day is holy;
neither be you grieved. 12;And all the people went their way to eat, and to drink,
and to send portions, and to make great mirth, because they had understood the
words, that were declared to them.

+/- September 28th. (Tishul /Ephraim 1st.)

They fasted at Mizpah

(1 Maccabees 3:46-54) 46:Then they assembled and went to Mizpah near
Jerusalem, because there was formerly, at Mizpah a place of prayer for Israel.
47:That day they fasted and wore sackcloth; they sprinkled ashes on their heads and
tore their closes. 48:They unrolled the scroll of the law, to learn about the things, for
which the Gentiles consulted the images of their idols.

49:They brought with them the priestly vestments, the first fruits, and the tithes; and
they brought forward the Nazirites who have completed the time of their vows.
50:And they cried aloud to Heaven: “What shall we do with these men,
and where should we take them?
51:For your sanctuary has been trampled on and profaned, and your priest are in
mourning and humiliation.

52:Noe the Gentiles have gathered together against us to destroy us. You know what they plot against us. 53:How shall we be able to resist them unless you help us?" 54:Then they blew the trumpets, and cried out loudly.

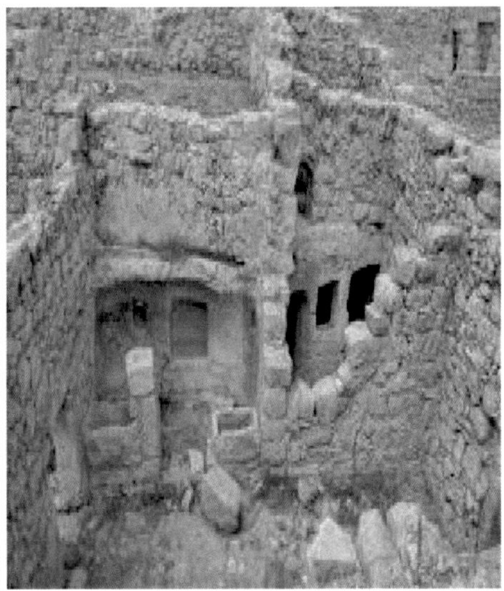

Above; Mizpah, where they stayed and fasted

+/- September 28th. (Tishul /Ephraim 1st.)

The winds were contrary:

(Acts 27:3-4) 4;And the next day we touched at Sidon. And Julius courteously entreated Paul, and gave him liberty to go to his friends to refresh himself. 4;And when we had launched from there, we sailed under Cyprus, because the winds were contrary.

+/- September 29th. (Tishul /Ephraim 2nd.)

The Second day, was called:
Yom Shaynee, God separated the waters:

(Genesis 1:6-8) 6;And God said, Let there be a firmament in the midst of the waters, and let it divide the waters from the waters. 7;And God made the firmament, and divided the waters which were under the firmament from the waters which were above the firmament: and it was so. 8;And God called the firmament Heaven. And the evening and the morning were the second day.

+/- September 29th. (Tishul /Ephraim 2nd.)

Laban was informed

(Genesis 31;22-23) 22:And it was told Laban on the third day that Jacob had fled. 23;And he took his brethren with him, and pursued after him seven days journey, when they overtook him on mount Gilead.

+/- September 29th. (Tishul /Ephraim 2nd.)

The year +/- 401 B.C.E. They learned about the Lords feast

(Nehemiah 8:13-15) 13;And on the second day were gathered together the chief of the fathers of all the people, the priests, and the Levites, to Ezra the scribe, even to understand the words of the law. 14;And they found written in the law which the Lord had commanded by Moses, that the children of Israel should dwell in booths in the feast of the seventh month.15;And that they should publish and proclaim in all their cities, and in Jerusalem, saying; Go forth to the mount, and fetch olive branches, and pine branches, and myrtle branches and palm branches and branches of thick trees, to make booths, as it is written.

+/- September 29th. (Tishul /Ephraim 2nd.)

Paul sailed to Lycia

(Acts 27:5) 27:And when we had sailed over the sea of Cilicia and Pamphylia, we came to Myra, a city of Lycia.

The Cove where they would have landed.   The ruins of Myra

+/- September 30th. (Tishul /Ephraim 3rd.)

The Third day called: Yom Shlee'shee,
God formed dry land and covered it

(Genesis 1:9-13) 9;And God said, Let the waters under the heaven be gathered together to one place, and let the dry land appear: and it was so. 10:And God called the dry land Earth; and the gathering together of the waters called he Seas: and God saw that it was good. 11;And God said, Let the earth bring forth grass, the herb yielding seed, and the fruit tree yielding fruit after his kind, whose seed is in itself, upon the earth: and it was so. 12;And the earth brought forth grass, and herb yielding seed after his kind, and the tree yielding fruit, whose seed was in itself, after his kind: and God saw that it was good. 13;And the evening and the morning were the third day.

365

And the Lord brought forth grass, flowers, and trees of all kinds and saw it was good.

+/- September 30th. (Tishul /Ephraim 3rd.)

The Fast of the seventh month turned to a Feast

(Zechariah 8:19) 19;This says the Lord of hosts; The Fast of the Fourth month, and the Fast of the Fifth, and the Fast of the **Seventh**, and the Fast of the tenth month, shall be to the house of Judah joy and gladness, and cheerful feasts; therefore love the truth and peace.

It was during the month of Elul

The year +/- 4977 B.C.E. The Birth of Abel

(Genesis 4:2) 2:Next she bore his brother Able.
Able became a keeper of the flocks, and Cane a tiller of the soil.

Chapter 10:October -Tishul /Ephraim

It is the 7th. month on the Hebrew calendar
In Hebrew this month is called:Tishul / Ephraim,
which means:Beginning / Gift
Tribe of Dan, means:(He has vindicated us)
The stone of (White Jade) represents this tribe.
Dan:(The 1st.) Son of Bilhah the hand maiden of Rachel.
(Was believed to have been born in this month.)
(Spirit of Truth)

+/-October 1st. (Tishul /Ephraim 4th.)

The Fourth day called: Yom Revee'ee

On the Day, God put the Sun in the sky

(Genesis 1:14-19) 14:And God said, Let there be lights in the firmament of the
heaven to divide the day from the night; and let them be for signs, and for seasons,
and for days, and years: 15:And let them be for lights in the firmament of the
heaven to give light upon the earth: and it was so. 16:And God made two great
lights; the greater light to rule the day, and the lesser light to rule the night: he made
the stars also. 17:And God set them in the firmament of the heaven to give light
upon the earth. 18:And to rule over the day and over the night, and to divide the
light from the darkness: and God saw that it was good. 19:And the evening and the
morning were the fourth day.

+/-October 1st. (Tishul /Ephraim 4th.)

Laban confronts Jacob

(Genesis 31:24-54) 24:And God came to Laban the Syrian in a dream that night,
and said to him, Take heed that you speak not to Jacob either good or bad. 25:Then
Laban overtook Jacob. Now Jacob had pitched his tent in the mount: and Laban
with his brethren pitched in the mount of Gilead. 26And Laban said to Jacob, What
have you done, that you hast stolen away unawares to me, and carried away my
daughters, as captives taken with the sword?

27:Why did you flee away secretly, and steal from me; and did not tell me you were going, I might have sent you away with mirth, and with songs, with tambourines, and with harp? 28;And you did not even let me to kiss my sons and my daughters, goodbye? You have now done foolishly in doing this. 29:It is in the power of my hand to hurt you: but the God of your father spoke to me last night, saying; Take you heed that you speak not to Jacob either good or bad. 30:And now, though you want to be gone, because you surly long after your father's house, yet why have you stolen my gods? 31:And Jacob answered and said to Laban, Because I was afraid: for I said; Peradventure you would take by force your daughters from me. 32:With whom soever you find your gods, let them not live: before our brethren, decide what ever is yours that I have with me, and take it with you.. For Jacob knew not that Rachel had stolen them. 33:And Laban went into Jacob's tent, and into Leah's tent, and into the two maidservants' tents; but he did not find them. Then went he out of Leah's tent, and entered into Rachel's tent. 34:Now Rachel had taken the images, and put them in the camel's furniture, and sat upon them. And Laban searched all the tent, but did nit find them. 35:And she said to her father, Let it not displease my lord that I cannot rise up before your; for the custom of women is upon me. And he searched, but found not the images. 36:And Jacob was enraged, and asked Laban: What is my trespass? what is my sin, that you have so fiercely pursued after me? 37:Now that you have ransacked all my things, have you found a single thing taken from your belongings?If so put it here before our kinsmen. And let them decide between us. 38:This twenty years have I been with you; your ewes and your she goats have not lost their young, and the rams of your flock, I have not eaten. 39:That which was torn from beast I did not bring to you; but I bare the loss of it; of my hand did you require it, whether stolen by day, or stolen by night. 40:This I was; in the day the drought consumed me, and the frost by night; and my sleep departed from mine eyes. 41:This have I been twenty years in your house; I served you fourteen years for your two daughters, and six years for your cattle: and you have changed my wages ten times. 42:Except the God of my father, the God of Abraham, and the fear of Isaac, had been with me, surely you would have sent me away now empty. God has seen my affliction and the labor of my hands, and rebuked you last night. 43:And Laban answered and said to Jacob: "These daughters are my daughters, and these children are my children, and these cattle are my cattle, and all that you see is mine. And what can I do this day for these my daughters, or for their children which they have born? 44:Now therefore come you, let us make a covenant, I and you; and let it be for a witness between me and you. 45:And Jacob took a stone, and set it up for a pillar. 46:And Jacob said to his brethren, Gather stones; and they took stones, and made an heap: and they did eat there upon the heap. 47:And Laban called it Jegar-sahadutha: but Jacob called it Galeed. 48:And Laban said, This heap is a witness between me and your this day. Therefore was the name of it called Galeed; 49:And Mizpah; for he said; "Let the Lord watch between me and you, when we are absent one from another. 50:If you shall afflict my daughters, or if you shall take other wives beside my daughters, no man is with us; see, God is our witness between me and you. 51:And Laban said to Jacob, Behold this heap, and behold this pillar, which I have cast between me and you. 52:This heap will also be a witness, and this pillar will be witness, that I will not pass over this heap to you, and that you shall not pass over this heap and this pillar to me, for harm.

53:The God of Abraham, and the God of Nahor, the God of their father, judge between us. And Jacob swore by the fear of his father Isaac. 54:Then Jacob offered sacrifice upon the mount, and called his brethren to eat bread: and they did eat bread, and stayed all night on the mount.

+/-October 1st. (Tishul /Ephraim 4th.)

Paul sailed to Italy

(Acts 27:6-7) 6:And there the centurion found a ship of Alexandria sailing into Italy; and he put us therein. 7:And when we had sailed slowly many days, and scarce were come over against Cnidus, the wind not suffering us, we sailed under Crete, over against Salmone;

+/- October 2nd. (Tishul /Ephraim 5th.)

The Fifth day called: Yom Khah'mee'shee God created the creatures of the waters and the air

(Genesis 1:20-23) 20:And God said, Let the waters bring forth abundantly the moving creature that has life, and fowl that may fly above the earth, in the open firmament of heaven. 21:And God created great whales, and every living creature that moves, which the waters brought forth abundantly, after their kind, and every winged fowl after his kind: and God saw that it was good. 22:And God blessed them, saying, Be fruitful, and multiply, and fill the waters in the seas, and let fowl multiply in the earth. 23:And the evening and the morning were the fifth day.

+/-October 2nd. (Tishul /Ephraim 5th.)

Laban said goodbye to his daughters and grand children(Genesis 31:55-32:5) 55:And early in the morning Laban rose up, and kissed his sons and his daughters, and blessed them: and Laban departed, and returned to his place. **32:1:**And Jacob went on his way, and the angels of God met with him. 2:And when Jacob saw them, he said: "This is God's encampment" and he called the name of that place Mahanaim. 3:And Jacob sent messengers before him to Esau his brother unto the land of Seir, the country of Edom. 4:And he commanded them, saying, This shall you speak to my lord Esau; your servant Jacob said this: I have sojourned with Laban, and stayed there until now, 5:and I have oxen, and asses, flocks, and menservants, and women servants: and I have sent to tell my lord, that I may find grace in your sight.

+/- October 2nd. (Tishul /Ephraim 5th.)

The year +/- 324 B.C. Esther was made Queen

(Esther 2:10-21)15:Now when the turn of Esther, the daughter of Abihail the uncle of Mordecai, who had taken her for his daughter, time had come to go in to the King, she asked for nothing but what Hegai the King's chamberlain, the keeper of the women, appointed. And Esther obtained favor in the sight of all them that looked upon her. 16:So Esther was taken into King Ahasuerus to his royal house in the tenth month, which is the month Tishul, on the second day, in the seventh year of his reign. 17:And the King loved Esther above all the other women, and she obtained grace and favor in his sight more than all the virgins; so that he set the royal crown upon her head, and made her queen instead of Vashti. 18:Then the King made a great feast for all his princes and his servants, even Esther's feast; and he made a release to the provinces, and gave gifts, according to the state of the King. 19:And when the virgins were gathered together the second time, then Mordecai sat in the King's gate; Esther had not told anyone of her family or her people. 20:As Mordecai had told her to do, for Esther did obey whatever Mordecai had told her, as she did, when she was being brought up by him. 21:In those days, while Mordecai sat in the King's gate, two of the King's chamberlains, Bigthan and Teresh, of those which kept the door, were wroth, and sought to lay hand on the King Ahasuerus. 22:And the thing was heard by Mordecai, who told to Esther the Queen; and Esther told the King of what was heard, by Mordecai's. 23:And when inquisition was made of the matter, it was found out; therefore they were both hanged on a tree: and it was written in the book of the chronicles before the King.

+/- October 3rd. (Tishul /Ephraim 6th.)

The Sixth day called: Yom Ha'shee'shee

God created the animals and the angles asked to make man in their Image

(Genesis 1:24-31) 24:And God said, Let the earth bring forth the living creatures of all kinds, cattle, and creeping thing, and beast of the earth after his kind: and it was so. 25:And God made the beast of the earth after his kind, and cattle after their kind, and every thing that creeps upon the earth after his kind: and God saw that it was perfect. 26:And the Elohim,(god head, or angels, who were in charge over the earth.) Said; let us make man in our image, after our own likeness: and let them have dominion over the fish of the sea, and over the fowl of the air, and over the cattle, and over all the earth, and over every creeping thing that creeps upon the earth. And God said; let it be so. 27:So the Angels created man in their own images, in the images of them did they created them; both male and female they created them. 28:And God blessed them, and God said to them, Be fruitful, and multiply, and replenish the earth, and subdue it: and have dominion over the fish of the sea, and over the fowl of the air, and over every living thing that moves upon the earth. 29:And God said, Behold, I have given you every herb bearing seed, which is upon the face of all the earth, and every tree, in the which is the fruit of a tree yielding seed; to you it shall be for food. 30:And to every beast of the earth, and to every fowl of the air, and to every thing that creeps upon the earth, where in there is life, I have given every green herb for food: and it was so. 31:And God saw every thing that he had made, and, behold, it was very good. And the evening and the morning were the sixth day.

+/- October 3rd. (Tishul /Ephraim 6th.)

Jacob sent peace offerings to Esau

(Genesis 32:6-20)6:And the messengers returned to Jacob, saying, We came to your brother Esau, and also he comes to meet your, and four hundred men with him.

7:Then Jacob was greatly afraid and distressed:and he divided the people that was with him, and the flocks, and herds, and the camels, into two bands; 8:And said, If Esau come to the one company, and strike it, then the other companies which are left shall escape. 9:And Jacob said, O God of my father Abraham, and God of my father Isaac, the Lord which said to me, Return to your country, and to your kindred, and there I will deal well with you. 10:I am not worthy of the least of all the mercies, and of all the truth, which you have showed to your servant; for with my staff I passed over this Jordan alone; and now I have become two bands. 11:Deliver me, I pray you, from the hand of my brother, from the hand of Esau: for I fear him, lest he will come and strike me, and the mothers with the children.

12:And you said, I will surely do you good, and make your seed as the sand of the sea, which cannot be numbered for multitude. 13:And he lodged there that same night; and took of that which came to his hand a present for Esau his brother; 14:Two hundred she goats, and twenty he goats, two hundred ewes, and twenty rams, 15:Thirty milch camels with their colts, forty kine, and ten bulls, twenty she asses, and ten foals. 16:And he delivered them to the hand of his servants, every drove by themselves; and said unto his servants, Pass over before me, and put a space between drove and drove. 17:And he commanded the foremost saying;"When Esau my brother meets you, and ask you, saying, Whose are you? and where are you going? and whose are these before you? 18:Then you shall say: They are your servant Jacob's; it is a present sent to his lord Esau: and, behold, also he is behind us." 19:And so he told the second, and the third, and all that followed the droves, saying, On this manner shall you say to Esau, when you find him. 20:And say also, Behold, your servant Jacob is behind us. For he said, I will appease him with the presents that go before me, and afterward I will see his face; peradventure he will accept of me.

+/-October 4th. (Tishul /Ephraim 7th.)

The Seventh day called: Yom Shabbat God rested and called the Day Holy

(Genesis 2:1-3)1:This the heavens and the earth were finished, and all the host of them. 2:And on the seventh day God ended his work which he had made; and he rested on the seventh day from all his work which he had made. 3:And God blessed the seventh day, and sanctified it: because that in it he had rested from all his work which God created and made.

+/-October 4th. (Tishul /Ephraim 7th.)

The year +/-327 B.C. The King requested Queen Vashti presence, at the Feast

(Esther 1:10-21) 10: On the seventh day, when the heart of the King was merry with wine, he commanded Mehuman, Biztha, Harbona, Bigtha, and Abagtha, Zethar, and Carcas, the seven chamberlains that served in the presence of Ahasuerus the King, 11:To bring Vashti the Queen before the King with the crown royal, to show the people and the princes her beauty: for she was fair to look on. 12:But the queen Vashti refused to come at the King's commandment by his chamberlains:

therefore was the King very wroth, and his anger burned in him. 13:Then the King said to the wise men, which knew the times, (for so was the King's manner toward all that knew law and judgment. 14:And the next to him was Carshena, Shethar, Admatha, Tarshish, Meres, Marsena, and Memucan, the seven princes of Persia and Media, which saw the King's face, and which sat the first in the kingdom.) 15:What shall we do to the queen Vashti according to law, because she has not performed the commandment of the King Ahasuerus by the chamberlains? 16;And Memucan answered before the King and the princes, Vashti the queen has not done wrong to the King only, but also to all the princes, and to all the people that are in all the provinces of the King Ahasuerus. 17:For this deed of the queen shall come abroad to all women, so that they shall despise their husbands in their eyes, when it shall be reported, The King Ahasuerus commanded Vashti the queen to be brought in before him, but she came not. 18:Likewise shall the ladies of Persia and Media say this day to all the King's princes, which have heard of the deed of the queen. This shall there arise too much contempt and wrath. 19:If it please the King, let there go a royal commandment from him, and let it be written among the laws of the Persians and the Medes, that it be not altered, That Vashti come no more before King Ahasuerus; and let the King give her royal estate to another that is better than she. 20:And when the King's decree which he shall make shall be published throughout all his empire, (for it is great,) all the wives shall give to their husbands honor, both to great and small. 21:And the saying pleased the King and the princes; and the King did according to the word of Memucan:

+/- October 5th. (Tishul /Ephraim 8th.)

The Year +/- 4885 B.C. The Creation of the perfect Man, (Adam and Lilith)

(Genesis 2:7) 7:And the Lord God formed man out of the dust of the ground. Both male and female and he breathed into their nostrils the breath of life; and mankind became living souls.

+/- October 6th. (Tishul /Ephraim 9th.)

They sailed to Fair Havens

(Acts 27:8) 8:And hardly passing it, came to a place which is called: The Fair Havens; close to where the city of Lassa was.

+/- October 7th. (Tishul /Ephraim 10th.)

Jacob wrestled with God

(Genesis 32:21-33:20) 21:So went the present over before him: and himself lodged that night in the company. 22:And he rose up that night, and took his two wives, and his two women servants, and his eleven sons, and passed over the ford Jabbok. 23:And he took them, and sent them over the brook, and sent over that he had. 24:And Jacob was left alone; and there wrestled a man with him until the breaking of the day. 25:And when he saw that he prevailed not against him, he touched the hollow of his thigh; and the hollow of Jacob's thigh was out of joint, as he wrestled with him.

26:And he said, Let me go, for the day breaking. And he said; I will not let you go, unless you bless me. 27:And he said to him, What is your name? And he said, Jacob. 28:And he said, "You shall be called Jacob no more, but Israel: for as a prince you have wrestled with God and Men and have prevailed." 29:And Jacob asked him, and said, Tell me, I beg you, your name. And he said, Why is it that you ask after my name? And he blessed him there. 30:And Jacob called the name of the place Penile: for I have seen God face to face, and my life is preserved. 31;And as he passed over Penuel the sun rose upon him, and he hobbled upon his thigh. 32:Therefore the children of Israel eat not of e sinew which shrank, which is upon the hollow of the thigh, to this day: because he touched the hollow of Jacob's thigh, in the sinew that shrank. **33:1:**And Jacob lifted up his eyes, and looked, and, behold, Esau came, and with him four hundred men. And he divided the children unto Leah, and unto Rachel, and unto the two handmaids. 2:And he put the handmaids and their children foremost, and Leah and her children after, and Rachel and Joseph furthest. 3:And he went over first to them, but had fallen to the ground, seven times, until he came near to his brother. 4:And Esau ran to meet him, and embraced him, and fell on his neck, and kissed him: and they wept. 5:And he lifted up his eyes, and saw the women and the children; and said, Who are these people with you? And he said, The children which God had graciously given your servant. 6:Then the handmaidens came near, they and their children, and they bowed themselves. 7:And Leah also with her children came near, and bowed themselves: and then came Joseph near and Rachel, and they bowed themselves. 8:And he said, What do you mean by all these animals, which I met? And he said, "These are to find grace in your sight my lord. 9:And Esau said, I have enough, my brother; keep that what you have to yourself. 10:And Jacob said, No, I beg you, if I have found grace in your sight, then receive my present at my hand: for therefore I have seen your face, as though I had seen the face of God, and you were pleased with me. 11:Take, I beg you, my blessing that is brought to you; because God had dealt graciously with me, and because I have enough. And he urged him, and he took it. 12:And he said, Let us take our journey, and let us go, and I will go before you. 13:And he said to him, My lord knows that the children,are young, and the flocks and herds with young are with me: and if men should overdrive them one day, all the flock will die. 14:Let my lord, I beg you, pass over before his servant: and I will lead on softly, according as the cattle that go's before me and the children be able to endure, until I come to my lord and to Seir. 15:And Esau said, Let me now leave with you some of the men that are with me. And he said, What need is it? let me find grace in your sight my lord. 16:So Esau returned that day on his way to Seir. 17;And Jacob journeyed to Succoth, and there he put up a tent for himself, and made booths for his cattle, therefore the name of the place, is called Succoth.

+/- October 7th. (Tishul /Ephraim 10th.)

(A Fast day) The year +/-1357 B.C. God spoke of Yom Kipper, the Holiest day of the year

Begins at dark on the 9th. Tishul and ends at dark on the 10th.

(Leviticus 23:27-32) 27:Also on the tenth day of this seventh month there shall be a day of atonement: it shall be an Holy Convocation to you; and you shall afflict your souls, and offer an offering made by fire to the Lord.

28:And you shall do no work in that same day: for it is a day of atonement, to make an atonement for you, before the Lord your God. 29:For what soever soul it be that shall not be afflicted in that same day, he shall be cut off from among his people. 30:And what soever soul it be that does any work in that same day, the same soul will I destroy from among his people. 31:You shall do no manner of work: it shall be a statute for ever throughout your generations in all your dwellings. 32:It shall be to you a sabbath of rest, and you shall afflict your souls: in the ninth day of the month at evening, until the evening of the tenth day, shall you celebrate and hold this sabbath.

+/- October 7th. (Tishul /Ephraim 10th.)

The year +/- 151 B.C. Judith gave all the things from Holofernes tent

(Judith 16:18-19) 18:The people went to Jerusalem to worship God; when they were purified, they offered there holocausts, free-will offerings, and gifts. 19:Judith dedicated, as a votive offering to God, all the things in Holofernes that the people had given her, as well as the canopy that she herself had taken from his bedroom.

+/- October 7th. (Tishul /Ephraim 10th.)

The year +/- 169 B.C. Heliodorus was flogged by Heaven

(2Maccabees 3;22-35)22:While they were imploring the almighty Lord to keep the deposit safe and secure for those who had placed them in trust. 23:Heliodorus went on with his plan. 24:but just as he was approaching the treasury with his bodyguards, an angel of the Lord manifested himself in such a way that those who have been bold enough to follow Heliodorus were panic stricken at God's power and ran away in terror. 25:There appeared to them a richly caparisoned horse, mounted by a dreadful rider. Charging furiously, the horse attacked Heliodorus with its front hoofs. The rider was seen wearing golden armor. 26;Then two other young men, remarkably strong, strikingly beautiful, and splendidly attired, appeared before him. Standing on each side of him, they flogged him unceasingly until they had given him innumerable blows. 27:Suddenly he fell to the ground, enveloped in great darkness. Men picked him up and laid him on a stretcher. 28:The man who a moment before had entered that treasury with a great retinue and his body guard was carried away helpless, having dearly experienced the sovereign power of God. 29:While he laid speechless and deprived of all hope and aid, due to an act of God's power, 30:the Hebrews praised the Lord who had marvelously glorified his holy place, and the temple, charged so shortly before with fear and commotion , was filled with joy and gladness, now that the Lord had manifested himself. 31;Soon some of the companions of Heliodorus begged Onias to invoke the Most High, praying that the life of this man who was about to expire might be spared. 32:Fearing that the King might think that Heliodorus had suffered some foul play at the hands of the Hebrews, the high priest offered a sacrifice for the man's recovery. 33:While the high priest was offering the sacrifice of atonement, the same young man in the same clothing again appeared and stood before Heliodorus. “Be very grateful to the high priest Onias,” They told him. “It is for his sake that the Lord has spared your life. 34:Since you have been scourged by Heaven, proclaim to all men the majesty of God's power.” When they had said this, they disappeared.

35:After Heliodorus had offered a sacrifice to the Lord and made most solemn vows to him who had spared his life, he said to Onias farewell, and returned with his soldiers to the King.

+/- October 7th. (Tishul /Ephraim 10th.)

The year +/- 163 B.C. Apollonius and his men took the city

(2Maccabees 5:25-27) 25:When this man arrived in Jerusalem he pretended to be peacefully disposed and waited, until the Holy day of the sabbath; then finding the Hebrews refraining from any kind of work, he ordered his men to parade fully armed. 26:All those who came out to watch the parade, he massacred, then running through the city with armed men, he cut down a large number of people. 27:But Judas Maccabees with about nine others withdrew to the wilderness where he and his companions lived like wild animals in the hills, continuing to eat what grew wild to avoid sharing the defilement.

+/- October 7th. (Tishul /Ephraim 10th.)

Jesus saw a poor widow put in two coins

(Luke 21:1-36)1:And he looked up, and saw the rich men casting their gifts into the treasury. 2;And he saw also a certain poor widow casting in two mites. 3:And he said, Of a truth I say to you, that this poor widow has cast in more than they all. 4:For all these have put in of their abundance casting in to the offerings of God: but she of her penury has cast in all that she had even to live on. 5;And as some spoke of the temple, how it was adorned with goodly stones and gifts, he said;:As for these things which you have seen, the days will come, in the which there shall not be left one stone upon another, that shall not be thrown down. 7;And they asked him, saying, Master, but when shall these things be? And what sign will there be when these things shall come to pass? 8;And he said, Take heed that you be not deceived: for many shall come in my name, saying, I am the Christ and the time draws near: go you not therefore after them. 9;But when you shall hear of wars and commotions, be not terrified: for these things must first come to pass; but the end is not by and by. 10;Then said he to them, Nation shall rise against nation, and kingdom against kingdom: 11;And great earthquakes shall be in divers places, and famines, and pestilences; and fearful sights, and great signs shall there be from heaven. 12;But before all these, they shall lay their hands on you, and persecute you delivering you up to the synagogues, and into prisons, being brought before Kings and rulers for my name's sake. 13;And it shall turn to you for a testimony. 14;Settle it therefore in your hearts, not to meditate before what you shall answer: 15;For I will give you a mouth and wisdom, which all your adversaries shall not be able to gainsay nor resist. 16;And you shall be betrayed both by parents, and brethren, and family, and friends; and some of you shall they cause to be put to death. 17;And you shall be hated of all men for my name's sake. 18;But there shall not an hair of your head perish. 19;In your patience possess you your souls. 20;And when you shall see Jerusalem compassed with armies, then know that the desolation thereof is near. 21;Then let them which are in Judea flee to the mountains; and let them which are in the midst of it depart out; and let not them that are in the countries enter there into. 22;For these be the days of vengeance, that all things which are written may be fulfilled. 23;But woe to them that are with child, and to them that give suck, in those days! for there shall be great distress in the land, and wrath upon this people. 24;And they shall fall by the edge of the sword, and shall be led away captive into all nations: and Jerusalem shall be trodden down of the Gentiles, until the times of the Gentiles be fulfilled. 25;And there shall be signs in the sun, and in the moon, and in the stars; and upon the earth distress of nations, with perplexity; the sea and the waves roaring. 26:Man's hearts failing them for fear, and for looking after those things which are coming on the earth: for the powers of heaven shall be shaken. 27;And then shall they see the Son of man coming in a cloud with power and great glory. 28;And when these things begin to come to pass, then look up, and lift up your heads; for your redemption draws near. 29;And he spoke to them a parable; Behold the fig tree, and all the trees; 30;When they now shoot forth, you see and know of your own selves that summer is now near at hand. 31;So likewise you, when you see these things come to pass, know you that the kingdom of God is near at hand. 32;Verily I say to you, This generation shall not pass away, till all be fulfilled. 33;Heaven and earth shall pass away: but my words shall not pass away. 34;And take heed to yourselves, lest at any time your hearts be overcharged with surfeiting, and drunkenness, and cares of this life, and so that day come upon you unawares. 35;For as a snare shall it come on all them that dwell on the face of the whole earth. 36:Watch you therefore, and pray always, that you may be accounted worthy to escape all these things that shall come to pass, and to stand before the Son of man.

Note: The name of this type of coin is called "as"
Later it was changed to penny.
One coin was equal to a days pay, for a laborer.

+/- October 8th. (Tishul /Ephraim 11th.)

Jacob set up a alter

(Genesis 33:18-20) 18;And Jacob came to Salem, a city of Shechem, which is in the land of Canaan, when he came from Paddan-aram; and pitched his tent before the city. 19:And he bought a parcel of a field, where he had spread his tent, at the hand of the children of Hamor, Shechem's father, for an hundred pieces of silver. 20:And he erected there an altar, and called it Elohim-Israel.

+/- October 9th. (Tishul /Ephraim 12th.)

The year +/- 1941 B.C. Prince Mastema spoke to Go about Abraham

(Book of Jubilees 17:19-22)19:In the year during the first month on the twelfth day of the month, in this jubilee there were voices in heaven regarding Abraham, that he was faithful in everything that he had been told. 20:That the Lord loved him, and that in every difficulty he was faithful. Then Prince Mastema came and said before God; "Abraham does indeed love his son Isaac and finds him more pleasing than anyone else. 21;Tell him to offer him as a sacrifice on an altar. 22:Then you will see whether he performs this order and will know whether he is faithful in everything through which you test him.

+/- October 11th. (Tishul /Ephraim 14th.)

They spoke against Moses and Aaron,

(Numbers 16:1-17) 1:Now Korah, the son of Izhar, the son of Kohath, the son of Levi, and Dathan and Abiram, the sons of Eliab, the son of Pallu, son of Reuben took 2:two hundred and fifty men, who were leaders in the community, members of the council and men of note. They stood before Moses, 3:and they gathered themselves together against Moses and against Aaron, and said unto them, you take too much upon you, seeing all the congregation are holy, every one of them, and the Lord is among them: wherefore then lift you up yourselves above the congregation of the Lord? 4:And when Moses heard it, he fell upon his face.

5:Then he spoke to Korah and to all his company, saying, Even tomorrow the Lord will show who are his, and who is holy; and will cause him to come near unto him: even him whom he has chosen will he cause to come near to him. 6:This do; Take you censers, Korah, and all his company; 7:And put fire therein, and put incense in them before the Lord tomorrow, and it shall be that the man whom the Lord does choose, he shall be holy: you take too much upon you, you sons of Levi. 8:And Moses said to Korah, Hear, I pray you, you sons of Levi. 9:It seems but a small thing to you, that the God of Israel has separated you from the congregation of Israel,to bring you near to himself to do the service of the tabernacle of the Lord, and to stand before the congregation to minister to them?

10:And he has brought you near to him and all your brethren the sons of Levi with you: and seek you the priesthood also? 11:For which cause both you and all your company are gathered together against the Lord: and what is Aaron, that you murmur against him? 12:And Moses sent to call Dathan and Abiram, the sons of Eliab: which said, We will not come up. 13:Is it a small thing that you have, brought us up out of a land that flows with milk and honey, to kill us in the wilderness, except you make yourself a prince over us? 14:Moreover you have not brought us into a land that flows with milk and honey, or given us inheritance of fields and vineyards: will you put out the eyes of these men? We will not come up,

15:and Moses was very angry, and said to the Lord, except not you their offering: I have not taken one ass from them, nor have I hurt one of them. 16:And Moses said to Korah, have you and all your company come before the Lord, tomorrow with Aaron and I. 17;And take every man his censer, and put incense in them, and bring you before the Lord every man his censer, two hundred and fifty censers; you also, and Aaron, each of you his censer.

+/- October 11th. (Tishul /Ephraim 14th.)

Saul was transformed into another man

(1Samuel 10:6-16) 6:And the Spirit of the Lord will come upon you, and you shall prophesy with them, and shall be turned into another man. 7:And let it be, when these signs are come to you, that you do as occasion serve you; for God is with you. 8:And you shall go down before me to Gilgal; and behold, I will come down to you, to offer burnt offerings, and to sacrifice, sacrifices of peace offerings: seven days shall you stay, till I come to you, and show you what you shall do.

9:And it was so that when he had turned his back to go from Samuel, God gave him another heart: and all those signs came to pass that day. 10:And when they came closer to the hill, behold, a company of prophets met him; and the Spirit of God came upon him, and he prophesied among them. 11;And it came to pass, when all that knew him before time saw that, behold, he prophesied among the prophets, then the people said one to another, What is this that is come to the son of Kish? Is Saul also among the prophets?

12:And one of the same place answered and said, But who is their father? Therefore it became a proverb, Is Saul also among the prophets? 13:And when he had made an end of prophesying, he came to the high place. 14:And Saul's uncle said to him and to his servant, Where did you go? And he said, To seek the asses: and when we saw that they were no where, we came to Samuel. 15:And Saul's uncle said, Tell me, I ask you, what did Samuel say to you. 16:And Saul said to his uncle, He told us plainly that the asses were found. But of the matter of the kingdom, where of Samuel spoke, he told him not.

+/- October 11th. (Tishul /Ephraim 14th.)

They made for them self's booths

(Nehemiah 8:16-17) 16:So the people went forth, and brought them, and made themselves booths, every one upon the roof of his house, and in their courts, and in the courts of the house of God, and in the street of the water gate,
and in the street of the gate of Ephraim.

17:And all the congregation of them that were come again out of the captivity made
booths, and sat under the booths: for since the days of Jeshua, the son of Nun unto
that day had not the children of Israel done so. And there was very great gladness.

Below on the left: a booth set up in the back yard, on the right A booth put up in the desert.

Above: Booths set up in Jerusalem on the streets, on the right the inside look of a booth. Every year God told his people to live in these shelters for seven days. To remember when they left Egypt and wondered through the desert, and lacked for nothing. For he was with them.

+/- October 11th. (Tishul /Ephraim 14th.)

Paul said they should stay in Haven

(Acts 27:9-12) 9:They sailed to Haven Now when much time was spent, and when sailing was now dangerous, because the fast was now already past, Paul admonished them, 10:and said to them: Sirs, I perceive that this voyage will be with hurt and much damage, not only of the lading and ship, but also of our lives.11:Nevertheless the centurion believed the master and the owner of the ship, more than those things which were spoken by Paul. 12:And because the haven was not commodious to winter in, the more part advised to depart thence also, if by any means they might attain to Phenice, and there to winter; which is an haven of Crete, and lies toward the south west and north west.

+/- October 12th. (Tishul /Ephraim 15th.)

The year +/- 1358 B.C. The feast of Booths / Tabernacles: last for eight days

(Leviticus 23:33-44) 33:And the Lord spoke to Moses, saying; 34:Speak to the children of Israel, saying, The fifteenth day of this seventh month shall be the feast of tabernacles for seven days unto the Lord. 35:On the first day shall be an holy convocation: you shall do no servile work on it. 36:Seven days you shall offer an offering made by fire to the Lord: on the eighth day, shall be an holy convocation to you; and you shall offer an offering made by fire to the Lord: it is a solemn assembly; and you shall do no servile work on it. 37;These are the feasts of the Lord, which you shall proclaim to be a holy convocations, to offer an offering made by fire to the Lord, a burnt offering, and a meat offering, a sacrifice, and drink offerings, every thing upon his day. 38:Beside the sabbaths of the Lord, and beside your gifts, and beside all your vows, and beside all your freewill offerings, which you give unto the Lord. 39:Also in the fifteenth day of the seventh month, when you have gathered in the fruit of the land, you shall keep a feast to the Lord seven days: on the first day shall be a sabbath, and on the eighth day shall be a sabbath. 40:And you shall take you on the first day the boughs of goodly trees, branches of palm trees, and the boughs of thick trees, and willows of the brook; and you shall rejoice before the Lord your God seven days. 41;And you shall keep it a feast unto the Lord seven days in the year. It shall be a statute for ever in your generations: you shall celebrate it in the seventh month. 42:You shall dwell in booths seven days, all that are Israelites born shall dwell in booths. 43;That your generations may know that I made the children of Israel to dwell in booths, when I brought them out of the land of Egypt. I am the Lord your God. 44:And Moses declared to the children of Israel, all the feasts of the Lord.

+/- October 12th. (Tishul /Ephraim 15th.)

The year +/- 1358 B.C. Korah, Dathan, and Abiram: were swallowed up by the ground

(Numbers 16:18-40) 18:And they took every man his censer, and put fire in them, and laid incense thereon, and stood in the door of the tabernacle of the congregation with Moses and Aaron. 19:And Korah gathered all the congregation against them, to the door of the tabernacle of the congregation: and the glory of the Lord appeared to all the congregation. 20:And the Lord spoke to Moses and to Aaron, saying; 21:Separate yourselves from among this congregation, that I may consume them in a moment. 22:And they fell upon their faces, and said, O God, the God of the spirits of all flesh, shall one man sin, and will you be angry with all the congregation? 23:And the Lord spoke to Moses, saying; 24:Speak to the congregation, saying, Get you up from about the tabernacle of Korah, Dathan, and Abiram. 25:And Moses rose up and went unto Dathan and Abiram; and the elders of Israel followed him. 26:And he spoke to the congregation, saying, Depart, I pray you, from the tents of these wicked men, and touch nothing of theirs, lest you be consumed in all their sins. 27:So they got up from the tabernacle of Korah, Dathan, and Abiram, on every side: and Dathan and Abiram came out, and stood in the door of their tents, and their wives, and their sons, and their little children. 28:And Moses said, Hereby you shall know that the Lord has sent me to do all these works; for I have not done them of mine own mind. 29:If these men die the common death of all men, or if they be visited after the visitation of all men; them the Lord has not sent me. 30:But if the Lord make a new thing, and the earth open her mouth, and swallow them up, with all that appertain to them, and they go down quick into the pit, then you shall understand that these men have provoked the Lord. 31:And it came to pass,as he had made an end of speaking all these words, that the ground caved in under them: 32;And the earth opened her mouth, and swallowed them up, and their houses, and all the men that pertained to Korah, and all their goods. 33:They, and all that pertained to them, went down alive into the pit, and the earth closed upon them: and they perished from among the congregation. 34;And all Israel that were round about them fled at the cry of them: for they said, Lest the earth swallows us up also.35:And there came out a fire from the Lord, and consumed the two hundred and fifty men that offered incense. 36;And the Lord spoke to Moses, saying; 37;Speak to Eleazar the son of Aaron the priest, that he take up the censers out of the burning, and scatter you the fire yonder; for they are hallowed. 38;The censers of these sinners against their own souls, let them make them broad plates for a covering of the altar: for they offered them before the Lord, therefore they are hallowed: and they shall be a sign to the children of Israel. 39;And Eleazar the priest took the brass censers, wherewith they that were burnt had offered; and they were made broad plates for a covering of the altar: 40;To be a memorial to the children of Israel, that no stranger, which is not of the seed of Aaron, come near to offer incense to the Lord; that he be not as Korah, and as his company,as the Lord said to him by the hand of Moses.

+/- October 12th. (Tishul /Ephraim 15th.)

They brought the ark up to Jerusalem

(1Kings 8:1-9) 1:Then Solomon assembled the elders of Israel, and all the heads of the tribes, the chief of the fathers of the children of Israel, to King Solomon in Jerusalem, that they might bring up the ark of the covenant of the Lord out of the city of David, which is Zion. 2:And all the men of Israel assembled themselves to King Solomon at the feast in the month Ephraim, which is in the seventh month. 3:And all the elders of Israel came, and the priests took up the ark. 4:And they brought up the ark of the Lord, and the tabernacle of the congregation, and all the holy vessels that were in the tabernacle, even those did the priests and the Levites bring up. 5:And King Solomon, and all the congregation of Israel, that were assembled to him, were with him before the ark, sacrificing sheep and oxen, that could not be told nor numbered for multitude. 6:And the priests brought in the ark of the covenant of the Lord to his place to the oracle of the house, to the most holy place even under the wings of the cherubims. 7:For the cherubims spread forth their two wings over the place of the ark, and the cherubims covered the ark and the staffs there of above. 8:And they drew out the staffs, that the ends of the staffs were seen out in the holy place before the oracle, and they were not seen without: and there they are to this day. 9:There was nothing in the ark except the two tables of stone, which Moses put there at Horeb, when the Lord made a covenant with the children of Israel, when they came out of the land of Egypt.

+/- October 12th. (Tishul /Ephraim 15th.)

Solomon prayed to the Lord

(2Chronicles 5:1-7:8) 1:Then all the work that Solomon had done for the house of the Lord was finished: and Solomon brought in all the things that David his father had dedicated; and the silver, and the gold, and all the instruments, put he among the treasures of the house of God. 2:Then Solomon assembled the elders of Israel, and all the heads of the tribes, the chief of the fathers of the children of Israel, to Jerusalem, to bring up the ark of the covenant of the Lord out of the city of David, which is Zion. 3:Wherefore all the men of Israel assembled themselves to the King at the feast which was in the seventh month on the fifteenth day. 4:And all the elders of Israel came; and the Levites took up the ark. 5:And they brought up the ark, and the tabernacle of the congregation, and all the holy vessels that were in the tabernacle, these did the priests and the Levites bring up. 6:Also King Solomon, and all the congregation of Israel that were assembled to him before the ark, sacrificed sheep and oxen, which could not be told nor numbered for multitude. 7:And the priests brought in the ark of the covenant of the Lord to his place, to the oracle of the house, into the most holy place, even under the wings of the cherubims. 8:For the cherubims spread forth their wings over the place of the ark, and the cherubims covered the ark and the staffs thereof above. 9:And they drew out the staffs of the ark, that the ends of the staffs were seen from the ark before the oracle; but they were not seen without. And there it is to this day. 10:There was nothing in the ark save the two tables which Moses put in at Horeb, when the Lord made a covenant with the children of Israel, when they came out of Egypt. 11:And it came to pass, when the priests had come out of the holy place, (for all the priests that were present were sanctified, and did not then wait by course. 12:Also the Levites which were the singers, all of them of Asaph, of Heman, of Jeduthun, with their sons and their brethren, being arrayed in white linen, having cymbals and psalteries and harps, stood at the east end of the altar, and with them an hundred and twenty priests sounding with trumpets:) 13:It came even to pass, as the trumpeters and singers were as one, to make one sound to be heard in praising and thanking the Lord; and when they lifted up their voice with the trumpets and cymbals and instruments of music, and praised the Lord, saying; For he is good; for his mercy endures for ever: at that the house was filled with a cloud, even the house of the Lord. 14:So that the priests could not stand to minister by reason of the cloud:

for the glory of the Lord had filled the house of God. **6:1:**Then said Solomon, The
Lord has said that he would dwell in the thick darkness. 2:But I have built an house
of habitation for you, and a place for your dwelling forever. 3:And the King turned
his face, and blessed the whole congregation of Israel: and all the congregation of
Israel stood. 4:And he said, Blessed be the Lord God of Israel, who has with his
hands fulfilled that which he spoke with his mouth to my father David, saying,
5:Since the day that I brought forth my people out of the land of Egypt I chose no
city among all the tribes of Israel to build an house in, that my name might be there;
neither chose I any man to be a ruler over my people Israel. 6:But I have chosen
Jerusalem, that my name might be there; and have chosen David to be over my
people Israel. 7:Now it was in the heart of David my father to build an house for the
name of the Lord God of Israel. 8:But the Lord said to David my father, Inasmuch
as it was in your heart to build an house for my name, you did well in that it was in
your heart. 9:Not with standing, you shall not build the house; but your son which
shall come forth out of your loins, he shall build the house for my name. 10:The
Lord therefore had performed his word that he had spoken: for I am risen up in the
room of David my father, and am set on the throne of Israel, as the Lord promised,
and have built the house for the name of the Lord God of Israel. 11:And in it have I
put the ark, wherein is the covenant of the Lord, that he made with the children of
Israel. 12:And he stood before the altar of the Lord in the presence of all the
congregation of Israel, and spread forth his hands.

13:For Solomon had made a brazen scaffold, of five cubits long, and five cubits
broad, and three cubits high, and had set it in the midst of the court: and upon it he
stood, and knelt down upon his knees before all the congregation of Israel, and
spread forth his hands toward heaven. 14:And said, O Lord God of Israel, there is
no God like you in the heaven, or in the earth; which keeps covenant, and shows
mercy to your servants, that walk before you with all their hearts. 15:You which has
kept with your servant David my father that which you have promised him; and
spoke the words with your mouth, and has fulfilled it with your hand, as it is this
day. 16:Now therefore, O Lord God of Israel, keep with your servant David my
father that which you have promised him, saying, There shall not fail your a man in
my sight to sit upon the throne of Israel; yet so that your children take heed to their
way to walk in my law, as you have walked before me. 17:Now then, O Lord God
of Israel, let your word be verified, which you have spoken to your servant David.
18:But will God indeed dwell with men on the earth? Behold, heaven and the
heaven of heavens cannot contain you; how much less this house which I have built!
19:Have respect therefore to the prayer of your servant, and to his supplication, O
Lord my God, to listen to the cry's and the prayers which your servant prays before
you. 20:That your eyes may be open upon this house day and night, upon the place
whereof you have said that you would put your name there; to listen to the prayer
which your servant prays toward this place. 21:Hearken therefore to the
supplications of your servant, and of your people Israel, which they shall make
toward this place: hear you from your dwelling place, even from heaven; and when
you hear, forgive. 22:If a man sin against his neighbor, and an oath be laid upon him
to make him swear, and the oath come before your altar in this house. 23:Then hear
you from heaven, and do, and judge your servants, by requiting the wicked, by
recompensing his way upon his own head; and by justifying the righteous,

by giving him according to his righteousness. 24:And if your people Israel be put to the worse before the enemy, because they have sinned against you; and shall return and confess your name, and pray and make supplication, before you in this house. 25:Then hear you from the heavens, and forgive the sin of your people Israel, and bring them again to the land which you gave to them and to their fathers. 26:When the heaven is shut up, and there is no rain, because they have sinned against you;yet if they pray toward this place, and confess your name, and turn from their sin, when you do afflict them. 27;Then hear you from heaven, and forgive the sin of your servants, and of your people Israel, when you have taught them the good way, wherein they should walk; and send rain upon your land, which you have given to your people for an inheritance. 28:If there be dearth in the land, if there be pestilence, if there be blasting, or mildew, locusts, or caterpillars; if their enemies besiege them in the cities of their land; whatsoever sore or whatsoever sickness there be. 29:Then what prayer or what supplication soever shall be made of any man, or of all your people Israel, when every one shall know his own sore and his own grief, and shall spread forth his hands in this house. 30:Then hear you from heaven your dwelling place, and forgive, and render to every man according to all his ways, whose heart you know; (for you only, know the hearts of the children of men) 31:That they may fear you, to walk in your ways, so long as they live in the land which you gave to our fathers. 32:Moreover concerning the stranger, which is not of your people Israel, but is come from a far country for your great name's sake, and your mighty hand, and your stretched out arm; if they come and pray in this house. 33:Then hear you from the heavens, even from your dwelling place, and give according to all that the stranger ask of you; that all people of the earth may know your name, and fear you, as does your people Israel, and may know that this house which I have built is called by your name. 34:If your people go out to war against their enemies by the way that you shall send them, and they pray to you toward this city which you have chosen, and the house which I have built for your name.

35:Then hear you from the heavens their prayer and their supplication, and maintain their cause. 36:If they sin against you, (for there is no man which does not sin) and when you are angry with them, and deliver them over before their enemies, and they carry them away captives to a land far off or near. 37:Yet if they think to themselves in the land where they are carried captive, and turn and pray to you in the land of their captivity, saying, We have sinned, we have done amiss, and have dealt wickedly; 38:If they return to you with all their heart and with all their soul in the land of their captivity, whither they have carried them captives, and pray toward their land, which you gave to their fathers, and towards the city which you have chosen, and toward the house which I have built for your name. 39:Then hear you from the heavens, even from your dwelling place, their prayer and their supplications, and maintain their cause, and forgive your people which have sinned against you. 40:Now, my God, let, I ask you, your eyes be open, and let your ears be attentive to the prayers, that are made in this place. 41:Now therefore arise, O Lord God, into your resting place, you, and the ark of your strength: let your priests, O Lord God, be clothed with salvation, and let your saints rejoice in goodness. 42:O Lord God, turn not away the face of your anointed: remember the mercies of David your servant. **7:1:**Now when Solomon had made an end of praying, the fire came down from heaven, and consumed the burnt offering and the sacrifices;

and the glory of the Lord filled the house. 2:And the priests could not enter into the house of the Lord, because the glory of the Lord had filled the Lord's house. 3:And when all the children of Israel saw how the fire came down, and the glory of the Lord upon the house, they bowed themselves with their faces to the ground upon the pavement, and worshiped, and praised the Lord, saying; For he is good; for his mercy endures forever. 4:Then the King and all the people offered sacrifices before the Lord. 5:And King Solomon offered a sacrifice of twenty and two thousand oxen, and an hundred and twenty thousand sheep, so the King and all the people dedicated the house of God. 6;And the priests waited on their offices: the Levites also with instruments of music of the Lord, which David the King had made to praise the Lord, because his mercy endures for ever, when David praised by their ministry; and the priests sounded trumpets before them, and all Israel stood. 7:Moreover Solomon hallowed the middle of the court that was before the house of the Lord: for there he offered burnt offerings, and the fat of the peace offerings, because the bronze altar which Solomon had made was not able to receive the burnt offerings, and the meat offerings, and the fat. 8:Also at the same time Solomon kept the feast seven days, and all Israel with him, a great congregation, from the entering in of Hamath to the river of Egypt.

+/- October 12th. (Tishul /Ephraim 15th.)

The year +/- 146 B.C. Demetrius heard that Alexander had made friends with the Hebrews

(1Maccabees 10;21-24) 21:Jonathan put on the sacred vestments on the fifteenth day of the seventh month of the year one hundred and sixty at the feast of Booths, and he gathered an army and procured many arms. When Demetrius heard of these things, he was distressed and said; 23:Why have we allowed Alexander to get ahead of us by gaining the friendship of the Hebrews and this strengthening himself?" 24:I also will wright them conciliatory words and offer dignities and gifts, so that they may be an aid to me.

+/- October 12th. (Tishul /Ephraim 15th.)

Note: It is believed that Jesus was in Jerusalem, every year at this time.

(As it is written in the law) (Leviticus 23:42-43) 42:You shall dwell in booths seven days; all that are Israelites born shall dwell in booths. 43:That your generations may know that I made the children of Israel to dwell in booths, when I brought them out of the land of Egypt: I am the Lord your God.

+/- October 12th. (Tishul /Ephraim 15th.)

Paul sailed for Clauda

(Acts 27:13-18) 13:And when the south wind blew softly, supposing that they had obtained their purpose, loosing thence, they sailed close by Crete. 14:But not long after there arose against it a tempestuous wind, called Euroclydon. 15:And when the ship was caught, and could not bear up into the wind, we let her drive. 16:We passed along the sheltered side of an island named Clauda, and managed with some difficulty to get the dinghy under control. 17:They hoisted it aboard, then used cables to under gird the ship. Because of their fear that they would run aground on the shoal of Syrtis, they lowered the drift anchor, and were carried along in this way.

+/- October 13th. (Tishul /Ephraim 16th.)

The year +/- 1358 B.C. God sent a plague on his people

(Numbers 16:41-50) 41:But the next day all the congregation of the children of Israel murmured against Moses and against Aaron, saying:You have killed the people of the Lord. 42:And it came to pass, when the congregation was gathered against Moses and against Aaron, that they looked toward the tabernacle of the congregation: and, behold, the cloud covered it, and the glory of the Lord appeared. 43:And Moses and Aaron came before the tabernacle of the congregation. 44:And the Lord spoke to Moses, saying; 45:Get you up from among this congregation, that I may consume them as in a moment. And they fell upon their faces. 46:And Moses said to Aaron, Take a censer, and put fire therein from off the altar, and put on incense, and go quickly to the congregation, and make an atonement for them: for there is wrath gone out from the Lord; the plague has begun. 47:And Aaron took as Moses commanded, and ran into the midst of the congregation; and, behold, the plague had begun among the people: and he put on incense, and made an atonement for the people. 48:And he stood between the dead and the living; and the plague stayed. 49;Now they that died in the plague, were fourteen thousand and seven hundred, beside them that died about the matter of Korah. 50:And Aaron returned to Moses at the door of the tabernacle of the congregation, and the plague stayed.

+/- October 13th. (Tishul /Ephraim 16th.)

They lightened the ship

(Acts 27:18) 18:And we being exceedingly tossed with a tempest, the next day they lightened the ship, by throwing the cargo over board.

+/- October 14th. (Tishul /Ephraim 17th.)

The year +/- 1358 B.C. Aaron's name was written on the rod of Levi

(Numbers 17:1-7) 1:And the Lord spoke to Moses, saying; 2:Speak to the children of Israel, and take of every one of them a rod according to the house of their fathers, of all their princes according to the house of their fathers twelve rods: write you every man's name upon his rod. 3:And you shall write Aaron's name upon the rod of Levi: for one rod shall be for the head of the house of their fathers. 4:And you shall lay them up in the tabernacle of the congregation before the testimony, where I will meet with you. 5:And it shall come to pass, that the man's rod, whom I shall choose, shall blossom: and I will make to cease from me the murmurings of the children of Israel, where by they murmur against you. 6:And Moses spoke to the children of Israel, and every one of their princes gave him a rod apiece, for each prince one, according to their fathers' houses, even twelve rods: and the rod of Aaron, was among their rods. 7:And Moses laid up the rods before the Lord in the tabernacle of witness.

+/- October 14th. (Tishul /Ephraim 17th.)

The third day they threw overboard the tackling

(Acts 27:19) 19:And the third day we cast overboard with our own hands the tackling of the ship

+/- October 15th. (Tishul /Ephraim 18th.)

The year +/- 1358 B.C. The staff of Levi was chosen

(Numbers 17:8-18:32) 8:And it came to pass, that on the next day Moses went into the tabernacle of witness; and, behold, the rod of Aaron for the house of Levi was budded, and brought forth buds, and bloomed blossoms, and yielded almonds. 9:And Moses brought out all the rods from before the Lord to all the children of Israel: and they looked, and took every man his rod. 10:And the Lord said to Moses, Bring Aaron's rod again before the testimony, to be kept for a token against the rebels; and you shall surly take away their murmurings from me, so they will not die. 11:And Moses did so, as the Lord commanded him, so did he. 12:And the children of Israel spoke unto Moses, saying, Behold, we die, we perish, we all perish. 13:Who soever comes near unto the tabernacle of the Lord shall die: shall we be consumed with dying?

18:1;And the Lord said to Aaron; You and your sons and your father's house with you shall bear the iniquity of the sanctuary: and you and your sons with you shall bear the iniquity of your priesthood. 2:And your brethren also of the tribe of Levi, the tribe of your father, bring with you, that they may be joined unto you, and minister to you: but you and your sons with you shall minister before the tabernacle of witness. 3:And they shall keep your charge, and the charge of all the tabernacle, only they shall not come near the vessels of the sanctuary, or the altar, that neither they, nor you also, should die. 4:And they shall be joined to you, and keep the charge of the tabernacle of the congregation, for all the service of the tabernacle: and a stranger shall not come near to you. 5:And you shall keep the charge of the sanctuary, and the charge of the altar: that there be no wrath any more upon the children of Israel. 6:And I, behold, I have taken your brethren the Levites from among the children of Israel: to you they are given as a gift for the Lord, to do the service of the tabernacle of the congregation. 7:Therefore you and your sons with you shall keep your priest's office for every thing of the altar, and within the vale; and you shall serve: I have given your priest's office unto you as a service of gift: and any stranger that comes near shall be put to death.

8:And the Lord spoke to Aaron, Behold, I also have given you the charge of mine heave offerings of all the hallowed things of the children of Israel; to you have I given them by reason of the anointing, and to your sons, by an ordinance for ever. 9:This shall be thine of the most holy things, reserved from the fire: every oblation of theirs, every meat offering of theirs, and every sin offering of theirs, and every trespass offering of theirs, which they shall render to me, shall be most holy for you and for your sons. 10:In the most holy place shall you eat it; every male shall eat it: it shall be holy to you. 11:And this is yours; the heave offering of their gift, with all the wave offerings of the children of Israel: I have given them to you, and to your sons and to your daughters with you, by a statute forever: every one that is clean in your house shall eat of it. 12:All the best of the oil, and all the best of the wine, and of the wheat, the first fruits of them, which they shall offer to the Lord, them have I given you. 13:And what soever is first ripe in the land, which they shall bring to the Lord, shall be yours; every one that is clean in your house shall eat of it. 14:Every thing devoted in Israel shall be yours. 15:Every thing that opens the matrix in all flesh, which they bring to the Lord, whether it be of men or beasts, shall be yours: nevertheless the firstborn of man shall you surely redeem, and the first born of unclean beasts shall you redeem. 16:And those that are to be redeemed from a month old shall you redeem, according to your estimation, for the money of five shekels, after the shekel of the sanctuary, which is twenty gerahs. 17:But the first born of a cow, or the first born of a sheep, or the first born of a goat, you shall not redeem; they are holy: you shall sprinkle their blood upon the altar, and shall burn their fat for an offering made by fire, for a sweet savor to the Lord. 18:And the flesh of them shall be thine, as the wave breast and as the right shoulder are thine.

19:All the heave offerings of the holy things, which the children of Israel offer to the Lord, have I given you, and your sons and your daughters with you, by a statute for ever: it is a covenant of salt for ever before the Lord unto you and to your seed with you. 20:And the Lord spoke to Aaron; You shall have no inheritance in their land, neither shall you have any part among them: I am your part and your inheritance among the children of Israel. 21:And, behold, I have given the children of Levi all the tenth in Israel for an inheritance, for their service which they serve, even the service of the tabernacle of the congregation. 22:Neither must the children of Israel from now on come near the tabernacle of the congregation, lest they bear sin, and die. 23:But the Levites shall do the service of the tabernacle of the congregation, and they shall bear their iniquity: it shall be a statute forever throughout your generations, that among the children of Israel they have no inheritance. 24:But the tithes of the children of Israel, which they offer as an heave offering to the Lord, I have given to the Levites to inherit: therefore I have said to them, Among the children of Israel they shall have no inheritance.

25:And the Lord spoke to Moses, saying; 26:This say to the Levites, say to them, When you take of the children of Israel the tithes which I have given you from them for your inheritance, then you shall offer up an heave offering of it for the Lord, even a tenth part of the tithe. 27:And this your heave offering shall be reckoned to you, as though it were the corn of the threshing floor, and as the fulness of the wine-press. 28:This you also shall offer an heave offering to the Lord of all your tithes, which you receive of the children of Israel; and you shall give thereof the Lord's heave offering to Aaron the priest. 29:Out of all your gifts you shall offer every heave offering of the Lord, of all the best thereof, even the hallowed part thereof out of it. 30:Therefore you shall say to them, When you have heaved the best thereof from it, then it shall be counted unto the Levites as the increase of the threshing floor, and as the increase of the wine-press. 31:And you shall eat it in every place, you and your households: for it is your reward for your service in the tabernacle of the congregation. 32:And you shall bear no sin by reason of it, when you have heaved from it the best of it: neither shall you pollute the holy things of the children of Israel, lest you die.

+/- October 15th. (Tishul /Ephraim 18th.)

Jesus taught in the temple

(John 7:14-36) 14:Now about the midst of the feast Jesus went up to the temple, and taught. 15:And the Jews marveled, saying, How does this man know these letters, having never learned? 16:Jesus answered them, and said, My doctrine is not mine, but he who has sent me. 17:If any man will do his will, he shall know of the doctrine, whether it be of God, or whether I speak of myself. 18:He that speaks of himself seeks his own glory: but he that seeks his glory that sent him, the same is true, and no unrighteousness is in him. 19:Did not Moses give you the law, and yet none of you keeps the law? Why are you going about to kill me? 20:The people answered and said, “You have a devil in you who is trying to kill you?” 21:Jesus answered and said to them, I have done one work, and you all marvel. 22:Moses therefore gave to you circumcision; (not because it is of Moses, but of the fathers;) and you on the sabbath day circumcise a man. 23;If a man on the sabbath day receive circumcision, that the law of Moses should not be broken; are you angry at me, because I have made a man completely whole on the sabbath day? 24:Judge not according to the appearance, but judge righteous judgment. 25;Then said some of them of Jerusalem, “Is not this he, whom they seek to kill? 26;But, look, he speaks boldly, and they say nothing to him. Do not the rulers know indeed, that this is the very Christ?” 27;Howbeit we know this man where he is: but when Christ comes, no man knows where he is. 28Then Jesus called out in the temple as he taught, saying: You both know me, and you know where I am: and I have not come of myself, but from he that has sent me, who is true, whom you do not know. 29:But I know him: for I am from him, and he has sent me. 30;Then they sought to take him: but no man laid hands on him, because his hour has not yet come. 31:And many of the people believed on him, and said, When Christ comes, will he do more miracles than these which this man has done? 32:The Pharisees heard that the people murmured such things concerning him; and the Pharisees and the chief priests sent officers to take him. 33:Then said Jesus to them, Yet a little while am I with you, and then I will go back to him who has sent me. 34:You shall seek me, and shall not find me,and where I am, going you cannot come. 35:Then said the Jews among themselves, Where will he go, that we shall not find him? Will he go to the dispersed among the Gentiles, and teach the Gentiles? 36:What manner of saying is this that he said? You shall seek me, and shall not find me, and where I am, going you cannot come?

+/- October 18th. (Tishul /Ephraim 21th.)

God speaks through Haggai

(Haggai 2:1-9) 1:In the seventh month, on the one and twentieth day of the month, came the word of the Lord by the prophet Haggai, saying; 2:Speak now to Zerubbabel the son of Shealtiel, governor of Judah, and to Joshua the son of Josedech, the high priest, and to the residue of the people, saying, 3:Who is left among you that saw this house in her first glory? and how do you see it now? Is it not in your eyes in comparison of it as nothing? 4:Yet now be strong, O Zerubbabel, says the Lord; and be strong, O Joshua, son of Josedech, the high priest; and be strong, all you people of the land, says the Lord, and work: for I am with you, says the Lord of hosts. 5:According to the word that I covenanted with you when you came out of Egypt, so my spirit remains among you, do not fear. 6:For this says the Lord of hosts; Yet once, it is a little while, and I will shake the heavens, and the earth, and the sea, and the dry land. 7;And I will shake all nations, and the desire of all nations shall come: and I will fill this house with glory, says the Lord of hosts. 8:The silver is mine, and the gold is mine, says the Lord of hosts. 9:The glory of this latter house shall be greater than of the former, says the Lord of hosts: and in this place will I give peace, says: the Lord of hosts.

+/- October 19th. (Tishul /Ephraim 22nd.)

The eighth day Solemn assembly

(Leviticus 23:36)36: Seven days you shall offer an offering made by fire to the Lord: on the eighth day shall be an holy convocation to you; and you shall offer an offering made by fire to the Lord: it is a solemn assembly; and you shall do no servile work on it.

+/- October 19th. (Tishul /Ephraim 22nd.)

Job sacrificed to God

(Job 1:3-5) 3:His substance also was seven thousand sheep, and three thousand camels, and five hundred yoke of oxen, and five hundred she asses, and a very great household; so that this man was the greatest of all the men of the east. 4:And his sons went and feasted in their houses, every one on his day from the oldest to the youngest; and sent and called for their three sisters to eat and to drink with them. 5:And it was so, when the days of their feasting were gone, that Job sent and sanctified them, and rose up early in the morning, on the eighth day and offered burnt offerings according to the number of them all: for Job said, It may be that my sons have sinned, and cursed God in their hearts. This did Job continually.

+/-October 19th. (Tishul /Ephraim 22nd.)

God asked Solomon, what he wanted

(2Chronicles 1:7-12) 7:In that night did God appear to Solomon, and said to him, Ask what I shall give you. 8:And Solomon said to God, You have showed great mercy to David my father, and have made me to reign in his stead. 9:Now, O Lord God, let your promise to David my father be established: for you have made me King over a people like the dust of the earth in multitude.

10:Give me now wisdom and knowledge, that I may go out and come in before this people: for who can judge these your people, that is so great? 11:And God said to Solomon, Because this was in your heart, and you have not asked for riches, wealth, or honor, nor the life of your enemies, neither did you asked for long life; but have asked for wisdom and knowledge for yourself, that you may judge my people, over whom I have made you King. 12;Wisdom and knowledge is granted to you; and I will give you riches, and wealth, and honor, such as none of the Kings have had that have been before you, neither shall there any after you have the like.

+/-October 19th. (Tishul /Ephraim 22nd.)

The last day of the feast, during the sacred Assembly

(John 7:37-53) 37:In the last day, that great day of the feast, Jesus stood and cried, saying; If any man thirst, let him come to me, and drink. 38:He that believes on me, as the scripture has said, out of his belly shall flow rivers of living water. 39:(But this spoke he, of the Spirit, which they that believe on him should receive: for the Holy Ghost was not yet given because that Jesus was not yet glorified.) 40:Many of the people therefore, when they heard this saying, said, Of a truth this is the Prophet. 41:Others said, This is the Christ. But some said; Shall Christ come out of Galilee? 42:Has not the scripture said, That Christ comes of the seed of David, and out of the town of Bethlehem, where David was? 43:So there was a division among the people because of him. 44:And some of them would have taken him; but no man laid hands on him. 45:Then came the officers to the chief priests and Pharisees; and they said to them, Why have you not brought him? 46:The officers answered,"Never man spoke like this man." 47:Then answered them the Pharisees, Are you also deceived? 48:Have any of the rulers or of the Pharisees believed on him? 49;But this people who knows not the law are cursed. 50:Nicodemus said to them, (he had come to Jesus by night, being one of them,) 51:Does our law judge any man, before it hears him, and know what he has done? 52:They answered and said to him, Are you also from Galilee? Search, and look: for out of Galilee has there never came a prophet. 53:And every man went to his own house.

+/-October 20th. (Tishul /Ephraim 23th.)

Solomon sent the people away to their tents

(2 Chronicles 7:10-11)10:And on the three and twentieth day of the seventh month he sent the people away into their tents, glad and merry in heart for the goodness that the Lord had showed to David, and to Solomon, and to Israel his people. 11:Then Solomon finished the house of the Lord, and the King's house: and all that came into Solomon's heart to make in the house of the Lord, and in his own house, he prosperously effected.

+/-October 20th. (Tishul /Ephraim 23th.)

(John 8:1-11) A woman caught in adultery was brought to Jesus

(John 8:1-11) 1:Jesus went to the mount of Olives. 2:And early in the morning he came again to the temple, and all the people came to him; and he sat down, and taught them. 3:And the scribes and Pharisees brought to him a woman who was caught in adultery; and when they had thrown her in front of him. 4:They said to him, Master, this woman was caught in adultery, in the very act. 5:Now Moses in the law commanded us, that such should be stoned: but what do you say we should do with her? 6:This they said, tempting him, that they might have to accuse him. But Jesus stooped down, and with his finger wrote on the ground, (Names and dates of those who were around him, who have done this very same crime,) as though he did not hear what they were saying. 7:So when they continued asking him, he lifted up himself, and said to them, Let he who has not guilty of this sin, who is among you, be the first to cast a stone at her.

8:And again he stooped down, and wrote on the ground. 9:And when they heard what he said, they were being convicted by their own conscience, went out one by one, beginning at the eldest, even to the last: and Jesus was left alone, and the woman standing in the midst. 10:When Jesus had lifted up himself, and saw none but the woman, he said to her, Woman, where are those your accusers? Is there no man to condemned you? 11:She said, No man, my Lord. And Jesus said to her, Neither do I condemn you, go and sin no more.

+/-October 21st. (Tishul /Ephraim 24th.)

The year +/- 400 B.C. They were fasting with sackcloth

(Nehemiah 9:1-10:39) 1:Now in the twenty and fourth day of the month of Tishul the children of Israel were assembled with fasting, and wearing sackcloth's, and having dirt upon their heads. 2:And the seed of Israel separated themselves from all strangers, and stood and confessed their sins, and the iniquities of their fathers.
3:And they stood up in their place, and read in the book of the law of the Lord their God one fourth part of the day; and another fourth part they confessed, and worshiped the Lord their God. 4:Then stood up upon the stairs, of the Levites, Jeshua, and Bani, Kadmiel, Shebaniah, Bunni, Sherebiah, Bani, and Chenani, and cried with a loud voice to the Lord their God. 5:Then the Levites, Jeshua, and Kadmiel, Bani, Hashabniah, Sherebiah, Hodijah, Shebaniah, and Pethahiah, said, Stand up and bless the Lord your God forever and ever: and blessed be your glorious name, which is exalted above all blessing and praise. 6:You, only you, alone are the Lord God; you have made the heavens, and the heaven of heavens, with all their host, the earth, and all things that are in them, the seas, and all that is them, and you preserved them all; and the host of heaven worship you. 7:You are the Lord God, who did choose Abram, and brought him forth out of Ur of the Chaldeans, and gave him the name of Abraham, 8:And found his heart faithful before you, and made a covenant with him to give the land of the Canaanites, the Hittites, the Amorites, and the Perizzites, and the Jebusites, and the Girgashites, to give it, I say to his seed, and have performed your words; for you are righteous:
9:And did see the affliction of our fathers in Egypt, and heard their cry by the Red sea. 10:And showed signs and wonders upon Pharaoh, and on all his servants, and on all the people of his land, for you knew that they dealt proudly against them. So did you get you a name, as it is this day. 11:And you didst divide the sea before them, so that they went through the midst of the sea on the dry land; and their persecutors you threw into the deeps, as a stone into the mighty waters.
12:Moreover you led them in the day by a cloudy pillar; and in the night by a pillar of fire, to give them light in the way where they should go. 13:You came down also upon mount Sinai, and spoke with them from heaven, and gave them right judgments, and true laws, good statutes and commandments: 14:And made known to them your holy sabbath, and commanded them precepts, statutes, and laws, by the hand of Moses your servant. 15:And gave them bread from heaven for their hunger, and brought forth water for them out of the rock for their thirst, and promised them that they should go in to possess the land which you had sworn to give them. 16:But they and our fathers dealt proudly, and hardened their necks, and hearkened not to your commandments, 17:and refused to obey, neither were mindful of your wonders that you didst among them; but hardened their necks,

and in their rebellion appointed a captain to return to their bondage: but you are a God ready to pardon, gracious and merciful, slow to anger, and of great kindness, and forsook them not. 18:Yes, when they had made them a molten calf, and said, This is your God that brought you up out of Egypt, and were guilty of great many sins. 19:Yet you in your manifold mercies forsook them not in the wilderness: the pillar of the cloud departed not from them by day, to lead them in the way; neither the pillar of fire by night, to show them light, and the way which they should go. 20:You gave also your good spirit to instruct them, and did not with hold your manna from their mouth, and gave them water for their thirst. 21:Yes, for forty years did you sustain them in the wilderness, so that they lacked nothing; their clothes never grew old, and their feet did not swelled. 22:Moreover you gave them kingdoms and nations, and did divide them into corners, so they possessed the land of Sihon, and the land of the King of Heshbon, and the land of Og, King of Bashan. 23:Their children also multiplied, like the stars of heaven, and brought them into the land, concerning which you had promised to their fathers, that they should go in to possess it. 24:So the children went in and possessed the land, and you subdued before them the inhabitants of the land, the Canaanites, you gave them into their hands, with their Kings, and the people of the land, that they might do with them as they would. 25:And they took strong cities, and a fat land, and possessed houses full of all goods, dug wells, vineyards, and olive yards, and fruit trees in abundance, so they did eat, and were filled, and became fat, and delighted themselves in your great goodness. 26:Nevertheless they were disobedient, and rebelled against you, and cast your law behind their backs, and slew your prophets which testified against them to turn them back to you, and they wrought great provocations.

27:Therefore you delivered them into the hand of their enemies, who oppressed them, and in the time of their trouble, when they cried to you, you heard them from heaven; and according to your manifold mercies you sent them saviors, who saved them out of the hand of their enemies. 28:But after they had rest, they did evil again before you: therefore left you them in the hand of their enemies, so that they had the dominion over them: yet when they returned, and cried unto you, you heard them again from heaven; and many times did you deliver them according to your mercies, 29:And testified against them, that you might bring them again to your law: yet they dealt proudly, and hearkened not to your commandments, but sinned against your judgments, (which if a man do, he shall live in them;) and with drew the shoulder, and hardened their neck, and would not hear. 30:Yet many years did you forbear them, and testified against them by your spirit in your prophets: yet would they not give ear: therefore you gave them into the hand of the people of the lands. 31:Nevertheless for your great mercies' sake you did not utterly consume them, nor forsake them;for you are a gracious and merciful God. 32:Now therefore, our God, the great, the mighty, and the terrible God, who keeps the covenant and mercy, let not all the trouble seem little before you, that has come upon us, on our kings, on our princes, and on our priests, and on our prophets, and on our fathers, and on all your people, since the time of the Kings of Assyria to this day. 33:In all that has come upon us; for you kept faith while we have done evil. 34:Neither have our Kings, our princes, our priests, or our fathers, kept your laws, nor listened to your commandments and your testimonies, of which you reminded them. 35:For they have not served you in their kingdom, and in your great goodness that you gave them, and in the large and fat land which you gave before them, neither turned they from their wicked works. 36:Behold, we are servants this day, and for the land that you gave to our fathers to eat the fruit thereof and the good thereof, behold, we are servants in it. 37:And it yielded much increase to the Kings whom you have set over us because of our sins: also they have dominion over our bodies, and over our cattle, at their pleasure, and we are in great distress. 38:And because of all this we make a sure covenant and write it, and our princes, Levites, and priests, seal to it. **10:1:**Now those that sealed were, Nehemiah, the Tirshatha, the son of Hachaliah, and Zidkijah, 2:Seraiah, Azariah, Jeremiah, 3:Pashur, Amariah, Malchijah, 4:Hattush, Shebaniah, Malluch, 5:Harim, Meremoth, Obadiah, 6:Daniel, Ginnethon, Baruch, 7:Meshullam, Abijah, Mijamin, 8:Maaziah, Bilgai, Shemaiah: these were the priests. 9:And the Levites: both Jeshua the son of Azaniah, Binnui of the sons of Henadad, Kadmiel, 10:And their brethren, Shebaniah, Hodijah, Kelita, Pelaiah, Hanan, 11:Micha, Rehob, Hashabiah, 12:Zaccur, Sherebiah, Shebaniah, 13:Hodijah, Bani, Beninu. 14:The chief of the people; Parosh, Pahathmoab, Elam, Zatthu, Bani, 15:Bunni, Azgad, Bebai, 16:Adonijah, Bigvai, Adin, 17:Ater, Hizkijah, Azzur, 18:Hodijah, Hashum, Bezel, 19:Hariph, Anathoth, Nebai, 20:Magpiash, Meshullam, Hezir, 21:Meshezabeel, Zadok, Jaddua, 22:Pelatiah, Hanan, Anaiah, 23:Hoshea, Hananiah, Hashub, 24:Hallohesh, Pileha, Shobek, 25:Rehum, Hashabnah, Maaseiah, 26:And Ahijah, Hanan, Anan, 27:Malluch, Harim, Baanah. 28:And the rest of the people, the priests, the Levites, the porters, the singers, the Nethinims, and all they that had separated themselves from the people of the lands unto the law of God, their wives, their sons, and their daughters, every one having knowledge, and having understanding. 29:They cleaved to their brethren, their nobles, and entered into a curse, and into an oath, to walk in God's law, which was given by Moses the servant of God, and to observe and do all the commandments of the Lord, our Lord and his judgments and his statutes. 30:And that we would not give our daughters to the people of the land, nor take their daughters for our sons.

31:And if the people of the land bring ware or any victuals on the sabbath day to sell, that we would not buy it of them on the sabbath, or on the holy day: and that we would leave the seventh year, and the exaction of every debt. 32:Also we made ordinances for us, to charge ourselves yearly with the third part of a shekel for the service of the house of our God. 33:For the show bread, and for the continual meat offering, and for the continual burnt offering, of the sabbaths, of the new moons, for the set feasts, and for the holy things, and for the sin offerings to make an atonement for Israel, and for all the work of the house of our God. 34:And we cast the lots among the priests, the Levites, and the people, for the wood offering, to bring it into the house of our God, after the houses of our fathers, at times appointed year by year, to burn upon the altar of the Lord our God, as it is written in the law. 35:And to bring the first fruits of our ground, and the first fruits of all fruit of all trees, year by year, to the house of the Lord. 36:Also the firstborn of our sons, and of our cattle, as it is written in the law, and the first-lings of our herds and of our flocks, to bring to the house of our God, to the priests that minister in the house of our God. 37:And that we should bring the first fruits of our dough, and our offerings, and the fruit of all manner of trees, of wine and of oil, to the priests, to the chambers of the house of our God; and the tithes of our ground to the Levites, that the same Levites might have the tithes in all the cities of our tillage. 38:And the priest the son of Aaron shall be with the Levites, when the Levites take tithes: and the Levites shall bring up the tithe of the tithes to the house of our God, to the chambers, to the treasure house. 39:For the children of Israel and the children of Levi shall bring the offering of the corn, of the new wine, and the oil, unto the chambers, where are the vessels of the sanctuary, and the priests that minister, and the porters, and the singers: and we will not forsake the house of our God.

All three of these men are in mourning.

Above on the left :A man out side of Jerusalem, fasting and wearing sackcloth. Above right: A man whom is called: Daniel, whom is fasting and wearing sackcloth and covered ashes. Below: A man who showed up at Vatican city, fasting bare foot and wearing sackcloth. The Pope came out to meet him.

+/-October 21st. (Tishul /Ephraim 24th.)

Jesus spoke to the Pharisees

(John 8:12-59) 12;Then Jesus spoke again, saying; I am the light of the world he that follows me shall not walk in darkness, but shall have the light of life. 13:The Pharisees then said to him; "You bear record of yourself; therefore your record is not true. 14:Jesus answered and said to them, Though I bear record of myself, yet my record is true: for I know where I came from, and where I am going; but you cannot tell where I came, or where I am going. 15:You judge after the flesh; I judge no man. 16:And yet if I judge, my judgment is true: for I am not alone, for I and the Father who has sent me are one. 17:It is also written in your law, that the testimony of two men is true. 18:I am one that bear witness of myself, and the Father that sent me bears witness of me. 19:Then said they to him, Where is your Father? Jesus answered, You neither know me, nor my Father:if you had known me, you would have known my Father also. 20:These words Jesus spoke in the treasury, as he taught in the temple: and no man laid hands on him; for his hour has not yet come. 21:Then Jesus said again to them, I go my way, and you shall seek me, and shall die in your sins: where I go, you cannot come. 22:Then the Hebrews said; "Will he kill himself? Because he said, Where I go, you cannot come." 23:And he said to them, You are from beneath;(the earth) I am from above:(the Heavens) you are of this world; I am not of this world. 24:I said therefore to you, that you shall die in your sins: for if you do not believe that I am he, you shall die in your sins. 25:Then said they to him, Who are you? And Jesus said to them, Even the same that I said to you from the beginning. 26:I have many things to say and to judge of you: but he that sent me is true; and I speak to the world, those things which I have heard from him.

27:They understood not that he spoke to them of the Father. 28:Then Jesus said to them, When you have lifted up the Son of man, then you shall know that I am he and that I do nothing of myself; but only as my Father has told me, I speak these things. 29;And he that sent me is with me: the Father has not left me alone; for I do always those things that please him. 30;As he spoke these words, many believed on him. 31:Then Jesus said to those Hebrews which believed on him, If you continue in my word, then are you my disciples indeed; 32:And you shall know the truth, and the truth shall make you free. 33:They said to him, We be Abraham's seed, and were never in bondage to any man: why do you say, You shall be made free? 34:Jesus answered them, Verily, verily, I say to you, Who soever commits sin is the servant of sin. 35:And the servant does not abide in the house forever: but the Son will abide forever. 36:If the Son therefore shall make you free, you shall be free indeed. 37:I know that you are Abraham's seed; but you seek to kill me, because my word has no place in you. 38:I speak that which I have seen with my Father: and you do that which you have seen with your father. 39:They answered and said to him, Abraham is our father. Jesus said to them, If you were Abraham's children, you would do the works of Abraham. 40:But now you seek to kill me, a man that has told you the truth, which I have heard from God: that Abraham had not. 41:You say you do the deeds of your father. Then they said to him; We were not born of fornication; we have one Father, even God. 42:Jesus said to them, If God were your Father, you would love me: for I proceeded forth and came from God; neither came I on my own, but he sent me. 43:Why do you not understand my speech?

Why can you not hear my words. 44:You are of your father the devil, and the lusts of your father you will do. He was a murderer from the beginning, and abode not in the truth, because there is no truth in him. When he speaks a lie, he speaks of his own: for he is a liar, and the father of it. 45:And because I tell you the truth, you do not believe me. 46:Which of you convicts me of sin? And if I say the truth, why do you not believe me? 47:He that is of God hears God's words: you will not hear them, because you are not of God. 48:Then answered the Hebrews, and said to him; "We say truly that you are a Samaritan, and has a devil in you? 49:Jesus answered, I have not a devil; but I honor my Father, and you do dishonor me. 50:And I seek not mine own glory: there is one that seeks and judges. 51:Verily, truly, I say to you, If a man keep my saying, he shall never see death. 52:Then said the Hebrews said to him, Now we know that you have a devil. Abraham is dead, and the prophets; and you say, If a man keep my saying, he shall never taste of death. 53:Are you greater than our father Abraham, which is dead? And the prophets who are dead: who do you make yourself to be? 54:Jesus answered, If I honor myself, my honor is nothing: it is my Father that honors me; of whom you say, that he is your God. 55:Yet you have not known him; but I know him: and if I should say, I know him not, I shall be a liar like you: but I know him, and keep his sayings. 56:Your father Abraham rejoiced when he had seen, the day of my coming. 57:Then the Hebrews said to him; You are not even fifty years old yet, and have you seen Abraham? 58;Jesus said to them, Verily, truly, I say to you, Before Abraham was, I was. 59;Then they took up stones to cast at him: but Jesus hid himself, and went out of the temple, going through the midst of them, and so passed by.

+/-October 23rd. (Tishul /Ephraim 26th.)

Paul spoke to the men

(Acts 27:20-21) 20:And when neither sun nor stars in many days appeared, and no small tempest lay on us, all hope that we should be saved was then taken away. 21:But after long abstinence Paul stood up in the midst of them, and said, Sirs, you should have listened to me, and not have left Crete, and would not have brought this harm and loss upon us.

+/-October 24th. (Tishul /Ephraim 27th.)

Paul gave encouraging words

(Acts 27:22-25) 22:And now I exhort you to be of good cheer: for there shall be no loss of any man's life among you, but of the ship. 23:For there stood by me this night an angel of God, whose I am, and whom I serve. 24:Saying; fear not, Paul; you must be brought before Caesar: and, look, God has given you all them that sail with you. 25:Wherefore, sirs, be of good cheer: for I believe God, that it shall be even as it was told me. 26:Howbeit we must be cast upon a certain island.

+/-October 26th. (Tishul /Ephraim 29th.)

They wished for day break

(Acts 27:27-32) 27:But when the fourteenth night had come, as we were driven up and down in Adria, about midnight the midshipmen deemed that they drew, near to some country, 28:and sounded, and found it twenty fathoms: and when they had gone a little further, they sounded again, and found it fifteen fathoms. 29:Then fearing lest we should have fallen upon rocks, they cast four anchors out of the stern, and wished for the day. 30:And as the midshipmen were about to flee out of the ship, when they had let down the boat into the sea, under color as though they would have cast anchors out of the fore ship. 31:Paul said to the centurion and to the soldiers, Except these stay in the ship, you cannot be saved. 32:Then the soldiers cut off the ropes of the boat, and let the boat fall off.

+/-October 27th. (Tishul /Ephraim 30th.)

Paul was bitten by a snake

(Acts 27:33-28:6) 33:And while the day was coming on, Paul talked them all into taking some meat, saying, This day is the fourteenth day that you have stayed and continued fasting, having taken nothing. 34:Wherefore I pray you to eat some meat: for this is for your health: for there shall not an hair fall from the head of any of you.

35:And when he had spoken these words, he took bread, and gave thanks to God in presence of them all: and when he had broken it, he began to eat. 36:Then were they all of good cheer, and they also took some meat. 37:And we were in all in the ship two hundred threescore and sixteen souls. 38;And when they had eaten enough, they lightened the ship, and cast out the wheat into the sea. 39:And when it was day, they knew not the land: but they discovered a certain creek with a shore, into the which they were minded, if it were possible, to thrust in the ship.

40:And when they had taken up the anchors, they committed themselves to the sea, and loosed the rudder bands, and hoisted up the mainsail to the wind, and made toward shore.41:And falling into a place where two seas met, they ran the ship aground; and the forepart stuck fast, and remained unmovable, but the hinder part was broken with the violence of the waves.

42:The soldiers' counsel was to kill the prisoners, lest any of them should swim out, and escape. 43:But the centurion, willing to save Paul, kept them from their purpose; and commanded that they which could swim should cast themselves first into the sea, and get to land. 44:And the rest, some on boards, and some on broken peaces of the ship. And so it came to pass, that they escaped all safe to land.

28:1: And when they were all on land, then they knew that the island was called Melita. 2:And the barbarous people showed us kindness: for they kindled a fire, and received us every one, because of the present rain, and because of the cold. 3:And when Paul had gathered a bundle of sticks, and laid them on the fire, there came a viper out of the heat, and fastened on his hand. 4:And when the barbarians saw the venomous beast hang on his hand, they said among themselves, No doubt this man is a murderer, whom, though he had escaped death by the sea,
yet vengeance will not let him live. 5:And he shook the snake into the fire, and felt no harm. 6:So when they looked, and he had not swollen, or fallen down dead suddenly: but after they had watched while, and saw no harm come to him, they changed their minds, and said that he was a god.

+/-October 28th. (Heshvan/Bul 1st.)

The year +/- 1 A.D. Mary brought a lamb for a sin offering

Mary the wife of Joseph, the Mother of Jesus, brought her sin offering according to the Mosaic law. **As it is written in: (Leviticus 12:1-8)** 1:And the Lord spoke to Moses, saying, 2:Speak to the children of Israel, saying, If a woman have conceived seed, and born a man child: then she shall be unclean seven days; according to the days of the separation for her infirmity shall she be unclean. 3:And in the eighth day the flesh of his foreskin shall be circumcised. 4:And she shall then continue in the blood of her purifying three and thirty days; she shall touch no hallowed thing, nor come into the sanctuary, until the days of her purifying be fulfilled. 5:But if she bear a maid child,_then she shall be unclean two weeks, as in her separation: and she shall continue in the blood of her purifying threescore and six days.6:And when the days of her purifying are fulfilled, for a son, or for a daughter, she shall bring a Lamb of the first year for a burnt offering, and a young Pigeon, or a Turtledove, for a sin offering, to the door of the tabernacle of the congregation, to the priest. 7:Who shall offer it before the Lord, and make an atonement for her; and she shall be cleansed from the issue of her blood. This is the law for her that has given birth to a male or a female. 8:And if she cannot afford to bring a Lamb, then she shall bring two Turtle doves, or two young Pigeons; the one for the burnt offering, and the other for a sin offering: and the priest shall make an atonement for her, and she shall be clean.

+/-October 28th. (Heshvan/Bul 1st.)

Publius took in the men from the ship wreck

(Acts 28:7) 7:In the same quarters were possessions of the chief man of the island, whose name was Publius; who received us, and lodged us three days courteously.

+/-October 28th. (Heshvan/Bul 1st.)

Constantine saw a vision at Milvian bridge

He look in to the sky and saw "Eν Τούτῳ Νίκα",*En toutō níka,*
in Latin it reads : in hoc signo vinces, In this sign you (shall) conquer

(It is believed during the month of Tishul, which is also known as: New Beginning) God took Eve out of Adam

(Genesis 2:21-25) 21:And the Lord God caused a deep sleep to fall upon Adam, and he slept: and he took one of his ribs, and closed up the flesh instead thereof. 22:And the rib, which the Lord God had taken from man, made he a woman, and brought her to the man. 23:And Adam said, This is now bone of my bones, and flesh of my flesh: she shall be called Woman, because she was taken out of Man. 24:Therefore shall a man leave his father and his mother, and shall cleave to his wife: and they shall be one flesh. 25:And they were both naked, the man and his wife, and were not ashamed.

(Please note In the original writings it is written as: Mate not Wife)

(During the first week of the month of October)

(Ezra 3:1-7) They came together as one, 1:And when the seventh month had come, and the children of Israel were in the cities, the people gathered themselves together as one man to Jerusalem. 2:Then stood up Jeshua the son of Jozadak, and his brethren the priests, and Zerubbabel the son of Shealtiel, and his brethren, and build the altar of the God of Israel, to offer burnt offerings thereon, as it is written in the law of Moses the man of God. 3;And they set the altar upon his bases; for fear was upon them because of the people of those countries: and they offered burnt offerings thereon to the Lord, even burnt offerings morning and evening. 4:They kept also the feast of tabernacles, as it is written, and offered the daily burnt offerings by number, according to the custom, as the duty of every day required. 5:And afterward offered the continual burnt offering, both of the new moons, and of all the set feasts of the Lord that were consecrated, and of every one that willingly offered a freewill offering to the Lord. 6:From the first day of the seventh month began they to offer burnt offerings to the Lord. But the foundation of the temple of the Lord was not yet laid. 7:They gave money also to the masons, and to the carpenters; and meat, and drink, and oil, to them of Zion, and to them of Tyre, to bring cedar trees from Lebanon to the sea of Joppa, according to the grant that they had of Cyrus king of Persia.

(During the second week of October/Tishul)

(Book of Jubilees 11:18-21) 18:And in the three and thirtieth Jubilee, in the first of the year in the second week, Peleg took to himself a wife, whose name was Lomna, the daughter of Sina'ar and bore him a son in the fourth year, in the second week, and she called his name Reu; for he said; "Behold the children of men have become evil though the wicked purpose of building for themselves a city and a tower in the land of Shinar. 19: "For they departed from the land of Ararat eastward to Shinar for in his days they built the city and the tower, saying; "Go to, let us ascend thereby into heaven" 20:And they began to build and in the fourth week they made brick with fire, and the bricks served them for stone, and the clay with which they cemented them together with asphalt which comes out of the sea, and out of the fountains of waters in the land of Shinar. 21:And they built on it for forty three years.

(During the third week of October)

(October /Tishul) David became King of Hebron

(2 Samuel 2:11) 11:And the time that David was King in Hebron, over the house of Judah for: seven years and six months.

Nimrod started to build the Towers of Babel

(Genesis 11:3-4)3:And they said one to another, Go to, let us make brick, and burn them thoroughly. And they had brick for stone, and slime had they for mortar. 4:And they said, Go to, let us build us a city and a tower, whose top may reach to heaven; and let us make us a name, lest we be scattered abroad upon the face of the whole earth. So they started making bricks.

(It was also during the month of October/Tishul)
Hananiah the prophet died

(Jeremiah 28:17)17:So Hananiah the prophet died the same year in the seventh month.

Ishmael and ten men killed Gedaliah

(2Kings 25:25-26) 25:But it came to pass in the seventh month, that Ishmael the son of Nethaniah, the son of Elishama, of the seed royal, came, and ten men with him, and struck Gedaliah, so that he died, and the Jews and the Chaldeans that were with him at Mizpah. 26:And all the people, both small and great, and the captains of the armies arose, and came to Egypt: for they were afraid of the Chaldeans.

The Death of King Herod

(In the Hebrew year of +/- **3756)** It is believed that; King Herod died in the month of Tishul/Ephraim

Ishmael escaped from Johanan

(Jeremiah 41:1-18)1:Now it came to pass in the seventh month, that Ishmael the son of Nethaniah the son of Elishama, of the seed royal, and the princes of the King, he had ten men with him, came to Gedaliah, the son of Ahikam at Mizpah; and there they did eat bread together in Mizpah. 2:Then arose Ishmael the son of Nethaniah, and the ten men that were with him, and struck Gedaliah, the son of Ahikam, the son of Shaphan with the sword, and killed him, whom the King of Babylon had made governor over the land. 3:Ishmael also killed all the Jews that were with him, even with Gedaliah, at Mizpah, and the Chaldeans that were found there, and the men of war. 4:And it came to pass the second day after he murdered Gedaliah, and no man knew of it, 5:That there came eighty men with their beards shaved off,clothes in rags, and with gashes on their bodies came from Shechem, from Shiloh, and from Samaria, bringing food offerings and incense for the house of the Lord. 6:And Ishmael the son of Nethaniah went forth from Mizpah to meet them, weeping all along as he went: and it came to pass, as he met them, he said unto them, Come to Gedaliah the son of Ahikam. 7:And it was so, when they came into the midst of the city, that Ishmael the son of Nethaniah killed them, and threw them into the midst of the pit, he and the men that were with him. 8:But ten men were found among them that said to Ishmael, do not kill us: for we have treasures in the field, of wheat, and of barley, and of oil, and of honey. So he stopped, and did not kill them, along with their brethren. 9:Now the pit wherein Ishmael had cast all the dead bodies of the men, whom he had slain because of Gedaliah, was it which Asa the King had made for fear of Baasha King of Israel: and Ishmael the son of Nethaniah filled it with them that were slain. 10:Then Ishmael carried away captive all the residue of the people that were in Mizpah, even the King's daughters, and all the people that remained in Mizpah, whom Nebuzaradan the captain of the guard and Ishmael the son of Nethaniah, he also carried away captive, and departed to go over to the Ammonites. 11:But when Johanan the son of Kareah, and all the captains of the forces that were with him, heard of all the evil that Ishmael, the son of Nethaniah had done. 12:Then they took all the men, and went to fight with Ishmael the son of Nethaniah, and found him by the great waters that are in Gibeon.

13:Now it came to pass, that when all the people which were with Ishmael saw Johanan the son of Kareah, and all the captains of the forces that were with him, then they were glad. 14:So all the people that Ishmael had carried away captive from Mizpah cast about and returned, and went to Johanan the son of Kareah. 15:But Ishmael the son of Nethaniah escaped from Johanan with eight men, and went to the Ammonites. 16:Then took Johanan the son of Kareah, and all the captains of the forces that were with him, all the remnant of the people whom he had recovered from Ishmael the son of Nethaniah, from Mizpah, after that he had slain Gedaliah the son of Ahikam, even the mighty men of war, and the women, and the children, and the eunuchs, whom he had brought again from Gibeon. 17:And they departed, and dwelt in the habitation of Chimham, which is by Bethlehem, to go to enter into Egypt, 18:Because of the Chaldeans: for they were afraid of them, because Ishmael the son of Nethaniah had killed Gedaliah the son of Ahikam, whom the King of Babylon made governor in the land.

Believed to be the month Joseph was born

(Ezekiel 37:15-28) 15:The word of the Lord, came again to me, saying, 16:Moreover, you son of man, take you one stick, and write upon it, For Judah, and for the children of Israel his companions: then take another stick, and write upon it, For Joseph, the stick of Ephraim, and for all the house of Israel his companions: 17:And join them one to another unto one stick; and they shall become one in your hand. 18:And when the children of your people shall speak to you, saying; Will you not show us what you mean by these? 19:Say to them; This is what the Lord God says; Behold, I will take the stick of Joseph, which is in the hand of Ephraim, and the tribes of Israel his fellows, and will put them with him, even with the stick of Judah, and make them one stick, and they shall be one in mine hand. 20:And the sticks where on you wright shall be in your hand before their eyes. 21:And say to them, This says the Lord God; Behold, I will take the children of Israel from among the heathen, whither they be gone, and will gather them on every side, and bring them into their own land. 22:And I will make them one nation in the land upon the mountains of Israel; and one King shall be King to them all: and they shall be no more two nations, neither shall they be divided into two Kingdoms any more at all. 23:Neither shall they defile themselves any more with their idols, nor with their detestable things, nor with any of their transgressions: but I will save them out of all their dwelling places, wherein they have sinned, and will cleanse them: so shall they be my people, and I will be their God. 24:And David my servant shall be King over them; and they all shall have one shepherd: they shall also walk in my judgments, and observe my statutes, and do them. 25:And they shall dwell in the land that I have given to Jacob my servant, wherein your fathers have dwelt; and they shall dwell therein, even they, and their children, and their children's children forever: and my servant David shall be their prince forever. 26:Moreover I will make a covenant of peace with them; it shall be an everlasting covenant with them: and I will place them, and multiply them, and will set my sanctuary in the midst of them for evermore. 27:My tabernacle also shall be with them: yes, I will be their God, and they shall be my people. 28:And the heathen shall know that I the Lord do sanctify Israel, when my sanctuary shall be in the midst of them for evermore.

(October /Tishul)

The year +/- 306 B.C. A sinful man became King

(1Maccabees. 1:10-13) 10:There sprang from these a sinful off-shoot, Antiochus Epiphanies, son of King Antiochus, once a hostage at Rome. He became King in the year one hundred and eighty seven of the kingdom of the Greeks. 11:In those days there appeared in Israel men who were breakers of the law, and they seduced many people, saying; "Let us go and make alliance with the Gentiles all around us; scene we separated from them, many evils have come upon us. 12:The proposal was agreeable; 13:some of the people promptly went to the King, and he authorized them to introduce the way of living, of the Gentiles.

The year +/- 294 B.C. Antiochus plundered Egypt

(1Maccabees 6:16-18) 6:When his kingdom seemed secure, Antiochus proposed to become King of Egypt, so as to rule over both kingdoms.17;He invaded Egypt with a strong force, with chariots, elephants, and with a large fleet. 18;To make war on Ptolemy, King of Egypt. Ptolemy was frightened at his presence and fled, leaving many casualties.19;The fortified cities of the land of Egypt were captured, and Antiochus plundered the land of Egypt.

Extra notes for (October /Tishul)
On page 362, (October 7th.)
(Ancient Hebrew learning center)

Jacob: sent up his tents and booths outside the town of Salem, on Mount Zion. Later this town would be called Jerusalem. Thought to be after after Shechem died, Jacob bought the city at a great cost of livestock from the people, who were living there at the time.

It was during the month of Tishul
The year +/- 4779 B.C.E. The Birth of Cane

(Genesis 4:1) 1:Then Adam knew his wife Eve, and she bore conceived and bore a son, then called him Cane, "I have produced a man with the help of the Lord."

October 29th /Heshvan/Bul 2nd. +/- 312 C.E.

Constantine entered Rome

The fallowing year. Then Constantine and Licinius issued the edict of Milan. which made Christianity an officially recognized and tolerated religion in the Roman Empire. In the last 6 years of his life he was very sick and was scared of what God would do to him after his death. So he wrote a law that it was illegal to worship any other God than the God of the Christians.

October 31st. /Heshvan/Bul 4th.

The year +/- 1517 C.E. The Bible was given to the common person

A German monk and professor of theology, Dr. Martin Luther, courageously published the simple, straightforward truth of the Bible. On October 31, 1517, the Bible came into the hands of the common people once again.

Chapter 11:November - Heshvan / Bul

It is the 8th. month on the Hebrew calendar.
In Hebrew this month is called: Heshvan / Bul,
which means: Rain / Sealed
Tribe of Naphtali, means:(In a wrestling match, he has wrestled)
The stone of (Amethyst Quarts) represents this tribe.
Naphtali,(The 2nd.) Son of Bilhah the hand maiden of Rachel.
(Was believed to have been born in this month.)
(Spirit of Wrath)

+/- November 5th. (Heshvan/Bul 9th.)

The year +/- 160 B.C. Now after forty days

(2Maccabees 5:5-7) 5:But when a false rumor circulated that Antiochus was dead, Jason gathered fully a thousand men and suddenly attacked the city. As the defenders on the wall were forced back and the city was finally being taken, Menelaus took refuge in the citadel. 6:Jason then slaughtered his fellow citizens without mercy, not realizing that triumph over one's own kindred was the greatest failure, but imagining that he was winning a victory over his enemies, not his fellow countrymen. 7:Even so, he did not gain control of the government, but in the end received only disgrace for his treachery, and once again took refuge in the country of the Ammonites.

+/- November 6th. (Heshvan/Bul 10th.)

The year +/- 3229 B.C. They entered the Ark.

(Genesis 7:1-9) 1:And the Lord said to Noah, Come you and all your house into the ark; for you have I seen righteous before me in this generation. 2:Of every clean beast you shall take to you by seven, males and fourteen females: and of beasts that are not clean, two by two, both males and females. 3:Of fowls also of the air by sevens, the males and the females;

to keep seed alive upon the face of all the earth. 4:For in seven days, and I will cause it to rain upon the earth forty days and forty nights; and every living substance that I have made I will destroy, from off the face of the earth. 5:And Noah did according to all that the Lord commanded him. 6:And Noah was six hundred years old when the flood of waters was upon the earth. 7:And Noah went in, along with his sons, his wife, and his sons wives with him, into the ark, because of the waters of the flood. 8:Of clean beasts, and of beasts that are not clean, and of fowls, and of every thing that creeps upon the earth, 9:There went in two by two unto Noah, and into the ark, the males and the females, as God had commanded Noah.

Above left, is a model of Noah's Ark. On the right, is 1 of the 14 counter weights, Noah used to help keep the ark balanced during the flood.

The counter weights (14 in all), were found in the Lost City, not far from where the ark landed. On it is the mark of Nimrod, the first conquer of men.

Before the flood started: Noah lived next to the Awali river, close to the Al Shouf forest, located in modern day Lebanon.

Please note: Nimrod was the son of Cush, the grand son of Ham and the great- grandson of Noah.

Later he would be killed by Esau. On the 14th. of Nissan. Found in the (Book of Jasper 27:1-17)

+/- November 7th. (Heshvan/Bul 11th.)

The day Rachel died

(Genesis 48:7)7:And as for me, when I came from Padan, Rachel died by me in the land of Canaan on the way, when yet there was but a little way to come to Ephrath: and I buried her there in the way of Ephrath; the same is near to Bethlehem.

Rachel's sarcophagus is now in Bethlehem, it is approximately, 5 miles from Jerusalem.

+/- November 7th. (Heshvan/Bul 11th.)

Jephthah's daughter was sacrificed to the Lord

In accordance to the law, as it is written in:**(Leviticus 27:28-29)**

This is the first of 4 days of mourning and dance for Rachel,

(Which was believed to have been her name)

(Judges 11:39-40) 39;And it came to pass at the end of two months, that she returned to her father, who did with her according to his vow to the Lord, which he had vowed: and she knew no man. And it was a custom in Israel. 40: That the daughters of Israel went yearly to lament and dance for the daughter of Jephthah, the Gileadite four days each year.

+/- November 7th. (Heshvan/Bul 11th.)

They went and took wives from the daughters of Shiloh

(Judges 21:19-25) 19:Then they said, Behold, there is a feast of the Lord in Shiloh yearly in a place which is on the north side of Bethel, on the east side of the highway that goeth up from Bethel to Shechem, and on the south of Lebonah. 20:Therefore they commanded the children of Benjamin, saying; Go and lie in wait in the vineyards, 21:And see, and, behold, if the daughters of Shiloh come out to dance in dances, then you come out of the vineyards, and catch you every man his wife of the daughters of Shiloh, and go to the land of Benjamin. 22:And it shall be, when their fathers or their brethren come to us to complain, that we will say to them, Be favorable to them for our sakes: because we reserved not to each man his wife in the war: for you did not give to them at this time, that you should be guilty. 23:And the children of Benjamin did so, and took them wives, according to their number, of them that danced, whom they caught: and they went and returned to their inheritance, and repaired the cities, and dwelt in them. 24:And the children of Israel departed thence at that time, every man to his tribe and to his family, and they went out from thence every man to his inheritance. 25:In those days there was no King in Israel: every man did that which was right in his own eyes.

+/- November 8th. (Heshvan/Bul 12th.)

Rebekah's Birthday

(According to the Ancient Hebrew learning center) The day of Rebekah's birth, the daughter of Bethuel the Syrian of Padanaram, the sister to Laban the Syrian. Rebekah who became the wife of Isaac.

+/- November 11th. (Heshvan/Bul 15th.)

Between the years +/- 925-904 B.C. Jeroboam hand was withered

(1Kings 12:32-13:10) 32:And Jeroboam ordained a feast in the eighth month, on the fifteenth day of the month, to duplicate the feast that is in Judah, and he offered upon the altar. So did he in Bethel, sacrificing to the calves that he had made: and he placed in Bethel the priests of the high places which he had made. 33:So he offered upon the altar which he had made in Bethel the fifteenth day of the eighth month,

even in the month which he had devised of his own heart; and ordained a feast to
the children of Israel, and he offered upon the altar, and burnt incense. **13:1:**And,
behold, there came a man of God out of Judah by the word of the Lord to Bethel:
and Jeroboam stood by the altar to burn incense. 2:And he cried out against the altar
the word of the Lord, and say; "O altar, altar, the Lord says; Behold, a child shall be
born to the house of David, Josiah by name; who shall slaughter upon you the
priests of the high places who offer sacrifice upon you, and he shall burn human
bones upon you." 3:And he gave a sign the same day, saying; This is the sign which
the Lord has spoken; Behold, the altar shall be rent, and the ashes that are upon it
shall be poured out. 4:And it came to pass, when King Jeroboam heard the saying of
the man of God, which had cried against the altar in Bethel, that he put forth his
hand from the altar, saying, Lay hold on him. And his hand, which he put forth
against him, dried up, so that he could not pull it in again to him. 5:Moreover, the
alter broke up and the ashes from it were; strewn about the sign the man of God had
given as the word of the Lord. 6:And the King answered and said to the man of
God, entreat now the face of the Lord your God, and pray for me, that my hand may
be restored to me again. And the man of God besought the Lord, and the King's
hand was restored to him again, and became as it was before. 7:And the King said to
the man of God, Come home with me, and refresh yourself, and I will give you a
reward. 8:And the man of God said to the King, If you will give me half of your
house, I would not go with you, nor will I eat bread nor drink water in this place.
9:For so was it charged me by the word of the Lord, saying, Eat no bread, nor drink
water, nor return again, by the same way that you came. 10:So he went another way,
and returned not by the way that he came to Bethel.

+/- November 12th. (Heshvan/Bul 16th.)

Between the year +/- 925-904 B.C. The prophet was killed by a Lion

(1Kings 13:11-26) 11:Now there dwelt an old prophet in Bethel; and his sons came
and told him all the works that the man of God had done that day in Bethel: the
words which he had spoken to the King, them they told also to their father. 12:And
their father said to them, What way did he go? For his sons had seen the way the
man of God went, which came from Judah. 13:And he said to his sons, Saddle me
the ass. So they saddled him the ass: and he rode thereon, 14:And went after the
man of God, and found him sitting under an oak: and he said to him; Are you the
man of God that came from Judah? And he said, I am. 15:Then he said to him,
Come home with me, and eat bread. 16:And he said, I may not return with you, nor
will I go in with you: neither will I eat bread nor drink water with you in this place.
17:For it was said to me by the word of the Lord, You shall eat no bread nor drink
water there, nor turn again to go by the way that you came. 18:He said to him, I am
a prophet also as you are; and an angel spoke to me by the word of the Lord, saying,
Bring him back with you to your house, that he may eat bread and drink water. But
he lied unto him. 19:So he went back with him, and did eat bread in his house, and
drank water. 20:And it came to pass, as they sat at the table, that the word of the
Lord came to the prophet that brought him back. 21:And he cried to the man of God
that came from Judah, saying, This is what the Lord says; because you have
disobeyed the words of the Lord,and have not kept the commandment which the
Lord your God has commanded you.

22:But came back, and have eaten bread and drank water in the place, of the which the Lord did say to you; Do not eat any bread, or drink any water from this place; your carcase shall not come to the sepulcher of your fathers. 23:And it came to pass, after he had eaten bread, and after he had drank, that he saddled for him the ass, for the prophet whom he had brought back. 24:And when he was gone, a lion met him by the way, and killed him: and his carcase was cast in the way, and the ass stood by it, the lion also stood by the carcase. 25:And, behold, men passed by, and saw the carcase cast in the way, and the lion standing by the carcase: and they came and told it in the city where the old prophet dwelt. 26:And when the prophet that brought him back from the way heard therefore he said; It is the man of God, who was disobedient to the word of the Lord: therefore the Lord has delivered him to a lion, which had torn him into peaces, and killed him, according to the word of the Lord, which he had spoken to him.

+/- November 13th. (Heshvan/Bul 17th.)

The year +/- 3229 B.C. The Day the Great Flood started

(Genesis 7:11-12)11:In the six hundredth year of Noah's life, in the second month, the seventeenth day of the month, the same day were all the fountains of the great deep broken up, and the windows of heaven were opened. 12:And the rain was upon the earth, forty days and forty nights.

+/- November 19th. (Heshvan/Bul 23rd.)

After the work was done, David held a feast,

(2Chronicles 7:10)10;And on the three and twentieth day of the seventh month he sent the people away to their tents, glad and merry in heart for the goodness that the Lord had showed to David, and to Solomon, and to Israel his people.

+/- November 23rd. (Heshvan/Bul 27th.)

The Year +/- 3228 B.C. Noah and his family left the Ark

(Genesis 8:14-9:19) 14:And in the second month, on the seven and twentieth day of the month, was the earth dried. 15:And God spoke to Noah, saying, 16:Go forth out of the ark, you, and your wife, and your sons, and your sons, wives with you. 17:Bring forth with you every living thing that is with you, all of the flesh, all of the fowl, and cattle, and of every living thing, the creeping things that creep upon the earth; that they may breed abundantly in the earth, and be fruitful, and multiply upon the earth. 18:And Noah went forth, and his sons, and his wife, and his sons, wives with them. 19:Every beast, every creeping thing, and every fowl, and what soever creeps upon the earth, after their kinds, went forth out of the ark. 20:And Noah build an altar to the Lord; and took of every clean beast, and of every clean fowl, and offered burnt offerings on the altar. 21:And the Lord smelled a sweet savor; and the Lord said in his heart, I will never again curse the ground any more for man's sake; for the imagination of man's heart is evil from his youth; neither will I again strike anymore every thing living, as I have done. 22:While the earth remains, the time of seed and harvest, and cold and heat, and summer and winter, and day and night shall not cease.

9:1: And God blessed Noah and his sons, and said to them, Be fruitful, and
multiply, and replenish the earth. 2:And the fear of you and the dread of you shall be
upon every beast of the earth, and upon every fowl of the air, upon all that moves
upon the earth, and upon all the fishes of the sea; into your hand are they delivered.
3:Every moving thing that lives shall be meat for you; even as the green herb have I
given you all things. 4:But flesh with the life there of, which is the blood, you shall
you not eat. 5:And surely your blood of your lives will I require; at the hand of
every beast will I require it, and at the hand of man; at the hand of every man's
brother will I require the life of man.6:Who so sheds another man's blood, by man
shall his blood be shed: for in the image of God made he man. 7:And you, be shall
be fruitful, and multiply; bring forth abundantly in the earth, and multiply therein.
8:And God spoke to Noah, and to his sons with him, saying; 9:And I, behold, I
establish my covenant with you, and with your seed after you. 10:And with every
living creature that is with you, of the fowl, of the cattle, and of every beast of the
earth with you; from all that go out of the ark, to every beast of the earth. 11:And I
will establish my covenant with you; neither shall all flesh be cut off any more by
the waters of a flood; neither shall there any more be a flood to destroy the earth.

12:And God said, This is the token of the covenant which I make between me and
you and every living creature that is with you, for perpetual generations. 13:I do set
my bow in the cloud, and it shall be for a token of a covenant between me and the
earth. 14:And it shall come to pass, when I bring a cloud over the earth, that the bow
shall be seen in the cloud. 15:And I will remember my covenant which is between
me and you and every living creature of all flesh; and the waters shall no more
become a flood to destroy all flesh. 16:And the bow shall be in the cloud; and I will
look upon it, that I may remember the everlasting covenant between God and every
living creature of all flesh that is upon the earth. 17:And God said to Noah, This is
the token of the covenant, which I have established between me and all flesh that is
upon the earth. 18:And the sons of Noah, that went forth of the ark, were Shem, and
Ham, and Japheth: and Ham is the father of Canaan. 19:These are the three sons of
Noah: and of them was the whole earth overspread.

(More about Noah and his family) From the: Babylonian Talmud, the Book of Jubilees, Sibyl Oracles of Greece,

Noah's wife's name was **Naamah**, which means: (**Beautiful or Pleasant.**)
His children were: 1st Son **Shem** and his wife; **Sedeqetelebab**, who name means: (**From the East.**) 2nd. Son **Ham** and his his wife: **Ne'eltama'uk**, who name means: (**Magi, or watcher of the stars.**) 3rd Son **Japheth** and his wife: **Adataneses**, also called: (**Tse-da-qah Ley-vav**) who name means: **(Correctness of mind.**)

(The seven Laws God gave to Noah)

1:Establish courts of Law. **2:**Do not Lie or commit Blasphemy. **3:**Do not commit Idolatry. **4:**Do not commit Incest or adultery. **5:**One man is not to strike another with his hands or to shed his another mans blood, for he is made in the image of God. **6:**Do not commit robbery or steal. **7:**Do not eat the flesh of any animal while it is yet alive.

**Above are what is believed to be the remains of Noah's Ark.
Below a picture of the inside of the Ark.**

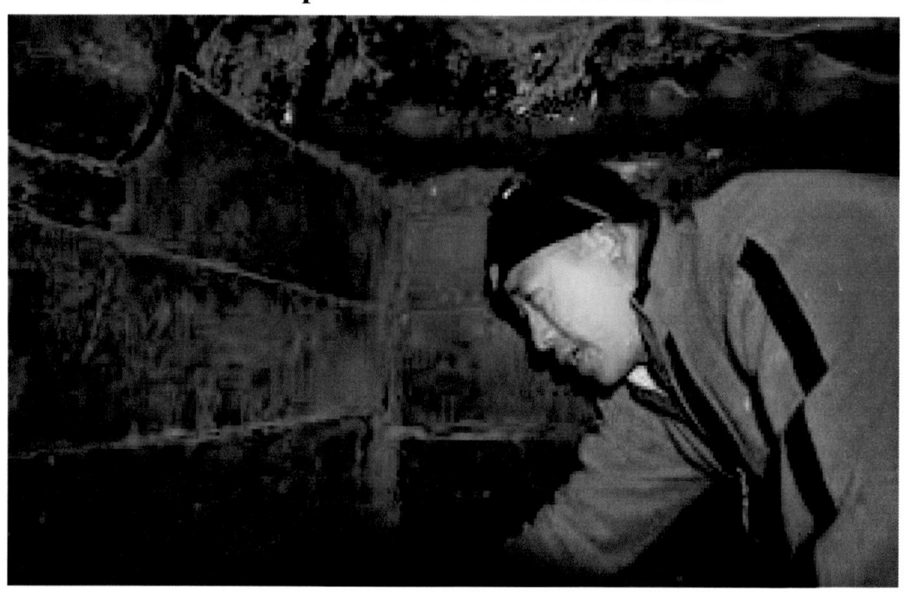

+/- November 25th. (Heshvan/Bul 29th.)

The year +/- 40A.D. Michael went to war, against the Dragon in Heaven

(Revelation 12:7-9) 7:And there was war in heaven: Michael and his angels fought against the Dragon; and the Dragon and his angels fought, 8:And prevailed not; neither was their place found any more in heaven for them. 9:And the great dragon was cast out, that old serpent, called the Devil, and Satan, which deceives the whole world: he was cast out down to the earth, and his angels were cast out with him.

+/- November 27th. (Kislev / Chislev 1st.)

The year +/-1 B.C.E. The Birthday of John the Baptist,

(Luke 1:57-58) 57:Now Elizabeth's full time came that she should be delivered; and she brought forth a son. 58:And her neighbors and her cousins heard how the Lord had showed great mercy upon her; and they rejoiced with her.

+/- November 30th. (Kislev / Chislev 4th.)

The Lord spoke through Zechariah

(Zechariah 7;1-14) 1:And it came to pass in the fourth year of King Darius, that the word of the Lord came to Zechariah in the fourth day of the ninth month, in Chislev. 2:When they had sent Sherezer and Regemmelech to the house of God, and their men, to pray before the Lord. 3:And to speak to the priests which were in the house of the Lord of hosts, and to the prophets, saying, Should I weep in the fifth month, separating myself, as I have done these so many years?

4:Then came the word of the Lord of hosts said to me. 5:Speak to all the people of the land, and to the priests, saying, When you fasted and mourned in the fifth and seventh month, even those seventy years, did you at all fast to me, or for yourselves? 6:And when you did eat, and when you did drink, did you not eat, and drink for yourselves? 7:Should you not hear the words which the Lord has cried by the former prophets, when Jerusalem was inhabited and in prosperity, and the cities thereof round about her, when men inhabited the south and the plain?

8:And the word of the Lord came to Zechariah, saying; 9:This speaks the Lord of hosts, saying, Execute true judgment, and show mercy and compassion every man to his brother. 10:And oppress not the widow, nor the fatherless, the stranger, nor the poor; and let none of you imagine evil against his brother in your heart. 11:But they refused to listen, and turned their backs on me, and stopped their ears, so that they would not hear.

12:Yes, they made their hearts as an adamant stone, lest they should hear the law, and the words which the Lord of hosts had sent in his spirit by the former prophets, therefore came a great wrath from the Lord of hosts. 13:Therefore it is come to pass, that as he cried, and they would not hear; so they cried, and I would not hear, says the Lord of hosts.

14:But I scattered them with a whirlwind among all the nations whom they knew not. This the land was desolate after them, that no man passed through nor returned: for they laid the pleasant land desolate.

(It was also in the month of November / Kislev)

The house of the Lord was finished after seven years

(1Kings 6:38) 6:And in the eleventh year, in the month Bul, which is the eighth month, that the house was finished throughout all the parts thereof, and according to all the fashion of it. So was he seven years in building it.

The year +/- 156 B.C. The King was informed of evil being done

(1Maccabees 6:20-27) 20:So in the year one hundred and fifty they assembled and stormed the citadel, for which purpose he constructed catapults and other devices. 21:Some of the besieged escaped, joined by impious Israelites, 22:they to the King and said; "How long will you fail to do justice and avenge our kinsmen? 23;We agreed to serve your father and to follow his orders and obey his edicts. 24:And for this the sons of our people have become our enemies; they have put to death as many of us as they could find and have plundered our estates. 25:They have acted aggressively not only against us, but throughout their whole territory. 26:Look! They have now besieged the citadel in Jerusalem in order to capture it, and they have fortified the sanctuary and Bethzur. 27:Unless you quickly forestall them, they will even do worse things than these, and you not be able to stop them. 28:When the king heard this he was angry, and he called together all his Friends,and the Officers of his army, and the Commanders of the Calvary.

The Lord said return to me and I will return to you

(Zechariah 1:1-6)1:In the eighth month, in the second year of Darius, came the word of the Lord to Zechariah, the son of Berechiah, the son of Iddo the prophet, saying: 2:The Lord has been surly displeased with your fathers. 3:Therefore you will say to them, This says the Lord of hosts; Return you to me, says the Lord of hosts, and I will return to you, says the Lord of hosts. 4:Be you not as your fathers, to whom the former prophets have cried, saying, This is what the Lord of hosts has to say; Turn you now from your evil ways, and from your evil doings: but they would not hear, nor listen to me, says the Lord. 5:Your fathers, where are they now? And the prophets, do they live forever? 6:But my words and my statutes, which I commanded my servants the prophets, did they not take hold of your fathers? And they returned and said, Like as the Lord of hosts thought to do to us, according to our ways, and according to our doings, so has he dealt with us.

The vineyards outside of Shiloh

(Spoke of on page 405) A city in the Ephraim hill country, where the young single daughters of Shiloh would dance.

Here are two other pictures of the land today around Shiloh

Above: Shiloh is built on the the top of the hill.

Chapter 12: December / Kislev / Chislev

It is the 9th. month on the Hebrew calendar
In Hebrew this month is called:Kislev/ Chislev,
which means:(Trust-Faith /Festival of Lights)
Tribe of Gad, means:(In luck)
The stone of (Chrysoprase) represents this tribe.
Gad:(The 1st.)Son of Zilpah, the hand maiden of Leah,
(Was believed to have been born in this month.)
(Spirit of Discernment)

+/- December 4th. (Kislev/ Chislev 8th.)

The Birth of John, son of Zachariah,
who would come to be called John the baptist

(Luke 1:59-80) 59:And it came to pass, that on the eighth day they came to
circumcise the child; and they called him Zachariah, after the name of his father.
60:And his mother answered and said, Not so, but he shall be called John. 61:And
they said to her, There is none of your kindred that is called by this name. 62:And
they made signs to his father, how he would have him called. 63:And he asked for a
writing table, and wrote, his name is John. And they all marveled. 64:And his mouth
was opened immediately, and he once again could speak and he said his name is
John, and praised God. 65:And fear came on all that dwelt round about them: and
all these sayings were noised abroad throughout all the hill country of Judea.
66:And all they that heard them laid them up in their hearts, saying, What manner of
child shall this be! And the hand of the Lord was with him. 67:And his father
Zachariah was filled with the Holy Ghost, and prophesied, saying; 68:Blessed be the
Lord God of Israel; for he has visited and redeemed his people. 69:And has raised
up an horn of salvation for us in the house of his servant David; 70:As he spoke by
the mouth of his holy prophets, which have been since the world began. 71:That we
should be saved from our enemies, and from the hand of all that hate us. 72:To
perform the mercy promised to our fathers, and to remember his holy covenant.

73:The oath which he swore to our father Abraham, 74:That he would grant to us, that we being delivered out of the hand of our enemies might serve him without fear. 75:In holiness and righteousness before him, all the days of our life. 76:And your, child, shall be called the prophet of the Highest: for you shall go before the face of the Lord to prepare his ways. 77:To give knowledge of salvation to his people by the remission of their sins. 78:Through the tender mercy of our God; whereby the day spring from on high has visited us, 79:To give light to them that sit in darkness and in the shadow of death, to guide our feet into the way of peace. 80:And the child grew, and waxed strong in spirit, and was in the deserts till the day of his showing to Israel.

+/- December 11th. (Kislev / Chislev 15th.)

The year +/- 161 B.C. The King erected pagan alters

(1Maccabees 1:54-58) 54:On the fifteenth of the month Chislev, in the year one hundred and forty-five, the King erected the horrible abomination upon the alter of holocaust, and in the surrounding cities of Judah they build pagan alters. 55:They also burnt incense at the doors of houses and in the streets. 56:Any scrolls of the law which they found they tore up and burnt. 57:Whoever was found with a scroll of the covenant, and whoever observed the law, was condemned to death by royal decree. 58:So they used their power against Israel, against those who were caught, each month in the cities.

+/- December 14th. (Kislev/ Chislev 18th.)

The year +/- 396 B.C. The men of Judah and Benjamin came together

(Ezra 10:1-8)1:Now when Ezra had prayed, and when he had confessed, weeping and casting himself down before the house of God, there assembled to him out of Israel a very great congregation of men and women and children: for the people wept very sore. 2:And Shechaniah the son of Jehiel, one of the sons of Elam, answered and said to Ezra, We have trespassed against our God, and have taken strange wives of the people of the land: yet now there is hope in Israel concerning this thing. 3:Now therefore let us make a covenant with our God to put away all the wives, and such as are born of them, according to the counsel of my lord, and of those that tremble at the commandment of our God; and let it be done according to the law. 4:Arise; for this matter belongs to you, we also will be with you; be of good courage, and do it. 5:Then arose Ezra, and made the chief priests, the Levites, and all Israel, to swear that they should do according to this word. And they all swore. 6:Then Ezra rose up from before the house of God, and went into the chamber of Johanan the son of Eliashib: and when he came closer, he did not eat any bread, nor drink any water, for he mourned because of the transgression of them that had been carried away. 7:And they made proclamation throughout all of Judah and Jerusalem to all the children of the captivity, that they should gather themselves together to Jerusalem, 8:And that who soever would not come within three days, according to the counsel of the princes and the elders, all his substance should be forfeited, and himself separated from the congregation of those that had been carried away.

+/- December 16th. (Kislev / Chislev 20th.)

The year +/- 396 B.C. The men who took strange wife's

(Ezra 10:9-16) 9:Then all the men of Judah and Benjamin gathered themselves together to Jerusalem within three days. It was in the ninth month, on the twentieth day of the month; and all the people sat in the street of the house of God, trembling because of this matter, and for the great rain. 10:And Ezra the priest stood up, and said to them, You have transgressed, and have taken strange wives, to increase the trespass of Israel. 11:Now therefore make confession to the Lord God of your fathers, and do his pleasure: and separate yourselves from the people of the land, and from the strange wives. 12:Then all the congregation answered and said with a loud voice, As you have said, so must we do. 13:But the people are many, and it is a time of much rain, and we are not able to stand out side, neither can this work be done one day or two, for many have done this transgress. 14:Let now our rulers of all the congregation stand, and let all them which have taken strange wives in our cities come at appointed times, and with them the elders of every city, and the judges thereof, until the fierce wrath of our God for this matter be turned from us. 15:Only Jonathan the son of Asahel and Jahzeiah the son of Tikvah were employed about this matter, and Meshullam and Shabbethai the Levite helped them. 16:And the children of the captivity did so. And Ezra the priest, with certain chief of the fathers, after the house of their fathers, and all of them by their names, were separated, and sat down, on the first day of the tenth month to examine the matter.

+/- December 18th. (Kislev / Chislev 22nd.)

Jesus heals a man who was blind from birth

(John 9:2-10:21) 2:And as Jesus passed by and he saw a man which was blind from birth. 2:And his disciples asked him, saying, Master, who's sin caused this? Was it this man, or his parents, that he was born blind? 3:Jesus answered, Neither has this man sinned, nor his parents: but that the works of God should be made manifest in him. 4:I must work the works of him that sent me, while it is day: the night comes, when no man can work. 5:As long as I am in the world, I am the light of the world. 6:When he had spoke these words, he spit on the ground, and made clay from the spit, and he anointed the eyes of the blind man with the clay. 7:And said to him, Go, wash in the pool of Siloam, (which is by interpretation, Sent.) He went his way therefore, and washed, and started seeing. 8:The neighbors therefore, and they which before had seen him that he was blind, said, Is not this he that sat and begged? 9:Some said, This is he: others said; He is like him, but he said, I am he. 10:Therefore said they to him, How were your eyes opened? 11:He answered and said, A man who is called Jesus made clay, and anointed mine eyes, and said to me, go to the pool of Siloam, and wash: and I went and washed, and I received sight. 12:Then said they to him, Where is he? He said, I know not. 13:They brought him to the Pharisees and said;that for a time was blind. 14:And it was the sabbath day when Jesus made the clay, and opened his eyes. 15;Then again the Pharisees also asked him how he had received his sight. He said to them, He put clay upon mine eyes, and I washed, and now I can see. 16:Therefore said some of the Pharisees, This man is not of God, because he keeps not the sabbath day. Others said, How can a man that is a sinner do such miracles?

And there was a division among them. 17:They say to the blind man again, What do you say about him, that he has opened your eyes? He said; He is a prophet. 18:But the Jews did not believe concerning him, that he had been blind, and received his sight, until they called the parents of him that had received his sight. 19:And they asked them, saying, Is this your son, who you say was born blind? How then, can he see now? 20:His parents answered them and said, We know that this is our son, and that he was born blind. 21:But by what means he now sees, we know not; or who has opened his eyes, we know not: he is of age; ask him: he shall speak for himself. 22:These words were spoken from his parents, because they feared the Jews: for the Jews had agreed already, that if any man did confess that he was Christ, he should be put out of the synagogue. 23:Therefore said his parents, He is of age; ask him. 24;Then again called they the man that was blind, and said unto him, give God the praise: we know that this man is a sinner. 25:He answered and said, Whether he be a sinner or no, I know not: one thing I know, that, whereas I was blind, now I see. 26:Then said they to him again, What did he do to you? How did he open your eyes? 27:He answered them, I have told you already, and you did not hear: wherefore would you hear it again? will you also be his disciples? 28:Then they reviled him, and said, You are one of his disciples; but we are Moses' disciples. 29:We know that God spoke to Moses: as for this fellow, we know not from where he comes from. 30;The man answered and said to them, Why worry about this, a marvellous thing, that you know not from where he is from, and yet he has opened mine eyes. 31:Now we know that God hears not sinners: but if any man be a worshiper of God, and does his will, him he will hear. 32:Since the world began was it not heard that any man opened the eyes of one that was born blind. 33:If this man were not of God, he could do nothing. 34:They answered and said to him, You were altogether born in sins, and do you teach us? And they cast him out. 35:Jesus heard that they had cast him out; and when he had found him, he said to him, Do you believe on the Son of God? 36:He answered and said, Who is he, Lord, that I might believe on him? 37:And Jesus said to him: You have both seen him, and it is he who is speaking with you now. 38:And he said, Lord, I believe. And he worshiped him. 39:And Jesus said, For judgment I am come into this world, that they who do not, may see; and that they who see can see, be made blind. 40:And some of the Pharisees which were with him heard these words, and said to him, Are we blind also? 41;Jesus said to them, If you were blind, you would have no sin: but now you say, We see; therefore your sin stays with you.

10:1: Verily, truly, I say to you, He that entered not by the way of the door into the sheepfold, but climbs up some other way, the same is a thief and a robber. 2:But he that enters in by the door is the shepherd of the sheep. 3:To him the porter opens; and the sheep hear his voice: and he calls his own sheep by name, and leads them out. 4:And when he puts forth his own sheep, he goeth before them, and the sheep follow him: for they know his voice. 5:And a stranger will they not follow, but will run from him: for they do not know the voice of strangers. 6:This parable spoken by Jesus to them: but they understood not what things they were which he spoke to them. 7:Then said Jesus to them again, Verily, truly, I say to you, I am the door of the sheep. 8:All that ever came before me are thieves and robbers: but the sheep did not hear them. 9:I am the door: by me if any man enter in, he shall be saved, and shall go in and out, and find pasture.

10:The thief comes not, but for to steal, and to kill, and to destroy: I am come that they might have life, and that they might have it more abundantly. 11:I am the good shepherd: the good shepherd gives his life for the sheep. 12:But he that is an hireling, and not the shepherd, whose own the sheep are not, sees the wolf coming, and he leaves the sheep, and flees: and the wolf catch's them, and scatters the sheep. 13:The hireling flees, because he is an hireling, and cares not for the sheep. 14:I am the good shepherd, and I know my sheep, and am known by my sheep. 15:As the Father knows me, even so know I the Father: and I lay down my life for the sheep.16:And other sheep I have, which are not of this fold: them also I must bring, and they shall hear my voice; and there shall be one fold, and one shepherd. 17:Therefore my Father loves me, because I lay down my life, that I might take it up again. 18:No man takes it from me, but I lay it down of myself. I have power to lay it down, and I have power to take it again. This commandment have I received from my Father. 19:There was a division therefore again among the Jews for these sayings. 20:And many of them said: He has a devil, and he is mad; why do you listen to him? 21:Others said, These are not the words of him that has a devil. Can a devil open the eyes of the blind?

+/- December 20th. (Kislev / Chislev 24th.)

The year +/- 518 B.C. The Lord told Haggai to speak to the priest

(Haggai 2:10-19) 10:In the four and twentieth day of the ninth month, in the second year of Darius, came the word of the Lord by Haggai the prophet, saying; 11:This says the Lord of hosts; Ask now the priests concerning the law, saying; 12:If one bear holy flesh in the skirt of his garment, and with his skirt do touch bread, or pottage, or wine, or oil, or any meat, shall it be holy? And the priests answered and said, No. 13:Then said Haggai; If one that is unclean by a dead body touch any of these, shall it be unclean? And the priests answered and said, It shall be unclean, true. 14:Then answered Haggai and said; So is this people, and so is this nation before me, says the Lord; and so is every work of their hands; and that which they offer there is unclean. 15:And now, I pray you, consider from this day and upward, from before a stone was laid upon a stone in the temple of the Lord.16:Since those days were, when one came to an heap of twenty measures, there were but ten: when one came to the vat to draw out fifty vessels out of the press, there were but twenty. 17:I struck you with blasting and with mildew and with hail in all the labors of your hands; yet you turned not back to me, says the Lord. 18:Consider now from this day and upward, from the four and twentieth day of the ninth month, even from the day that the foundation of the Lord's temple was laid, consider it. 19:Is the seed yet in the barn? Yes, as yet the vine, and the fig tree, and the pomegranate, and the olive tree, has not brought forth their fruit: from this day will I bless you?

+/- December 20th. (Kislev / Chislev 24th.)

The year +/- 516 B.C. The Lord sent Haggai to speak with Zerubbabel

(Haggai 2:20-23) 20;And again the word of the Lord came to Haggai in the four and twentieth day of the month, saying, 21;Speak to Zerubbabel, governor of Judah, saying, I will shake the heavens and the earth;

22:And I will overthrow the throne of kingdoms, and I will destroy the strength of the kingdoms of the heathen; and I will overthrow the chariots,

+/- December 21st. (Kislev/ Chislev 25th.)

The year +/-161 B.C. They defiled the Lords temple

(1Maccabees 1:59-63) 59:On the twenty-fifth day of Chislev, and each month after they sacrificed on the alter erected over the alter of holocausts. Women who have had their children circumcised were put to death, in keeping with the decree, 61:with the babies hung from their necks; their families, and those who did the circumcision were also killed. 62:But many in Israel were determined and resolved in their hearts not to eat anything unclean. 63:They preferred to die rather than to be defiled with unclean food or to profane the holy covenant; (That all male children among you be circumcised at eight days of age) so they were killed A terrible affliction, was upon Israel in those days.

The Law of circumcision

(Genesis 17:9-14) 9:And God said to Abraham, You shall keep my covenant therefore, you, and your seed after you in their generations. 10:This is my covenant, which you shall keep, between me and you and your seed after you; Every man child among you shall be circumcised. 11:And you shall circumcise the flesh of your foreskin; and it shall be a token of the covenant between me and you. 12:And he that is eight days old shall be circumcised among you, every man child in your generations, he that is born in the house, or bought with money of any stranger, which is not of your seed. 13:He that is born in your house, and he that is bought with your money, must needs be circumcised: and my covenant shall be in your flesh for an everlasting covenant. 14:And the uncircumcised man child whose flesh of his foreskin is not circumcised, that soul shall be cut off from his people; for he has broken my covenant.

+/- December 21st. (Kislev/ Chislev 25th.)

The year +/-118 B.C. The Feast of Dedication; References:

(1Maccabees 4:52-59, Bikkurim1:6, Rosh HaShanah 1:3, Taanit 2:10, Megillah 3:4 & 3:6, Moed Katan 3:9, Bava Kama 6:6, Josephus book called the Jewish Antiquities XII, The Babyloian Talmud 21b, Hanukkah sometimes called; Chanukah, is also know as :The Feast of Dedication to the Lords temple, and The Festival of lights. It is a eight day festival commemorating the re-dedication of the Holy temple, (the second Temple), in Jerusalem at the time of the Maccabean Revolt of the 2nd.centry. B.C.E.

+/- December 21th. (Kislev / Chislev 25th.)

The year +/-158 B.C. The Dedication of the Lords temple

(1Maccabees 4:52-59)52:Early in the morning on the twenty fifth day of the ninth month, that is the month of Chislev in the year one hundred and forty-eight. 53:They arose and offered sacrifices according to the law on the new altar of holocausts,that they had made.

54:On the anniversary of the day on which the Gentiles had defiled it, on the very day it was reconsecrated with songs, flutes, and cymbals. 55:All the people prostrated themselves and adored and praised Heaven, who had given them success. 56:for eight days they celebrated the dedication of the altar and joyfully offered holocausts, and sacrifices of deliverance and praise. 57:They ornamented the facade of the temple with gold crowns and shields; they repaired the gates and the priest's chambers and furnished them with doors. 58:there was a great joy among the people now that the disgrace of the Gentiles was removed. 59:then Judas and his brothers and the entire congregation of Israel, decreed that the days of the dedication of the alter should be observed with joy and gladness on the anniversary ever year for eight days, from the twenty-fifth day of the month of Chislev.

+/- December 21st. (Kislev / Chislev 25th.)

Jesus at the feast of Dedication

(John 10:22-42)22:And it was at Jerusalem the feast of the dedication, and it was winter. 23:And Jesus walked in the temple in Solomon's porch. 24:Then came the Jews round about him, and said to him, how long will you make us wonder? If you are the Christ, tell us plainly.

25:Jesus answered them; I told you, and you did not believe: the works that I do in my Father's name, they bear witness of me. 26:But you believe not, because you are not of my sheep, as I said to you.27:My sheep hear my voice, and I know them, and they follow me. 28:And I give to them eternal life; and they shall never perish, neither shall anyone be able to pluck them out of my hand. 29:My Father, which gave them me, is greater than all; and no one is able to pluck them out of my Father's hand. 30:I and my Father are one.

31:Then the Jews took up stones again to stone him. 32; Jesus answered them, Many good works have I showed you from my Father; for which of those works do you stone me?

33;The Jews answered him, saying, it is not for good works we stone you; but for blasphemy; and because that you, being a man, make yourself a God.

34;Jesus answered them, Is it not written in your law, I said, You are gods? 35;If he called them gods, to whom the word of God came, and the scripture cannot be broken; 36;Say you of him, whom the Father has sanctified, and sent into the world; You speak blasphemes; because I said, I am the Son of God? 37;If I do not do the works of my Father, do not believe in me. 38;But if I do, though you do not believe me, believe the works: that you may know, and believe, that the Father is in me, and I in him.

39;Therefore they sought again to take him: but he escaped out of their hand, 40;And went away again beyond Jordan into the place where John at first baptized; and there he stayed. 41;And many resorted to him, and said, John did no miracle: but all things that John spoke of this man were true. 42;And many believed on him there.

+/- December 23rd. (Kislev / Chislev 27th.)

The year +/- 3229 B.C. After forty days the Rain of the Great flood stopped:

(Genesis 8:1-2)1:And God remembered Noah, and every living thing and all the cattle that was with him in the ark; and God made a wind to pass over the earth, and the waters began to subside. 2:The fountains also of the deep and the windows of heaven were stopped, and the rain from heaven was restrained.

+/- December 25th. (Kislev / Chislev 29th.)

The year +/- 3328 B.C. Noah send out a dove and she returned

(Genesis 8:8-9) 8;Also he sent forth a dove from him, to see if the waters were abated from off the face of the ground; 9;But the dove found no rest for the sole of her foot, and she returned to him into the ark, for the waters were on the face of the whole earth: then he put forth his hand, and took her,
and pulled her to him in the ark.

+/- December 25th. (Kislev / Chislev 29th.)

Between the years +/- 3140-3115 B.C.

Believed to be Nimrods Birthday

(Genesis 10:8) 8;And Cush begot Nimrod: he began to be a mighty one in the earth. The great grandson of Noah through his son Ham. It is believed by the Babylonians that Nimrod was born on this day, he was the first conquer of men. He was also the builder of the Towers of Babel, (Archeologist found that there were four towers in all, not one.)

Above are: The ruins of Nimrods strong hold

Above: The remains of the tower of Babel, built by Nimrod.

+/- December 25th. (Kislev / Chislev 29th.)

The year +/- 331 C.E. Constantine the great declared this to be Jesus Birthday:

Constantine was born on (February 27th. 272 C.E.) and became one of the Emperors of Rome on (March 1st. 307 C.E.). In a dream he had,he saw a sign in Heaven, (In hoc signo vinces, Under this sign you will conquer,) Note: It was very similar to the sign of Nimrod. After a battle for Rome on the October 28th. 312 C.E. When his brother-in-law was killed. He became the sole Emperor of Rome. Helena, the mother of Constantine was a christian, but Constantine was 42 before he would finely declared himself to be a christian in 314 C.E. Towards the the last 6 years of his life he became very sick so being afraid of what was to come. He decided to bring acceptance and coexistence to his people. In (+/-331 C.E.) He declared that the 25th of December, which was the day, the pagans celebrated their sun god's birthday. Was and would be both; Apollo, (The Roman sun god) and Jesus the (true) son of God's birthday. And it became a common day of celebration.
Then after 6 years he outlawed the celebration and worship of Apollo. So it was accepted as the birthday of Jesus, from that time forward.
Constantine died on the 22nd of May, 337 C.E.

(It was also during the month of December / Chislev) Nehemiah ask about the Hebrews:

(Nehemiah 1:1-11)1:The words of Nehemiah the son of Hachaliah. And it came to pass in the month Chislev, in the twentieth year, as I was in Shushan the palace,
2:That Hanani, one of my brethren, came, with him was some men of Judah; and I asked them concerning the Hebrews that had escaped,

which were left of the captivity, and concerning Jerusalem. 3:And they said to me, The remnant that are left of the captivity there in the province are in great affliction and reproach: the wall of Jerusalem also is broken down, and the gates thereof are burned with fire. 4;And it came to pass, when I heard these words, that I sat down and wept and mourned for days, and fasted and prayed before the God of heaven, 5;And said, I pray to you , O Lord God of heaven, the great and terrible God that keeps covenant and mercy for them that love him and observe his commandments: 6;Let your ear now be attentive, and your eyes open, that you may hear the prayer of your servant, which I pray before you now, day and night, for the children of Israel, your servants, and confess the sins of the children of Israel, which we have sinned against you: both I and my father's house have sinned. ;We have dealt very corruptly against you, and have not kept the commandments, nor the statutes, nor the judgments, which you commanded your servant Moses. 8:Remember, I beg you, the word that you commanded your servant Moses, saying, if you transgress, I will scatter you abroad among the nations: 9:But if you turn to me, and keep my commandments, and do them; though them who were cast out to the uttermost, part of the heaven, yet will I gather them from there, and will bring them back to the place that I have chosen to set my name there. 10:Now these are your servants and your people, whom you have redeemed by your great power, and by your strong hand. 11:O Lord, I beseech you, let now thine ear be attentive to the prayer of your servant, and to the prayer of your servants, who desire to fear your name: and prosper, I pray you, your servant this day, and grant him mercy in the sight of this man. For I was the King's cup bearer.

The Philistines took the ark of God

(1Samuel 4:1-5:12) 4:1: And the word of Samuel came to all Israel. Now Israel went out against the Philistines to battle, and pitched beside Ebenezer: and the Philistines pitched in Aphek. 2:And the Philistines put themselves in array against Israel: and when they joined battle, Israel was smitten before the Philistines: and they slew of the army in the field about four thousand men. 3:And when the people had come into the camp, the elders of Israel said, Why has the Lord struck this day before the Philistines? Let us fetch the ark of the covenant of the Lord out of Shiloh to us, that, when it comes among us, it may save us out of the hand of our enemies. 4:So the people went to Shiloh, so that they might bring from there the ark of the covenant of the Lord of hosts, which dwells between the cherubims: and the two sons of Eli, Hophni and Phinehas, were there with the ark of the covenant of God.5:And when the ark of the covenant of the Lord came into the camp, all Israel shouted with a great shout, so that the earth rang again. 6;And when the Philistines heard the noise of the shout, they said; What does this noise mean, of this great shout in the camp of the Hebrews? And they understood that the ark of the Lord had come into the camp. 7:And the Philistines were afraid, for they said; God has come into the camp. And they said, Woe to us! For there has not been such a thing for a long time. 8:Woe to us! Who shall deliver us out of the hand of this mighty God? This is the God that struck the Egyptians with all the plagues in the wilderness. 9:Be strong, and pull yourselves together like men, O you Philistines, that you be not servants to the Hebrews, as they have been to you: pull yourselves together like men, and fight. 10:And the Philistines fought, and Israel was struck, and they fled every man to his own tent: and there was a very great slaughter;

for there fell of Israel thirty thousand footmen. 11:And the ark of God was taken; and the two sons of Eli, Hophni and Phinehas, were slain. 12:And there ran a man of Benjamin out of the army, and came to Shiloh the same day with his clothes rent, and with earth upon his head.13:And when he came, look, Eli sat upon a seat by the wayside watching: for his heart trembled for the ark of God. And when the man came into the city, and told it, all the city cried out. 14:And when Eli heard the noise of the crying, he said, What dose this noise of this tumult mean? And the man came in hastily, and told Eli. 15:Now Eli was ninety and eight years old; and his eyes were dim, that he could not see. 16;And the man said to Eli, I am he that came out of the army, and I fled today out of the army. And he said, What is there done, my son? 17:And the messenger answered and said, Israel is fled before the Philistines, and there has been also a great slaughter among the people, and your two sons also, Hophni and Phinehas, are dead, and the ark of God is taken. 18:And it came to pass, when he made mention of the ark of God, that he fell from off the seat backward by the side of the gate, and he broke his neck, and he died: for he was an old man, and heavy. And he had judged Israel forty years. 19:And his daughter in law, Phinehas' wife, was with child, near to be delivered: and when she heard the tidings that the ark of God was taken, and that her father in law and her husband were dead, she bowed herself and travailed; for her pains came upon her. 20:And about the time of her death the women that stood by her said to her, Fear not; for you have born a son. But she answered not, neither did she regard it. 21:And she named the child Ichabod, saying, The glory is departed from Israel: because the ark of God was taken, and because of her father in law and her husband. 22:And she said, The glory is departed from Israel: for the ark of God is taken.

5:1: And the Philistines took the ark of God, and brought it from Ebenezer to Ashdod. 2:When the Philistines took the ark of God, they brought it into the house of Dagon, and set it by Dagon. 3;And when the men of Ashdod arose early on the next day, behold, Dagon was fallen upon his face to the earth before the ark of the Lord. And they took Dagon, and set him in his place again. 4:And when they again rose early on the fallowing morning, behold, Dagon had fallen upon his face to the ground before the ark of the Lord; and the head of Dagon and both the palms of his hands were cut off upon the threshold; only the stump of Dagon was left to him. 5;Therefore neither the priests of Dragon, nor any that come into Dagon's house, tread on the threshold of Dagon in Ashdod to this day. 6;But the hand of the Lord was heavy upon them of Ashdod, and he destroyed them, and struck them with hemorrhoids, even Ashdod and the coasts thereof. 7:And when the men of Ashdod saw that sit was so, they said, The ark of the God of Israel shall not abide with us: for his hand is sore upon us, and upon Dagon our god. 8:They sent therefore and gathered all the lords of the Philistines to them, and said, What shall we do with the ark of the God of Israel? And they answered, Let the ark of the God of Israel be carried about to Gath. And they carried the ark of the God of Israel a little closer. 9:And it was so that, after they had carried it about, the hand of the Lord was against the city with a very great destruction: and he struck the men of the city, both small and great, and they had hemorrhoids broke out on them. 10:Therefore they sent the ark of God to Ekron. And it came to pass, as the ark of God came to Ekron, that the Ekronites cried out, saying, They have brought about the ark of the God of Israel to us, to slay us and our people.

11:So they sent and gathered together all the lords of the Philistines, and said, Send away the ark of the God of Israel, and let it go again to his own place, that it slay us not, and our people: for there was a deadly destruction throughout all the city; the hand of God was very heavy there. 12:And the men that died not were smitten with the hemorrhoids:and the cry of the city went up to heaven.

Also during: (December / Kislev)

Jehoiakim King of Judah burned the scroll:

(Jeremiah 36:9-32) 9:And it came to pass in the fifth year of Jehoiakim the son of Josiah King of Judah, in the ninth month, that they proclaimed a fast before the Lord to all the people in Jerusalem, and to all the people that came from the cities of Judah to Jerusalem. 10:Then read Baruch in the book the words of Jeremiah in the house of the Lord, in the chamber of Gemariah the son of Shaphan the scribe, in the higher court, at the entry of the new gate of the Lord's house, in the ears of all the people. 11:When Micaiah the son of Gemariah, the son of Shaphan, had heard out of the book all the words of the Lord. 12:Then he went down to the King's house, into the scribe's chamber: and saw, all the princes sitting there, even Elishama the scribe, and Delaiah the son of Shemaiah, and Elnathan the son of Achbor, and Gemariah the son of Shaphan, and Zedekiah the son of Hananiah, and all the princes. 13:Then Micaiah declared to them all the words that he had heard, when Baruch read the book in the ears of the people. 14:Therefore all the princes sent Jehudi the son of Nethaniah, the son of Shelemiah, the son of Cushi, to Baruch, saying, Take in your hand the roll wherein you have read in the ears of the people, and come. So Baruch the son of Neriah took the roll in his hand, and came to them.

15;And they said to him, Sit down now, and read it in our ears. So Baruch read it in their ears. 16:Now it came to pass, when they had heard all the words, they were afraid both one and other, and said to Baruch, We will surely tell the King of all these words. 17:And they asked Baruch, saying, Tell us now, How did you write all these words from his mouth? 18:Then Baruch answered them, He said all these words to me with his mouth, and I wrote them with ink in the book. 19;Then said the princes to Baruch, Go, hide yourself, you and Jeremiah; and let no man know where you are.20:And they went in to the King into the court, but they laid up the roll in the chamber of Elishama the scribe, and told all the words in the ears of the King. 21:So the King sent Jehudi to fetch the roll: and he took it out of Elishama the scribe's chamber. And Jehudi read it in the ears of the King, and in the ears of all the princes which stood beside the King. 22:Now the King sat in the winter house in the ninth month: and there was a fire on the hearth burning before him. 23:And it came to pass, that when Jehudi had read three or four leaves, he cut it with the penknife, and cast it into the fire that was on the hearth, until all the roll was consumed in the fire that was on the hearth. 24:Yet they were not afraid, nor rent their garments, neither the King, nor any of his servants that heard all these words. 25:Nevertheless Elnathan and Delaiah and Gemariah had made intercession to the King that he would not burn the roll: but he would not hear them. 26:But the King commanded Jerahmeel the son of Hammelech, and Seraiah the son of Azriel, and Shelemiah the son of Abdeel, to take Baruch the scribe and Jeremiah the prophet, but the Lord hid them. 27;Then the word of the Lord came to Jeremiah, after that the King had burned the roll, and the words which Baruch wrote at the mouth of Jeremiah, saying, 28:Take you again another roll, and write in it all the former words that were in the first roll, which Jehoiakim the King of Judah has burned. 29:And you shall say to Jehoiakim King of Judah, This says the Lord; You have burned this roll, saying, Why have you written therein, saying, The King of Babylon shall certainly come and destroy this land, and shall cause to cease from thence man and beast? 30:Therefore this says the Lord of Jehoiakim, King of Judah; He shall have none to sit upon the throne of David: and his dead body shall be cast out in the day to the heat, and in the night to the frost. 31:And I will punish him and his seed and his servants for their iniquity; and I will bring upon them, and upon the inhabitants of Jerusalem, and upon the men of Judah, all the evil that I have pronounced against them; but they would not listen. 32:Then took Jeremiah another roll, and gave it to Baruch the scribe, the son of Neriah; who wrote therein from the mouth of Jeremiah all the words of the book which Jehoiakim King of Judah had burned in the fire: and there were added besides to them many like words.

Extra Writers notes: About the Julian calendar

In the Ancient Hebrew calendar there were 30 days for each month and 360 days for a year. In around 36 B.C. They found that there was 365 days in a year. So began the Julian calendar. So eventually the Hebrews added a new month called 2nd. Adar. Every 6 years the would add the thirteenth month to their calendar, to accommodate for the extra 5 days. What I have done is gone back to the original beginning of the year that God had given to Moses, with 30 days for each month then added the extra 5 days at the end of the month of Adar, to make a 365 day year.

About the Names of the Months:

After putting all the names of the months together, I found they spelled out a message, about the coming of the Messiah Starting with Nissan -Abib, being the first month and going through to Adar the last month of the Hebrew year.

The months translate into English as:

Their flight a night to remember, a time of **healing** for the **olive**. **Brigh**t is the **hidden giver of the vine**. The **Holy Father**, has set a spiritual **wedding,** to be held at the beginning of the **feast of booths**. He has called all to **repentance** and will give them a new **beginning**. A holy gift, that is coming after the **rain that has been sealed.** Have **faith** and **trust** in him who will declare that he is; The son of God, during the **festival of lights**. He is the good **tree of life,** who's enduring **strength** will never fail.

About the Names of the Tribes:

The names of the twelve tribes: After putting the names of the twelve tribes together starting with Joseph, and ending with Zebulum. It speaks of what is to come. **It translates as: He has given and he has taken away. Sent out from the Father's right hand his first born, look a son. He has heard** (our cries.) **He will become attached** (to us.) **We will give grateful praise** (for) **he has vindicated us. In a wrestling mach, he has wrestled. In luck, in our good fortune they call us blessed. His reward will be** (a) **bridegroom's gift.**

More about Adam and Lilith

More about Adam and Lilith: Adam and Lilith were formed in Hebron. The year +/- **(4885 B.C.E.)** Then after a argument between Lilith and Adam. Lilith stated when we come together as one, we should both have equal say in the matter. Adam said no I am stronger so I should be in control of what we do. So Lilith left him and went and laid with a fallen angel (who's name I will not wright) during the month of Elul, (September). God sent three angels to talk with her who's names were: Sanvi, Sansanvi, and Semangelaf and have her come back to Adam in Hebron. She refused saying: If she return I would have to be under Adam. And that she had already had been with another, they told her that God would forgive her, if she would just returned. After she overpowered them she ran away and prayed to the one who she had sex with, and went to the angel whom she had laid with ask him to give her wings to fly away. Then in the month of Bul, (November) he transformed her into a Demon,and gave her wings and feet like a owl. She was given power over new born infants. Male children for 8 days and female children for 40 days.

So God then moved Adam to the Garden of Eden, (Fertile plane) which is about 200 miles south of modern Baghdad. He then brought all the animals there for him to name, and he had others females to come and see if any were a match for him. When he saw that none were a match, he put Adam to sleep, then took a rib from Adam and made a mate for him. In the month of Ephraim, (October). Note: (This was a year after Lilith had left him). When Adam first saw her he said: Chavah, which means breath. Once they were kicked out of the garden, he called her name Eve. (Mother of life.) After they were kicked out of the Garden of Eden , they were sent back west to Hebron, where she gave birth to Cane and Awen, in the year +/- **(4789 B.C.E.).**

Then the next year she gave birth to Abel and Azura, +/- **(4788 B.C.E.)** Before they gave their sacrifices cane overheard his parents (Adam and Eve) speaking about it being time to have their Son and Daughters (marry) so they decided that Cane would marry Azura, and Abel would marry Awen.

This made Cane very angry because he wanted to marry Awen, not Azura. Later that day Cane and Abel went down to give their burnt offerings to the Lord. When Cane's sacrifice was not excepted he was even more angry.
They went down to the field to fight; (as they often did) when Cane struck Able with a rock and killed him. After this he took his sister Awen down to the forest and married her. Later God spoke with him about Able. +/- **(4776 B.C.E.)**

The fallowing year +/- **(4775 B.C.E.)** Seth was born. When he got older he was married to Azura, though when he was told to marry her he did not want to marry her. He was around 12 years of age.+/- **(4763 B.C.E.)**

Please note: (After 1150 they started removing Lilith from the writings, and in the 1500's removed or forbid many of the sacred writings from the Bibles. Because it was different from some of the doctrines that they had established. For more on finding these dates in the Bible, they are found in the book of;
Genesis from (1:26-31) (2:7-25)

More about Esther

Hadassah: is what Esther's name was in Hebrew, Esther is a variant of the name of the Babylonian goddess Ishtar.

About the Language that Jesus spoke:

Many times as I have read the transcripts I wondered if they were correct about the language that Jesus spoke. So while I was in Jerusalem I started asking some of the Jewish Rabbis about this. The modern Hebrew language is still the same language they spoke for over 4000 years. Though their letters are now written in a Arabic alphabet. It is like saying we speak Greek because we use Greek letters in English.

The Ancient Hebrew letters are know as Hebrewic writings, used by Moses and before. Were it was changed around +/- **(2100 B.C.E).** Also know as Phoenician Hebrew, Then about +/- **(1950 B.C.E.)** to Wadi-El-Hhol, Hebrew.
Then in +/- **(1830 B.C.E)** to Babyloian block style letters. In +/- **(1450 B.C.E.)** to Siniatic. In +/-**(1200B.C.E)** It changed to Middle Semitic, which is also know as (Plaeo-Hebrew). Then between +/- **(1050-950 B.C.E.)** to Tel-Zayit.
In around +/- **(400 B.C.E.)** it changed to Late Semitic, Also known as Arabic letters. Today they still use Arabic letters in writing their language.
But they still speak Hebrew.

Note: About Jesus calling out on the Cross

While on the cross it is written; That he called out; **Eli, Eli, lama sabachthani?** which was though to be; My God, my God, why have you forsaken me. But it was written he would never cry out. And the people there, (who spoke the language said): He is calling on Elijah, (Mathew 27:47, Mark 15:35). While I was studying at the Ancient Hebrew Learning Center, at the University of Jerusalem. I inquired about this matter, and found that during that time period the Hebrews used Arabic letters but spoke in Hebrew. (Like: Spanish, German, or French using the same letters we use in English.) But they speak in there own language. So I inquired how it would translate from Hebrew to English? Here it is: Elijah, Elijah, why have you gone from my (left) side? Some said he was calling on Elijah, and others then said: Let us see whether Elijah will come to save him. See: (Mathew 17:3, and Mark 9:4) Also the Arabic language was not spoken by all the Jewish people, but Hebrew was.

What is the difference between: B.C. and A.D. and C. E.

B.C. Stands for: (Before Christ Era). It is suppose to be (Before Jesus was born) But years ago the powers to be, looking at the books of Mathew, Mark and John had one passover date and Luke had another. So the powers that be decided to go between the two. Now we know that Jesus was born in the Hebrew year 3754, known to us as 6 **B.C.** Because of the census taken were every 14 years, and Herod's death was in 4 **B.C**. two years after the census was taken. **A.D**. is short for in Latin: (Anno Domini Norsti Le'sous Christi). In the year of our Lord Jesus Christ. After finding out the dates were wrong, they simply started to call it **C.E**. (Common Era.) So with this in mind these dates are set at the actual time line with 6 B.C. being 1 **A.D.** This book shows that change to be more accurate.

The Lords prayer translated from Hebrew to English:

Our Father who is in heaven above, Holiest is your name. Let your kingdom come to be and your will be done here on earth, as it is done in heaven above. Give us this day are daily bread, and forgive us of our trespasses, as we have already forgiven those, who have trespassed against us. Do not let us be led off the lightened path which you have set before me in to temptation, but deliver us from evil and the fallen one.

Later this was added by the Catholic Church:

For yours is the Kingdom, and the Power and Glory for ever and ever Amen.

God told Moses: Tell Aron to bless the children of Israel, in the way; (Numbers 6:24-26)

24:The LORD bless thee, and keep thee:

25:The LORD make his face to shine upon thee, and be gracious unto thee:

26:The LORD lift up his countenance upon thee, and give thee peace.

Note: This was translated from Hebrew to Greek then to English. When translated from the original writings: In ancient Hebrew, they would have understood it to mean this:

(Numbers 6:24-26)
24:He who Exists, will kneel before you presenting gifts, as a parent towards a child,and will guard you with a hedge of protection.

25:He who Exists, will illuminate the wholeness of his being towards you bringing order, and he will provide you with love, substance and friendship.

26:He who Exists, will left up his wholeness of being and look upon you, and he will set in place all your needs to be whole and complete.

Note: The Hebrews Calendar was created

+/- 175 years after the Death of Adam and Eve +/- 4110 years B.C. During the life of Enoch who was +/-153 years of age at the time. Enoch died at 365 years old.

The year +/- 1437 B.C. The killing of the new born male children

Pharaoh Ramses II, after hearing from his wise men of the prophecy:
That a male child will be born to the Hebrews, who will set free all of the slaves from the land of Egypt. Pharaoh sent out a order throughout the land spoken of in: **(Exodus 1:22)** 22:And Pharaoh charged all his people, saying, Every son that is born you shall cast into the river, and every daughter you shall keep alive.

More about King David died after forty years of being King, for 33 of them he was King over Jerusalem. Below is picture of the

sign over the entrance of King David's tomb in Jerusalem
Below: Mounted on the side of the entrance

Above: Kings Davids tomb.   Below: King David's court yard

Extra: Pictures of Saint Peters tomb

Peter's place and manner of death are also mentioned by Tertullian ch.(160-220) in Scorpiane in: Chapter 11. Where the death is said to have take place during the Christian persecutions by Nero. Tacitus: vs.(56-117) describes the persecution of Christians in his writings, though he does not specifically mention Peter._12:"They were torn by dogs and perished, some were nailed to crosses, and others were doomed to be burned to death." Furthermore, Tertullian also says these events took place in the imperial gardens near the Circus of Nero. No other area would have been available for public persecutions after the great fire of Rome took place and destroyed the Circus Maximus and most of the rest of the city in the year 64 C.E.

The Great fire of Rome

Note: Nero set fire to Rome on the +/-18th. Of July 64 C.E. In hopes of rebuilding a bigger and better city. So he would be remembered. But after the people became enraged and wanted to kill him, he soon turned and blamed, the Christians for the act.

To learn more about what God commanded us to do, and what is now being taught in the modern Churches. Please be sure to read:

What God Commanded, & What Man Decided.

By: Sir William L. Smith Ph.D.
The Son of Edward

Please note: There were more dates that I found that I did not recorded in this book. So that the readers might find them on their own.

For it is written in: **(Proverbs 25:2)** It is the Glory of God to conceal a matter, But the honor of Kings to search out a matter.

Please note: The pictures that are in this book are for visual effect only, some were taken from free stock photos and others were pictures taken on site. So that the reader may have a better understanding of where the events had taking place during the time. The scriptures that are in this book, are only to provide a quick reference for the reader. Even though the translations from many different Bibles and other books were used. It is hoped that this will give a better understanding of the importance of the dates, in which the events had taken place.

A thought about the Six Days of Creation

After many years of studies and research this is the conclusion of what I have found. Most people I have spoken to have heard of the 6 days of creation, that are spoken of in the Bible. Almost all christian have the belief that the 6 days of creation were six twenty four hour days, we now have here on Earth. Others think the six days are 6000 years, as spoke of in Psalm 90:4: A thousand years in your sight are like a day that has just gone by, or like a watch in the night, and again in:(2 Peter) It is written: But do not forget this one thing, dear friends: With the Lord a day is like a thousand years, and a thousand years are like a day. Be that what it may, God spoke of the six days in which he created the Heavens and Earth, then at the end of each day God went back home to the Heavens above the heavens. When Jesus spoke to the people, he spoke of the Heavens above the Earth where the Angels are, but where God lives, is in the Heavens above the heavens, also know as the land called Eternity. Where it is written a day is like 1,000 years in the second Heaven. Where the Prince tried to set his thrown higher than God's. God was not gone a day from Heaven, but closer to a thousand years. Using this formula to the days we have or had during the time of Moses 360 days in a year, it breaks down to this: 1 day to God is (1k x1k x 360)= 360,000,000 years to us here on earth. Giving a clearer understanding of what was being told to the people by God. Now knowing we are at the end of the eighth day, it makes more since of what was written in the Ancient Scrolls.

The Beginning Elul 17th. - September 14th.

2,880,000,000 B.A. (+/- 10k)

The Date the Hebrews believe the Universe was called into Existence; God put his hand together and blew into them and said Let there be light, and the light was formed, then God said let the light separate and go into the darkness, and it did. There was a large explosion, the noise we still hear today in space. Now called (The big bang theory). Then God called forth all the host of Heaven, Wisdom, Understanding, Knowledge, Discernment, he called forth the first born Prince (M*****) the bright morning Star, (Whom became known as the fallen one), then Michel, Gabriel, Raphael, Tyre and all the other Angels and heavenly host. He went out threw the Heavens he had created, building and bringing forth life to all that is there. It was towards the end of the first day that God came over the earth that is called his foot stool and spoke the words, (Let it begin). Note: After he spoke God left and went back to his home, in the third Heaven until the next day. At the end of each day he went back to the Heavens above the heavens, to the place where he would rest. Then return the next day to work again until the seventh day came, and then he rested for that day and called it Holy. God comes from the Heavens above the heavens, that we call the land of Eternity. Along with him came; The Great Architect, (from whom all things were made), and the Holy Spirit, also know as the bringer of life, the Great Comforter, and the Giver of Gifts. Note: It is written that God gave us Faith, Hope and Love see (1Chorinthians 13:13)

Faith: is also know as the one we call (the Son) (the lamb of God) The Lord Jesus
Hope: is also know as the one we call (the Spirit of Truth) The Holy Ghost.
Love: is also know as the one we call (the Holy One) (God Almighty) The Father.

And the Greatest of these is Love.

God hovered over the Earth

The 1st Day 2,699,750,000 B.A. (+/- 100k)

(Genesis 1:2-5) The Beginning. 2:And the earth was without form, and void; and darkness was upon the face of the deep. And the Spirit of God hovered over the face of the waters. 3:And God spoke, Let it begin and the earth started to take form. 4:And God saw it form and it was pleasing to him and said that it was good: and God divided the light from the darkness. 5:And God called the light Day, and the darkness he called Night. And there was evening and morning. This the very first day. Note (As written in the old Torah, it is written as: Let there be order, in modern Bibles it is: Let there be light.

God separated the waters:

The 2nd. Day 2,339,750,000 B.A. (+/-100k)

(Genesis 1:6-8) 6;And God came over the earth again and said, Let there be a firmament in the midst of the waters, and let it divide the waters from the waters. 7;And God made the firmament, and divided the waters which were under the firmament from the waters which were above the firmament: and it was so. 8;And God called the firmament Heaven. And the evening and the morning were the second day. Note: God formed the sky and the clouds, and separated them from the waters.

God formed the land and Mountains, and covered them

The 3rd. Day 1,979,750,000 B.A. (+/-100k)

(Genesis 1:9-13) 9:And God said, Let the waters under the heaven be gathered together to one place, and let the dry land appear: and it was so. 10:And God called the dry land Earth; and the gathering together of the waters called he Seas: and God saw that it was good. 11:And God said, Let the earth bring forth grass, the herb yielding seed, and the fruit tree yielding fruit after his kind, whose seed is in itself, upon the earth: and it was so. 12:And the earth brought forth grass, and herb yielding seed after his kind, and the tree yielding fruit, whose seed was in itself, after his kind: and God saw that it was good. 13;And the evening and the morning were the third day.

God put the Sun in the Sky

The 4th. Day 1,619,750,000 B.A. (+/- 100k)

(Genesis 1:14-19) 14:And God said, Let there be lights in the firmament of the heaven to divide the day from the night; and let them be for signs, and for seasons, and for days, and years: 15:And let them be for lights in the firmament of the heaven to give light upon the earth: and it was so. 16:And God made two great lights; the greater light to rule the day, and the lesser light to rule the night: he made the stars also. 17:And God set them in the firmament of the heaven to give light upon the earth. 18:And to rule over the day and over the night, and to divide the light from the darkness: and God saw that it was good. 19:And the evening and the morning were the fourth day. (Note: It is written in the old Aramaic writings that the Heavens gave one of its own to watch over the earth.) The Sun shall watch over (Govern) the Day and the Moon shall watch over the night, and shine with the glory of the Sun. (To watch over or govern in Ancient Hebrew is the same as the word God, Master, or someone in Authority, whom God created or placed over someone or place.

God created the Creatures of the Waters and the Air

The 5th. Day 1,259,750,000 B.A. (+/- 100k)

(Genesis 1:20-23) 20:And God said, Let the waters bring forth abundantly the moving creature that has life, and fowl that may fly above the earth, in the open firmament of heaven. 21:And God created great whales, and every living creature that moves, which the waters brought forth abundantly, after their kind, and every winged fowl after his kind: and God saw that it was good. 22:And God blessed them, saying, Be fruitful, and multiply, and fill the waters in the seas, and let fowl multiply in the earth. 23:And the evening and the morning were the fifth day. (God put live in the waters and in the shy.)

God created the Animals of the Earth, then the Angles asked God: "Let us make man in our Image"

The 6th. Day 899,750,000 B.A. (+/- 100k)

(Genesis 1:24-31) 24:And God said, Let the earth bring forth the living creatures of all kinds, cattle, and creeping thing, and beast of the earth after his kind: and it was so. 25:And God made the beast of the earth after his kind, and cattle after their kind, and every thing that creeps upon the earth after his kind: and God saw that it was perfect. 26:And the Elim,(A God head, also known as angels, who were in charge over the earth, looked to God the Father and Said); Let us make man in our image, after our own likeness: and let them have dominion over the fish of the sea, and over the fowl of the air, and over the cattle, and over all the earth, and over every creeping thing that creeps upon the earth. And God said; let it be so. 27:So the Angels created man in their own images, in the images of them did they created them; both male and female they created them. 28:And God blessed them, and God said to them, Be fruitful, and multiply, and replenish the earth, and subdue it: and have dominion over the fish of the sea, and over the fowl of the air, and over every living thing that moves upon the earth. 29:And God said, Behold, I have given you every herb bearing seed, which is upon the face of all the earth, and every tree, in the which is the fruit of a tree yielding seed; to you it shall be for food. 30:And to every beast of the earth, and to every fowl of the air, and to every thing that creeps upon the earth, where in there is life, and I have given every green herb for food: and it was so. 31:And God saw every thing that he had made, and, behold, it was very good. And the evening and the morning were the sixth day. **Note:** It is written that the gods or also now called angels who asked God, Let us make man in our Image, so God blessed them and said: be fruitful and multiply.

God rested and called the Day Holy

The 7th. Day +/- 540,000,000 B.A. (+/- 100k)

(Genesis 2:1-3)1:This the heavens and the earth were finished, and all the host of them. 2:And on the seventh day God ended his work which he had made; and he rested on the seventh day from all his work which he had made.

3:And God blessed the seventh day, and sanctified it: because that in it he had rested from all his work which God created and made.

God was angry and Bared his mighty right Arm

The 8th. Day +/- 180,000,000 B.A. (+/-100k)

God returned to Heavens to find that Prince M***** had tried to put his thrown and Laws, higher that Gods Laws. Written in the Book of Bershit (also called a arrow shot to a target, or to the point) writings, Upon the return of Elohim to the heavens he had created. He was angered when he saw what was done, and he bared his mighty right arm and with one swing of his sword 95% of the demons (angels who turned away from him) fell to the Earth, then prince M***** begged for him to leave the rest so that Gods will can be done on the earth. So God stopped, and the war in Heaven started, between those who were true to God and those who had fallowed Prince M*****. **Note:** The word Devil, Satin, Dragon and accuser is also used to describe the Evil ones who fallowed the prince. Note: It was during the eight day when the angels started trying to form mankind.

The Prince was cast down from Heaven

Prince M***** was cast from Heaven and when he saw where he was he was cast, he became angered. As spoken of in (Isaiah 14:12) How you have fallen from heaven, morning star, son of the dawn! You have been cast down to the earth, you who once laid low the nations As spoken by Jesus in (Luke 10:18) He said to them, "I watched Satan fall from heaven like a lightning flash. Then Gods angels went to war in Heaven, (Removed from some of the modern Bibles)
John 5:17: Jesus spoke saying Truly, truly I say to you Even unto this day a war rages in Heaven and "My Father is always healing even on the Sabbath day, and I too am working." 18: For this reason they tried all the more to kill him.

Also Note: The Catholic Church added the word (Satan) to the Great Dragon, even though they were and are two different creatures.

Towards the end of the 8th. Day

on +/- October 5, 4885 B.C.E.

God created the First Perfect Man and called him; Adam

The Lords Feast and Fast Days

Feast Days; Every Saturday, New (or) Full Moons, March 9th. 10th, days of Prim, April 1st. New Year, Evening of the 13th Passover, and unleavened bread, last for seven days, fifty days after the first Saturday after the passover is the feast of weeks it always starts on a Sunday, it is in June and last for (7 days) the only feast that changes year to year, July 17th. Aug. 1st. Sept 28th. The Original New Year, 30th. Oct 12th. 19th. Feast of Booths - Tabernacles , last for eight days,

Fast Days: In June 16th. Praying for Ester. In August 7th. The Destruction of the Lords Temple. In October 6th. A day of sadness for sins, 7th. The Day of Atonement, In November 7th. Jephthah's daughter was sacrificed to the Lord